MW00650730

THE BAD JESUS

The Bible in the Modern World, 68

THE BAD JESUS
THE ETHICS OF NEW TESTAMENT ETHICS

Hector Avalos

SHEFFIELD PHOENIX PRESS

2015

Copyright © 2015 Sheffield Phoenix Press

Published by Sheffield Phoenix Press
Department of Biblical Studies, University of Sheffield
Sheffield S3 7QB

www.sheffieldphoenix.com

A CIP catalogue record for this book
is available from the British Library

Typeset by CA Typesetting Ltd
Printed on acid-free paper by Lightning Source

ISBN-13 978-1-909697-73-7 (hbk)
978-1-909697-79-9 (pbk)

CONTENTS

Acknowledgments

No book, even if there is only one listed author, is truly the product of a single person. This book is no exception. There were assistants at many crucial points.

First among them is my wife, Cynthia Avalos. Not only did she attentively meet all the needs of a busy author, but she proofread drafts of the manuscript and acted as a good sounding-board for my ideas. My colleague, Dr Robin Veldman, Assistant Professor of Religious Studies at Iowa State, read my chapter on environmental ethics and offered some helpful suggestions. Alison Church and Brenda Tyrrell, my diligent research assistants at Iowa State University, gathered a lot of the materials that I used and helped to proofread the manuscript. The personnel at Iowa State University's Interlibrary Loan department of Parks Library were efficient in securing even the most obscure materials that I needed.

David Clines of Sheffield Phoenix Press was patient and generous with his time as I prepared my manuscript. I am also indebted to him and others at Sheffield Phoenix for their expert suggestions on some issues.

Alejandro Botta of the Boston University School of Theology graciously shared his research on Elephantine.

As usual, I must thank Rusty, our omniscient pet squirrel, along with his friends, Skippy, Woody and Chip, whose antics provided needed entertainment when writers' fatigue subjugated me.

All are, hereby, absolved from any transgressions committed within these pages.

NOTE TO READERS

Our discussions of the Bible translations and exegesis of the Greek and Hebrew scriptures necessitate the use of various versions. But, unless noted otherwise, all of our biblical quotations are from the Revised Standard Version, as presented in Herbert G. May and Bruce M. Metzger, *The New Oxford Annotated Bible with Apocrypha* (New York: Oxford University Press, 1977). For the Greek, Aramaic and Hebrew text, we depend on the following:

Greek: Kurt Aland *et al.*, *The Greek New Testament* (Stuttgart: Deutsche Bibelgesellschaft/United Bible Societies, 4th rev. edn, 1998).

Hebrew: K. Elliger and W. Rudolph (eds.), *Biblia hebraica stuttgartensia* (Editio minor; Stuttgart: Deutsche Bibelgesellschaft, 1983).

We use foreign words in our main text as sparingly as possible, and when deemed necessary to understand our arguments. However, more complete extracts in foreign languages have been provided for scholars in footnotes, when the foreign language sources were available to me and/or when I deemed it sufficiently important.

ABBREVIATIONS

AAR	American Academy of Religion
AB	Anchor Bible
ABD	David Noel Freedman (ed.), *The Anchor Bible Dictionary* (New York: Doubleday, 1992)
AfO	*Archiv für Orientforschung*
AMT	Reginald C. Thompson, *Assyrian Medical Texts* (London: J. Bale, Sons and Danielsson, 1924)
ANET	James B. Pritchard (ed.), *Ancient Near Eastern Texts Relating to the Old Testament* (Princeton, NJ: Princeton University Press, 1950)
ANF	Anti-Nicene Fathers
ANRW	Hildegard Temporini and Wolfgang Haase (eds.), *Aufstieg und Niedergang der römischen Welt: Geschichte und Kultur Roms im Spiegel der neueren Forschung* (Berlin: W. de Gruyter, 1972–)
AP	A. Cowley, *Aramaic Papyri of the Fifth Century B.C.* (repr., Osnabrück: Otto Zeller, 1967 [1923])
BARev	*Biblical Archaeology Review*
BASOR	*Bulletin of the American Schools of Oriental Research*
BBB	Bonner biblische Beiträge
BDAG	W. Bauer, F.W. Danker, W.F. Arndt and F.W. Gingrich, *Greek–English Lexicon of the New Testament and Other Early Christian Literature*
BDF	Friedrich Blass, A. Debrunner and Robert W. Funk, *A Greek Grammar of the New Testament and Other Early Christian Literature* (Cambridge: Cambridge University Press, 1961)
Bib	*Biblica*
BibInt	*Biblical Interpretation: A Journal of Contemporary Approaches*
BK	*Bibel und Kirche*
BM	British Museum
BN	*Biblische Notizen*
BR	*Bible Review*
BSac	*Bibliotheca Sacra*
BT	*The Bible Translator*
BTB	*Biblical Theology Bulletin*
BWL	*Babylonian Wisdom Literature* (Oxford: Clarendon Press, 1960)
BZAW	Beihefte zur *ZAW*
BZNW	Beihefte zur *ZNW*
CAD	Ignace I. Gelb *et al.* (eds.), *The Assyrian Dictionary of the Oriental Institute of the University of Chicago* (Chicago, IL: Oriental Institute, 1964–)
CBQ	*Catholic Biblical Quarterly*
CFA	John Scheid, *Commentarii Fratrum Arvalium qui supersunt: Le copies épigraphiques des protocoles annuels de la Confrérie Arvale (21 AV.-31 AP. J.-C)* (Roma Antica, 4; Rome: École Française de Rome Sopritendenza Archaeologica di Roma, 1998)

CH	Code of Hammurabi
CIL	*Corpus inscriptionum latinarum*
ClQ	*Classical Quarterly*
DCH	D.J.A. Clines (ed.), *Dictionary of Classical Hebrew* (Sheffield: Sheffield Phoenix Press, 1993–2011)
EA	El Amarna Letters
EstBíb	*Estudios bíblicos*
ETL	*Ephemerides theologicae lovanienses*
EvQ	*Evangelical Quarterly*
EvT	*Evangelische Theologie*
ExpTim	*Expository Times*
FAT	Forschungen zum Alten Testament
FRLANT	Forschungen zur Religion und Literatur des Alten und Neuen Testaments
GMary	*Gospel of Mary*
HSS	Harvard Semitic Studies
HTR	*Harvard Theological Review*
HUCA	*Hebrew Union College Annual*
IDB	George Arthur Buttrick (ed.), *The Interpreter's Dictionary of the Bible* (4 vols.; Nashville, TN: Abingdon Press, 1962)
IEJ	*Israel Exploration Journal*
Int	*Interpretation*
JAAR	*Journal of the American Academy of Religion*
JAOS	*Journal of the American Oriental Society*
JBL	*Journal of Biblical Literature*
JCS	*Journal of Cuneiform Studies*
JECS	*Journal of Early Christian Studies*
JETS	*Journal of the Evangelical Theological Society*
JJS	*Journal of Jewish Studies*
JNES	*Journal of Near Eastern Studies*
JQR	*Jewish Quarterly Review*
JR	*Journal of Religion*
JRS	*Journal of Roman Studies*
JSJ	*Journal for the Study of Judaism in the Persian, Hellenistic and Roman Period*
JSNT	*Journal for the Study of the New Testament*
JSNTSup	*Journal for the Study of the New Testament*, Supplement Series
JSOT	*Journal for the Study of the Old Testament*
JSOTSup	*Journal for the Study of the Old Testament*, Supplement Series
JSP	*Journal for the Study of the Pseudepigrapha*
JSS	*Journal of Semitic Studies*
JTS	*Journal of Theological Studies*
LCL	Loeb Classical Library
LE	Laws of Eshnunna
LGBTQI	Lesbian, Gay, Bisexual, Transgender, Queer and Intersexed community
LH	Laws of Hammurabi
LKA	Erich Ebeling, *Literarische Keilschrifttexte aus Assur* (Berlin: Akademie Verlag, 1931)
LXX	Septuagint (Greek versions of the Hebrew Bible)
MT	Masoretic Text
NAB	New American Bible

NIDB	Katharine Doob Sakenfeld (ed.), *New Interpreter's Dictionary of the Bible* (Nashville, TN: Abingdon Press, 2006–2009)
NIGTC	The New International Greek Testament Commentary
NIV	New International Version
NJB	*New Jerusalem Bible*
NovT	*Novum Testamentum*
NPNF¹	Philip Schaff (ed.), *The Nicene and Post-Nicene Fathers* (Series 1; 14 vols.; 1886–89; repr., Peabody, MA: Hendrickson, 1994)
NRSV	New Revised Standard Version
NTC	*New Testament Commentary* (Grand Rapids, MI: Baker Academic)
NTS	*New Testament Studies*
OPSNKF	Occasional Publications of the Samuel Noah Kramer Fund
OTE	*Old Testament Essays*
OTP	James Charlesworth (ed.), *Old Testament Pseudepigrapha*
PDM	'Papyri Demoticae Magicae', in Hans Dieter Betz (ed.), *The Greek Magical Papyrus in Translation including The Demotic Spells* (Chicago, IL: University of Chicago Press, 2nd edn, 1992)
PG	J.-P. Migne (ed.), *Patrologia cursus completa… Series graeca* (166 vols.; Paris: Petit-Montrouge, 1857–83)
PGM	K. Preisendanz (ed.), *Papyri graecae magicae*
PL	J.-P. Migne (ed.), *Patrologia cursus completus Series prima [latina]* (221 vols.; Paris: J.-P. Migne, 1844–65)
PRSt	*Perspectives in Religious Studies*
RA	*Revue d'assyriologie et d'archéologie orientale*
RB	*Revue biblique*
REB	*Revised English Bible*
ResQ	*Restoration Quarterly*
RevQ	*Revue de Qumran*
RSV	Revised Standard Version
RV	Revised Version
SAA	State Archives of Assyria
SBL	Society of Biblical Literature
SBLABS	Society of Biblical Literature Archaeology and Biblical Studies
SBLDS	SBL Dissertation Series
SBLEJL	SBL Early Judaism and Its Literature
SBLSS	SBL Semeia Studies
SciRel	*Sciences Religieuses*
SM	Sermon on the Mount
SNTSMS	Society for New Testament Studies Monograph Series
SP	Sermon on the Plain
ST	*Studia theologica*
StudRel	*Studies in Religion*
TA	Tel Alalakh Tablets
TAD	Bezalel Porten and Ada Yardeni, *Textbook of Aramaic Documents from Ancient Egypt* (4 vols.; Jerusalem: Hebrew University of Jerusalem, 1989–1999)
TDNT	Gerhard Kittel and Gerhard Friedrich (eds.), *Theological Dictionary of the New Testament* (trans. Geoffrey W. Bromiley; 10 vols.; Grand Rapids, MI: Eerdmans, 1964–)

TLOT	Ernst Jenni and Claus Westermann (eds.), *Theological Lexicon of the Old Testament* (trans. M.E. Biddle; 3 vols.; Peabody, MA: Hendrickson, 1997)
TRu	*Theologische Rundschau*
TS	*Theological Studies*
TU	Texte und Untersuchungen
TynBul	*Tyndale Bulletin*
VT	*Vetus Testamentum*
VTSup	*Vetus Testamentum*, Supplements
WMANT	Wissenschaftliche Monographien zum Alten und Neuen Testament
WTJ	*Westminster Theological Journal*
WUNT	Wissenschaftliche Untersuchungen zum Neuen Testament
ZA	*Zeitschrift für Assyriologie*
ZAW	*Zeitschrift für die alttestamentliche Wissenschaft*
ZNW	*Zeitschrift für die neutestamentliche Wissenschaft*
ZPE	*Zeitschrift für papyrologie und epigraphic*

Chapter 1

INTRODUCTION

This book began as an effort to address more thoroughly a recurrent and puzzling experience I encounter in biblical scholarship. I first mentioned this experience in my previous book, *Slavery, Abolitionism, and the Ethics of Biblical Scholarship.*[1] If one reads almost any treatise on Christian ethics written by academic biblical scholars, one finds something extremely peculiar: *Jesus never does anything wrong.* This oddity even flies in the face of Jesus' own reply to the man asking about how to secure eternal life: 'And Jesus said to him, "Why do you call me good? No one is good but God alone"' (Mk 10.18). The Gospels record others judging Jesus as immoral: 'the Son of man came eating and drinking, and they say, "Behold, a glutton and a drunkard, a friend of tax collectors and sinners!"' (Mt. 11.19).[2]

Allen Verhey's chapter, 'The Gospels and Christian Ethics', in *The Cambridge Companion to Christian Ethics* (2012) represents a view that I typically encounter: 'Jesus has always been acknowledged as somehow normative for moral reflection and formation in the church. How could it be otherwise?'[3] At first sight, 'normative for moral reflection' allows for the possibility of moral censure or criticism of Jesus, but that is normally not the case. Instead, any moral reflection usually leads to conclusions such as those expressed by Rudolf Schnackenburg, a prominent New Testament ethicist, in his *The Moral Teaching of the New Testament*:

> The Early Church, and with it, Christianity, throughout the centuries was profoundly convinced that the greatest of Jesus' achievements in the moral sphere was the promulgation of the chief commandment of love of God and

---

1. Hector Avalos, *Slavery, Abolitionism, and the Ethics of Biblical Scholarship* (Sheffield: Sheffield Phoenix Press, 2011), pp. 1-2.

2. John Kilgallen ('Was Jesus Right to Eat with Sinners and Tax Collectors?' *Bib* 93 [2013], pp. 590-600) argues that Jesus was justified by the repentance of those with whom he ate, as in the case of Zacchaeus, who agreed to repay those whom he had cheated (Lk. 19.8). See also Mary J. Marshall, 'Jesus: Glutton and Drunkard?', *Journal for the Study of the Historical Jesus* 3 (2005), pp. 47-60.

3. Allen Verhey, 'The Gospels and Christian Ethics', in *The Cambridge Companion to Christian Ethics* (ed. Robin Gill; Cambridge: Cambridge: Cambridge University Press, 2nd edn, 2012), pp. 41-53 (41).

one's neighbour. The message of Christian *agapē*, the model and highest expression of which is the mission of the Son of God to redeem the sinful human race, brought something new into the world, an idea and reality so vast and incomprehensible as to be the highest revelation of God, and quite inconceivable apart from revelation.[4]

For Schnackenburg, Jesus represents the acme of human ethical development. The rest of the book finds nothing but praise for Jesus, and not a whit of criticism.

Perhaps this unrelenting praise of Jesus' ethics can be expected because Schnackenburg was a Catholic priest with an openly Christian commitment. But if one examines the work of Richard Horsley, who spent most of his career at the University of Massachusetts, a public secular university, there is not much difference. For example, the worst thing about Jesus in Horsley's *Jesus and the Spiral of Violence* is this assessment:

> It would be difficult to claim that Jesus was a pacifist. But he actively opposed violence, particularly institutionalized oppressive and repressive violence, and its effects on a subject people. Jesus was apparently a revolutionary, but not a violent political revolutionary... Jesus preached and catalyzed a social revolution... 'Love your enemies' turns out to be not the apolitical pacific stance of one who stands above the turmoil of his day, nor a sober counsel of nonresistance to evil or oppression, but a revolutionary principle. It was a social revolutionary principle insofar as the love of enemies would transform local social-economic relations.[5]

For Horsley, even when this new revolutionary principle is threatening to the ruling social order, that threat is a good thing because it will help liberate people from oppression.

So it looks as if prominent scholars with open religious commitments and scholars with seemingly secular commitments can agree that Jesus never did anything wrong. This uniformly benign picture of Jesus' ethics is peculiar because when historians study Alexander the Great or Augustus Caesar, they note the good and the bad aspects of their actions.[6] When academic biblical scholars study Moses or David and other biblical figures,

---

4. Rudolf Schnackenburg, *The Moral Teaching of the New Testament* (trans. J. Holland-Smith and W.J. O'Hara; London: Burns and Oates, 1975), pp. 90-91.

5. Richard A. Horsley, *Jesus and the Spiral of Violence: Popular Jewish Resistance in Roman Palestine* (Minneapolis: Fortress Press, 1993), p. 326.

6. In particular, Alexander the Great had a hagiographic phase, represented by William W. Tarn, who authored a two-volume biography, *Alexander the Great* (Cambridge: Cambridge University Press, 1948). Such hagiographic treatments came under sharp criticism with the work of Harvard historian, Ernst Badian. See further Frank Holt, 'Alexander the Great Today: In the Interest of Historical Accuracy?', *Ancient History Bulletin* 13 (1999), pp. 111-17; Albert B. Bosworth and Elizabeth J. Baynham (eds.), *Alexander the Great in Fact and Fiction* (New York: Oxford University Press, 2000).

they might note their flaws.[7] Today, Gandhi and Martin Luther King, icons of peace and justice, have had biographies that painfully detail their personal flaws.[8]

Even the god of the Old Testament has been subjected to some ethical scrutiny, though not as frequently as could be the case. R. Norman Whybray, a noted biblical scholar, admits:

> The dark side of God is a subject that has received astonishingly little attention from Old Testament scholars. The standard Old Testament theologies, monographs, about the Old Testament doctrine of God, articles about particular passages, even commentaries are almost silent on the matter…even those that make reference to them have tended to play down such passages or sought to explain them away with a variety of arguments.[9]

Similarly, J. Cheryl Exum, who has pioneered feminist and literary approaches to the Bible, states that her approach:

> [R]ather than privileging God as a character beyond reproof, showing love, mercy and concern for all, treats God as a character to be subjected to the same judicious analysis and evaluation as all the other characters. Like

7. Joel Baden, *The Historical David: The Real Life of an Invented Hero* (New York: HarperOne, 2013); Baruch Halpern, *David's Secret Demons: Messiah, Murderer, Traitor, King* (Grand Rapids, MI: Eerdmans, 2001). For moral evaluations of other Old Testament figures, see Michael James Williams, *Deception in Genesis: An Investigation into the Morality of a Unique Biblical Phenomenon* (Studies in Biblical Literature, 32; Frankfurt: Peter Lang, 2001); Mary E. Mills, *Biblical Morality: Moral Perspectives in Old Testament Narratives* (Burlington, VT: Ashgate, 2001); Mikael Sjöberg, *Wrestling with Textual Violence: The Jephthah Narrative in Antiquity and Modernity* (The Bible in the Modern World, 4; Sheffield: Sheffield Phoenix Press, 2006).

8. For Gandhi, see Joseph Lelyveld, *Great Soul: Mahatma Gandhi and his Struggle with India* (New York: Alfred A. Knopf, 2011), especially p. 43, where it speaks of Gandhi's abusive behavior toward his wife. For some criticisms by a fellow civil rights colleague of Martin Luther King's personal and adulterous conduct, see Ralph David Abernathy, *And the Walls Came Tumbling Down: An Autobiography* (New York: Harper & Row, 1989), especially pp. 470-75.

9. R. Norman Whybray, '"Shall Not the Judge of the Earth Do What is Just?" God's Oppression of the Innocent in the Old Testament', in *Shall Not the Judge of the Earth Do What is Right? Studies in the Nature of God in Tribute to James L. Crenshaw* (ed. David Perchansky and Paul L. Redditt; Winona Lake, IN: Eisenbrauns, 2000), pp. 1-19 (2); R. Norman Whybray, 'The Immorality of God: Reflections on Some Passages in Genesis, Job, Exodus and Numbers', *JSOT* 21 (1996), pp. 89-120. See also Hector Avalos, 'Yahweh is a Moral Monster', in *The Christian Delusion: Why Faith Fails* (ed. John Loftus; Amherst, NY: Prometheus, 2010), pp. 209-36. For examples of evangelical Christian approaches, see Christian Hofreiter, 'Genocide in Deuteronomy and Christian Interpretation', in *Interpreting Deuteronomy: Issues and Approaches* (ed. David G. Firth and Philip S. Johnston; Downers Grove, IL: InterVarsity Press, 2012), pp. 240-62; Iain Provan, *Seriously Dangerous Religion: What the Old Testament Says and Why it Matters* (Waco, TX: Baylor University Press, 2014).

them, he has good and bad points, which is what makes him interesting. I am not saying that the Bible should not be used as a source of solace, assurance, and even empowerment. I am saying that those who use it this way have an agenda that is usually more pastoral than scholarly, and such a readerly position makes critical feminist scholarship as it is practiced elsewhere in the academy difficult.[10]

However, few scholars have applied Whybray's and Exum's insights when it comes to Jesus or the New Testament.[11]

One of the few scholars who has issued strong criticisms of Jesus' ethics is J. Harold Ellens, who wrote an article titled 'The Violent Jesus' for his multi-volume work on religion and violence.[12] Ellens remarks that Jesus had 'fits of violence' and that they 'happened more frequently than Christian tradition is willing to acknowledge'.[13] When discussing Jesus' use of the whip in the temple in Jn 2.15, Ellens remarks that Jesus

> picked up a riding crop or bullwhip and started to abuse those most available, expending his long anguished anger, his weariness with the spiritual mediocrity of human life, and his obsessive need to feel the power of his delusional vision of the triumphal Son of Man realized in the here and now.[14]

Although Ellens's use of psychoanalysis has been criticized, he provides an alternative vision of a Jesus who is not always morally upright or even emotionally stable.[15]

10. J. Cheryl Exum, 'Trusting in the God of their Fathers: A Response to the Articles by Robert Knetsch and Amanda Benckhuysen', in *Strangely Familiar: Protofeminist Interpretations of Patriarchal Biblical Texts* (ed. Nancy Calvert-Koyzis and Heather E. Weir; Atlanta, GA: Society of Biblical Literature, 2009), pp. 49-55 (54).

11. One of the exceptions is James A. Metzger, 'Where has Yahweh Gone? Reclaiming Unsavory Images of God in New Testament Studies', *Horizons in Biblical Theology* 31 (2009), pp. 51-76.

12. J. Harold Ellens, 'The Violent Jesus', in *The Destructive Power of Religion: Violence in Judaism, Christianity, and Islam* (ed. J. Harold Ellens; 4 vols.; Westport, CT: Praeger, 2004), III, pp. 15-37.

13. Ellens, 'The Violent Jesus', p. 16. I would not go as far as characterizing Jesus as a sort of psychopath suffering finally from some 'affective stupor' ('affektiven stupor') that cost him his life, as does Berthold Block, *Jesus und seine Jünger: Wege im Wahn: Beobachtungen zu Bibel, Kirche, Christenthum* (Forum Religionskritik, 9; Münster: LIT, 2009), especially p. 8, where my quote is found.

14. Ellens, 'The Violent Jesus', p. 32. See also Stephen Voorwinde, *Jesus' Emotions in the Gospels* (London: T. & T. Clark, 2011).

15. See, for example, the criticisms of Thomas R. Yoder Neufeld, *Killing Enmity: Violence and the New Testament* (Grand Rapids, MI: Baker Academic, 2011), pp. 68-70. For other examples of psychological and psychoanalytic approaches to the Bible, see J. Harold Ellens and Wayne G. Rollins (eds.), *Psychology and the Bible: A New Way to Read the Scriptures* (4 vols.; Westport, CT: Praeger, 2004); Helen Efthimiades-Keith,

Ed P. Sanders, who is famous for exposing Christian biases in New Testament scholarship, also has attempted a more humanized view of Jesus.[16] When speaking of the possibility that Jesus was in error about the timing of the eschaton, Sanders remarked:

> Naturally, many people, in the academy as well as in the church, wish to prevent Jesus from making an error, even one of timing; and so apocalyptic eschatology is an aspect of Judaism that many New Testament scholars would like to see eliminated from Christianity.[17]

Jack T. Sanders goes so far as to assert that 'Jesus provides no guide for ethics today', and he denied that the love commandment was central to New Testament ethics.[18] Rather, Sanders thought that Jesus lived in an eschatological milieu that is irrelevant today. He considered the epistle of James to offer a more promising ethical base because it 'best points beyond the disappointment of eschatological hopes to the real world and to everyday problems'.[19] However, Sanders did not voice any ethical criticisms of Jesus' own words or deeds.

Nil Guillemette expresses another apparent criticism when he notes that Jesus does not seem to follow literally some of his own commandments, including calling the Pharisees fools (Mt. 23.17) after he had prohibited using such terms of abuse in Mt. 5.22. To solve such problems, Guillemette advocates '*absolute* fidelity and at the same time *non-literal* fidelity'.[20] For Guillemette, 'Jesus does not give directives, but rather direction'.[21] In other words, Guillemette is still trying to reconcile Jesus' deeds with his own pronouncements, which he thinks still should be followed today. But Guillemette is not willing to accuse Jesus of being a

The Enemy Within: A Jungian Psychoanalytic Approach to the Book of Judith (Biblical Interpretation, 67; Leiden: E.J. Brill, 2004); Martin Leiner, 'Neutestamentliche Exegese zwischen "Psycholatrie" und "Psychophobie"', *EvT* 65 (2005), pp. 148-54; Agustín Caballero Arenciba, *Psicoanálisis y Biblia: El psicoanálisis aplicado a la investigación de textos bíblicos* (Salamanca: Universidad Pontificia de Salamanca, 1994).

16. On Christian biases in the study of Judaism in the New Testament, see Ed P. Sanders, *Paul and Palestinian Judaism: A Comparison of Patterns of Religion* (Philadelphia, PA: Fortress Press, 1977).

17. Ed P. Sanders, 'Jesus, Ancient Judaism, and Modern Christianity: The Quest Continues', in *Jesus, Judaism, and Christian Anti-Judaism: Reading the New Testament after the Holocaust* (ed. Paula Fredriksen and Adele Reinhartz; Louisville, KY: Westminster/John Knox Press, 2002), pp. 31-55 (44).

18. Jack T. Sanders, *Ethics in the New Testament* (London: SCM Press, 1986), p. xiv.

19. Sanders, *Ethics in the New Testament*, p. xiv.

20. Nil Guillemette, 'The Sermon on the Mount: Feasible Ethics?, *Landas* 9 (1995), pp. 209-36 (222). Guillemette's italics.

21. Guillemette, 'The Sermon on the Mount', p. 235.

hypocrite who does not practice what he preaches. One wonders if Guillemette would use the word 'hypocrite' for anyone else who does not practice what he or she preaches.

Non-Christian scholars have voiced criticisms of how Jesus has been viewed in Christian ethics. Adele Reinhartz notes the reluctance of many scholars to see Jesus in a bad ethical light. Insofar as questions of Jesus' anti-Judaism in the Gospel of John are concerned, Reinhartz remarks: 'Many scholars do, however, attempt to reconcile or, one might even say, to explain away the apparent anti-Jewish rhetoric of both the text and its portrayal of Jesus'.[22]

Compared to what Charles F. Dole (1845–1927) was writing back in 1908, it looks as if New Testament scholarship has regressed in its ability to humanize Jesus. Dole's book, *What We Know about Jesus* (1908) is as refreshing today as it was then, though it is still very unfamiliar to many modern New Testament ethicists. Dole was a Unitarian minister who hoped that the world had gone beyond the divinization of Jesus in modern critical scholarship. He remarks:

> The new judgment of the Bible inevitably touches the person of Jesus. We cannot continue lightly to take for granted certain easy assumptions about him. Whereas the world has worshiped him as a God for many centuries, the whole modern tendency is to think of him as a man... The deity of Jesus, not his humanity, took pretty nearly the whole emphasis. Now that all will allow that Jesus was a real man, it is high time to try to find out what it is to be a man. To be a man is to suffer limitations; it is not to know everything, but often to be misinformed; it is to share in the ideas of one's own time and people...[23]

Dole soon left no doubt that viewing Jesus as a man meant being frank about his flaws, ethically and otherwise. For example, when discussing the Gospel of John, Dole observed:

> [T]he general portraiture of Jesus in the Fourth Gospel hardly impresses us as winning or lovable. We are constantly disturbed by the language of egoism and self-assertion continuously put into Jesus' mouth... All this portraiture, judged by our highest standards of conduct, is unworthy of the best type of man, not to say a good God.[24]

Dole also rebuffs Jesus for not showing the Pharisees 'any sympathy', and so anticipated many of the discussions one sees today about anti-Judaism in

---

22. Adele Reinhartz, 'The Gospel of John: How "The Jews" Became Part of the Plot', in Fredriksen and Reinhartz (eds.), *Jesus, Judaism, and Christian Anti-Judaism*, pp. 99-116 (111).

23. Charles F. Dole, *What We Know about Jesus* (Chicago, IL: Open Court, 1908), p. vii.

24. Dole, *What We Know about Jesus*, pp. 15-16.

the New Testament.[25] Dole explicitly denounces Jesus' actions in the temple in Jn 2.15, and remarks: 'as a man, Jesus had not warrant to lift the whip over men and to destroy their property'.[26]

Overall, Dole rejected attempts to idolize Jesus or render him a paradigm of modern ethics. For Dole, 'Our actual ideal, on the contrary, is that of a patriot, a husband and father, a man of affairs, a man of the world, in the highest sense of the word'.[27] Discussions of the ethics of Jesus by Dole in 1908 illuminate the peculiarity of the modern academic study of Jesus' ethics. From a purely historical viewpoint, Jesus is a man and not a god. *Jesus should have flaws*. Dole acknowledged that in 1908, but most modern New Testament ethicists do not.

So how is it that most current academic biblical scholars still do not consider anything that Jesus does as wrong or evil? The answer, of course, is that most biblical scholars, whether in secular academia or in seminaries, still see Jesus as divine, and not as a human being with faults. Their Christology is high enough to exempt Jesus from any evil sentiments or ethical malpractice.[28] The feminist scholar Mary Daly argues, as I do, that '[a] great deal of Christian doctrine has been docetic, that is, it has not seriously accepted the fact that Jesus was a limited human being'.[29]

Most New Testament scholars are affiliated with religious institutions and are part of what I have called an ecclesial-academic complex that has no counterpart in any other areas of the humanities. For example, most, if not all, scholars of Greek religion are not part of some Greek religious movement or organization. Despite biases that always exist in the study of the classics, it is fair to say that few have any personal stake in whether Zeus or Tiberius was good or bad because those entities don't constitute any sort of authority for their actions. That is not the case with Jesus, who is still viewed as the paradigmatic authority for most Christian scholars.

Such scholars are still studying Jesus through the confessional lenses of Nicea or Chalcedon rather than through an historical approach that we would use with other human beings. In fact, Luke Timothy Johnson, a well-known NT scholar at Emory University, remarks:

> We can go further and state that the basic 'historical' claims of the Nicene Creed are well supported: 'He was born of the virgin Mary, suffered under Pontius Pilate, was crucified, died, and was buried'...in essence, what the

---

25. Dole, *What We Know about Jesus*, p. 22.

26. Dole, *What We Know about Jesus*, p. 24.

27. Dole, *What We Know about Jesus*, p. 78.

28. For a study of early Christology, see Charles H. Talbert, *The Development of Christology during the First Hundred Years and Other Essays in Early Christian Christology* (Supplements to Novum Testamentum, 140; Leiden: E.J. Brill, 2011).

29. Mary Daly, *Beyond God the Father* (Boston, MA: Beacon Press, 1973), p. 69.

most universally used Christian creed asserts about the human person Jesus is historically verifiable.[30]

Although Johnson realizes that many of the supernatural claims about Jesus cannot be validated historically, he adds that '[t]he only real validation for the claim that Christ is what the creed claims him to be, that is, light from light, true God from true God, is to be found in the quality of life demonstrated by those who make his confession'.[31] Johnson, of course, assumes that this 'quality of life' based on imitating Jesus must be completely good.

Basic Elements of the Argument

In a previous book, *The End of Biblical Studies* (2007), I showed how the main subfields of biblical scholarship are permeated with religionist assumptions that present themselves as objective descriptive scholarship.[32] Such fields include archaeology, history, textual criticism, literary aesthetics, and translation. Examining those fields shows how biblical scholarship is preoccupied with retaining the Bible's relevance when its own findings paradoxically show the opposite.[33]

I followed that book with *Slavery, Abolitionism, and the Ethics of Biblical Scholarship* (2011), which examined how modern biblical scholarship was still preoccupied with mitigating or defending ideas and practices involving slavery in the Bible.[34] Modern biblical scholarship still functions largely as a defense of biblical slavery. In that book, I did examine Jesus' views on imperialism and slavery, but I soon realized that Jesus' views on other issues may be equally or more offensive to modern codes of ethics.

I decided to engage in a broader exploration of Jesus' ethics as a vehicle to critique the religionist and Christian orientation of modern biblical scholarship. Briefly, my broader argument has the following interrelated elements:

1. Biblical scholarship is still primarily a religionist apologetic enterprise despite claims to be engaging in historico-critical and descriptive scholarship.
2. A more specific Christian orientation is clearly revealed in the manner in which the ethics of Jesus are predominantly viewed as

30. Luke Timothy Johnson, *The Real Jesus: The Misguided Quest for the Historical Jesus and the Truth of the Traditional Gospels* (New York: HarperSanFrancisco, 1996), pp. 126-27.

31. Johnson, *The Real Jesus*, p. 168.

32. Hector Avalos, *The End of Biblical Studies* (Amherst, NY: Prometheus, 2007).

33. For a defense of relevance, see W.A. Meeks, 'Why Study the New Testament?', *NTS* 51 (2005), pp. 155-70.

34. Avalos, *Slavery*.

benign and paradigmatic, even among supposedly secular academic scholars.

3. However, many of the fundamental ethical principles announced or practiced by Jesus actually would be antithetical to those we otherwise describe as 'acceptable' or 'good' by some of the most widely accepted standards of ethics today.

4. Accordingly, such a predominantly benign view of Jesus' ethics signals a continuing acceptance of Jesus as divine or as morally supra-human, and not as the flawed human being who should be the real subject of historico-critical study.

Each element of my thesis requires a few preliminary remarks. A religionist orientation refers to one that attempts to preserve or promote the value of religion, which I define as a mode of life and thought that presupposes the existence of, and relationship with, supernatural beings and/or forces. I will not enter here into the debate over the proper definition of religion, but I have defended my definition elsewhere.[35] Alternatively phrased, a religionist orientation argues that religion is essential for human life and/ or generally conducive to human welfare and social advances. In its Christian form, a religionist orientation holds that the Bible is generally a good guide for ethics today.[36] By referring to the 'continuing acceptance of Jesus as divine or as morally supra-human' I intend to include scholarship that, while not accepting Jesus as divine, still regards him as heralding a superior system of ethics. As I will show in the case of medical ethics, protecting a benign image of Jesus' ethics sometimes involves de-supernaturalizing him.

When I claim that many of Jesus' ethical principles and practices described in the New Testament would be antithetical to those encoded in the sets of ethics that are widely accepted today, I am speaking primarily of those enshrined in the United Nations' Universal Declaration of Human Rights (UDHR), which has an arguable position as the consensus of most nations today. For example, one can say that there is widespread agreement

---

35. Most recently in Hector Avalos, 'Religion and Scarcity: A New Theory for the Role of Religion in Violence', in *The Oxford Handbook of Religion and Violence* (ed. Mark Juergensmeyer, Margo Kitts and Michael Jerryson; New York: Oxford University Press, 2013), pp. 554-70. A discussion of the role of biblical studies in secular universities may be found in William Arnal, 'What Branches Grow out of this Stony Rubbish? Christian Origins and the Study of Religion', *StudRel/SciRel* 39 (2010), pp. 549-72 (551).

36. A critique of the religionist and supernaturalist stance of New Testament studies is offered by Zeba Crook, 'On the Treatment of Miracles in New Testament Scholarship', *StudRel/SciRel* 40 (2011), pp. 461-78. Religionist defenses for New Testament studies include Harold W. Attridge, 'Can We Trust the Bible?', *Reflections* 92.1 (2005), pp. 4-9; Meeks, 'Why Study the New Testament?'

with Article 4, which states: 'No one shall be held in slavery or servitude; slavery and the slave trade shall be prohibited in all their forms'.[37] As Francis Adeney notes, there is also the Declaration of Human Rights by the World's Religions (1998), which is based on the UDHR.[38] Since the UDHR has been formally adopted by so many nations, it is best to view it as the most accepted expression of global ethics.

For my purposes, modern western ethics also includes the notion of equality, insofar as all human beings are thought to be equal in terms of life, liberty, and the pursuit of happiness. This idea is included in Article 1 of the Universal Declaration: 'All human beings are born free and equal in dignity and rights. They are endowed with reason and conscience and should act towards one another in a spirit of brotherhood.'[39] Democracy or republicanism is viewed as the ideal form of government in modern western ethics. Laws based on the consent of the governed are key to the entire legal structure of modern society. Article 21(1) of the Universal Declaration embodies this concept: 'Everyone has the right to take part in the government of his country, directly or through freely chosen representatives.'[40]

I speak of ethical principles enunciated or practiced by Jesus with full cognizance that Jesus is largely (or even completely) the construct of later writers in the New Testament. I am well aware of all the historical problems that beset anyone attributing any particular action or idea to Jesus.[41]

---

37. United Nations, *The Universal Declaration of Human Rights, 1948*. [Online: http://www.un.org/en/documents/udhr/.]

38. See Frances Adeney, 'Comparative Religious Ethics', in Joel B. Green (ed.), *Dictionary of Scripture and Ethics* (Grand Rapids, MI: Baker Academic, 2011), pp. 152-57 (154). For the text of the draft, see the letter by Arvind Sharma, 'Universal Declaration of Human Rights by the World's Religions', *Journal of Religious Ethics* 27 (1999), pp. 539-44. A revised version is online: http://gcwr2011.org/pdf/UDHRWR_en.pdf. For a study of the impact of the UDHR, see Louis Henken, 'Religion, Religions, and Human Rights', *Journal of Religious Ethics* 26 (1998), pp. 229-39. For a human rights focus in New Testament studies, see Adrian Long, *Paul and Human Rights: A Dialogue with the Father of the Corinthian Community* (Sheffield: Sheffield Phoenix Press, 2009).

39. United Nations, *Universal Declaration of Human Rights, 1948*. For a general philosophical treatment of inequality, see Amartya Sen, *Inequality Reexamined* (New York: Oxford University Press, 1992).

40. United Nations, *Universal Declaration of Human Rights, 1948*.

41. The literature on the 'historical' Jesus is enormous, but the more recent skeptical approaches to historicity may be found in Richard Carrier, *On the Historicity of Jesus: Why We Might have Reason to Doubt* (Sheffield: Sheffield Phoenix Press, 2014); Thomas L. Thompson and Thomas S. Verenna (eds.), *'Is This Not the Carpenter?' The Question of the Historicity of the Figure of Jesus* (London: Equinox, 2012); Raphael Lataster, *There was No Jesus, There is No God: A Scholarly Examination of the Scientific, Historical and Philosophical Evidence and Arguments for Monotheism* (Charleston, SC: CreateSpace Independent Publishing Platform, 2013). A defense of Jesus' historicity from what I would call a 'minimalist historical Jesus' view, is that of the

I have already commented on these problems in *Health Care and the Rise of Christianity* (1999), which argued that many followers of Christianity may have been attracted by certain benefits that Christianity offered when compared to other health-care options in the Greco-Roman world.[42] In particular, the emphasis on faith in healing mitigated cost and did not impose burdens, such as traveling to distant shrines or obtaining costly medicinal substances, that other health-care options emphasized. I devoted an entire chapter in *The End of Biblical Studies* to the flaws and circularity of both conservative and liberal (e.g., Jesus Seminar) reconstructions of Jesus.[43]

For the record, I am an agnostic when it comes to the historical Jesus. I am not a so-called 'Jesus mythicist', nor am I concerned in this book with the question of Jesus' resurrection. I do affirm that we do not have sufficient data from the actual time of Jesus to fully corroborate any particular portrayal of Jesus that one finds in the Gospels.[44] For me, the inability to reconstruct any 'original' or 'real' Jesus is a philosophical problem as well as an historical one. Without direct access to the original Jesus, all we would have are the earliest traditions about what Jesus said and did. Identifying the earliest traditions about Jesus would not prove that Jesus said or did anything. Only having direct access to the original Jesus would allow modern scholars to accurately compare the extant representations with any 'original'. That access is not historically possible, and that is why the 'earliest' traditions about Jesus should not be equated with the 'original' or 'actual' historical Jesus.[45] Assertions about what anyone would or would not make up about Jesus in 'a Jewish context' are not compelling because we don't have a complete picture of the Judaisms at the time of Jesus.[46] Radical innova-

self-described agnostic scholar, Bart Ehrman, *Did Jesus Exist?: The Historical Argument for Jesus of Nazareth Scholarship* (New York: HarperOne, 2013). For some representative works that challenge the usual criteria for historicity, see Rafael Rodriguez, 'Authenticating Criteria: The Use and Misuse of a Critical Method', *Journal for the Study of the Historical Jesus* 7 (2009), pp. 152-67.

42. Hector Avalos, *Health Care and the Rise of Christianity* (Peabody, MA: Hendrickson, 1999).

43. Avalos, *The End of Biblical Studies*, pp. 185-218.

44. See my discussion of the circularity in determining what Jesus said or taught in Avalos, *The End of Biblical Studies*, pp. 198-209, which includes a critique of the criteria for determining Jesus' words and language used by Jesus presented in Stanley Porter, *The Criteria for Authenticity in Historical-Jesus Research: Previous Discussions and New Proposals* (Sheffield: Sheffield Academic Press, 2000). Similar objections of circularity could be made for the criteria proposed in the essays found in Bruce Chilton and Craig E. Evans (eds.), *Authenticating the Words of Jesus* (Boston, MA and Leiden: E.J. Brill, 2002).

45. See my more elaborate arguments in Avalos, *The End of Biblical Studies*, especially pp. 69-72, 203-209.

46. One example is James F. McGrath (*The Burial of Jesus: History and Faith*

tions are possible and have been posited for other featues of Jesus that supposedly don't accord with the Judaism of the time.

Since we only have diverse representations of any supposed original
form of Jesus' teachings, then scholars ultimately pick and choose what
representation agrees with their opinion of Jesus' historical teachings. There
is no inherent reason, for example, why the violent Jesus is any less 'original' than the peaceful Jesus. Since some Jews in the first century favored
apocalyptic approaches and others may have favored 'wisdom' or 'cynic'
approaches to life, there is no way of knowing which approach any 'real
Jesus' favored. Once one chooses one of these alternative portraits, one can
discount those representations that do not agree as deviations, additions or
corruptions. But the very existence of such radically different possible portraits of Jesus is evidence that there is something inherently wrong with the
methodology of most historical Jesus research.

Nonetheless, the fact remains that most biblical scholars still view Jesus'
ethics as benign and normative for today despite all the problems with
ascertaining what Jesus actually said or did in history. Indeed, none of the
diversity in Jesus' portraits has deterred scholars from attributing a uniformly benign set of ethics to Jesus. My contention is that such diversity
and historical problems are addressed much like theologians address other
problems in the Bible. They use a diverse set of hermeneutical tools to preserve the benignity of Jesus and to eliminate or sanitize anything that may
be offensive today.

My argument here is not that any supposed historical Jesus was good or
bad. My subject matter is the portraits in the New Testament of a man called
Jesus.[47] As such, my approach echoes that of Frank Matera, who remarked
that his study of Matthew focused on 'the ethical teachings of Jesus as presented by the Evangelist Matthew rather than upon the historical Jesus'.[48]

[Englewood, CO: Patheos Press, 2011], p. 63): 'a "crucified Messiah"…is simply not
something that anyone in a Jewish context in that time would make up'.

47. See also Susan E. Meyers (ed.), *Portraits of Jesus: Studies in Christology*
(WUNT, 2.321; Tübingen: Mohr Siebeck, 2012). Less satisfactory are references to any
'remembrances' of Jesus that suppose that the remembrances are accurate or correspond
to any 'historical Jesus'. See James D.G. Dunn, *Jesus Remembered: Christianity in the
Making, Volume 1* (Grand Rapids, MI: Eerdmans, 2003); James D.G. Dunn, *Beginning
from Jerusalem: Christianity in the Making, Volume 2* (Grand Rapids, MI: Eerdmans,
2008).

48. Frank Matera, *New Testament Ethics: The Legacies of Jesus and Paul* (Louisville,
KY: Westminster/John Knox Press, 1996), p. 36. See also R.K. McIver, *Mainstream or
Marginal? The Matthean Community in Early Christianity* (Friedensauer Schriftenreihe,
Reihe A: Theologie, 12; Frankfurt: Peter Lang, 2012). For similar approaches to John,
see Jan G. van der Watt and Ruben Zimmerman (eds.), *Rethinking the Ethics of John:
'Implicit Ethics' in the Johannine Writings* (Kontexte und Normen neutestamentlicher

My project aims to explore how modern New Testament ethicists attempt to sanitize and protect those portraits, regardless of how historical they may be. Whether Jesus did or said anything claimed in the Gospels is not as important as the fact that those portrayals have become normative for modern Christians. Otherwise, I can agree with Kurt Noll, who argues that 'any quest for a historical Jesus is irrelevant to an understanding of the earliest social movements that evolved into the religion now called Christianity'.[49]

My lack of interest in reconstructing the ethics of the historical Jesus does not mean that there are no methodological advances that can be achieved by humanizing the portrayed ethics of Jesus. The removal of the hagiographic approach to Jesus' ethics can generate new insights into the sources of the ethics attributed to Jesus. In particular, I will show how often Jesus' so-called innovations are a continuation of ethics of Near Eastern, Jewish and Greco-Roman traditions.[50] Other times, I will show how Jesus can be seen as regressive relative to earlier 'advances' in features called innovative in Jesus. In the final analysis, this study aims to show that there is no reason to regard anything Jesus taught or did as authoritative for modern ethics.

Insofar as I believe that theism is itself unethical and has the potential to destroy our planet, I identify myself with what is called 'the New Atheism'.[51] For my purposes, the New Atheism describes a post September 11, 2001 (9/11) phenomenon, which viewed that event as illustrative of the potential of religion to bring global war and even the destruction of our ecosphere.[52] For that reason, what is distinctive about the New Atheism is

Ethik/Contexts and Norms for New Testament Ethics, 3; WUNT, 2.291; Tübingen: Mohr Siebeck, 2012).

49. Kurt L. Noll, 'Investigating Earliest Christianity without Jesus', in Thompson and Verenna (eds.), *'Is This Not the Carpenter?*, pp. 163-84 (167).

50. For a study of how the Roman empire was portrayed by Christian apologists, see Jörg Rüpke, *Von Jupiter zu Christus: Religionsgeschichte im römischer Zeit* (Darmstadt: Wissenschaftliche Buchgesellschaft, 2011).

51. See Jaco Gericke, 'A Fourth Paradigm? Some Thoughts on Atheism in Old Testament Scholarship', *OTE* 25 (2012), pp. 518-33. The main initial expositions of the New Atheism are in Richard Dawkins, *The God Delusion* (New York: Bantam, 2006); Sam Harris, *The End of Faith: Religion, Terror, and the Future of Reason* (New York: W.W. Norton, 2004), and Christopher Hitchens, *god is not Great: How Religion Poisons Everything* (New York: Twelve Books, 2007). Unfortunately, Dawkins, Harris, and Hitchens, among other New Atheists, are untrained in biblical studies, and so perpetuate much misinformation about the Bible and its cultural context.

52. According to Victor Stenger (*The New Atheism: Taking a Stand for Science and Reason* [Amherst, NY: Prometheus, 2009], p. ii), who describes himself as a New Atheist, the New Atheism was motivated primarily by 9/11 and began with 'a series of six best-selling books that took a harder line against religion than had been the custom among secularists'. Harris (*The End of Faith*, p. 323) states that he 'began writing this book on September 12, 2001', which clearly shows the link between 9/11 and the rise

a type of secular apocalypticism, but one based on scientific grounds rather than on supernatural revelation. The New Atheism features a more vocal and anti-theist stance (rather than just passively atheist stance) as embodied in the writings of Richard Dawkins, Sam Harris and Christopher Hitchens. Although not as well known as these writers, there also has emerged a group of biblical scholars who, while not necessarily describing themselves as 'New Atheists', do openly identify themselves as atheist, secular or agnostic (e.g., Kenneth Atkinson Robert Cargill, Richard Carrier, Bart Ehrman, James Linville and Gerd Lüdemann). James Crossley, the British New Testament scholar, rightly notes that 'a number of scholars have now been defined by themselves or others as "secular", "atheist", or "agnostic" in work that has received a notable degree of scholarly and public attention'.[53] But perhaps the most salient feature of the New Atheism is that it has gone beyond the basic philosophical and scientific arguments against God and the Bible. The New Atheism emphasizes the immorality of religious thinking itself. It challenges the ethics of Christianity and the Bible, in particular.

Alternatively, some may group me with 'the New Secularism', a term recently championed by Roland Boer.[54] However, I differ from Boer's New Secularism in that I do not see any 'emancipatory' uses for the Bible.[55] I affirm that liberation means liberation from the use of any ancient text for modern ethics.[56] The religionist and secularist divide is one that is very

of the New Atheism. On the New Atheism among ethnic minorities, see Hector Avalos, 'The Hidden Enlightenment: Humanism among US Latinos', *Essays in the Philosophy of Humanism* 20 (2012), pp. 3-14.

53. James G. Crossley, 'Can John's Gospel be Used to Reconstruct a Life of Jesus? An Assessment of Recent Trends and a Defence of a Traditional View', in Thompson and Verenna (eds.), *'Is This Not the Carpenter?'*, pp. 163-84 (167). See also James G. Crossley, *Jesus in an Age of Terror: Scholarly Projects for a New American Century* (London: Equinox, 2008); James G. Crossley, *Jesus in an Age of Neoliberalism: Quests, Scholarship, and Ideology* (London: Equinox, 2012), p. 136.

54. An elaboration of the 'New Secularism' is offered by Roland Boer, *Rescuing the Bible* (Blackwell Manifestos; Malden, MA: Blackwell, 2007), especially pp. 6-32; Roland Boer (ed.), *Secularism and Biblical Studies* (London: Equinox, 2010); Roland Boer, *Marxist Criticism of the Bible* (Sheffield: Sheffield Academic Press, 2003). See also Jacques Berlinerblau, *The Secular Bible: Why Nonbelievers Must Take Religion Seriously* (Cambridge: Cambridge University Press, 2005); idem, *How to be Secular: A Call to Arms for Religious Freedom* (New York: Houghton Mifflin Harcourt, 2012); Randall Reed, *A Clash of Ideologies: Marxism, Liberation Theology and Apocalypticism* (Princeton Theological Monograph Series; Eugene, OR: Pickwick Press, 2009). Despite the title, Reed offers significant attention to the increasing role of secularist scholars within the Society of Biblical Literature.

55. Boer (*Rescuing the Bible*, p. 32) has 'supporting emancipatory uses' of the Bible as one of his five features of the New Secularism.

56. Hector Avalos, 'The End of Biblical Studies as a Moral Obligation', in *Secularism and Biblical Studies* (ed. Roland Boer; London: Equinox, 2010), pp. 85-100.

apparent in the Society of Biblical Literature, the largest organization of professional biblical scholars in the world.[57]

Although most standard works in New Testament ethics were written before there was a conscious interaction with the New Atheism, some scholars recognize that the New Atheists are forcing Christian scholars to address ethical issues. In his comments about Jesus' eschatology, Ken Esau, a pacifist Christian scholar, remarks, 'the New Atheists have played a significant role in pressing Christians to deal with this issue more directly'.[58] So, perhaps, one can view atheist biblical scholars as 'Second Wave New Atheists' to contrast with the non-biblical scholars that dominated the first wave. Readers should view the present work as the first systematic New Atheist challenge to New Testament ethics by a biblical scholar.[59]

New Testament Ethics in Historical Context

According to one textbook definition, '[e]thics…deals with what is right or wrong in human behavior and conduct'.[60] Within biblical studies per se, Eckart Otto, one of the foremost biblical ethicists, provides another: 'Ethics, as a theory of morals, considers maxims of conduct from the viewpoint of the normative good, seeking its philosophical foundations and consequences of good action'.[61]

Charles H. Cosgrove refers to one possible view of New Testament ethics as entailing 'a historical treatment of earliest Christian morality in its original environment as reflected in the writing that make up the NT'.[62]

---

57. See John J. Collins, 'Faith, Scholarship, and the Society of Biblical Literature', in *Foster Biblical Scholarship: Essays in Honor of Kent Harold Richards* (ed. Frank Ritchel Ames and Charles William Miller; Atlanta, GA: Society of Biblical Literature, 2010), pp. 64-81; Ronald Hendel, 'Farewell to the SBL: Faith, Reason, and Biblical Studies', *BARev* 36 (2010), pp. 28, 74; Hector Avalos, 'The Ideology of the Society of Biblical Literature and the Demise of an Academic Profession', *SBL Forum* (April 2006). Online: http://www.sbl-site.org/publications/article.aspx?ArticleId=520.

58. Ken Esau, 'Disturbing Divine Behavior: Seibert's Solution to the Problem of the Old Testament God', *Direction: A Mennonite Brethren Forum* 40 (2011), pp. 168-78 (178). Online: http://www.directionjournal.org/40/2/disturbing-scholarly-behavior-seiberts.html.

59. In this regard, the present work is different from that of Bart Ehrman, *God's Problem: How the Bible Fails to Answer our Most Important Questions—Why We Must Suffer* (New York: HarperCollins, 2008), which centers on issues of theodicy, and is not a critique of the religionism in the field of New Testament ethics itself.

60. Jacques P. Thiroux and Keith W. Krasemann, *Ethics: Theory and Practice* (Upper Saddle River, NJ: Prentice–Hall, 2009), p. 2.

61. Eckart Otto, 'Law and Ethics', in *Religions of the Ancient World* (ed. Sarah Iles Johnson; Cambridge, MA: Harvard University Press, 2004), pp. 84-97 (84).

62. Charles H. Cosgrove, 'New Testament Ethics', in Green (ed.), *Dictionary of Scripture and Ethics*, pp. 548-52 (548).

By 'New Testament ethicists', I refer primarily to those who have written general surveys of the New Testament ethics (e.g., Richard Burridge, Joel B. Green, Richard Hays, Frank Matera, Russell Pregeant, Wolfgang Schrage, Allen Verhey), and especially those that include the word 'ethics' or 'moral(ity)' in the titles of their works. However, there are other works that don't include the word 'ethics' or 'moral(ity)', and yet are heavily focused on ethics or on more restricted areas of ethics (e.g., ecological ethics, gender) that will be included (e.g., Elisabeth Schüssler Fiorenza, Joanna Dewey, Elaine Wainwright). A second feature in what I denominate 'New Testament ethicists' is their association with academia, whether secular or religious. Their works are represented to be academic works. Accordingly, I will not include the recent work by Joseph Ratzinger (Pope Benedict XVI), as he does not claim to be doing historical-critical ethics in the same way.[63]

The vast majority of treatises on the ethics of Jesus are the product of Christian scholars. There is nothing particularly surprising about this fact, especially given that the biblical scholarship was born within the Jewish and Christian communities for whom the Bible is an authoritative text. After all, the sciences and many of the liberal arts originally were thought to be in the service of the church. Astronomy, for example, was useful in calculating important dates in the Christian calendar. The study of music was encouraged because of its use in ecclesiastical liturgy.

By the late nineteenth century there was an active effort to introduce more critical and scientific methods to the study of the history of the biblical materials in their Near Eastern context. These efforts were facilitated by the discoveries in Mesopotamia and Egypt that illuminated the continuities between other ancient Near Eastern texts (e.g., The Code of Hammurabi, *The Epic of Gilgamesh*) and the Bible. New discoveries of papyri and archaeological work had similar effects on the study of the New Testament.

Also in the late nineteenth century a new culture of 'professionals' was emerging across the sciences and humanities. According to Burton J. Bledstein, an acute historian of academia, the culture of professionalism in

---

63. The main works of interest here include Joseph Ratzinger, Pope Benedict XVI, *Jesus of Nazareth: From the Baptism in the Jordan to the Transfiguration* (trans. Adrian Walker; New York: Doubleday, 2007); idem, *Jesus of Nazareth: Part 2. Holy Week. From the Entrance into Jerusalem to the Resurrection* (trans. P.J. Whitmore; San Francisco: Ignatius, 2011). On the alleged theological tendentiousness of the English edition versus the original German edition, see Marianne Sawicki, 'Review of Jesus of Nazareth by Joseph Ratzinger', *Fourth R* 20.6 (2007), pp. 20-22. For the German editions, see Joseph Ratzinger, *Jesus von Nazareth*. I. *Von der Taufe im Jordan zur Verklärung* (Freiburg: Herder, 2007). For a study of Ratzinger's views on Jesus, see Adrian Pabst and Angus Addison (eds.), *The Pope and Jesus of Nazareth: Christ, Scripture and the Church* (London: SCM Press, 2009).

America began around the end of the Civil War, amidst a struggle to validate an emerging middle class.[64] Indeed, in the 1860s through 1880s, we have already this partial but impressive list of new organizations:[65]

1864	American Ophthalmological Society
1868	American Otological Society
1876	American Chemical Society
1880	American Society of Chemical Engineers
1880	Society of Biblical Literature and Exegesis
1883	American Ornithologists Union
1883	American Society of Naturalists
1884	American Climatological Society
1885	American Institute of Electrical Engineers
1888	Geological Society of America
1888	American Pediatric Society

Right in the middle of this growth is the Society of Biblical Literature and Exegesis, which later shortened its name to the Society of Biblical Literature.[66]

The members of the Society of Biblical Literature also wanted a profession that was somewhat independent of church control. Charles Cosgrove explains that '[o]nly in the past 150 years or so has "New Testament ethics" been a subject distinct from theology or separate from the task of giving practical instructions to the church'.[67] Some scholars were growing fonder of the critical methods germinating in Europe, particularly in England and Germany. The response of American biblical scholars was mixed. In particular, they wanted to be part of the 'research' oriented approaches that had come to America from Germany.[68] Nonetheless, the first members

64. Burton J. Bledstein, *The Culture of Professionalism: The Middle Class and the Development of Higher Education in America* (New York: Norton & Norton, 1976). See also Alvin W. Gouldner, *The Future of Intellectuals and the Rise of the New Class* (New York: Oxford University Press, 1979).

65. Bledstein, *The Culture of Professionalism*, pp. 85-86.

66. See Ernest W. Saunders, *Searching the Scriptures: A History of the Society of Biblical Literature, 1880–1980* (Chico, CA: Scholars Press, 1982); Stephen D. Moore and Yvonne Sherwood, *The Invention of the Biblical Scholar: A Critical Manifesto* (Minneapolis: Fortress Press, 2011); Timothy K. Beal, *The Rise and Fall of the Bible: The Unexpected History of an Accidental Book* (Boston, MA: Houghton Mifflin, 2011); Keith Ward, *The Word of God? The Bible after Modern Scholarship* (London: SPCK, 2010).

67. Cosgrove, 'New Testament Ethics', p. 548. But see C. Kavin Rowe, 'New Testament Theology: The Revival of a Discipline. A Review of Recent Contributions to the Field', *JBL* 125 (2006), pp. 393-410.

68. See Michael C. Legaspi, *The Death of Scripture and the Rise of Biblical Studies* (New York: Oxford University Press, 2010). Although Legaspi actually concentrates on the importance of Johann David Michaelis (1717–1791), he still discusses some broader developments. See also Richard D. Crane, 'Michael Legaspi's *The Death of Scripture*

were all ministers. Despite the claim to more objective and historical approaches, a report of the 1887 meeting says that 'Many of the papers disclose conservative to moderate positions with reference to critical study of the scriptures'.[69]

At the same time, many treatises on the ethics of Jesus were partly born out of a perceived crisis about the applicability of biblical ethics in the modern world. This perceived crisis can be seen in Henry Churchill King's *The Ethics of Jesus* (1910), wherein King remarked: 'Singularly violent attacks are being made just now, in some quarters, even upon the ethics of Jesus.'[70] One of Churchill's concerns was that the emphasis on the eschatological orientation of Jesus' ethics made them 'impracticable' for today.[71] Other teachings, and particularly those in Luke, were 'as hard on the conscience as the wonderstories of the Bible are difficult for the reason'.[72]

If we fast-forward to the twenty-first century, one sees relatively more independence in biblical scholarship from church control. In part, this independence is the result of biblical studies becoming part of many public and secular universities. However, when compared to all other fields, biblical scholarship has preserved a larger amount of religionism in its basic methodology and aims even in secular academia. If one compares biblical studies to classical studies, for instance, classicists do not see themselves as serving faith communities who still worship Zeus. Classicists do not use theological assumptions in their methods, and neither do any of the other humanities or social sciences. Chemistry is chemistry regardless of whether one is a Muslim or Christian. In short, biblical studies still retains an earlier religionist stance that has been shed by every other discipline in academia.

Within biblical studies, ethics has retained such religionism even more. That is easy to see in almost any manual of New Testament ethics. *Jesus and the Ethics of the Kingdom* (1987), co-authored by Bruce Chilton and J.I.H. McDonald, says outright that the book is part of a series that aims 'to bridge the gap between biblical scholarship and the larger enterprise of Christian theology'.[73] Richard Hays affirms that 'the primary goal' of his treatise, *The Moral Vision of the New Testament*, is '*to engage in the theological problem of how the New Testament ought to shape the ethical norms*

---

and the Birth of Biblical Studies: A Review Essay', *PRSt* 39 (2012), pp. 395-404. An older, but still useful, history is that of Jerry Wayne Brown, *The Rise of Biblical Criticism in America, 1800–1870: The New England Scholars* (Middletown, CT: Wesleyan University Press, 1969).

69. Saunders, *Searching the Scriptures*, p. 11.

70. Henry Churchill King, *The Ethics of Jesus* (New York: Macmillan, 1910), p. 4.

71. King, *The Ethics of Jesus*, p. 5.

72. King, *The Ethics of Jesus*, pp. 4-5.

73. Bruce D. Chilton and J.I.H. McDonald, *Jesus and the Ethics of the Kingdom* (Grand Rapids, MI: Eerdmans, 1987), p. ix.

and practices of the church in our time'.[74] Lisa Sowle Cahill tells readers that '[t]he essential and enduring relevance of the New Testament for ethics lies in its heightening of the human ability to recognize humanity in others, especially others over whom one may wield power'.[75]

Richard Longenecker's *New Testament Social Ethics for Today* (1984) defines New Testament ethics as:

> [P]rescriptive principles stemming from the heart of the gospel (usually embodied in the example and teachings of Jesus), which are to be applied to specific situations by the direction and enablement of the Holy Spirit, being always motivated and conditioned by love.[76]

Frank Matera's *New Testament Ethics* (1996), tells us,

> While outsiders will inevitably admire certain aspects of the moral teachings of Jesus and Paul and dispute others, I do not believe that they can fully appreciate this ethic since they do not participate in the faith life of the believing community. In this respect, the moral vision of the New Testament is primarily for the church.[77]

These sorts of approaches are very much unlike any other academic historical study of the ethics of other cultures.

I do not know of any scholars studying Greek ethics, for instance, who aim to solve the theological problem of how the *Iliad* ought to shape the ethical norms of Zeus worshipers today. One can argue that this is because there are no Zeus worshipers today. However, I do not know of anyone in academia who would take the worship of Zeus seriously in modern times, let alone take seriously trying to apply the ethics of ancient Greek works for those modern worshipers even if they existed. I don't know of any classical scholars who say that 'outsiders' cannot ever fully appreciate Greek ethics since they do not participate in the faith life of the faith communities of the Greek gods.

Of course, this is not to deny that Greeks did have some good ideas that we can still use. Many ideas about democracy and even some rights for

74. Richard B. Hays, *The Moral Vision of the New Testament: A Contemporary Introduction to New Testament Ethics* (New York: HarperOne, 1996), p. 9; Hays's italics. For a similar Christian orientation, see Thomas B. Matson, *Biblical Ethics: A Guide to the Ethical Message of the Scriptures from Genesis through Revelation* (repr., Macon, GA: Mercer University Press, 1991 [1967]).

75. Lisa Sowle Cahill, *Sex, Gender and Christian Ethics* (Cambridge: Cambridge University Press, 1996), p. 129.

76. Richard N. Longenecker, *New Testament Social Ethics for Today* (Grand Rapids, MI: Eerdmans, 1984), p. 15. A similar view is expressed by Russell Pregeant, *Knowing Truth, Doing Good: Engaging New Testament Ethics* (Minneapolis: Fortress Press, 2008), p. 365.

77. Matera, *New Testament Ethics*, p. 10.

slaves can first be found in Greek literature. But, in the broader study of Greek ethics, such utility for Greek ideas is also coupled with criticism or acknowledgment that some Greek ideas were detrimental for modern life. For example, one finds vigorous discussions of how Aristotle influenced some of the most injurious ideas about hierarchy and slavery in western civilization.[78] One looks almost in vain for any similar critiques of Jesus' ethics.[79]

In fact, much of modern Christian ethics has not deviated from the basic strategy employed by Augustine's *On Christian Doctrine* when dealing with objectionable texts:

> In the first place, then, we must show the way to find out whether a phrase is literal or figurative. And the way is certainly as follows: Whatever there is in the Word of God that cannot, when taken literally, be referred either to purity or life or soundness of doctrine, you may set down as figurative. Purity of life has reference to the love of God and one's neighbor; soundness of doctrine to the knowledge of God and one's neighbor.[80]

In other words, Augustine declares as 'figurative' anything he finds morally objectionable, and literally what he finds as ethically laudable. I have argued elsewhere that 'fundamentalism' is usually a philosophically empty charge made by those who wish to dismiss the ethical problems resulting from a plain and literal reading of texts.[81] Augustine has many modern followers among biblical scholars who insist that God can do no wrong even if the biblical texts seem to say just that. Thus, Paul Redditt tells readers: 'It is one thing for an exegete to expose "ungodlike" attitudes and behaviors

---

78. See Robert Schlaifer, 'Greek Theories of Slavery from Homer to Aristotle', *Harvard Studies in Classical Philology* 47 (1936), pp. 165-204; Lewis Hanke, *Aristotle and the American Indians: A Study in Race Prejudice in the Modern World* (Bloomington, IN: Indiana University Press, 1959).

79. One that approximates this objective is Peter Craffert, 'New Testament Studies—Preventing or Promoting Human Society?', *Religion and Theology* 14.3-4 (2007), pp. 161-205.

80. Augustine, *On Christian Doctrine* 3.10.14 (NPNF[1] II, pp. 560-61). Latin (PL 34.71): 'Demonstrandus est igitur prius modus inveniendae locutionis, propriane an figurata sit. Et iste omnino modus est, ut quidquid in sermone divino neque ad morum honestatem, neque ad fidei veritatem proprie referri potest, figuratum esse cognoscas. Morum honestas ad diligendum Deum et proximum, fidei veritas ad cognoscendum Deum et proximum pertinet.' See also Jace R. Broadhurst, *What is the Literal Sense? Considering the Hermeneutic of John Lightfoot* (Eugene, OR: Pickwick, 2012).

81. Hector Avalos, 'Six Anti-Secularist Themes: Deconstructing Religionist Rhetorical Weaponry', *Bible and Interpretation* (November 2010). Online: http://www.bibleinterp.com/opeds/anti358029.shtml.

Among those who argue against what are often called 'fundamentalists' is Christian Smith, *The Bible Made Impossible: Why Biblicism is Not Truly Evangelical Reading of Scripture* (Grand Rapids, MI: Brazos, 2011).

attributed to God in biblical texts. It is quite another thing to assume that they should be included in a valid picture of God's character.'[82]

Metacriticism of Biblical Scholarship

This book represents what some biblical scholars are characterizing as the metacriticism of biblical scholarship.[83] In 2011 the Society of Biblical Literature officially recognized a unit with the title, 'The Metacriticism of Biblical Scholarship', which has the following mission:

> This unit critically evaluates suppositions in and underlying biblical scholarship, including how an explicitly non-religious approach differs from what is even now represented as historical-critical scholarship, especially when compared to other secular disciplines within the Humanities (history, classical studies) and the Social Sciences (e.g., anthropology, sociology).[84]

Metacriticism represents a deepening introspective and self-critical orientation within biblical studies. Metacriticism of biblical scholarship reflects the divide between secularist and faith-oriented biblical studies.[85]

Despite a theological orientation, biblical ethics often represents itself as an academic endeavor that is no less descriptive than the fields that I have examined in my previously mentioned book, *The End of Biblical Studies* (2007). For example, John Barton approves of the leadership of Eckart Otto, a premier biblical ethicist today, 'in aiming primarily to present a descriptive, historical account of ethical beliefs and practices in ancient Israel as evidenced in the Old Testament'.[86] When it comes more specifi-

82. Paul Redditt, 'The God who Loves and Hates', in *Shall Not the Judge of the Earth Do What is Right? Studies in the Nature of God in Tribute to James L. Crenshaw* (ed. David Perchansky and Paul Redditt; Winona Lake, IN: Eisenbrauns, 2000), pp. 175-90 (189).

83. Metacriticism may be part of what Stephen D. Moore and Yvonne Sherwood ('Biblical Studies "after" Theory: Onwards Towards the Past. Part Three: Theory in the First and Second Waves', *BibInt* 18 [2010], pp. 191-225) describe as a 'second wave' of theory enthusiasm, which 'would offer meta-critical analyses of our disciplinary pasts that would radically dismantle the default categories in which we operate as biblical scholars' (p. 225).

84. Society of Biblical Literature. Online: http://www.sbl-site.org/meetings/Congresses_CallForPaperDetails.aspx?MeetingId=23&VolunteerUnitId=588.

85. John Dart, 'Scholars and Believers: Growing Pains at the SBL', *Christian Century* 128.7 (2011), pp. 34-38.

86. John Barton, *Understanding Old Testament Ethics: Approaches and Explorations* (Louisville, KY: Westminster/John Knox Press, 2003), p. 173. See also Eckart Otto, *Theologische Ethik des Alten Testaments* (Stuttgart: Kohlhammer, 1994); idem, 'Of Aims and Methods in Hebrew Bible Ethics', in *Ethics and Politics in the Bible* (ed. Douglas A. Knight; Semeia, 66; Atlanta, GA: Society of Biblical Literature, 1995), pp. 161-71. On the idea of studying the 'implicit ethics' of the New Testament, see the essays in Ruben

cally to the New Testament, Richard B. Hays, of Duke University, remarks that '[t]he first task of New Testament ethics is to describe the content of the individual writings of the New Testament canon'.[87] Similarly, Leander Keck remarked that, '"New Testament ethics" is the ethics of the New Testament texts, period'.[88]

The present work will show that the claim to be engaging in a descriptive historical-critical study of New Testament ethics does not withstand scrutiny. Of course, such has been said of those who deny that the ethics of Jesus are relevant today. For example, Jack T. Sanders recalled how his claim about the irrelevance of Jesus' ethics was criticized by his reviewers as presenting his own 'claim about the general inapplicability of the New Testament to ethics "masked in the form of a historical study"'.[89]

Nonetheless, the study of New Testament ethics, and particularly those reflected by Jesus, is almost completely preoccupied with showing the superiority of Jesus' ethics. Most studies believe that all of Jesus' actions were good and are still good and relevant today. Even when such studies speak of actions that parallel those found objectionable in other religious or political figures, Jesus somehow gets a pass or there is no reflection on the negative consequences of what Jesus thought or did.

Some advocates of metacriticism view biblical studies as part of a larger ecclesial-academic complex that is in crisis in public universities, particularly in the United States. Economically, universities are in a major period of downsizing. This downsizing is related in dolorous detail by Frank Donoghue, *The Last Professors: The Corporate University and the Fate of the Humanities* (2008). According to Donoghue, 'the last academic year in which 50 percent of students graduated with a traditional liberal arts major was 1969–70'.[90] Students now flock to business majors instead. Because of the declining popular demand for humanities programs, it is even more difficult now to make a plea for adding a biblical scholar, when the society is clamoring for alternative fuels experts or business entrepreneurs. Although

Zimmermann, Jan G. van der Watt, and Susanne Luther (eds.), *Moral Language in the New Testament: The Interrelatedness of Language and Ethics in Early Christian Writings* (WUNT 2.296; Tübingen: Morh Siebeck, 2010).

87. Hays, *The Moral Vision*, p. 13. Douglas A. Knight ('Old Testament Ethics', *Christian Century* 99.2 [1982], p. 58) says: 'biblical ethics is primarily a descriptive discipline'. Per contra, Bruce C. Birch (*Let Justice Roll Down: The Old Testament Ethics and Christian Life* [Louisville, KY: Westminster/John Knox Press, 1991], p. 25) says: '...nor do I believe that ethics should be primarily descriptive'.

88. Leander E. Keck, 'Rethinking "New Testament Ethics"', *JBL* 115 (1996), pp. 3-16 (4).

89. Sanders, *Ethics in the New Testament*, p. x.

90. Frank Donoghue, *The Last Professors: The Corporate University and the Fate of the Humanities* (New York: Fordham University Press, 2008), p. 91.

Robert N. Watson argues that the humanities actually are profitable university departments, the truth is that biblical studies brings in little money to most universities.[91]

At the same time, there is the growth of for-profit universities catering specifically to a consumerist mindset. The University of Phoenix, which enrolls 400,000 undergraduates and 78,000 graduate students, now has the largest enrollment of any American university. According to Donoghue, 'in 2000–2001, the entire for profit, postsecondary industry graduated 28,000 Business and Management A.A.s [Associate of Arts] and B.A.s, 11,500 A.A.s and B.A.s in the health professions, and not a single English major'.[92] More importantly, the University of Phoenix has no program in biblical studies. Jobs in biblical studies face extinction if this trend holds in public universities.

On a social level, biblical studies is deemed a ministerial program by faculty members in other departments. In other words, a principal problem in academia is that biblical studies are not viewed as secular enough. Unfortunately, many biblical scholars reinforce a religionist perception of biblical studies. When not touting the supposed ethical superiority of the Bible, some professors of biblical studies may also be busy attending to pastoral duties in their churches. They do not treat the Bible as another ancient document such as Homer's *Iliad* or *The Epic of Gilgamesh*.

Demographic changes must be taken into account. I teach both biblical studies and US Latino Studies. US Latinos (aka Hispanics), numbering over 50 million people, are people living in the United States whose roots come from the Spanish-speaking countries of Latin America. Latinos are the largest ethnic agglomeration in the United States. Latinos are also part of perhaps one of the greatest revolutions in the history of Christianity insofar as their rate of conversion from Catholicism to Protestantism may exceed what happened in Europe in the sixteenth century when Protestantism first arose.[93] These changes are already affecting everything from the recent presidential elections to the cultural fabric of small towns in the American Midwest.[94]

The growth of these groups is also affecting the literary canon. In the 1940s 'American literature' meant mostly that composed by New Englanders. By extension, literature meant 'Shakespeare' and other greats of the

---

91. Robert N. Watson, 'Bottom Line Shows Humanities Really Do Make Money', *Chronicle of Higher Education* (21 March 2010). Online: http://today.ucla.edu/portal/ut/bottom-line-shows-humanities-really-155771.aspx.

92. Donoghue, *The Last Professors*, p. 92.

93. See Hector Avalos (ed.), *Introduction to the U.S. Latina and Latino Religious Experience* (Leiden and Boston, MA: Brill, 2004); idem, *Strangers in our Own Land: Religion in U.S. Latina/o Literature* (Nashville, TN: Abingdon Press, 2007).

94. Ann V. Millard and Jorge Chapa, *Apple Pie and Enchiladas: Latino Newcomers in the Rural Midwest* (Austin, TX: University of Texas Press, 2001).

British Isles. Today, my Latino students want to know as much about Gloria Anzaldúa and Rudolfo Anaya as they want to know about Shakespeare, if they want to know the latter at all. The current generation of students in America also is increasingly 'minimalist'. Students wish to do the minimum required to receive the credentials needed for the real purpose of a college education: making money.

More alarmingly, fewer students are willing to learn ancient languages (e.g., Hebrew, Greek) indispensable to biblical studies. Large enrollments in introductory classes on the Bible mean little for the future profession of biblical scholarship if those students reject careers as biblical scholars. Where will the next generations of biblical scholars come from when few undergraduates are taking anything beyond popular introductory Bible courses?

To survive in public academia, biblical scholars must address the larger issues that are now being discussed on a more philosophical level. These issues involve the role of academics in constructing canons that are meant to further the interests of an academic professorial class. Drawing on Pierre Bourdieu's concept of 'cultural capital', the literary critic John Guillory characterizes cultural capital thus: 'If there exists a form of capital which is specifically symbolic or cultural, the production, exchange, distribution, and consumption of this capital presupposes the division of society into groups that can be called classes.'[95]

Guillory argues that constructing a canon creates 'cultural capital' because mastering a particular set of books distributes power in a society. It has little to do with literary quality, which itself is a social construct. Furthermore, those who construct the canon are not the authors, but rather the mass media (e.g., Oprah Winfrey's book club) and the professoriate, who create the curriculum and select what they deem to be representative works.

So, from a Guilloryian perspective, Shakespeare's works are read not because they necessarily have any higher literary value than many other works we could name, but because 'knowing Shakespeare' might function as a credential in elite circles. Indeed, when asked what differentiated the Bible from Shakespeare, Phyllis Trible, the renowned biblical scholar, could only reply, 'I ask myself that question, and if I had a clear answer, I'd give it to you'.[96] In fact, biblical scholars forget how new the study of English literature is in our university curricula. As Gerald Graff reminds us, in 1895 it was possible, even at Yale, to go through four years of college without hearing the name of a single English author or the title of a single

---

95. John Guillory, *Cultural Capital: The Problem of Literary Canon Formation* (Chicago, IL: University of Chicago Press, 1993), p. viii.

96. Phyllis Trible, 'Wrestling with Scripture [interview with Hershel Shanks]', *BARev* 32 (2006), pp. 46-52, 76-77 (49).

English classic.[97] Indeed, biblical aesthetics often is another form of bibliol-atry (i.e., we must the study the Bible because of its supposed superior lit-erary beauty).

Furthermore, this effort to promote biblical literacy depends on the illu-sion that there is such a thing as 'THE Bible'. Consider the fact that the text of our New Testament is a hypothetical reconstruction that is identical to no single manuscript extant in the first few centuries of Christianity. Our canon could have been made of many combinations and included books that we do not consider part of 'biblical studies'. Therefore, 'the Bible' is partly the construction of scholars (ancient or modern), and today the power to define the Bible still resides mostly with ecclesiastical authorities, as well as with academic biblical scholars.[98] So, even if believers hold 'the Bible' to be rel-evant, it is because clerics and scholars have not divulged how much of it is constructed by scholars.

Organization of this Study

The organization of this study should be placed in the context of debates about what the proper center of New Testament ethics should be.[99] Basically, one can identify two positions: (1) A Christocentric position, which argues that Jesus is the center for the study of New Testament ethics; (2) A non-Christocentric position, which argues that New Testament ethics describes the ethics in the New Testament, and not just those of Jesus. Richard A. Burridge and Richard Longenecker would represent the first position, while Richard Hays and Frank Matera would represent this second position.

Frank Matera, for example, emphasizes that 'the primary object of New Testament ethics should be the writings of the New Testament rather than a historical reconstruction of the ethical teachings of Jesus, the early church, Paul, and so on'.[100] In fact, he went as far as proposing that 'this may be an opportune time to reassess cherished assumptions about the ethical teach-ings of Jesus'.[101] Yet, it is clear that reassessing has little to do with finding any flaws in Jesus' ethical teachings.

---

97. Gerald Graff, *Professing Literature: An Institutional History* (Chicago, IL: Uni-versity of Chicago Press, 1987).

98. See also Andrew K.M. Adam, *Faithful Interpretation: Reading the Bible in a Postmodern World* (Minneapolis: Fortress Press, 2006).

99. A useful review of the field of New Testament ethics from 1993–2009 is offered by Friedrich W. Horn, 'Ethik und Neuen Testaments 1993–2009: Teil I', *TRu* 76 (2011), pp. 1-36; idem, 'Ethik und Neuen Testaments 1993–2009: Teil II', *TRu* 76 (2011), pp. 180-221. The first part is useful for the ethics of Jesus, while the second part is more about Pauline ethics.

100. Matera, *New Testament Ethics*, p. 7.

101. Matera, *New Testament Ethics*, p. 7.

In contrast to Matera, Richard A. Burridge, author of *Imitating Jesus: An Inclusive Approach to New Testament Ethics* (2007), argues that Jesus must be the center of the study of Christian ethics. As he phrases it:

> [M]any other studies concentrate simply on the ethics of the New Testament writers, partly because of the difficulty of reconstructing the historical Jesus, and partly for the good literary reason of beginning with the final form of the text. However we want to assert that the key to understanding the New Testament has to be the person of Jesus, and that therefore he is the correct person and place with which to begin as well as to end.[102]

Although Burridge acknowledges the problems of using the New Testament for modern ethics, he ultimately concludes that 'to be truly biblical is to be inclusive in any community which wants to follow and imitate Jesus'.[103] In other words, Jesus is still a model, especially of inclusivity. Burridge also points to no real problems with Jesus' ethics.

Each of these positions can organize their discussion either diachronically or synchronically. A *diachronic* approach might start with the ethics of Jesus, and then move to those of Paul, and then other writers of the early Church. In *The Ethics of the New Testament*, Wolfgang Schrage begins with a study of the eschatological ethics of Jesus, and then he moves to the Synoptic Gospels, and from there to the Pauline and non-Pauline epistles, and finally to Revelation.[104] There may be a concomitant interest in redactional criticism to determine the earliest strata of New Testament traditions. A synchronic approach might especially focus on specific themes rather than a general chronological order. As Frank Matera notes, Ceslas Spicq organized his *Théologie morale du Nouveau Testament* without much attention to redaction, and with much emphasis on the canonical forms of the text. His themes included 'New Being and New Life', 'Grace and Glory', and 'Love of God and Love of Neighbor'.[105]

The organizational approach used in this work is 'Jesucentric', insofar as it focuses on the ethics of Jesus, and not those of other New Testament writers.[106]

---

102. Richard A. Burridge, *Imitating Jesus: An Inclusive Approach to New Testament Ethics* (Grand Rapids, MI: Eerdmans, 2007), p. 4. On the imitation of moral models and the concept of 'situation ethics' in Roman culture, see Rebecca Langlands, 'Roman *exempla* and Situation Ethics: Valerius Maximus and Cicero *de Officis*', *JRS* 101 (2011), pp. 100-122.

103. Burridge, *Imitating Jesus*, p. 409.

104. Wolfgang Schrage, *The Ethics of the New Testament* (trans. David E. Green; Philadelphia, PA: Fortress Press, 1988). For a recent study of Pauline ethics, see Martin Meiser (ed.), *The Torah in the Ethics of Paul* (Library of New Testament Studies, 473, European Studies on Christian Origins; London: T. & T. Clark, 2012).

105. Matera, *New Testament Ethics*, p. 5. Ceslas Spicq, *Théologie morale du Nouveau Testament* (2 vols.; Paris: J. Gabalda, 1965).

106. For a defense of the term 'Jesucentric', particularly because it focuses on the

But the present study is not an exhaustive treatise on the ethics of Jesus, nor is it a treatise on New Testament ethics. Rather, this book presents a series of case studies meant to illustrate the extent to which religionism, and more particularly a Christian bias, still permeates what are otherwise supposed to be historical-critical descriptive studies of the ethics of Jesus. At times, the case studies consist of detailed exegetical explorations meant to expose the flaws of ethical discussions that purport to be based on sound linguistic analyses. My study is also synchronic insofar as I concentrate on different ethical topics rather than the historical development of Jesus' ethics. That is not to say that I have no interest or discussion of such matters, but just that it is not my primary concern. But I will present examples that show how modern ethicists use or abuse source criticism, redaction criticism, textual criticism, rhetorical criticism and other modern historico-critical tools to protect the ethics of Jesus.

The chapters in this book follow a loose thematic progression. Chapters two through six treat Jesus in the context of the bases of human interrelations, such as love, hate, violence against others, violence against the self, and social hierarchies (imperialism and slavery). Chapters 7 through 10 address Jesus' attitudes toward more specific groups of people (e.g., Jews, women, the poor, and disabled). Chapters 11 through 13 treat Jesus in relationship to broader phenomena and institutions, such as science/magic, the biosphere/ecology, and Jesus' use and abuse of the Hebrew scriptures.

Since this book is not intended to be a comprehensive treatise on New Testament ethics, there are major areas left without discussion. Perhaps the most important of these omissions is the appeal to Jesus' teachings in debating LGBTQI issues. I do mention the work of scholars (e.g., Deryn Guest, Ken Stone) who are issuing pleas to go beyond the male–female dichotomy permeating biblical scholarship. In general, however, I see many scholars who advocate on behalf of the LGBTQI community trying to make Jesus more friendly to that community than the text allows.[107] Overall, my argument is that liberation movements are best served by abandoning the use of any ancient text or figure to authorize modern ethics.

My study focuses on the ethics of Jesus manifested in the form of the text accepted as canonical by orthodox Christianity. I am interested in the sources or earliest strata of any traditions only to the extent that they have been used by Christian scholars to mitigate or excuse Jesus' behavior. I

---

human person rather than his theological title, see Alexander J.M. Wedderburn, *The Death of Jesus: Some Reflections on Jesus-Traditions and Paul* (WUNT, 2.299; Tübingen: Mohr Siebeck, 2013), pp. 44-45.

107. One example is the recent argument made by Matthew Vines, *God and the Gay Christian: The Biblical Case in Support of Same-Sex Relationships* (New York: Convergent Books, 2014).

am interested in non-canonical texts about Jesus only to the extent that they offer some comparative perspective. Non-canonical texts also allow us to interrogate why New Testament ethicists do not regard them as having high value for determining the ethics of Jesus. In short, these non-canonical texts reaffirm my larger argument that New Testament ethics is primarily an apologetic and theological enterprise, and not a historical one.[108]

This is not a compendium of metaethics. However, most treatises on New Testament ethics rarely interact or address the metaethical issues that their own conclusions and procedures pose. In that regard, the concluding chapter will explore the larger metaethical questions that relying on biblical ethics poses. In particular, it will interrogate the extent to which it is ethical to rely on a text or some revered figure, ancient or modern, to formulate ethics. It will also explore the circular and self-referential nature of all theistic ethics, and how that is contrary to any form of democratic government.

Subsidiary agendas will be detected and form an organic part of my argument. First, I certainly intend to give a voice to non-Christian ancient Near Eastern cultures that may have been dismissed as not as ethically innovative or as humane as Christianity. I have long contended that bibliolatry has effectively silenced the texts of many ancient Near Eastern cultures that also could be praised as innovative or as ethically advanced if they had the army of modern apologists that Christianity does. The silencing of those texts is itself part of a Christian textual imperialism.

Second, I emphasize that most biblical scholarship is itself part of an imperialist enterprise bent on preserving the authority of a text that has set its fundamental policies. Third, I aim to show that 'ethnic' biblical scholarship is as useful as ethnic chemistry or ethnic physics.[109] Ethnicity and life experiences may explain why one scholar notices or becomes interested in certain issues in biblical scholarship, but the conclusion must ultimately be validated by empirical evidence regardless of the ethnicity. Philosophically, the most significant dividing line for me is between secular and non-secular, while my ethnicity (I am usually identified as Mexican American or Hispanic/Latino) is not used to justify any of my main conclusions.[110]

---

108. See Bart Ehrman, *Lost Christianities: The Battles for Scripture and the Faiths We Never Knew* (New York: Oxford University Press, 2005).

109. An example of 'ethnic' biblical exegesis is found in Randall C. Bailey, Tatsiong Benny Liew and Ferndando Segovia (eds.), *They were All Together in One Place: Toward Minority Biblical Criticism* (SBL Semeia Studies, 57; Atlanta, GA: Society of Biblical Literature, 2009).

110. See further, Hector Avalos, 'In Praise of the Evil Kings: Latino Ethnic Identity and Biblical Scholarship', *Bible and Interpretation* (December 2013). Online: http://www.bibleinterp.com/articles/2013/12/ava378004.shtml; Julie Kelso, 'Us versus Them:

Fourth, I seek to transcend the disciplinary boxes into which many scholars are usually placed. Many usually identify me as a scholar of the Hebrew Bible and the ancient Near East, the areas in which I received my doctorate. The question naturally will arise therefore as to what I am doing in New Testament studies, and more particularly in New Testament ethics. My principal response is that I have never thought of myself as restricted to one 'testament', and I certainly do not think traditional canons should matter much any more. What I present here are interests that I have had since my earliest academic formation.

The religious tradition in which I was raised expected me to be competent in both testaments, at least as a layperson. My undergraduate degree in anthropology also included a minor in classics, which encouraged familiarity with Greco-Roman cultures and literature. The first paper I delivered to the Society of Biblical Literature (in 1982) was on New Testament textual criticism. My graduate courses at Harvard included one on the New Testament with Krister Stendahl. In 1999, I published *Health Care and the Rise of Christianity*, which was read by many scholars of the Bible and early Christianity as a sympathetic portrayal of the role of Christian health care in the growth of Christianity.[111] Whatever my training and expertise may be thought to be, it is the evidence presented that ultimately will show whether or not my conclusions are sound.

Summary

If one relied on most modern treatises of New Testament ethics, Jesus had no bad ideas, and never committed any bad deed. This cannot possibly be sustained if Jesus is viewed as a real historical human figure. If Jesus was a human being, he must have had some ideas that are ethically objectionable, or, at least, morally questionable. If Jesus was a human being, he must have had flaws, inconsistencies and hypocrisy in his moral system, just as does every other human being.[112] If his followers, ancient or modern, believe that those ideas are applicable to their lives and to the lives of others, then it also raises the question of whether any of Jesus' bad ideas also had bad

On Biblical (Studies) Identity Production', *The Bible and Critical Theory* 4 (2008), pp. 1-4. Ronald Hendel, 'Mind the Gap: Modern and Postmodern Biblical Studies', *JBL* 133 (2014), pp. 422-43 (433-34), where Hendel mentions the misguided nature of interpretations that seek justification in the interpreter's ethnicity.

111. See reviews of *Health Care and the Rise of Christianity* by Abigail Rian Evans, *Theology Today* 58 (2002), pp. 576-77; W. Brian Shelton, *JECS* 9 (2001), pp. 286-87; Mark W. Hamilton, *ResQ 43* (2001), pp. 125-26.

112. On hypocrisy as an inherent element in human behavior, see Robert Kurzban, *Why Everyone (Else) is a Hypocrite: Evolution and the Modular Mind* (Princeton, NJ: Princeton University Press, 2012).

consequences. If Jesus had some bad ideas, then imitating Jesus' bad ideas could be a bad practice today. Given how much time historically has been spent on lauding the Good Jesus, this book centers on illuminating 'the Bad Jesus'.

Chapter 2

THE UNLOVING JESUS: WHAT'S NEW IS OLD

In an interview published in the April 2012 issue of the popular evangelical Christian periodical, *Christianity Today*, Amy-Jill Levine, a prominent professor of New Testament studies at Vanderbilt University, was asked: 'So what is truly original about Jesus?' Her response was:

> He's the only person I can find in antiquity who says you have to love your *enemy*. But you have to look at the entire person to see his distinctiveness. Other people told parables. Other people referred to God as Father. Other people debated how to follow Torah. Other people lost their lives on Roman crosses. Other people proclaimed God's justice will be breaking in, and that we can live as if we've got one foot in that world to come.

> But the way Jesus puts it together makes him distinctive: the striking images that he gives, the loyalty he engendered from his followers such that they were willing to leave their homes and families to follow him and give up their lives for him. In that particular time he was able to give fellow Jews hope that some of them did not find elsewhere. To look at any one aspect of his tradition does not give us the full impacts that he would have made on his followers.[1]

What is remarkable about this response is that it comes from a self-identified Jewish scholar who would not be expected to adopt so uncritically some of the claims made by Christian apologists for Jesus' innovative ethics. Indeed, one can argue that crediting Jesus with innovation reaches back to the New Testament where the scribes represent Jesus' ability to exorcise through his own authority as a novel doctrine: 'And they were all amazed, so that they questioned among themselves, saying, "What is this? A new teaching! With authority he commands even the unclean spirits, and they obey him"' (Mk 1.27). Justin Martyr (ca. 100–165 CE), the early Church Father, represents Jesus as emphasizing innovation in Mt. 5.46: 'If ye love ye that love you, what new thing [τί καινόν] do ye?'[2]

---

1. David Neff, 'Jesus through Jewish Eyes', *Christianity Today* (April 2012), pp. 52-54 (54).
2. Justin Martyr, *The First Apology* 1.15.9 (ANF, I, p. 167).

John P. Meier is one of the few modern Christian scholars who has a very nuanced and cautious position on the role of love in Jesus' ministry. He concludes that 'the historical Jesus never directly connects his individual halakic pronouncements to some basic or organizing principle of love'.[3] Otherwise, the idea that Jesus was an ethical innovator, especially in the role of love, is standard in works by Christian literati and scholars.[4] As mentioned, Rudolf Schnackenburg thought that '[t]he message of Christian *agapē*, the model and highest expression of which is the mission of the Son of God to redeem the sinful human race, brought something new into the world, an idea so vast and incomprehensible as to be the highest revelation of God'.[5] Burridge, who admits the problems of reaching consensus on the historical Jesus, still proclaims: 'At the heart of Jesus' ethics is the double command, to love God and one's neighbour, given in response to a question abut the greatest commandment (Mk 12.28-34)... The centrality of love in Jesus' ethics extends to the love of enemies'.[6]

Burridge is referencing the oft-cited directive first found in Lev. 19.18, which reads in whole: 'You shall not take vengeance or bear any grudge against the sons of your own people, but you shall love your neighbor as yourself: I am the LORD'.[7] However, as Harry M. Orlinsky, the prominent scholar of Hebrew, has deftly noted, the Hebrew term (רֵעֲךָ) translated as 'your neighbor' is actually best understood as 'your fellow Israelite'.[8] The

---

3. John P. Meier, *A Marginal Jew: Rethinking the Historical Jesus, Volume 4: Law and Love* (New Haven, CT: Yale University Press, 2009), p. 655. For a more laudatory view of Jesus' love, see Daniel J. Harrington, *Jesus, the Revelation of the Father's Love: What the New Testament Teaches us* (Huntington, IN: Our Sunday Visitor, 2010).

4. Mary Wollstonecraft (*A Vindication of the Rights of Women* [repr., Köln: Könneman, 1998 [1792], p. 19) suggested that Jesus was a 'dangerous innovator'.

5. Schnackenburg, *The Moral Teaching of the New Testament*, p. 90.

6. Burridge, *Imitating Jesus*, pp. 50-51. Similarly, Lúcás Chan and James F. Keenan (eds.), *Biblical Ethics in the Twenty-First Century: Developments, Emerging Consensus, and Future Directions* (Mahwah, NJ: Paulist Press, 2013), p. 57: 'The heart of Jesus' teaching is still the double command of love'. For a far more cautious assessment of the role of the love commands in the ministry of the 'historical Jesus', see Meier, *Law and Love*; Per Bilde, *The Originality of Jesus: A Critical Discussion and Comparative Attempt* (Göttingen: Vandenhoeck & Ruprecht, 2013).

7. For the dating and other issues pertaining to this text, see Jacob Milgrom, *Leviticus 1–16* (AB, 3; New York: Doubleday, 1991), p. 27; Esther Eshel, 'Leviticus, Book of', in *Encyclopedia of the Dead Sea Scrolls* (ed. Lawrence Schiffman and James VanderKam; 2 vols.; New York: Oxford University Press, 2000), I, pp. 488-93. A more technical report may be found in Emanuel Tov, '4QLev [c,e,g] (4Q25, 26a, 26b)', in *Pomengranates and Golden Bells: Studies in Biblical, Jewish, and Near Eastern Ritual, Law, and Literature in Honor of Jacob Milgrom* (ed. David P. Wright, David N. Freedman and Avi Hurvitz; Winona Lake, IN: Eisenbrauns, 1995), pp. 257-66.

8. Harry M. Orlinsky, 'Nationalism-Universalism and Internationalism in Ancient Israel', in *Translating and Understanding the Old Testament: Essays in Honor of*

verse's final instruction to love your fellow Israelite as yourself, therefore, follows logically on the instruction not to hate 'any of the sons of your own people' (בני עמך) in the first half of the verse. Similarly, John P. Meier concludes that:

> There is no good reason to think that, when Jesus cited, Lev. 19.18b, 'you shall love your neighbor as yourself', he meant anything other than what the Hebrew text means by *rēaʿ*, namely, a fellow Israelite who belongs to the cultic community that worships Yahweh alone as the one true God (as proclaimed in Deut. 6.4-5).[9]

Indeed, Lev. 19.18 does not obligate universal love, but, in fact, is premised on privileging love for fellow Israelites over love for non-Israelites.[10]

J. Ian H. McDonald, a biblical ethicist at the University of Edinburgh, is more emphatic about how Jesus' ethics differed from those of other cultures:

> The distinctiveness of this new praxis is not to be underestimated. While Graeco-Roman moral teaching expressed the beauty and obligations of friendship, the general consensus was that one should hate (= not love) one's enemies. Even the Jewish tradition could take the form of love for the 'sons of light' and hatred for 'all the sons of darkness'. Covenental language in itself need not be interpreted to include love for God's enemies. Jesus took faith praxis beyond such boundaries into awareness of the need to meet anger with understanding and violence with non-aggression, and thus the practical means of reintegrating the estranged.[11]

The religiocentricity and ethnocentricity of such ethical claims by McDonald are not difficult to detect.[12] The entire Greco-Roman world supposedly

Herbert Gordon May (ed. Harry Thomas Frank and William L. Reed; Nashville, TN: Abingdon Press, 1970), pp. 206-236 (210-11).

9. Meier, *Law and Love*, p. 651.

10. An unconvincing proposal to translate this verse as 'You should care for persons in your surroundings the same way as you would like them to take care of you!' is offered by Bob Becking, 'Love Thy Neighbour...' in *'Gerechtigkeit und Recht zu üben' (Gen 18,19): Studien zur altorientalischen und biblischen Rechtsgeschichte, zur Religionsgeschichte Israels und zur Religionssoziologie. Festschrift für Eckart Otto zum 65. Geburtstag* (ed. Reinhard Achenbach and Martin Arneth; Beihefte zur Zeitschrift für Altorientalische und Biblische Rechtsgeschichte, 13; Wiesbaden: Harrassowitz Verlag, 2009), pp. 182-87 (185). Becking offers no sound linguistic parallels for his speculative reading.

11. J. Ian H. McDonald, *The Crucible of Christian Morality: Religion in the First Christian Centuries* (New York: Routledge, 1998), p. 105.

12. Even some works ostensibly written to extol the contributions of Greco-Roman culture ultimately reflect a Christian attitude of superiority towards them. Thus, Gregory S. Aldrete and Alicia Aldrete, *The Long Shadow of Antiquity: What have the Greeks and the Romans Done for us?* (London: Continuum, 2012), p. 240, note that the Romans had a vision of the afterlife, but that it could only be enjoyed by a few. On the other hand, Christianity democratized heaven because it was meant 'for all believers'. Of course, that still means that one has to be in the in-group to achieve a life in heaven, and Jesus

has a consensus 'that one should hate (= not love) one's enemies'. Yet, McDonald does not even bother to offer any supporting documentation. The fact is that some scholars of Greco-Roman religion have found the opposite to be true. Runar Thorsteinsson's study of *agapē*, and his comparison with Stoicism, concludes that 'the moral teaching of Roman Christianity does not teach unconditional universal humanity. It is conditioned by adherence to a particular religion.'[13] Thorsteinsson finds that it is Stoicism that is universal in its ideas of human kinship, not Christianity.

Even when some New Testament ethicists admit that the Hebrew Bible and pre-Christian Jewish tradition already have injunctions to love the enemy, it is still claimed that Jesus brought an innovation nonetheless. Willard Swartley tells readers:

> Since the Torah calls for kindness and help to the enemy in need (Exod. 23.4-5; Deut. 22.1-4), Jesus' love command is not altogether novel, William Klassen contends. But Marius Reiser's close study of both the Greek and Jewish ethical traditions argues the opposite. While in both traditions one can find injunctions not to retaliate in kind…the explicit positive initiative to love *enemies* is unique to Jesus… The theme of 'love' toward injurers, however, applies only to local personal conflict (*Testaments of the Twelve Patriarchs*) not to situations of socio-political oppression by outsiders.[14]

Swartley's distinctions between loving in the context of a 'local personal conflict' and loving in the context of 'socio-political' oppression are difficult to understand and not clearly made by Jesus or by other non-Christian writers. Otherwise, why was Jesus credited with an innovation that can also be read into other non-Christian writers?

Loving the Enemy in the Ancient Near East

The raw historical record shows that loving the enemy is not an innovation at the time of Jesus. It is certainly not true, as Levine claims, that Jesus is the

said that 'many are called but few are chosen' (Mt. 22.14), a text Aldrete and Aldrete never mention in this discussion.

13. Runar M. Thornsteinsson, *Roman Christianity and Roman Stoicism: A Comparative Study of Ancient Morality* (New York: Oxford University Press, 2010), p. 206. Julia Kindt (*Rethinking Greek Religion* [Cambridge: Cambridge University Press, 2012]) also notes how Christianity has perpetuated misconceptions of Greek religion. For a Christian perspective, see Tuomas Rasimus, Troels Engberg-Pedersen and Ismo Dunderberg (eds.), *Stoicism and Early Christianity* (Grand Rapids, MI: Baker, 2010).

14. Willard M. Swartley, *Covenant of Peace: The Missing Peace in New Testament Theology and Ethics* (Grand Rapids, MI: Eerdmans, 2006), p. 58. Swartley cites William Klassen, *Love of Enemies: The Way to Peace* (Philadelphia, PA: Fortress Press, 1984), pp. 12-66; Marius Reiser, 'Love of Enemies in the Context of Antiquity', *NTS* 47 (2001), pp. 411-27.

only person 'in antiquity who says you have to love your *enemy*'. Already in a collection of Mesopotamian texts known as the *Counsels of Wisdom* one finds this advice: 'Requite with kindness your evil doer. Maintain justice to your enemy. Smile on your adversary.'[15] In *The Instruction of Amenemope*, an Egyptian wisdom text perhaps composed in the Ramesside period (ca. fourteenth to eleventh centuries BCE), one finds this advice: 'Don't raise an outcry against one who attacks you; Nor answer him yourself.'[16] Why can't such advice apply to those attacking the victim in a personal conflict and in a case of socio-political oppression by outsiders?

Non-Christian writings from before the time of Jesus, as well as those contemporary with Jesus, enunciate the love of enemies. In his treatise on Exodus, for instance, Philo tries to explain the reasons for the instruction given in Exod. 23.4: 'If you meet your enemy's ox or his ass going astray, you shall bring it back to him.' According to Philo, 'It is an excess of gentleness if in addition to not harming an enemy one even tries to be of help. In the second place, it is a prohibition and shaming of greed. For he who is not willing to harm an enemy, whom else will he wish to harm for his own profit?'[17] Later in his discussion, Philo links this sort of attitude toward the animals of enemies to a wider human kinship: 'For who would disregard any human being with whom he has a single natural kinship, when he has been taught by the divine Law and is accustomed not to disregard even a beast?'[18] If so, then this undermines the idea that love of enemies pertains only to local personal conflicts, as Philo's ideas can be extended to outsiders and they make no distinction between local conflict and some larger oppression by outsiders.

In the *Community Rule/Manual of Discipline* (1QS 10.17-18) from Qumran, one finds a speaker saying the following about his enemies: 'I shall not repay anyone with an evil reward; with goodness I shall pursue the man. For to God belongs the judgement of every living being.'[19] Although this is an

---

15. Wilfred G. Lambert, *Babylonian Wisdom Literature* (Oxford: Clarendon Press, 1960), p. 101, ll. 42-44. The Akkadian text may be found in Lambert, *Babylonian Wisdom Literature*, p. 100, ll. 42-44: a-na e-piš li-mut-ti-ka damiqta ri-ib-šu/a-na rag-gi-ka mi-šá-ra [ki]l-ᵉla¹-áš-šú/a-na ṣir-ri-ka [ka-ba]t-ta-ka [li-i]m-mir-šú. I use slashes to separate the lines as divided by Lambert. See also W.G. Lambert, 'Morals in Ancient Mesopotamia', *JEOL* 15 (1955–58), pp. 184-96. For other comments on this text, see Gordon M. Zerbe, *Non-Retaliation in Early Jewish and New Testament Texts: Ethical Themes and Social Contexts* (Sheffield: JSOT Press, 1993), pp. 34-35.

16. Miriam Lichtheim, *Ancient Egyptian Literature* (3 vols.; Berkeley, CA: University of California Press, 1976), II, p. 150; for dating see p. 147.

17. Philo, *Quaest. in Exod.* 2.11 (Marcus, LCL).

18. Philo, *Quaest. in Exod.* 2.12 (Marcus, LCL).

19. Florentino García Martínez, *The Dead Sea Scrolls Translated: The Qumran Texts in English* (Leiden: E.J. Brill, 1994), p. 16. According to the Hebrew edition of Eduard

instance of what I call 'deferred violence', it does show that Jesus' instructions in Mt. 5.38 had possible precedents at Qumran.[20]

A more elaborate argument for extending kindness to enemies is found in ancient Greek war narratives. For example, there was an assembly in ancient Syracuse (Sicily) to discuss what to do with the Athenians whom they had just defeated. According to Diodorus Siculus (first century BCE), there was a three-way debate. A man named Diocles argued that the defeated Athenians should be tortured to death. Another man, named Hermocrates, voiced support for moderation. Finally, an elder named Nikolaus, who had lost two sons in the war with the Athenians, gave an extended speech outlining reasons for mercy. In part, Nikolaus says:

> Good it is indeed that the deity involves in unexpected disasters those who begin an unjust war [τοὺς ἀδίκου πολέμου]... Do not, therefore begrudge our country the opportunity of being acclaimed by all mankind, because it surpassed the Athenians not only in feats of arms but also in humanity [φιλανθρωπία]...the spirits of civilized men are gripped I believe, most perhaps by mercy, because of the sympathy [ὁμοπάθειαν] that nature has implanted in all.[21]

Nikolaus's arguments, though ultimately unsuccessful with the Syracusans, demonstrate well-developed philosophical Greek tradition that considered the value of kindness, even to enemies. The whole notion of philanthropy (φιλανθρωπία) was not just about being kind to friends or strangers, but also to enemies, as Nikolaus's speech shows.[22]

Levine's reference to people willing to leave their families for Jesus is also not that extraordinary in the ancient world. There were many well-known and well-documented historical figures who were able to persuade multitudes to leave their families to follow them. That was the case with Alexander the Great, who was able to lead thousands of men to near the ends of the known world. One could argue that these men were making an investment in riches and glory that perhaps they thought Alexander's victories could attain for them. As I will show later, this is not so different from Galilean disciples who also thought they might obtain some more

---

Lohse [*Die Texte aus Qumran: Hebräisch und Deutsch* (Munich: Kösel, 2nd edn, 1981], p. 38: לוא אשיב לאיש גמול רע בטוב ארדף גבר כיא את את אל משפט כול חי.

20. So Edmund Sutcliffe, 'Hatred at Qumran', *RevQ* 2 (1960), pp. 345-56. See also M.K.M. Tso, *Ethics in the Qumran Community: An Interdisciplinary Investigation* (WUNT, 2.292; Tübingen: Mohr Siebeck, 2010); Alex P. Jassen, 'The Dead Sea Scrolls and Violence: Sectarian Formation and Eschatological Imagination', *BibInt* 17 (2009), pp. 12-44.

21. Diodorus Siculus, *Historia* 13.21-24 (Oldfather, LCL).

22. See further, David J. Leigh, 'Forgiveness, Pity, and Ultimacy in Ancient Greek Culture', *Ultimate Reality and Meaning* 27 (2004), pp. 152-61.

permanent heavenly or utopian benefit if they really believed Jesus could do what he claimed.

Lesser-known teachers, who were not rich nor promising great material rewards, also had loyal followers. One example is from the Stoic philosopher, Epictetus:

> And how shall I free myself? Have you not heard over and over again that you ought to eradicate desire utterly, direct your aversion toward the things that lie within the sphere of moral purpose, and these things only, that you ought to give up everything, your body, your property, your reputation, your books, turmoil, office, freedom from office?[23]

Despite demands to rid oneself of possessions, such philosophers found followers because those followers were looking for benefits that were not necessarily material. So, why would that make Jesus so distinctive? As I will show, there were probably profoundly negative consequences for women and children left behind by followers of these leaders, but those negative consequences are usually not the subject of reflection by Christian scholars who laud the ethics of Jesus.

Love can Entail Violence

As most students of New Testament Greek realize, there are three main Greek words that have been translated as 'love' in English.[24] Love centered on sexual passion is usually *erōs* (ἔρως). However, this word does not occur in the New Testament. The verb *phileō* (φιλέω), which is found in the New Testament, can refer to the love of attention or to love between family members (e.g., Mt. 6.5; 10.37). The highest form of love mentioned in the New Testament is often said to reflect the Greek word *agapē* (ἀγάπη). A main exponent of this idea was Anders Nygren in his *Agape and Eros*.[25] For

23. Epictetus, *The Discourses* 4.4.33-34 (Oldfather, LCL).

24. Fundamental studies of 'love' in the New Testament include Ceslas Spicq, *Agape in the New Testament* (trans. Sister Marie Aquinas McNamara, OP and Sister Mary Honoria Richter, OP; 3 vols.; St. Louis, CO: B. Herder Book Company, 1963–66); Spicq actually includes more detailed philological study in his earlier work, *Agapè: Prolégomènes a une étude de théologie néo-testamentaire* (Leiden: E.J. Brill, 1955). For a more recent brief survey, see William Klassen, 'Love (NT and Early Jewish)', *ABD*, IV, pp. 381-96. Also useful is David Shepherd, '"Do you Love me?" A Narrative-Critical Reappraisal of ἀγαπάω and φιλέω in John 21.15-17', *JBL* 129 (2010), pp. 777-92. Fernando F. Segovia, *Love Relationships in the Johannine Tradition: Agapē/Agapan in 1 John and the Fourth Gospel* (SBLDS, 58; Chico, CA: Society of Biblical Literature, 1982).

25. Anders Nygren, *Agape and Eros* (trans. Philip S. Watson; Philadelphia, PA: Westminster Press, 1953). For a similar benign view, applied to modern ethical problems, see Gene Outka, *Agape: An Ethical Analysis* (New Haven, CT: Yale University Press, 1972).

Nygren, *agapē* was selfless love, and it typified Christianity, in opposition to the Old Testament. Even after new research showing some of the Greek and Near Eastern roots of *agapē*,[26] most Christian theologians and scholars of the New Testament continue to affirm that Christian love was one of the most essential and valuable gifts bestowed upon the world by Christianity.[27] So momentous is this supposedly new concept that some scholars have even tried to explain its development sociologically.[28]

Agapē is the word used, in one of the most famous love passages: 'For God so loved the world that he gave his only Son, that whoever believes in him should not perish but have eternal life' (Jn 3.16). And, of course, *agapē* is the Greek word used in what are portrayed as Jesus' new commandments.

> A new commandment I give to you, that you love one another; even as I have loved you, that you also love one another. By this all men will know that you are my disciples, if you have love for one another (Jn 13.34-35).

First Corinthians, a letter usually attributed to the apostle Paul, likewise extols the value of *agapē* in the famous passage about the virtues of love:

> Love is patient; love is kind; love is not envious or boastful or arrogant or rude. It does not insist on its own way; it is not irritable or resentful; it does not rejoice in wrongdoing, but rejoices in the truth. It bears all things, believes all things, hopes all things, endures all things. Love never ends. But as for prophecies, they will come to an end; as for tongues, they will cease; as for knowledge, it will come to an end (1 Cor. 13.4-8; NRSV).

Yet, the suspicion that the rhetoric of 'love' could be self-serving is evidenced by New Testament itself, as in 1 John:

26. Of special importance are the articles by Oda Wischmeyer, 'Vorkommen und Bedeutung von *Agape* in der Ausserliche Antike', *ZNW* 69 (1978), pp. 212-38; idem, 'Traditiongeschichtlich Untersuchung der Paulinischen Aussagen über die Liebe (*Agape*)', *ZNW* 74 (1983), pp. 222-36. Wischmeyer shows that, contrary to some previous conclusions, *agapē* was used in Ancient Greek, but she argues that it received a whole new semantic development in Christianity, particularly with Paul.

27. For examples of scholars still influenced, implicitly or explicitly, by an idealized view of *agapē*, see Glen H. Stassen, 'The Fourteen Triads of the Sermon on the Mount (Matthew 5:21–7:12)', *JBL* 122 (2003), pp. 267-308 (282). For one critique of Nygren, see Lowell D. Streiker, 'The Christian Understanding of Platonic Love: A Critique of Anders Nygren's *Agape and Eros*', *Chicago Studies* 47 (1964), pp. 331-40.

28. Eugen Schoenfeld, 'An Illusive Concept in Christianity', *Review of Religious Research* 30 (1989), pp. 236-45; Paul Rigby and Paul O'Grady, '*Agape* and Altruism: Debates in Theology and Social Psychology', *JAAR* 57 (1989), pp. 719-37. For the argument that the concept of loving one's enemies constituted the principal part of Jesus' social revolution, see Horsley, *Jesus and the Spiral of Violence*.

> We know love by this, that he laid down his life for us—and we ought to lay down our lives for one another. How does God's love abide in anyone who has the world's goods and sees a brother or sister in need and yet refuses help? Little children, let us love, not in word or speech, but in truth and action (1 Jn 3.16-18; NRSV).[29]

The author of this letter undertakes elaborate discussions on what love really meant, which presumes that he did not deem it clear to his addressees. The author's concept of *agapē* did not agree with those he was trying to persuade. Those criticized by the author apparently were using the rhetoric of love, but not performing actions that suited the author's definition of it. In more recent times Friedrich Nietzsche remarked: 'Not their love of humanity, but the impotence of their love, prevents the Christians of to-day—burning us.'[30]

Indeed, emerging particularly in the last half century is the realization that 'love' can sometimes be part of the discourse of master–slave or lord–vassal relationships. Far from being mutual or self-less, *agapē* may describe behavior that entails violence, not to mention other hierarchical behaviors. Part of the reason for this change is that previous scholars had been too eager to divorce the New Testament use of *agapē* from corresponding words and concepts found in the Hebrew Bible. After all, Christianity was often thought to be bringing something radically new.

The word 'love' often designates the attitude and set of behaviors that a Lord expects from his vassal in the ancient Near East. Especially instructive in this regard are the Assyrian lord-vassal 'treaties' of Esarhaddon (ca. 681–669 BCE), king of Assyria.[31] One commandment to a vassal, for example, reads: '(You swear) that you will love Ashurbanipal, the crown prince, son

---

29. See comments in David Rensberger, *The Epistles of John* (Louisville, KY: Westminster/John Knox Press, 2001), pp. 58-59; Rudolf Schackenburg, *The Johannine Epistles: Introduction and Commentary* (trans. Reginald and Ilse Fuller; New York: Crossroad, 1992), p. 184.

30. Friedrich Nietzsche, *Beyond Good and Evil* (trans. Helen Zimmern; Amherst, NY: Prometheus, 1989), p. 91.

31. The common designation for these documents is 'treaties', though this is most misleading if meant to convey some sort of mutuality. These documents were more like acknowledgments of surrender and capitulation. There was not much choice for the vassal about whether or not to accept many stipulations because the superior party dictated the stipulations and did not ask for the vassal's consent to impose them. Again, the slave–master mentality is what is fundamental, and the kinship rhetoric is what is fictionalized. See further, Amnon Altman, 'How Many Treaty Traditions Existed in the Ancient Near East?', in *Pax Hethitica: Studies on the Hittites and their Neighbours in Honour of Itamar Singer* (ed. Yoram Cohen, Amir Gilan and Jared L. Miller; Wiesbaden: Harrasowitz, 2010), pp. 18-36; idem, *The 'Historical Prologues' of Hittite Vassal Treaties: An Inquiry into the Concepts of Hittite Interstate Law* (Ramat-Gan: Bar-Ilan University Press, 2004); Simo Parpola and Kazuko Watanabe, *Neo-Assyrian Treaties and Loyalty Oaths* (SAA, 2; Helsinki: Helsinki University Press, 1988).

of Esarhaddon, king of Assyria, your lord as (you do) yourselves.'[32] Like-wise, a vassal is commanded to 'fight and (even) die for him [the lord]'.[33] The demands found in this Assyrian vassal treaty, of course, are not that dif-ferent from what Jesus commanded his own disciples: 'If any one comes to me and does not hate his own father and mother...yes, and even his own life [ψυχήν], he cannot be my disciple' (Lk. 14.26). Curses were applied to those who did not obey the Assyrian king's commandments.

The hint that lord–vassal language is important in understanding the New Testament concept of love was already noted over fifty years ago by the brilliant Harvard Near Eastern scholar, William L. Moran, who said: 'if the old sovereign-vassal terminology of love is as relevant as we think it is, then what a history lies behind the Christian test of true *agapē*—"If you love me, you will keep my commandments!"'[34] Nonetheless, Moran's insight, while bringing a new understanding, have remained confined largely to the Hebrew Bible. The similarity of New Testament language to lord–vassal treaties, when commented upon, is often expressed only obliquely.[35]

More recently, Susan Ackerman has made a case that the Hebrew words *'ahēb*, a verb, and *'ahābâ*, the related noun, which are usually translated into Greek with the relevant forms of *agapē*, almost always reflect an inequality in power in the Hebrew Bible.[36] She argues that, while there may be overlap

---

32. Donald J. Wiseman, *The Vassal Treaties of Esarhaddon* (London: British School of Archaeology in Iraq, 1958), pp. 49-50, ll. 266-68: The Assyrian crucial clause is ki-i nap-šat-ku-nu la tar-'a-ma-ni (= 'you will love [Ashurbanipal]...as you do your own lives').

33. Wiseman, *The Vassal Treaties*, pp. 33-34, ll. 50-51.

34. William L. Moran, 'The Ancient Near Eastern Background of the Love of God in Deuteronomy', *CBQ* 25 (1963), pp. 77-87 (87). For a more expanded study of lord–vassal language, see Klaus Baltzer, *The Covenant Formulary in Old Testament, Jewish, and Early Christian Writings* (trans. David E. Green; Philadelphia, PA: Fortress Press, 1971). For a study of how Assyrian imperial ideology and rhetoric was transmitted to, and adapted by, Hebrew authors, see Shawn Zelig Aster, 'Transmission of Neo-Assyrian Claims of Empire to Judah in the Late Eighth Century B.C.E.', *HUCA* 79 (2007), pp. 1-44; Peter Machinist, 'Assyria and its Image in the First Isaiah', *JAOS* 103 (1983), pp. 719-37. On obedience as a feature of discipleship, see Mathew Palachuvattil, *'The One Who Does the Will of the Father': Distinguishing Character of Disciples According to Matthew: An Exegetical and Theological Study* (Tesi Gregoriana, Serie Teologia, 154: Rome: Editrice Pontificia Università Gregoriana, 2007).

35. Thus, Luke T. Johnson (*The Writings of the New Testament: An Introduction* [Philadelphia, PA: Fortress Press, 1986], p. 186) notes that the Beatitudes bear some similarities to the blessings and curses of Deuteronomy 27–28, but he does not elaborate on how this structure was part of lord–vassal terminology. Spicq (*Agapè: Prolégomènes*, pp. 122-24), mentions some of the hierarchical nature of related words, but never devel-ops the connection with lord–vassal treaties.

36. Susan Ackerman, 'The Personal is Political: Covenental and Affectionate Love ['ĀHĒB, 'AHĂBÂ] in the Hebrew Bible', *VT* 52 (2002), pp. 437-58. For an earlier treatment

between interpersonal 'love' and 'political' love, the former still indicates a one-sided use of the word. Thus, Jacob is described as loving Rachel (Gen. 29.18, 20 and 30), but it is never said that Rachel loved Jacob. The same is true in the description of numerous other relationships between men and women.

Ackerman believes that *'āhēb / 'ᵃhābâ* is an action performed by the superior party relative to an inferior party (male > female, parent > child, Yahweh > human being, etc.). Only once is it said that a man (Solomon) loves Yahweh (1 Kgs 3.3), whereas the reverse is the norm (Yahweh loves X). In cases where gods seem to be the object of human love in Jeremiah (2.25 and 8.2), Ackerman interprets that as a satirical reversal that reflects Jeremiah's view of those gods as inferior to human beings.

While I am convinced that Ackerman seems to have found a pattern, it does leave another question: Why is it only the superior party that is described as performing this act? This is especially puzzling because, as Moran had noted, it was usually the inferior party who owed 'love' to the master in the relationship. I believe that this puzzle can be solved if we add one more element to this hierarchical and political view of love. The element is individual privileging. Love functions as a manner to express status differences in which a superior party selects an object of love, who can only return gratitude, affection and service in return. Inferior parties cannot or do not select their superiors, masters or parents.

The idea that the superior party selects the inferior one is repeatedly found in the Hebrew Bible, as in Deut. 7.6: 'For you are a people holy to the LORD your God; the LORD your God has chosen you to be a people for his own possession, out of all the peoples that are on the face of the earth.' This selection can be acknowledged as simply arbitrary: 'As it is written, "Jacob I loved, but Esau I hated"' (Rom. 9.13).

If one compares the Hebrew Bible to the New Testament, there is actually a reversal in the latter. Far from indicating mutuality or even lack of self-interest, *agapē* has often become even more hierarchical, demanding and servile in the New Testament relative to that in the Hebrew Bible. Although Nygren does not locate *agapē* in the context of Near Eastern imperial rhetoric, his translator, Philip Watson, actually seems to acknowledge the slavish nature of *agapē* when he says:

> But the love of man for God of which the New Testament speaks is of quite a different stamp. It means whole-hearted surrender to God, whereby man becomes God's willing slave, content to be at His disposal, having entire trust and confidence in Him, and desiring only that His will be done.[37]

of love as political in the Hebrew Bible, see J.A. Thompson, 'The Significance of the Verb *Love* in the David-Jonathan Narratives in 1 Samuel', *VT* 24 (1974), pp. 334-38.

37. Nygren, *Agape and Eros*, p. viii. See also Bultmann's comments on the servile

More importantly, New Testament notions of *agapē* also obligate and even enjoin violence. One example is placed on the lips of Jesus:

> I will no longer talk much with you, for the ruler of this world is coming. He has no power over me; but I do as the Father has commanded me, so that the world may know that I love the Father. Rise, let us be on our way (Jn 14.30-31).

As becomes apparent at the crucifixion, Jesus' demonstration of his love for the Father means the willingness to be tortured and be killed.

In fact, love means that a friend should be willing to die for his comrade (Jn 15.13). Jesus says that 'He who loves his life loses it, and he who hates his life in this world will keep it for eternal life' (Jn 12.25).[38] Paul Ramsey, one of the foremost Christian ethicists of the twentieth century, also acknowledges that love for one's neighbor has been used to argue for the necessity of war.[39] We have already seen how Luke sees love for Jesus as entailing hatred for one's parents, and parallels the idea that the servant's love for the master is paramount. Matthew 10.34-37 says that love for Jesus entails violence among family members. Nor is the notion of *agapē* very inclusive. While Jesus commands disciples to 'love one another', the benefits of salvation are only available for those that obey Jesus' view of God. Note this passage: 'Jesus said to him, "I am the way, and the truth, and the life; no one comes to the Father, but by me"' (Jn 14.6).

While Paul expounds on the virtues of love in 1 Corinthians 13, he elsewhere recommends violence upon the body for the sake of salvation.[40] Thus, Paul issues the following instruction concerning a man who commits a sexual sin: 'you are to deliver this man to Satan for the destruction of the flesh, that his spirit may be saved in the day of the Lord Jesus' (1 Cor. 5.5). Most readers fail to appreciate that Paul is likely speaking of the literal killing or death of the person.[41] The author reflects again the idea that the spirit is much more important than the body, and so any violence that results in

---

nature of *agapē* in Rudolf Bultmann, *Theology of the New Testament* (trans. Kendrick Grobel; 2 vols.; New York: Charles Scribner's Sons, 1951–1955), I, pp. 262-63, 343-45.

38. On love in John, see Segovia, *Love Relationships in the Johannine Tradition*.

39. Paul Ramsey, 'Justice in War', in *The Essential Paul Ramsey: A Collection* (ed. William Werpehowski and Stephen D. Crocco; New Haven, CT: Yale University Press, 1994), pp. 60-67 (64): '[L]ove for neighbors threatened by violence, by aggression, or tyranny, provided the grounds for admitting the legitimacy of the use of military force.'

40. On 1 Corinthians 13, see Emanuel Miguens, '1 Corinthians 13:8-13 Reconsidered', *CBQ* 37 (1975), pp. 76-97.

41. Hans Conzelmann (*I Corinthians: A Commentary on the First Epistle to the Corinthians* [trans. James Leitch; Hermeneia; Philadelphia, PA: Fortress Press, 1975], p. 97) remarks: 'The destruction of the flesh can hardly mean anything but death.'

bettering the spirit is a form of love. 'Love' meant love toward someone's soul, not necessarily toward their body.[42]

The view of *agapē* in 1 Peter shows how easily violence and 'love' can be combined:

> Honor all men. Love the brotherhood. Fear God. Honor the emperor. Servants, be submissive to your masters with all respect, not only to the kind and gentle but also to the overbearing. For one is approved if, mindful of God, he endures pain while suffering unjustly (1 Pet. 2.17-19).

Here it is honorable to suffer, and love can entail suffering on behalf of a religious group.

The history of post-biblical interpretation shows that love could also be interpreted in such a way as to allow almost any act of violence. One can see how this works in the writings of the preeminent theologian of western Christendom, Augustine. In his *Reply to Faustus*, Augustine attempts to answer non-Christian objections to the violence in the Bible.[43] Faustus, an unbeliever, cites examples in which a violent act does not seem compatible with love, as in the case where Moses cooperated with Yahweh in the killing of some three thousand Israelites because they had committed idolatry with the Golden Calf (Exod. 32.30-35).

Augustine, however, sees this as an instance of love because idolatry hurts the soul, whereas Moses only hurt the bodies of the idolaters. Indeed, the idea that the soul could benefit by punishing the body has roots in the teachings of Jesus: 'Do not fear those who kill the body but cannot kill the soul; rather fear him who can destroy both soul and body in hell' (Mt. 10.28). Such a pneumatocentric view, which privileges any immaterial part of a human being over the physical part, is at the root of many instances of corporeal violence.[44]

Augustine makes a similar argument in his commentary on the Sermon on the Mount.[45] Therein he explains that physical punishment (*vindicta*) is not incompatible with love. Beating a child, for example, is an act of love. The proper attitude of the recipient of punishment, therefore, should

---

42. See also Jennifer Glancy, 'Boastings of Beatings (2 Corinthians 11.23-25)', *JBL* 123 (Spring 2004), pp. 99-135; N. Clayton Croy, '"To Die is Gain" (Philippians 1.19-26): Does Paul Contemplate Suicide?', *JBL* 122 (2003), pp. 517-31. For a critical look at Paul's notions of inclusion, see Denise Kimber Buell and Caroline Johnson Hodge, 'The Politics of Interpretation: The Rhetoric of Race and Ethnicity in Paul', *JBL* 123 (2004), pp. 235-51.

43. Augustine, *Reply to Faustus* 22.79 (NPNF[1], IV, pp. 303-304).

44 For the view that 'spirit' was in fact a material entitity in the Pauline corpus, see Troels Engberg-Pedersen, *Cosmology and Self in the Apostle Paul: The Material Spirit* (New York: Oxford University Press, 2010).

45. Augustine, *Sermon on the Mount* 1.20.63 (NPNF[1], VI, p. 27).

be happiness. He then cites examples of Elijah who punished with death the worshipers of Baal, the rival of Yahweh, so that the living might 'be struck with salutary fear'.[46] In other words, the creation of fear, otherwise called terrorism, is a just and legitimate instrument for God and his prophet.

Likewise, for Augustine, turning the other cheek can still allow retaliative violence. The idea that 'love' of God should entail the willingness to endure physical violence without retaliation can be traced back to Jesus' injunction to turn the other cheek. However, Augustine says that it is intentionality and inward disposition that makes the difference. Thus, we can intend to turn the other cheek, but our external bodily response need not match that inward disposition.[47]

In order to illustrate the difference between inward dispositions and outward actions, Augustine specifically cites an apocryphal story in which a servant strikes the apostle Thomas. Thomas curses the man, who is then mauled by a lion. However, since Thomas secured a pardon for the servant in the next world, then this violent retaliation in this world should not be seen as evil. Augustine concludes, concerning Thomas: 'Inwardly he preserved a kindly feeling, while outwardly he wished the man to be punished as an example.'[48]

Walter Wink argues that the sort of striking Jesus has in mind is more of a slap, which qualifies as an insult rather than as a real act of violence, an argument I will analyse more thoroughly in a following chapter.[49] Hugo Grotius (1583–1645), the reputed father of international law, has an even more ingenious explanation for Jesus' injunction of turning the other cheek. Grotius explains that a specific statement restricts a more general statement. In the case of turning the other cheek, we ought to interpret this as literally as possible, meaning that Christ is encouraging non-retaliation only in the case where one is struck on those specific body parts, namely the cheeks.[50]

Therefore, Jesus does not prohibit retaliation when someone strikes any other body parts. In fact, the selection of 'cheeks' for this injunction shows that Jesus intended non-retaliation for the lightest sort of injury possible

---

46. Augustine, *Sermon on the Mount* 1.20.64 (NPNF[1], VI, p. 27).

47. Augustine, *Reply to Faustus* 22.76-79 (NPNF[1], IV, pp. 301-304).

48. Augustine, *Reply to Faustus* 22.79 (NPNF[1], IV, p. 304). This episode about Thomas is also mentioned in Augustine's *Sermon on the Mount* 1.20.65 (NPNF[1], VI, p. 28). In both passages, Augustine alludes to the non-canonical status of the story.

49. Walter Wink, *Engaging the Powers: Discernment and Resistance in a World of Domination* (Minneapolis: Fortress Press, 1992), pp. 175-76.

50. Grotius, *Law of War* 1.2.8.3. Following Hugo Grotius, *The Law of War and Peace* (trans. Francis W. Kelsey; Indianapolis: Bobb-Merrill Company, 1925). The internal numeration for our citations is as follows: Book.Chapter. Section.Paragraph. For the Latin text, see William Whewell (ed.), *Hugonis Grottii De Jure Belli et Pacis Libri Tres* (Cambridge: Cambridge University Press, 1853).

rather than for more severe injuries (e.g., severing a limb, or potential life-threatening injury). Basing himself on supposed Hebrew customs, Grotius also opines that 'turning the cheek' could be entirely figurative. In addition, Grotius argues that Christ is not addressing magistrates, who may have duties to retaliate when the larger national body is attacked.

Grotius's legalistic mind was able to counter at least two other arguments used by pacifists. Jesus' injunction to walk an extra mile, Grotius argues, shows that Jesus is simply choosing actions that would least inconvenience a Christian. It would be different if Jesus had obliged us to walk a thousand miles. Jesus' injunction (Mt. 5.40//Lk. 6.29) to turn over a cloak when someone demands only a coat comes under Grotius's scalpel as well.[51] Grotius notes that a coat or a cloak should not be held equivalent to means of subsistence. War, therefore, is permissible for defense of one's food supply or country under Jesus' injunctions. Grotius also believes that the injunction about the cloak only refers to not pursuing some sort of lawsuit in court.[52]

Among modern authors, one also finds that love can explain acts of the most brutal violence. One example comes from Reuben A. Torrey (1856–1928), one of the contributors to *The Fundamentals*, a series of tracts that helped popularize the name 'fundamentalist'.[53] Torrey argues that 'The extermination of the Canaanite children was not only an act of mercy and love to the world at large; it was an act of love and mercy to the children themselves'.[54] The reason is that, if these children grew up, then they probably would end up suffering an eternity in hell. Slaughtering them in infancy ensures that their souls would go to heaven. Clearly, the slaughter, under this logic, is a loving act.

The Golden Rule: Love as Tactical

The so-called 'Golden Rule' bears particular importance in discussions about the teachings of Jesus. In the Matthean version, the rule reads as follows: 'So whatever you wish that men would do to you, do so to them; for this is the law and the prophets' (Mt. 7.12). As is the case with many other

51. Michael G. Steinhauser ('The Violence of Occupation: Matthew 5:40-41 and Q', *Toronto Journal of Theology* 8 [1992], pp. 28-37) argues that the Lucan version is older and reflects a specific context in which taking items of clothing was part of the Roman military occupation of Palestine.

52. Grotius, *Law of War*, 1.2.8.3 and 4. Grotius anticipates a current argument that Matthew 5.40, whose context seems to be a Jewish court of law, is later than the context of the parallel saying in Lk. 6.29.

53. See further, Roger Martin, *R.A. Torrey: Apostle of Certainty* (Murfreesboro, TN: Sword of the Lord, 1976).

54. Reuben A. Torrey, *Difficulties in the Bible: Alleged Errors and Contradictions* (Chicago, IL: Moody Press, n.d.), p. 60.

key passages, what seems obvious at first sight in this passage becomes complicated once examined in light of ancient cultures. Indeed, it should be noted that the Golden Rule is not unique or original to Christianity. One can trace its various versions to Greek authors hundreds of years before Jesus. Marcus Borg, a well-known member of the Jesus Seminar, claims that he finds a similar rule in Buddhist scriptures.[55]

There are various ways to read this rule.[56] The first interpretation is that it represents a completely disinterested action, and so is the true paradigm of love. This interpretation is the one favored by many modern Christian interpreters, especially those with pacifist leanings. A second interpretation emphasizes a reciprocal or neutral stance, in which equality is more of an economic transaction. A third interpretation is that the Golden Rule is based on self-interest.[57] This interpretation has antecedents in Greek authors who see a more Machiavellian strategy to vanquish the enemy. Thus, Thucydides speaks of the wisdom of one who 'vanquishes his foe by generosity'.[58] Being good to an enemy may oblige the enemy to return the favor.

So which interpretation is the one favored by the Gospel writer? At first glance, it may seem as though the disinterested interpretation is indicated. However, this would not seem compatible with the violence that Jesus plans for the enemies of Christians at the last judgment in Matthew 25.

> Then he will say to those at his left hand, 'Depart from me, you cursed, into the eternal fire prepared for the devil and his angels; for I was hungry and you gave me no food, I was thirsty and you gave me no drink, I was a stranger and you did not welcome me, naked and you did not clothe me, sick and in prison and you did not visit me.' Then they also will answer, 'Lord, when did we see thee hungry or thirsty or a stranger or naked or sick or in prison, and did not minister to thee?' Then he will answer them, 'Truly, I say to you, as you did it not to one of the least of these, you did it not to me.' And they will go away into eternal punishment, but the righteous into eternal life (Mt. 25.41-46).

It is here that one sees, then, another view of the nature of Christian love, at least in Matthew. However, there is also good reason to suppose that the idea can be traced back to the earliest sources. Gordon Zerbe, author of an extensive treatise on non-retaliation in the New Testament, notes, 'As in

---

55. Marcus Borg, *Jesus and Buddha: The Parallel Sayings* (Berkeley, CA: Seastone, 1999), pp. 14-15. Borg quotes Dhammapada 10.1. for his Buddhist source.

56. See further, Alan Kirk, '"Love your Enemies", the Golden Rule, and Ancient Reciprocity (Luke 6:27-35)', *JBL* 122 (2003), pp. 667-86. Kirk follows Marshall Sahlins (*Stone Age Economics* [Chicago, IL: Aldine, 1972], p. 39) in proposing three types of reciprocity (general reciprocity, balanced reciprocity, and negative reciprocity).

57. See Jeffrey Wattles, *The Golden Rule* (New York: Oxford University Press, 1996), especially pp. 64-66.

58. *Thucydides* 4.19.2 (Smith, LCL): καὶ ἀρετῇ αὐτὸν νικήσας.

many early Jewish texts non-retaliation and good deeds in response to persecutors in Q is [*sic*] grounded in the hope of eschatological vindication and judgement.'[59]

One can trace the roots of Matthew 25 further back into Egypt, where a similar scene occurs. *The Book of the Dead* refers to a compilation of materials that took final form in the Twenty-Sixth Dynasty of Egypt (685–525 BCE), though one can trace it to the beginning of the New Kingdom and before. Thus, it is older than any existing manuscript of the Bible. As a guidebook for the journey into the afterlife, *The Book of the Dead* is one of the first texts in history to provide an extensive list of specific actions that were valued by the gods. As preparation for this journey, a person is supposed to list actions the gods would find acceptable:

> I have acted rightly in Egypt.
> I have not cursed a god…
> I have done what people speak of,
> What the gods are pleased with…
> I have given bread to the hungry,
> water to the thirsty,
> clothes to the naked,
> a ferryboat to the boatless.
> I have given divine offerings to the gods.[60]

As in the case of the Matthean judgment scene, *The Book of the Dead* judges individuals by the extent to which they helped those experiencing the same triad of sufferings (hungry, thirsty, naked).

The idea that love has a utilitarian value reappears in the work of modern pacifists. Thus, William Klassen urges that Christians use love to 'win' over enemies.[61] In any case, Matthew indicates that Christians can afford to love the enemy now because Jesus will torture the enemies of Christians at the end of time. The judgment described in Matthew 25, after all, does not differ much from an act of revenge. At the very least, the author or editor of Matthew did not seem to see any incompatibility between the Golden Rule that he included in Matthew 7 and the revenge that Jesus was to mete out in Matthew 25.

The Parochialism of New Testament Ethics

Why do so many New Testament scholars believe that Jesus was an innovator? As already indicated, part of the answer is pure religiocentrism and ethnocentrism. However, there is also evidence that some of this notion

59. Zerbe, *Non-Retaliation in Early Jewish and New Testament Texts*, p. 210.
60. Lichtheim, *Ancient Egyptian Literature*, II, p. 128.
61. Klassen, '"Love Your Enemy"', pp. 147-71.

has to do with how New Testament ethicists are trained. One expects most New Testament scholars to be acquainted with Greco-Roman and Jewish literature of the Second Temple period. There are, of course, some New Testament scholars who are well trained in ancient Near Eastern literature (e.g., Adela Yarbro Collins). But the vast majority of the primary works in New Testament ethics still display a parochialism in the comparative set of data from ancient Near Eastern sources. That lack of either acquaintance or unwillingness to engage with that literature explains the predominance of the idea that Jesus was an innovator.

Consider 'state of the art' surveys of New Testament studies, which often lack chapters or essays dealing with ancient Near Eastern parallels other than Greco-Roman. For example, not a single chapter in *The Face of New Testament Studies: A Survey of Recent Research* edited by Scot McKnight and Grant R. Osborn is devoted to parallels from the ancient Near East.[62] The indices of works cited in New Testament scholarship likewise offer a good metric of the extent to which New Testament ethicists utilize any pre-Hellenistic Near Eastern Literature from Anatolia (Hittites), Egypt, Mesopotamia, Phoenicia or Ugarit. I have collected some basic information from the indices of major works in New Testament ethics in the Appendix, but observe for now that none of the listed works that identify their sources ever cite pre-Hellenistic Near Eastern sources.

In particular, the citation indices of Richard Hays's *Moral Vision of the New Testament* cites no sources from ancient Anatolia, Egypt, Phoenicia, Mesopotamia or Ugarit.[63] Elisabeth Schüssler Fiorenza's classic work, *In Memory of Her*, cites no extrabiblical sources at all.[64] It is no wonder that the Jesus-as-ethical-innovator trope persists with this lack of awareness of his predecessors.

Summary

In contrast to the claims of many Christian ethicists, Jesus is not an innovator in ethics, and certainly not in his approach to love. At the least he is not the originator of the concept of loving your enemy, which is already found in both Jewish and ancient Near Eastern sources centuries before Jesus came on the scene. The lack of any interest in, or awareness of, ancient Near

---

62. Scot McKnight and Grant R. Osborn (eds.), *The Face of New Testament Studies: A Survey of Recent Research* (Grand Rapids, MI: Baker, 2004). Similarly, Ron Cameron and Merrill P. Miller (eds.), *Redescribing Christian Origins* (SBL Symposium, 28; Atlanta, GA: Scholars Press, 2004).

63. Hays, *The Moral Vision*, p. 496.

64. Elisabeth Scüssler Fiorenza, *In Memory of Her: A Feminist Reconstruction of Christian Origins* (New York: Crossroad, 1983), pp. 353-57.

Eastern cultures by many prominent New Testament ethicists may be one reason that they continue to tout innovations and novelties for Jesus.

Nor is the concept of love that simple. The English word, love, in the New Testament actually translates a set of Greek words that are themselves complex and are often used to translate Hebrew words. Love can be altruistic, and it can be a thoroughly imperialistic term. Any requirement to love one's enemy must be balanced by Jesus' belief in deferred violence, which is rarely mentioned by New Testament ethicists. Jesus obligates you to give up your own life for that of your master, whom you are supposed to love above all. Jesus, as the innovator of a thoroughly selfless and altruistic love ethic, is mainly the creation of Christian ethicists.

Chapter 3

The Hateful Jesus: Luke 14.26

Even if not all New Testament ethicists agree on whether love is the central message of Jesus' ethics, there seems to be a general agreement that Jesus certainly did not advocate hate. Otto Michel (1903–1993), author of the *TDNT* article on 'hate', denies that Jesus intended any real hatred and contrasts him with a presumably more hateful Judaism: 'Jesus lays on his disciples the obligation of love for all men, even enemies. He knows no holy hatred against men. He thus brings to light an irresolvable discord in the OT and especially in Judaism.'[1] Such comments by Michel not only show a theological bias in his lexicography, but also betray the sort of Christian supersessionism critiqued by E.P. Sanders, among many others.[2]

Yet, New Testament scholars usually admit that the word 'hate', in the most negative sense one might attribute to it, existed in the biblical texts. Thus, Edmund Sutcliffe observes the following with respect to the Hebrew Bible:

> [T]here is the real malicious hatred by which man wishes evil to his enemy and even desires and, if possible, accomplishes his destruction. Thus Esau hated his brother Jacob because he had surreptitiously obtained his father's blessing and in his hatred determined to slay him... It is a hatred that is seated in both feelings and in the will, and it is a hatred of persons.[3]

Sutcliffe's description of 'hate' involves (1) an intent to harm the object of hatred and (2) an emotive or affective component.[4] For the purposes of my

---

1. Otto Michel, 'μισέω', *TDNT*, IV, pp. 683-94 (693). For Michel's ties to the Nazi regime that may explain some of his approaches to lexicography and biblical studies, see Gisela Dachs, 'Otto Michel: Freund der Juden?', *Zeit Online* (22 January 2012). Online: http://www.zeit.de/2012/04/Judaistik-Theologe-Michel. See also Anders Gerdmar, *Roots of Theological Antisemitism: Biblical Interpretation and the Jews, from Herder and Semmler to Kittel and Bultmann* (Leiden: E.J. Brill, 2009).

2. Sanders, 'Jesus, Ancient Judaism, and Modern Christianity', pp. 31-55. For responses to Sanders, see James M. Hamilton, 'N.T. Wright and Saul's Moral Bootstraps: New Light on "The New Perspective"', *Trinity Journal* 25 (2004), pp. 139-55.

3. Edmund Sutcliffe, 'Hatred at Qumran', *RevQ* 2 (1960), pp. 345-56 (345).

4. For a sociological study of hatred, see Jack Levin and Gordana Rabrenovic, *Why we Hate* (Amherst, NY: Prometheus, 2004).

argument, I will regard Sutcliffe's description as the 'literal' meaning of 'hate'. It is this view of hatred that New Testament scholars most often deny to Jesus, even though he should have felt such hatred as much as any other human being on certain occasions.

Of course, the idea that Jesus preaches only love, but not hatred, inevitably has to address places where Jesus explicitly used the word, 'hate', or committed actions that would be seen as cruel or hateful if performed by anyone else. So, how do New Testament ethicists address those texts? Usually, one encounters two approaches: (a) Ignore the texts; (b) Claim that actions or words that might otherwise appear hateful are really not so. The latter strategy often combines appeals to other languages, as well as to theological rationales that often are not represented as what they are.

Jesus Commands Hate

Discussions of Lk. 14.26 within New Testament scholarship show how denials of Jesus' 'hate speech' usually do not reckon fully with the nature of the linguistic evidence. Often these discussions reflect theological rationales that are being substituted for linguistic and historical ones. Luke 14.26, perhaps the most prominent example of 'hate speech' by Jesus, reads:

> If any one comes to me and does not hate his own father and mother and wife and children and brothers and sisters, yes, and even his own life, he cannot be my disciple (Lk. 14.26).

> Εἴ τις ἔρχεται πρός με καὶ οὐ μισεῖ τὸν πατέρα ἑαυτοῦ καὶ τὴν μητέρα καὶ τὴν γυναῖκα καὶ τὰ τέκνα καὶ τοὺς ἀδελφοὺς καὶ τὰς ἀδελφάς, ἔτι τε καὶ τὴν ψυχὴν ἑαυτοῦ, οὐ δύναται εἶναί μου μαθητής.

Although the text seems as clear an expression of literal hate as any text found anywhere, Christian apologists have attempted to erase or lessen its negative connotations.

Among those who completely or virtually ignore Lk. 14.26 is Stephen Voorwinde, who wrote an entire book on *Jesus' Emotions in the Gospels* (2011), which contains chapters or sections devoted to love, compassion, grief, amazement, indignation, but none to hate.[5] Allen Verhey does not mention Lk. 14.26 in the scriptural index of his *Remembering Jesus*.[6] Wayne Meeks also omits Lk. 14.26 from his scriptural index of his book, *The Origins of Christian Morality*.[7] Matera's *New Testament Ethics* does quote the

---

5. Luke 14.26 does not appear in Voorwinde's index (*Jesus' Emotions*, p. 240) of biblical citations.

6. Allen Verhey, *Remembering Jesus: Christian Community, Scripture and the Moral Life* (Grand Rapids, MI: Eerdmans, 2002), p. 520.

7. Wayne A. Meeks, *The Origins of Christian Morality: The First Two Centuries* (New Haven, CT: Yale University Press, 1993), p. 262.

verse once, but relates it only to the cost of discipleship: 'The first of these sayings (Lk. 14.26) echoes what Jesus told the three would-be disciples at the beginning of the journey about the need to leave family behind.'[8] Similarly, Richard B. Hays cites it once in a sentence about how 'the demands of radical discipleship in the synoptic Gospels are potentially disruptive of family order'.[9] As I will discuss further below, to say 'potentially disruptive of family order' is already sanitizing what Jesus commanded if taken literally.

Burridge, whose entire project is devoted to the ethics of Jesus, hardly addresses Lk. 14.26 at all. Burridge cites the verse twice. In the first instance, Burridge mentions it within a broader discussion about the demands of following Jesus: 'The call must take priority over family relationships (Mt. 10.37-38//Lk. 14.26).'[10] In the second instance, he cites it within a broader rejection of a literal understanding of some of Jesus' more radical demands: 'Does Jesus expect his disciples to cut off their hands or feet, or pluck out their eyes (Mk 9.43-48), or to "hate father or mother" (Lk. 14.26)'?'[11]

The Jewish Annotated New Testament simply remarks '*Hate*, hyperbolic (See Prov. 13.24) but consistent with Luke's interest in severing familial and economic ties…'.[12] There is no argument offered for why it is 'hyperbolic' and no reason given why such language is attributed to the author rather than to Jesus. I. Howard Marshall, whose commentary on Luke centers on issues of Greek philology, refers readers to the Hebrew word שנא (*śn'*) and to other Greek words he thinks are comparable (e.g., ἀφίημι, ἀρνέομαι). Marshall then assures readers that '[t]he thought is, therefore, not of psychological hate, but of renunciation'.[13] For support, Marshall simply refers to Michel's article on 'hate' in *TDNT*.

The Good News Bible erases the word 'hate' altogether, and renders the verse as follows: 'Whoever comes to me cannot be my disciple unless he loves me more than he loves his father and his mother, his wife and his

8. Matera, *New Testament Ethics*, p. 81.

9. Hays, *The Moral Vision*, p. 196. See also Rekha M. Chennattu, *Johannine Discipleship as a Covenant Relationship* (Peabody, MA: Hendrickson, 2006); Leif Vaage, 'En otra casa: El discipulado en Marcos como asceticismo domestico', *EstBib* 63.1 (2005), pp. 21-42; Anni Hentschel, *Diakonia im Neuen Testament: Studien zur Semantik unter besonderer Berücksichtigung der Rolle von Frauen* (WUNT, 2.226; Tübingen: Mohr Siebeck, 2007); John N. Collins, *Diakonia: Re-interpreting the Ancient Sources* (New York: Oxford University Press, 1990).

10. Burridge, *Imitating Jesus*, p. 48.

11. Burridge, *Imitating Jesus*, p.58.

12. Amy-Jill Levine and Marc Zvi Brettler (eds.), *The Jewish Annotated New Testament* (New York: Oxford University Press, 2011), p. 132.

13. I. Howard Marshall, *The Gospel of Luke: A Commentary on the Greek Text* (New International Greek Testament Commentary; Exeter: Paternoster Press, 1978), p. 592.

children, his brothers, and his sisters and himself as well.' In other words, the *Good News Bible* transfers Mt. 10.37 to Lk. 14.26. Carson Brisson approves of the alleged Matthean redaction: 'By substituting love for hate, it avoids the misunderstanding that could arise from the harshness of the hyperbolic "hate" in Luke's text.'[14] Edmund Sutcliffe also believes that, in the case of Lk. 14.26, 'the meaning is given clearly in another text…Matthew 10,37'.[15]

All of these scholars, even when they bother to mention Lk. 14.26, assume that 'hate' in that verse cannot be understood in its harshest sense and offer no detailed exegetical reasons why they believe so. As such, these scholars do not differ much from so-called fundamentalist Christians who also believe it is not literal. Thus, John Vernon McGee, a 'fundamentalist' Christian broadcaster and commentator, says: 'The verses are simply saying that we should put God first. A believer's devotedness to Jesus Christ should be such that, by comparison, everything else is hated.'[16]

Indeed, the main defense for Jesus offered by New Testament ethicists is that Jesus was speaking comparatively. More specifically it is alleged that Lk. 14.26 expresses a comparison of degree (i.e., 'more than'). One may label this 'the comparative interpretation', which can be summarized more schematically as: 'Hate X = Love Y [= Jesus] more than X [= family] in Lk. 14.26'. As mentioned, this interpretation of Lk. 14.26 is often justified by assuming that a parallel saying in Mt. 10.37 ('He who loves father or mother more than me is not worthy of me; and he who loves son or daughter more than me is not worthy of me') constitutes the proper meaning of Lk. 14.26.

If one applies more rigorous linguistic procedures, it is necessary to examine the basic relevant grammatical structure of a crucial portion of Lk. 14.26:

Verb +	Object(s) of verb +	Reflexive pronoun
Hate	the father…	('his own…')
μισεῖ	τὸν πατέρα	ἑαυτοῦ…

This construction highlighted consists of a transitive verb in the third person masculine singular (μισεῖ, from the verb μισέω, pronounced *miseō*) with a direct object indicated by the accusative case (τὸν πατέρα…), and followed by a masculine reflexive pronoun in the genitive case indicating possession (e.g., 'his own father'). 'Father', the first direct object of *miseō*, is

---

14. Carson Brisson, 'Luke 14:25-27', *Int* 61 (2007), pp. 310-12 (311).

15. Sutcliffe, 'Hatred at Qumran', p. 346.

16. J. Vernon McGee, *Thru the Bible with J. Vernon McGee* (5 vols.; Pasadena, CA: Thru the Bible Radio, 1988), IV, p. 311.

followed by six others: 'mother and wife and children and brothers and sisters, yes, and even his own life'.

The main problem with interpreting the grammatical structure, *miseō* + object of hate, as a comparative expression is that it is no such thing grammatically. Greek has very specific modes of constructing comparative expressions, and no indicators of comparison are present here.[17] In fact, in Mt. 10.37 one finds an explicit example of a Greek comparative construction: Ὁ φιλῶν πατέρα ἢ μητέρα ὑπὲρ ἐμὲ οὐκ ἔστιν μου ἄξιος. Here, the preposition ὑπέρ ('above', 'more') informs readers of such a comparison. In contrast, there are no explicit verbs, particles or prepositions associated with comparison in Lk. 14.26.[18]

At the same time, there are cogent reasons for not using Mt. 10.37 to establish the meaning of Lk. 14.26. One reason is quite simple: *One cannot assume that Luke's readers had read Matthew at the time Luke was written.* At the time Luke was being written, the New Testament, as we know it, did not exist. It was not complete, and that applies to all four Gospels. Therefore, it is implausible for the author of Luke to use a powerful word such as *miseō*, and then hope that someone would have read Matthew in order to explain what Luke meant. Rather, one would expect that Luke will use words that the audience will understand *from the way that those words are used in the language of the reader.* The Greek word *miseō* has as consistent and as strong a meaning as any word in the entire Greek lexicon. It does not vary or is not subject to as much flexibility as other words may be.

Matthew's reading can also be explained without having to change the meaning of the word *miseō* in Luke. Matthew may not have liked the strong and harsh tone of Lk. 14.26, and so he changed it. Indeed, the Catholic biblical scholar Joseph Fitzmyer explicitly says so: 'Matthew has softened the demand of Jesus by his redactional wording "loves...more than me"'.[19] Some scholars suspect that Matthew changed, added or used other sources relative to Luke.[20] As I will show further below, the Gospel of Thomas may also indicate that Mt. 10.34-37 is reflecting an independent tradition. Similarly, the fact that the *Good News Bible* substitutes 'love' for 'hate' in Lk. 14.26 does not mean that the definition of the word 'hate' has changed; it just

17. On comparative expressions, see BDF, paragraphs 60-62.

18. For this use of ὑπέρ, see meaning B in BDAG, p. 1031a: 'w. acc. marker of a degree beyond that of a compared scale of extent, in the sense of excelling, surpassing, *over and above, beyond, more than*' (italic emphasis BDAG).

19. Joseph A. Fitzmyer, *The Gospel According to Luke X–XXIV* (AB, 28A; Garden City, NY: Doubleday, 1985), p. 1063.

20. So Ulrich Luz, *Matthew 8–20: A Commentary* (trans. James E. Crouch; Hermeneia; Minneapolis: Fortress Press, 2001), p. 112, where he says that 'the original saying was formulated in a more radical, viz., in an antithetical way: "Whoever does not hate father and mother..."'.

means that the *Good News Bible* has disregarded or changed the meaning of *miseō* in Lk. 14.26 altogether. Accordingly, Matthew's supposed redaction does not redefine the word *miseō* in Greek; Matthew may be simply changing the meaning of Luke altogether by providing different words.

Lexicography as Apologetics

Lexicography has been a primary instrument to mitigate the hateful teachings of Jesus. In many cases, blatant theological rationales are substituted for linguistic methods to determine the meaning of words. One illustration is the article on *miseō* written by Otto Michel in *TDNT*, still one of the most authoritative lexicons in New Testament studies. It is worth quoting at length a passage from that article explaining why *miseō* should not be interpreted in Lk. 14.26 as it is interpreted virtually everywhere else in the New Testament:

> No challenge is offered to the supremacy of the law of love. It is worth noting that Rev. 2.6 speaks of hatred for the works of the Nicolaitans, not of hatred for the men themselves. When Jesus presents the requirements for discipleship, He certainly says that the disciple must renounce the natural and legal ties which bind him to his relatives (Lk. 14.26; Mt. 10.37), and to his own life (Jn 12.25). But here, too, the reference is not to a psychologically conditioned shunning of men explicable in human terms. It is to the unconditional and exclusive character of the claim of Jesus, which will not stop at even the most important of earthly bonds, including the Law itself. There is in the NT a holy repudiation and abnegation (μισεῖν), but it is embraced and interpreted by love as the power and content of the new world of God. Because the love of God in Christ sanctifies and cleanses, holy hate is forbidden. A repudiation which does not derive from love, or lead to love, cannot appeal to the NT. The NT overcomes all possible forms of hate between man and man, including religious. It teaches, however, a holy repudiation of wickedness and a commitment to Christ with no human reservations or conditions.[21]

Note how few linguistic data are presented for the conclusions. In fact, in adducing Rev. 2.6 because it provides an example of 'hatred for the works of the Nicolaitans, not of hatred for the men themselves', Michel blatantly disregards the fact that the direct objects of the word μισέω in Lk. 14.26 are human beings (father, mother, etc.), and not works. Otherwise, Michel's reasoning is completely circular:

    A. In Lk. 14.26 *miseō* cannot mean literal hate
    B. Because the New Testament does not teach hate;
    C. And since the New Testament does not teach hate,
    D. In Lk. 14.26 *miseō* cannot mean literal hate.

21. Michel, 'μισέω', p. 693.

Likewise, there is little else but Michel's theological speculation to establish, for example, that '[b]ecause the love of God in Christ sanctifies and cleanses, holy hate is forbidden'.[22] Other comments bear a pastoral flavor, including the claim that 'a repudiation of which is not derived from love, or lead to love, cannot appeal to the NT'.[23] I will return to examine some of the more seemingly linguistic arguments offered by Michel below.

In any case, one still needs to establish the most accurate meaning of the Greek word *miseō* translated 'hate'. There are at least two basic lexicographical procedures for establishing the meaning of words in any ancient language: (A) seek contrastive expressions involving the word in question; (B) compare translations into other languages.[24] If one uses Procedure A, then in every instance where one finds '*miseō* + object of hate' in the New Testament or Septuagint there is every reason to take it as the opposite of love. For example:[25]

> **Judg. 14.16**: And Samson's wife wept before him, and said, 'You only *hate* [μεμίσηκας] me, you do not *love* [οὐκ ἠγάπηκας] me'.

> **Amos 5.15**: *Hate* [μισέω] evil and *love* [ἀγαπάω] good...

> **Lk. 16.13**: No servant can serve two masters; for either he will *hate* [μισήσει] the one and *love* [ἀγαπήσει] the other, or he will be devoted to the one and despise the other. You cannot serve God and mammon.

> **1 Jn 2.10-11**: He who *loves* [ἀγαπῶν] his brother abides in the light, and in it there is no cause for stumbling. But he who *hates* [μισῶν] his brother is in the darkness and walks in the darkness, and does not know where he is going, because the darkness has blinded his eyes.

In every case, '*miseō* X' means the absence of any love for X, the opposite of 'to love' (ἀγαπάω/*agapaō*), and/or even hostility toward X.[26] Never does '*miseō* + X' indisputably mean 'to love Y more than X' in any other Greek biblical text where hate and love are paired. In fact, *miseō* is interpreted as the opposite of love virtually everywhere *miseō* and love are paired or encountered separately in Greek biblical texts.

22. Michel, 'μισέω', p. 693.
23. Michel, 'μισέω', p. 693.
24. For a general treatment on the issues of establishing the meaning of words, see R.R.K. Hartmann (ed.), *Lexicography: Principles and Practice* (New York: Academic Press, 1983); Arthur Mettinger, *Aspects of Semantic Opposition in English* (New York: Oxford University Press, 1994).
25. Quoting Judg. 14.16 and Amos 5.15 as cited in the Septuagint, the Greek translation of the Hebrew Bible. My italics. For an edition, see Alfred Rahlfs, *Septuaginta... Editio minor* (Stuttgart: Deutsche Bibelgesellschaft, 1979). On the use of the Septuagint by early Christians, see Martin Hengel, *The Use of the Septuagint as Scripture: Its Prehistory and the Problems of its Canon* (Grand Rapids, MI: Baker Academic, 2004).
26. See also Fitzmyer, *Luke X–XXIV*, p. 1063.

Luke 16.13 is particularly instructive because it shows the usage of the word *miseō* by presumably the same author of Lk. 14.26: 'No slave can serve two masters; for a slave will either hate the one and love the other, or be devoted to the one and despise the other. You cannot serve God and wealth' (Lk. 16.13). The author clearly indicates here that 'hate = absence of love'. One *cannot* have both love and hate for the same person. You either love one or the other. In 1 Jn 2.10-11 the author is contrasting 'loves his brother' (ὁ ἀγαπῶν τὸν ἀδελφὸν αὐτοῦ) in v. 10 with 'hates his brother' (ὁ δὲ μισῶν τὸν ἀδελφὸν αὐτοῦ) in v. 11 because the adversative conjunction (δέ/'but') usually introduces an opposing statement. And 1 Jn 2.11 offers a similar grammatical construction with a form of *miseō* + human beings as direct objects, just as is found in Lk. 14.26.

Thus, one can develop a basic linguistic and semantic rationale for my literal interpretation of *miseō* in Lk. 14.26:

> A. Since *miseō* is interpreted literally as the opposite of 'to love' *every-where* in the Greek scriptures when these words are paired,
> B. And since there is no other indication that *miseō* is not literal in Lk. 14.26,
> C. Then *miseō* probably means literally the opposite of 'to love' in Lk. 14.26.
> D. The opposite of 'to love' is 'to hate'.

Despite a clear Greek linguistic rationale for taking the word literally in Lk. 14.26, New Testament ethicists have tried to appeal to other sources of evidence, and these sources range from Semitic texts (especially in Hebrew, Aramaic and Akkadian) to contextual and theological rationales that are presented as historical and linguistic ones. I now turn to examine those sources in more detail.

The Use of Greco-Roman Sources

Otto Michel and Darrell Bock appeal to Epictetus (55–135 CE), the Stoic philosopher, to support his comparative interpretation. As Bock remarks in his commentary on Lk. 14.26: 'The idiom is known in Greek (see Epictetus 3.3.5). See also O. Michel.'[27] Both Bock and Michel cite the work of J. Denney for support.[28] J. Denney is perhaps the earliest scholar to cite Epictetus to support a non-literal rendering of Lk. 14.26.[29] However, neither Michel nor Bock quote Epictetus directly, and a close examination of the passage cited shows the weakness of Bock's claim. As it is, Denny

---

27. Darrell L. Bock, *The NIV Application Commentary: Luke* (Grand Rapids., MI: Zondervan, 1996), p. 401 n. 2.

28. Michel, 'μισέω', p. 690 n. 24.

29. J. Denny, 'The Word "Hate" in Luke xiv.26', *ExpTim* 20 (1909), pp. 41-42.

is actually comparing Epictetus to a passage in Shakespeare's *History of Henry VI: Part II* (Act 5, Scene 2), about the love of valor over the love of self, and not to a grammatical structure in Lk. 14.26.

In any case, note what Epictetus actually says: 'This is why the good is preferred above every form of kinship. My father is nothing to me, but only the good.'[30] What Bock means by 'the idiom' that is supposedly analogous to that in Lk. 14.26 is unclear. Epictetus certainly does not use the word *miseō* to express preference for the good (*agathos*) over kinship. Epictetus shows that a person could choose some good principle over family, but it does not show that he used the word *miseō* to express such a choice. In fact, Epictetus confirms that he does not use *miseō* in the way that Bock suggests.

Moreover, Epictetus concedes that maintaining kinship relationships could be redefined as good, and so no choice would be necessary. Note this statement: 'If, however, we define the good as consisting in a right moral purpose [ἐὰν δ' ἐν ὀρθῇ προαιρέσει θῶμεν], then the mere preservation of the relationships of life becomes a good.'[31] That statement is much more positive about the value of maintaining family relations than what is advised by Jesus. Jesus defines hatred of one's family as a good thing as long as one follows Jesus. Epictetus, on the other hand, defines a familial relationship as one that has a good moral purpose, without any stipulations about follow-ing Epictetus. In sum, this passage in Epictetus has absolutely no bearing on the meaning of *miseō*, which Epictetus does not use here in any case.[32]

Love and Hate as Comparative in Hebrew

Some scholars realize that they cannot make their case on the basis of Greek linguistics. Thus, Christopher M. Hays admits, 'Μισέω does not mean "love less" and often (but not always) carries the real emotional vehe-mence of the modern term "hate".'[33] Therefore, he attempts to appeal to 'Semitic usage' to make the case for an alternative and less objectionable

30. Epictetus, *Discourses* 3.3.5 (Oldfather, LCL): Διὰ τοῦτο πάσης οἰκειότητος προκρίνεται τὸ ἀγαθόν. οὐδὲν ἐμοὶ καὶ τῷ πατρί, ἀλλὰ τῷ ἀγαθῷ.

31. Epictetus, *Discourses* 3.3.8 (Oldfather, LCL): ἐὰν δ' ἐν ὀρθῇ προαιρέσει θῶμεν, αὐτὸ τὸ τηρεῖν τὰς σχέσεις ἀγαθὸν γίνεται καὶ λοιπὸν ὁ τῶν ἐκτός τινων ἐκχωρῶν οὗτος τοῦ ἀγαθοῦ τυγχάνει. For comments on the value of the family in Epictetus, see Julia Annas, 'Epictetus on Moral Perspectives', in *The Philosophy of Epictetus* (ed. Theodore Scaltsas and Andrew S. Mason; New York: Oxford University Press, 2007), pp. 140-52.

32. For parallels with the New Testament, see Douglas S. Sharp, *Epictetus and the New Testament* (London: Charles H. Kelley, 1914). Sharp does not list Lk. 14.26 or *miseō* in his index of parallels to Epictetus.

33. Christopher M. Hays, 'Hating Wealth and Wives? An Examination of Disciple-ship Ethics in the Third Gospel', *TynBul* 60 (2009), pp. 47-68 (54).

meaning: 'behaving toward someone or something in a negligent or delete-rious fashion, which might otherwise imply hate'.[34] Such arguments rely on the well-known premise that New Testament authors often retain or reflect Semitic usage, especially from Hebrew and Aramaic.[35] Thus, Craig Evans explicitly tells readers that, in Lk. 14.26, '*If anyone does not hate...* may be an example of the Semitic expression of preference by means of antith-esis—"I love A and hate B" meaning "I prefer A to B" (cf. Gen. 29.30ff; Rom 9.13), which has been altered, but correctly interpreted in its Matthean form (Mt. 10.37).'[36]

At the center of these arguments is the meaning of the West Semitic root שׂנא (*śn'*) that is attested in, among other ancient Semitic languages, Hebrew, Aramaic, Moabite and Phoenician.[37] *The Dictionary of Classical Hebrew* lists its first meaning as 'personal, **hate**, with a wide range of intensity, from the strongly, emotional **hate, loathe**, to the milder despise, shun...**take an aver-sion to**, and the even milder **have enough of, be weary of** (Pr 25^{17})'.[38] As I will attempt to show, even those cases where *DCH* understands *śn'* to bear a milder meaning (e.g., Prov. 25.17) do not preclude a more intense or harsher understanding. Most scholars agree that its Akkadian equivalent is *zêru*.[39]

As pointed out already, the Hebrew *śn'* is regarded as the direct opposite of 'love' (אהב) in a number of texts, including Judg. 14.16 and Amos 5.15. Such oppositional usage continues at Qumran, as in the *Community Rule/Manual of Discipline* (1QS 1.9-10): 'and to love all the sons of light...and to hate all the sons of darkness' (ולאהוב כול בני אור...ולשׂנוא כול בני חושך).[40]

34. Hays, 'Hating Wealth and Wives?', pp. 54-55.

35. For example, Samuel Tobias Lachs ('Hebrew Elements in the Gospels and Acts', *JQR* 71 [1980], pp. 31-43 [40-41]) sees Hebrew poetic elements in Lk. 14.26; Michel says ('μισέω', p. 685): 'We have here a Hebraism as in the requirement for disciple-ship... Luke 14.26.'

36. Craig Evans, *St. Luke* (TPI New Testament Commentaries; Philadelphia, PA: Trin-ity Press International, 1990), p. 577 (italics Evans). Similarly, E. Jenni, 'שׂנא', *TLOT*, III, pp. 1277-79. To be fair, Evans (*St. Luke*, p. 577) adds: 'But in view of the sweeping nature of v. 33 and the addition of wife (cf. a similar addition in Mark in 18.29, it may express Luke's rigorous outlook.' Yet note the sanitizing of 'hate' by the adjective, 'rig-orous', when we could just as well describe Luke's view as 'hateful'. Evans also attri-butes such a hateful view to Luke, while attributing the loving passages to the historical Jesus, and not to the author of the Gospels.

37. See E. Lipinski, 'שׂנא', *TDOT*, XIV, pp. 164-74; Jenni, 'שׂנא', pp. 1277-79.

38. See 'שׂנא', *DCH*, VIII, pp. 167-71 (167). Bold emphases are those of *DCH*.

39. Lipinski, 'שׂנא', *TDOT*, XIV, p. 164. For *zêru*, see *CAD*, XXI, pp. 97-99.

40. Martínez (*The Dead Sea Scrolls Translated*, p. 3) has the oppositional pair as 'love...detest'. For the Hebrew text, I depend on Lohse, *Die Texte aus Qumran*, p. 4. See also Sutcliffe, 'Hatred at Qumran', pp. 345-56; Krister Stendahl, 'Hate, Non-Retaliation, and Love: 1QS x. 17-20 and Rom. 12:19-21', *HTR* 55 (1962), pp. 343-55.

Thus, 'love' and 'hate' can be viewed as literal opposites in all periods of the pre-Christian Hebrew language in which the words are attested together.

In any case, Gen. 29.30-31 is thought to offer a good analogy to Lk. 14.26 according to Craig Evans's commentary on Luke.[41] In particular, the LXX version of Gen. 29.30-31 appears to undermine my case for such drastic contrasts between love and hate:

> καὶ εἰσῆλθεν πρὸς Ραχηλ· ἠγάπησεν δὲ Ραχηλ μᾶλλον ἢ Λειαν· καὶ ἐδούλευσεν αὐτῷ ἑπτὰ ἔτη ἕτερα. Ἰδὼν δὲ κύριος ὅτι μισεῖται Λεια, ἤνοιξεν τὴν μήτραν αὐτῆς· Ραχηλ δὲ ἦν στεῖρα.

> So Jacob went in to Rachel also, and he loved Rachel more than Leah, and served Laban for another seven years. When the LORD saw that Leah was hated, he opened her womb; but Rachel was barren (Gen. 29.30-31).

It is true that the construction μισεῖται Λεια (passive indicative of μισέω + subject) is the semantic equivalent of the μισέω + direct object of Lk. 14.26.

However, reading μᾶλλον ἢ Λειαν as expressing a comparison of degree (i.e., 'more than') is not necessarily correct or definitive. Here is a case where μᾶλλον can apply to cases of 'exclusivistic comparisons'. In BDAG, one finds at least three major meanings for μᾶλλον.[42] In particular, note meaning 3c, where the construction μᾶλλον ἢ is specifically addressed. This construction excludes what follows from the action of the previous verb. Thus, it should be translated 'instead of' or 'rather than'. It is an *exclusionary* comparative expression rather than a comparison of degree.

Thus, when describing Moses's decision to choose his suffering people over the sinful life he could have had in Egypt, Heb. 11.25 remarks: 'choosing rather to share ill-treatment with the people of God than to enjoy the fleeting pleasures of sin' (μᾶλλον ἑλόμενος συγκακουχεῖσθαι τῷ λαῷ τοῦ Θεοῦ ἢ πρόσκαιρον ἔχειν ἁμαρτίας ἀπόλαυσιν). Given the high esteem accorded to Moses by the author of Hebrews (e.g., Heb. 3.2-5; 11.27), it would be odd for that author to mean that Moses merely preferred to suffer with his people *more than* he liked to live sinfully in Egypt. Instead the author of Hebrews more likely means that Moses chose his people to the exclusion of a sinful life in Egypt, which is exactly what the biblical narratives show (cf. Heb. 3.16). Similarly, the clause in Gen. 29.30 can be acceptably translated as 'He loved Rachel instead of Leah' = 'He loved Rachel, not Leah'.

Corroborative evidence comes from the Hebrew, which the Greek version was presumably attempting to translate (though this claim must be

41. Evans, *St. Luke*, p. 577.
42. BDAG, 'μᾶλλον', pp. 613-14.

stated with caution).[43] The MT bears the following construction: ויאהב גם את
רחל מלאה. In particular, Bruce K. Waltke and M. O'Connor view the Hebrew
construction in Gen. 29.30 as 'comparison of exclusion', and translate it:
'He loved Rachel *rather than* Leah.'[44] Accordingly, Gen. 29.30 does not
constitute a definitive example where μισέω expresses a comparison of
degree as it is alleged for Lk. 14.26. The verse can be understood to mean
that Jacob loved Rachel, and hated (or had no love for) Leah. If so, then
Jesus in Lk. 14.26 could be understood to say: 'hate your father...but love
me'.

Romans 9.13, which is cited by Evans as analogous to Lk. 14.26, may
be explained in the same manner. The text reads: 'As it is written: "Jacob I
loved, but Esau I hated"' (καθὼς γέγραπται, Τὸν 'Ιακὼβ ἠγάπησα, τὸν
δέ 'Ησαῦ ἐμίσησα). The author of Romans, of course, is referencing Mal.
1.2-3, which the MT represents as: ואהב את יעקב ואת עשו שנאתי. The use of
the Greek adversative conjunction δέ in τὸν δέ 'Ησαῦ ἐμίσησα signals
an opposition to the previous clause. A proper paraphrase could be: 'I have
loved Jacob, but I have not loved (= hated) Esau.' There is no comparison
of degree implied or stated here grammatically either in Hebrew or Greek.
It is perfectly understood in Hebrew and Greek that Yahweh has love for
Jacob, and has no love for Esau. Such rhetoric may originate in real hatred
between Edom and Israel, as is reflected in Ps. 137.7: 'Remember, O LORD,
against the Edomites the day of Jerusalem, how they said, "Rase it, rase it!
Down to its foundations!"' (cf. Jer. 49.7-22; Obadiah).[45] Thus, neither Gen.
29.30 nor Rom. 9.13 refutes a literal and non-comparative understanding
of Lk. 14.26.

The use of *śn'* in Prov. 13.24, which *The Jewish Annotated New Testament* deemed to be a hyperbolic expression analogous to that in Lk. 14.26,

---

43. On the problems of Septuagintal translation techniques, see Johann Cook, 'The
Translation of a Translation: Some Methodological Considerations on the Translation of
the Septuagint', in Melvin K.H. Peters (ed.), *XII Congress of the International Organization for Septuagint and Cognate Studies, Leiden 2004* (Septuagint and Cognate Studies,
54; Atlanta, GA: Society of Biblical Literature, 2006), pp. 29-40; John A. Beck, *Translators as Storytellers: A Study in Septuagint Translation Technique* (Studies in Biblical Literature, 25; New York: Peter Lang, 2000).

44. Bruce K. Waltke and M. O'Connor, *An Introduction to Biblical Hebrew Syntax*
(Winona Lake, IN: Eisenbrauns, 1990), p. 265, paragraph 14.4e. Italics are those of
Waltke and O'Connor.

45. On the conflicts between Edom and Israel that may be behind such rhetoric, see
Juan Manuel Tebes, '"You shall not abhor an Edomite for he is your brother": The Tra-
dition of Esau and the Edomite Genealogies from an Anthropological Perspective',
Journal of Hebrew Scriptures 6 (2006), pp. 2-30 (4). Online: http://www.jhsonline.
org/Articles/article_56.pdf. See also Diana V. Edelman (ed.), *You Shall Not Abhor an
Edomite for he is your Brother: Edom and Seir in History and Tradition* (SBLABS, 3;
Atlanta, GA: Scholars Press, 1995).

need not be hyperbolic at all.[46] Proverbs 13.24 reads: 'He who spares the rod hates his son, but he who loves him is diligent to discipline him.' First, and as in other cases examined in both Hebrew and Greek, Prov. 13.24 also considers 'love' to be the opposite of 'hate'. Second, the passage offers an example of something a father does if he loves his son, and something a father does if he hates his son. Such an expression might be no more hyperbolic than descriptions of other expected loving (e.g., hugging, kissing) or hateful actions (e.g., raping) by a parent.

For example, consider this analogy: 'He who hates his son does not hug his son, but he who loves his son hugs his son.' Nothing about hugging a son would lead us to expect that the author is speaking hyperbolically because the author may be referencing a literal action that he expects of a father who loves his son. Otherwise, there is no reason to assume that Proverbs cannot literally mean what it says in terms of the actions expected of a loving or hateful father. Nothing about using a rod precludes a literal or non-hyperbolic meaning for love and hate in this proverb.

In Prov. 25.17, *śn'* may, indeed, bear the sense of 'have enough of, be weary of', as suggested by *DCH*. Proverbs 25.17 reads: 'Let your foot be seldom in your neighbor's house, lest he become weary of you and hate you.' Nothing in this context precludes the stronger meaning and nothing requires a milder meaning without more information about the context. After all, visiting a neighbor may involve activities that could arouse hatred. *The Instruction of Any*, an Egyptian wisdom text dating from the Twenty-First or Twenty-Second Dynasty (ca. eleventh–eighth centuries BCE), perceives potential problems: 'Do not enter the house of anyone,/ Until he admits you and greets you;/Do not snoop around in his house,/ Let your Eye observe in silence,/Do not speak of him outside.'[47] Note also the Tenth Commandment: 'You shall not covet your neighbor's house; you shall not covet your neighbor's wife, or his manservant, or his maidservant, or his ox, or his ass, or anything that is your neighbor's' (Exod. 20.17; cf. Prov. 3.29).

Emotivist versus Non-Emotivist Views

Equally important is the acknowledgment of the emotive and psychological dimensions of *śn'*. For example, in Lev. 19.17: 'You shall not hate your brother in your heart [לֹא־תִשְׂנָא אֶת־אָחִיךָ בִּלְבָבֶךָ], but you shall reason with your neighbor, lest you bear sin because of him.' Here, the hate is particularly situated in 'the heart' (בלבב), the very part of the body that is explicitly

---

46. *The Jewish Annotated New Testament*, p. 132.

47. Lichtheim, *Ancient Egyptian Literature*, II, p. 136. I use slashes to divide the poetic lines as divided by Lichtheim.

associated with the emotions in Hebrew anthropology.[48] Acknowledging that love (אהב) can have an emotive component is important because some scholars believe that אהב and שׂנא may not have emotive aspects when used in legal or diplomatic contexts.

Perhaps the most important proponent of such a non-emotivist view is found in William L. Moran's aforementioned and widely influential article, where he explored how Near Eastern covenants use the word 'love' as a technical term entailing loyalty and other characteristics desired in political relations, especially from a vassal to a superior party.[49] Moran believed that it was this sort of covenantal use that typified Deuteronomy, as when it commanded that one love God in Deut. 6.4. In fact, Moran emphatically stated that 'the distinctive deuteronomic view, which nowhere draws on the image of parental or conjugal love, was guided by another and different love relationship'.[50]

Bruce Wells, who has done substantial work on ancient Near Eastern legal terminology, follows Moran when he remarks: 'The terms "to love" (Hebrew *'āhab*; Akkadian *râmu*) and "to hate" (Hebrew *śānē*; Akkadian *zêru*), when used in legal contexts in the ancient Near East, function as technical legal terms.'[51] Tiana Bosman, who favors the use of cognitive linguistics in Hebrew lexicography, also follows Moran when she remarks: 'Within the Deuteronomistic History the well known command "love the

48. See Fritz Stoltz, 'לב', *TLOT*, II, pp. 638-42 (639). A comprehensive study of the heart as the seat of the emotions is that of Angel Gil Mondrego, 'Estudio de lēb/āb en el Antiguo Testamento: análisis sintagmático y paradigmático' (Doctoral dissertation; 2 vols.; Madrid: Universidad Complutense de Madrid, 1990), which states (II, p. 725): 'La mayor parte de los sintagmas en los que aparece se refieren al mundo psicológico, campo mental-volitivo, emociones, sentimientos, actitudes, estados, pasiones, interioridad ético-religiosa.' See also Thomas Krüger, *Das Menschliche Herz und die Weisung Gottes* (Zürich: Theologischer Verlag Zürich, 2009); André Wénin, 'Coeur et affectivité humaine dans le premier Testament', *Theologica* 36 (2011), pp. 31-46; Renate Egger-Wenzel and Jeremy Corley (eds.), *Emotions from Ben Sira to Paul* (Berlin and Boston, MA: W. de Gruyter, 2012).

49. William L. Moran, 'The Ancient Near Eastern Background of the Love of God in Deuteronomy', *CBQ* 25 (1963), pp. 77-87. For another scholar who sees no incompatibility between 'love' and 'subordination', see Nathan Jastram, 'Male as Male and Female: Created in the Image of God', *Concordia Theological Quarterly* 68.1 (2004), pp. 5-96.

50. Moran, 'The Ancient Near Eastern Background', p. 78. See also Udo Rüterswörden, 'Die Liebe zu Gott im Deuteronomium', in *Die deuteronomistischen Geschichtswerke: Redaktions und religiongeschichtliche Perspektiven zu 'Deuteronomismus'—Diskussion in Tora und Vorderen Propheten* (ed. Markus Witte, Konrad Schmid, Dorish Prechel, Jan Christian Gertz and Johannes F. Diehl; BZAW, 365; Berlin: W. de Gruyter, 2006), pp. 229-38.

51. Bruce Wells, 'The Hated Wife in Deuteronomic Law', *VT* 60 (2010), pp. 131-46 (136).

Lord your God with all your heart, and with all your soul, and with all your might" should rather be translated into "be/remain loyal to your God…".'[52]

Moran's view has been challenged by Jacqueline E. Lapsley, who argues that the term, even when used in legal settings, can retain its affective aspect.[53] Lapsley objects that 'Moran and others speak of covenantal love as "loyalty", but they strip that loyalty of affect, whereas loyalty can, and often does, have a very strong affective quality'.[54] Lapsley adds that 'The ethical implications of Deuteronomic love are thus linked to the narrative structure of the Pentateuch as a whole and, indeed, cannot be understood outside of this framework (as I think Moran tried to do)'.[55] Wells remains unconvinced by Lapsley's arguments: 'Lapsley wishes to attribute more emotive aspects to these terms rather than interpreting them in a strictly legal sense, but she does not seem to take the non-biblical evidence sufficiently into account.'[56]

I believe that Lapsley has a viable argument, especially when it comes to familial and marital relations. One example is in *The Epic of Gilgamesh*, where Gilgamesh offers advice to Enkidu about how to behave in the Netherworld, which apparently has rules that reverse those in the normal world. Note Gilgamesh's advice (*Epic of Gilgamesh* 12.23-26):

> You must not kiss the wife you love,
> You must not strike the wife you hate.
> You must not kiss the son you love,
> You must not strike the son you hate.[57]

52. See Tiana Bosman, 'A Critical Review of the Translation of the Hebrew Lexeme אהב', *Old Testament Essays* 18 (2005), pp. 22-34 (31). I will also omit further discussion of Bosman's reliance on cognitive linguistics and an emphasis on 'valency patterns' for *'āhēb*, as I am not sure that these approaches differ that much from the approaches I see used by other scholars.

53. Jacqueline E. Lapsley, 'Feeling our Way: Love for God in Deuteronomy', *CBQ* 65 (2003), pp. 350-69.

54. Lapsley, 'Feeling our Way', p. 354. For wide-ranging treatments of love in the ancient Near East, see the essays in John H. Marks and Robert M. Good (eds.), *Love and Death in the Ancient Near East: Essays in Honor of Marvin H. Pope* (Guilford, CT: Four Quarters, 1987). See also Yochanan Muffs, 'Joy and Love as Metaphorical Expressions of Willingness and Spontaneity in Cuneiform, Ancient Hebrew, and Related Literatures: Investitures in the Midrash in the Light of Neo-Babylonian Royal Grants', in *Christianity, Judaism, and other Greco-Roman Cults: Studies for Morton Smith at Sixty. Part 3, Judaism Before 70* (ed. Jacob Neusner; Leiden: E.J. Brill, 1975), pp. 1-36.

55. Lapsley, 'Feeling our Way', p. 356.

56. Wells, 'The Hated Wife', p. 136 n. 21.

57. A.R. George, *The Babylonian Gilgamesh Epic: Introduction, Critical Edition and Cuneiform Text* (2 vols.; New York: Oxford University Press, 2003), I, p. 729. George's edition of the Akkadian text reads: aš-šat-ka šá ta-ram-mu la ta-na-ši[q]/ aš-šat-ka šá ta-ze-ru la ta-maḫ-ḫaṣ/ma-rat-ka šá ta-ram-mu la ta-na-šiq/ ma-rat-ka šá ta-ze-ru la ta-maḫ-ḫaṣ. I have used slashes to indicate George's line divisions.

As in the Hebrew and Greek instances noted before, Akkadian can explicitly contrast 'love' (*ta-ram-mu*) and 'hate' (*ta-ze-ru*). The emotivist components are indicated by the words 'kiss' (*ta-na-šiq*) and 'strike' (*ta-maḫ-ḫaṣ*).

In the Hebrew Bible, one finds an emotive component in the word 'hate' in a story that also may involve a divorce context. According to 2 Samuel 13, Amnon lusts after his half-sister, Tamar. Tamar proposes that he ask the king for permission to marry her, but Amnon is in no mood to wait for an answer, and rapes her instead. The description of Amnon's attitude is instructive for determining the emotivist component of 'hate':

> But he would not listen to her; and being stronger than she, he forced her, and lay with her. Then Amnon hated her with very great hatred; so that the hatred with which he hated her was greater than the love with which he had loved her. And Amnon said to her, 'Arise, be gone'. But she said to him, 'No, my brother; for this wrong in sending me away is greater than the other which you did to me'. But he would not listen to her (2 Sam. 13.14-16).

From Tamar's viewpoint, the crime here may have been Amnon's virtual divorce (per dismissal) of his sister, especially if raping her obligated him to marry her (cf. Deut. 22.28-29). Note that there is the presence of שׂנא + a verb indicating dismissal (לשׁלחני and לכי) in vv. 15-16. However, it seems very clear that Amnon dismisses his sister because he came to hate her with as much, or more, affective and emotional intensity as he had previously loved her. And, unlike Lk. 14.26 and other cases discussed above, 2 Sam. 13.15 bears an explicit comparative construction in Hebrew (וישׂנאה אמנון שׂנאה גדולה ...מאד כי גדלה השׂנאה).[58] So, such constructions with *śn'* certainly were available to Hebrew writers when they wanted to make comparisons of degree.

Another text used to establish that שׂנא bears no emotive components, but simply means less preferred or demoted, is found in Deuteronomy 21:

> If a man has two wives, the one loved and the other disliked, and they have borne him children, both the loved and the disliked, and if the first-born son is hers that is disliked, then on the day when he assigns his possessions as an inheritance to his sons, he may not treat the son of the loved as the first-born in preference to the son of the disliked, who is the first-born, but he shall acknowledge the first-born, the son of the disliked, by giving him a double portion of all that he has, for he is the first issue of his strength; the right of the first-born is his (Deut. 21.15-17).

Daniel Block admits that 'to love' and 'to hate' are opposites, but yet claims that '[t]he latter term need not be interpreted as "hatred, antipathy toward". As in Mal. 1.2-3, it may mean simply "to be indifferent toward, to neglect,

---

58. See also *TAD* D23.1.13 (Sheikh Fadl Cave Inscription, fifth c. BCE) in which a man pursuing his love interest declares: 'I love her abundantly' (אוהב אני אותה מאוד).

or disregard"'.[59] However, there is no reason to assume that Block understands the word 'hate' in Mal. 1.2-3 correctly (see discussion above).

Bruce Wells opines that in Deut. 21.15-17, '[a] hated wife is one who
either has been demoted within the household to a lower status than what
she previously held or has been divorced and sent away from the husband's
household'.[60]

Wells also remarks: 'Raymond Westbrook has shown…that the term
"hate" (Hebrew; Akkadian) when used in a legal context, represents an
unjustified motivation for the action with which it is associated'.[61] Yet,
the instances cited for evidence do not preclude the possibility that hate is
deemed a sufficient motive for seeking a divorce. Indeed, there is no reason
that, just as in many modern cultures, the society recognizes the problem of
being married to someone that is intensely disliked.

The fact that 'hate' need not be just a technical word for divorce is shown
by a Neo-Assyrian marriage document (656 BCE) from Nimrud that is also
cited by Porten and Botta.[62] The document describes an agreement between
a man named Milki-ramu and Amat-Aṣṭarti, a woman who gives her daughter, Ṣubētu, in marriage to him. The crucial portion reads:

> If Ṣubētu does not conceive and bear (children), she shall buy a slave girl
> in her stead and set her in her place and (so) bring sons into existence. The
> sons (will be) her sons. If she loves the slave-girl, she shall keep (her), if
> she *hates* her, she shall *sell* her.

> If Subetu *hates* Milki-ramu she shall *leave* (him), if Milki-ramu hates his
> wife (?), he shall pay (back the dowry) to her two-fold.[63]

59. Daniel I. Block, *The NIV Application Commentary: Deuteronomy* (Grand Rapids,
MI: Zondervan, 2012), p. 497 n. 17. On the meaning of 'hate' in Malachi, see also Redditt, 'The God who Loves and Hates', pp. 175-90.

60. Wells, 'The Hated Wife', p. 135. Note that *Yeb.* 23a interprets this perhaps as 'forbidden to marry' (שׂנואה בנישׂואיה שׂנואה).

61. Bruce Wells, 'Sex, Lies, and Virginal Rape: The Slandered Bride and False Accusation in Deuteronomy', *JBL* 124 (2005), pp. 41-72 (59).

62. H.Z. Szubin and B. Porten, 'The Status of a Repudiated Spouse: A New Inter-
pretation of Kraeling 7 (TAD B3.8)', *Israel Law Review* 35 (2001), pp. 46-78 (56-57);
Alejandro F. Botta, 'Hated by the Gods and your Spouse: The Legal Use of שׂנא in Ele-
phantine and its Ancient Near Eastern Context', in *Law and Religion in the Eastern
Mediterranean: From Antiquity to Early Islam* (ed. Anselm Hagedorn and Reinhard G.
Kratz; New York: Oxford University Press, 2013), pp. 105-128 (112).

63. ND 2307, lines 41-50: šum-ma ᵐⁱṣu-[bi-(e)-tú l]a? [t]a-a-ri/la tú-ú-la-[d]a GEMÉ
ta-laq-qi/e-si qa-an-ni-šá ina š[ub-t]i-šá ta-ša-kan/DUMU. MEŠ tú-šab-šá DU[MU.MEŠ?]
DUMU.MEŠ-ša/šum-ma ta-ra-[x x (x)] ta-ha-ṣi-ni/šum-ma ta-ze-e-[r]a ta-da-aᵎ-ši/
šum-ma ᵐⁱṣu-bi-t[ú a-n]a mil-ki-ra-mu/ta-ze-e-ra [x-x]-ra-ma/šum-ma mil-ki-ra-[m]u ᶜMI-
šú?ᶜ e-zi-ra/e-ṣip-ši SUM-an. I follow the transliteration and translation of J.N. Postgate,
Fifty Neo-Assyrian Legal Documents (Warminster: Aris and Phillips, 1976), pp. 105-
106. B. Parker ('The Nimrud Tablets, 1952: Business Documents', *Iraq* 16 [1954], pp.

Note that love and hate are treated as opposites, and not as expressive of comparison of the two sexual partners of Milki-ramu. In fact, it is stated that if Ṣubētu 'hates' (ta-ze-e-[r]a) the slave girl, she will sell her. Thus, this case at least shows that 'hate' need not involve simply preferring one of two sexual partners. Rather, 'hate' is the apt description for an emotional act that can lead to the expulsion or demotion of a wife.

Otto Michel does not necessarily deny the emotive components in Deut. 21.15, but he claims that this passage allows him to treat Luke's usage of *miseō* as comparative. Michel says:

> The antonyms ἀγαπᾶν/μισεῖν take on a special flavour in Mt. 6.24; Lk. 16.13, where, in dependence on Dt. 21.15-17 and [Exod. R.] 51 (104), they mean 'to prefer' ('to be faithful to') and 'to slight' ('to despise'). We have here a Hebraism as in the requirement for discipleship... Luke 14.26.[64]

Michel does not really specify why the antonyms in these texts should be treated as having a 'special flavour' other than because he believes that they are dependent on Deut. 21.15-17 and *Exod. R.*

In fact, Michel says quite the opposite just a few pages previously where, concerning Deut. 21.15, he remarks: 'The opp[osite] of "to hate" in the OT is always "to love." Of two wives it may be that a man loves one and hates the other...or that love turns to hate.'[65] Yet, why is it not even conceivable to Michel that, just as he has proposed could be the case in Deut. 21.15, Jesus may be saying the same thing in Lk. 14.26? That is to say, why can't Jesus be demanding that you conjure up hatred or that love should turn to hatred for one's family?

Perhaps it is because Michel has already decided that Jesus 'knows no holy hatred against men'.[66] Thus, one finds theology rather than linguistics or history at work in Michel's argument.

Does Hate = Divorce at Elephantine?

Perhaps second in importance to the use of Hebrew texts is the use of Aramaic texts in determining the meaning of *miseō* in Lk. 14.26.[67] Of particular

---

29-58, especially p. 39 for the translation and p. 55 for the cuneiform copy) translates lines 45-50 as 'if she [Subietu] curses, strikes, if she is furious (and) treats her (the hand-maid) improperly, if Subietu (with) Milki-ramu is at enmity (lit. is furious) and (…) if Milki-ramu (with her) is at enmity (even then) if he divorces her, he is to give'.

64. *TDNT*, IV, p. 690. I use *Exod. R.* for Michel's 'Ex. r.' as the abbreviation of *Exodus Rabbah*.

65. *TDNT*, IV, p. 685.

66. *TDNT*, IV, p. 690.

67. On the general use of Aramaic in biblical studies see Stephen A. Kaufman, 'Recent Contributions of Aramaic Studies to Biblical Hebrew Philology and the Exegesis of the

significance have been the Jewish Aramaic documents from Elephantine.[68] Presumably, they offer parallels to Jewish understandings of the word in the fifth century BCE that may have continued into the first century. There are principally three marriage documents at issue, and they are designated as *TAD* B2.6 (ca. 449 BCE), B3.3 (449 BCE), and B3.8 (420 BCE) in the standard edition of Porten and Yardeni, who label each of them as a 'Document of Wifehood'.[69] Another document, *TAD* B2.4 (459 BCE), is labeled as a 'Grant of Usufruct to Son-in-Law', but it also bears an instance of the use of *śn'*.[70]

As to the usage of *śn'*, an illustrative case is found in *TAD* B2.6, which outlines the agreement concerning the marriage of Eshor, a royal builder or architect, and Miptahiah, the daughter of Mahseiah, an Aramean from Syene in Egypt. The crucial portion reads:

> Tomorrow o[r] (the) next day, should Miptahiah stand up in an assembly and say: 'I *hated* Eshor my husband', silver of hatred is on her head. She shall PLACE UPON the balance-scale and weigh out to Eshor silver, 6[+1] (= 7) shekels, 2 q(uarters), and all that she brought in her hand she shall take out, from straw to string, and go away wherever she desires without suit or without process.

> Tomorrow or (the) next day, should Eshor stand up in an assembly and say: 'I *hated* my [wif]e Miptahiah', her mohar [will be] lost (= forfeit) and all that she brought in in her hand she shall take out, from straw to string, on one day in one stroke and go away wherever she desires without suit or without process (*TAD* B2.6.22-29).

מחר א[ו]יום אחרן תקום מפתחיה בעדה ותאמר שנאת לסאחור בעלי כסף

שנאה בראשה תתב על מוזנא ותתקל לאסחור כסף שקלן 3 +3 + 1 ר 2

וכל זי הנעלת בידה תהנפק מן חם עד חוט ותהך לה אן זי צבית ולא

Hebrew Bible', in *Congress Volume Basel 2001* (ed. André Lemaire; VTSup, 80; Leiden and Boston, MA: Brill, 2000), pp. 43-54. For a more extensive defense of the Aramaic background on Jesus' words, see Maurice Casey, 'The Role of Aramaic in Reconstructing the Teaching of Jesus', in *Handbook for the Study of the Historical Jesus* (ed. Tom Holmén and Stanley Porter; 4 vols.; Leiden: E.J. Brill, 2011), II, pp. 1343-75.

68. For the standard edition, see Bezalel Porten and Ada Yardeni, *Textbook of Aramaic Documents from Ancient Egypt* (4 vols.; Jerusalem: Hebrew University of Jerusalem, 1989–1999). See also Alejandro Botta, *The Aramaic and Egyptian Legal Traditions at Elephantine: An Egyptological Approach* (New York: T. & T. Clark, 2009); Baruch A. Levine, 'On the Origins of the Aramaic Legal Formulary at Elephantine', in *Christianity, Judaism, and Other Greco-Roman Cults: Studies for Morton Smith at Sixty. Part 3, Judaism before 70* (ed. Jacob Neusner; Leiden: E.J. Brill, 1975), pp. 37-54.

69. For example, *TAD*, II, p. 63. My italics. Capitals those of *TAD*.

70. *TAD*, II, p. 28.

ידין לא דבב

מחר או יום אחרן יקום אסחור בעדה ויאמר שנאת [לאנ]תתי מפטחיה

מהרהן י[באד וכל זי הנעלת בידה תהנפק מן חם עד חוט ביום חד

בכף חדה ותהך לה אן זי צבית ולא זי דין ולא דבב

Both the husband and wife can exercise the right to divorce each other, and the procedure consists, in part, of (1) standing up in the assembly, and (2) stating (here in more general form): 'I *śn'* my spouse'.

The root *śn'* was translated as 'divorce' by some of the earliest editors of the Elephantine papyri, including A.E. Cowley.[71] However, there is no universal agreement today on the meaning of *śn'*. One can identify at least four positions (and their representatives) with respect to the meaning of *śn'* at Elephantine:

A. Botta: 'שׂנא cannot mean anything but divorce.'[72]
B. Porten: 'signifies repudiation or rejection, the effect of which is tantamount to a breach of contract due to demotion of status within an existing relationship.'[73]
C. Westbrook: 'The term "hate" is therefore in addition to the divorce formula which expresses not the divorce itself (for which there is another technical term) but some extra dimension thereof...the verb invariably appears in combination with a verb of action, providing the motivation for that action.'[74]

---

71. A. Cowley, *Aramaic Papyri of the Fifth Century BC* (repr., Osnabrück: Otto Zeller, 1967 [1923]). Cowley (*Aramaic Papyri*, p. 28) remarks concerning his translation of AP 9.8: 'שׂנא, as in 15.23, is a legal term for "divorce".' Similarly, Ludwig Blau (*Die jüdische Ehescheidung und der jüdische Scheidebrief: Eine historische Untersuchung, Erster Teil* [Strasburg: K.J. Trübner, 1911], p. 20), remarks: 'Das "Ich hasse" (שׂנאת) ist hier, wie Cowley dem Sinne nach richtig übertragen hat, mit "Ich scheide mich" identisch und der "Preis des Hasses" ist nichts anderes als "Scheidungsgeld". Der Hass ist nicht spezifiziert...die Ehegatten sind nicht gehalten, besondere Gründe für ihre Abneigung beizubringen.' For another equation of 'hate' with 'divorce', see Joseph A. Fitzmyer, 'A Re-Study of an Elephantine Marriage Contract (*AP* 15)', in *Near Eastern Studies in Honor of William Foxwell Albright* (ed. Hans Goedicke; Baltimore, MD: The Johns Hopkins University Press, 1971), pp. 137-68.

72. Botta, 'Hated by the Gods', pp. 105-128 (125).

73. Szubin and Porten, 'The Status of a Repudiated Spouse', p. 56. See also Bezalel Porten, 'Elephantine', in *A History of Ancient Near Eastern Law* (ed. Raymond Westbrook; 2 vols.; Leiden: E.J. Brill, 2003), II, pp. 863-81 (876).

74. Raymond Westbrook, 'The Prohibition on Restoration of Marriage in Deuteronomy 24:1-14', in *Studies in Bible* (ed. Sarah Japhet; Scripta Hierosolymitana, 31; Jerusalem: Magnes Press, 1986), pp. 386-405 (401).

D. Nutkowicz: 'This root, commonly attested in West-Semitic languages, always has the meaning "to hate, to show aversion towards someone/ something".'[75]

One can also divide the positions as to whether they acknowledge a primarily emotive meaning (Nutkowicz, Lapsley), or whether it is primarily a legal meaning (Botta, Wells, Porten) in divorce documents.

Botta and Nutkowicz have better cases than Porten as to whether the word relates to demotion or divorce. Botta is successful in showing that *śn'* is not just about a demotion in status for a spouse that remains married. I think that Nutkowicz makes a better argument in showing that *śn'* accurately entails an emotional state that usually precedes divorce, but does not itself mean 'divorce'. Indeed, there need not be a stark dichotomy between a purely legal and an emotivist understanding. There are good reasons to prefer a hybrid or synthetic meaning in legal contexts, which can combine both the emotive and technical aspects.

One problem with Botta's proposal for rendering *śn'* as a technical term for 'divorce' is that it depends, in part, on viewing as a hendiadys the combination of *śn'* + verb indicating flight/abandonment.[76] Yet, the mere fact that two verbs appear together does not necessarily render them as a hendiadys. A verbal hendiadys in Akkadian has a very specific meaning, as is noted by John Huehnergard: 'Verbal hendiadys is the use of two verbs, co-ordinated either with –*ma* or asyndetically (i.e., without a conjunction), in which the first verb qualifies or restricts the meaning of the second.'[77] One example Huehnergard offers is 'atūr-ma wardam ana bēliya aṭrud "I sent the slave to my lord again"'.[78] Here, the verb *târum*, which means to 'return', can also mean 'to do something again' and so modifies the verb *ṭarādum* ('to send').

Otherwise, verbs connected with –*ma* are perfectly understood as meaning 'and' or 'and also' and serve to coordinate clauses.[79] So, there is nothing to preclude a translation that reckons with the possibility that an individual really left his or her spouse because of real hatred. Nor is there anything that precludes the verb from describing the emotion of hatred that Botta and others already believe to be the primary meaning of the root in many contexts outside of marriage or divorce law.

---

75. Hélène Nutkowicz, 'Concerning the Verb *SN'* in Judaeo-Aramaic Contracts from Elephantine', *JSS* 52 (2007), pp. 211-25.

76. Botta, 'Hated by the Gods', p. 115.

77. John Huehnergard, *A Grammar of Akkadian* (Atlanta, GA: Scholars Press, 1997), p. 125 (14.5).

78. Huehnergard, *A Grammar of Akkadian*, p. 125. For another study of sequences indicated by –*ma*, see also Eran Cohen, 'Akkadian –*ma* in Diachronic Perspective', *ZA* 90 (2000), pp. 207-26 (221).

79. Huehnergard, *A Grammar of Akkadian*, 7.4, p. 49.

Furthermore, there are other expressions of divorce that do not restrict themselves to a hendiadys or use more than two verbs in a sequence. For example, in *TAD* B2.6.26-29: 'Tomorrow or (the) next day, should Eshor stand up in an assembly and say: "I hated my [wif]e Miptahiah", her mohar [will be] lost (= forfeit) and all that she brought in her hand she shall take out…and go away.' Here the sequence of verbs in the divorce procedure can also be described as follows: (1) stand up (יקום); (2) say (יאמר); (3) I hate (שֹנאת); (4) take out (תהנפק); (5) go away (תהך). There are also cases where *śn'* does not appear with a coupled verb of flight, and cases where it explicitly describes the opposite of love in narratives involving marital discord (e.g., Judg. 14.16).

A completely legal and non-emotive understanding of *śn'* still leaves unexplained why that word, which usually does precede other verbs in divorce proceeding, cannot express literal 'hate' as the first step of a multistep divorce announcement or proceeding in *TAD* B2.6 (or B2.4, B3.3 and B3.8).[80] After all, anger as a motive for divorce is acknowledged in *Ket.* 81b: 'Still, whenever a husband had occasion to be angry with his wife, he would say to her, "Take your *kethubah* and go"' (ועדיין כשכועס עליה אומר לה טלי כתובתיך וצאי).[81] So, what prevents *śn'* from literally meaning 'I really loathe my spouse, and for that reason I am divorcing her?' And if individuals at Elephantine did want to express their motive for divorce as consisting of literal hatred or loathing, then what other word would they have used or how would they have phrased it?

Hating a City

As evidence for *śn'* having only the technical meaning of 'divorce', Botta appeals to the Laws of Eshnunna 30: 'If a man hated [*i-ze-er-a*] his city and his master and fled [*it-ta-ah-bi-it*], another indeed took his wife: whenever he returns to his wife he shall have no claim.'[82] As Botta phrases it: '[B]oth

---

80. The role of *śn'* in *TAD* B3.8 is actually more difficult to discern. The spouses (Ananiah and his wife Jehoishma) are apparently prohibited from using the wives of friends or colleagues in a lawsuit against each other. In particular, B3.8.36-39 (*TAD*, II, p. 82) says: 'Ananiah shall not be able to do (i.e., refuse) to Jehoishma his wife the law of [one] or two of his colleagues' wives and if he not do thus (i.e., if he refuse), [it is] hatred.' If so, 'hatred' may still describe the reason for the refusal (i.e., out of hatred). See further, Emil G. Kraeling, *The Brooklyn Museum Aramaic Papyri: New Documents from the Fifth Century B.C. from the Jewish Colony at Elephantine* (New Haven, CT: Yale University Press, 1953), p. 219.

81. Unless noted otherwise, all of my citations/quotations of the Babylonian Talmud follow *Hebrew-English Edition of the Babylonian Talmud* (ed. Harry Freedman and Isidore Epstein; repr., London: Soncino Press, 1988–1994 [1935–1962]).

82. Following Reuven Yaron (*The Laws of Eshnunna* [Jerusalem: Magnes Press, 2nd

verbs are used together in several ancient Near Eastern legal traditions and should be understood as a common hendiadyc pair to denote the break of the bond.'[83] However the verb transliterated as *it-ta-aḫ-bi-it* is contestable here (i.e., *ittabit* v. *ittaḫbit*), and it is difficult to know if any hendiadys is regular on the basis of this instance.[84]

LE 30 also figures in the arguments presented by John J. Collins for understanding *śn'* as a purely technical term. Concerning LE 30, Collins remarks: 'The point is not that he fled his city because of aversion but that he repudiated it for whatever reason. (The laws list no circumstances in which a man is justified in leaving his city and his master).'[85] Collins believes that LE 30 is analogous to LH 136: 'If a man deserts his city and flees, and after his departure his wife enters another's house—if that man should then return and seize his wife, because he repudiated his city and fled, the wife of the deserter will not return to her husband.'[86]

Yaron does argue that in LE 30 'there seems to be no ground for assuming that "hatred" had to find expression in some overt act prior to the flight'.[87] However, Yaron clarifies that both LE 30 and LH 136 appear to refer to 'the husband's malicious absence', which does not rule out an emotive component at all.[88] Yaron further remarks that in LE 30, 'the absence is malicious, motivated by hatred of "king and country"'.[89]

Indeed, there is evidence that 'hating a city' can have an affective component and summarizes prior actions. For example, in the Amarna Letters (fourteenth century BCE), one finds a long complaint by Rib-Hadda, king of Byblos, to his Egyptian overlord concerning the lack of assistance the former is receiving from the latter.[90] Among other things, Rib-Hadda resents

edn, 1988], p. 23 n. 15 and p. 61). Martha T. Roth (*Law Collections from Mesopotamia* [Atlanta, GA: Scholars Press, 2nd edn, 1997]), p. 62) translates *izēr* as 'repudiates'.

83. Botta, 'Hated by the Gods', p. 115.

84. Some scholars prefer the variant, it-ta-bit-it. The latter may derive from *nabatum/na'butum* ('to flee') or *abatum* ('to destroy'?), which would change the situation described in the law. See Yaron (*The Laws of Eshnunna*, p. 61) for text-critical comments on manuscripts. See also Botta, 'Hated by the Gods', p. 115 n. 51. For *na'butum*, see Huehnergard, *A Grammar of Akkadian*, p. 508.

85. John J. Collins, 'Marriage, Divorce and Family in Second Temple Judaism', in *Families in Ancient Israel* (ed. Leo G. Perdue, Joseph Blenkinsopp, John J. Collins and Carol Meyers; Louisville, KY: Westminster/John Knox Press, 1997), pp. 104-162 (118-19).

86. Roth, *Law Collections*, p. 107.

87. Yaron, *The Laws of Eshnunna*, p. 208 n. 119. Botta ('Hated by the Gods', p. 115) approves of Yaron's conclusion here.

88. Yaron, *The Laws of Eshnunna*, p. 208.

89. Yaron, *The Laws of Eshnunna*, p. 206.

90. See further, Louise M. Pryke, 'The Many Complaints of Rib Addi of Byblos', *JAOS* 131 (2011), pp. 411-22.

that his overlord is supplying provisions to other kings but nothing to him (EA 126.14-16). Rib-Hadda wants Egypt to send troops to rescue him from his enemies, including the Hittites who are setting fire to his homeland, but none are sent (EA 126.23-24). In the midst of these complaints, Rib-Hadda exclaims (EA 126.44-45): 'If the king hates his city, then let him abandon it' (šum-ma LUGAL za-ir URU.KI-šu ù i-zi-ba-ši).[91]

The letter from Rib-Hadda shows that 'hating a city' has an emotive component. Note also that 'hating' is coupled with 'abandoning' a city in EA 126. That is to say, it is perfectly natural that one thing to do when hating a thing or a person is to distance oneself. Rib-Hadda's exasperation is not just with a lack of loyalty, but also expresses the emotional pain resulting from that lack of loyalty. In any case, the word 'hate' is not describing some unspecified or arbitrary motive, as Collins argues in the case of LE 30, but rather 'hating a city' summarizes a list of very specific complaints that are cited as evidence for that potential hatred. From the point of view of Rib-Hadda, those specific actions by his overlord do constitute evidence of a possible aversion to Rib-Hadda or to his city.

A similar use of *zêru* is found in a letter from Amarna (EA 158), where Aziru, the king of Amurru, implies that Tutu, his overlord, is permitting malicious talk against Aziru. Since Aziru cannot seem to tell where he stands with Tutu, he declares: '[But i]f the king, my lord, does not love me [la i-ra-am-ma-an-ni], but rather hates me [i-zé-i-ra-an-ni], then what should I say?'[92] Here, there is an explicit contrast, as seen in Hebrew and Greek usages, between love and hate. Aziru offers evidence for concluding that Tutu might hate, and not love, Aziru.

Given the laconic nature of legal codes, there is nothing to preclude a list of prior indications or actions behind the statement that 'a man hated his city'

---

91. William L. Moran, *The Amarna Letters* (Baltimore, MD: The Johns Hopkins University Press, 1992), p. 206. For the Akkadian edition, I depend on Shlomo Izre'el, *The Amarna Tablets*. Online: http://www.tau.ac.il/humanities/semitic/EA115-162.html. J.A. Knudtzon (*Die El-Amarna Tafeln mit Einleitung un Erläuterungen* [2 vols.; repr., Osnabruck: Otto Zeller, 1964 (1915)], I, p. 541) translates this passage as: 'Wenn der König seine Stadt hasst, so verlasse ich sie.' In his French edition, William L. Moran (*Les Lettres d'El Amarna* [trans. Dominique Collon and Henri Cazelles; Paris: Cerf, 1987], p. 340) translates the passage as: 'Si le roi déteste sa ville qui'il l'abandonne donc.'

92. My translation of EA 158.36-37. For the Akkadian transliteration, I depend on Shlomo Izre'el, *Amurru Akkadian: A Linguistic Study* (HSS, 41; 2 vols.; Atlanta, GA: Scholars Press, 1991), II, p. 21: ù ⌜šum⌝-ma⌝ LUGAL EN-ia la i-ra-am-an-ni ù i-zeŭ-i-ra-an-ni. Izre'el (*Amurru Akkadian*, II, p. 23) translates as: 'If? the king, my lord, does not like me, but hates me…'. Moran (*Amarna Letters*, p. 244, l. 36) translates: '[But i]f the king, my lord, does not love me and rejects me…' (italics Moran's). My translation is closer to that of *CAD*, XXI, p. 98: 'if the king my lord does not love, but dislikes me…'. See also Knudtzon (*Die El-Amarna Tafeln*, I, p. 645): [A]b[e]r we[n]n der Kön[ig, mei]n [H]e[rr], m[ich] nicht liebt, sondern mich hasst…'.

in LE 30. These hateful actions may be known to the city's administrators prior to rendering such an opinion about the man's hatred. One could make an analogous argument for LH 136 because there is nothing to preclude any emotive components to why the man 'hated' his city. For all we know, there may be some background to this hatred that is simply not elaborated upon in legal codes. However, the Amarna letters indicate that 'hate' can be a 'summary word', which entails both preceding legal and emotive components.

Hate as a Motive for Divorce

Westbrook's claim that *śn'* expresses the motive for a divorce is cogent. Westbrook argues that in a construction with two verbs (i.e., 'hate' + verb indicating flight/abandonment), 'hate' provides the motivation, and the second verb (e.g., as in 'you are not my husband') is the one that indicates the actual divorce action. As Westbrook notes: 'The formula of the declaration was "You are not my wife/husband".'[93] As Westbrook also observes, this type of construction appears earlier in conditional statements, such as this one from the bilingual (Sumerian and Akkadian) *ana ittišu* series. Specifically in *ana ittišu* 7.4.1-5, one finds: 'If a woman hates her husband, and said "You are not my husband", into the river they shall throw her.'[94]

Botta sees this law differently: 'the series *ana ittišu* 7 iv 1–5…reads: "if a wife hated her husband and said, 'you are not my husband'". This formula is exactly the same as the one used by husband and wife in *TAD* B3.8: 21, 24, and there is no question that in *ana ittišu* we are facing a divorce formula.'[95] While it may be true that 'hated' is used in a divorce formula, it is not necessary to conclude that 'hate' is the word for divorce or even part of a hendiadys meaning divorce. Given that a formula for marriage can be expressed simply as 'let her be a wife' or the like in Mesopotamian and Aramaic legal traditions, then it seems reasonable that its opposite (e.g., 'you are not my wife' or 'she is not my wife'; cf. היא לא אשתי in Hos. 2.2/MT 2.4) could be sufficient to express a divorce.[96]

93. Raymond Westbrook, 'Old Babylonian Period', in *A History of Ancient Near Eastern Law* (ed. Raymond Westbrook; 2 vols.; Leiden: E.J. Brill, 2003), I, pp. 361-430 (388).

94. I depend on the edition of Benno Landsberger (ed.), *Die Serie ana ittišu* (Rome: Pontifical Biblical Institute, 1937), p. 103: šum-ma aš-ša-ta mu-us-sa i-zi-ir-ma ul mu-ti at-ta iq-ta-bi a-na na-a-ri i-na-ad-du-šu.

95. Botta, 'Hated by the Gods', p. 112.

96. For example, Martha Roth, *Babylonian Marriage Agreements 7th–3rd Centuries B.C.* (Neukirchen–Vluyn: Butzon & Bercker Kevelaer, 1989), 2.6: 'lu aš-šá-tum [at]-[ti]'; Roth 26.6: 'lu aš-šá-tum ši-i'. Texts in this source by Roth will be designated as Roth + number assigned by Roth in this edition (e.g., Roth 26). BM 42470.6 (Cornelia Wunsch, *Urkunden zum Ehe-, Vermögens- und Erbrecht aus verschiedenen neubabylonischen Archiven* [Dresden: Islet, 2003], p. 14, no. 3, line 6): 'lu-ú aššatu ši-i'. Compare

Accordingly, the construction in *ana ittišu* 7.4.1-5 is perfectly understandable as consisting of three clauses as follows:

A: First protasis: If a woman hates her husband, AND
B: Second protasis: She pronounces the divorce formula;
C: Apodosis: She will be thrown into a river.

Indeed, in the very next law in the series *ana ittišu* (7.4.8-12), 'hate' is omitted, implying that the husband needs no motivation at all: 'If a man tells his wife "You are not my wife", he shall pay half a mina of silver.'[97] One can analyse this law as consisting of two clauses, a single protasis and a single apodosis:

A. Protasis: If a man tells his wife 'You are not my wife';
B. Apodosis: He shall pay half a mina of silver.

But if 'hate' is part of a hendiadys expressing divorce, then why was 'hate' omitted in this law? These two examples show that the crucial divorce action is to declare that 'you are not my spouse', while 'hate' may be sometimes added as a motivation, as Westbrook has argued. There seems to be something additional expressed by 'hate' that also results in the woman being thrown into the river.

The series *ana ittišu* (3.4.40-43) shows that 'hate' is neither the word for divorce nor part of a hendiadys expressing divorce: 'If [a son] hates his father, he shall forfeit all that he brought [into the household].'[98] Here, there is no divorce and the word 'hate' is still used. Nor is there a hendiadys. The word 'hate' seems to tell us all we need to know to explain the result. Presumably, the son forfeits any profit or goods that he contributed to his father's household.

Supplementary evidence for an emotivist understanding of 'hate' in divorce cases may be found in LH 142-43:

If a woman hates her husband [šumma sinništrum mussa izērma], and declares 'You will not take me', [ul taḫḫazanni iqtabi] her circumstances shall be examined. If [it is determined that] she is chaste and there is no fault, but that her husband has strayed and disparages her greatly, then that woman will bear no penalty; she shall take her dowry and go to her father's household. If she is not not chaste, but has strayed, and she maligns her husband, they shall seize her dowry and they will cast her into the river.[99]

---

this to הי אנתתי in *TAD* B3.3.3. On Hosea, see M.J. Geller, 'The Elephantine Papyri and Hosea 2, 3', *JSJ* (1977), pp. 139-48.

97. Landsberger, *Die Serie ana ittišu*, p. 103: šum-ma mu-tú a-na áš-ša-ti-sú ul aš-ša-ti at-ta iq-ta-bi ½ ma-na kaspa-i-šaq-qal.

98. Landsberger, *Die Serie ana ittišu*, pp. 49-50: šúm-ma a-ba-šu iz-zi-ir i-na min-ma šá ú-še-ri-bu-šú i-tel-li.

99. Roth, *Law Collections*, p. 108. My translation and bracketed transcriptions.

Although there is debate as to whether the verb *aḫāzu* relates to marriage or to having sexual intercourse, the fact remains that her 'hate' was viewed as sufficient motive, barring any other impropriety on her part, to divorce her husband or at least leave her husband.[100]

In LH 142, the 'hate' declared cannot be a matter of preferring her husband over another husband (as in a comparison of degree alleged for Leah and Rachel). The additional motivation for 'you will not take me' (*ul taḫḫazanni*) is also very consistent with a woman who detests her husband so much that she is not willing to have sexual intercourse with him. The notion of hating a spouse is also consistent with the wife's statement that the husband will not continue to retain the wife (or remain married) if we understand the durative meaning of the verb more literally. If so, then we can schematize the relevant stipulations for this divorce as follows:

A:　If a woman declares that she hates her husband; and
B:　The woman (hates him so much that) she declares the cessation of intercourse with him;
C:　Furthermore, the city elders find no impropriety on her part; and
D:　The husband keeps maligning her unjustly, then
E:　That woman will not be penalized, and
F:　She can take her dowry, and
G:　She can go back to her father's household.
H:　But if (in addition to A and B) she is not chaste, and
I:　She maligns her husband;
J:　They shall cast her into the river.

Again, there is no reason to deny that 'hate' here means a fully emotive and affective dislike that the woman is expressing. The cessation of marital relations would be fully consistent with such an emotional hatred.

John J. Collins rejects Westbrook's formulation, and appeals to Deut. 24.1-3, where the biblical author discusses the case of a man who wishes to remarry his wife after divorcing her.[101] In particular, Deut. 24.2-3 states concerning that woman: 'if she goes and becomes another man's wife, and the latter husband dislikes her and writes her a bill of divorce and puts it in her hand and sends her out of his house, or if the latter husband dies, who took her to be his wife…'. Collins argues that '[t]he very fact that *to hate* can stand alone in the context of divorce shows that it has become a

---

100. Wells ('Sex, Lies, and Virginal Rape', p. 59 n. 58) considers these laws as relating to a betrothed woman, and not a fully married one. So, *aḫāzu* relates to 'taking' in the sense of fully marrying the husband. Roth (*Law Collections*, p. 108) views these laws as cases where the woman is fully married, and *aḫāzu* refers to her refusal 'to have marital relations' with her husband.

101. Collins, 'Marriage, Divorce and Family', p. 119. On Deut. 24.1-3 as a case of palingamy (remarriage), see Bernard S. Jackson, 'The "Institutions" of Marriage and the Divorce in the Hebrew Bible', *JSS* 56 (2011), pp. 221-51 (241).

technical term, and this is confirmed by the expressions, "law of hatred" and "silver of hatred"'.[102] Yet, the Hebrew verb *śn'* does not stand alone because it is joined with at least two other verbs, כתב ('writes') and נתן ('gives'), in the clause, 'and writes her a bill of divorce and puts it in her hand' (וכתב לה ספר כריתת ונתן בידה).

The fact that an object related to divorce can be used in a genitival relationship does not invalidate an emotivist view of hate. For example, the phrase 'blood money' (τιμὴ αἵματος), which is also a genitival phrase in Mt. 27.6, refers to the money returned by Judas to the priests after the crucifixion of Jesus. That money was involved in an act in which blood was literally shed. So, why can't 'silver of hatred' refer to an act in which silver was involved in an act in which hatred was literally displayed or in an act for which hate served as a motivation? Accordingly, Collins's examples do not refute Westbrook's claim that hate offers a motive for divorce, but it is not itself the technical word for divorce.

Porten, who rejects the notion that *śn'* by itself means divorce, points to a text from Alalakh, which reads: 'if Bitta-malki hates him and leaves him'.[103] Such a conditional clause is evidence that 'hate' need not be the single motive for divorce. Lipinski's translation assumes an affective component: 'If Bitta-malki has taken a dislike to him (i.e., her husband) and has left him.'[104] Corroboration that 'hate' is only one of a number of possible reasons for divorce comes from a demotic text cited by both Porten and Botta: 'If I expel you as wife, be it that I hate you, be it that I prefer another woman as wife instead of you.'[105] Clearly, there were at least two alternatives presented here as motives for divorce: (a) hate; or (b) the desire for another woman. Thus, 'hate' cannot be merely a standard word for divorce, but rather also reflects a real motivation (dislike, hatred) that may be expected to justify such an action.

Malachi may display perhaps the most definitive case where *śn'* is not the word for 'divorce': 'For I hate divorce, says the LORD the God of Israel, and covering one's garment with violence, says the LORD of hosts. So take heed

102. Collins, 'Marriage, Divorce and Family', p. 119.

103. TA 94, ll. 17-19: 'šum-ma [ᵐ??d]u-ᵈIM ᶠbi-it-ta-ma-al-ki [i-z]é-er-šu u i-zi-bu-šu'. A copy of the text was published by D.J. Wiseman, 'Supplementary Copies of Alalakh Tablets', *JCS* 8 (1954), pp. 1-30, and the copy appears on plate 7. I follow the transliteration of Wells ('The Hated Wife', p. 137 n. 26), who translates this as: 'if PN (husband) hates and divorces PN2 (wife)'. I follow Lipinski in reading the Akkadian suffix (-šu) as indicating a masculine object.

104. Edward Lipinski, 'The Wife's Right to Divorce in the Light of an Ancient Near Eastern Tradition', *Jewish Law Annual* 8 (1981), pp. 9-27 (19).

105. Following the translation of Szubin and Porten, 'The Status of a Repudiated Spouse', p. 57. See also P.W. Pestman, *Marriage and Matrimonial Property in Ancient Egypt* (Papyrologica Lugdono-Batava, 39; Leiden: E.J. Brill, 1961), p. 61.

to yourselves and do not be faithless' (Mal. 2.16). The MT has שנא, and not a first person singular form here. The RSV rendition ('I hate') does not reflect the MT. The Qumran version (4QXIIa, ii.4-7) bears: כי אם שׂנתה שׁלח, which can be rendered as 'but if you hate [her], divorce [her]'.[106] That also accords with the LXX reading, which has ἀλλὰ ἐὰν μισήσας ἐξαποστείλῃς. Adela Y. Collins believes that this text may have 'originally expressed an unqualified rejection of divorce', and was emended by Qumran scribes and the LXX to conform to Deut. 24.1.[107] But the point remains that any emendation still presupposes that *śn'* is not the word for divorce. The emendation also supports the idea that, at the time of Qumran, 'hate' was a motivation for divorce.[108]

Demotic magical papyri corroborate what is entailed in hating a spouse to the point of divorce. In a text (PDM xiv.366-375) from the London–Leiden Demotic Papyrus, one finds a spell with the incipit, 'the method of separating of man from a woman and a woman from her husband'.[109] The crucial portion reads:

> Put the fire behind his heart and the flame in his place of sleeping, the… fire of hatred never [ceasing] to enter into his heart at any time, until he casts NN, the daughter of NN, out of his house(s), she carrying (?) hatred to his heart [mst n ḥt-f], she carrying quarreling to his face. Give him nagging, squabbling, fighting, and quarreling between them at all times, until they are separated from each other, without having been at peace forever and ever.[110]

106. Following the translation of Adela Yarbro Collins, *Mark: A Commentary* (Hermeneia: Minneapolis: Fortress Press, 2007), p. 460. For the Hebrew text, I follow Eugene Ulrich, *The Biblical Qumran Scrolls: Transcriptions and Textual Variants* (Leiden: E.J. Brill, 2010), p. 624. Beth Glazier-McDonald (*Malachi: The Divine Messenger* [SBLDS, 98; Atlanta, GA: Scholars Press, 1987], p. 82) translates Mal. 2.16 as: 'For one who divorces because of aversion', says Yahweh, the God of Israel, 'thereby covers his garment with violence…'. On the meaning of 'hate' in Malachi, see also Redditt, 'The God who Loves and Hates', pp. 175-90.

107. Collins, *Mark: A Commentary*, p. 460.

108. See also the discussion in Meier, *Law and Love*, p. 147; P. Marucci, *Parole di Gesù sul divorzio* (Aloisiana, 16; Pubblicazioni della Pontificia Facoltà Teologica dell' Italia Meridonale, Sezione S. Luigi; Naples: Morcelliana, 1982), p. 81.

109. See Hans Dieter Betz (ed.), *The Greek Magical Papyri in Translation Including the Demotic Spells* (Chicago, IL: University of Chicago Press, 1992), p. 217.

110. PDM lxi. 197-216 = PGM LXI.39-71, following the translation of Betz, *Greek Magical Papyri*, p. 217. For the demotic transliteration, I depend on the standard demotic edition of Francis L. Griffith and Herbert Thompson, *The Demotic Magical Papyrus of London and Leiden* (3 vols.; London: H. Grevel, 1904), II, pp. 93-94, col. XIII, ll. 1-10. On the language of the text, see Janet H. Johnson, 'The Dialect of the Demotic Magical Papyrus of London and Leiden', in *Studies in Honor of George R. Hughes* (ed. Janet H. Johnson and Edward F. Wente; Ancient Oriental Civilization, 39; Chicago, IL: Oriental

Another demotic magic spell reflects an effort to create dissension between husband and wife: 'Lizard, lizard,/as Helios and all the gods have hated you, so let NN, hate her husband for all time and//her husband hate her.'[111]

Even more instructive is an Egyptian magical papyrus in Greek, which uses the word *miseō*. Dating from the fifth century, this papyrus was published by Dierk Wortmann, and records the efforts of a man named Theon to capture the heart of a woman named Euphemia.[112] In particular, Theon addresses the possibility that she has another lover, as follows:

> But if she has another one at her bosom, move her to push him away and forget him and hate him, but me she shall be fond of and love with affection and grant me her favors, and she shall do nothing against my will (PGM CI.49-52).[113]

> εἰ δὲ καὶ ἕτερον ἔχι ἐν κόλποις, ἐκῖνον μὲν ὑπεκθέσθω καὶ {καὶ} ἐπιλαθέσθω καὶ μισήσῃ, ἐμὲ δὲ φιλήσῃ καὶ ἀγαπήσῃ καὶ στοργήσῃ καὶ τὰ αὐτῆς ἐμοῖ χαρίσητε καὶ μηδὲν παρὰ ἐμὴ{ν}ν γνώμην πράξῃ.[114]

This papyrus shows again that *miseō* is the opposite of love (as both ἀγαπάω and φιλέω). The papyrus also shows that pushing away (ἐκῖνον μὲν ὑπεκθέσθω) is naturally associated with hating, and does not always just involve a legal procedure. Diogenes Laertius also records the case of a man named Thrasonides, who 'although he had the mistress in his power, abstained from her because she hated him'.[115] Here, again, 'hate' is not a legal term but an expression of emotion that can lead to other actions (e.g., abstention from sexual relations).

So, perhaps the legal and demotic and Greek magical papyri are reflecting what was common knowledge in their culture (and in ours): *real emotional hatred can lead to divorce*. Equally important, the text evidences the belief that love and hate could be generated through magic rituals, which

Institute, 1977), pp. 105-32. Pestman (*Marriage and Matrimonial Property*, p. 64 n. 4) translates ll. 8-9 as: 'till he N.N. throws the daughter of N.N. out of his house...because she has become *hated* in his heart and means fight before his face' (Pestman's italics).

111. Betz, *Greek Magical Papyri*, pp. 291-92 (92). Also useful are the various wisdom texts, including *The Instruction of Any*, which says: 'Do not control your wife in her house/When you know she is efficient... It is a joy when your hand is with her,/There are many who don't know this./If a man desists from strife at home,/He will not encounter it its beginning' (Lichtheim, *Ancient Egyptian Literature*, II, p. 143).

112. Dierk Wortmann, 'Neue magische Texte', *Bonner Jahrburcher* 168 (1968), pp. 85-102.

113. Following the translation of Betz, *Greek Magical Papyri*, p. 309. Note that he translates φιλήσῃ as 'fond of' and ἀγαπήσῃ as 'love with affection'.

114. Following the edition of Wortmann, 'Neue magische Texte', p. 90, lines 49-52.

115. Diogenes Laertius, *Zeno* 7.130 (Hicks, LCL): Θρασωνίδην, καίπερ ἐν ἐξουσίᾳ ἔχοντα τὴν ἐρωμένην διὰ τὸ μισεῖσθαι ἀπέχεσθαι αὐτῆς.

are also part of making covenants in the ancient Near East.[116] These beliefs help explain why Jesus can command love and hate for family even if that is not the natural inclination. In cautioning scholars against using data from Mesopotamia and Elephantine to construct a very legalist view of 'hate', Pestman remarks: 'As long as further data are lacking, we prefer "to hate" as "not to love", in the larger sense, not the supposed limited one of the legal systems just mentioned.'[117] I agree.

Expressing Preference

In general, it is not compelling to appeal to ancient Near Eastern texts to show that *miseō* in Lk. 14.26 merely expresses preference (i.e., prefer Jesus over family). Ancient Near Eastern texts were perfectly capable of expressing comparative descriptions of a wife's status without the use *śn'*. In the Alalakh tablets, one finds a case (TA 92) where a woman named Naidu is married to a noble named Irihalpa. TA 92.19-20 specifies that 'Naidu will be the superior' (Na-i-du-ma rabû(bu)-ti) even when she has borne a son after her husband, Irihalpa, has had sons by another woman.[118] Nowhere in the Alalakh tablets do we see 'love' and 'hate' used to express preferences or comparisons of degree with wives or people.[119]

In the Neo-Babylonian marriage agreements collected by Martha Roth, we find a contract that bears the following stipulation: 'Should Harri-menna release Nahdi-Esu his wife, and have another wife live (in the house) in preference to her [šá-ni-tum ana UGU-ḫi-šú], he will give her five minas of silver in addition to her dowry.'[120] Preference is expressed not by the use of 'love'

---

116. See Rüdiger Schmitt, *Magie im Alten Testament* (AOAT, 313; Münster: Ugarit-Verlag, 2004), especially pp. 326-32 where Deut. 21.1-9 is discussed.

117. Pestman, *Marriage and Matrimonial Property*, p. 64.

118. Following Donald J. Wiseman, *The Alalakh Tablets* (London: British Institute of Archaeology at Ankara, 1953), pp. 54-55. See also Wells, 'The Hated Wife', p. 138.

119. The only case I have found where 'love' and 'hate' may express preference at Alalakh involves property in TA 7, where a king renders a decision about the property rights of Abban and his sister, Bittati. The relevant portion (AT 7.20-24) says: 'Thus says the king, "from the property, let Abban choose and take the part he prefers [ša i-ra-am-mu], and the part which he does not prefer [ša i-zi-ir-ru] let Bittatti take"'. Here, 'prefer' may be better than a literal translation of 'love' and 'hate'. See further, Wiseman, *The Alalakh Tablets*, pp. 34-35. For another possible instance with property, see *The Epic of Gilgamesh* 11.26: [m]a-ak-ku-ru ze-er-ma na-piš-ti bul-liṭ ('Abandon riches and seek survival'): following the edition of George, *The Babylonian Gilgamesh Epic*, I, pp. 704-705. This is important to note because Michael ('μισέω', p. 693) makes a distinction between hating works and hating people in Rev. 2.6 ('hatred for the works of the Nicolaitans, not of hatred for the men themselves') in order to mitigate the harshness of *miseō*.

120. Roth, *Babylonian Marriage Agreements*, 34.28-30.

and 'hate', but by a prepositional phrase that can be more literally rendered 'a second (wife) over her' (šá-ni-tum ana UGU-ḫi-šú).[121] A variant of the latter construction is found in Roth 26.12-16: 'Should Guzanu release Kassa and take a second wife in preference to her (aš-ša-tum šá-ni-tum ana UGU-ḫi-šú ir-te-šu), he will pay six minas of silver and she may go back to her parental home.'[122] In the Neo-Babylonian documents collected by Cornelia Wunsch, one also finds a reference to a 'primary wife' (<DA>M! rabiti[ti]).[123] So, as at Alalakh, one could also identify the preferred wife by using the adjective 'great' or 'primary', and one need not use 'hate' or 'love'.

Hate in the Gospel of Thomas

Some New Testament ethicists use extracanonical gospels to support benign interpretations of Jesus, but they seem silent or dismissive when such a gospel supports a negative interpretation of Jesus. In particular, John Dominic Crossan believes that the Gospel of Thomas derives from the earliest stratum (ca. fifties to seventies CE) of the primary documents for reconstructing the life of Jesus.[124] For Crossan, the early dating for Lk. 14.26 is corroborated by parallels in the Gospel of Thomas, and these form part of the evidence that 'Jesus will tear the hierarchical or patriarchal family in two along the axis of domination and subordination'.[125] Acting against domination and subordination is presumably good. Burridge believes that the Gospel of Thomas is later than the canonical gospels but accepts that it can be useful as evidence that the historical Jesus combined a 'mission of preaching and teaching with a ministry of healing and accepting people, especially those outside the normal social and religious groups'.[126]

Indeed, the Gospel of Thomas records 'hate' in the two places in which it bears parallels to the canonical gospels, namely, Logion 55 and Logion 101. In particular, *Gos. Thom.* 55 bears: ⲡⲉϫⲉ ⲓ̅ⲥ̅ ϫⲉ ⲡⲉⲧⲁⲙⲉⲥⲧⲉ ⲡⲉϥⲉⲓⲱⲧ... ('Jesus said, whoever does not hate his father...'). The Coptic word ⲙⲟⲥⲧⲉ

---

121. On prepositional phrases with ana/ina + muḫḫum, see Huehnergard, *Grammar of Akkadian*, 12.3, p. 100.

122. Roth, *Babylonian Marriage Agreements*, p. 92.

123. BM 33795, reverse line 4 as edited in Wunsch, *Urkunden zum Ehe*, p. 21, no. 5, reverse line 4. Wunsch (*Urkunden zum Ehe*, p. 22) translates <DA>M! rabiti[ti] as 'Ranghöchste'.

124. John Dominic Crossan, *The Historical Jesus: The Life of a Mediterranean Jewish Peasant* (New York: HarperCollins, 1991), pp. 427-28. For other studies of the Gospel of Thomas, see *Thomasine Traditions in Antiquity: The Social and Cultural World of the Gospel of Thomas* (ed. Jon M. Asgeirsson, April D. DeConick and Risto Uro; Nag Hammadi and Manichean Studies, 59; Leiden: E.J. Brill, 2006).

125. Crossan, *The Historical Jesus*, p. 300.

126. Burridge, *Imitating Jesus*, p. 39.

(*moste*) is certainly the equivalent of Greek *miseō*, as indicated by Coptic biblical translations.[127]

Equally important, the Gospel of Thomas may support the claim that the sayings in Lk. 14.26 and Mt. 10.37 are independent of each other because the Gospel of Thomas preserves both. That is to say, Mt. 10.37 may not be 'redacting' Lk. 14.26 at all, but rather recording an independent tradition. Indeed, a parallel to Mt. 10.37 (and to Lk. 12.51-53) is found in *Gos. Thom.* 16, which says:

> Perhaps people think that I have come to cast peace upon the earth, but they do not know that I have come to cast dissension upon the earth, fire, sword (and) war. For there will be five in one house: three against two and two against three, the father against the son, and the son against the father, and they will stand as solitary ones.[128]

So, if Mt. 10.37 really explains what Lk. 14.26 meant, then it is odd that the Gospel of Thomas did not simply substitute the Matthean version in all of its Logia, since it has something akin to the Matthean version. If the Gospel of Thomas is dependent on both Luke and Matthew, then it still shows that this extra-canonical gospel may not regard Mt. 10.37 and Lk. 14.26 as alternate versions of each other, but as separate traditions.[129] That is why one must be cautious in proposing that Matthew is redacting Luke here.[130]

In any case, even Coptic scholars who believe that the Coptic verb ⲙⲟⲥⲧⲉ (*moste*) means 'hate' in other contexts make an exception here on bases that are either borrowed from New Testament scholars or not independently argued on the basis of Coptic usage. For example, Uwe-Karsten Plisch, who authored commentary on the Coptic Gospel of Thomas, says:

> Hate is not to be understood here in an emotional sense; it rather indicates the fundamental opposite of unconditional priority and unconditional dismissal. The absolute radicalism of unconditional priority and unconditional dismissal. The absolute radicalism of this demand becomes especially transparent in the context of Near Eastern family and clan traditions.[131]

---

127. W.E. Crum (*A Coptic Dictionary* [Oxford: Clarendon Press, 1939], p. 187) sees ⲙⲟⲥⲧⲉ as the equivalent of Greek μισεῖν, and lists some relevant biblical passages. See also Joaquim Acevedo (ed.), *A Simplified Coptic Dictionary (Sahidic Dialect)* (Cachoeira, Brazil: Seminario Adventista Latino-Americano de Teologia, 2001), p. 52.

128. Uwe-Karsten Plisch, *The Gospel of Thomas: Original Text with Commentary* (Stuttgart: Deutsche Bibelgesellschaft, 2008), p. 70.

129. See further James M. Robinson, Paul Hoffmann and John S. Kloppenborg (eds.), *The Critical Edition of Q* (Louvain: Peeters, 2000), pp. 380-87.

130. For redactional studies of Lk. 14.26 and Mt. 10.34-37 in light of the Gospel of Thomas, see Wolfgang Schrage, *Das Verhältnis des Thomas-Evangeliums zur synoptischen Tradition und zu den koptischen Evangeliensübersetzungen* (BZNW, 29; Berlin: Alfred Topelmann, 1964), especially p. 58; Crossan, *The Historical Jesus*, pp. 300-301.

131. Uwe-Karsten Plisch, *The Gospel of Thomas: Original Text with Commentary*

3. The Hateful Jesus: Luke 14.26

There is no evidence from Coptic adduced to make such a judgment. That the Coptic verb, *moste*, is the opposite of love is evidenced by a Coptic magical invocation (Cologne 10235), wherein a practitioner wants power 'in every work of mine—every one, whether love or hate [ⲛⲉ ⲉⲓⲧⲉ ⲙⲟⲥⲧⲉ], whether favor or condemnation, whether binding or loosing, whether killing or vivifying'.[132]

Plisch seems to be adopting the rationales that have been used in New Testament scholarship to mitigate the intensity of *miseō*. As I will show below, violent attitudes toward the family are very much a part of 'Near Eastern family and clan traditions'.

To be fair, some critical scholars have acknowledged the anti-familial nature of some of Jesus' earliest injunctions.[133] However, the problem remains that any interpretation that sees Jesus as essentially loving and peaceful will center on choosing one text, whether early or late, as representative of the preaching of Jesus. But if one assumes that the anti-familial passages are indeed closer to the historical Jesus, then it is the advocates of a more violent and hateful portrayal of Jesus who may have a greater claim to approximating any 'essential' message of Jesus.

The Statistics of Hate and Love

In order to demonstrate why 'love' should be treated literally, while 'hate' should be treated non-literally in Lk. 14.26, some scholars have invoked what I would call 'canonical statistics'. The basic argument is that Lk. 14.26, even if it is literal, should not have priority over the much larger number of passages where Jesus preaches love or where New Testament authors preach love. Fred B. Craddock's commentary on Luke illustrates this rationale:

> To the call to cross bearing heard earlier at 9.23, is joined the almost frightening demand to hate one's family and one's own life (v. 26). To hate is a Semitic expression meaning to turn away from, to detach oneself from. There is nothing of that emotion we experience in the expression 'I hate you'. Were that the case, then verse 26 alone would cancel all the calls to

(Stuttgart: Deutsche Bibelgesellschaft, 2008), p. 139. For arguments against tracing Jesus' sayings back to some specific context or coherent social program, see William Arnal, 'Just How Radical were the First Followers of Jesus? Q and the Use of Jesus' Sayings', *Fourth R* 23 (2010), pp. 8-20.

132. See Marvin Meyer and Richard Smith, *Ancient Christian Magic: Coptic Texts of Ritual Power* (New York: HarperCollins, 1994), pp. 210-11 (211). For the Coptic edition of the text, I depend on Manfred Weber, 'Ein koptischer Zaubertexte aus der Kölner Papyrussamlung', *Enchoria* 2 (1972), pp. 55-63, especially p. 56, l. 32.

133. See Elizabeth A. Clark, 'Antifamilial Tendencies in Ancient Christianity', *Journal of the History of Sexuality* 5 (1995), pp. 356-80.

love, to care, to nourish, especially one's own family (1 Tim. 5.8) found throughout both Testaments.[134]

As such, Lk. 14.26 is treated as a statistical anomaly within the canon. This argument is primarily theological rather than linguistic or historical.

First, Craddock's appeal to 1 Tim. 5.8 is puzzling as Luke may not have full cognizance of anything said by the author of Timothy. Craddock, of course, is assuming, anachronistically, that both Timothy and Luke should be read together in some canon that did not exist at the time of Luke. So, because Timothy and other biblical writers teach love, then Jesus cannot have meant 'hate' in Luke. In any case, Craddock is misinformed on the meaning of 'hate' in Semitic languages.

Second, the number of times that one word occurs relative to another does not change the meaning of the respective words. So, for example, even if 'hate' may occur once, while love occurs one hundred times, that numerical difference would not prove that the meaning of 'hate' is other than the opposite of love.

Otherwise, Craddock's argument appears to be a moral one—for example, Jesus could not possibly have meant 'hate your father' as that would seem immoral.

This very same approach is taken by Paul Redditt when discussing the various scholarly views concerning God's hatred for Esau: 'These views for the most part operate on the assumption that God must act morally, an assumption that this article ultimately will affirm.'[135] However, that procedure imposes the modern scholar's morality upon the author when most Christian ethicists insist that they derive their morality from the biblical author's words. Moreover, one could change the meaning of all texts that we find immoral for us. Linguistic meanings must be established on linguistic grounds, not moral grounds.

Recontextualizing Strategies

Since the meaning of *miseō* in Lk. 14.26 seems to be clear on linguistic grounds, sometimes New Testament ethicists will resort to 'recontextualization' or 'modernization' to maintain the value of this text. John Howard Yoder, a leading pacifist author, says:

> Modern psychologizing interpretation of Jesus has been bothered largely with whether the word *hate* here should be taken seriously or not. This is certainly to miss the point of the passage. The point is rather that in a society characterized by very stable, religiously undergirded family ties,

---

134. Fred B. Craddock, *Interpretation Bible Commentary: Luke* (Louisville, KY: John Knox Press, 1990), pp. 181-82.
135. Redditt, 'The God who Loves and Hates', p. 179.

> Jesus is here calling into being a community of voluntary commitment,
> willing for the sake of its calling to take upon itself the hostility of a given
> society.[136]

Yoder's violence to the plain meaning of the text is as arbitrary as any encountered from fundamentalists. Indeed, how does one come to understand 'the point' of a passage except by understanding the meaning of the words in a passage? If *hate* is the opposite of love, as can be amply demonstrated, then why can't the point of the passage be that you must hate your family to follow Jesus? Instead, Yoder invents his own 'point', which has nothing to do with anything mentioned in the text or context.

And why does Yoder invert the object of hate so that the passage becomes centered on a 'community' taking upon itself 'the hostility of a given society'? Grammatically, the direct object of the verb, 'to hate', are parents and family. So, why does Yoder not see parents and family as the community that becomes the object of Jesus' hostility? Indeed, one can just as well argue that Yoder is denying the victimization of the family by Jesus. Likewise, why does Yoder suppose that Jesus cannot be doing both, creating a so-called 'voluntary' organization *and* asking joiners to hate their families? As in the case of other pacifistic readings, Yoder's claim ends up as nothing less than an effort to maintain the value of violent texts and hate speech by claiming that Jesus did not mean what he said.

This also leads to another question: If Jesus wanted to make the point that you should actually *hate* your family, what other stronger word would he have used? Yoder asks readers to believe that Luke or Jesus chose the strongest possible word expressing the opposite of love, when it was not necessary to do so at all. As mentioned, Greek was perfectly able to express the types of comparative expressions that Yoder and his like-minded scholars allege for Lk. 14.26.

Deuteronomy as Background

By rejecting the hagiographic and 'dehumanizing' approach to the ethics of Jesus, it is possible to find new insights into the nature of Jesus' demands to hate one's family. As mentioned, William Moran wrote a seminal article on love in Deuteronomy that portrayed the love of God as more like the loyalty that was owed a lord by a vassal, rather than describing some affection. At that end of that article he made the following tantalizing remark: 'If so, and if the old sovereign vassal terminology of love is as relevant as we think it is, then what a history behind the Christian test of true agapē—"If you

---

136. John Howard Yoder, *The Politics of Jesus* (Grand Rapids, MI: Eerdmans, 1972), p. 45.

love me, keep my commandments".'[137] More recently, Caryn A. Reeder has explored enmity within the family in Deuteronomy, Greco-Roman culture and the New Testament.[138] While she engages in apologetic arguments for the value of violent biblical texts, she does offer some important discussions about the pervasive nature of intra-family conflicts in ancient Israel and the Greco-Roman world. I concur that Deuteronomy is a plausible context for understanding Jesus' demands as portrayed by Luke.

Jesus' statements should be understood in terms of both lord–vassal terminology, and in the inducement of hatred for family that is described in Deuteronomy. Indeed, few New Testament ethicists see that Jesus is often portrayed as continuing many of the demands to love Yahweh found in Deuteronomy 13:

> If your brother, the son of your mother, or your son, or your daughter, or the wife of your bosom, or your friend who is as your own soul, entices you secretly, saying, 'Let us go and serve other gods', which neither you nor your fathers have known, some of the gods of the peoples that are round about you, whether near you or far off from you, from the one end of the earth to the other, you shall not yield to him or listen to him, nor shall your eye pity him, nor shall you spare him, nor shall you conceal him; but you shall kill him; your hand shall be first against him to put him to death, and afterwards the hand of all the people. You shall stone him to death with stones, because he sought to draw you away from the LORD your God, who brought you out of the land of Egypt, out of the house of bondage. And all Israel shall hear, and fear, and never again do any such wickedness as this among you (Deut. 13.6-11).

Not only is violence demanded upon the family members who worship other gods, but the author expects that love can be extinguished on demand ('nor shall your eye pity him'; ולא תחוס עינך עליו), and hatred or lack of pity is induced against family members upon command. According to Josephus, God expects that one overcome any feelings of pity for anyone God hates, as in the case of the Amalekites: 'For God so hated the race of the Amalekites that He had ordered to spare not even the infants, to whom is more natural that pity be shown.'[139] Given such understandings of hate in

137. Moran, 'The Ancient Near Eastern Background', p. 87. See also Maarten J.J. Menkens and Steve Moyise (eds.), *Deuteronomy in the New Testament* (Library of New Testament Studies, 358; London: T. & T. Clark, 2007); Eckart Otto, 'The History of the Legal-Religious Hermeneutics of the Book of Deuteronomy from the Assyrian to the Hellenistic Period', in Hagedorn and Kratz (eds.), *Law and Religion in the Eastern Mediterranean*, pp. 211-50. On the influence of Deuteronomy on extra-canonical Jewish literature (e.g., Jubilees), see David Lambert, 'Did Israel Believe that Redemption Awaited its Repentance? The Case of Jubilees 1', *CBQ* 68 (2006), pp. 631-50.

138. Caryn A. Reeder, *The Enemy in the Household: Family Violence in Deuteronomy and Beyond* (Grand Rapids, MI: Baker Academic, 2012).

139. Josephus, *Ant.* 6.138 (Thackeray and Marcus, LCL): ὁ μὲν Θεὸς οὕτως ἐμίσησε

the Hebrew Bible and in Josephus, Jesus could have expected family members to overcome any love for family and turn it into genuine and emotional hatred.

Similarly, Jesus' demands ultimately reach back to the expectations that Near Eastern lords placed on their vassals or followers. As previously mentioned, Esarhaddon, the king of Assyria, demanded the following of his vassals: 'You will love Ashurbanipal, the crown-prince, son of Esarhaddon, king of Assyria, your lord, as (you do) your own life' (ki-i nap-šat-ku-nu la tar-'a-ma-ni).[140] Note that the Assyrian word for 'life' here is *napištum*, which is cognate with Hebrew שֶׁפֶנ (*nephesh*), the word usually translated in the Septuagint with the Greek ψυχή (*psyche*). The latter term is precisely the one used in Lk. 14.26 to translate 'life' in the clause, '[hate]...even his own life' (καὶ τὴν ψυχὴν ἑαυτοῦ). So Moran was certainly on the right track in connecting the language used by Jesus in the New Testament with the covenantal language of the ancient Near East.

The Semantic Logic of Love and Hate

While the linguistic arguments adduced against a literal meaning of hate are themselves indicative of the apologetic nature of New Testament ethics, few pause to consider the even greater logical problems that such a non-literalist position generates. Indeed, the comparative interpretation of Lk. 14.26 actually creates a number of logical and semantic problems. For example, if we accept the proposition that 'hate X' actually means 'to love Y more than X', then we should note the odd reading generated by such an equation in Amos 5.15: 'Hate evil' = 'Love good more than evil'. However, it is clear that the author of Amos 5.15 is exhorting listeners to not love evil at all.

The arbitrary nature of Jesus apologetics in Lk. 14.26 can also be gauged by an unwillingness to treat occurrences of 'love' in the same figurative or comparative manner. That is to say, few, if any, of the same interpreters that want to treat 'hate' comparatively in Lk. 14.26 will do so for 'love'. One could just as well posit that 'love X' = 'To hate Y more than X'. Indeed, there is a great circularity at work in saying that Jesus cannot mean hate in Lk. 14.26 because he preaches 'love' elsewhere. So, why not argue that Jesus probably did not mean 'love' literally elsewhere because he clearly meant 'hate' in Lk. 14.26?

τὸ τῶν 'Αμαληκιτῶν ἔθνος, ὡς μηδὲ νηπίων φείσασθαι κελεῦσαι πρὸς ἃ μᾶλλον ἔλεος γίνεσθαι πέφυκε.

140. Wiseman, *The Vassal Treaties of Esarhaddon*, pp. 49-50, ll. 266-268. My adapted translation, as Wiseman's rendition (which is also plausible) of *napšatkunu* with the term 'yourselves' does not illuminate the Hebrew cognate that is often translated with the Greek ψυχή in the Septuagint.

There were alternate ways of describing leaving one's family that did not utilize a charged word such as *miseō*, which only would confuse readers if Jesus meant something less than what *miseō* commonly meant. Indeed, Christian ethicists seem to overlook the semantic logical problems that their defense of Jesus creates. If Jesus really meant to say 'hate', what other word would he have used? Why use the word with the harshest meaning, when others were available? Josephus, for example, represents Zerubbabel as speaking of what men will do for the love of a woman. According to Zerubbabel, 'we even leave our fathers and our mothers' (ἐγκαταλείπομεν δὲ καὶ πατέρας καὶ μητέρας).[141] If Josephus can express leaving father and mother with the word ἐγκαταλείπω, then surely Matthew did not have to use such a hateful word as *miseō* to express the same action. The use of *miseō* best makes sense if Jesus literally meant what he said.

Summary

There are no compelling linguistic or historical reasons to deny that the Greek word *miseō* in Lk. 14.26 means what it means everywhere else we encounter it in the Greek scriptures. There are no convincing reasons to deny the humanity of Jesus by removing his ability to hate, as well as to love. Those who deny a literal meaning for *miseō* have presented no cases where any comparative meaning for *miseō* is clear or required on either philological or contextual grounds. All the comparative evidence from the ancient Near East (Elephantine, Laws of Hammurabi, Coptic magical papyri, etc.) consistently shows that the linguistic equivalents of Greek *miseō* mean the opposite of love in its fully emotive sense. The act expressed by *miseō* entails rejection, repudiation, and can result in divorce among other actions. But *miseō* is not the word for those actions.

Iit is therefore reasonable to conclude that the word *miseō* in Lk. 14.26 means what Sutcliffe thought it meant: '[T]he real malicious hatred by which man wishes evil to his enemy and even desires and, if possible, accomplishes his destruction.'[142] The targets of such destruction could include idolatrous family members in Deuteronomy 13, where it is commanded that family members extinguish any natural loving feelings. If Jesus knew and followed such a tradition, then it should not be surprising that Jesus would demand the same, especially as he also indicates that he will ultimately destroy, burn or torture those who did not cater to his followers even if they happen to be the family members of his followers (Mt. 25.41-46; cf. Deut. 32.41-42).

---

141. Josephus, *Ant.* 11.52 (Thackeray, LCL).
142. Sutcliffe, 'Hatred at Qumran', p. 345.

Moreover, New Testament scholars are still largely evading the ethical issues that are raised even if *miseō* meant no more than the demand that followers of Jesus prefer him over their families. Those who deny that Jesus meant 'hate' in the most emotive and harshest sense do so because they think it would be unethical for Jesus to do such a thing. Yet, these same New Testament ethicists seem to have no problem accepting as ethical Jesus' demands that followers bestow their total allegiance to him even in preference over their own families.

How would we judge a modern religious leader who said that we should prefer him over our families? Why would we not treat such a person as an egomaniacal cult leader who does what all cult leaders do: transfer allegiance from one's family to him or her. In other words, that demand would be viewed as unethical in itself.

In the end, Jesus was not erasing some patriarchal or hierarchical social structure, as is argued by Crossan and others. Rather, Jesus was perpetuating a well-known tradition of leadership that was ultimately based on ancient Near Eastern master–servant and lord–vassal relationships, which demanded that the lord receive the total allegiance of any subordinates even at the expense of their own lives and families. Labeling his demand as a call for 'radical discipleship' appears to be another euphemistic attempt by New Testament ethicists to whitewash the hegemonic, despotic, egomaniacal and unethical view of submission that Jesus was demanding.

Chapter 4

THE VIOLENT JESUS

Judging by the titles of many treatises on the Jesus' ethics, Jesus is the ultimate advocate of peace. Joseph A. Grassi's *Jesus is Shalom: A Vision of Peace from the Gospels* (2006), Mark Bredin's *Jesus, Revolutionary of Peace: A Nonviolent Christology in the Book of Revelation* (2003), and Willard M. Swartley's *Covenant of Peace: The Missing Peace in New Testament Theology and Ethics* (2006) all help to perpetuate this portrait of Jesus.[1] Many Christian groups, including the Amish, Mennonites and Quakers, assume that a peaceful Jesus is the most historically authentic Jesus.[2] As Gordon Zerbe observes in the case of the non-retaliatory teachings ascribed to Jesus in Mt. 5.38-48 (cf. Lk. 6.27-36), '[m]ost interpreters have concluded that the basic elements of the Gospel texts derive from authentic teachings of Jesus'.[3]

In contrast, I argue that Jesus is sometimes portrayed as endorsing violence and as actually committing violence. Willard Swartley, an advocate of a non-violent Jesus, observes that there are at least twenty-four texts in the New Testament that are used by those who think that Christians are allowed to participate in war, and at least fifteen of those are associated with Jesus' teachings and deeds in the synoptics.[4] As I will explain, some instances of the supposed advocacy of non-violence on the part of Jesus can actually be considered as advocacy of deferred violence. Other instances of supposed

1.   Joseph A. Grassi, *Jesus is Shalom: A Vision of Peace from the Gospels* (Mahwah, NJ: Paulist Press, 2006); Mark Bredin, *Jesus, Revolutionary of Peace: A Nonviolent Christology in the Book of Revelation* (Waynesboro, GA: Paternoster, 2003), Willard M. Swartley, *Covenant of Peace: The Missing Peace in New Testament Theology and Ethics* (Grand Rapids, MI: Eerdmans, 2006). See also Lisa Sowle Cahill, *Love your Enemies: Discipleship, Pacifism, and Just War Theory* (Minneapolis: Fortress Press, 1994); Peter J. Riga, 'Christ and Nonviolence', *Emmanuel* 118 (2012), pp. 301-305.

2.   See, for example, Eric A. Seibert, *Disturbing Divine Behavior: Troubling Old Testament Images of God* (Minneapolis: Fortress Press, 2009), pp. 191-92.

3.   Zerbe, *Non-Retaliation*, p. 20.

4.   Swartley, *Covenant of Peace*, pp. 46-47. The passages in the Synoptics are listed by Swartley as Lk. 22.36-38, Mk 12.37-17, Mt. 10.34-35//Lk.12.51, Lk. 7.2-10//Mt. 8.5-10, Lk. 11.21-22, Mk 12.1-9, Mk 13.7-13, Lk. 3.14, Lk. 14.31-32, Mk 9.42, Mt. 23, Mt. 26.52, Mt. 11.12//Lk. 16.15, Mk 8.34-35, Lk. 12.39-40//Mt. 24.34-44.

non-violence rest on dubious readings of the immediate literary context or broader cultural context of the texts in question.

My definition of violence is an adaptation of one used in a previous book: '*Violence is the act of modifying and/or inflicting pain upon a living body in order to express or impose power differentials.*'[5] In this definition, killing would be the ultimate method to impose a power differential because it completely eliminates the power of the target. My definition is more restricted than other definitions that have been enunciated. This is important because some Christian apologists object that a widened definition of violence explains why Jesus is being viewed as more violent than previous definitions would allow.

Actual physical violence is not necessary to be defined as 'violence' in these widened definitions. For example, Thomas R. Yoder Neufeld references Robert MacAfee Brown's definition of violence as centering on a 'violation of personhood' as an example of a wide definition of violence that may also involve economic and attitudinal components in the larger society.[6] In these widened definitions, the putative victims can decide what is violent to them, and so Jesus could be accused of being violent depending on whose perspective one adopts. My aim is to show that Jesus could be seen as violent even under more restrictive definitions of violence accepted by most pacifistic apologists for Jesus' supposed peaceful ideology.

Matthew 10.34-37: Jesus' Violent Purpose

The most explicit affirmation that Jesus views himself as coming to bring war, not peace to the earth, is found in the following passage in Matthew.

> Do not think that I have come to bring peace on earth; I have not come to bring peace, but a sword. For I have come to set a man against his father, and a daughter against her mother, and a daughter-in-law against her mother-in-law; and a man's foes will be those of his own household. He who loves father or mother more than me is not worthy of me; and he who loves son or daughter more than me is not worthy of me; and he who does not take his cross and follow me is not worthy of me. He who finds his life will lose it, and he who loses his life for my sake will find it (Mt. 10.34-37).

Jesus' rhetoric is not only blatantly violent, but it violates all precepts of honoring father and mother (Exod. 20.12), and loving your neighbor (Lev. 19.18), evinced in the Hebrew Bible.

---

5.   Hector Avalos, *Fighting Words: The Origins of Religious Violence* (Amherst, NY: Prometheus, 2005), p. 19. I have changed 'human body' to 'living body' to include violence against non-human species.

6.   See Robert MacAfee Brown, *Religion and Violence* (Philadelphia, PA: Westminster, 2nd edn, 1987), p. 7; Neufeld, *Killing Enmity*, p. 2.

Some ethicists just ignore this passage in their treatment of New Testament violence. For example, Leo Lefebure begins one of his essays on New Testament violence by claiming that 'Jesus proclaimed a gospel of peace', and then cites some prooftexts that leave out Mt. 10.34.[7] Otherwise, there are two main strategies that have been used to mitigate or eliminate any violent sentiments on the part of Jesus. The first strategy is to argue that this is figurative language. Thus, in his *Christian Attitudes toward War and Peace*, Roland H. Bainton explains the use of the word 'sword' must be 'metaphorical' because Luke used a different word.[8] Simon Joseph remarks that '[m]ost scholars rightly regard this saying as symbolic or metaphorical'.[9]

Richard Hays bears a similar approach, and he rejects any notion that this passage justifies violence:

> In this context, the 'sword' of verse 34 is a metaphor for the division that will occur between those who proclaim the good news of the kingdom and those who refuse to receive it. The meaning of the saying is explicated in verses 35-36: 'For [*gar*] I have come to set man against his father, and a daughter against her mother, and a daughter-in-law against her mother-in-law; and one's foes will be members of one's own household...'. To read this verse as a warrant for the use of violence by Christians is to commit an act of extraordinary hermeneutical violence against the text.[10]

The ethical premises of Hays's analysis are problematic. He apparently has no problem with the very real pain that people can suffer when their families are in conflict. Hays presumably sees emotional and mental distress in this case as justified because Jesus' 'good news' is worth it.[11] Moreover, Hays does not address why Jesus cannot have in mind a more literal directive such as Deuteronomy where those who do not follow the preferred religion should be killed even if they are family members: 'nor shall your eye pity him, nor shall you spare him, nor shall you conceal him; but you shall kill him' (Deut. 13.8-9).[12]

---

7. Leo Lefebure, 'Violence in the New Testament and the History of Interpretation', in *Fighting Words: Religion, Violence, and the Interpretation of Sacred Texts* (ed. John Rennard; Berkeley, CA: University of California Press, 2012), pp. 75-100 (75).

8. Roland H. Bainton, *Christian Attitudes toward War and Peace: A Historical Survey and Critical Re-evaluation* (Nashville, TN: Abingdon Press, 1960), p. 56. See also Philip E. Friesen, *The Old Testament Roots of Nonviolence: Abraham's Personal Faith, Moses' Social Vision, Jesus' Fulfillment, and God's Work Today* (Eugene, OR: Wipf & Stock, 2010).

9. Simon J. Joseph, *The Nonviolent Messiah: Jesus, Q, and the Enochic Tradition* (Minneapolis: Fortress Press, 2014), p. 26.

10. Hays, *The Moral Vision*, pp. 332-33.

11. A critique of Hays's stance on violence by an advocate of 'just war theory' may be found in Nigel Biggar, 'Specify and Distinguish! Interpreting the New Testament on "Non-Violence"', *Studies in Christian Ethics* 22 (2009), pp. 164-84.

12. See also Reeder, *The Enemy in the Household*.

The other apologetic strategy is redactional. The offensive part of the verse or the entire verse is declared to be a later editorial edition, and not anything Jesus said. An example of this is The Jesus Seminar's edition of the Gospels, which comments as follows on this passage:

> The claim that Jesus deliberately creates conflict would seem to contradict other sayings of Jesus in which he recommends unqualified love (for example, Mt. 5.43-48). In this saying, Jesus also refers to himself in the first person, something the Fellows doubt that he did. For that reason, and because the saying is based on something the prophet Micah said, the Fellows concluded that these sentences were formulated by the Christian community.[13]

As I have argued above, any attribution of any saying to Jesus already assumes that one knows what Jesus would have said or thought. Without some objective means to know what Jesus said or did, any such attribution is completely subjective and circular. For example, the Fellows, as members of the Jesus Seminar refer to themselves, doubt that Jesus said what is recorded in Mt. 10.34.

One reason is their own doubt ('something the Fellows doubt that he did') of what Jesus would have done. How is this better than an opposing reason—for example, 'Jesus also refers to himself in the first person, something the Fellows believe that he did'. And are the Fellows' doubts a sufficient reason for anything?

Another reason is equally circular, namely, that Jesus is recorded to have preached 'unqualified love' elsewhere. But how did the Fellows determine that it is the loving Jesus that is authentic rather than the more violent one? If this saying is so starkly contraposed to the love sayings, then why does the redactor not see that? Denying that Jesus uttered this logion because it alludes to Mic. 7.5-6 is also circular. Given that quoting, or alluding to, the Hebrew Bible was common in Jewish exegesis of the time, how did the Fellows determine that Jesus could not allude to that passage?[14]

However, perhaps the most common strategy is to misread Jesus' purpose clause ('For I have come to set a man against his father...') as a result clause, which is not what the grammar of Jesus' language indicates at all. The relevant clauses in Mt. 10.34-35 are purpose clauses, as indicated by the infinitives, βαλεῖν and διχάσαι, after ἦλθον, an intransitive verb of motion, in the Greek expression Μὴ νομίσητε ὅτι ἦλθον βαλεῖν εἰρήνην ἐπὶ τὴν γῆν. οὐκ ἦλθον βαλεῖν εἰρήνην ἀλλὰ μάχαιραν. ἦλθον γὰρ διχάσαι ἄνθρωπον κατὰ τοῦ πατρὸς αὐτοῦ. This is rightly translated as

13. Robert Funk, Roy W. Hoover and the Jesus Seminar, *The Five Gospels: What Did Jesus Really Say* (New York: HarperCollins, 1997), p. 174.

14. See Matthias Henze (ed.), *Biblical Interpretation at Qumran: Studies in the Dead Sea Scrolls and Related Literature* (Grand Rapids, MI: Eerdmans, 2005).

'Do not think that I have come to bring peace on earth; I have not come to bring peace, but a sword. For I have come to set a man against his father...' (Mt. 10.34-35).

As Daniel Wallace notes, purpose clauses can be expressed by a '[s]imple or "naked" infinitive (usually following an [intransitive] verb of motion'.[15] A close parallel to the use of the infinitive in Mt. 10.34 is found in Mt. 5.17: 'Think not that I have come to abolish the law and the prophets; I have come not to abolish them but to fulfil them'/Μὴ νομίσητε ὅτι ἦλθον καταλῦσαι τὸν νόμον ἢ τοὺς προφήτας. Οὐκ ἦλθον καταλῦσαι ἀλλὰ πληρῶσαι. In both cases one finds the negative purpose expression, οὐκ ἦλθον καταλῦσαι (Mt. 5.17) and οὐκ ἦλθον βαλεῖν (Mt. 10.34), followed by the adversative conjuction, ἀλλὰ, and then positive purpose clauses, ἦλθον...πληρῶσαι (Mt. 5.17) and ἦλθον γὰρ διχάσαι (Mt. 10.34). Accordingly, Jesus did not say that his mission would simply result in family strife. Jesus *is saying* that a primary *purpose* of his mission is to create violence within families, and the mention of the sword is consistent with that violent sentiment.

Matthew 5.38-42: Don't Victimize Me, Please

Although many Christian ethicists extol the love of enemies as an innovation in ethics, they also realize that this directive could encourage more victimization and violence. Consider the paradigmatic passage where Jesus advises his disciples to abrogate the ancient tradition of *Lex talionis* in Matthew:

> You have heard that it was said, 'An eye for an eye and a tooth for a tooth'. But I say to you, Do not resist one who is evil. But if any one strikes you on the right cheek, turn to him the other also; and if any one would sue you and take your coat, let him have your cloak as well; and if any one forces you to go one mile, go with him two miles. Give to him who begs from you, and do not refuse him who would borrow from you (Mt. 5.38-42).[16]

Jerome Rausch is among many scholars who see the problem with Jesus' directives when interpreted literally:

> And yet, if we read it as a contradiction to primitive justice, we notice that it can be read as a contradiction to all justice. That is, turn the other cheek, never demand one's rights. However, if rights are never demanded, one

15. Daniel B. Wallace, *The Basics of New Testament Syntax: An Intermediate Greek Grammar* (Grand Rapids, MI: Zondervan, 2000), p. 256. On the increasing standardization of verbs of motion (e.g., 'came'/ἦλθον) + infinitives in purpose clauses in the New Testament, see BDF, p. 197, paragraph 390.

16. For the argument that these logia do not reach back to Jesus, see J. Sauer, 'Traditionsgeschichtliche Erwägungen zu den synoptischen und paulinischen Aussagen über Feindesliebe und Wiedervergeltungsverzicht', *ZNW* 76 (1985), pp. 102-25.

can argue—and it has been argued—those rights cease to exist. Those who govern become autocrats and those who are governed become sheep.[17]

Accordingly, Walter Wink attempts to mitigate the nature of the physical act described in Mt. 5.39 as follows:

> A blow by the right fist in that right-handed world would land on the *left* cheek of the opponent. An open-handed slap would also strike the left cheek. To hit the right cheek with the fist would require using the left hand, but in that society the left hand was used only for unclean tasks. Even to gesture with the left hand at Qumran carried the penalty of ten days' penance. The only way one could naturally strike the right cheek with the right hand would be with the back of the hand. We are dealing with insult, not a fistfight.[18]

Wink is an advocate of what he calls 'the third way', which endorses neither passivity nor violence as a response to violence.[19] Rather, he endorses what he calls 'active nonviolent resistance'.

Yet, one could also build a plausible case that Jesus meant to encourage complete nonresistance, regardless of the brutality. First, Jesus himself did not resist when struck in the Gospel of John:

> When he had said this, one of the officers standing by struck Jesus with his hand [ἔδωκεν ῥάπισμα], saying, 'Is that how you answer the high priest?' Jesus answered him, 'If I have spoken wrongly, bear witness to the wrong; but if I have spoken rightly, why do you strike me [τί με δέρεις;]?' (Jn 18.22-23).

Note also how the author of 1 Peter, who, when encouraging slaves to obey even cruel masters, added this reasoning:

> For to this you have been called, because Christ also suffered for you, leaving you an example, that you should follow in his steps. He committed no sin, no guile was found on his lips. When he was reviled, he did not revile in return; when he suffered, he did not threaten; but he trusted to him who judges justly (1 Pet. 2.21-23).

17. Jerome Rausch, 'The Principle of Nonresistance and Love of Enemy in Mt 5, 38-48', *CBQ* 28 (1966), pp. 31-41 (36).

18. Wink, *Engaging the Powers*, pp. 175-76; Wink's italics. The discussion of this passage by Nancey Murphy ('When Jesus Said "Love your Enemies" I Think He Probably Meant Don't Kill Them'", *PRSt* 40 [2013], pp. 123-29 [128]) adopts Wink's conclusion without exploring any alternative interpretations. For an negative evaluation of Wink's general approach from an evangelical perspective, see Chloe Lynch, 'How Convincing is Walter Wink's Interpretations of Paul's Language of the Powers?', *EvQ* 83.3 (2011), pp. 251-66.

19. See Walter Wink, *Jesus and Nonviolence: A Third Way* (Minneapolis: Fortress Press, 2003). For an early statement of this proposal, see Walter Wink, 'Neither Passivity nor Violence: Jesus' Third Way (Matt 5:38-42//Luke 6:29-30)', *Forum* 7 (1991), pp. 5-28.

How could this author misunderstand Jesus so blatantly if Wink's readings are correct? First Peter shows that many early Christians did believe Jesus' tolerance for, or encouragement of, victimization was real.[20]

Second, the Greek word ῥαπίζω ('to strike') may also have stronger and more violent connotations, as in the retelling of the story of Micaiah (1 Kgs 22.24) in Josephus. According to the latter, a rival prophet tested Micaiah's prophetic authenticity by devising the following test for Ahab, who wanted to know if he would be successful in his proposed battle against the Syrians.

> Let him right now, when I strike him [ῥαπισθείς], disable my hand as Jadaos caused the right hand of King Jeroboam to wither when he wish to arrest him. For I suppose you must have heard that the thing happened. According when he struck [πληξάντος] Michaias and suffered no harm as a result, Achab took courage...(Josephus, Ant. 8.408).

Note that both ῥαπίζω and πλήσσω are synonyms. The action described by the latter verb can be lethal, as in Josephus's retelling of the story of the woman of Tekoa (2 Sam. 14.6). That woman had two sons, and 'one of them was struck by the other and killed' (πληγέντα ἀποθανεῖν).[21] Therefore, it is not clear whether Jesus is describing only a slap because ῥαπίζω, whose nominal form (ῥαπίς) means 'rod', could also involve hitting someone with a weapon. As BDAG notes, 'almost always in non-biblical authors "strike with a club or rod"... Mt. 26.67 could have this meaning'.[22] It is also possible that the word σιαγών does not mean just 'cheek', but also jaw. That meaning is attested in the LXX (Judg. 15.14-17).[23] While there are clearly cases in the New Testament where 'slapping' is the meaning, one cannot simply dismiss an understanding that involves hitting the face more violently, perhaps even with an instrument. After all, Jesus explicitly juxtaposed his new directive against the ones requiring severe injuries to teeth and eyes (Exod. 21.24), and a simple slap would not be equivalent to those injuries.

There are too many other unknown factors to provide a definite answer to what Jesus meant here. Wink, for example, claims that in 'that society the left hand was used only for unclean tasks', but he provides no data to support this contention. In fact, there are priestly procedures that call for the use of the left hand as in the following: 'Then the priest shall take some of the log of oil, and pour it into the palm of his own left hand' (Lev. 14.15), and so what does 'in that society' mean? When Philo discussed which side of

20. On this passage in 1 Peter, see also Darrin W. Snynder Belousek, *Atonement, Justice, and Peace: The Message of the Cross and the Mission of the Church* (Grand Rapids, MI: Eerdmans, 2012), p. 36.

21. Josephus, *Ant.* 7.183 (Thackeray and Marcus, LCL).

22. BDAG, 'ῥαπίζω', p. 903b.

23. BDAG, 'σιαγών', p. 922a.

Adam was used to make Eve, he seems to value both sides equally: 'Truly our sides are twin in all their parts and are made of flesh.'[24] The author of 2 Corinthians did not seem to discriminate between left and right hands, when he remarks: 'with the weapons of righteousness for the right hand and for the left' (2 Cor. 6.7).

Whatever one thinks of Wink's proposals, the fact is that Jesus was not doing much different than others had already envisioned. Josephus tells us that women are more powerful than men because men will do anything for love. Josephus specifically remarks: 'I once saw a king being slapped by his concubine' (παλλακῆς δ' αὐτοῦ ῥαπιζόμενον).[25] There was no ostensible retaliation by the king. Jesus was preaching something that others were probably already doing for love.

Matthew 26.48-56: Non-Interference with Planned Violence

Starkly juxtaposed to Jesus' self-described violent mission in Mt. 10.34 is his statement to a disciple who drew a sword to strike off the ear of a slave belonging to the high priest who is depicted as a leader of the group coming to arrest Jesus in Matthew 26:

> Now the betrayer had given them a sign, saying, 'The one I shall kiss is the man; seize him'. And he came up to Jesus at once and said, 'Hail, Master!' And he kissed him. Jesus said to him, 'Friend, why are you here?' Then they came up and laid hands on Jesus and seized him. And behold, one of those who were with Jesus stretched out his hand and drew his sword, and struck the slave of the high priest, and cut off his ear. Then Jesus said to him, 'Put your sword back into its place; for all who take the sword will perish by the sword. Do you think that I cannot appeal to my Father, and he will at once send me more than twelve legions of angels? But how then should the scriptures be fulfilled, that it must be so?' At that hour Jesus said to the crowds, 'Have you come out as against a robber, with swords and clubs to capture me? Day after day I sat in the temple teaching, and you did not seize me. But all this has taken place, that the scriptures of the prophets might be fulfilled'. Then all the disciples forsook him and fled (Mt. 26.48-56).

The passage ostensibly shows that Jesus advocates a nonviolent approach to conflict. That is one reason many pacifistic scholars labor to place it in the mouth of the historical Jesus.

Some scholars appeal to redaction to demonstrate that an earlier, and presumably more 'authentic', Jesus was nonviolent, but this redactional criticism can be selective. Thus, Willard Swartley argues that

---

24. Philo, *Leg. All.* 2.21 (Colson and Whitaker, LCL).
25. Josephus, *Ant.* 11.54 (Thackeray and Marcus, LCL).

> Interestingly, unlike other Synoptic accounts (cf. Mt. 26.51; Lk. 22.50-51), in Mark Jesus does not rebuke his disciples for striking out in violence. It does not really require rebuke—the act of violence rebukes itself. For the act of striking out in violence to defend the Messiah from arrest reveals that the one who draws the sword does not truly know the Messiah he sets out to defend.[26]

Swartley's reasoning is both circular and unsupported by any evidence. To say that the author omitted Jesus' rebuke because one of his disciples does not 'truly know the Messiah' presupposes that the Messiah is already peaceful. But why could it not be that the disciple drew his sword precisely because he knew Jesus did not always object to defensive violence? And what is the evidence that an act of violence 'rebukes itself' for Mark? If that were true, then why did the other Gospel writers feel the need to add Jesus' rebuke?

Although Jesus does instruct one of his disciples to put away his sword, that instruction cannot serve as evidence of a non-violent ideology or theology. In fact, the very remarks that God could send 'twelve legions of angels' if Jesus so requested means that Jesus accepts the concept that God has a military force ready to take violent action at his command. If Jesus' theology is completely non-violent, then why does he envision God even having an angelic military force divided into legions in the first place?

Equally important is the overarching reason that Jesus offers for his non-retaliatory instruction. Jesus instructs his disciples to desist from violence so that he might suffer the violence scripture had predicted ('all this has taken place, that the scriptures of the prophets might be fulfilled'). Jesus is not rejecting violence at all. Rather, his non-retaliatory instruction is meant to avoid interrupting the violent divine plan in which he is participating. This is real violence to which he is submitting, and which he is accepting. The violence that is about to be perpetrated against him is simply a mechanism for facilitating the greater violence that God will bring against his enemies. Indeed, a few verses later, Jesus exclaims: 'But I tell you, hereafter you will see the Son of man seated at the right hand of Power, and coming on the clouds of heaven' (Mt. 26.64). That verse harkens back to the judgment scene of great violence that Jesus described in Mt. 25.41-46.

The parallel passage in Jn 18.36 ('if my kingship were of this world, my servants would fight, that I might not be handed over to the Jews; but my kingship is not from the world') may be read in a similar way. Adele Reinhartz already grasped the broader violence that this verse references when she remarks: 'But the Gospel preaches that Jesus' kingdom is ultimately more powerful, more enduring, and more violent by virtue of its divine mandate and its cosmic scope.'[27]

---

26. Swartley, *Covenant of Peace*, p. 113.
27. Adele Reinhartz, 'Love, Hate, and Violence in the Gospel of John', in *Violence in*

Few pacifist scholars notice that the story of Jesus' arrest is very similar to that of Vitellius, who reigned for eight months as Rome's emperor in the year 69.

In particular, the account of Tacitus bears a few parallels to the capture of Jesus. According to that account, Vitellius sought to hide from the advancing forces of Vespasian, who succeeded him. A tribune named Julius Placidus finds Vitellius and drags him out into the light, where Vitellius presented a 'grievous sight as he was led away'.[28] Tacitus tells us that 'even the meanest of his slaves had slipped away or else avoided meeting him'.[29] In the case of Jesus, some of his disciples deserted or denied him. Having been an emperor, Vitellius now found himself in a situation where 'many cried against him, not one shed a tear'.[30] The crowds taunted Jesus, the king of kings, without mercy after his arrest. More importantly, Tacitus reports the following:

> One of the soldiers from Germany met him and struck at him in rage, or else his purpose was to remove him the quicker from insult or he may have been aiming at the tribune—no one could tell. He cut off the tribune's ear and was once run through. Vitellius was forced at the point of the sword to lift his face and offer to his captors' insults... His only utterance marked his spirit as not ignoble, for when the tribune insulted him, he replied, 'Yet I was your emperor'. Then he fell under a shower of blows; and the people attacked his body after he was dead with the same base spirit with which they had fawned on him when he lived.[31]

Aside from the similarity in the incident involving the lopped ear of an official, there are other broader similarities that one could transform into a manifesto for nonviolence. As in the case of Jesus, Tacitus explicitly notes that Vitellius did not resist, and only uttered an innocuous phrase. Tacitus cites Vitellius's gracious response as an explicit indication of his character. Indeed, we could read into the arrest of Jesus a stereotypical account of the arrest of a leader regarded in favor by the author. Vitellius is humble and non combative. Yet, there are no New Testament scholars turning Tacitus's account of Vitellius's arrest and execution into some anti-violence manifesto on the part of Vitellius.

the New Testament (ed. Shelly Matthews and E. Leigh Gibson; New York: T. & T. Clark, 2005), pp. 109-23 (121).

28. Tacitus, *Histories* 3.84 (Jackson, LCL): 'foedum spectaculum'.

29. Tacitus, *Histories* 3.84 (Jackson, LCL): 'etiam infimis servitiorum aut occursum eius declinantibus'. For a study of Tacitus's historical approach, see Ronald Mellor, *Tacitus' Annals* (Oxford Approaches to Classical Literature; New York: Oxford University Press, 2011).

30. Tacitus, *Histories* 3.84 (Jackson, LCL): 'multis increpantibus, nullo inlacrimate'.

31. Tacitus, *Histories* 3.84-85 (Jackson, LCL).

Luke 9.52-56: Rebuking Violence

Part of the portrait of the anti-violent Jesus is constructed on the basis of texts where he seemingly rebukes violence. One example is the following:

> And he sent messengers ahead of him, who went and entered a village of the Samaritans, to make ready for him; but the people would not receive him, because his face was set toward Jerusalem. And when his disciples James and John saw it, they said, 'Lord, do you want us to bid fire come down from heaven and consume them?' But he turned and rebuked them. And they went on to another village (Lk. 9.52-56).

Dale C. Allison sees this as an example of a radical departure from prior retributive ideologies. As he phrases it: 'There is at this point no harmony between old and new. Jesus' unelaborated rebuke seemingly implies that violent vengeance is wrong at all times and places.'[32] But if one thinks that Jesus is an innovator or marks some radical departure from previous traditions, then one would be wrong. The *Testament of Abraham*, a Jewish work dated to the first or second century, has a story similar to that of Lk. 9.52-56. In that pseudepigraphical work, which Dale C. Allison knows well, Abraham is taken on a tour of the world in an airborne chariot piloted by the archangel Michael.[33] When Abraham sees robbers at work, he commands wild beasts to destroy them, and wild beasts do so. Abraham then sees a couple engaging in illicit sex, and Abraham requests that the earth swallow them up. The next instance of wrongdoing witnessed by Abraham bears repeating at length:

> And he saw in another place men breaking into a house and carrying off the possessions of others, and he said, 'LORD, LORD, command that fire come down from heaven and consume them'. And as he was speaking fire came down from heaven and consumed them. And immediately a voice came down from heaven to the Commander-in-Chief, speaking thus, 'O Michael, Commander-in-Chief, command the chariot to stop and turn Abraham away, lest he should see the entire inhabited world. For if he were to see all those who pass their lives in sin, he would destroy everything that exists. For behold, Abraham has not sinned and he has no mercy on sinners. But I made the world, and I do not want to destroy any one of them; but I delay the death of the sinner until he should convert and live' (*T. Abr.* 10.10-15).[34]

This episode shows that rebuking an episode of violence does not entail rebuking all violence. God allows the destruction of people in the first two instances, but not in the third. God does not reject the use of all violence

---

32. Dale C. Allison, 'Rejecting Violent Judgment: Luke 9:52-56 and its Relatives', *JBL* 121 (2002), pp. 459-78 (476).

33. See Dale C. Allison, *The Testament of Abraham* (Commentaries on Early Jewish Literature; Berlin: W. de Gruyter, 2003).

34. *OTP*, I, pp. 887-88.

every time, but God does advocate something akin to 'deferred violence' insofar as he wishes to delay violence, not eliminate it completely.[35] Similarly, Jesus' rebuke of violence in Lk. 9.52-53 is consistent with the advocacy of deferred violence, not non-violence.

Deferred Violence versus Non-Violence

Part of the problem with discussing non-violence attributed to Jesus is that many more specifically pacifist writers do not make a distinction between non-violence and deferred violence. In the most absolute terms, non-violence should refer to the repudiation of violence in any form and under any circumstances. By 'deferred violence', I refer to violence meant to be performed at a future time, usually because of expediency. In these cases, violence may be refused or put aside for the time being. This delay may give the false impression that an advocate of deferred violence is an advocate of non-violence. Christian pacifists often automatically count an appeal against violence by Jesus without accounting for the fact that Jesus means to delay, rather than absolutely refuse, the use of violence.

A pre-Christian instance of deferred violence is found in a work known as *The Instruction of Any*, which may have been composed during the New Kingdom in Egypt: 'Don't rush to attack your attacker/Leave him to the god;/Report him daily to the god,/Tomorrow being like today, and you will see what the god does,/When he injures him who injures you.'[36] Here the author is not advocating non-violence. Rather the author is advocating that the victim refrain from violence because his god will avenge him later. It would be inaccurate to count the author of *Any* as an advocate of non-violence on the basis of the first clause without also taking account of what he said in the last two clauses. A good analogy might be if I advise my little brother to not retaliate against a more powerful foe because later I will come and avenge him on his behalf.

In New Testament studies, Krister Stendahl was among the first to grasp the importance of explaining non-retaliatory instructions on the basis of an expected future eschatological revenge.[37] Stendahl observed how some texts at Qumran could enjoin non-retaliation in a manner similar to texts found in the New Testament. One reason is that the authors of those texts

35. Allison (*Testament of Abraham*, p. 220) argues that the passage 'sets scripture against scripture' insofar as the Testament chooses biblical passages that speak of mercy rather than destruction of sinners. However, Allison never examines the ethics of God allowing the first two instances of killing sinners. Nor does Allison address the ethics of deferred violence.

36. Lichtheim, *Ancient Egyptian Literature*, II, p. 142. The slashes preserve the lines of poetry as divided by Lichtheim.

37. Stendahl, 'Hate, Non-Retaliation, and Love'.

thought that God's vengeance on their behalf was imminent. As Stendahl remarks, '[i]n such a situation one can afford to practice non-retaliation toward the enemies—the enemies of the righteous which are by definition also the enemies of God'.[38]

An illustrative case is Rom. 12.14, which is often invoked as an example of Christian love toward enemies: 'Bless those who persecute you; bless and do not curse them.' However, Paul also advocates deferred violence. Christians must do what is expedient while awaiting the final overthrow of the Roman empire or whatever non-Christian empire is in force, as indicated in Rom. 12.19: 'Vengeance is mine; I will repay, says the Lord.' The tactical and utilitarian aspect of this advice in Rom. 12.14 becomes clearer in verse 20: 'if your enemy is hungry, feed him; if he is thirsty, give him drink; for by so doing you will heap burning coals upon his head.' The latter clause about heaping 'burning coals upon his head' is an allusion to Prov. 25.21-22, where the vengeful nature of the metaphor is very apparent.[39]

The expression in Romans and Proverbs recalls one in the Babylonian *Counsels of Wisdom*, where there existed the concept that a god could repay a victimizer with good or evil on behalf of a victim who dealt kindly in return, for example 'Shamash will repay with evil' (i-ra-ab-šú lu[m-n]u).[40] Once read as a whole, the directive to be generous to an opponent becomes an instrument of deferred violence against the opponent. The kinder one is to the opponent, the more violence will be deserved by the opponents when God repays them.[41]

The fact that Jesus is preaching deferred violence is clear from his statements later in Matthew 25.

> When the Son of man comes in his glory, and all the angels with him, then he will sit on his glorious throne. Before him will be gathered all the nations, and he will separate them one from another as a shepherd separates the sheep from the goats, and he will place the sheep at his right hand, but the goats at the left. Then the King will say to those at his right hand, 'Come, O blessed of my Father, inherit the kingdom prepared for you from the foundation of the world; for I was hungry and you gave me food, I was thirsty and you gave me drink, I was a stranger and you welcomed me, I was naked and you clothed me, I was sick and you visited me, I was in prison and you came to me'. Then the righteous will answer him, 'LORD,

38. Stendahl, 'Hate, Non-Retaliation, and Love', p. 344.

39. See also Stanislav Segert, '"Live Coals Heaped on the Head"', in Marks and Good (eds.), *Love and Death in the Ancient Near East*, pp. 159-64.

40. *BWL*, p. 100, l. 60; Akkadian in *BWL*, p. 100, l. 60. See further Segert, '"Live Coals Heaped on the Head"', p. 163. Segert's representation of the *Counsels of Wisdom* is misleading insofar as the line quoted concerning Shamash does not pertain directly to the enemy who has been requited with kindness.

41. See further, Zerbe, *Non-Retaliation*, pp. 251-54.

when did we see thee hungry and feed thee, or thirsty and give thee drink? And when did we see thee a stranger and welcome thee, or naked and clothe thee? And when did we see thee sick or in prison and visit thee?' And the King will answer them, 'Truly, I say to you, as you did it to one of the least of these my brethren, you did it to me'. Then he will say to those at his left hand, 'Depart from me, you cursed, into the eternal fire prepared for the devil and his angels; for I was hungry and you gave me no food, I was thirsty and you gave me no drink, I was a stranger and you did not welcome me, naked and you did not clothe me, sick and in prison and you did not visit me'. Then they also will answer, 'LORD, when did we see thee hungry or thirsty or a stranger or naked or sick or in prison, and did not minister to thee?' Then he will answer them, 'Truly, I say to you, as you did it not to one of the least of these, you did it not to me'. And they will go away into eternal punishment, but the righteous into eternal life (Mt. 25.31-46).

Whence comes the idea that Christ is obligated to avenge wrongs done to his followers? I agree with Stendahl, who suggests that the idea is already found in Deuteronomy 32.[42] As in the case of Matthew 24, Deut. 32.36 describes Yahweh's besieged people after allowing them to suffer: 'For the LORD will vindicate his people and have compassion on his servants, when he sees that their power is gone, and there is none remaining, bond or free.' Eventually, Yahweh decides to avenge his servants:

See now that I, even I, am he, and there is no god beside me; I kill and I make alive; I wound and I heal; and there is none that can deliver out of my hand. For I lift up my hand to heaven, and swear, As I live for ever, if I whet my glittering sword, and my hand takes hold on judgment, I will take vengeance on my adversaries, and will requite those who hate me. I will make my arrows drunk with blood, and my sword shall devour flesh—with the blood of the slain and the captives, from the long-haired heads of the enemy. Praise his people, O you nations; for he avenges the blood of his servants, and takes vengeance on his adversaries, and makes expiation for the land of his people (Deut. 32.39-43).

As does Christ in Matthew 25, Yahweh in Deuteronomy 32 promises to avenge his servants. As gruesome and violent as Deuteronomy 32 is, Christ goes much further. Christ does not only wish to kill those who harmed his servants. Christ wants to torture them eternally with fire, one of the most horrific ways to destroy a body.

Once one views Mt. 5.38 in light of Mt. 25.39-46, one understands that its rationale for refraining from violence is very much like that of *The Instruction of Any*:

A. An instruction to victim to refrain from violence in the present followed by a
B. Promise of future vengeance upon the perpetrator.

42. Stendahl, 'Hate, Non-Retaliation, and Love', p. 344.

The main structural difference otherwise is that *The Instruction of Any* compresses the time between A and B, while Matthew has inserted a lot of material in between these two events.

In the introduction to their anthology on violence in the New Testament, Shelly Matthews and E. Leigh Anderson remark: 'More troubling than studies of violence in the Bible that ignore the New Testament are those that lift up the New Testament as somehow containing the antidote for Old Testament violence.'[43]

Indeed, the quality and quantity of the violence in the New Testament is far beyond what usually had been expressed in the Hebrew Bible and other ancient Near Eastern literature. If anything, Jesus is innovative in extending and intensifying violence. In the Hebrew Bible, divine violence usually is reserved for one's normal lifetime on the earth (cf. Deut. 28.15-68). Very few works of ancient Near Eastern literature promise an eternal torture for those who do not follow a god's wishes. Other times, one finds references to living in the netherworld, but as a sort of prisoner. It is Jesus who emphasizes, more than anyone else before him, the idea that those who displease him should suffer an eternal torture. So the quality of the violence (burning) and the eternal duration of the violence are infinitely greater than almost any precedent I know.[44]

Mark 13/Matthew 24–25: Eschatological Violence

Matthew 25 is an instance of eschatological violence that is weighing on the conscience of many modern biblical scholars. As Tina Pippin remarks, '[a]pocalyptic discourses and literature have often been embarrassments for New Testament scholars, like some bad relative with a prison record'.[45] David J. Neville frames the problem as follows:

> There is a discrepancy at the heart of the New Testament. Briefly stated, the discrepancy is this: although the canonical Gospels present a fairly uniform picture of Jesus as an advocate of peace and practitioner of nonretaliation, certain texts within these same Gospels and in other parts of the New

43. Matthews and Gibson (eds.), *Violence in the New Testament*, p. 3. See also Jack Nelson-Pallmeyer, 'Another Inconvenient Truth: Violence within the "Sacred Texts"', *Fourth R* 20 (2007), pp. 9-15. A more comparative approach may be found in Harold A. Drake (ed.), *Violence in Late Antiquity: Perceptions and Practices* (Burlington, VT: Ashgate, 2006).

44. Something close is what is described in Plato's *Phaedo* 113d-114b, whose description of the afterlife bears resemblances to the story of Lazarus and the Rich Man (Lk. 16.20-31).

45. Tina Pippin, *Apocalyptic Bodies: The Biblical End of the World in Text and Image* (London: Routledge, 1999), p. 20.

Testament apparently anticipate a future arrival, or *parousia*, of Jesus in the guise of a violent avenger.[46]

At the same time, there is a debate about whether ensuring obedience through rewards and punishments is a proper system of morality. In his discussion of Matthew's eschatology, Richard Hays affirms that '[t]he motivation for obedience to God is grounded repeatedly in the rewards and punishments that await everyone at the final judgment'.[47] David Neville, on the other hand, objects to Hays and states: 'Promises of rewards and threat of punishment are not the best means to a mature, well-integrated moral reality.'[48] Accordingly, there is a renewed urgency in addressing the ethical problems posed by eschatological violence and theodicy.[49]

Since the subject of eschatological violence is now so complex and diverse, I will concentrate in the present chapter on issues where theological argumentation, rather than purely historico-critical methodology, is still utilized by biblical scholarship. In particular, Eric Seibert devotes a portion of his book, *Disturbing Divine Behavior*, to explaining eschatological violence. Seibert generally sees three possible responses that aim to preserve a non-violent eschatology of Jesus:

> Option 1: Jesus' Teaching about Eschatological Violence Does not Reflect His Views of God… Option 2: 'Jesus' Teachings' about Eschatological Judgment Do Not Originate with Jesus… Option 3: Jesus' Teachings about Eschatological Judgment are Less Violent (and Less Problematic) than they Appear.[50]

I will use Seibert's categories to explain why none of them offers a viable defense for a non-violent Jesus.[51]

Option 1 is a wholly theological argument, and so is unsuitable in any historical study of the Bible. A main proponent is I. Howard Marshall in his

---

46. David J. Neville, *A Peaceable Hope: Contesting Violent Eschatology in the New Testament Narratives* (Grand Rapids, MI: Baker Academic, 2013), p. 1. See also David J. Neville, 'Moral Vision and Eschatology in Mark's Gospel: Coherence or Conflict?', *JBL* 127 (2008), pp. 359-84.

47. Hays, *The Moral Vision*, p. 106.

48. Neville, *A Peaceable Hope*, p. 18.

49. Some works that address the ethical dimensions of eschatology include Bruce Barber and David J. Neville (eds.), *Theodicy and Eschatology* (Adelaide: ATF Press, 2005); Christfried Böstrich, *Eschatologie und Ethik im frühen Christentum: Festschrift für Günter Haufe zum 75. Geburstag* (Greifswalder theologische Forschungen, 11; New York: Peter Lang, 2006); Dale C. Allison, 'The Eschatology of Jesus', in *The Encylopedia of Apocalypticism: Volume 1. The Origins of Apocalypticism in Judaism and Christianity* (ed. John J. Collins; New York: Continuum, 1998), pp. 267-302.

50. Seibert, *Disturbing Divine Behavior*, pp. 248-51.

51. For another critique of Seibert, this one from within the Christian pacifist tradition, see Esau, 'Disturbing Divine Behavior'.

Beyond the Bible: Moving from Scripture to Theology (2004), which argues that Jesus was an accommodationist in his teachings insofar as he some-times used imagery that his audience would understand even when it might be misleading.[52] Marshall argues, for example, that some of the eschatolog-ical parables with violent imagery belong 'to a time in a society that was accustomed to such things in real life and saw no incongruity in portraying divine judgment in that way. But we can no longer think of God in that way, even if this is imagery used by Jesus.'[53]

There are many reasons why this sort of argumentation is unsuitable in critical biblical scholarship, but the most obvious reason is its circularity. It presumes that we can determine which teachings about God are truly reflected in Jesus' words, and which are not. Marshall judges Jesus' true teachings by whether they agree with Marshall's view of God. But Mar-shall's view of God is completely circular: 'I believe the true God acts in Manner X because I believe the true God acts in Manner X.' He is saying nothing that we can verify to be true historically.

Option 2 (Jesus' Teachings about Eschatological Judgment Do Not Orig-inate with Jesus) is advocated by, among others, Jack Nelson-Pallmeyer, who claims that 'Jesus' original sayings were not apocalyptic and the apoc-alyptic edge, including threats of divine retribution, was added later by others'.[54] However, Nelson-Pallmeyer's proposals take us to the equally problematic and untestable claims about what the 'historical' Jesus really said. Judging the historical Jesus is virtually impossible without having independent historical evidence of what the 'original' Jesus really thought about anything.[55] That is why even identifying the earliest traditions within the redactional history of the New Testament will not help.

As mentioned, the 'earliest' tradition about Jesus should not be confused with 'original' or 'actual' historical Jesus.[56] Since we only have diverse rep-resentations of any supposed original form of Jesus' teachings, then New Testament ethicists pick and choose what representation agrees with their opinion of Jesus' historical teachings. There is no inherent reason, for exam-ple, why the violent Jesus is any less 'original' than the peaceful Jesus.

---

52. I. Howard Marshall, *Beyond the Bible: Moving from Scripture to Theology* (Grand Rapids: Baker Academic, 2004), especially p. 66.

53. Marshall, *Beyond the Bible*, p. 67.

54. Jack Nelson-Pallmeyer, *Jesus against Christianity: Reclaiming the Missing Jesus* (Harrisburg, PA: Trinity Press International, 2001), p. 227. See also Garry W. Trompf, *Early Christian Historiography: Narratives of Retribution* (London: Equinox, 2007).

55. For the view that judgment sayings were authentic, see Brian H. Gregg, *The His-torical Jesus and the Final Judgment Sayings in Q* (WUNT, 2.207; Tübingen: Mohr Sie-beck, 2006).

56. See my more elaborate arguments in Avalos, *The End of Biblical Studies*, espe-cially pp. 69-72, 203-209.

Violent apocalypticism was certainly an option available to the 'historical' Jesus in the first century. The Dead Sea Scrolls, most of which predate the time of Jesus, already witness a number of texts that depict a violent apocalyptic conflict between the human and demonic forces of good and evil, and often do so within the context of real locations and peoples. For example, in the *War Scroll* (1QM), one finds an impending apocalyptic battle that involves historical people and places such as Moab and Jerusalem (1QM 1.1-3). Later in the text, it describes the nature of God's impending judgment of the nations:

> The heroes of the army of his angels are enlisted with us; the war hero is in our congregation; the army of his spirits, with our infantry and our cavalry. They are like clouds and dew to cover the earth... Get up hero, take your prisoners, oh glorious one, collect your spoil, wonder-worker! Place your hand on the neck of your foes...and may your sword consume the flesh (1QM 12.8-9, 19.2-4).[57]

This imagery does not differ much from that of Mt. 25.31-46 or Rev. 19.11-21. If these violent apocalyptic traditions are attested by the time of Jesus, then what would have prevented Jesus from adopting them? If these apocalyptic traditions were available at the time of Jesus, and if some Gospel writers indicate that he was using them, then why must apocalypticism be regarded as an expansion, redaction or corruption of his 'original' preaching by later editors?

Option 3 (Jesus' Teachings about Eschatological Judgment are Less Violent Than they Appear) is disputable. Aside from the judgment described at the return of Christ (Mt. 25.31-46), the ultimate eschatological punishment is hell. Seibert emphasizes that there is a diversity of opinion as to the nature of hell. For support, Seibert cites the work of Edward Fudge, among others.[58] It is true that opinions on the nature of hell range from a state of emotional and mental torment to actual and eternal physical suffering. Otherwise, views divide themselves into the usual literal versus figurative options deployed with other ethically problematic passages.[59]

---

57. Following Martínez, *The Dead Sea Scrolls Translated*, p. 114. See also Jean Duhaime, *The War Texts: 1QM and the Related Manuscripts* (Companion to the Qumran Scrolls, 6; New York: T. & T. Clark, 2007).

58. See Edward William Fudge and Robert A. Peterson, *Two Views of Hell: A Biblical and Theological Dialogue* (Downers Grove, IL: InterVarsity Press, 2000).

59. Neville ('Moral Vision and Eschatology in Mark's Gospel, p 362 n. 11) says: 'I am not convinced that the Apocalypse of John envisages literal eschatological vengeance, even if John's use of violent imagery is responsible for interpreting along those lines'. Neville is arguing specifically against John J. Collins ('The Zeal of Phinehas: The Bible and the Legitimation of Violence', *JBL* 122 [2003], pp. 3-21 [16]), who remarks that 'The expectation of vengeance is also pivotal in the book of Revelation'.

Of particular interest to Seibert are Christian writers who advocate con-
ditionalism, which holds that immortality is conditional and hell may refer
to annihilation of a person, and not their eternal existence in hell.[60] Part of
the textual support comes from Jesus' statement in Mt. 10.28: 'And do not
fear those who kill the body but cannot kill the soul; rather fear him who can
destroy both soul and body in hell.' Yet, the idea that the evil are destroyed
in hell is also juxtaposed to Jesus' reference to 'eternal punishment' [κόλα-
σιν αἰώνιον] in Mt. 25.46.

The premise that annihilation of existence is somehow a better alternative to an eternal fiery torture does not exculpate Jesus from a violent
eschatology. After all, one of the main goals of violence and genocide is the
destruction of persons. Arguing that Jesus deserves a higher moral praise
because he merely advocates destroying persons, rather than torturing them,
is like arguing that human beings who extinguish the lives of other human
beings are somehow morally superior to those who torture human beings. It
is true that torture, as opposed to killing without torture, may lengthen the
amount of temporal suffering, but neither act would remain morally unobjectionable. Both would be viewed as violent or impermissible acts by the
United Nations.[61]

According to Seibert, acknowledging that God may use violence after
the judgment of humanity does not negate a nonviolent view of God. As
Seibert phrases it:

> But for the sake of argument, let us assume that the eschatological divine
> punishment that conditionalists envision does involve some measure of
> violence. What then? How would this affect the way we describe God's
> character? At the very least, we would need to acknowledge that God may
> resort to violence at the end of time. This would require us to be a bit more
> nuanced when speaking about God's non-violent nature. Still, our descrip-
> tion of God as one who does not engage in violence in *historical* times still
> stands. Even if we operate on the premise that eschatological judgment
> involves some degree of divine violence, it does not fundamentally alter
> our previous description or the value of using this description to evalu-
> ate disturbing divine behavior in the Old Testament since the problematic

---

60. See for example, Edward William Fudge, *A Biblical and Historical Study of the
Doctrine of Final Punishment* (Eugene, OR: Wipf & Stock, 2011); Edward William
Fudge and Peter Cousins, *The Fire that Consumes: The Biblical Case for Conditional
Immortality* (Carslile: Paternoster Press, 1994). For Stoic ideas about a final conflagra-
tion, see Ricardo Salles, Ἐκπύρωσις and the Goodness of God in Cleanthes', *Phronesis*
50 (2005), pp. 56-78.

61. In particular, torture is addressed by Article 5 of the *Universal Declaration of
Human Rights*: 'No one shall be subjected to torture or to cruel, inhuman or degrading
treatment or punishment.' Online: http://www.un.org/en/documents/udhr. Genocide is
addressed by Article 2 of the United Nations' *Convention on the Prevention and Punishment of the Crime of Genocide* at http://www.hrweb.org/legal/genocide.html.

portrayals included there reportedly 'took place' in historical time. Maximally then, this position suggests that God uses violence only outside of the space–time continuum, only for a limited period of time, and only for the sake of final punishment. Therefore, if one accepts the conditionalists' view of eternal punishment, it is still possible to maintain that the God Jesus reveals acts nonviolently in historical time and is, therefore, fundamentally nonviolent even in the face of Jesus' teachings about eschatological judgment.[62]

Yet, a distinction between historical violence and violence 'outside of the space–time continuum' is not based on any evidence from Jesus' own teachings. Jesus did not make a clear distinction between history and non-history, or speak of anything outside of the space–time continuum, which is a modern Einsteinian view of the cosmos.

Events in the future may be just as real as events in the past for Jesus. For example, Mt. 25.31 states: 'When the Son of man comes in his glory, and all the angels with him, then he will sit on his glorious throne.' Elsewhere, this Gospel says that angels ministered to Jesus while he was on earth (Mt. 4.6), and Jesus seems to make factual claims about the behavior of angels in Mt. 22.30. These entities seem to exist in real time and history for the author and for Jesus. So why would coming back with angels to execute a violent judgment be any less historical or real for Jesus?

Indeed, early Christians seem to expect that they would see Christ return in real time and history as is presupposed in the discussion in 1 Thessalonians 4 about whether the dead will be able to witness the return of Christ. The author responds: 'For this we declare to you by the word of the Lord, that we who are alive, who are left until the coming of the Lord, shall not precede those who have fallen asleep' (1 Thess. 4.15). The rest of the response assumes that real people will be meeting Christ in a real sequence, not outside some space–time continuum. Similarly, Rev. 1.7 says: 'Behold, he is coming with the clouds, and every eye will see him, every one who pierced him; and all tribes of the earth will wail on account of him.'[63] What is unhistorical about that expectation, given that New Testament authors believed that Jesus was literally pierced, and given that clouds and eyes exist in real time and history?

Seibert's solutions create more ethical problems than they solve. For example, he does not explain why annihilating someone in a final judgment is somehow ethically superior to torturing them. Seibert also has not addressed the distinction between non-violence and deferred violence. Indeed, Seibert

---

62. Seibert, *Disturbing Divine Behavior*, pp. 253-54; Seibert's italics

63. See also Thomas R. Hatina, 'Who Will See "The Kingdom of God Coming with Power" in Mark 9, 1—Protagonists or Antagonists?', *Bib* 86 (2005), pp. 20-34. According to Hatina, the one who will see Jesus are particularly his antagonists, who will be judged.

is engaging more in theology than in historico-critical analysis. Seibert has to contradict himself because he views the Bible as describing God's character accurately while disavowing the Bible's theological accuracy when it bears portrayals of God with which he disagrees. Seibert has offered no historically verifiable reasons why Jesus could not have espoused a violent eschatology, and he confuses the 'earliest' traditions with the 'original' traditions about Jesus. So perhaps the 'real' and 'historical' Jesus is a man that Seibert and like-minded Christian ethicists would not find to be ethical or righteous at all.

Similarly, Neville's affirmation that eschatological rewards and punishments are not the best means to construct a moral reality also fails to address the fact that this is the system behind all New Testament eschatology, as is noted by Richard Hays.[64] Neville's acceptance of the idea that apocalyptic judgment scenes reflect only God's prerogative, and so do not provide warrants for human moral practices, also fails to address the very premise that God should construct a moral system in this manner in the first place.[65] Neville does not seem to even contemplate the idea that all ethical statements about God are self-referential. Saying that it is God's prerogative to perform Action X is still Neville's opinion of how God behaves, and has no evidentiary value for how God, if he exists, behaves. In the end, it is Neville and his like-minded cohorts who are endorsing the idea that rewards and punishments are a proper incentive for moral action. Attributing that prerogative to God does not change the nature of that moral system.

John 2.15: Whipping up Pacifism

Since pacifism often has been identified as paradigmatic for Jesus' character, then a passage such as Jn 2.13-19 presents a significant challenge. N. Clayton Croy sums up the challenge posed by this passage to the image of a peaceful Jesus as follows:

> If medieval and Renaissance artists are any indication, the so-called temple cleansing must be one of the most important episodes in the life of Jesus. But some readers of John's account have felt unease with the image of a violent, whipcracking Jesus.[66]

64. Hays, *The Moral Vision*, p. 106.

65. Neville, *A Peaceable Hope*, p. 19, is adopting the arguments of Swartley, *Covenant of Peace*, p. 90 n. 120.

66. N. Clayton Croy, 'The Messianic Whippersnapper: Did Jesus Use a Whip on People in the Temple (John 2:15)?', *JBL* 128 (2009), pp. 555-68 (556). For a general survey of Jerusalem at the time of Jesus, see Lee I. Levine, *Jerusalem: Portrait of the City in the Second Temple Period (538 B.C.E.–70 C.E.)* (Philadelphia, PA: Jewish Publication Society, 2002).

John 2.13-19 itself reads:

> The Passover of the Jews was at hand, and Jesus went up to Jerusalem. In the temple he found those who were selling oxen and sheep and pigeons, and the money-changers at their business. And making a whip of cords, he drove them all, with the sheep and oxen, out of the temple; and he poured out the coins of the money-changers and overturned their tables. And he told those who sold the pigeons, 'Take these things away; you shall not make my Father's house a house of trade'. His disciples remembered that it was written, 'Zeal for thy house will consume me'. The Jews then said to him, 'What sign have you to show us for doing this?' Jesus answered them, 'Destroy this temple, and in three days I will raise it up' (Jn 2.13-19).[67]

For my purposes, the most crucial verses are 14-15, which the Greek text presents as follows:

καὶ εὗρεν ἐν τῷ ἱερῷ τοὺς πωλοῦντας βόας καὶ πρόβατα καὶ περι-στερὰς καὶ τοὺς κερματιστὰς καθημένους, καὶ ποιήσας φραγέλ-λιον ἐκ σχοινίων πάντας ἐξέβαλεν ἐκ τοῦ ἱεροῦ, τά τε πρόβατα καὶ τοὺς βόας, καὶ τῶν κολλυβιστῶν ἐξέχεεν τὸ κέρμα καὶ τὰς τραπέζας ἀνέτρεψεν.

According to the plain reading of the passage, Jesus uses violence against people who are otherwise going about their business in a peaceful manner. They are not attacking Jesus, nor are they threatening to attack Jesus physically. Rather, Jesus does not like them engaging in the particular business of selling animals and money changing, and so he decides to expel them from the temple. If any dissenting Catholic entered the Vatican today, and started to drive out worshippers with a whip and vandalize the sanctuary, such a person might be labeled as a terrorist or a vandal with no right to engage in such actions.

Historically, there have been many scholars who have seen Jesus' actions as violent, but all of them justify any violence. Raymond Brown, a major modern interpreter of the Gospel of John, remarks: 'Seemingly Jesus used the whip on the merchants.'[68] Timothy Wardle, who characterizes Jesus' actions as a 'demonstration', admits that Jesus drove out both the mon-eychangers and their animals, but issues no negative ethical evaluation of Jesus' actions.[69]

---

67. For a more extensive study of this passage and comparison to parallel accounts in other Gospels, see Raymond E. Brown, *The Gospel According to John 1–XII* (AB, 29; Garden City, NY: Doubleday, 1983), pp. 114-25. For the view that Jesus viewed himself and his movement as the embodiment of the eschatological temple, see Nicholas Perrin, *Jesus the Temple* (Grand Rapids, MI: Baker Academic, 2010).

68. Brown, *The Gospel According to John I–XII*, p. 115.

69. Timothy Wardle, *The Jerusalem Temple and Early Christian Identity* (WUNT, 2.291; Tübingen: Mohr Siebeck, 2010), pp. 172-80 (172). For another study, see Jacob

Burridge admits that '[w]ith regard to violence, Jesus does make "a whip of cords" to drive the money changers out of the temple (2.15). However, when Peter draws a sword to cut off the high priest's servant's ear in the garden, Jesus rebukes him and heals the man (18.10-11)'.[70]

Burridge's ethical warrants for such a rationale are somewhat confusing. Apparently, violence by a perpetrator in one case is justified if there is another case where the same perpetrator objects to violence. In more schematic form: Person A can injure one person with a whip in Instance X if Person A objects to violence in Instance Y. However, would we really excuse violence in this way if it were anyone else? That is to say, would we excuse a man who, at least hypothetically, assaulted his wife with a whip one New Year's Eve because on Christmas Day he had prevented one of his sons from cutting off the ear of his daughter?

With a rare exception, I have found no current Christian biblical scholar or ethicist who argues that Jesus was wrong to use violence or wrong to do anything he did.[71] For example, one may see Jesus' actions as another sign of his intolerance towards other religious views of the temple.[72] Or one could view him as a religious thug who disrupted the economy of the merchants; the latter may have included poor people trying to make a living.

In fact, it is usually the opposite. Most Christian scholarship has either given tacit approval to the actions of Jesus or it has empathically denied that Jesus even committed any acts of violence suggested by a plain reading of the text.[73]

Chanikuzhy (ed.), *Jesus, the Eschatological Temple: An Exegetical Study of Jn 2, 13-22 in the Light of pre-70 CE. Eschatological Temple Hopes and the Synoptic Temple Action* (Contributions to Biblical Exegesis and Theology, 58; Leuven: Peeters, 2012).

70. Burridge, *Imitating Jesus*, p. 331.

71. One exception, as mentioned, is Ellens, 'The Violent Jesus', III, pp. 15-37.

72. On intolerance in the New Testament, see Gerd Lüdemann, *Intolerance and the Gospel: Selected Texts from the New Testament* (Amherst, NY: Prometheus, 2008). An attack on polytheism's religious tolerance is offered by C. Kavin Rowe, *The World Turned Upside Down: Reading Acts in the Graeco-Roman Age* (New York: Oxford University Press, 2009), especially pp. 163-66. For a critical response to Rowe, see Matthew Levering, 'God and Greek Philosophy in Contemporary Scholarship', *Journal of Theological Interpretation* 4 (2010), pp. 169-85 (176-82). Rowe's response to Levering may be found in C. Kavin Rowe, 'God, Greek Philosophy, and the Bible: A Response to Matthew Levering', *Journal of Theological Interpretation* 5 (2011), pp. 69-80.

73. Others just factually mention Jesus' violent actions without comment. Jarl Henning Ulrichsen ('Jesus—Der neue Tempel? Ein kritischer Blick auf Die Auslegung von Joh 2, 313-22', in *Neotestamentica et Philonica: Studies in Honor of Peder Borgen* [ed. David E. Aune, Torrey Seland and Jarl Henning Ulrichsen; Leiden: E.J. Brill, 2002], pp. 202-214 [206]): 'macht Jesus eine Geissel aus Stricken...und treibt damit alle aus dem Tempel hinaus, nicht nur die Verkäufer und Geldwechsler, sondern auch die Tiere'.

Ronald Sider, a self-described pacifist, attempts to devalue this text by claiming that 'Jesus certainly did not kill the moneychangers. Indeed I doubt he even used the whip on them.'[74] He provides no documentation for the claim that Jesus did not use a whip, and yet he does not hesitate to declare as historical the pacifistic statements of Jesus. Sider also seems to indicate that such violence short of killing is acceptable. This again shows that many self-described pacifists are no less arbitrary than fundamentalists in choosing what counts as a true representation of Jesus.

Similarly, Croy concludes that 'Jesus did not apply the whip to persons in the temple precincts. If that interpretation is correct, it is thoroughly consonant with the broadly attested tradition of a non-violent Jesus'.[75] More recently, Andy Alexis-Baker concludes that Jesus did not even strike any animals with a whip, which was made of materials too soft to injure anyone or any animal.[76]

If we look at the evidence these scholars present, such a nonviolent interpretation is not so clear. The following are the main pieces of evidence presented by Croy, who is largely followed by Alexis-Baker.

A. The temple would not have allowed weapons in its precinct.
B. Textual criticism casts doubt on whether Jesus' instrument was a whip.
C. Any whip was made out of materials too soft to injure anyone.
D. The Greek grammar indicates that only the animals were struck, if they were struck at all.
E. The internal logic of the story suggests a non-violent action was sufficient to drive out the offenders.

Croy's claim that the temple would not have allowed weapons is based principally on a passage in the Mishnah. As Croy phrases his reasoning:

> Historically, as commentators have often noted, weapons were forbidden in the temple area. The Mishnah forbids one to bring a staff (מַקֵּל, *maqqēl*) into the temple (*m. Ber.* 9.5). While the Roman soldiers under Pilate's command certainly had *flagella*, Jews would not likely possess them and certainly not in the temple precincts. If Jesus had wielded such an instrument in a crowd at the Passover festival, his behavior would have been tolerated by neither Jews nor Romans. His arrest would likely have been immediate.[77]

74. Ronald Sider, *Christ and Violence* (repr., Eugene, OR: Wipf & Stock, 2001 [1979]), p. 47. Brooke Foss Westcott (*The Gospel According to St. John* (repr., Grand Rapids, MI: Eerdmans, 1971 [1881], p. 41) sees the whip 'as a symbol of authority and not as a weapon of offence'.

75. Croy, 'The Messianic Whippersnapper', pp. 567-68.

76. Andy Alexis-Baker, 'Violence, Nonviolence and the Temple Incident in John 2:13-15', *BibInt* 20 (2012), pp. 73-96.

77. Croy, 'The Messianic Whippersnapper', p. 556.

Already there is a problem. Croy seemingly disregards decades of scholarship cautioning against using Mishnaic literature to corroborate the historicity of events at the time of Jesus. As Philip Alexander observes: 'Many New Testament scholars are still guilty of massive and sustained anachronism in their use of Rabbinic sources. Time and again we find them quoting *texts from the 3rd, 4th, or 5th centuries AC, and even later, to illustrate Jewish teachings in the 1st century.*'[78] Indeed, the Mishnah is a late source, and some of its regulations and descriptions of the temple are contradicted by those we find in other sources (e.g., Josephus) that are supposedly closer to the time when the temple was still standing before 70 CE.[79]

In fact, the very passage that Croy cites includes other items that would not necessarily be consonant with the episode in John 2. The Mishnaic passage states: 'A man should not enter the temple with his staff or with his shoes on or with his money bag [ובפונדתו] or with his dust on his feet.'[80] The Aramaic פונדה/פונדא is defined as a 'money bag, hollow belt' by Jastrow.[81] If so, then it is difficult to understand how moneychangers were carrying their money into the temple. Of course, there could be many ways to interpret what constituted a פונדה/פונדא, but the passage cited by Croy demonstrates how we cannot simply assume that Mishnaic rules were always applicable in Herod's temple.

---

78. Philip S. Alexander, 'Rabbinic Judaism and the New Testament', *ZNW* 74 (1983), pp. 237-46 (244), italics Alexander's. For a more cautious approach to the use of Rabbinic materials for interpreting the Gospel of John, see John Christopher Thomas, 'The Fourth Gospel and Rabbinic Judaism', *ZNW* 82 (1991) pp. 159-82. For a defense of the use of Rabbinic texts in New Testament exegesis, see Miguel Pérez Fernandez, 'Rabbinic Texts in the Exegesis of the New Testament', *Review of Rabbinic Judaism* 7 (2004), pp. 95-120; Bruce D. Chilton and Jacob Neusner, *Classical Christianity and Rabbinic Judaism: Comparing Theologies* (Grand Rapids, MI: Baker, 2004).

79. The prominent archaeologist of Herodian architecture, Ehud Netzer (*The Architecture of Herod the Great Builder* [Grand Rapids, MI: Baker Academic, 2008], p. 136) remarks: 'The descriptions in the Mishnah and the works of Josephus sometimes correspond with, and in many cases supplement, one another, but occasionally they are contradictory or there are discrepancies within the abundant information provided, giving rise to further difficulties.' For recent biographies of Herod the Great, see Jerry Knoblet, *Herod the Great* (Lanham, MD: University Press of America, 2004); Manuel Vogel, *Herodes: König der Juden, Freund der Römer* (Biblische Gestalten, 5; Leipzig: Evangelische Verlangstalt, 2002). For a study of the temple among early Christians, see Wardle, *The Jerusalem Temple*.

80. Ber. 54a (= Ber. 9.5), following Freedman and Epstein (eds.), *Hebrew-English Edition of the Babylonian Talmud*.

81. Marcus Jastrow, *A Dictionary of the Targumim, the Talmud Babli and Yerushalmi and the Midrashic Literature* (2 vols.; repr., Brooklyn, NY: Shalom, 1967 [1903]), II, p. 1143a.

More importantly, Josephus's account of the destruction of the offensive eagle statue set up by Herod demonstrates that Croy's reliance on the Mishnah is misguided. Josephus's account shows that zealous Jews had no problem bringing weapons to the temple when they thought their temple was being desecrated. According to Josephus (*Ant.* 17.151), Herod had erected a great golden eagle over the great gate of the temple. When Herod died, some Jewish scholars counseled some youth to destroy the eagle. Josephus relates what happened next:

> At mid-day, therefore, the youths went up to the roof of the temple and pulled down the eagle and cut it up with axes before many people who gathered in the temple. And the officer of the king—for the attempt had been reported to him—, suspecting that something more serious was involved than was being done, came up with a force large enough to meet the crowd of men who were intent upon pulling down the image that had been set up.[82]

Note that the youths were able to carry axes (πελέκεσιν) into the temple precincts, and so the Mishnaic prohibition mattered little here. There did not seem to be any sort of security checks for weapons, nor did the authorities act as quickly as Croy would have us believe.

Another episode in Josephus concerning the Sicarii shows that it was not difficult to smuggle weapons into the temple. The Sicarii, whose diverse origins and nature has been more thoroughly investigated recently, were Jewish rebels who use daggers or swords in their efforts against the Romans.[83] Josephus saw them as terrorists who killed even fellow Jews who sympathized with the Romans. In fact, Josephus specifically blames them for the fall of Jerusalem. For my purposes, the episode in question concerns their activities surrounding their assassination of Jonathan, the high priest:

> With daggers concealed under their clothes they mingled with the people about Jonathan and assassinated him. As the murder remained unpunished, from that time forth the brigands with perfect impunity used to go to the city during the festivals and, with their weapons similarly concealed, mingle with the crowds. In this way, they slew some... They committed these murders only in other parts of the city but even some cases in the temple; for there too they made bold to slaughter their victims for they did not regard even this as a desecration.[84]

---

82. Josephus, *Ant.* 17.155-56 (Thackeray and Marcus, LCL): καὶ μέσης ἡμέρας ἀνελθόντες κατέσπων τε καὶ πελέκεσιν ἐξέκοψαν τὸν ἀετόν, πολλῶν ἐν τῷ ἱερῷ διατριβόντων. καὶ ὁ στρατηγὸς τοῦ Βασιλέως (ἀγγέλεται γὰρ ἡ ἐπιχείρησις πρὸς αὐτόν) ἀπὸ μείζονος διανοίας ἢ ἐπράσσετο ὑπολαβὼν ἄνεισι χεῖρα πολλὴν ἀγόμενος, ὁπόσοι ἀνθέξοιεν τῷ πλήθει τῶν πειρωμένων καθαιρεῖν τὸ ἀνάθημα.
83. For a recent treatment of the Sicarii, see Mark Andrew Brighton, *The Sicarii in Josephus's Judean War: Rhetorical Analysis and Historical Observations* (Early Judaism and its Literature, 27; Atlanta, GA: Society of Biblical Literature, 2009).
84. Josephus, *Ant.* 20.164-66 (Thackeray and Marcus, LCL).

This episode clearly contradicts the idea that temple guards would have intervened immediately before any real trouble occurred, and it shows that weapons were not so easily detected. In addition, Jews who thought the temple was already desecrated would have had no trouble disregarding any supposed regulations about the permissibility of weapons in the temple precincts.

The fact that Jesus may have regarded any temple regulations as not in force is indicated by Lk. 19.46, where Jesus gives one motivation as follows: 'It is written, "My house shall be a house of prayer"; but you have made it a den of robbers.' John portrays the disciples as connecting Jesus' use of violence to a biblical text (Ps. 69.9). Thus, Jesus' actions could very well parallel those of the youths who attacked the golden eagle and those of Sicarii who smuggled their edged weapons into the temple. Just as they saw it permissible to bring weapons into the temple when the temple had been desecrated, Jesus may have thought it permissible to use a weapon when he thought the temple had been desecrated. Normal laws and conduct in the temple may not apply while the temple is desecrated.

As Josephus relates it, the reaction from the authorities first involved a report to the officer of the king, who then raised a force to counter what Josephus describes as a 'crowd of men', which numbered at least forty. Thus, it does not appear as if the guards were ready to act on the spot, but rather they had to be gathered after a report to the main officer was received.

Such delayed reactions are also attested during large festivals, such as Passover. This is important to note because Alexis-Baker cites Josephus (*Ant.* 20.106) to argue that 'unrest during Jewish festivals was so commonplace that the Roman authorities prepared for it by sending in extra soldiers to "quell any uprising that might occur"'.[85] Josephus is here referring to the actions of Ventidius Cumanus, the Roman procurator (48–52 CE) at the time.

Yet, in the very passage that Alexis-Baker cites, Josephus also clarifies that great restraint was urged even when crowds threatened to riot. Josephus says that on the fourth day of Passover, a Roman soldier uncovered his genitals, and that enraged Jewish onlookers, who saw it as blasphemy against God. Some Jews began to insult Cumanus because they saw him as having instigated the soldier's actions. But Cumanus did not attack or seize any potential rioters right away. Instead, he 'merely admonished them to put an end to this lust for revolution, and not to set disorders ablaze during the festival'.[86] It is only after the Jews did not desist, that he ordered the army to act, causing thousands of deaths among the fleeing throngs who were caught in the narrow passages of the precincts.

---

85. Josephus, *Ant.* 20.106 (Feldman, LCL); Alexis-Baker, 'The Temple Incident', p. 88 n. 34.

86. Josephus, *Ant.* 20.109-10 (Feldman, LCL).

Surprisingly, neither Croy nor Alexis-Baker discuss a later episode in John, where the biblical author explains that the temple guards did not always act as expeditiously against Jesus as the religious authorities might have wished: 'The officers then went back to the chief priests and Pharisees, who said to them, "Why did you not bring him?" The officers answered, "No man ever spoke like this man!"' (Jn 7.45-46). In this case, Jesus had been preaching during a festival at the temple to the chagrin of the authorities. Given that the author of John portrays temple officials as offering deference to Jesus, then the lack of action by the temple guards in John 2 may be for similar reasons. Certainly, John 7 is much more relevant than citing a Mishnaic tract written hundreds of years later.

The entire idea that Jewish temple guards or Roman guards would have acted immediately is also belied by the fact that the passage in John says no such action occurred. Even without the use of weapons, the actions by Jesus should have led to an immediate arrest or action by any temple guards. He had, at the very least, significantly disrupted the temple economy, and had committed acts of vandalism. Yet, for all that trouble, Jesus elicits a very pacifistic reaction from the Jews: 'The Jews then said to him, "What sign have you to show us for doing this?"' So, if anything, it is Jesus who should be viewed as violent, and the Jews who should be viewed as pacifists in this episode.

Croy also employs textual criticism. He rightly notes that some early papyri, such as p⁶⁶ and p⁷⁵, have ὡς φραγέλλιον. Such a reading could mitigate the nature of Jesus' whip because 'as a whip' could be interpreted as something less than a whip, or perhaps not a whip at all. However, it is difficult to account for the wide range of witnesses, including the major uncials, Vaticanus and Sinaiticus, that don't have that conjunction. Croy opts for a hypothesis that it was accidentally omitted. As he phrases his reasoning:

> It would be hard to account for the *deliberate* omission of ὡς since that would make the image harsher. On the other hand, the word ὡς might have been *accidentally* omitted through parablepsis, the scribe's eye inadvertently skipping just two letters from the final sigma in ποιήσας to the sigma in ὡς, resulting in a reading that, although secondary, was perfectly intelligible.[87]

Therefore, Jesus should be described as making something that was 'as a whip' (καὶ ποιήσας ὡς φραγέλλιον), and not necessarily a whip per se. For Croy, something less than a whip is added to explain that a real whip is not made out of weak cords.

It is certainly possible that homeoteleuton was responsible for removing the conjunction. What is curious is that Croy cannot contemplate ('since that would make the image harsher') the possibility that a scribe intended a

---

87. Croy, 'The Messianic Whippersnapper', p. 557; Croy's emphasis.

harsher image of Jesus, and so removed ὡς. And if a more benign Jesus is what the scribes had in mind by adding ὡς, then it is just as reasonable to posit that the earlier and more 'original' reading was the harsher and more violent one. Metzger remarks, 'On the other hand, it is probable that copyists introduced the word in order to soften somewhat the bald statement that Jesus made a whip of cords; "he made a kind of whip of cords"'.[88] Such mitigation of Jesus' harsher portrayal resembles the manner in which Mt. 10.37 might have lessened the impact of Lk. 14.26.

However, even if the earlier reading has ὡς, that would not necessarily render φραγέλλιον less of a whip. The conjunction does not necessarily lessen the full and literal identity of what follows it. For example, in 1 Thess. 2.6, the clause, 'we might have made demands as apostles of Christ' does not mean 'we might have made demands as though we were almost apostles of Christ'.[89] Likewise, in Mt. 14.5, ὡς προφήτην αὐτὸν εἶχον is translated rightly 'they held him to be a prophet' (RSV), not 'they held him as though he were almost a prophet'. So, whether the conjunction was present or not becomes irrelevant in refuting the claim that Jesus made a whip.

If Jesus did make a whip, then Croy argues that it would not have been capable of injuring or inflicting pain. He reasons:

> The instrument was fashioned (ποιήσας) on the spot from materials that were available. The latter did not likely include leather thongs, bone fragments, or bits of metal. Moreover, John describes the whip as constructed ἐκ σχοινίων, 'from cords'. Originally these were rushes or reeds, akin to rattan or wicker material. This material might have been available as the animals' bedding or perhaps was already fashioned into ropes or traces. Otherwise, σχοινία may refer to ropes of other material, as in the case of the lines used to attach a skiff to a larger, seagoing ship in Acts 27.32, the only other NT usage... In either case, the whip wielded by Jesus was clearly a makeshift tool, scarcely equal to the Roman instrument of torture.[90]

Croy's list of materials is too poorly documented to say that such a whip could not be strong enough to injure anyone or not be equal to a Roman instrument of torture. The reference to these items being 'originally' out of rushes or reeds obscures the fact that they could be made of materials that were very strong. As it is, Croy seems to be confusing the Greek word, σχοῖνος, which refers to 'a rush' or 'reed', with σχοινίον, which is a rope or cord in classical Greek.[91]

88. Bruce M. Metzger, *A Textual Commentary on the Greek New Testament* (New York: United Bible Societies, 1975), pp. 202-203.

89. See also Joseph A. Fitzmyer, *The Letter to Philemon: A New Translation with Introduction and Commentary* (AB, 34C; New York: Doubleday, 2000), p. 114.

90. Croy, 'The Messianic Whippersnapper', p. 557.

91. See Henry George Liddell and Robert Scott, *Greek-English Lexicon* (repr., London: Oxford University Press, 1968 [1889]), p. 787. See also Christopher A. Faraone,

The Septuagintal use of σχοινία had a wide range, but it could refer to something strong enough to bring down a city: 'If he withdraws into a city, then all Israel will bring ropes [σχοινία] to that city, and we shall drag it into the valley, until not even a pebble is to be found there' (2 Sam. 17.13). Similarly, Herodotus says that Ephesus was attacked 'by attaching a rope [σχοινίον] to the city wall from the temple of the goddess, standing seven furlongs away from the ancient city'.[92] As Croy mentions, Acts 27.32 ('Then the soldiers cut away the ropes [τὰ σχοινία] of the boat, and let it go') indicates that these ropes were heavy and strong enough to hold a boat in place. There is no other indication in the New Testament that σχοινίον is anything less than a very strong item.

Grammatically, Croy is assuming erroneously that the material that follows the preposition ἐκ in the clause, ποιήσας φραγέλλιον ἐκ σχοινίων, is meant to describe the *only* material that constituted the device made. Other expressions with the form, ποιέω + ἐκ + X material, are not meant to restrict the material only to that mentioned after the preposition. For example, in Jn 9.6, Jesus makes mud out of both dirt and spit, and yet John mentions only the spittle after the preposition in the clause: καὶ ἐποίσεν πηλὸν ἐκ τοῦ πτύσματος. Similarly, Herodotus describes Egyptian boats as 'made out of acacia' (ἐστὶ ἐκ τῆς ἀκάνθης ποιεύμενα).[93] However, Herodotus clearly does not restrict the materials of those boats only to acacia because he also speaks of the sails and the caulk as made out of byblus.[94] So, what follows the preposition may describe the primary material, but it does not necessarily restrict it only to that material.

Given the fact that hundreds, if not thousands, of animals had to be managed in the temple area, it is not certain why Croy would automatically dismiss the availability of whips or raw materials needed to manage such animals in the precincts. As Bruce D. Chilton observes, 'Jesus is here portrayed as using the very objects which would need to be there to control the animals, so as to expel them and their vendors.'[95] If you need whips, then these might include those made out of leather, bone bits, or metal that should have been readily available in a marketplace. Jesus was also a 'carpenter' or

'The Wheel, the Whip and Other Implements of Torture: Erotic Magic in Pindar Pythian 4.213-29', *Classical Journal* 89 (1993), pp. 1-19.

92. Herodotus 1.26 (Godley, LCL).

93. Herodotus 2.96 (Godley; LCL).

94. A common boat could be made out of a dozen different species of trees as illustrated archaeologically by Lea Lofenfeld Winkler and Ramit Frankel, *The Boat and the Sea of Galilee* (trans. Ora Cummings; New York: Gefen, 2007), pp. 65-70.

95. Bruce D. Chilton, '[ὡς] φραγέλλιον ἐκ σχοινίων (John 2.15)', in *Templum Amicitiae: Essays on the Second Temple presented to Ernst Bammel* (ed. William Horbury; JSOTSup, 48; Sheffield: Sheffield Academic Press, 1991), pp. 330-44 (340-41).

craftsman, and so one can just as well suppose that the author can attribute some ingenuity to Jesus.

Croy next tackles the question of what Jesus whipped even if he whipped anything at all. Croy argues that the clause, πάντας ἐξέβαλεν ἐκ τοῦ ἱεροῦ, τά τε πρόβατα καὶ τοὺς βόας, expresses a partitive appositive, wherein 'all' is defined solely by the correlative expression, τά τε πρόβατα καὶ τοὺς βόας. In other words, 'all' really refers only to the sheep and the goats. As Croy phrases it:

> The whole would be πάντας, to which τά τε πρόβατα καὶ τοὺς βόας would stand in apposition, giving the constituent parts, that is, 'he drove *all* out of the temple, namely, the "all" consisting of *both the sheep and the cattle*'.[96]

Part of Croy's evidence consists of appealing to Edwin Abbott's exhaustive grammatical study of John. Croy quotes Abbott as follows:

> Edwin Abbott's thorough study of Johannine grammar devotes ten pages to appositional constructions in John. Numerous types and examples are discussed. With reference to John 2.15, Abbott opines that 'in a writer so fond of parenthesis as Jn the meaning might be, 'He cast them all out of the temple—both the sheep and the oxen [did he cast out]—and he poured forth the money'.[97]

Croy, however, has misrepresented Abbott's position. In his main text, Abbott actually said:

> John is referring to a previous statement that Jesus 'found in the Temple those that were selling oxen and sheep and doves'. What follows may mean that Jesus (ii.15) 'drove all [of them] out of the Temple, *both sheep and oxen* (πάντας ἐξέβαλεν ἐκ τοῦ ἱεροῦ, τά τε πρόβατα καὶ τοὺς βόας)', i.e., the men and what they sold, indicating that 'all [of them]' included their belongings, 'sheep sellers and ox sellers, sheep, and oxen'.[98]

What Croy is quoting is a footnote, where Abbott is discussing the merits of the Authorized and Revised Versions. In that discussion, Abbott uses the word 'parenthesis', not 'apposition', to describe another possible interpretation found in the RV: 'and he made a scourge of cords, and cast all out of the temple, both the sheep and the oxen; and he poured out the changers' money, and overthrew their tables'.

Abbott differentiates an appositional phrase from a parenthetic phrase when he speaks of 'a parenthesis, or a statement out of its chronological

---

96. Croy, 'The Messianic Whippersnapper', p. 561; Croy's italics..

97. Croy, 'The Messianic Whippersnapper', p. 561.

98. Edwin Abbott, *Johannine Grammar* (London: A. & C. Black, 1906), p. 37. See also Chanikuzhy, *Jesus, the Eschatological Temple*, p. 249; Abbott's emphasis..

place, of the nature of an afterthought'.[99] This is not quite the same as an appositive expression. Similarly, Robertson says of a parenthetical clause: 'Such a clause, inserted in the midst of the sentence without proper syntactical connection, is quite common in the N.T.'[100] If so, then Abbott is declaring that τά τε πρόβατα καὶ τοὺς βόας reflects a parenthetical insertion that emphasizes that oxen and sheep are also *included*, but not that 'all' is *limited to* oxen and sheep. Admittedly, parentheses are difficult to identify, but Abbott's opinion is corroborated by his statement in the main text of his discussion.[101]

If Abbott's statement does not provide definitive support, then what about the parallels of τε...καὶ that Croy cites? According to Croy:

> Given the abundance of close grammatical parallels (the above list is selective), it is likely that the construction in Jn 2.15 is a partitive appositive. The whole would be πάντας, to which τά τε πρόβατα καὶ τοὺς Βόας would stand in apposition, giving the constituent parts, that is, 'he drove *all* out of the temple, namely, the "all" consisting of *both the sheep and the cattle*'.

Let me now examine the parallels collected by Croy:[102]

> Lk. 22.66: 'the elders of the people, both chief priests and [τε...καί] scribes'
> Acts 8.38: 'both of them, Philip and [τε...καί] the eunuch, went down into the water'
> 1 Esd. 6.26: 'the holy vessels...both the gold ones and [τε...καί] the silver ones'
> 4 Macc. 15.26: 'two ballots, one bearing death and [τε...καί] one deliverance'
> Mt. 22.10: '*all* whom they found, both good and [τε...καί] bad'
> Acts 19.10: '*all* the residents of Asia, both Jews and [τε...καί] Greeks'
> Rom. 3.9: '*all*, both Jews and [τε...καί] Greeks, are under the power of sin'
> Rev. 19.18: 'the flesh of *all* people, free and [τε...καί] slave, both small and [τε...καί] great'
> 3 Macc. 1.1: 'he gave orders to *all* his forces, both infantry and [τε...καί] cavalry'.

The fact is that these are not really the 'close grammatical parallels' that Croy portrays.[103] None of them have πάντας + verb + τε...καί. Even

---

99. Abbott, *Johannine Grammar*, pp. 348-49.

100. A.T. Robertson, *A Grammar of the Greek New Testament in the Light of Historical Research* (Nashville, TN: Broadman Press, 1934), p. 433.

101. See further, J.W. Johnston, *The Use of Πᾶς in the New Testament* (Studies in Biblical Greek, 11; New York: Peter Lang, 2004).

102. Croy, 'The Messianic Whippersnapper', p. 561; Croy's emphasis. Following the English biblical translations of Croy.

103. The same applies to the grammatical manuals that Croy cites. For example, Croy ('The Messianic Whippersnapper', p. 560 n. 26) cites J.D. Denniston (*The Greek Particles* [Oxford: Clarendon Press, 2nd edn, 1959) 'for the Greek particles in general'. But

Chilton, who is cited for support elsewhere by Croy, remarks: 'That construction, ἅπαξ λεγόμενον, in the Fourth Gospel, is what makes the phrase seem odd as an apposition, with the result that the sense of the passage has appeared problematic'.[104]

In none of the cases listed by Croy does τε...καί separate items that would otherwise be included under πάντας from some other group that would be included by a plain reading. For example, in Rev. 19.18, great and small and free and slave exhausts the meaning of 'all' people because the society is composed of great and small, slave and free. It does not separate the groups labeled great/small or free/slave from some other group that might be included in 'all people'.

Likewise, in Mt. 22.10 'both good and [τε...καί] bad' exhaust the constituents of 'all whom they found' because only people, not animals, had been previously mentioned in the broader pericope, and people can be categorized completely by the adjectives good and bad. So, in Mt. 22.10, τε... καί does separate the good and the bad from some other group of people (or type of entity) that could also be included based on the preceding discussion in the pericope. At the very least, it is ambiguous whether τε...καί refers only to the sheep and oxen, or also includes their owners.

Croy and Alexis-Baker betray another bias when they appeal to the synoptic Gospels. In his collection of grammatical parallels, Croy cites Luke and Matthew for support in understanding Jn 2.15. Yet, Matthew, Mark and Luke all make it very clear that Jesus expelled the people engaged in commerce.

Mt. 21.12
And Jesus entered the temple of God and drove out all who sold and bought in the temple [καὶ ἐξέβαλεν πάντας τοὺς πωλοῦντας καὶ ἀγοράζοντας ἐν τῷ ἱερῷ], and he overturned the tables of the money-changers and the seats of those who sold pigeons.

Mk 11.15
And they came to Jerusalem. And he entered the temple and began to drive out [ἤρξατο ἐκβάλλειν τοὺς πωλοῦντας καὶ τοὺς ἀγοράζοντας ἐν τῷ

---

the relevant discussion by Denniston (*The Greek Particles*, p. 515) does not pertain to appositional or epexegitcal uses of τε...καί, and so does not help to resolve our issue in Jn 2.15.

104. Chilton, '[ὡς] φραγέλλιον ἐκ σχοινίων (John 2.15)', pp. 330-44 (333). Neufeld (*Killing Enmity*, p. 61) seems to misunderstand the unique nature of this Greek construction in Jn 2.15 when he states: 'Normal Greek grammar suggests that John, the only evangelist to mention the whip, understands Jesus as physically shooing the animals out of the temple precincts'. Neufeld (*Killing Enmity*, p. 61) also makes much of the fact that John is the only one of the Gospels to mention both the animals and the whip, and so the whip must have been meant only for the animals. But he fails to explain the parallel use of πάντας in Mt. 21.12 and Jn 2.15.

ἱερῷ] those who sold and those who bought in the temple, and he over-turned the tables of the money-changers and the seats of those who sold pigeons.

Lk. 19.45
And he entered the temple and began to drive out those who sold [ἤρξατο ἐκβάλλειν τοὺς πωλοῦντας].

Croy does not explain why John changed the meaning of the Synoptics so that now only the animals were driven out.[105] If Jesus wanted to purify the temple, why would he drive out the animals, but leave untouched the persons who were desecrating the temple?

A similar bias occurs when Croy addresses the agreement between πάντας, a masculine accusative pronoun, and the animals, which are grammatically of different genders. The masculine pronoun would best fit the men whom Jesus cast out. Croy is correct to note that agreement between pronouns and their referents can be varied, especially if the referents are of mixed genders. Croy cites all sorts of sources to support the argument that πάντας need not refer to the human beings in terms of grammatical agreement. Croy omits Mt. 21.12 from the discussion of verbal parallels here. But only Jn 2.15 and Mt. 21.12 have πάντας in their parallel stories, and it is clear that Matthew means the human offenders, not the animals. Why John would not include human beings is unclear despite all the syntactical problems.

The context provided by John is conducive to a more violent interpretation. In Jn 2.17, the disciples explain Jesus' actions as follows: 'Zeal for thy house will consume me'. In other instances where 'zeal' is used to describe a believer's actions, violence is often explicitly referenced. For example, Yahweh's zeal is said to be violent : 'How long, O LORD? Wilt thou be angry for ever? Will thy jealous wrath burn like fire? Pour out thy anger on the nations that do not know thee, and on the kingdoms that do not call on thy name!' (Ps. 79.5-6).[106] In Psalm 69, the very one cited by John, we also see violent intentions by the suppliant in vv. 23-24: 'Let their eyes be darkened,

---

105. For a recent study of the relationship of John to the Synoptics, see Tobias Nicklas, 'Die johanneische "Tempelreinigung" (Joh 2, 12-22) für Leser der Synoptiker', *Theologie und Philosophie 80* (2005), pp. 1-16. For a study of the episode in Mark, see Solomon Hong-fai Wong, *The Temple Incident in Mark 11, 15-10: The Disclosure of Jesus and the Marcan Faction* (New Testament Studies in Contextual Exegesis, 5; Frankfurt: Peter Lang, 2009).

106. See also Susanna Braund and Glenn W. Most (eds.), *Ancient Anger: Perspectives from Homer to Galen* (Yale Classical Studies, 32; Cambridge: Cambridge University Press, 2003). On Jesus' anger in extrabiblical traditions, see Kristi Upson-Saia, 'Holy Child or Holy Terror? Understanding Jesus' Anger in the Infancy Gospel of Thomas', *Church History* 82.1 (2013), pp. 1-39. Saia claims that stories of Jesus' bad behavior were invented by opponents, and subsequently absorbed by his followers.

so that they cannot see; and make their loins tremble continually. Pour out thy indignation upon them, and let thy burning anger overtake them.'

The fact that at least some Jews are portrayed as accusing Jesus of using violence against the temple is clear from Acts 6.13-14: 'This man never ceases to speak words against this holy place and the law; for we have heard him say that this Jesus of Nazareth will destroy this place, and will change the customs which Moses delivered to us.' Although the biblical author portrays this as a false accusation, one could just as easily argue that the author was preserving an 'authentic' Jesus tradition about threatening divine violence against the temple.

Nevertheless, Neufeld argues that Jesus' 'prophetic words of condemnation are far graver and more fearsome than any use of a whip made of the straw lying around'.[107] As mentioned, the claim that the whip was made of straw is dubious. Moreover, Jesus does not see prophetic condemnations as sufficient to intimidate many of his opponents. After all, Jesus complained that prophets were routinely killed (Mt. 5.12), which implies that those who heard them were not intimidated by their words, however strong or authoritative they may have been. In Jn 4.44, Jesus complains that a prophet receives no honor in his own land, which does not seem to indicate that his supposedly fearsome words intimidated many people.

Croy provides an additional argument for the lack of necessity in using a whip on the people who owned the livestock: 'As for the sellers of the sheep and oxen, even if the whip had not been applied to them directly, they would likely have followed their livestock. In this way, Jesus' driving out of the animals would have simultaneously effected the removal of the sellers.'[108] Croy's supposition is much too speculative, and he apparently thinks that the sellers will passively accept the disruption of their livelihoods. But, as Origen had already surmised, anyone who seeks to disrupt the marketplace can expect business owners to respond violently.[109] So a whip would have been a handy weapon to have. After all, why would Jesus expect anyone to give up the very business that sustained them just because he requested it?

A similar story of disrupting temple trade is found in Acts 19, where Paul is said to be endangering the livelihood of a silversmith named Demetrius.

---

107. Neufeld, *Killing Enmity*, p. 61.

108. Croy, 'The Messianic Whippersnapper', pp. 562-63.

109. Origen, *Commentary on John* 10.146, following Origen, *Commentary on the Gospel According to John, Books 1–10* (trans. Ronald E. Heine; The Fathers of the Church: A New Translation; Washington, DC: Catholic University of America Press, 1989), p. 289: 'And who, if he is struck with a whip of cords and is being driven out by one they supposed to be worthless, would not seize him and cry out and work vengeance with his own hand, especially since he has so large a multitude of those who seemed to be insulted as well to cooperate in such acts against Jesus?' Origen, however, allegorizes this episode and so preserves a peaceful view of Jesus.

The reaction to Paul's dismissal of the reality and powers of Artemis, the goddess worshipped by Demetrius, was as follows:

> When they heard this they were enraged, and cried out, 'Great is Artemis of the Ephesians!' So the city was filled with the confusion; and they rushed together into the theater, dragging with them Gaius and Aristarchus, Macedonians who were Paul's companions in travel. Paul wished to go in among the crowd, but the disciples would not let him; some of the Asiarchs also, who were friends of his, sent to him and begged him not to venture into the theater (Acts 19.28-31).

Similarly, what one expects in Jerusalem is not for temple traders to surrender themselves meekly to the whims of Jesus.

Even if we accept the validity of the claim that Jesus did not use a whip on human beings, one does not see a Neufeld or Croy condemning the very act of abusing the property of others or disrupting the livelihoods of the people selling their merchandise. Would these New Testament scholars see it as a peaceful act if someone entered their churches and overturned their altars or benches even if he did not hurt anyone physically? If that person described them as participating in some perverted worship while destroying their property, would they be as willing to say that this person was simply acting prophetically or would they apply a wider definition of violence to those actions?

My purpose is not to solve the problem of the syntax of Jn 2.15. Croy's understanding, on purely linguistic grounds, is possible. On historical grounds, the argument is less well grounded, especially since so much of it is built on speculations about what the temple would or would not be like at the time of Jesus. Mishnaic tracts are not good historical evidence for the rules governing the temple at the time of Jesus, especially when there are conflicting views in Josephus. We do not know what temple guards would or would not have done, and Jn 7.45 invokes a motivation for the actions of temple officials that Croy never considers.

Given all of this discussion, we can just as well propose an alternative version of why John introduced the whip into this story. None of the Synoptics explained how Jesus could have expected to drive out anyone who made their livelihood without encountering opposition or violence. John could have added the whip to explain how Jesus accomplished that feat. One cannot expect those whose entire livelihood could depend on the income from such trade to be cowered by a mild-looking whip. Readers would have been familiar enough with Roman whips to know that they could inflict damage, and so John did not need to add more details about its construction. The business people could be persuaded to flee precisely because Jesus had a visible and nasty instrument in his hand. Given that John tries to link Jesus' actions to Psalm 69, why should we think that Jesus' zeal should be any less violent than that of Yahweh? Could it not be the case that Jesus' violent zeal was viewed as a fulfillment of his Messianic expectations, just as the disciples realized?

In the end, the point is not so much that Jn 2.15 can only be interpreted violently or peacefully. The point is that so much of biblical ethics, and the broader biblical scholarship, is still focused on avoiding a portrait of Jesus that might be objectionable to many audiences. There is no reason why Jesus could not have been overcome by zeal, and committed a violent act.[110] The god of the Hebrew Bible is repeatedly shown mixing love and violence, and so why should Jesus be any different if he is supposed to be the embodiment of that god in the Gospel of John? Viewed in this manner, Jesus indeed continues a long tradition of a divine being who can combine love and wrath.

Acts 9: Jesus Assaults Saul

New Testament ethicists normally do not describe Jesus as assaulting people. In fact, the debate over Jn 2.15 shows how far some scholars are willing to go to absolve Jesus of any thought of injuring human beings or animals. In Acts 9, however, it is difficult not to describe what happens to Saul on the way to Damascus as an assault. According to the relevant portion of that narrative:

> But Saul, still breathing threats and murder against the disciples of the Lord, went to the high priest and asked him for letters to the synagogues at Damascus, so that if he found any belonging to the Way, men or women, he might bring them bound to Jerusalem. Now as he journeyed he approached Damascus, and suddenly a light from heaven flashed about him. And he fell to the ground and heard a voice saying to him, 'Saul, Saul, why do you persecute me?' And he said, 'Who are you, LORD?'; And he said, 'I am Jesus, whom you are persecuting; but rise and enter the city, and you will be told what you are to do'. The men who were traveling with him stood speechless, hearing the voice but seeing no one. Saul arose from the ground; and when his eyes were opened, he could see nothing; so they led him by the hand and brought him into Damascus. And for three days he was without sight, and neither ate nor drank (Acts 9.1-9).

Jesus need not use his own body directly to assault Saul. The very divine presence is itself dangerous, as is very clear from the theophanic narratives that we have from the Hebrew Bible (cf. Exod. 19.12; 33.20).[111]

---

110. Voorwinde (*Jesus' Emotions*, p. 163) connects a consuming zeal with Jesus' own death which consumed him: 'Zeal is more than anger. It is the ardour of red-hot passion... It eats him up... He has zeal that will consume him literally and totally.'

111. See further, H.W.F. Saggs, *The Encounter with the Divine in Mesopotamia and Israel* (London: Athlone Press, 1978).

In her study of this episode, Brittany Wilson argues that the narrative reflects the emasculation or 'unmanning' of Saul, insofar as blindness was viewed as a deficiency in one's manhood. Wilson remarks, 'In Acts 9, Paul's "unmanning" initiates his status as a man who obeys Jesus and who models this obedience for other believers.'[112] While Wilson acknowledges that Jesus 'exerts power over Saul by blinding him', she does not characterize this as an improper action or discuss the ethics of such an assault.[113] By and large, the same applies to others who comment on the passage.[114] They may acknowledge the violence but they either leave it without ethical evaluation or assume it is justified.

When compared to a similar legend in the Greco-Roman world, the encounter between Jesus and Saul was far more violent. The story of Romulus is narrated in Plutarch's *Lives*. Plutarch writes that a patrician named Julius Proculus went to the forum to relate his encounter with Romulus, a founder of Rome who had died about seven hundred years earlier. Plutarch says that Romulus,

> Solemnly swore by the most sacred emblems before all the people that, as he was travelling on the road, he had seen Romulus coming to meet him, fair and stately to the eye as never before, and arrayed in bright and shining armour. He himself, then, affrighted at the sight, had said: 'O, King what possessed thee, or what purpose hadst thou, that thou has left us patricians a prey to unjust and wicked accusations, and the whole city sorrowing without out end at the loss of its father?' Whereupon Romulus had replied: 'It was the pleasure of the gods, O Proculus, from whom I came, that I should be with mankind only a short time, and that after founding a city destined to be the greatest on earth for empire and glory, I should dwell again in heaven. So, farewell, and tell the Romans that if they practice self-restraint, and add to it valour, they will reach the utmost heights of human power.'[115]

The parallels with Saul's encounter with Jesus are unmistakable, and that includes a revelation while on the road, a reference to the bright and shining appearance of Romulus and Jesus, a question posed by Romulus and Saul, and a sort of directive given by both Jesus and Romulus. Jesus also dwelt for only a brief period on earth, and then returned to heaven.[116] What is different in the case of Saul is the violent nature of the encounter. All theophanies need not be violent, as that of Romulus shows. Jesus is portrayed

---

112. Brittanny Wilson, 'The Blinding of Paul and the Power of God: Masculinity, Sight, and Self-Control in Acts 9', *JBL* 133 (2014), pp. 367-87 (387).

113. Wilson, 'The Blinding of Paul', p. 383.

114. For another study, see Dennis Hamm, 'Paul's Blindness and its Healing: Clues to Symbolic Intent (Acts 9, 22 and 26)', *Bib* 71 (1990), pp. 64-65.

115. Plutarch, *Romulus* 28.1-3 (Perrin, LCL).

116. See Richard C. Miller, 'Mark's Empty Tomb and Other Translation Fables in Classical Antiquity', *JBL* 129 (2010), pp. 759-76 (esp. 762-64 and 773).

in Acts 9 as a punitive lord, who acquires followers through violence and extortion. He will blind you to gain obedience from you, and heal you when you become his obedient slave.

Summary

If any historical Jesus was faithfully following the Hebrew scriptures, then he inherited a tradition in which Yahweh can use violence to accomplish his purposes. Jesus accepted those scriptures as sacred despite their endorsement of genocide, the slaughter of women and children (e.g., Deut. 7.1-5, 1 Sam. 15.1-3), and the devastation of the environment as part of Yahweh's judgment (Deut. 28.15-56). Yahweh's violent behavior mimics that of ancient Near Eastern kings and imperialists. Accepting as sacred any scripture that at any time endorses genocide is itself sufficient to brand Jesus as unethical. Instead of repudiating those traditions or being opposed to them, Jesus actually expanded the violence relative to the Hebrew Bible. Any cases where Jesus seems to oppose the violent traditions of the Hebrew Bible (e.g., Mt. 5.39-44) are misleading because they do not take into account his advocacy of deferred violence. The god of the Hebrew Bible could harm those who disobeyed him, but that harm usually was imposed during one's earthly lifetime. Jesus' view of violence is infinitely greater in quality and quantity because he is portrayed as eternally burning and torturing those who opposed his religious beliefs and his empire otherwise known as the Kingdom of God.

Chapter 5

THE SUICIDAL JESUS: THE VIOLENT ATONEMENT

While the previous chapter examined Jesus' view of violence against others, this chapter focuses on Jesus' view of violence against himself. The idea that Jesus committed violence against himself is voiced by Jürgen Moltmann, a Christian theologian, when he remarked: 'Jesus did not suffer passively from the world in which he lived, but incited it against himself by his message and the life he lived.'[1] In particular, this chapter explores how Jesus saw his mission as part of 'the atonement', the definition of which is too varied to explain for the moment. I will explore how the New Testament depicts Jesus' attitudes about self-violence without making any final claims about whether the historical Jesus had those views or not. This chapter also investigates how the increasing sensitivity toward violence in modern biblical studies extends to soteriology.[2] Indeed, the role of violence in God's plan of salvation has come under renewed scrutiny from pacifists, feminists, and postcolonialist streams.[3]

---

1. Jürgen Moltmann, *The Crucified God: The Cross of Christ as the Foundation and Criticism of Christian Theology* (trans. R.A. Wilson and John Bowden; New York: Harper & Row, 1974), p. 51. See also comments on Moltmann's views in Joanne C. Brown and Rebecca Parker, 'For God So Loved the World?', in *Christianity, Patriarchy, and Abuse: A Feminist Critique* (ed. Joanne C. Brown and Carole R. Bohn; New York: Pilgrim Press, 1989), pp. 1-30 (18-19).

2. See Belousek, *Atonement, Justice, and Peace*; Derek Tidball, David Hilborn and Justin Thacker (eds.), *The Atonement Debate: Papers from the London Symposium on the Theology of the Atonement* (Grand Rapids, MI: Zondervan, 2008); Peter Schmiechen, *Saving Power: Theories of Atonement and Forms of the Church* (Grand Rapids, MI: Eerdmans, 2005).

3. A recent defense of the penal substitution theory can be found in Steve Jeffrey, Michael Ovey and Andrew Sach, *Pierced for our Transgressions: Rediscovering the Glory of Penal Substitution* (Wheaton, IL: Crossway Books, 2007). A response may be found in Derek Flood, 'Substitutionary Atonement and the Church Fathers: A Reply to the Authors of *Pierced for our Transgressions*', *EvQ* 82 (2010), pp. 142-59. For another argument that early church accepted penal substitution, see Peter Ensor, 'Justin Martyr and Penal Substitutionary Atonement', *EvQ* 83 (2011), pp. 217-32. See also Scot McKnight, *Jesus and His Death: Historiography, the Historical Jesus, and Atonement Theory* (Waco, TX: Baylor University Press, 2005).

Ever since the publication of Gustaf Aulén's *Christus Victor* (1931) many scholars have popularized a triadic paradigm of atonement theories: (1) The Christus Victor model, which sees Jesus as an innocent victim in a larger cosmic struggle between good and evil; (2) the satisfaction theory associated with St Anselm of Canterbury, which requires the sacrifice of a god-man; and (3) the moral influence theory associated with St Abelard (1079–1142), who claims that the death of Jesus shows the love of God for human beings, who then may be moved to repent once they realize the loving nature of that sacrifice.[4] St Abelard's theory was already motivated, at least in part, by the ethical problems posed by the idea that God would demand such a violent method of salvation.[5]

According to J. Denny Weaver, one of the leading voices against the claim that the atonement is fundamentally violent, the Christus Victor model,

> used the image of cosmic battle between good and evil, between the forces of God and those of Satan. In the fray, God's son Jesus was killed, an apparent defeat of God and victory by Satan. However, Jesus' resurrection turned the seeming defeat into a great victory, which forever established God's control of the universe and freed sinful humans from the power of sin and Satan.[6]

Aulén called this the 'classical' theory of the atonement because he thought it actually represented early Christianity the best. In this theory, God does not demand or receive any sort of violent sacrifice.

The Christian theologian at the center of Christian soteriology is St Anselm of Canterbury (1033–1109), whose idea of substitutionary atonement has been highly influential. Its main thesis, expounded primarily in his *Cur Deus Homo* (ca. 1098), has been repeated many times, but briefly it argues that God's infinite honor has been so violated by human sin that only an infinite payment can remunerate the deity.[7] Only an infinite being such as God, and not a human being, can possibly repay such a debt. Yet, God should

---

4.   Victor Aulén, *Christus Victor: A Historical Study of the Three Main Types of Atonement* (trans. Jaroslav Pelikan; New York: Macmillan, 1969 [1931]). J. Denny Weaver (*The Nonviolent Atonement* [Grand Rapids, MI: Eerdmans, 2001], p. 14) specifically credits Aulén with 'lending credibility to a threefold taxonomy of atonement models'.

5.   Weaver, *The Nonviolent Atonement*, pp. 18-19.

6.   Weaver, *The Nonviolent Atonement*, pp. 14-15. Other critiques of the violent atonement may be found in Stephen Finlan, *Options on Atonement in Christian Thought* (Collegeville, MN: Liturgical Press, 2007); idem, *Problems with Atonement: The Origins of, and Controversy about, the Atonement Doctrine* (Collegeville, MN: Liturgical Press, 2005); Christian A. Eberhart, *The Sacrifice of Jesus: Understanding Atonement Biblically* (Minneapolis: Fortress Press, 2011).

7.   For an English edition, see St Anselm of Canterbury, *Proslogium, Monlogium, in Behalf of the Fool by Gaunilon, and Cur Deus Homo* (Chicago, IL: Open Court, 1903).

not be obligated to repay something that is owed by human beings. Jesus, as both god and man, solves the problem. Therefore the violent and sacrificial death of Jesus, the god-man, was necessary to reconcile God and humanity.

My aim here is not to defend Anselm's theory. Rather, I show that some passages in the New Testament do portray Jesus as engaged in a sort of self-sacrifice that was meant to achieve God's favor and reconciliation with Jews and/or the larger human community. That self-sacrifice did serve to appease God or secure God's favor in some form. The evidence for a satisfaction or substitutionary idea of Jesus' atonement is strong enough that even Tim Gorringe, who rejects Anselm's theory, admits: 'The New Testament can certainly be read as supporting satisfaction theory. What I have tried to argue is that it does not *have* to be read in this way, and that there is much that points in other directions.'[8] I will show that Gorringe, and like-minded scholars, must resort to theological speculation to make such a case.

I will also critique at least two different strategies that may be identified among New Testament scholars who address the role of violence in the atonement. The first strategy virtually ignores specific texts in which violence was part of, or necessary for, any atoning work of Jesus. Instead, the arguments for nonviolence usually appeal to some theological rationale or involve a plea for reinterpreting or recontextualizing the atonement. The second strategy does address specific texts, but it relies on theological assumptions to erase the plain meaning of texts that clearly presuppose violence as necessary or desirable to effect the atonement.

J. Denny Weaver's Nonviolent Atonement

As mentioned, J. Denny Weaver is one of the most vocal advocates of a nonviolent view of the atonement. In *The Nonviolent Atonement* (2001), Weaver made an extensive case for abandoning Anselm's view of a sub-stitutionary atonement, and embracing a form of the Christus Victor model of the atonement, which required no violence and denied any culpability to God for killing Christ. Rather, Jesus was an innocent victim. In his plea for a non-violent view of the atonement, Weaver summarizes the dominant form of atonement theology as follows:

> Atonement theology starts with violence, namely the killing of Jesus. The commonplace assumption is that something good happened, namely salvation of sinners, when or because Jesus was killed. It follows that the doctrine of atonement then explains how and why Christians believe the death of Jesus—the killing of Jesus—resulted in salvation of sinful humankind.[9]

8. Tim Gorringe, *God's Just Vengeance* (Cambridge: Cambridge University Press, 1996), p. 81.
9. Weaver, *The Nonviolent Atonement*, p. 2.

Weaver is only one of many other biblical scholars who deny that Jesus ever saw himself as a sacrifice or endorse the use of violence to restore any broken relationship between God and humanity.

In terms of biblical scholarship and exegesis, the work of Weaver leaves much to be desired. For example, Weaver seems uninterested in addressing in any detail the specific passages that have been used to argue for a satisfaction theory of atonement. In fact, his book has no scriptural index. His argument consists mostly of reciting some of the historical developments that purport to show that Anselm's theory is a late development, and in summarizing some of the problems feminists and other marginalized segments of biblical scholarship have voiced with the idea of atonement.

Jesus as a Willing Sacrificial Victim

The evidence that Jesus either saw himself as a martyr or was seen as a martyr is overwhelming in the New Testament. By 'martyr', I refer to someone who gives his or her life on behalf of a greater cause or on behalf of others. Thus, there should be little controversy about the fact that Jesus endorsed the idea that violence was a necessary or beneficial part of God's plan for Israel or the world. Jon Levenson has argued cogently that Jesus' self-identification as a willing sacrificial victim is part of a long tradition that can be traced at least as far back as the story of Abraham and Isaac.[10] Jesus' statements concerning the self-sacrificial mission of the Son of Man are perfectly consistent with the idea that sacrificing oneself for a greater good should be encouraged.

The identity of the Son of Man has been the subject of great debate in New Testament scholarship, and I do not intend to rehearse that issue here.[11] Whether the historical Jesus saw himself as the Son of Man or not, the point remains that Jesus is portrayed as endorsing or accepting the idea that the

10. Jon Levenson, *The Death and Resurrection of the Beloved Son: The Transformation of Child Sacrifice in Judaism and Christianity* (New Haven, CT: Yale University Press, 1993). For a Christian response to Levenson, see William C. Placher, 'Christ Takes our Place: Rethinking Atonement', *Int* 53 (1999), pp. 5-20. See also Jintae Kim, 'The Concept of Atonement in Hellenistic Thought and 1 John', *Journal of Greco-Roman Christianity and Judaism* 2 (2001–2005), pp. 100-116; idem, 'The Concept of Atonement in Early Rabbinic Thought and the New Testament', *Journal of Greco-Roman Christianity and Judaism* 2 (2001–2005), pp. 117-45.

11. See Larry W. Hurtado and Paul L. Owen, '*Who is This Son of Man? The Latest Scholarship on a Puzzling Expression of the Historical Jesus* (London and New York: T. & T. Clark, 2011); Thomas Kazen, 'The Coming Son of Man Revisited', *Journal for the Study of the Historical Jesus* 5 (2007), pp. 155-74; Derbert Burkett, *The Son of Man Debate: A History and Evaluation* (SNTMS, 107; Cambridge: Cambridge University Press, 1999).

Son of Man had to endure violence to carry out his divine mission. For the moment, I follow Adela Yarbro Collins, who views the origin of the 'Son of Man' in the Gospels as ultimately deriving from Dan. 7.13.[12] Mark portrays Jesus as identifying himself with this figure: 'Again the high priest asked him, "Are you the Christ, the Son of the Blessed?" And Jesus said, "I am; and you will see the Son of man seated at the right hand of Power, and coming with the clouds of heaven"' (Mk 14.61-62).

The archetypal scene of human sacrifice in the Hebrew Bible is that of Isaac in Genesis 22.[13] Abraham is depicted as involved in a test of loyalty by his divine master. God asks Abraham to sacrifice his son, Isaac, who does not realize what his father intends. After Abraham shows his willingness to kill his son, the meaning of the ordeal is revealed by the angel of God: 'Do not lay your hand on the lad or do anything to him; for now I know that you fear God, seeing you have not withheld your son, your only son, from me' (Gen. 22.12). The idea of 'fearing God' is well known from covenant language in which a vassal or slave is supposed to act because he fears what his master might do in retaliation (cf. Deut. 28.15-68; Prov. 24.21).

The idea of offering Yahweh the firstborn seems to be normal in Exod. 13.2: 'Consecrate to me all the first-born; whatever is the first to open the womb among the people of Israel, both of man and of beast, is mine.' Yahweh also commands: 'The first-born of your sons you shall give to me. You shall do likewise with your oxen and with your sheep: seven days it shall be with its dam; on the eighth day you shall give it to me' (Exod. 22.29-30). Child sacrifice is the ultimate test of obedience to Yahweh in Ezekiel: 'Moreover I gave them statutes that were not good and ordinances by which they could not have life; and I defiled them through their very gifts in making them offer by fire all their first-born, that I might horrify them; I did it that they might know that I am the LORD' (Ezek. 20.25-26).[14]

The notion that child sacrifice worked magically to avert the wrath of Yahweh or to gain his favor is indicated by the story of Jephthah, who vowed to sacrifice whoever came out of his house if Yahweh would grant him victory over the Ammonites. Yahweh did give the Ammonites into Jephthah's

---

12. Adela Yarbro Collins, 'Son of Man', in *NIDB*, V, pp. 341-48.

13. See Leroy A. Huizenga, *The New Isaac: Tradition and Intertextuality in the Gospel of Matthew* (Supplements to Novum Testamentum, 131; Leiden: E.J. Brill, 2009).

14. The claim that this passage concerns animal sacrifice, not human sacrifice, is defended by Scott Walker Hahn and John Seitze Bergsma, 'What Laws were "Not Good"? A Canonical Approach to the Theological Problem of Ezekiel 20:25-26', *JBL* 123 (2004), pp. 201-218. Per contra, see Levenson, *The Death and Resurrection of the Beloved Son*, p. 5; Moshe Greenberg, *Ezekiel 1–20* (AB, 22; Garden City, NY: Doubleday, 1983), p. 369. Hahn and Bergsma ultimately depend on apologetic and theological arguments to make their case.

hand (Judg. 11.32), and his daughter came out to greet him. Thus, Jephthah 'did with her according to his vow which he had made' (Judg. 11.39). There is no moral objection voiced to Jephthah's actions. Even if the vow is regarded as foolish, it is assumed that the vow should be carried out. More importantly, the story assumes that Yahweh honored the vow, and did not intervene on behalf of Jephthah's daughter (cf. the case of Isaac, where God intervened to save the lad).[15]

Second Samuel 21 contains a pericope about a famine in the land of Israel that lasted three years. In 2 Sam. 21.1, Yahweh gives his reason for not heeding David's repeated prayers to alleviate the famine: 'There is bloodguilt on Saul and on his house, because he put the Gibeonites to death.' When David asked the Gibeonites what he could do to appease them, they responded: '"Let seven of his sons be given to us, so that we may hang them up before the LORD at Gibeon on the mountain of the LORD" And the king said, "I will give them"' (2 Sam. 21.6). So, David took seven of Saul's sons, and handed them over to the Gibeonites, who 'hanged them on the mountain before the LORD, and the seven of them perished together. They were put to death in the first days of harvest, at the beginning of barley harvest' (2 Sam. 21.9). The pericope ends by noting that 'after that God heeded supplications for the land' (2 Sam. 21.14).

In fact, human sacrifice can be honored by Yahweh even when performed by a non-Israelite. Note the case of the Moabite king who sacrificed his eldest son in 2 Kings:

> When the king of Moab saw that the battle was going against him, he took with him seven hundred swordsmen to break through, opposite the king of Edom; but they could not. Then he took his eldest son who was to reign in his stead, and offered him for a burnt offering upon the wall. And there came great wrath upon Israel; and they withdrew from him and returned to their own land (2 Kgs 3.26-27).

Despite the debates about when child sacrifice was eliminated in ancient Israel, it is clear that child sacrifice was meant to retain or gain the favor of the god to whom the sacrifice was offered. It is also clear that Yahweh is portrayed as honoring these sacrifices on at least some occasions.

By the Late Second Temple period, Jewish literature contained explicit endorsements of the benefits of martyrdom and self-sacrifice. One illustrative example occurs in Pseudo-Philo, a Jewish work dated to 'around the time of Jesus' by Daniel J. Harrington.[16] In an episode about the sacrifice of Jephthah's daughter (Judges 11), Jephthah is portrayed as regretful

---

15. So noted by J. Cheryl Exum, 'Feminist Criticism: Whose Interests are Being Served?', in *Judges and Method: New Approaches in Biblical Studies* (ed. Gale A. Yee; Minneapolis: Fortress Press, 2nd edn, 2007), pp. 65-89 (74).

16. Daniel J. Harrington, 'Pseudo-Philo', *OTP*, II, p. 299.

about fulfilling his vow to sacrifice his daughter, here named Seila, as he had promised Yahweh. Jephthah had vowed to sacrifice whoever stepped out of his house in order to defeat the Ammonites who were oppressing the Israelites. However, Seila urges her father not to revoke his vow as follows:

> And Seila his daughter said to him, 'And who is there who would be sad in death, seeing the people freed? Or do you not remember what happened during the days of our fathers when the father placed the son as a holocaust, and he did not refuse him but gladly gave his consent to him and the one being offered was ready and the one who was offering was rejoicing?…and if I did not offer myself willingly for sacrifice, I fear that my death would not be acceptable or I would lose my life in vain (Pseudo-Philo 40.2-3).[17]

The efficacy of any self-sacrifice here is directly linked to the level of willingness on the part of the victim. In addition, such a sacrifice could be seen as a joyous occasion because it would have a greater liberatory effect for a larger number of fellow Jews.[18] While the Ammonites are the ones named in the story, there can be little doubt that Jews living in the Roman empire would have seen a similar rationale to martyrdom in liberating Jews from Roman oppression.

Josephus treated the direct or indirect suicides of figures mentioned in the Hebrew Bible as noble. In regard to Samson, Josephus speaks of 'the grandeur of his end'.[19] According to Josephus, Mattathias, the Maccabean hero, told his sons to be prepared to die for the laws when rebelling against Antiochus (*Ant.* 12.281-82). Josephus touts freedom from slavery and oppression as a worthy motive for choosing death even when the victims are fighting against Jews. When the people of Gaza were about to be defeated by Alexander Jannaeus around 100 BCE, Josephus describes how the inhabitants of that town killed their own children and wives. For the people of Gaza, death was 'the means by which they were compelled to deliver them from slavery to their foes'.[20]

Given the purpose and nobility of self-sacrifice attested in the Hebrew Bible and in some Second Temple Jewish authors, it would not be surprising that Jesus is portrayed by the evangelists as offering his life on behalf of the Jews in order to liberate them from Roman oppression. The first

---

17. *OTP*, II, p. 353.

18. See also Marie-Francoise Baslez, '*Hellenismus-Ioudaismos*: Cross-Approaches of Jewish-Greek Literature of Martyrdom', *Henoch* 32 (2010), pp. 19-33; Jintae Kim, 'The Concept of Atonement in the Qumran Literature and the New Covenant', *Journal of Greco-Roman Christianity and Judaism* 7 (2010), pp. 98-111.

19. Josephus, *Ant.* 5.317 (Thackeray and Marcus, LCL): τὴν τελευτὴν μεγαλόφρονος.

20. Josephus, *Ant.* 13.364 (Thackeray and Marcus, LCL): τῆς ὑπὸ τοῖς ἐχθροῖς αὐτοὺς δουλείας οὕτως ἀπαλλάττειν ἠναγκασμένοι.

announcement of the 'good news' by Jesus in Mk 1.15 exclaims: 'The time is fulfilled, and the kingdom of God is at hand; repent, and believe in the gospel.' Indeed, Jesus makes liberation specific to his mission: 'The Spirit of the Lord is upon me, because he has anointed me to preach good news to the poor. He has sent me to proclaim release to the captives and recovering of sight to the blind, to set at liberty those who are oppressed' (Lk. 4.18).

Mark 10.45: Self-Sacrifice as a Ransom

Death seems to be the divine destiny for the Son of Man in Mk 10.45: 'For the Son of man also came not to be served but to serve, and to give his life as a ransom for many.' The Greek expression, καὶ δοῦναι τὴν ψυχὴν αὐτοῦ λύτρον ἀντὶ πολλῶν has attracted much debate.[21] According to *TDNT*, 'λύτρον is esp[ecially] the money paid to ransom prisoners of war, but it is then used for slaves, or for release from a bond. The word is infrequently used cultically for the payment made to a deity to which man has incurred indebtedness.'[22] An illuminating example of how a ransom may be offered for someone deserving death is found in the famous case of the ox that gores:

> When an ox gores a man or a woman to death, the ox shall be stoned, and its flesh shall not be eaten; but the owner of the ox shall be clear. But if the ox has been accustomed to gore in the past, and its owner has been warned but has not kept it in, and it kills a man or a woman, the ox shall be stoned, and its owner also shall be put to death. If a ransom is laid on him, then he shall give for the redemption of his life whatever is laid upon him (Exod. 21.28-30).

In the LXX, the word 'ransom' (λύτρα; MT: פִדְיֹן) in v. 30 refers to a monetary payment that may be substituted for the life of the man otherwise legally deserving of death.

It is important to understand that a ransom could be paid to Yahweh, as in the case of the firstborn:

> You shall set apart to the LORD all that first opens the womb. All the firstlings of your cattle that are males shall be the LORD's.

> Every firstling of an ass you shall redeem with a lamb, or if you will not redeem it you shall break its neck. Every first-born of man among your sons you shall redeem (Exod. 13.12-13).

21. See J. Christopher Edwards, *The Ransom Logion in Mark and Matthew: Its Reception and its Significance for the Study of the Gospels* (WUNT, 2.327; Tübingen: Mohr Siebeck, 2012); Greg H.R. Horsley, *New Documents Illustrating the History of Christianity, Volume 3: A Review of the Greek Inscriptions and Papyri Published in 1978* (Grand Rapids, MI: Eerdman, 1983), pp. 72-75.

22. *TDNT*, IV, p. 340.

The redemption consists of substituting a lamb, which is offered to Yahweh, instead of the human firstborn. The LXX uses the verb λυτροῦν to describe the act of redemption expressed by the Hebrew verb פדה.

Non-Christian inscriptions attest to the idea of paying a ransom to a god for sins committed. Note the inscription that G.H.R. Horsley translates as: 'Alexander son of Thalouse with Julius and his sister paid to the god Men of Diodotus a ransom | for things known and unknown. Year 233.'[23] The inscription may be speaking of sins committed intentionally ('known') or unintentionally ('unknown'), but uncertainties remain about the nature of the ransom. If the grammar of that inscription renders it difficult to establish the existence of ransom paid to a deity, a mosaic from the Mount of Olives (VII) seems clearer in speaking of a certain Symeon who 'built and decorated an oratory for "our *despotes* Christ", ὑπὲρ λύτρου τῶν αὐτοῦ ἁμαρτιῶν κ(αὶ) ἀναπαύσεως τῶν αὐτοῦ ἀδελφ(ῶν)'.[24] Here, there seems to be no question that Symeon offers a ransom for the purpose of receiving forgiveness from sins.

The concept expressed in Mk 10.45 is very similar to that evidenced in 4 Maccabees (first century), where there is a discussion about how 'the holy ones' mentioned in Deut. 33.2 were martyrs for a great good.[25] According to 4 Macc. 17.20-21: '[T]hrough them our enemies did not prevail against our nation, and the tyrant was punished and our land purified, since they became, as it were, a ransom [ἀντίψυχον] for the sin of our nation.'[26] Jon Levenson explains:

> Isaac in 4 Maccabees, both is and is not thus a spiritual forebear of Jesus as reinterpreted by Paul and inherited by Christians. Isaac is a forebear of Jesus in that, as a martyr, he helps bring reconciliation and redemption. He is not a forebear in that his death is not *uniquely and exclusively* redemptive.[27]

In any case, the Greek word, ἀντίψυχον, in 4 Maccabees seems parallel to how ἀντίλυτρον is used in 1 Tim. 2.5-6: 'For there is one God, and there is one mediator between God and men, the man Christ Jesus, who gave himself as a ransom [ἀντίλυτρον] for all, the testimony to which was borne at the proper time.'

Jesus' death is understood as both a sacrifice and as a preplanned event according to Paul: 'Christ died for our sins in accordance with the scriptures' (1 Cor. 15.3). The author of Hebrews apparently also understands Jesus'

23. See Horsley, *New Documents*, p. 72.
24. Horsley, *New Documents*, p. 74.
25. For the date, see H. Anderson, *OTP*, II, pp. 533-34.
26. *OTP*, II, p. 563.
27. Levenson, *The Death and Resurrection of the Beloved Son*, p. 189; his emphasis..

death as a self-offering sacrifice.[28] Jesus portrays his own capture as part of his prophesied fate: 'Day after day I was with you in the temple teaching, and you did not seize me. But let the scriptures be fulfilled' (Mk 14.49). Elsewhere in Mark, one finds the following discussion about Jesus' mission:

> And they asked him, 'Why do the scribes say that first Elijah must come?' And he said to them, 'Elijah does come first to restore all things; and how is it written of the Son of man, that he should suffer many things and be treated with contempt? But I tell you that Elijah has come, and they did to him whatever they pleased, as it is written of him' (Mk 9.11-13).

Luke ties Jesus' fate more closely to Isaiah's 'Suffering Servant':

> He said to them, 'But now, let him who has a purse take it, and likewise a bag. And let him who has no sword sell his mantle and buy one. For I tell you that this scripture must be fulfilled in me, "And he was reckoned with transgressors"; for what is written about me has its fulfillment' (Lk. 22.36-37).

The Suffering Servant is a figure that appears in Second Isaiah in a series of passages usually called the Servant Songs (e.g., Isa. 42.1-4, 49.1-6, 50.4-9). Luke is tying Jesus most closely to the Servant Song in Isa. 52.13–53.12.[29] The identity of the Servant has been contested, and I will not rehearse the arguments here. The point is that there was a link made between the experiences of the Servant and Jesus. In fact, some New Testament scholars see Isaiah 53 as a foundational text to explain Jesus' mission.[30]

Whether Jesus thought of himself as a martyr, or his martyrdom was invented to explain some unforeseen death, the consistency in the portrayal cannot be ignored. Moreover, as Arthur Droge and James Tabor observe:

> If it is not always easy to distinguish between 'suicide' and 'martyrdom', between killing oneself and provoking one's own death, then the Jews in the Fourth Gospel were not wrong when they described Jesus' 'going away'

28. See Guido Telscher, *Opfer aus Barmherzigkeit: Hebr 9, 11-28 im Kontext biblischer Sühnetheologie* (Forschung zur Bibel, 112; Würzburg: Echter, 2007).

29. For general treatments of Isaiah 53, see Bernd Janowski and Peter Stuhlmacher (eds.), *The Suffering Servant: Isaiah 53 in Jewish and Christian Sources* (trans. Daniel P. Bailey; Grand Rapids, MI: Eerdmans, 2004); William H. Bellinger and William R. Farmer (eds.), *Jesus and the Suffering Servant: Isaiah 53 and Christian Origins* (Harrisburg, PA: Trinity Press International, 1998); Frederick Hägglund, *Isaiah 53 in the Light of Homecoming after Exile* (FAT, 31; Tübingen: Mohr-Siebeck, 2008); David J.A. Clines, *I, He, We, and They: A Literary Approach to Isaiah 53* (JSOTSup, 1; Sheffield: JSOT Press, 1976).

30. For example, Patrick Fabien, 'L'interprétation de la citation d'Is 53, 7-8 en Ac 8, 23-33', *RB* 117.4 (2010), pp. 550-70. See also David C. Mitchell, 'Firstborn *Shor* and *Rem*: A Sacrificial Josephite Messiah in 1 Enoch 90.37-38 and Deuteronomy 33.17', *JSP* 15.3 (2006), pp. 211-28.

as a death threat. Indeed the author of the Fourth Gospel makes this explicit by having Jesus declare, 'No one takes [my life] from me, but I lay it down of my own free will. I have the power to lay it down, and I have the power to take it again' (Jn 10.18).[31]

Jesus gives at least one motive for his willingness to die: 'Greater love has no man than this, that a man lay down his life for his friends [ὑπὲρ τῶν φίλων αὐτοῦ]' (Jn 15.13). Jesus is no radical innovator here, as a similar sentiment is recorded by Diogenes Laertius:

> They tell us that the wise man will for reasonable cause make his own exit from life, on his country's behalf or for the sake of his friends [ὑπὲρ φίλων], or if he suffer intolerable pain, mutilation, or incurable disease.[32]

Self-sacrifice on behalf of others can be considered an act of love by Jesus and by some non-Christian philosophers. Since self-sacrifice is a form of violence (a violence against the self), then it is clear that Jesus is portrayed as glorifying self-violence. Given the abundance of evidence for Jesus' portrayal as a sort of planned sacrifice, then it is important to understand how pacifist scholars address the evidence.

Sacrifice as Service: Transformation or Denial?

Since sacrificial language cannot be completely erased from the Gospels, some scholars argue that Jesus somehow has transformed the entire concept of sacrifice into something more benign and nonviolent. For example, James G. Williams admits that the word, λύτρον, in Mk 10.45 is 'an unmistakably sacrificial word that would be readily understood as such'.[33] Yet, he argues that the very same word 'was used to break out of a sacrificial worldview'.[34] Williams also argues that 'in most of the instances where clearly, heavily freighted sacrificial language is used, the sacrificial meaning is transformed'.[35]

For Williams, Mk 10.45 ('the Son of man also came not to be served but to serve') demonstrates that Jesus' kingship consists of service. Williams remarks, 'as the king becomes a servant, sacrifice is transformed into service'.[36] Williams accomplishes this transformation by redefining 'sacrifice' as follows:

---

31. Arthur J. Droge and James D. Tabor, *A Noble Death: Suicide and Martyrdom among Christians and Jews in Antiquity* (New York: HarperCollins, 1992), p. 118.

32. Diogenes Laertius, *Zeno* 7.130 (Hicks, LCL).

33. James G. Williams, *The Bible, Violence and the Sacred: Liberation from the Myth of Sanctioned Violence* (New York: HarperCollins, 1991), p. 224.

34. James G. Williams, 'King as Servant, Sacrifice as Service: Gospel Transformations', in Swartley (ed.), *Violence Renounced*, pp. 178-99 (193).

35. Williams, 'King as Servant', p. 195.

36. Williams, 'King as Servant', p. 193.

> The ransom, *lytron*, that which looses, unbinds, liberates, is derived from
> sacrificial usage, but this is not a substitution—a sacrifice standing-in-stead-
> of—of one for all that God imposes on humans, who must in turn render the
> ransom to God to satisfy the divine command or to appease divine wrath.
> Of course, from the standpoint of 'world', i.e., ordinary mimesis, it *is* sacri-
> fice, as are not only the offerings of victims in ritual, but all executions also.
> But from the standpoint *sub specie Dei*, or the kingdom of God, it is God's
> free offering of release to human beings through Jesus as the divine son,
> Son of God, Son of man—the king who rules through serving. The ordinary
> world of mimesis is exposed for what is through the suffering, death, and
> resurrection of the divine son.[37]

Williams is basing a substantial portion of his claims on René Girard's
theory of mimetic violence, which I address more fully below. For now, it is
sufficient to remark that nothing in Mk 10.45 can be construed to mean that
the biblical author aims to expose the fallacy of mimetic violence.

Williams deems this sort of servitude as benign and nonviolent, when
there is nothing in the text to indicate that servitude is meant to be nonviolent. Rather, servitude or slavery was a very violent institution. For
Jesus, it is Yahweh or God who is the ultimate sovereign to whom all,
including the Son of Man, must pledge allegiance. Rather than expressing
a nonviolent approach to rulership, Jesus suggests that any rise to power
or privilege in the Kingdom of Yahweh must be preceded by a loyalty test
and by a willingness to prove one's willingness to be a slave to the ultimate master. That loyalty test could include a willingness to submit to
violence.

To understand this potentially violent path to privilege in the Kingdom
of God, one must realize that the saying in 10.45 is preceded by a series of
conversations about how to enter the Kingdom of God. In Mk 10.17 a rich
man had asked: 'Good Teacher, what must I do to inherit eternal life?' Jesus
gave the rich man a loyalty test, and instructed him as follows after certi-
fying in Mk 10.19-20 that the Rich Man followed the Mosaic commandments: 'You lack one thing; go, sell what you have, and give to the poor,
and you will have treasure in heaven; and come, follow me' (Mk 10.21). For
Jesus to demand that the Rich Man give up his possessions to follow him is
a sort of loyalty test that does not require violence. Giving up possessions
to follow Jesus, however, still means that Jesus demands a servitude centered on Jesus' agenda.

The disciples then begin to wonder how they can ever enter into the
Kingdom of Heaven, and Peter specifically notes that his disciples had
already met Jesus' loyalty test by giving up 'everything' (Mk 10.24-28). At
this point, Jesus says:

---

37. Williams, 'King as Servant', p. 193.

> Truly, I say to you, there is no one who has left house or brothers or sisters or mother or father or children or lands, for my sake and for the gospel, who will not receive a hundredfold now in this time, houses and brothers and sisters and mothers and children and lands, with persecutions, and in the age to come eternal life. But many that are first will be last, and the last first (Mk 10.29-31).

Whether Jesus thinks of 'service' as a sacrifice or not, it is clear that the service is to be rendered to him or on his behalf ('for my sake'). At the same time, suffering or deprivation is a prologue to a greater reward later.

As Jesus and his disciples depart that scene, Jesus makes another comment that details how any rising of the Son of Man, an act that denotes another step toward exaltation in the Kingdom of God, will be preceded by violence:

> Behold, we are going up to Jerusalem; and the Son of man will be delivered to the chief priests and the scribes, and they will condemn him to death, and deliver him to the Gentiles; and they will mock him, and spit upon him, and scourge him, and kill him; and after three days he will rise (Mk 10.33-34).

Since the disciples understand that suffering and violence will eventually result in Jesus' exaltation, James and John ask whether they also will receive an exalted place alongside him. Up to now, there is no hint that James and John expect suffering to be a condition to gain any exalted position in the Kingdom of Heaven:

> And James and John, the sons of Zebedee, came forward to him, and said to him, 'Teacher, we want you to do for us whatever we ask of you'. And he said to them, 'What do you want me to do for you?' And they said to him, 'Grant us to sit, one at your right hand and one at your left, in your glory' (Mk 10.35-37).

It is at this point that Jesus clarifies that their request will necessitate a greater loyalty test that will involve more requirements, even violent ones, compared to what Jesus asked of the Rich Man. Note Jesus' reply:

> But Jesus said to them, 'You do not know what you are asking. Are you able to drink the cup that I drink, or to be baptized with the baptism with which I am baptized?' And they said to him, 'We are able'. And Jesus said to them, 'The cup that I drink you will drink; and with the baptism with which I am baptized, you will be baptized; but to sit at my right hand or at my left is not mine to grant, but it is for those for whom it has been prepared' (Mk 10.38-40).

That 'the cup' is linked to his violent death is suggested in the following passage:

> And as they were eating, he took bread, and blessed, and broke it, and gave it to them, and said, 'Take; this is my body'. And he took a cup, and when

> he had given thanks he gave it to them, and they all drank of it. And he said
> to them, 'This is my blood of the covenant, which is poured out for many.
> Truly, I say to you, I shall not drink again of the fruit of the vine until that
> day when I drink it new in the kingdom of God' (Mk 14.22-25).

Later, Jesus again mentions 'blood' and 'the cup' when referring to his violent suffering: 'And he said, "Abba, Father, all things are possible to thee;
remove this cup from me; yet not what I will, but what thou wilt"' (Mk
14.36).[38] Jesus describes how he himself is fulfilling a loyalty test:

> And Jesus called them to him and said to them, 'You know that those who
> are supposed to rule over the Gentiles lord it over them, and their great men
> exercise authority over them. But it shall not be so among you; but who-
> ever would be great among you must be your servant, and whoever would
> be first among you must be slave of all. For the Son of man also came not
> to be served but to serve, and to give his life as a ransom for many' (Mk
> 10.42-45).

Williams seemingly accepts the false dichotomy that Jesus presents just
prior to the latter's remarks in Mk 10.45. Jesus presents a false dichotomy
because he suggests that Gentiles have a more dictatorial form of exercising
power than what he is presenting. Jesus continues a tradition of imperialists
presenting their rule as more benign than those of the empires they seek to
replace. Jesus engages in disparaging 'the Gentiles' as if their imperialism
is somehow worse.[39] The fact is that the biblical traditions of power exercised by Yahweh or his regents on earth can be viewed as no less oppressive, coercive or dictatorial than what is found among 'the Gentiles'.

Nor is Jesus' view of servitude for kings very novel or revolutionary.
The idea of God as the ultimate sovereign, even of human kings, already is
found in the Hebrew Bible. Serving Yahweh could mean serving an Israelite
king or a foreign king, such as Nebuchadnezzar who is also deemed God's
servant (Jer. 27.6-8). Serving Yahweh could mean being a good slave to a
temple priest (e.g., Samuel at the Temple at Shiloh) or servant to an Israelite
king. The idea of servitude by a human ruler was well known among Gentiles according to Philo of Alexandria:

> Let us hear the voice of Sophocles in words which are as true as any Del-
> phic Oracle: 'God and no mortal is my Sovereign' [θεὸς ἐμὸς ἄρχων,
> θνητὸς οὐδείς]. For in very truth he who has God alone for his leader,
> he alone is free, though to my thinking he is also the leader of all others,

---

38. On the proper translation of αἷμα in sacrificial terms, see P. Ellingsworth, 'We
Must Have Blood', *BT* 60 (2009), pp. 5-9.

39. On Jesus' interest in the Gentiles, see Michael F. Bird, 'Jesus and the Gentiles
after Jeremias: Patterns and Prospects', *Currents in Biblical Research* 4 (2005), pp.
83-105; Joachim Jeremias, *Jesus' Promise to the Nations* (Naperville, IL: A.R. Allenson,
1958).

having received the charge of earthly things from the great, the immortal King, whom he, the mortal, serves as viceroy.[40]

Philo credits the Greeks, and not his own Jewish tradition, with emphasizing this idea.[41] Philo of Alexandria already knows of a topos in which statesmen are viewed as the servants of the people they rule: 'the true statesman knows quite well that the people has the power of a master, yet he will not admit that he is a slave [οὐχ ὁμολογήσει δοῦλον]'.[42] Today, one still finds the idea of serving the ruled or constituents among many politicians.

Given these observations, it is difficult to understand how Williams can come to this conclusion about *lytron*:

> I think Mark probably intends to say, in effect, 'The human condition is such that only the price of the Son of Man's suffering and death will have the effect of loosening the bonds of the sacred social structure, enabling human beings to see what their predicament is and the kind of faith and action that will bring liberation'. In other words, sacrificial language is used necessarily, in order to break out of a sacrificial view of the world. In this sense, the Son of Man as 'a ransom for many' is the Son of Man as a revelatory way, a means of access to community and nonviolence.[43]

But, if that is the case, one would not know it from reading Mark. The climax of the crucifixion centers on the identity of Jesus: 'And when the centurion, who stood facing him, saw that he thus breathed his last, he said, "Truly this man was the Son of God!"' (Mk 15.39). The Kingdom of God is meant, at best, to liberate Jesus' followers from the Roman empire, but not to liberate them from servitude or violence. If anything, Jesus envisions his disciples as enduring violence after his crucifixion, and so it is unclear why Williams believes Jesus to be the definitive end of mimetic violence.

It is also unclear why one must use sacrificial language 'in order to break out of a sacrificial view of the world'. It is one thing to use sacrificial language in order to reject sacrifice, and it is another to use sacrificial language under the assumption that sacrifice is efficacious or a proper method of atonement. In Mk 10.45 everything indicates that a violent substitutionary atonement is efficacious, and nothing in the text denies or rejects it as a proper method. Nothing in the text climaxes in some final unmasking of mimetic violence. Rather, it perpetuates the idea that his followers must also

---

40. Philo, *Omn. Prob. Lib.* 19-20 (Colson, LCL).

41. For a general assessment of Philo's philosophy, see Mireille Hadas-Lebel, *Philo of Alexandria: A Thinker in the Jewish Diaspora* (trans. Robyn Fréchet; Studies in Philo of Alexandria, 7; Leiden: E.J. Brill, 2012). See also Roland Deines and Karl-Wilhelm Niebuhr (eds.), *Philo und das Neue Testament. Wechselseitige Wahrnehmungen. 1. Internationale Symposium zum Corpus Judeo-Hellenisticum. 1-4 Mai 2003, Eisenach/Jena* (WUNT, 2.172; Tübingen: Mohr Siebeck, 2004).

42. Philo, *Jos.* 67 (Colson, LCL).

43. Williams, *The Bible, Violence and the Sacred*, p. 224.

suffer violence just as he did.[44] They all must drink of his cup if they ever want to advance in God's empire.

2 Corinthians 5.18: Anselm Unrefuted

As mentioned, Gustaf Aulén (1879–1977) was one of the first modern scholars who led the assault against Anselm's theory of atonement.

> It is precisely the work of salvation wherein Christ breaks the power of evil that constitutes the atonement between God and the world; for it is by it that He removes the enmity, takes away the judgment which rested on the human race, and reconciles the world to Himself, not imputing on them trespasses (2 Cor. v.18).[45]

For Aulén, the key passage for his argument is 2 Cor. 5.18, the importance of which he describes as follows:

> The classic idea of the atonement has never found more pregnant expression than in the great passage of 2 Cor. v. 18f.: 'All things are of God, who reconciled us to Himself through Christ, and gave us the ministry of reconciliation; to wit, that God was in Christ reconciling the world unto Himself, not reckoning unto them their trespasses, and having committed unto us the word of reconciliation'.[46]

However, nothing in 2 Cor. 5.18-19 refutes the idea that violence against Christ was part of God's plan of reconciliation. Even if one accepts the idea that God was willing to sacrifice his beloved son on behalf of human sinners, that does not remove the ethical problems of Aulén's 'classical' model of the atonement. For even in that model, violence was apparently the method by which God chose to effect any reconciliation. It still retains a violent view of God's entire method of atonement.

René Girard: Sacrificing Apologetics

René Girard has been one of the main proponents of the idea that Christianity's ideology helps to minimize or eliminate violence.[47] Born in Avi-

---

44. Indeed, the centrality of blood shedding for the forgiveness of sins continued to be extolled after the crucifixion, as pointed out by Hermann V.A. Kuma, *The Centrality of Αἷμα (Blood) in the Theology of the Epistle to the Hebrews: An Exegetical and Philological Study* (Lewiston, NY: Edwin Mellen Press, 2012). See also Gunnar Samuelsson, *Crucifixion in Antiquity: An Inquiry into the Background and Significance of the New Testament Terminology of Crucifixion* (WUNT, 2.310; Tübingen: Mohr Siebeck, 2011).

45. Aulén, *Christus Victor*, p. 71. Aulén uses 'v.18' for '5.18'.

46. Aulén, *Christus Victor*, p. 73.

47. See Scott Cowdell, *René Girard and Secular Modernity: Christ, Culture and Crisis* (Notre Dame, IN: University of Notre Dame Press, 2013).

gnon, France in 1923, Girard has been most closely associated with Stanford University. His influence towers above that of most theologians and philosophers who have theorized about violence. Some biblical scholars and scholars of religion have accepted Girard's theories as an advance in the understanding of violence.[48] Indeed, Girard's theory of violence has been so widely discussed in biblical studies that it is important to understand the claims he makes, and why they are flawed.[49] Others decry Girard's theories as nothing but thinly disguised Christian apologetics. Thus, Marilyn Katz opines: 'Girard's theory...has not commanded wide acceptance by specialists in the fields of either Anthropology or Classics.'[50]

The basis of Girard's influence in religious studies rests chiefly on his *Violence and the Sacred*, which was first published in 1972.[51] Girard, in general, sees religion as an essential component of humanity. He claims that 'of all social institutions, religion is the only one to which science has been unable to attribute a genuine objective, a real function'.[52] Moreover, Girard claims that 'there is no society without religion because without religion society cannot exist'.[53] At the same time, he proclaims that 'we are reluctant to admit that violence and the sacred are one and the same thing'.[54]

---

48. For an example of acceptance, see Ted Grimsrud, 'Scapegoating No More: Christian Pacifism and New Testament Views of Jesus' Death', in *Violence Renounced: René Girard, Biblical Studies and Peacemaking* (ed. Willard M. Swartley; Telford, PA: Pandora Press; Scottdale, PA: Herald Press, 2000), pp. 49-69.

49. For a collection of studies on Girard's impact on biblical studies, see Andrew J. McKenna (ed.), 'René Girard and Biblical Studies', *Semeia* 33 (1985); for an example of Girard's influence in the study of specific portions of the Bible, see Hans J.L. Jensen, 'Desire, Rivalry and Collective Violence in the "Succession Narrative"', *JSOT* 55 (1992), pp. 39-59.

50. Marilyn A. Katz, 'Problems of Sacrifice in Ancient Cultures', in *The Bible in Light of Cuneiform Literature* (ed. William W. Hallo, Bruce Williams Jones and Gerald L. Mattingly; Scriptures in Context, III; Lewiston, NY: Edwin Mellen Press, 1990), pp. 89-201 (97). See also Luc de Heusch, *Sacrifice in Africa: A Structuralist Approach* (trans. Linda O'Brien and Alice Morton; Bloomington, IN: Indiana University Press, 1985), pp. 15, 17.

51. René Girard, *Violence and the Sacred* (trans. Patrick Gregory; Baltimore, MD: The Johns Hopkins University Press, 1977). In all the citations of this work, we provide the original French text from *La violence et le sacré* (Paris: Bernard Grasset, 1972).

52. Girard, *Violence and the Sacred*, p. 92; *La violence*, p. 135: 'De toutes les institutions sociales, la religieux est la seule à laquelle la science n'a jamais réussi à attribuer un objet réel, une fonction veritable.'

53. Girard, *Violence and the Sacred*, p. 221; *La violence*, p. 303: 'Il n'y a pas de societé sans religion parce que sans religion aucune societé ne serait possible.'

54. Girard, *Violence and the Sacred*, p. 262; *La violence*, p. 303: 'nous répugnons à admettre l'identité de la violence et du sacré.'

As it pertains to conflict, Girard's initial premise is that 'there is…hardly any form of violence that cannot be described in terms of sacrifice'.[55] A society inflicts on a sacrificial victim the violence that would otherwise be turned towards the members of that society. Sacrifice becomes a preventive instrument against violence. Girard believes that religion 'invariably strives to subdue violence',[56] even if it sometimes paradoxically uses violence to end violence.

Girard argues that all sacrificial rituals require two substitutions. A community will identify a victim upon whom it will exhaust its aggression. However, such a victim, being a member of the community, usually will not actually be sacrificed. Instead, a ritual or surrogate victim from outside the community substitutes for the original victim, who then represents all the members of the community.[57] The outsider can also be seen as a monstrous double of the insider's surrogate victim. But what causes conflict and the need for sacrifice in the first place? Girard tells us that 'rivalry does not arise because of the fortuitous convergence of two desires on a single object; rather *the subject desires the object because the rival desires it*'.[58] This imitating of a desire Girard terms 'mimesis'. Conflicts arise because people want things because others want them. Desire is itself mimetic.

Although Girard's *Violence and the Sacred* does not make many explicit pronouncements about Christianity, his later works declare that Christianity is superior to other traditions in its ability to manage and expose violence.[59] Girard claims that, in contrast to scapegoating in non-Christian 'myths', in Christianity the victim is truly innocent, and the persecutors are guilty.[60] Girard adds that

> Our religious tradition [Judeo-Christianity] is more genuinely scientific than our science of mythology. The biblical revelation (exposure) of mythology is no 'mystical' insight. It rests on commonsensical observations. It requires no religious commitment to be understood. This anthropological vindication of the Judeo-Christian tradition is the foremost consequence of mimetic theory.[61]

55. Girard, *Violence and the Sacred*, p. 1; *La violence*, p. 1: 'n'y a guère de violence…qui ne puisse se décrire en termes de sacrifice.'

56. Girard, *Violence and the Sacred*, p. 20; *La violence*, p. 38: 'Le religieux vise toujours à apaiser la violence.'

57. Girard, *Violence and the Sacred*, p. 102.

58. Girard, *Violence and the Sacred*, p. 145 (Girard's emphasis); *La violence*, p. 204: 'La rivalité n'est pas le fruit d'une convergence accidentelle des deux désirs sur le même objet. *Le sujet désire l'objet parce que le rival lui-même le désire.*'

59. For example, René Girard, *Things Hidden since the Foundation of the World* (trans. Stephen Bann and Michael Metter; Stanford, CA: Stanford University Press, 1978).

60. René Girard, '*Violence Renounced:* Response by René Girard', in Swartley (ed.), *Violence Renounced*, pp. 312-13.

61. Girard, *Violence Renounced*, p. 313.

He predicts that '[i]f and when the Judeo-Christian deconstruction of mythology becomes common knowledge, the whole post-enlightenment culture of naïve contempt for our Judeo-Christian heritage will crash to the ground'.[62] Girard proclaims the uniqueness of the Hebrew Bible in that there 'God sides with the victims against their persecutors'.[63] In short, Girard reveals himself as a frank apologist for Christianity and the Bible.

While Girard has identified how one mechanism of violence works, Girard's theory has numerous flaws if it is meant to outline the most fundamental mechanisms for religious violence. Sacrifice is a secondary mechanism, not a fundamental one. Religious sacrifice depends on certain prior religious beliefs, which have created a need for sacrifice. Thus, religious sacrifice alone is meaningless unless there are prior religious presuppositions that lead to the very idea that sacrifice is the way to resolve issues.

Historically and empirically, Girard's theory has little merit. The anthropologist, Luc de Heusch, for instance, concludes that Girard's theory shows little acquaintance with the practice of sacrifice in many cultures.[64] De Heusch adds that Girard's theory 'is based on a dogmatic bias', and is 'a neo-Christian, somewhat heretical theology'.[65] There are few empirical and statistical data provided to see how many of the cultures or instances where sacrifice is offered work in the way that Girard claims.

Girard's theory also fails in its application to the very biblical texts he seeks to explain on the basis of his theory. He offers superficial and arbitrary readings of biblical texts. For example, he notes that Amos, Isaiah and Micah denounce the Hebrew sacrificial system. Girard adds that 'the eroding of the sacrificial system seems to result in the emergence of reciprocal violence'.[66] Such a conclusion is refuted by a mound of evidence. For example, reciprocal violence was enshrined in the Code of Hammurabi at least a thousand years earlier than any Hebrew prophets.[67] Yet, the Code of Hammurabi was thoroughly embedded in a culture that had an extensive sacrificial system.[68] Conversely, some of the most violent episodes described in

---

62. Girard, *Violence Renounced*, p. 314.

63. Girard, *Violence Renounced*, p. 319.

64. Heusch, *Sacrifice in Africa*, pp. 16-17.

65. Heusch, *Sacrifice in Africa*, pp. 16-17.

66. Girard, *Violence and the Sacred*, p. 43; *La violence*, p. 68: 'L'usure du système sacrificiel apparaît toujours comme une chute dans la violence reciproque'.

67. The relationship of the Code of Hammurabi to biblical law has been studied by David P. Wright, *Inventing God's Law: How the Covenant Code of the Bible Used and Revised the Code of Hammurabi* (New York: Oxford University Press, 2009). The Code of Hammurabi has laws that endorse reciprocal injury (Laws 196-205) together with a Preamble that touts the value of 'pure sacrifices' [*zībī ellūtim*] (CH iv. 22 in Roth, *Law Collections*, p. 79).

68. For a critique of Girard that integrates data from Mesopotamia, see Katz, 'Problems of Sacrifice in Ancient Cultures', pp. 89-201.

the Hebrew Bible occur in books (e.g. Deuteronomy 7 and 18) that advocate sacrifice.

Job, as read by Girard, becomes a moral farce. He tells us that 'God sides with the victims against their persecutors', and then uses Job as an example.[69] Girard forgets that the narrator says that God allows Satan to torture Job, who is held to be 'blameless and upright' (Job 1.1). God himself comments to Satan about Job: 'He still holds fast his integrity, although you moved me against him, to destroy him without cause' (Job 2.3). Thus, even God admits he is siding with the torturer and against the victim, Job. God admits that he is allowing Job to be tortured 'for no reason'.[70]

As it pertains to his work on the New Testament, Girard's work has also been criticized by those who otherwise accept the main thrust of his theories. John A. Darr, for example, outlines how, in analysing the passion narratives, Girard 'is clearly attempting to read these Gospels as a monolithic entity, or, in his words, as "the total" gospel'.[71] While Girard tells us that Christ's sacrifice had the effect of 'raising humankind once and for all above the culture of scapegoating',[72] one sees Jesus himself vowing to come back to exact revenge upon those that do not follow him (Mt. 25.31-46). In Mt. 10.34-37 Jesus says he came not to bring peace but a sword, which seems to contradict Girard's supposition about God's purposes. Thus, Girard picks-and-chooses proof-texts just as the so-called 'fundamentalists' do.

Overall, Girard is working with an essentialist paradigm that sees Christianity as the acme of peace and love, the latter being concepts that are misunderstood by Girard and many Christian apologists. Girard's reading of the Hebrew and Christian Scriptures is idiosyncratic and superficial, not to mention interlaced with unverifiable theological premises. Girard simply represents another Christian apologist seeking to minimize the violent premises on which Christianity is based and to tout Christianity as humankind's greatest achievement.[73]

---

69. Girard, *Violence Renounced*, p. 319. See also René Girard, *Job: The Victim of his People* (trans. Yvonne Freccero; Stanford, CA: Stanford University Press, 1987). For a sympathetic treatment of Girard's view of Job, see Baruch Levine, 'René Girard and Job: The Question of the Scapegoat', *Semeia* 33 (1985), pp. 125-33.

70. David J.A. Clines (*Job 1–20* [Word Biblical Commentary, 17; Nashville, TN: T. Nelson, 1989], p. 43) remarks concerning Job 2.3: '...now for the first time it is with a single word explicitly granted that Job has been "smitten for nothing" (חנם)'.

71. John A. Darr, 'Mimetic Desire, the Gospels, and Early Christianity', *BibInt* 1 (1993), pp. 357-67 (362).

72. Girard, *Violence Renounced*, p. 319.

73. Other assessments of Girard include Hent de Vries, *Religion and Violence: Philosophical Perspectives from Kant to Derrida* (Baltimore, MD: The Johns Hopkins University Press, 2002), which some may find to be more permeated by philosophical rhetoric than by historical applications.

Otherwise, Girard's theory is neither as novel as some would think, nor is it as effective empirically in explaining religious violence. There may be some cases where scapegoating provides a good explanation for violence. But Girard misses a more fundamental and persistent mechanism of religious violence—the perception, created by religious belief, of scarce resource that must be maintained or acquired through violence.[74]

Summary

The effort to minimize or eliminate the violent nature of Jesus' atoning self-sacrifice, especially by self-described Christian pacifists, is part of a theological agenda, and not anything that can be shown on historical or linguistic grounds. Even if one does not accept Anselm's view of the reason for why a god-man had to be sacrificed, it is clear that the New Testament is firmly within those Near Eastern traditions that viewed sacrifice as one method to avert divine wrath or to gain a deity's favor.

On the contrary, the New Testament view of atonement represents a retrogression relative to some other Near Eastern cultures that had replaced human death penalties with monetary or animal substitutes. For example, Hittite law systematically replaced death penalties with fines for many offenses. Thus, Law 166 of the Hittite Law Code demanded the death penalty for appropriating another man's farmland. But Law 167 says: 'But now they shall substitute one sheep for the man.'[75] In other words, the very symbol of the Christian substitutionary atonement had a preceding parallel in Hittite law. I do not know of any New Testament scholars celebrating the great ethical advances exemplified by these Hittite legal changes.

For Girard and many advocates of a nonviolent atonement, there is a human trajectory culminating in Jesus' atonement at which point mimetic violence is unmasked and somehow the world is better after that. These 'transformational' views of Jesus' atonement do not match what one observes in history. Violence did not fade away when Christianity spread and grew. As Christianity spread throughout the globe, so did violence, most prominently in the form of slavery. If the Girardian reading of the New Testament is accurate,

---

74. For a full exposition of how scarce resources are related to religious violence, see Avalos, *Fighting Words*.

75. Harry A. Hoffner, *The Laws of the Hittites: A Critical Edition* (Leiden: E.J. Brill, 1997), pp. 133-34. On the humanitarian ideas of the Hittites, see Alfonso Archi, 'L'humanité des Hittites', in *Florilegium Anatolicum: Mélanges offerts à Emmanuel Laroche* (ed. Ekrem Akurgal, Folke Josephson and Emmanuel Laroche; Paris: Boccard, 1979), pp. 37-48. See also Samuel Greengus, 'Some Issues Relating to the Comparability of Laws and Coherence of the Legal Tradition', in *Theory and Method in Biblical and Cuneiform Law: Revision, Interpolation, and Development* (ed. Bernard M. Levinson; Sheffield: Sheffield Academic Press, 1994), pp. 65-72.

then it was missed by most, if not all, those who practiced Christianity. If sacrificial language is somehow transformational, then that transformation is not evident in the last two thousand years of Christian history. Christian pacifists want a Jesus who fulfilled the Hebrew scriptures, except for all of the approved genocidal and biocidal violence found therein. If Christian pacifists truly rejected all violence or violent ideologies, they would reject the Bible itself. In short, there would be no such thing as 'Christian' pacifism.

Chapter 6

THE IMPERIALIST JESUS: WE ARE ALL GOD'S SLAVES

In his book, *The Politics of Jesus* (2006), Obery Hendricks claims that: '[t]he rhetoric of empire certainly is not consistent with the politics of Jesus'.[1] Hendricks is not the only one to make such a claim. Richard Horsley and Warren Carter, among many other prominent names, are also devoted to this anti-imperialist image of Jesus.[2] In this view, Jesus was fully aware of the problems of imperialism presented by the Roman empire in which he lived, and Jesus sought to correct the injustice and social ills that such imperialism wrought. Horsley, for example, remarks that

> [t]rying to understand Jesus' speech and action without knowing how Roman imperialism determined the conditions of life in Galilee and Jerusalem is like trying to understand Martin Luther King without knowing how slavery, reconstruction, and segregation determined the lives of African Americans in the United States.[3]

Since I devoted an entire book to the subject of biblical slavery where I discussed the attitudes of Jesus and other New Testament writers, I will not belabor that subject here.[4] I will make a few remarks about how New Testament scholars have sought to explain away Jesus' acceptance of, or passive stance toward, slavery. This chapter also explains how the portrayal of Jesus

1. Obery Hendricks, *The Politics of Jesus: Rediscovering the True Revolutionary Nature of Jesus' Teachings and How They Have Been Corrupted* (New York: Doubleday, 2006), p. 222.

2. Richard A. Horsley, *Jesus and Empire: The Kingdom of God and the New World Disorder* (Minneapolis: Fortress Press, 2003); Warren Carter, *Matthew at the Margins: A Sociopolitical and Religious Reading* (Maryknoll, NY: Orbis Books, 2000); idem, *Matthew and Empire: Initial Explorations* (Harrisburg, PA: Trinity Press International, 2001). See also Ian E. Rock, *Paul's Letter to the Romans and Roman Imperialism: An Ideological Analysis of the Exordium (Romans 1:1-17)* (Eugene, OR: Pickwick Press, 2012); Joerg Rieger, *Christ and Empire: From Paul to Postcolonial Times* (Minneapolis: Fortress Press, 2007); Lance B. Richey, *Roman Imperial Ideology and the Gospel of John* (Catholic Biblical Quarterly Monograph Series, 283; Washington, DC: Catholic Biblical Association of America, 2007).

3. Horsley, *Jesus and Empire*, p. 13.

4. Avalos, *Slavery*, pp. 96-156.

as an anti-imperialist serves a tried and true apologetic tactic of deflecting attention from the problems and destruction caused by Jesus-inspired Christian empires over the last two thousand years.

This chapter also examines how the promotion of the supposed anti-imperialist Jesus actually betrays a pro-imperialist Christian agenda on the part of biblical scholarship. As Bill Ashcroft and his coauthors observe, the British empire is now largely defunct, but 'cultural hegemony has been maintained through canonical assumptions about literary activity, and through attitudes toward postcolonial literature which identify them as off-shoots of English literature'.[5] Similarly, although Christian empires may no longer be as powerful as they once were, they still exert their cultural hegemony by extolling the ethical and aesthetic superiority of their biblical texts over those of other cultures. Many biblical scholars can be viewed as agents of that effort to maintain Christian cultural hegemony.

To understand this argument, one might begin with what Frederick Douglass, the famous African American abolitionist, saw better than most historians today when it came to the Christian historiography of slavery.

> Now that slavery is no more, and the multitude are claiming the credit of its abolition, though but a score of years have passed since the same multitude were claiming an exactly opposite credit, it is difficult to realize that an abolitionist was ever an object of popular scorn and reproach in this country.[6]

Douglass was commenting on the fact that many Christians who formerly supported slavery began to revise their own history when they joined the abolitionism bandwagon. Instead of admitting that they once supported slavery, many Christians now claimed that they had always been against it. Likewise, many anti-imperialist readings of Jesus and the New Testament may be nothing more than attempts to whitewash the fact that imperialism is so inscribed in the New Testament that later Christian imperialism was simply putting into effect what was there from the beginning.

In terms of literary history, the anti-imperialist view of Jesus is part of a broader trend in biblical studies that focuses on post-colonialist and anti-imperialist readings of the Bible.[7] Historically, this is part of the western

---

5. Bill Ashcroft, Gareth Griffiths and Helen Tiffin (eds.), *The Empire Writes Back: Theory and Practice in Postcolonial Literatures* (London: Routledge, 1989), p. 7.

6. Frederick Douglass, 'Great Britain's Example is High, Noble, and Grand...6 August, 1885', in *The Frederick Douglass Papers: Series One—Speeches, Debates and Interviews* (ed. John W. Blassingame and John R. McKivigan; 5 vols.; New Haven, CT: Yale University Press, 1979–92), V, p. 203. See also J. Byron, 'Paul and the Background of Slavery: The Status Questionis in New Testament Scholarship', *Currents in Biblical Research* 3 (2004), pp. 116-39.

7. For some examples of postcolonial approaches to biblical interpretation, see

response to the continued dismantling of European empires that began in the eighteenth century, and continued with independence movements in Latin American, India and Africa, among other places after World War II. The trend accelerated with the rise of what is called 'liberation theology' in the 1960s and 1970s.[8] In ancient Near Eastern studies, postcolonialist approaches gained some more fervor with the publication of Edward Said's *Orientalism* (1978).[9]

Despite its relatively recent advent, postcolonialist approaches already form a diverse phenomenon.[10] If postcolonialism refers to the socio-political situation that exists after the achievement of formal independence by nations, then the postcolonial experience of countries around the globe has not been uniform, and the achievement of freedom itself spans a variety of historical contexts.[11] In fact, the economic dependency of otherwise

Fernando F. Segovia and R.S. Sugirtharajah (eds.), *A Postcolonial Commentary on the New Testament Writings* (The Bible and Postcolonialism, 13; London: T. & T. Clark, 2007); Fernando Segovia and Stephen D. Moore, *Postcolonial Biblical Criticism: Interdisciplinary Intersections* (Bible and Postcolonialism; London: T. & T. Clark, 2005); R.S. Sugirtharajah, *Postcolonial Criticism and Biblical Interpretation* (New York: Oxford University Press, 2002); idem, *The Bible in Asia: From the Pre-Christian Era to the Postcolonial Age* (Cambridge, MA: Harvard University Press, 2013). See also W.L. Wimbush (ed.), *Theorizing Scripture: New Critical Orientations to a Cultural Phenomenon* (New Brunswick, NJ: Rutgers University Press, 2008); Simon Samuel, *A Postcolonial Reading of Mark's Story* (Library of New Testament Studies, 340; London: T. & T. Clark, 2007); Ronald Charles, 'Q as a Question from a Postcolonial Point of View', *Black Theology* 7 (2009), pp. 182-99.

8. For surveys of liberation theology, see David Tombs, *Latin American Liberation Theology* (Leiden: E.J. Brill, 2003); Hector Avalos, 'Liberation Theology', in *Encyclopedia Latina: History, Culture and Society in the United States* (ed. Ilan Stavans; 4 vols.; Danbury, CT: Grolier, 2005), II, pp. 435-37.

9. Edward Said, *Orientalism* (New York: Vintage Books, 1978). See also Ibn Warraq, *Defending the West: A Critique of Edward Said's Orientalism* (Amherst, NY: Prometheus Books, 2007). For how imperialism affected Judaism, see Seth Schwartz, *Imperialism and Jewish Society, 200 B.C.E. to 640 C.E.* (Princeton, NJ: Princeton University Press, 2001). For a critique of Schwartz, see Yaron Z. Eliav, 'The Matrix of Ancient Judaism: A Review Essay of Seth Schwartz's *Imperialism and Jewish Society 200 B.C.E. to 640 C.E*', *Prooftexts* 24 (2004), pp. 116-28.

10. See the essays in Anna Runesson (ed.), *Exegesis in the Making: Postcolonialism and New Testament Studies* (Biblical Interpretation, 103; Leiden: E.J. Brill, 2011). See also Stephen D. Moore and Yvonne Sherwood, 'After "After Theory", and Other Apocalyptic Conceits', *BibInt* 18 (2010), pp. 1-27; idem, 'The Secret Vices of the Biblical God', *BibInt* 8 (2010), pp. 87-113; idem, 'Biblical Studies "after" Theory', pp. 191-225.

11. Octavio Paz (*Sor Juana* [Cambridge, MA: Harvard University Press, 1988], pp. 14-15), for example, argues that New Spain 'was never a colony' in the same sense as the American colonies. American colonists, argues Paz, came here to escape religious orthodoxy, while in New Spain colonists came to expand orthodoxy.

politically independent nations is a form of colonialism, and so the term 'postcolonial' is a misnomer altogether.[12] Rather the modern world is more akin to the relations between an economically hegemonic core and an economically exploited and dependent periphery outlined by Immanuel Wallerstein.[13]

For the purpose of this book, I define postcolonial literature and scholarship as writings that scrutinize critically the colonial experience, whether past or present.[14] Thus postcolonialism here refers to a state of consciousness that does not accept colonialism as the proper political arrangement. Under this definition the writer may or may not be living in a colonial situation. Colonialism may be seen as any form of social, political or economic subjugation undertaken by a state and its allied institutions.

The rise of anti-imperialist portrayals of Jesus is also part of a reaction against the depoliticized portrayals of other scholars. For example, in his construction of the anti-imperialist Jesus, Horsley remarks that '[w]e can identify at least four major interrelated factors in this construction of a depoliticized Jesus—most recently in the guise of a wisdom teacher'.[15] Horsley is specifically referring to the scholars of the Jesus Seminar who advocate a Jesus resembling 'the vagabond Cynic philosophers, which has so intrigued liberal interpreters recently'.[16] For Horsley, Jesus has been domesticated and his political dimensions erased by scholars who view him as a modern hippie.

The more recent impetus for the anti-imperialist portrayal of Jesus centers on a protest against American imperialism, especially during the presidency of George W. Bush after September 11, 2001. Obery Hendricks, for example, devotes an entire chapter in *The Politics of Jesus* to showing how George W. Bush does not comply with the teachings of Jesus about

12. See Ashcroft *et al.* (eds.), *The Empire Writes Back*, pp. 6-7.

13. Immanuel Wallerstein, *The Modern World System: Capitalist Agriculture and its Origin in the European World-Economy in the Sixteenth Century* (New York: Academic Press, 1974); idem, *The Capitalist World Economy* (Cambridge: Cambridge University Press, 1979). For a critique of Wallerstein's theories as they apply to the ancient Near East, see Norman Yoffee, 'Mesopotamian Interaction Spheres', in *Early Stages in the Evolution of Mesopotamian Civilization: Soviet Excavations in Northern Iraq* (ed. Norman Yoffee and Jeffrey J. Clark; Tucson, AZ: University of Arizona Press, 1993), pp. 257-70.

14. I first proposed this definition in Hector Avalos, 'The Gospel of Lucas Gavilán as Postcolonial Biblical Exegesis', *Semeia* 75 (1996), pp. 87-105 (88). My definition is a variant of the definition offered by Elleke Boehmer (*Colonial and Postcolonial Literature: Migrant Metaphors* [New York: Oxford University Press, 1995], p. 3), who defines postcolonial literature as literature which 'critically scrutinizes the colonial relationship'.

15. Horsley, *Jesus and Empire*, p. 6.

16. Horsley, *Jesus and Empire*, p. 154 n. 6.

social justice.[17] Richard Horsley specifically refers to September 11, 2001 when assailing the idea that one can separate religion and politics.[18] Moreover, Horsley speaks about how 'The United States, an ostensibly Christian country, violates the holy ground of Islam in basing military forces in Saudi Arabia, forces that also prop up the unpopular Saudi regime that oppresses its own people'.[19] Other references suggest that the United States is the modern version of the oppressive Roman empire against which Jesus would struggle if he were alive today.

Rethinking 'Anti-Imperialism'

The most salient problem in seeing Jesus as anti-imperialist is simply the biased definition of 'anti-imperialism' being used by most of these New Testament scholars.[20] Such scholars describe as 'anti-imperialist' statements that seem to attack the Roman empire.[21] Yet, the mere attack on any particular empire does not define one as anti-imperialist. Anti-imperialism should be defined as an ideology that is against any empire, and that is certainly not what Jesus was championing. Attacking the Roman empire in the New Testament is usually for the purposes of replacing it with another empire called the Kingdom of God or the like.

Hans Morgenthau, the famed advocate of political realism, postulated that any entity that seeks a favorable change in power status is, in fact, pursuing an imperialist policy, defensive or not.[22] By extension, those who oppose any empire must seek to replace an opposing empire with their own

---

17. Hendricks, *The Politics of Jesus*, pp. 207-47 (chapter 6). For the observation that anti-imperialist scholarship was particularly vigorous during the administration of George W. Bush, see also Scot McKnight and Joseph B. Modica (eds.), *Jesus is Lord, Caesar is Not: Evaluating Empire in New Testament Studies* (Downers Grove, IL: InterVarsity Press, 2013), p. 19.

18. Horsley, *Jesus and Empire*, p. 8.

19. Horsley, *Jesus and Empire*, p. 4.

20. See Michael G. Smith, 'The Empire of Theory and the Empire of History—A Review Essay', *Christian Scholar's Review* 39 (2010), pp. 305-322. For the idea that 'Kingdom of God' has no single referent, see Norman Perrin, *Jesus and the Language of the Kingdom* (Philadelphia, PA: Fortress Press, 1976).

21. For some important studies of the Roman empire, see Ramsey MacMullen, 'The Power of the Roman Empire', *Historia* 55.4 (2006), pp. 471-81; Arthur M. Eckstein, *Mediterranean Anarchy, Interstate War, and the Rise of Rome* (Hellenstic Culture and Society, 48; Berkeley, CA: University of California Press, 2006); Christopher Kelly, *Ruling the Later Roman Empire* (Cambridge, MA: Harvard University Press, 2004); Jon E. Lendon, *Empire of Honor: The Art of Government in the Roman World* (New York: Oxford University Press, 1997).

22. See Hans Morgenthau, *Politics among Nations: The Struggle for Power and Peace* (ed. Kenneth Thompson; New York: McGraw-Hill, 1993), pp. 50-51.

empire. That is to say, everyone is pursuing a hegemony for their view and that often requires force. Even those who say they want a pluralistic society seek to overthrow a non-pluralistic society. Extending a pluralistic society may require imperialistic actions when opponents do not want to yield peacefully. Similarly, Americans pursuing an abolitionist society eventually required force, as the US Civil War demonstrated.

One can readily see that many of those scholars who claim that Jesus is an anti-imperialist also believe that Jesus intended to replace the Roman empire with the Kingdom of God. In his study of the eschatological politics of Mark, Tat-siong Benny Liew concludes:

> Mark's politics of parousia, by promising the utter destruction of both Jewish and Roman authorities upon Jesus' resurrected return, is one that mimics or duplicates the authoritarian, exclusionary, and coercive politics of his colonizers.[23]

Other scholars are more self-contradictory on the imperialistic nature of the Gospels. Consider these two sentences by D. Michael Cox:

> In sum, Matthew's Gospel embodies resistance to the claims of empire. The theological challenge argues for the sovereignty of the Lord over against the gods of the Romans and the conviction that Jesus, not the emperor, acts as God's anointed agent and the manifestation of divine presence.[24]

In his first sentence, Cox describes Matthew as embodying 'resistance to claims of empire'. But in the very next sentence, Cox speaks of the 'sovereignty of the Lord' and of Jesus being the agent of that sovereign. How is Matthew 'resisting' empire if he champions the 'sovereignty' of his lord? Indeed, Matthew is not against empire at all. Matthew is simply saying that he prefers a different empire, but it is an empire no less because it aims to exert its sovereignty over the world. Matthew prefers Jesus, not the Roman emperor, as the agent of that divinely appointed empire.[25]

---

23. Tat-siong Benny Liew, *Politics of Parousia: Reading Mark Inter(con)textually* (Leiden: E.J. Brill, 1999), pp. 148-49.

24. D. Michael Cox, 'The Gospel of Matthew and Resisting Imperial Theology', *PRSt* 36 (2009), pp. 25-48 (38). See also Joan E. Taylor, 'Pontius Pilate and the Imperial Cult in Roman Judaea', *NTS* 52.4 (2006), pp. 555-82.

25. See further, Barry D. Smith, *Jesus' Twofold Teaching about the Kingdom of God* (New Testament Monographs, 54; Sheffield: Sheffield Phoenix Press, 2009). Smith differentiates two 'historical contexts' (non-rejection and rejection) for Jesus' teachings about the Kingdom of God that he thinks will harmonize those teachings. However, the proposal suffers from the same problem afflicting all claims about the historical Jesus, and that is we have no means of knowing what the historical Jesus thought about anything, and so all claims about the historical Jesus are ultimately circular.

Moreover, most of Christian ethicists never acknowledge the 'anti-imperialist' rhetoric present in authors one usually thinks to be pro-Roman.[26] In a study of the speeches placed in the mouth of the enemy, Eric Adler explores how Polybius, Livy, Tacitus, and other renowned Roman authors expressed a subversive critique of the Roman empire.[27] By placing such criticisms in the mouths of the enemy, the authors can voice criticism, while not ostensibly validating it. One example is from Tacitus's description of the rebellion by a widowed queen of the Celtic Iceni tribe in Britain around 60 or 61 CE. According to Tacitus:

> The Britons began to discuss the evils of slavery, to compare their wrongs, their grievances. Nothing is gained by submission, they argued, except that heavier commands are laid on those who appear to be willing sufferers… On the battlefield it is the braver man who plunders his foe; but under the present circumstances it is largely unwarlike cowards who are stealing their homes, abducting their children, demanding levies from them; as though they can die in any cause except their country's.[28]

If these opinions belong to Tacitus, rather than to the indigenous Celts, then he was calling the Romans cowards, and excoriating them for abusing the indigenous people. In contrast, none of the Gospel writers ever have Jesus or anyone else criticize the genocide and dispossession of the Canaanites.

In another case, Sallust (ca. 86–35/34 BCE), the Roman politician and historian, records the words of Mithridates VI (134–63 BCE), the king of Pontus, who complains: 'Indeed, for the Romans there is a single age-old cause for instigating war on all nations, people, and kings: a deep-seated lust for empire and riches.'[29] One looks in vain for any clear statement from Jesus about the nature of war or the motives for Roman imperialism other than what is couched in terms of his preference for the Kingdom of God. If Jesus deserves high praise for his supposedly anti-imperialism, then New Testament ethicists ought to praise Sallust or Mithridates even more.

---

26. For a study of Mesopotamian anti-imperialism, see Tracy Davenport, 'An Anti-Imperialist Twist to the Gilgameš Epic', in *Gilgameš and the World of Assyria: Proceedings of the Conference at Mandelbaum House, The University of Sydney, 21-23 July 2004* (ed. Joseph Azize and Noel Weeks; Leuven: Peeters, 2007), pp. 1-23.

27. Eric Adler, *Valorizing the Barbarians: Enemy Speeches in Roman Historiography* (Austin, TX: University of Texas Press, 2011).

28. Tacitus, *Agricola* 15.3 (Hutton and Ogilvie, LCL). For a more thorough discussion, see Adler, *Valorizing the Barbarians*, pp. 119-39.

29. Sallust, *Epistula Mithridatis* (*Historiae* 4.69.5). Following the edition in Adler, *Valorizing the Barbarians*, p. 179. The Latin text follows Adler, *Valorizing the Barbarians*, p. 177: 'Namque Romanis cum nationibus populis regibus cunctis una et vetus causa bellandi est: cupido profunda imperi et divitiarum.'

Selective Anti-Imperialism

According to Richard Horsley, Jesus' anti-imperialist project 'pressed a program of social revolution to reestablish just egalitarian and mutually supportive social-economic relations in the village communities that constituted the basic form of people's life'.[30] To showcase Jesus' revolutionary agenda, Horsley provides a catalogue of all the ills that the Roman empire inflicted on the inhabitants it controlled. However, missing from the contrasts between the ideology of Jesus and the ideology of the Roman Empire is any substantive acknowledgment that the Roman empire was not much worse than the biblical visions of God's empire that Jesus' own scriptures highlighted.[31] In so doing, Horsley follows a long Christian apologetic tradition of denigrating non-Christian cultures and extolling the superiority of his own despite very similar practices and concepts.

One example is how Horsley describes Israel as being 'under Empire', by which he refers to domination by the Egyptian, Assyrian, Babylonian, and other empires. Readers are told that after the Exodus,

> the Israelites established an independent life in the hill country of Palestine, led by 'liberators' (*shophetim*) and 'prophets' (*nebi'im*) such as Deborah and Samuel...the freedom-loving Israelites persistently resisted efforts by David and his successors to consolidate power in an imperial monarchy.[32]

Missing from this summary is any mention of how these 'freedom-loving Israelites' were actually the ones who dispossessed and oppressed the indigenous peoples of Canaan.

In fact, every single one of the bad features of the Roman empire listed by Horsley finds a correspondence in Israelite actions toward their own conquered peoples. For example, Horsley speaks of how the Romans 'had a penchant for public display of lists of peoples they had subjected, particularly in remote regions such as Ethiopia, Arabia, and India'.[33] Fair enough, but is that really different from the lists one finds in Joshua 12 of all the indigenous conquered people? Note this passage:

> And these are the kings of the land whom Joshua and the people of Israel defeated on the west side of the Jordan, from Baal-gad in the valley of Lebanon to Mount Halak, that rises toward Seir (and Joshua gave their land to the tribes of Israel as a possession according to their allotments, in the hill country, in the lowland, in the Arabah, in the slopes, in the wilderness, and

---

30. Horsley, *Jesus and Empire*, p. 105.

31. The same may be said of the evaluation of the Roman empire by Klaus Wengst, *Pax Romana and the Peace of Jesus Christ* (trans. John Bowden; Philadelphia, PA: Fortress Press, 1987).

32. Horsley, *Jesus and Empire*, p. 16.

33. Horsley, *Jesus and Empire*, p. 21.

in the Negeb, the land of the Hittites, the Amorites, the Canaanites, the Per-
izzites, the Hivites, and the Jebusites): the king of Jericho, one; the king
of Ai, which is beside Bethel, one; the king of Jerusalem, one; the king of
Hebron, one; the king of Jarmuth, one; the king of Lachish, one; the king
of Eglon, one; the king of Gezer, one; the king of Debir, one; the king of
Geder, one; the king of Hormah, one; the king of Arad, one; the king of
Libnah, one; the king of Adullam, one; the king of Makkedah, one; the king
of Bethel, one; the king of Tappuah, one; the king of Hepher, one; the king
of Aphek, one; the king of Lasharon, one; the king of Madon, one; the king
of Hazor, one; the king of Shimron-meron, one; the king of Achshaph, one;
the king of Taanach, one; the king of Megiddo, one; the king of Kedesh, one;
the king of Jokne-am in Carmel, one; the king of Dor in Naphath-dor, one;
the king of Goiim in Galilee, one; the king of Tirzah, one: in all, thirty-one
kings (Josh. 12.7-24).

Some of these conquests seemingly delight in informing readers that everyone, including women and children, were exterminated, as in the following
account: 'And they put to the sword all who were in it, utterly destroying them; there was none left that breathed, and he burned Hazor with fire'
(Josh. 11.11). Yet, Horsley and other anti-imperialist scholars never seem to
criticize Jesus for not being morally outraged by these genocidal actions in
his scriptures.

Similarly, when alluding to the horrible terror and vengeance practiced
by the Roman empire, Horsley remarks that '[t]here is no way we can
understand such practices as crucifixion, mass slaughter and enslavement,
massacres of whole towns and annihilation of whole peoples other than
as purposeful attempts to terrorize subjected people'.[34] Yet, Jesus generally
upholds the sanctity of biblical texts that also endorse terrorism to dispos-
sess and oppress. For example, in Exodus 23:

> I will send my terror before you, and will throw into confusion all the
> people against whom you shall come, and I will make all your enemies
> turn their backs to you. And I will send hornets before you, which shall
> drive out Hivite, Canaanite, and Hittite from before you. I will not drive
> them out from before you in one year, lest the land become desolate and
> the wild beasts multiply against you. Little by little I will drive them out
> from before you, until you are increased and possess the land (Exod.
> 23.27-30).

Unlike the case of the Romans, whose terroristic purpose Horsley reasonably inferred, the biblical author has no problem explaining that terrorism is
the explicit purpose of these actions against indigenous peoples.

In fact, Rahab, the prostitute at Jericho who aids Joshua, may be seen as
the victim of effective terrorism when she describes why she is willing to
help the conquerors:

---

34. Horsley, *Jesus and Empire*, p. 27.

> Before they lay down, she came up to them on the roof, and said to the men,
> 'I know that the LORD has given you the land, and that the fear of you has
> fallen upon us, and that all the inhabitants of the land melt away before you.
> For we have heard how the LORD dried up the water of the Red Sea before
> you when you came out of Egypt, and what you did to the two kings of the
> Amorites that were beyond the Jordan, to Sihon and Og, whom you utterly
> destroyed. And as soon as we heard it, our hearts melted, and there was no
> courage left in any man, because of you; for the LORD your God is he who
> is God in heaven above and on earth beneath' (Josh. 2.8-11).

And, of course, biblical narratives indicate that more specific acts of brutality such as mutilation (Judg. 1.6-7) and massacres of whole towns (Jericho
on Joshua 6) or peoples (1 Sam. 15.1-3) were part of God's agenda. Otherwise, these actions were accepted without objection. Yet, one never sees
Horsley or other critics of Roman ethics denounce Jesus for not censuring
these acts of terrorism in the scriptures Jesus holds sacred.

The Benign Rhetoric of Imperialism

Many biblical ethicists reference the benign, liberative and peaceful proc-
lamations of Jesus as proof that Jesus is anti-imperialistic. One finds such
claims in the work of Richard Horsley, Seyoon Kim, Ronald Sider, Walter
Wink and John Yoder.[35] Yet all imperialists speak of how their hegemony will bring peace, prosperity and social improvement. Empires usually frame their agendas in benign terms and peaceful terms, and claim
that any violence is defensive or necessary.[36] Even Warren Carter, who
champions the anti-imperialistic view of Jesus, observes that '[i]mpe-
rial rule typically presents itself as benign, especially for its immediate
beneficiaries'.[37]

If one reads the accomplishments recorded in the *Res Gestae* of Caesar
Augustus (reigned 27 BCE–14 CE), we would find at least some of these
benign actions of the emperor being extolled:

> At the age of nineteen on my own responsibility and at my own expense
> I raised an army, with which I successfully championed the liberty of the
> republic when it was oppressed by the tyranny of a faction... I undertook
> many civil and foreign wars by land and sea throughout the world, and as
> victor I spared the lives of all citizens who asked for mercy. When for-
> eign people could safely be pardoned I preferred to preserve rather than to

35. Horsley, *Jesus and the Spiral of Violence*; Seyoon Kim, *Christ and Caesar: The
Gospel and the Roman Empire in the Writings of Paul and Luke* (Grand Rapids, MI:
Eerdmans, 2008); Sider, *Christ and Violence*; Wink, *Jesus and Nonviolence*; Yoder, *The
Politics of Jesus*.

36. See Wengst, *Pax Romana*, especially pp. 19-24.

37. Carter, *Matthew and Empire*, p. 90.

exterminate them…in my eleventh consulship I bought grain with my own money and distributed 12 rations apiece…these largesses of mine never reached fewer than 250,000 persons.[38]

Here we find that some of the benign actions expected of the emperor include mercy, selflessness (taking monetary expenses upon himself), and equality, insofar as his distributions of rations were '12 apiece'. His largesse was massive, reaching no fewer than a quarter of a million people. A merciful Jesus supposedly feeds masses of people just as Caesar claims to do (Mk 6.34-42; 8.1-10).

Christ as Emperor

Joseph D. Fantin recently addressed the question of whether 'Paul's use of κύριος involves a polemic against the living emperor and, by implication, his (and the Roman state's) claim of sovereignty over every aspect of the lives of those under his authority'.[39] Fantin was challenging the view of James D.G. Dunn, who postulates that the application of *kyrios* (κύριος), the Greek word for 'lord' and 'master', to anyone who exercised authority over others was so routine that it posed no threat to the emperor.[40] As Dunn phrases it, 'The sharp antithesis between "Caesar is Lord" and "Christ is Lord"…is not yet in evidence in Paul's time.' Dunn adds that '[i]t is also clear that the attribution of lordship to Jesus could not have been derived from or modeled on the cultic worship of his Hellenistic environment', and he appeals to the use of *mar*, the Aramaic word for Lord in 1 Cor. 16.22, to show the non-Hellenistic origin of the title.[41]

---

38. A. Brunt and J.M. Moore, *Res Gestae Divi Augusti: The Achievements of the Divine Augustus* (London: Oxford University Press, 1967), pp. 19, 25. See also Ronald T. Ridley, *The Emperor's Retrospect: Augustus' Res Gestae in Epigraphy, Historiography, and Commentary* (Dudley, MA: Peeters, 2003); Brian Bosworth, 'Augustus, the *Res Gestae*, and Hellenstic Theories of Apotheosis', *JRS* 89 (1999), pp. 1-18. For a general biography of Augustus, see David Shotter, *Augustus Caesar* (London: Routledge, 2nd edn, 2005). On how Tiberius used starvation as a tactic, see Anthony J. Woodman, 'Tiberius and the Taste of Power: The Year 33 in Tacitus', *ClQ* 56 (2006), pp. 175-89. Tiberius's use of starvation is not that different from Yahweh's tactics: 'You shall serve your enemies whom the LORD will send against you, in hunger and thirst, in nakedness, and in want of all things; and he will put a yoke of iron upon your neck, until he has destroyed you' (Deut. 28.48).

39. Joseph D. Fantin, *The Lord of the Entire World: Lord Jesus, a Challenge to Lord Caesar?* (Sheffield: Sheffield Phoenix Press, 2011), p. 6.

40. James D.G. Dunn, *The Theology of Paul the Apostle* (Grand Rapids, MI: Eerdmans, 1998), p. 247.

41. Dunn, *The Theology of Paul the Apostle*, pp. 247-48.

I have previously suggested that Jesus is very much parallel to the Roman emperor in many of his portrayals.[42] Wilhelm Bousset and other scholars have long held similar opinions.[43] Fantin makes a compelling case that the use of κύριος by Paul had a polemical intent, especially as he claimed that Christ was the supreme lord, and not just any lord. A prime example of such a claim is found in 1 Corinthians:

> For although there may be so-called gods in heaven or on earth—as indeed there are many 'gods' and many 'lords'—yet for us there is one God, the Father, from whom are all things and for whom we exist, and one Lord, Jesus Christ, through whom are all things and through whom we exist (1 Cor. 8.5-6).

Since only Caesar could have the status of supreme lord in the Roman empire, then its use by Paul indicates a challenge to the emperor's claim.

However, even if one does not accept Fantin's claim that Paul was being intentionally polemical, it is clear that Jesus is portrayed as a superior and imperial figure in many New Testament texts. For the moment, it is irrelevant whether such imperial descriptions of Jesus derive from Hellenistic or older Hebrew concepts. What matters is that Jesus does advocate imperialism and that early Christians view him as an imperialist. After all, there is strong evidence that Christians were, at the very least, perceived as preaching that another king had come to rival the Roman emperor. Consider this example in Acts:

> But the Jews were jealous, and taking some wicked fellows of the rabble, they gathered a crowd, set the city in an uproar, and attacked the house of Jason, seeking to bring them out to the people. And when they could not find them, they dragged Jason and some of the brethren before the city authorities, crying, 'These men who have turned the world upside down

42. Avalos, *Slavery*, pp. 141-44. For parallels of Jesus with a wide array of figures, see Craig S. Keener, 'Jesus and Parallel Jewish and Greco-Roman Figures', in *Christian Origins and Greco-Roman Culture: Social and Literary Contexts for the New Testament* (ed. Stanley E. Porter and Andrew W. Pitts; Texts and Editions for New Testament Study, 9; Leiden: E.J. Brill, 2012), pp. 85-111.

43. Wilhelm Bousset, *Kyrios Christos* (trans. John E. Steely; Nashville, TN: Abingdon Press, 5th edn, 1970). See also Loveday Alexander, 'Luke's Political Vision', *Int* 66 (2012), pp. 283-93; Larry W. Hurtado, *Lord Jesus Christ: Devotion to Jesus in Earliest Christianity* (Grand Rapids, MI: Eerdmans, 2003). For an attempt to reconcile Jewish and Christian ideas of a kingly Messiahship, see Shirley Lucas, *The Concept of the Messiah in the Scriptures of Judaism and Christianity* (Library of Second Temple Studies, 78; London: T. & T. Clark, 2011); Karl Bornhäuser, *Jesus imperator mundi (Phil. 3,17-21 und 2,5-12)* (Gütersloh: Bertelsmann, 1938); Adolf Deissmann, *Light from the Ancient East: The New Testament Illustrated by Recently Discovered Texts of the Greco-Roman World* (trans. Lionel R. Strachan; repr., Peabody, MA: Hendrickson, 1995 [1927]), especially pp. 348-63.

have come here also, and Jason has received them; and they are all acting against the decrees of Caesar, saying that there is another king, Jesus'. And the people and the city authorities were disturbed when they heard this (Acts 17.5-8).

The appearance of the dove (as a counterpoint to the Roman eagle) at Jesus' baptism may carry revolutionary overtones.[44] Other statements by early Christians see Christ as an emperor or view Christianity as a type of future or present empire.[45] In Acts 2.30, David prophetically envisions Jesus as one who would inherit 'his throne'. The coming new empire is plainly described by Paul:

> But each in his own order: Christ the first fruits, then at his coming those who belong to Christ. Then comes the end, when he delivers the kingdom to God the Father after destroying every rule and every authority and power. For he must reign until he has put all his enemies under his feet. The last enemy to be destroyed is death. 'For God has put all things in subjection under his feet'. But when it says, 'All things are put in subjection under him', it is plain that he is excepted who put all things under him. When all things are subjected to him, then the Son himself will also be subjected to him who put all things under him, that God may be everything to every one (1 Cor. 15.23-28).

Clearly, many early Christians saw Christ as an emperor, regardless of how Jesus saw himself historically.

So, why are Christians perceived as preaching that Christ is a parallel to the Roman emperor? Perhaps because Christ *is* sometimes patterned very clearly on the Roman emperor or other kings of the ancient Near East.[46] Early Christians addressed Jesus as *kyrios* and *dominus* (in Latin), the very word related to 'domination'. As Fantin points out, κύριος is a relational word that can apply to anyone who holds power over another. Jesus certainly expects that 'lord' entails obedience to him in Lk. 6.46: 'Why do you call me "Lord, Lord", and not do what I tell you?' (Τί δέ με καλεῖτε,

---

44. See Michael Peppard, 'The Eagle and the Dove: Roman Imperial Sonship and the Baptism of Jesus (Mark 1.9-11)', *NTS* 56.4 (2010), pp. 431-51. See also Daniel Johansson, '*Kyrios* in the Gospel of Mark', *JSNT* 33 (2010), pp. 101-124.

45. Joel Willitts, *Matthew's Messianic Shepherd-King: In Search of the Lost Sheep of the House of Israel* (Beihefte für die neutestamentliche Wissenschaft und die Kunde der alteren Kirche, 147; Berlin: W. de Gruyter, 2007), especially p. 108.

46. See Manfred Clauss, *Kaiser und Gott: Herrscherkult im römischer Reich* (Stuttgart and Leipzig: Teubner, 1999); Justin K. Hardin, *Galatians and the Imperial Cult: A Critical Analysis of the First-Century Social Context of Paul's Letter* (Tübingen: Mohr Siebeck, 2008); S.R.F. Price, *Rituals of Power: The Roman Imperial Cult in Asia Minor* (Cambridge: Cambridge University Press, 1985). See also N.T. Wright, *How God Became King: The Forgotten Story of the Gospels* (New York: Harper One, 2012).

Κύριε, κύριε, καὶ οὐ ποιεῖτε ἃ λέγω;).[47] Fantin further notes that earlier emperors, such as Augustus and Tiberius, rejected the term *dominus* for themselves.[48] Nonetheless, even if those early Christians are simply using *kyrios* for a lesser lord, rather than the supreme lord, they still viewed Jesus as exercising power over subordinates. The use of *kyrios* still shows a hierarchical view of Jesus.

Jesus is called the son of God. The Roman emperor is called *divi filius*, the Latin term for the 'son of a god' that is found on the coins of Augustus Caesar before Jesus began his ministry.[49] As Fantin notes, '[i]t has been suggested that *divus* is something less than *deus*. Thus, the Latin *deus* is the equivalent to the Greek θέος (god); *divus* corresponds to θεῖος (divine, from the gods)'.[50] Fantin argues that the Roman idea of 'divine' may not require that the being to whom this designation is applied be an omnipotent monotheistic deity. As he notes, 'if "divine" means that the emperor is comparable to the traditionally worshipped deities in Roman religion, the answer may be different'.[51]

According to most modern understandings of Jn 1.1, Jesus is the Word, and the Word is described as follows: 'In the beginning was the Word, and the Word was with God, and the Word was God' (RSV). If the most common understanding of this verse is viable, then Jesus was regarded as God or as a god by the author of John.[52] Even if one translates the last clause of that verse as 'the Word was divine', then it still would be consistent with how some emperors and other members of the Roman elite were described as achieving a *divus* or divine status.[53] As Fantin remarks, '[o]ther developments especially under Augustus support the notion that the emperor was divine'.[54]

---

47. For the view that this saying is part of Q, and a reliable source for the 'historical Jesus', see Simon J. Joseph, '"Why Do you Call me 'Master'…?" Q646, the Inaugural Sermon, and the Demands of Discipleship', *JBL* 132 (2013), pp. 955-72.

48. Fantin, *Lord of the Entire World*, p. 212.

49. S.R.F. Price, 'Gods and Emperors: The Greek Language of the Roman Imperial Cult', *Journal of Hellenic Studies* 104 (1984), pp. 79-95.

50. Fantin, *Lord of the Entire World*, p. 117.

51. Fantin, *Lord of the Entire World*, p. 120.

52. On the disputes over the meaning of an anarthrous predicate nominative Θεός means 'a god' or just 'divine', see Wallace, *The Basics of New Testament Syntax*, pp. 119-23. On the question of a Hellenistic and/or Semitic origin of the theology of this passage, see David Reed, 'How Semitic was John? Rethinking the Hellenistic Background to John 1:1', *Anglican Theological Review* 85 (2004), pp. 709-26.

53. Fantin (*Lord of the Entire World*, p. 118) cites CIL VI.2099.2.5-6, 2.14 (= CFA 94.2.5-6, 2.14), an inscription from 183 CE that 'mentions that there were sixteen individuals who achieved *divus* status'.

54. Fantin, *Lord of the Entire World*, p. 128.

Jesus demands that followers transfer allegiance from their families to him (Lk. 14.26). This is a very common imperial practice, and many new reigns began with the populace swearing an oath of allegiance to the new king. As mentioned previously, this practice reaches back to ancient Near Eastern kings (e.g., Esarhaddon). These sorts of oaths were also in use during Jesus' lifetime, as is illustrated by a Greek inscription dating to 3 BCE from Paphlagonia:

> I swear by Jupiter, Earth, Sun, by all the gods and goddesses, and by Augustus himself, that I will be loyal to Caesar Augustus and to his children and descendants all my life in word, in deed, and in thought, regarding friends whomever they so regard, and considering as enemies whomever they so adjudge; that in defense of their interests I will spare neither body [σώματος], soul [ψυχῆς], life [βίου], nor children [τέκνων], but will in every way undergo every danger in defense of their interests.[55]

This, of course, is reminiscent of Jesus' demands in Lk. 14.26, where Jesus insists: 'If any one comes to me and does not hate his own father and mother and wife and children [τὰ τέκνα], and brothers and sisters, yes, and even his own life [ψυχὴν], he cannot be my disciple.' As do all good despots, Jesus insists that allegiance to him, even at the cost of one's own life or family, is the supreme act of loyalty. Indeed, Jesus redefined his family as his followers (Mk 3.35, Mt. 10.37, Lk. 14.26).

The *familia caesaris*, the family or household of Caesar, was a very well-developed concept in the Roman empire.[56] The household of Caesar, regarded as the *pater familias*, consisted of slaves, freedmen, as well as officials. Those who had the closest or equal relationships to kings were called 'friends' or 'brothers'. In her summary of anti-imperial rhetoric in the New Testament, Judith Diehl notes that '[t]he emperor became the "Father of the Fatherland" (*pater patriae*), a competing idea to the Jewish and Christian belief that God is the "Father" of all'.[57] Jesus' references to the heavenly and royal Father who has an earthly family and earthly subjects are no less imperialistic than the *familia caesaris*. Just as the emperor wished for his

55. English translation follows Fantin, *Lord of the Entire World*, p. 236. My bracketed insertions of Greek. For the Greek, I depend on *ILS* 8781 = Hermann Dessau, *Inscriptiones Latinae Selectae, Volume 2, Part 2* (Chicago, IL: Ares, 1979), p. 1010.

56. See P.R.C. Weaver, *Familia Caesaris: A Social Study of the Emperor's Freedmen and Slaves* (Cambridge: Cambridge University Press, 1972); Susan Treggiari, 'Domestic Staff at Rome in the Julio-Claudian Period, 27 B.C. to A.D. 68', *Histoire Sociale* 3 (1973), pp. 241-55.

57. Judith A. Diehl, 'Anti-Imperial Rhetoric in the New Testament', in McKnight and Modica (eds.), *Jesus is Lord, Caesar is Not*, pp. 38-81 (44). See also Judith A. Diehl, 'Anti-Imperial Rhetoric in the New Testament', *Currents in Biblical Research* 10.1 (2011), pp. 9-52.

dominion to extend to the entire world, Jesus also wished that his kingdom spread to the entire world.

The Kingdom of God as an Empire

Whether Jesus saw himself as an emperor or not, most scholarship agrees that Jesus sees himself as an agent of the entity known as the Kingdom of God or Kingdom of Heaven.[58] That Kingdom of God/Heaven is portrayed as being just as imperialistic as the Roman empire. Ironically, Warren Carter, who otherwise sees Jesus as an opponent of empire, acknowledges as much:

> The Gospel envisions salvation as the end of this sinful world, the defeat of Rome, and the establishment of a new heaven and earth under God's sovereignty. But the irony must be noted. This bold vision of the completion of God's salvation and overthrow of Roman imperial power co-opts and imitates the very imperial worldview that it resists! For Rome and God, the goal is supreme sovereignty of the most powerful. For both, the scope or extent of their sovereignty is the cosmos. Both appeal to the divine will for legitimation. Both understand the establishment of their sovereignty to be through a chosen agent and by means of the violent overthrow of all resistance. Both offer totalizing perspectives. Both demand compliance. Both destroy enemies without room for the different or the noncompliant. Both recognize that those who welcome its sovereignty benefit from it. The Gospel depicts God's salvation, the triumph of God's empire over all things, including Rome, with the language and symbols of imperial rule.[59]

Despite Carter's admission of the similarity between the Kingdom of God and the Roman empire, he still regards Jesus' views as different and ethically superior.

The best reason that Warren offers for the Gospel's imperialistic rhetoric is that it is simply using the only language that is available. For Carter, the Gospel is framed in imperialistic terms because 'the imperial worldview is so prevalent that even this story of protest against imperial rule cannot escape its own cultural world. It has no other language to use.'[60] The problem with this argument is that one must deny the plain meaning

---

58. For general treatments of the Kingdom of God/Heaven, see Horsley, *Jesus and Empire*; Dennis Duling, 'Kingdom of God, Kingdom of Heaven', *ABD*, IV, pp. 49-69; Wendell Willis, *The Kingdom of God in 20th-Century Interpretation* (Peabody, MA: Hendrickson, 1987); Halvor Moxnes, *The Economy of the Kingdom: Social Conflict and Economic Relations in Luke's Gospel* (Philadelphia, PA: Fortress Press, 1988); George R. Beasley-Murray, *Jesus and the Kingdom of God* (Grand Rapids, MI: Eerdmans, 1986); Bruce D. Chilton, *The Kingdom of God in the Teaching of Jesus* (Philadelphia, PA: Fortress Press, 1984); M. Pamment, 'The Kingdom of Heaven According to the First Gospel', *NTS* 27 (1981), pp. 211-32.

59. Carter, *Matthew and Empire*, p. 89.

60. Carter, *Matthew and Empire*, p. 90.

of the rhetoric in order to extract an opposing meaning. Even if Jesus is using imperialistic language, Carter tells us that Jesus really meant an anti-imperialistic message in those same words.

The apologetic intent of Carter's argument becomes apparent when one realizes that the same can be said of Roman imperialistic language. Why can't one say that the Romans were actually subverting empire by using imperialistic language? Why can't one argue that despite how imperialistic the rhetoric of the Romans may seem, it was really meant to be anti-imperialistic. One can just as well say, as does Carter in the case of the Gospel, that the Roman empire used imperialistic language to express an anti-imperialistic message because '[i]t has no other language to use'.

When Jesus' imperialism is acknowledged it is frequently done so by euphemisms or circumlocutions. Christopher Bryan, who has opposed the more radically political portrayals of Jesus drawn by Horsley, states: 'I believe that Jesus stood foursquare with the biblical and prophetic attitudes toward political and imperial power represented by Nathan, Jeremiah, Daniel and Deutero-Isaiah; he would acknowledge such power, but he would also (and therefore) hold it accountable.'[61] The Hebrew prophets mentioned by Bryan certainly see a worldwide empire under Yahweh's control. Yet, Bryan never describes Jesus as an 'imperialist' as he does others who support imperial power.

The entire idea of a Kingdom of God can be traced back to the Hebrew Bible.[62] As Dale Patrick observes, 'Jesus did not coin the expression Kingdom of God, it was already in circulation during his time'.[63] For example, in 1 Chron. 28.5 one finds this statement: 'And of all my sons (for the LORD has given me many sons) he has chosen Solomon my son to sit upon the throne of the kingdom of the LORD over Israel.' Here, the Septuagint renders the Hebrew מלכות יהוה ('kingdom of the Lord') as βασιλείας κυρίου. In Chronicles, the kingdom of Yahweh basically refers to the worldly territory or to the nation of Israel (cf. Exod. 15.18; 19.6).

The arrival of monotheism, at least by the time of Deutero-Isaiah, was accompanied by the belief that one god created and owned the entire world. In Isaiah 45, for example, one finds an intimate link between creation, ownership, and dominion of the world:

> For thus says the LORD,who created the heavens (he is God!), who formed
> the earth and made it (he established it; he did not create it a chaos, he

---

61. Christopher Bryan, *Render to Caesar: Jesus, the Early Church and the Roman Superpower* (New York: Oxford University Press, 2005), p. 42.

62. See Dale Patrick, 'The Kingdom of God in the Old Testament', in Willis (ed.), *The Kingdom of God*, pp. 67-79. For an earlier treatment, see John Bright, *The Kingdom of God* (Nashville, TN: Abingdon Press, 1953).

63. Patrick, 'The Kingdom of God in the Old Testament', p. 72.

formed it to be inhabited!): 'I am the LORD, and there is no other... By myself I have sworn, from my mouth has gone forth in righteousness a word that shall not return: 'To me every knee shall bow, every tongue shall swear' (Isa. 45.18, 23).

Moreover, Yahweh's favored people or followers will share in the earthly power that God's ownership bestows. Thus, Dan. 7.27 states: 'And the kingdom and the dominion and the greatness of the kingdoms under the whole heaven shall be given to the people of the saints of the Most High; their kingdom shall be an everlasting kingdom, and all dominions shall serve and obey them.'

Isaiah envisions the following for Immanuel (who is identified with Jesus in Mt. 1.21-23): 'Of the increase of his government and of peace there will be no end, upon the throne of David, and over his kingdom, to establish it, and to uphold it with justice and with righteousness from this time forth and for evermore' (Isa. 9.7).[64] Isaiah also envisions a future trajectory in which the entire world will be enslaved to Yahweh and his chosen people:

> But the LORD will have compassion on Jacob and will again choose Israel, and will set them in their own land; and aliens will join them and attach themselves to the house of Jacob. And the peoples will take them and bring them to their place, and the house of Israel will possess them in the LORD's land as male and female slaves; they will take captive those who were their captors, and rule over those who oppressed them (Isa. 14.1-2).

What is described here should best be characterized as pacification through violent means rather than through some benign process. The expectation of a worldwide Kingdom of God continued during the Second Temple Jewish period.[65]

Indeed, an equally important feature is that the arrival of the Kingdom of God entailed horrible violence. The *Testament of Moses*, which John J. Collins dates in its present form to 'about the turn of the eras', announces the following phenomena associated with the arrival of the Kingdom of God:[66]

> Then his kingdom will appear throughout his whole of creation. Then the devil will have an end. Yea, sorrow will be led away with him. Then will be filled the hands of the messenger, who is in the highest places appointed. Yea, he will at once avenge them of their enemies. For the Heavenly One will arise from his kingly throne. Yea, he will go forth from his holy habitation with indignation and wrath on behalf of his sons. And the earth will tremble, even to its ends shall be it shaken. And the high mountains will be

---

64. Peter Stuhlmacher, *Die Geburt des Immanuel: Die Weihnachtsgeschichten aus dem Lukas- und Matthäusevangelium* (Göttingen: Vandenhoeck & Ruprecht, 2005).

65. See John J. Collins, 'The Kingdom of God in the Apocrypha and Pseudepigrapha', in Willis (ed.), *The Kingdom of God*, pp. 81-95.

66. Collins, 'The Kingdom of God in the Apocrypha and Pseudepigrapha', p. 89.

made low. Yea, they will be shaken, as enclosed valleys will they fall. The sun will not give light. And in darkness the horns of the moon will flee. Yea, they will be broken in pieces... For God Most High will surge forth, the Eternal One alone. In full view will he come to work vengeance on the nations. Yea, all their idols will he destroy. Then you will be happy, O Israel! And you will mount up above the necks and wings of an eagle. Yea, all things will be fulfilled. And God will raise you to the heights. Yea, he will fix you firmly in heaven of the stars, in the place of their habitations. And you will behold from on high. Yea, you will see your enemies on the earth (*T. Mos.* 10.1-10).[67]

Of course, this cosmic upheaval accompanying the Kingdom of God also reaches back to Near Eastern theophanies, such as those of Baal.

Given such a history, it would not be surprising if any historical Jesus had assimilated and used such violent and imperialistic concepts of the Kingdom of God. Indeed, there are numerous passages, especially in Matthew, in which Jesus seems to have no trouble assuming an imperialistic view of the Kingdom of God. For example, in the Matthean version of the Lord's prayer, one reads: 'Thy kingdom come. Thy will be done, On earth as it is in heaven' (Mt. 6.10). The desire of any emperor is that his or her will be done in whatever area is deemed to be the emperor's property or domain. Accordingly, Jesus' view of the ruler of the Kingdom of God does not differ from what Augustus Caesar or Esarhaddon might want. Doing the will of the divine emperor is important to Jesus: 'Not every one who says to me, "Lord, Lord", shall enter the kingdom of heaven, but he who does the will of my Father who is in heaven' (Mt. 7.21).

The fact that Jesus sees himself as an agent of this empire is apparent when he speaks to Simon Peter: 'I will give you the keys of the kingdom of heaven, and whatever you bind on earth shall be bound in heaven, and whatever you loose on earth shall be loosed in heaven' (Mt. 16.19). If Jesus does designate himself as 'the Son of Man', then he also speaks of himself as the regent of that Kingdom of God: 'Truly, I say to you, there are some standing here who will not taste death before they see the Son of man coming in his kingdom' (Mt. 16.28). Note that, when referring to the Son of God, Jesus speaks of 'his kingdom' (τῇ βασιλείᾳ αὐτοῦ). Jesus further compares the Kingdom of Heaven directly to 'a king who wished to settle accounts with his servants' (Mt. 18.23).

The Kingdom of Heaven is compared to a king again in Mt. 22.2: 'the kingdom of heaven may be compared to a king who gave a marriage feast for his son'. However, in this example, Jesus has no ethical problems with a king who decides to burn an entire city to punish a few murderers who come from that city. According to Mt. 22.7: 'The king was angry, and he sent his troops and destroyed those murderers and burned their city.' These sorts of

---

67. Following *OTP*, I, pp. 931-32.

retributive actions are not that different from what the Roman emperor did with Jerusalem or from what Esarhaddon did with cities where violators of his treaties lived.

As previously noted, all divine kings have human agents, just like every other empire sponsored by a deity in the ancient world. A full-fledged violent imperialist is certainly depicted in Revelation:

> Then I saw heaven opened, and behold, a white horse! He who sat upon it is called Faithful and True, and in righteousness he judges and makes war. His eyes are like a flame of fire, and on his head are many diadems; and he has a name inscribed which no one knows but himself. He is clad in a robe dipped in blood, and the name by which he is called is The Word of God. And the armies of heaven, arrayed in fine linen, white and pure, followed him on white horses. From his mouth issues a sharp sword with which to smite the nations, and he will rule them with a rod of iron; he will tread the wine press of the fury of the wrath of God the Almighty. On his robe and on his thigh he has a name inscribed, King of kings and Lord of lords (Rev. 19.11-16).

When Christian apologists are confronted with such imperialist passages, one recourse is 'representativism', or the claim that only some texts in the canon represent Jesus' true teachings. For example, Hendricks argues that the book of Revelation is not representative of Jesus' teachings when he remarks: 'I don't mean the scary, vengeful Book of Revelation Jesus who fire-and-brimstone preachers claim will burn up everyone except the Elect'.[68]

I don't argue that Revelation is representative of all early Christians. I do affirm that selecting Revelation as representative of Jesus' teachings is no less arbitrary than selecting Matthew or Mark. That is to say, how was it determined that the author of Revelation was not transmitting any ideas that the historical Jesus had? As demonstrated by the Dead Sea Scrolls and other Second Temple texts, violent apocalyptic rhetoric was certainly available in the time of Jesus, and so why could Jesus not have used it?

In any case, there are sufficient similarities in the crucial features (divine origin or character; demand of all encompassing allegiance; threats of violence for violators of his empire) of an emperor and those ascribed to Jesus in the New Testament to conclude that he was viewed as a sort of emperor or viewed himself as an agent of an empire called the Kingdom of God or the Kingdom of Heaven.

Even if Jesus did not see himself as an emperor, he certainly can be seen as an agent or advocate of imperialism. What Jesus was presumably advocating was no less imperialistic than the Roman empire when he spoke of the Kingdom of God.

68. Hendricks, *The Politics of Jesus*, p. 3.

Spiritualizing Imperialism

Spiritualizing the Kingdom of God refers to efforts to describe that Kingdom as a non-political entity, and as some sort of realm wherein the activities of that kingdom are undertaken through completely peaceful or spiritual means. For example, Seyoon Kim's *Christ and Caesar* (2008) responds to Richard Horsley and other advocates of more politically oriented anti-imperialist views of Jesus.[69] For Kim, Christ's kingship is purely soteriological and spiritual, and has no political or military connotations in the real world.

In general, Kim follows a representativist approach in *Christ and Caesar* that entails picking some texts as representative of the real Jesus. At the same time, Kim perpetuates the claim that being against the Roman empire is the same as being against imperialism. As I have argued, being against the Roman empire does not constitute proof of anti-imperialism, which is a term that should refer to being against empires in any form. Early Christians simply yearned to replace the Roman empire with their empire.[70] Even Kim acknowledges, 'Luke makes it clear that the Empire of Rome and the lordship of Caesar are to be replaced by the Kingdom of God and the Lordship of Jesus Christ'.[71] According to Kim, this empire is realized by 'healing the sick, restoring sinners to God, and building a community of love and service'.[72] However, Kim simply reproduces the rhetoric of all empires, which tend to see their mission as benign (à la *Res Gestae*).

Kim does not appreciate the fact that even in Luke, which Kim sees as a paradigm of New Testament Christology, Jesus may be seen as an advocate of 'deferred violence' because Jesus can command pacificism for the moment on the premise that he will return to violently avenge his followers (cf. Mt. 25.41-45). In Luke, Christ is to return in 'power and great glory' (Lk. 21.27), and he has no healing in mind for those who destroyed Jerusalem. A plain reading of Luke 21 should suffice to determine if real or spiritual retribution is meant:

> Then let those who are in Judea flee to the mountains, and let those who are inside the city depart, and let not those who are out in the country enter it; for these are days of vengeance, to fulfil all that is written. Alas for those who are with child and for those who give suck in those days! For great distress shall be upon the earth and wrath upon this people; they will fall by the edge of the sword, and be led captive among all nations; and Jerusalem will be trodden down by the Gentiles, until the times of the Gentiles are fulfilled (Lk. 21.21-24).

69. Kim, *Christ and Caesar*, pp. xiv, 21-24.

70. For a study of other Jewish voices seeking to overthrow the Romans, see Kenneth Atkinson, 'Anti-Roman Polemics in the Dead Sea Scrolls and Related Literatures: Their Later Use in John's Apocalypse', *Qumran Chronicle* 12 (2004), pp. 109-22.

71. Kim, *Christ and Caesar*, p. 191.

72. Kim, *Christ and Caesar*, p. 193.

The fact that Jesus sees these events as 'days of vengeance, to fulfil all that is written' shows that healing is far from his mind here. Luke suggests Jesus will return as a king, whose normal functions involve violent intervention on behalf of his followers. Jesus' view of revenge is really not that different from that of other imperialists past or present.

Romans 13.1-7: Imperialism is Godly

According to Kim, Rom. 13.1-7 'is the Achilles' heel for all anti-imperial readings of Paul'.[73] While I concentrate on the portrayal of Jesus as an imperialist in the Gospels, it is important to address the challenges to anti-imperialist readings of Jesus posed by this passage, which reads:

> Let every person be subject to the governing authorities. For there is no authority except from God, and those that exist have been instituted by God. Therefore he who resists the authorities resists what God has appointed, and those who resist will incur judgment.
>
> For rulers are not a terror to good conduct, but to bad. Would you have no fear of him who is in authority? Then do what is good, and you will receive his approval, for he is God's servant for your good. But if you do wrong, be afraid, for he does not bear the sword in vain; he is the servant of God to execute his wrath on the wrongdoer. Therefore one must be subject, not only to avoid God's wrath but also for the sake of conscience. For the same reason you also pay taxes, for the authorities are ministers of God, attending to this very thing. Pay all of them their dues, taxes to whom taxes are due, revenue to whom revenue is due, respect to whom respect is due, honor to whom honor is due (Rom. 13.1-7).

If Paul represents faithfully any early teaching of Jesus, then this teaching clearly does not show an anti-imperialistic orientation for Jesus. If anything, the author seems to fully support all sorts of empires.

At the same time, Kim uses that passage to show that Christ's kingdom could not have been understood as an earthly kingdom or in political terms. In Kim's own words:

> It is indeed remarkable that even while proclaiming the risen Lord Jesus' present and future reign as the Davidic Messiah over the nations (1.3-5; 15.12), Paul enjoins Christians to be subject to the Roman authorities, to honor them as 'ministers of God', and to pay taxes to them (13.1-7)... Paul does not speak at all of the Messiah's political reign, but rather emphatically presents Jesus' messianic work in terms of the eschatological act of redemption that consisted in his death of vicarious atonement for sins... Paul understands Jesus' Davidic Messiahship no longer in the traditional Jewish sense of political reign over nations but in a transformed sense of

---

73. Kim, *Christ and Caesar*, p. 36.

the reign of redemption from the powers of sin and death (cf. 2 Cor. 5.14-17, 21).[74]

Kim's discussion overlooks the flaws in the dichotomy between a spiritual and an earthly kingdom. It is indeed a false dichotomy because both could be synthesized.

One can see that Paul is not deleting real violence from his view of the Kingdom of Christ or God. In Romans 1, Paul laments the lack of proper worship to his god. Paul explains that idolatry was rampant: 'Claiming to be wise, they became fools, and exchanged the glory of the immortal God for images resembling mortal man or birds or animals or reptiles' (Rom. 1.22-23). In the next chapter, which Kim barely mentions at all, Paul describes what awaits those who do not repent.[75]

> We know that the judgment of God rightly falls upon those who do such things. Do you suppose, O man, that when you judge those who do such things and yet do them yourself, you will escape the judgment of God? Or do you presume upon the riches of his kindness and forbearance and patience? Do you not know that God's kindness is meant to lead you to repentance? But by your hard and impenitent heart you are storing up wrath for yourself on the day of wrath when God's righteous judgment will be revealed. For he will render to every man according to his works: to those who by patience in well-doing seek for glory and honor and immortality, he will give eternal life; but for those who are factious and do not obey the truth, but obey wickedness, there will be wrath and fury. There will be tribulation and distress for every human being who does evil, the Jew first and also the Greek, but glory and honor and peace for every one who does good, the Jew first and also the Greek. For God shows no partiality. All who have sinned without the law will also perish without the law, and all who have sinned under the law will be judged by the law (Rom. 2.2-12).

So, yes, God will save those who worship Him, but for those who do not 'there will be wrath and fury' (ὀργὴ καὶ θυμός). In addition, there will be tribulation and distress (θλῖψις καὶ στενοχωρία) for all the unrepentant.

None of this violence seems solely spiritual or figurative, but rather part of a sort of imperialistic project that would affect real people on this earth. For example, the combination of 'wrath and fury' also occurs in Rev. 19.15: 'From his mouth issues a sharp sword with which to smite the nations, and

---

74. Kim, *Christ and Caesar*, pp. 18-19.

75. Kim (*Christ and Caesar*, pp. 17-18) cites Romans 2 only twice in his scriptural index. In the first citation, on page 17, he includes Romans 2 in a scriptural range where 'Paul polemicizes against the Jewish (2.1–3.20; 3.27-30) rather than the Roman imperialistic hubris'. In the second citation, on p. 18, Kim is actually citing a quote from N.T. Wright (*Paul: In Fresh Perspective* [Minneapolis: Fortress Press, 2005], p. 77), which aims to show that 'the Jews share equally' in pagan practices. Kim never addresses the real violence seemingly promised to the unrepentant in Romans 2.

he will rule them with a rod of iron; he will tread the wine press of the fury of the wrath of God the Almighty' (καὶ αὐτὸς πατεῖ τὴν ληνὸν τοῦ οἴνου τοῦ Θυμοῦ τῆς ὀργῆς τοῦ Θεοῦ τοῦ παντοκράτορος). If that does not describe a violent imperialistic agenda, then what does? And what Paul describes in Romans 2 does not differ much from what is described in Revelation 19.

Indeed, Kim comments that in Revelation 19, 'Christ is the agent of God who establishes God's kingship on earth'.[76] If that is the case, then why does Paul's description of God's judgment sound so much like that of Revelation, whose author even Kim acknowledges as speaking of establishing Christ's kingdom on earth? Accordingly, Kim has not demonstrated that Paul's notion of the Kingdom of Christ is 'no longer in the traditional Jewish sense of political reign over nations but in a transformed sense of the reign of redemption from the powers of sin and death'.[77] Indeed, Paul does not speak only of salvation from the powers of sin and death. In Rom. 5.9, he says: 'Since, therefore, we are now justified by his blood, much more shall we be saved by him from the wrath of God' (σωθησόμεθα δι᾽ αὐτοῦ ἀπὸ τῆς ὀργῆς).[78] Paul seeks salvation also from the coming violence that God, as the Supreme Lord, will mete out to the unrepentant. Here, God does not differ at all from what an earthly lord would do to rebellious subjects.

What Kim apparently overlooks is that both spiritual and realistic views of God's dominion could co-exist. There need not be a stark dichotomy between a spiritual Kingdom of God and a political one that affects human beings on earth in some way. Even today, for example, Muslim Jihadists believe that there is a heavenly paradise and also an earthly kingdom for Allah. For these jihadists, the United States is the Great Satan that must be fought in a sort of apocalyptic battle, but also as a real political entity. Salvation consists of gaining entrance to paradise, but also of freedom from the real pagan practices that afflict Muslims around the world.

Why was Jesus not More Vocal against Slavery?

I devoted an entire book to the subject of slavery, including Jesus' attitudes toward it, and so I will not rehearse that topic here.[79] I will address the more relevant argument of why Jesus, the supposedly radical egalitar-

---

76. Kim, *Christ and Caesar*, p. 194.

77. Kim, *Christ and Caesar*, p. 19.

78. The RSV has added 'of God', which is not in the Greek text, after 'wrath'.

79. For another slightly skeptical and critical view of Jesus' (more precisely, Luke's) attitudes toward slavery, see Elizabeth V. Dowling, 'Luke–Acts: Good News for Slaves?', *Pacifica: Journal of the Melbourne College of Divinity* 24 (2011), pp. 123-40 (140).

ian and anti-imperialist thinker, did not speak up against slavery as explicitly and as forcefully as he could have. The common apologetic answer is that Jesus and other New Testament figures did not wish to appear too radical in their social agendas. Ben Witherington cites with approval the rationale Ralph P. Martin offers for Christianity's seeming apathy toward abolition: 'That would have required revolution, which in turn would have been a violation of the teaching of Jesus regarding nonviolence. In other words, it was not a legitimate moral option, never mind an effective or practical option for a tiny minority sect.'[80]

Richard Horsley goes much further in his explanation for why Christianity was not more vocal against slavery:

> Finally, over against apologists for Christianity working from liberal individualistic perspectives and assumptions, it must be recognized that taking a stand in favor of abolishing slavery in Greek and Roman antiquity would not have occurred to anyone. Slavery was part and parcel of the whole political-economic religious structure. The only way even of imagining a society without slavery would have been to imagine a different society.[81]

These rationales are not only incoherent with other statements about the revolutionary nature of Christianity, but also flounder when we consider other facts.

First, it is not necessarily true that requiring abolition, at least from Christians, would have necessitated some revolution or violence.[82] The Quakers required their members to give up slavery in America in the late eighteenth century. There was resistance, but not much revolution or violence within Quakerism. Christianity need not have required non-Christians to abolish slavery. It could have had an ethical impact if it even just prevented its own members from having slaves. After all, there was no Roman law that said Christians were *required* to have slaves.

Again, Paul had no trouble demanding that people stop being drunks and adulterers, which would require a social revolution, as we found out with prohibition in the United States. Lester Scherer acutely observed the relative

---

80. Ben Witherington, *The Letters to Philemon, the Colossians, and Ephesians: A Socio-Rhetorical Commentary on the Captivity Epistles* (Grand Rapids, MI: Eerdmans, 2007), p. 51 n. 2. See also Ralph P. Martin, *Ephesians, Colossians, and Philemon* (Atlanta, GA: John Knox Press, 1991), p. 138.

81. Richard A. Horsley, 'The Slave Systems of Classical Antiquity and their Reluctant Recognition by Modern Scholars', in *Slavery in Text and Interpretation* (ed. Allen D. Callahan, Richard A. Horsley and Abraham Smith; Semeia, 83/84; Atlanta, GA: Scholars Press, 1998), pp. 19-66 (59).

82. For similar conclusions, see Margaret Davies, 'Work and Slavery in the New Testament: Impoverishment of Traditions', in *The Bible in Ethics: The Second Sheffield Colloquium* (ed. John W. Rogerson, Margaret Davies and M. Daniel Carroll R.; JSOTSup, 207; Sheffield: Sheffield Academic Press, 1995), pp. 315-47 (346).

importance that Christians placed on slavery when compared to alcoholism and sexual conduct in his study of antebellum American churches: 'Self-proclaimed and widely recognized as the nation's "conscience" the churches appeared to be saying that drinking whiskey or enjoying sex without marriage was more scandalous than holding slaves.'[83]

Second, at least some early Christian beliefs were known to be revolutionary, and that did not stop Christians from continuing to voice those beliefs. Consider Acts 17.7 where Christians are described as 'acting against the decrees of Caesar, saying that there is another king, Jesus'. What could be more revolutionary than proclaiming that there was another emperor besides Caesar? By definition, the overthrow or substitution of another emperor would be 'revolutionary'. Yet, we are supposed to believe that not allowing Christians to hold slaves was too revolutionary.

If Seyoon Kim is correct, and these passages in Acts simply represent false charges of sedition, we can still find other instances where Jesus and early Christians clearly knew their teachings would generate social conflict.[84] Acts does not portray Paul as stopping his mission because his message was upsetting Jewish communities. Jesus says (Mt. 10.34-37) his purpose was to bring conflicts to families, the principal mode of human organization. Early Christians are portrayed as willing and able to upset the social order in many ways, and so slavery, one of the greatest of human tragedies, should have been challenged even more.

Third, Horsley's claim that abolition 'would not have occurred to anyone' is refuted by the existence of groups who were advanced ethically enough to eliminate slavery from their group. There is evidence that Locris and Phocis in ancient Greece prohibited slavery.[85] Philo tells us that among the Essenes,

> not a single slave [δοῦλος] is to be found among them, but all are free, exchanging services with each other, and they denounce the owners of slaves, not merely for their injustice in outraging the law of equality, but also for their impiety in annulling the statute of Nature, who mother-like has born and reared all men alike, and created them genuine brothers, not in mere name, but in every reality, though this kinship has been put to confusion by the triumph of malignant covetousness, which has wrought estrangement instead of affinity and enmity instead of friendship.[86]

---

83. Lester B. Scherer, *Slavery and the Churches in Early America* (Grand Rapids, MI: Eerdmans, 1976), p. 158.

84. Kim, *Christ and Caesar*, pp. 75-76.

85. Glenn R. Morrow, *Plato's Laws of Slavery in its Relation to Greek Law* (repr., New York: Arno Press, 1976 [1939]), p. 130 n. 8.

86. Philo, *Omn. Prob. Lib.* 79 (Colson, LCL).

Clearly the idea of abolition, or at least not having slaves, had occurred to a number of people. Before Christianity, there were already groups who were much more vocal in their denunciations of slavery. They already were appealing to a 'higher' law rather than expediency. The Essenes seemed to have no fear of 'revolution' in requiring that their own members be slave-free or by denouncing non-members who were slaveholders.

Fourth, these apologists seem to believe that Jesus demanded nonviolence, when he did not. As noted, in Mt. 10.34, Jesus says: 'Do not think that I have come to bring peace on earth; I have not come to bring peace, but a sword.' As I argued earlier, interpretations that labor to render this logion as figurative, or to read it as expressing a result rather than the purpose of Jesus' mission, are no more plausible than readings that take Jesus more literally.

Fifth, and contrary to Horsley, imagining a different society was very much alive in the ancient Near East and in the Bible. Horsley himself says that Paul 'had been commissioned to organize communities as beachheads of the alternative society that would come fully into existence at the parousia of Christ'.[87] After all, apocalyptic biblical literature is all about imagining different, and often utopian, societies. What is the book of Revelation if not the imagining of a different society? Plato's *Republic* is the imagining of a different society. Yet, the fact that Jesus or the New Testament could not imagine a society free of slavery should be seen as an indictment of a corpus for which radical egalitarianism is claimed.

Finally, it seems that these apologists want to have it both ways. On the one hand, they want to credit Jesus for introducing a revolutionary new ethical system, and yet they want to deny that Jesus could be revolutionary when it came to slavery. Apologists want to credit Jesus with energizing abolition movements, some of which were quite violent, and yet shy away from saying that Jesus and Christianity should have done the same thing earlier.

Summary

An anti-imperialist should designate someone who is against all empires, whether human or divine. Scholars are also cognizant of the range of views of the Kingdom by different New Testament writers.[88] However, New Testament ethicists routinely overlook the extent to which New Testament authors portray Jesus' Kingdom of God as an imperialistic project. The

---

87. Richard A. Horsley, 'Paul and Slavery: A Critical Alternative to Recent Readings', in Callahan, Horsley and Smith (eds.), *Slavery in Text and Interpretation*, pp. 153-200 (190).

88. For example, Perrin, *Jesus and the Language of the Kingdom*.

Kingdom of God is envisioned as an empire more powerful than any known on earth. Jesus is portrayed as an agent of that empire and as an enthusiastic champion of it. Therefore, Jesus cannot be characterized as anti-imperialist. Jesus' imperialistic ideology explains his lenient or approving attitude toward slavery, which influenced the spread of slavery in Christianity.

Chapter 7

THE ANTI-JEWISH JESUS:
SOCIO-RHETORICAL CRITICISM AS APOLOGETICS

In 1998, Howard Clark Kee, a widely respected New Testament scholar, and Irvin J. Borowsky, founder of the American Interfaith Institute, edited a volume titled, *Removing the Anti-Judaism from the New Testament*. The book was prompted by the belief that anti-Jewish statements in the New Testament or by later Christian interpreters have led to violence against Jews. Borowsky himself says so:

> Publishers readily agree that anti-Semitism is anti-Christian madness and yet consciously or subconsciously leave unchanged the anti-Judaism in Bibles and Sunday School curricula that was written decades ago. **The stakes are high. People have been murdered because of these words.**[1]

Whether it be Chrysostom in the fourth century, Martin Luther in the sixteenth, or Rudolf Kittel in the twentieth, one can trace a steady stream of anti-Judaism in Christian thought and culture. Yet, few New Testament ethicists wish to admit that such vehement anti-Jewish rhetoric within Christianity had its origin with Jesus, the putative founder of Christianity itself. And despite the dangers that Borowsky believes are posed by the anti-Judaism of Jesus or other Christian figures in the New Testament, he proposes the following:

> The solution to erasing this hatred is for bible societies and religious publishers to produce two editions, one for the public similar to the Contemporary English Version which reduces significantly this anti-Judaic potential, and the other edition for scholars taken from the Greek text.[2]

What is being proposed here is nothing short of a paternalistic deception. Borowsky and like-minded scholars believe that parts of the New Testament

---

1. Howard Clark Kee and Irvin J. Borowsky (eds.), *Removing the Anti-Judaism from the New Testament* (repr., Philadelphia, PA: American Interfaith Institute/World Alliance, 2000 [1998]), p. 20; Borowsky's bold emphasis. See also Frederick B. Davis, *The Jew and Deicide: The Origins of an Archetype* (Lanham, MD: University Press of America, 2003).

2. Kee and Borowsky, *Removing the Anti-Judaism*, p. 18.

endorse and promote hateful and violent speech against Jews, but instead of denouncing the ethics of Jesus and other New Testament Christian voices, they simply want to revise the ethics expressed, at least for the *hoi polloi*. The masses will get the sanitized Bible constructed for them by scholars, and only scholars will have the version that best corresponds to the original meaning.

Historically, all such efforts to address the anti-Judaism in the New Testament received new impetus because of the Nazi Holocaust.[3] Many scholars, and particularly Jewish scholars, rightly noted that the long history of anti-Judaism could not be dismissed as part of the causal chain that led to the Nazi Holocaust. Among historians, this position can be traced as far back as the works of Guenter Lewy and Gordon Zahn.[4] Principal current representatives of this position are Richard Steigmann-Gall and Daniel Goldhagen.[5]

Within biblical scholarship proper, one finds two basic positions concerning the historical responsibility for Christian anti-Judaism.[6] One position argues that any anti-Judaism is primarily the product of post-biblical Christian interpretation. Representative scholars include Paul Gager and Paula Fredriksen. The other position argues that anti-Judaism is already present in the New Testament writings. Amy-Jill Levine and Adele Reinhartz, for example, explore how the Gospels bear some responsibility for the anti-Judaism of later Christianity. I will argue more emphatically that anti-Judaism can be traced back to Jesus himself, at least as he is portrayed in the Gospels.

3. Alan T. Davies, *Anti-Semitism and the Christian Mind: The Crisis of Conscience after Auschwitz* (New York: Paulist Press, 1969); Daniel F. Moore, *Jesus, an Emerging Jewish Mosaic: Jewish Perspectives, Post Holocaust* (Jewish and Christian Texts in Contexts and Related Studies, 2; London: T. & T. Clark, 2011); Geza Vermes, *Jesus, the Jew: A Historian's Reading of the Gospels* (London: William Collins Sons & Co., 1973).

4. Guenter Lewy, *The Catholic Church and Nazi Germany* (New York: McGraw-Hill, 1964); Gordon Zahn, *German Catholics and Hitler's Wars: A Study in Social Control* (New York: Sheed and Ward, 1962). See also Dan Jaffé, *Jésus sous le plume des historiens juifs du XXᵉ siècle: Approche historique, perspectives historiographiques, analyses méthodologiques* (Paris: Cerf, 2009); Lars Kierspel, *The Jews and the World in the Fourth Gospel: Parallelism, Function and Context* (WUNT, 2.220; Tübingen: Mohr Siebeck, 2006); Anthony Le Donne, 'The Quest for the Historical Jesus: A Revisionist History through the Lens of Jewish-Christian Relations', *Journal for the Study of the Historical Jesus* 10 (2012), pp. 63-86.

5. Richard Steigmann-Gall, *The Holy Reich: Nazi Conceptions of Christianity, 1919–1945* (Cambridge: Cambridge University Press, 2003); Daniel Jonah Goldhagen, *Hitler's Willing Executioners: Ordinary Germans and the Holocaust* (New York: Vintage Books, 1997).

6. See Fredriksen and Reinhartz (eds.), *Jesus, Judaism, and Christian Anti-Judaism*, pp. 4-5.

Otherwise, one can identify at least three approaches to New Testament anti-Judaism, which I summarize succinctly as follows:[7]

1. Censorship, which refers to either decanonizing offensive texts or revising the translations. This is what Borowsky has in mind.
2. Attacking the historical accuracy of the polemic. Thus, the historical scribes and Pharisees were more benign and less greedy than portrayed. Sjef van Tillborg's *The Jewish Leaders in Matthew* (1972) would represent one scholar in this camp.[8]
3. Revising the identity of 'the Jews', which really refers to some more select group such as the Pharisees or Judaizing Christians. One example is Harvey Falk's *Jesus the Pharisee: A New Look at his Jewishness* (1985).[9]

I will not enter too deeply into the extensive debate about the meaning of 'Jews' in the New Testament. According to James A. Sanders, *hoi Ioudaioi*, the phrase most literally translated as 'the Jews', occurs about 192 times in the New Testament, with 71 of those occurrences in John, and 16 in the Synoptic Gospels.[10] Suffice it to say that some scholars are concerned about the use of translation to conceal anti-Judaism. Ruth Sheridan remarks: 'I am concerned about other more accommodating and conciliatory translations of οἱ Ἰουδαῖοι that may obscure the harsh anti-Judaism of the text, as though the "rights" of the text need to be defended or protected.'[11] For my

---

7. I am adapting the categories described by Luke T. Johnson, 'The New Testament's Anti-Jewish Slander and the Conventions of Ancient Polemic', *JBL* 108 (1989), pp. 419-41 (421-22).

8. Sjef van Tillborg, *The Jewish Leaders in Matthew* (Leiden: E.J. Brill, 1972). See also Ruth Sheridan, 'Issues in the Translation of οἱ Ἰουδαῖοι in the Fourth Gospel', *JBL* 132 (2013), pp. 671-95; Douglas R.A. Hare, *The Theme of Jewish Persecution of Christians in the Gospel According to St. Matthew* (Cambridge: Cambridge University Press, 1967); Donald A. Carson, 'The Jewish Leaders in Matthew's Gospel: A Reappraisal', *JETS* 25 (1982), pp. 161-74; Judson R. Shaver, 'Christian Anti-Semitism: Tracing the Roots to the Gospel', *Church* 20 (2004), pp. 15-19.

9. Harvey Falk, *Jesus the Pharisee: A New Look at his Jewishness* (New York: Paulist Press, 1985). See also Judith M. Lieu, *Christian Identity in the Jewish and Greco-Roman World* (New York: Oxford University Press, 2006).

10. James A. Sanders, 'The Hermeneutics of Translation', in Kee and Borowsky (eds.), *Removing the Anti-Judaism from the New Testament*, pp. 43-62 (59). See also Paul Spilsbury, *The Image of the Jew in Flavius Josephus' Paraphrase of the Bible* (Texte un Studien zum antiken Judentum; Tübingen: Mohr Siebeck, 1998); Steve Mason, 'Jews. Judaeans, Judaizing, Judaism: Problems of Categorization in Ancient History?', *JSJ* 38 (2007), pp. 457-512. For a diaporic approach to Jewish identity, see Ronald Charles, *Paul and the Politics of Diaspora* (Paul in Critical Contexts; Minneapolis: Fortress Press, 2014).

11. Sheridan, 'Issues in the Translation of οἱ Ἰουδαῖοι', p. 695.

purposes, the main ethical focus of this chapter is on how socio-rhetorical criticism is being used by those who think 'Jews' can or does refer to a collective group, whether it be all Jews or only a selected portion of them.

Abuse Me, Please: Luke T. Johnson's Apologetics

The use of socio-rhetorical criticism in Christian apologetics has been very visible in attempting to mitigate slavery in the New Testament.[12] Not surprisingly, socio-rhetorical criticism is being used to mitigate the anti-Judaism in the New Testament. Unlike the philological efforts to redefine 'Jew' or to erase 'Jews' as a literal translation, a socio-rhetorical approach could argue that changing the terminology or ethnic identifications of the Jews is not necessary at all. Rather, the socio-rhetorical context can better explain, or even justify, any perceived anti-Judaism in the New Testament.

One scholar using socio-rhetorical criticism in this manner is Luke T. Johnson, who believes that he can explain the anti-Jewish rhetoric in the New Testament without theological assumptions.[13] In fact, he criticizes those who use theologically oriented approaches as follows:

> These approaches are theologically motivated and are anachronistic. They isolate 'Christianity' over against 'Judaism' as though each was a well defined entity when the polemic was written. This static bifurcation matches (and in part derives from) the contemporary Jew-Christian polarity. It also obviously exacerbates the negative power of the rhetoric.[14]

However, by the time we reach the conclusion of the article, one begins to understand that Johnson's article is at least partly inspired by ecumenical theology. As Johnson remarks:

> Can this historical and literary analysis help the contemporary relationship of Jews and Christians? It ought to have at least this positive impact: grasping the conventional nature of the polemic can rob such language of its mythic force and therefore its capacity for mischief.[15]

As I will show, Johnson's claim that he is not appealing to theological assumptions cannot withstand scrutiny.

---

12. See the extensive critique of such a use by Ben Witherington and other scholars in Avalos, *Slavery*, pp. 119-24, 127-35.

13. Johnson, 'The New Testament's Anti-Jewish Slander', pp. 419-41. See also Luke T. Johnson, 'Anti-Judaism in the New Testament', in *Handbook for the Study of the Historical Jesus* (ed. Tom Holmén and Stanley E. Porter; 4 vols.; Leiden: E.J. Brill, 2011), II, pp. 1609-638.

14. Johnson, 'The New Testament's Anti-Jewish Slander', pp. 422-23.

15. Johnson, 'The New Testament's Anti-Jewish Slander', p. 441.

In general, Johnson's basic argument involves a version of a *tu quoque* ('you do, too') argument. He details cases where philosophers assailed each other with insults parallel to what we find Jesus uttering against Pharisees and Sadducees in the New Testament. Among Johnson's examples is Colotes, an Epicurean, who attacked the heroes of Plutarch, a priest of Apollo at Delphi and a defender of Platonism. According to Johnson, Colotes assails the philosophical heroes of Plutarch as 'buffoons, charlatans, assassins, prostitutes, and nincompoops'.[16] Johnson emphasizes how Jews insulted each other in ways similar to what we find in the New Testament. Indeed, he emphasizes 'the use of this language everywhere in the fragmented Judaism of the first century'.[17]

There was a strong tradition of Gentile anti-Judaism by the first century. In *Against Apion*, Josephus reports how Jews were characterized as liars and spreaders of diseases (2.29), not to mention that they worshipped the head of an ass (2.80). Jews could also engage in anti-Gentile rhetoric. Josephus says that Apion has been 'gifted with the mind of an ass and the impudence of a dog'.[18] Gentiles who dislike Jews are generally characterized as 'frivolous and utterly senseless specimens of humanity', who were 'accustomed from the first to erroneous ideas about the gods', and 'incapable of imitating the solemnity of our theology'.[19] At the same time, Jews could attack fellow Jews with equal zeal. Josephus says that the Hebrew race [τὸ γένος... Ἑβραίων] who rebelled against Rome were 'slaves, the dregs of society, and the bastard scum of the nation'.[20]

After collecting a catalog of examples of abusive rhetoric, Johnson comes to his conclusions about whether the anti-Jewish rhetoric in the New Testament is any worse than other abusive rhetoric of the time or inappropriate in its context. Johnson's conclusions bear repeating at length:

> First, the polemic is more intelligible. The great problem with the historical vindication approach is that it leaves the NT polemic unmotivated: If Jews were so blameless, why were Christians so nasty? But our survey shows the use of this language everywhere in the fragmented Judaism of the first century. Readers today hear the NT's polemic as inappropriate only because the other voices are silent. Historical imagination can restore them. Second, by the measure of Hellenistic conventions, and certainly by the measure of contemporary Jewish polemic, the NT's slander against fellow Jews is remarkably mild. Third, the conventional nature of the polemic means that its chief rhetorical import is connotative rather than denotative. The polemic

16. Johnson, 'The New Testament's Anti-Jewish Slander', p. 431.
17. Johnson, 'The New Testament's Anti-Jewish Slander', p. 441.
18. Josephus, *Against Apion* 2.86 (Thackeray, LCL): '*cor asini ipse potius habuisset et impudentiam canis*'.
19. Josephus, *Against Apion* 1.225 (Thackeray, LCL).
20. Josephus, *War* 5.443 (Thackeray, LCL).

signifies simply that these are opponents and such things should be said about them. The attempt either to convict first-century Jews of hypocrisy or vindicate them from it is irrelevant as well as futile. Fourth, recognizing that both messianist and non-messianist Jews use the rhetoric associated with Hellenistic philosophical schools helps establish the hypothesis that this is the appropriate context for analyzing their interrelationships.[21]

There are significant historical, ethical and philosophical problems with each of these conclusions.

Philosophically, and as mentioned above, Johnson's argument is basically another version of the *tu quoque* argument. In such an argument, a proponent attempts to show that a behavior, criticism or objection applies equally to the person issuing it. A well-known summary alludes to the 'pot calling the kettle black'. The problem with such a *tu quoque* argument is that a behavior, criticism or objection is not itself validated because it also applies to others. Just because everyone is being abusive, for example, does not mean that it is ethically justified or appropriate to be abusive. Thus it is ethically irrelevant that 'the historical imagination' can restore any voices that show 'the use of this language everywhere in the fragmented Judaism of the first century'.[22] No matter how many other voices were saying the same thing, the rhetoric could remain objectionable on ethical grounds.

Likewise, any anti-Judaism in the New Testament cannot be ethically excused just because non-Christians also are engaging in anti-Judaism, or just because Jews engage in anti-Gentilism. Any anti-Judaism would remain 'inappropriate' regardless of the use of such rhetoric by all sides. To understand this point, consider the following two statements:

A. 'Existence impels the Jew to lie, and to lie perpetually just as it compels the inhabitants of the northern countries to wear warm clothing.'
B. 'You are of your father the devil, and your will is to do your father's desires... When he lies, he speaks according to his own nature, for he is a liar and the father of lies.'

Rhetorically, both statements center on Jews being liars by nature. Both statements were in a cultural context where such rhetoric was often used of opponents. Both statements can satisfy all of the other features that Johnson deems important for characterizing the rhetoric as appropriate—or, at least, not inappropriate. By Johnson's logic, in both statements 'the polemic signifies simply that these are opponents and such things should be said about them'.[23]

Yet, I wonder that one would say that about Statement A once one learns this was said by Adolf Hitler, the foremost modern practitioner of

21. Johnson, 'The New Testament's Anti-Jewish Slander', p. 441.
22. Johnson, 'The New Testament's Anti-Jewish Slander', p. 441.
23. Johnson, 'The New Testament's Anti-Jewish Slander', p. 441.

anti-Jewish rhetoric.[24] Indeed there is not much difference between Hitler's statement and Statement B, which is uttered by Jesus in Jn 8.44-45.[25] That is why the attempt to set the anti-Jewish rhetoric in the context of the Hellenistic world, as though it is special only to that context, is irrelevant. Vitriolic rhetoric has existed in most of recorded history. Therefore, setting vitriolic rhetoric in Nazi Germany is really not different from setting it in the Greco-Roman era.[26] Such rhetoric strives to incite some action, whether human or divine, against the opponent.

On a factual level, it is not clear that, as Johnson claims, 'the NT's slander against fellow Jews is remarkably mild' by comparison with Hellenistic conventions.[27] For example, in none of the examples collected by Johnson is there even the rhetorical suggestion that opponents should be burned or tortured eternally. Yet, Jesus describes the consequences of not catering to his followers: 'And the King will answer them, "Truly, I say to you, as you did it to one of the least of these my brethren, you did it to me". Then he will say to those at his left hand, "Depart from me, you cursed, into the eternal fire prepared for the devil and his angels"' (Mt. 25.40-41).

The argument that such descriptions are 'connotative rather than denotative' is also unsupported or dubious. Indeed, it is demonstrably untrue that '[t]he polemic signifies simply that these are opponents and such things should be said about them'.[28] Despite Jesus' invectives elsewhere, he did not always deem terms of abuse so acceptable:

---

24. Adolf Hitler, *Mein Kampf* (trans. Ralph Manheim; Boston, MA: Houghlin Mifflin, 1971), p. 305. For the German text, see Adolf Hitler, *Mein Kampf* (Münich: Zentralverlag der NSDAP/Franz Eher Nachfolger, 1938), p. 335: 'Das Dasein treibt den Juden zur Lüge, und zwar zur immerwährenden Lüge, wie es den Nordländer zur warmen Kleidung zwingt.'

25. For a thorough examination of the textual history and the syntax of the genitives in the phrase, ὑμεῖς ἐκ τοῦ πατρὸς τοῦ διαβόλου, in Jn 8.44, see Émile Puech, 'Le diable, homicide, menteur et père du mensonge en Jean 8,44', *RB* 112 (2005), pp. 215-52. Puech ('Le diable', p. 250) concludes that the best translation is: 'Vous, vous avez pour père le Diable…'. See also Reimund Bieringer, Didier Pollefeyt and Frederique Vandecasteele-Vanneuville, *Anti-Judaism and the Fourth Gospel* (Louisville, KY: Westminster/John Knox Press, 2001).

26. A study of anti-Christian rhetoric may be found in Bart Wagemakers, 'Incest, Infanticide, and Cannibalism: Anti-Christian Imputations in the Roman Empire', *Greece and Rome* 57 (2010), pp. 337-54.

27. Johnson, 'The New Testament's Anti-Jewish Slander', p. 441.

28. Johnson, 'The New Testament's Anti-Jewish Slander', p. 441. Scot McKnight ('A Loyal Critic: Matthew's Polemic with Judaism in Theological Perspective', in *Anti-Semitism and Early Christianity: Issues of Polemic and Faith* [ed. Craig E. Evans and Donald A. Hagner; Minneapolis: Fortress Press, 1993], pp. 55-79 [78]) offers a similar conclusion: 'His [Matthew's] rhetoric may be unacceptable to modern sensitivities, but it was not to his Jewish world.'

> But I say to you that every one who is angry with his brother shall be liable
> to judgment; whoever insults his brother shall be liable to the council, and
> whoever says, 'You fool!' shall be liable to the hell of fire (Mt. 5.22).

Clearly, Jesus does not see even calling someone a fool (μωρέ) as signify-
ing 'simply that these are opponents and such things should be said about
them'.

The general purpose of rhetoric is also important. Although there were
diverse views on the general purpose of rhetoric, some Roman authors
thought that its main purpose was to incite an audience to take certain
actions. Note Cicero's rhetorical question: 'Who indeed does not know
that the orator's virtue is pre-eminently manifested either in rousing men's
hearts to anger, hatred, or indignation, or in recalling them from these same
passions to mildness and mercy?'[29] So, it is not true, at least for Cicero, that
insults are merely to identify opponents and nothing more. The insults are
meant ultimately to persuade the audience to take certain actions against
the targets of the insults. The author of Mt. 5.22 might be cognizant of such
a use of abusive rhetoric.

Even in the sources cited by Johnson, abusive rhetoric is not merely
considered some harmless pastime among opponents. For example, Johnson uses Philo's *Flaccus* to support the existence of anti-Gentilic rhetoric
among the Jews.[30] But Philo also relates how abusive rhetoric was used to
incite the Alexandrian populace against the Jews during the time of Flaccus,
the prefect of Egypt appointed by Tiberius in 32 CE. Flaccus was a primary
actor in the massacre of Jews in Alexandria in 38 CE during the reign of
Caligula.[31] Eventually, Flaccus experiences a political demise that he attributes to his anti-Judaism. As Philo tells it, Flaccus confesses how he utilized xenophobic rhetoric against Jews: 'I cast on them the slur that they
were foreigners without civic rights, though they were inhabitants with full
civic rights'.[32] In another instance, Philo describes how a certain Isidorus

---

29. Cicero, *De Oratore* 1.12.53 (Sutton and Rackham, LCL): 'Quis enim nescit, max-
imam vim exsistere oratoris in hominum mentibus vel ad iram, aut ad odium, aut ad
dolorem incitandis, vel ab hisce eisdem permotionibus ad lenitatem misericordiamque
revocandis?' See also Kathryn Tempest, *Cicero: Politics and Persuasion in Ancient Rome*
(New York: Continuum, 2011); David A. DeSilva, 'The Strategic Arousal of Emotions in
the Apocalypse of John: A Rhetorical-Critical Investigation of the Oracles to the Seven
Churches', *NTS* 54 (2008), pp. 90-114; Matthew Leigh, 'Quintilian on the Emotions
[Institutio Oratoria 6 preface and 1-2]', *Journal of Roman Studies* 94 (2004), pp. 123-40.

30. Johnson, 'The New Testament's Anti-Jewish Slander', p. 435.

31. See further, Pieter W. van der Horst, *Philo's Flaccus: The First Pogrom. Introduction, Translation, and Commentary* (Leiden: E.J. Brill, 2003); D.R. Schwartz, 'Philo and
Josephus on the Violence in Alexandria in 38 C.E.', *Studia Philonica Annual* 24 (2012),
pp. 149-66.

32. Philo, *Flacc.* 17.138-39 (Colson, LCL).

employed 'vocalists' [φωνασκεῖν], who specialized in the art of yelling in marketplaces, to incite a mob against Flaccus himself in a gymnasium. Philo says that these vocalists 'filled the building and launched accusations against Flaccus with no foundation inventing against him things which had never happened and spinning long lying screeds of ribald doggerel'.[33] Yes, rhetoric can kill.

Within the New Testament, authors sometimes position a hostile speech just prior to some violent actions against Christians. At Philippi, Paul is confronted by an angry mob, which proceeds as follows:

> And when they had brought them to the magistrates they said, 'These men are Jews and they are disturbing our city. They advocate customs which it is not lawful for us Romans to accept or practice'. The crowd joined in attacking them; and the magistrates tore the garments off them and gave orders to beat them with rods (Acts 16.20-22).

Similarly, in Acts 21 another speech precedes violence against Paul:

> When the seven days were almost completed, the Jews from Asia, who had seen him in the temple, stirred up all the crowd, and laid hands on him, crying out, 'Men of Israel, help! This is the man who is teaching men everywhere against the people and the law and this place; moreover he also brought Greeks into the temple, and he has defiled this holy place'... Then all the city was aroused, and the people ran together; they seized Paul and dragged him out of the temple, and at once the gates were shut. And as they were trying to kill him, word came to the tribune of the cohort that all Jerusalem was in confusion. He at once took soldiers and centurions, and ran down to them; and when they saw the tribune and the soldiers, they stopped beating Paul. Then the tribune came up and arrested him, and ordered him to be bound with two chains. He inquired who he was and what he had done. Some in the crowd shouted one thing, some another; and as he could not learn the facts because of the uproar, he ordered him to be brought into the barracks. And when he came to the steps, he was actually carried by the soldiers because of the violence of the crowd; for the mob of the people followed, crying, 'Away with him!' (Acts 21.27-36).

The speech resulted in the city being 'aroused' (v. 30; ἐκινήθη), and so satisfies the very purpose that Cicero cites for rhetoric ('ad iram...incitandis').

In this case the rhetoric contributed to the violence against Paul. Rhetorically, the accusations made by the Jews against Paul include: (1) teaching men everywhere against the people and the law and this place; (2) bringing Greeks into the temple; (3) defiling the temple. Paul, therefore, probably was characterized as lawless or by other terms that Johnson says were used against opponents. But would this mean that Paul's opponents just wanted to identify him as their opponent, or was the rhetoric meant to describe Paul in a way that violence or some other action could be taken against him?

33. Philo, *Flacc.* 17.138-39 (Colson, LCL).

Johnson also misunderstands the imprecatory nature of at least some of the rhetoric used. Some abusive utterances can be categorized as belonging to the magical tradition insofar as the very act of uttering them has effects in the real world.[34] Other such utterances were specifically forbidden in Jewish law. One illustration involves Paul in Acts 23:

> And the high priest Ananias commanded those who stood by him to strike him on the mouth. Then Paul said to him, 'God shall strike you, you white-washed wall! Are you sitting to judge me according to the law, and yet contrary to the law you order me to be struck?' Those who stood by said, 'Would you revile God's high priest?' And Paul said, 'I did not know, brethren, that he was the high priest; for it is written, "You shall not speak evil of a ruler of your people"' (Acts 23.2-5).

The author indicates that there were some utterances that were so grievous as to be punishable offenses.

In the end, Johnson's argument for a more benign view of the slanderous and abusive rhetoric in the New Testament cannot be sustained. It is simply untrue that 'grasping the conventional nature of the polemic can rob such language of its mythic force and therefore its capacity for mischief'.[35] The 'conventional nature' of this rhetoric shows that it was used to incite mischief and violence. It is not true that interlocutors in such rhetoric just saw it as a way to identify opponents. Rather, many, including Jesus, saw it as a cause for arrest or other punitive measures. And it is ethically absurd to hold abusive rhetoric as ethically appropriate once we realize how everyone used such rhetoric. Such abusive rhetoric is ethically inappropriate regardless of how many people may use it then or now, as the examples from *Mein Kampf* show.

When is Anti-Judaism not Anti-Judaism?

Closely allied with the strategy of questioning the meaning of *Ioudaioi* and the propriety of abusive language is the discussion of whether one can label what Jesus said as 'anti-Judaism' or 'anti-Semitism'. These terms have a long and complicated history in western scholarship. For my purposes, I use the term anti-Judaism/anti-Jewish when rhetoric attacks the legitimacy or character of Judaism as a religion and/or as an ethnic group. Etymologically Judaism referred to a territorial identification but it usually coincided in the ancient world with a religious identity, as well. I use anti-Semitism

---

34. On curses, see Brian Britt, *Biblical Curses and the Displacement of Tradition* (Sheffield: Sheffield Phoenix Press, 2011); Leroy A. Huizenga, 'The Confession of Jesus and the Curses of Peter: A Narrative-Christological Approach to the Text-Critical Problem of Mark 14:62', *NovT* 53 (2011), pp. 244-66.

35. Johnson, 'The New Testament's Anti-Jewish Slander', p. 441.

when rhetoric attacks Semites as the entire sphere of Semitic speaking peoples, including Jews and Arabs. Historically, of course, the word has been used only to refer to anti-Judaism. But the fact is that Jews form only a small percentage of Semitic speaking people, and it is a matter of semantic logic to reserve anti-Semitism only for those who are against all Semitic people because there would be no other word left to use for such an all-encompassing hatred.

In any case, Richard Burridge believes that 'anti-Semitic' is not appropriate for language that is used in disputes within a group. He appeals to 'the Dead Sea Scrolls, which use even harsher language about the Jewish leaders in Jerusalem—yet no one calls them "anti-Semitic"'.[36] Burridge adds:

> Severe criticism is tolerated within a family alone, and, as with all families and communities, today only Jewish comedians (or Rabbis!) are allowed to tell Jewish jokes, and likewise for the Irish or whoever; as [Amy-Jill] Levine concedes, 'The analogy to the ethnic joke is somewhat apt'. Matthew is part of an argument going on within Judaism as he seeks to explain the theological problem for Jewish Christians of why Israel rejected her teacher, the fulfillment of her scriptures and her hopes, of why the kingdom has gone to the Gentiles, and why Jerusalem was destroyed.[37]

Verhey also uses this in-the-family analogy, and acknowledges that 'family quarrels, of course, are frequently ugly and they were in this case'.[38]

Burridge's claims are flawed on many levels. First, he offers no support for his generalization that 'severe criticism is tolerated within a family alone'. As mentioned, Jesus had injunctions against using the word 'fools' against one's brother (Mt. 5.22). There were codified rules against Jews insulting Jewish priests. So the idea that such abuse is necessarily tolerated within a family is demonstrably untrue.

Second, Burridge is oblivious to debates about the nature of ethnic comedy, and the extent to which it is harmful or ethically inappropriate, within or outside of a 'family'. Consider the work of Simon Weaver, a theorist of rhetoric who examines 'the ways in which racist humor acts as racist rhetoric, has a communicative impact, is persuasive, and can affect impressions of truth and ambivalence'.[39] He specifically studied how the Danish cartoon controversy illustrates the fact that abusive humor has an inherent polysemy that can lead to plausible offensive interpretations that, in turn, lead to violence. Because of that polysemy, it is inherently misguided to argue that one interpretation of that humor is wrong and another is right.

---

36. Burridge, *Imitating Jesus*, pp. 195.
37. Burridge, *Imitating Jesus*, pp. 195-96.
38. Verhey, *Remembering Jesus*, p. 437.
39. Simon Weaver, *The Rhetoric of Racist Humor: US, UK, and Global Race Joking* (Burlington, VT: Ashgate, 2011), p. 1.

Even individuals who engage in ethnic humor about their own ethnic group may be engaging in a counterproductive activity. The counterproductive aspects of ethnic humor by Jewish insiders has been particularly critiqued by Ruth Wisse, Martin Peretz Professor of Yiddish Literature and professor of comparative literature at Harvard University, in *No Joke: Making Jewish Humor* (2013).[40] Similarly Weaver observes the following concerning black comedians who use ethnic humor: 'While the humour of black comedians is important and often crucial for the explosion of stereotypes and expression of anti-racism, we should not forget that such discourse is always incongruous and thus ambiguous and double edged in its outcome.'[41] Because humor is so often polysemic and contextual, it is relatively easy for one group to take offense and another not to take such offense.

Many Greco-Roman ideas of humor do not support Burridge's claims. In his *Nichomachean Ethics*, Aristotle specifically addresses the dangers of humor. When discussing the behavior of an educated man (πεπ-αιδευμένος), Aristotle remarks: 'Hence a man will draw the line at some jokes; for raillery is a sort of vilification, and some forms of vilification are forbidden by law; perhaps some forms of raillery ought to be prohibited also.'[42] It is clear, therefore, that Greco-Roman ideas about abusive language and humor are too diverse to make the sorts of generalizations that Burridge enunciates.

Third, Burridge's view of what constitutes 'the family' within which such abusive language is tolerated is too amorphous to be of any practical use. For example, if such language is tolerated only within 'the Jewish family', then should Jesus' pronouncements against non-Jews be censured? Would Burridge tolerate abusive language by Christians against Muslims because they can all be viewed as part of the 'Abrahamic family of religions'? The Muslims who reacted violently against the Danish cartoons certainly did not see themselves as part of any larger Abrahamic 'family' to which the Danes historically could belong.[43] Would all such language be tolerated if we simply redefined 'the family' as 'the human family'?

---

40. Ruth Wisse, *No Joke: Making Jewish Humor* (Princeton, NJ: Princeton University Press, 2013).

41. Weaver, *The Rhetoric of Racist Humor*, p. 132.

42. Aristotle, *Nicomachean Ethics* 4.8.9 (Rackham, LCL): οὐ δὴ πᾶν ποιήσει. τὸ γὰρ σκῶμμα λοιδόρημά τί ἐστιν, οἱ δὲ νομοθέται ἔνια λοιδορεῖν κωλύουσιν. ἔδει δ᾽ ἴσως καὶ σκώπτειν.

43. On the Danish cartoons controversy, see David E. DeCosse, 'The Danish Cartoons Reconsidered: Catholic Social Teaching and the Contemporary Challenge of Free Speech', *TS* 71 (2010), pp. 101-132; Geoffrey B. Levey and Tariq Modood, 'Liberal Democracy, Multicultural Citizenship, and the Danish Cartoon Affair', in *Secularism,*

Fourth, Burridge does not contemplate the option that such abusive language should be wrong whether it is within the family or outside of the family. Otherwise, by that logic one might also be asked to tolerate domestic verbal abuse because it is happening within a household not between households. A husband might be able to call his wife all sorts of abusive names as long as it stays within the family. Certainly, there is something very ethically questionable with such thinking about abuse.

Fifth, such a position raises other ethical problems that may betray an imperialistic agenda on the part of modern Christian ethicists. Burridge seems to argue that modern ethicists can determine what others should find offensive. Scot McKnight, in fact, thinks Matthew's rhetoric is the opposite of anti-Semitic: 'Matthew's gospel, however harsh and unpleasant to modern sensitivities, is not anti-Semitic. It is, on the contrary, a compassionate but vigorous appeal to nonmessianic Judaism to respond to the Messiah.'[44] Both Burridge and McKnight represent Christian ethicists who allow themselves to determine how the 'other' should feel or think about particular insults issued by Jesus.

McKnight is especially operating on questionable ethical and logical grounds. After all, why could it not be that what sounds 'compassionate' to modern sensitivities is actually harsh and unpleasant? In other words, why treat 'harsh and unpleasant' as possibly being the opposite of what they appear to be, and yet not contemplate the possibility that what appears 'compassionate' may also be the opposite of what it seems? And why restrict ourselves only to modern sensitivities, when the Gospels themselves tell us how offensive Jesus' words and deeds were to the sensitivities of the Jews of that time? The term compassionate can only be justified on theological grounds, as it could just as well be said that what the Jews did to Jesus or Paul, however harsh and unpleasant to modern sensitivities, is not anti-Jesus or anti-Pauline. Rather those are 'compassionate' actions on the part of nonmessianic Jews.

When Did Christian Anti-Judaism Begin?

The question of whether Jesus engaged in anti-Judaism or not logically relates to the question of when Christian anti-Judaism began. If anti-Judaism can be attributed to the founder of Christianity, then anti-Judaism is there from the beginning. If anti-Judaism is the result of some later development, then the founder of Christianity is absolved. As mentioned, there is a division among scholars on this question. The religious and theological nature

Religion and Multicultural Citizenship (ed. Geoffrey B. Levey and Tariq Modood; Cambridge: Cambridge University Press, 2009), pp. 216-42.

44. McKnight, 'A Loyal Critic', p. 77.

of this division is apparent in that most of those attributing anti-Judaism to Jesus are self-identified Jewish scholars, while those blaming later Christian interpreters are self-identified Christian scholars.

Paula Fredriksen is a scholar who denies that Jesus engaged in anti-Judaism. She briefly outlines the history of Christian anti-Judaism thus:

> Christian antipathy toward Jews and Judaism began when Christian Hellenistic Jewish texts, such as the letters of Paul and the Gospels, began to circulate among total outsiders, that is, among Gentiles without any connection to the synagogue and without any attachment to Jewish traditions of practice and interpretation. At that point, the intra-Jewish polemics preserved in these texts began to be understood as condemnations of Judaism *tout court*. The next stage intensified the process, by taking this outsider's perspective to the text of the Septuagint. By the early second century, the engagement of intellectuals enriched the controversy by putting it on a philosophical basis, thereby integrating what otherwise might have remained secondhand name-calling into comprehensive, rational, total worldviews. Christian theologies of many different sorts were thereby born.[45]

This historical assessment contradicts much of what Fredriksen claims in her own article, not to mention what is within the quoted passage.

First, Fredriksen apparently does not count the very words of Jesus in passages such as Jn 8.44 as showing 'Christian antipathy toward Jews and Judaism'. If Jesus did say such a thing, then how could such antipathy begin only when such texts began circulating among total outsiders?[46] Of course, there is a legitimate question about whether the historical Jesus did say such things. I cannot prove that Jesus did say those things. But Fredriksen offers us nothing to prove that Jesus did not say those things, especially in light of the fact that she admits that there are 'intra-Jewish polemics preserved in these texts'. If Jews of Jesus' time were abusing each other in this manner, then is it at least possible that Jn 8.44 may preserve an 'authentic' oral tradition about what Jesus said? And if those intra-Jewish polemics do go back to Jesus himself, then why could one not say that anti-Jewish antipathy or polemics in Christianity began with Jesus?[47]

Second, there is nothing about condemning Judaism *tout court* that requires some post-Jesus development. The idea of collective characterization of entire groups is certainly found in pre-Christian Jewish traditions. In Deuteronomy one finds the following characterizations and actions encompassing entire ethnic groups:

45. Paula Fredriksen, 'The Birth of Christianity and the Origins of Christian Anti-Judaism', in Fredriksen and Reinhartz (eds.), *Jesus, Judaism, and Christian Anti-Judaism*, pp. 8-30 (28). Fredriksen's italics.

46. See further, J.R. Shaver, 'Christian Anti-Semitism: Tracing the Roots to the Gospel', *Church* 20 (2004), pp. 15-19.

47. See further Puech, 'Le diable', pp. 215-52.

> No Ammonite or Moabite shall enter the assembly of the LORD; even to the tenth generation none belonging to them shall enter the assembly of the LORD for ever; because they did not meet you with bread and with water on the way, when you came forth out of Egypt, and because they hired against you Balaam the son of Beor from Pethor of Mesopotamia, to curse you (Deut. 23.3-4).

Evil moral attitudes could also be viewed as inherent, as in Jeremiah:

> And if you say in your heart, 'Why have these things come upon me?' it is for the greatness of your iniquity that your skirts are lifted up, and you suffer violence. Can the Ethiopian change his skin or the leopard his spots? Then also you can do good who are accustomed to do evil (Jer. 13.22-23).

Despite debates about the questions of the extent to which 'race' and 'racism' existed in the ancient world, there is little question that people could be viewed as inherently evil or bear other moral characteristics on the basis of their ancestry or genealogy.[48]

There is also evidence that sects could view themselves as so separate from other Jews that they could speak of other co-ethnic members in the third person. Note this complaint in Isaiah: 'For thou art our Father, though Abraham does not know us and Israel does not acknowledge us; thou, O LORD, art our Father, our Redeemer from of old is thy name' (Isa. 63.16).[49] Clearly, the speaker presumes some historical relationship to Abraham and Israel, but yet speaks of Abraham and Israel as not acknowledging the speaker's group. Once such a differentiation is made, it would not take but another step to use other derogatory descriptors that the speaker could apply to Abraham and Israel, as collective entities.

The idea of collective punishment is pre-Christian, and could involve entire ethnic groups and religions. At the grandest scale, such collective punishment is inflicted on all life in Noah's Flood in Genesis 6–7, which would count as a case of biocide or ecocide. Collective punishment is encoded in the Decalogue: 'I the LORD your God am a jealous God, visiting the iniquity of the fathers upon the children to the third and the fourth generation of those who hate me, but showing steadfast love to thousands of those who love me and keep my commandments' (Exod. 20.5-6).

48. Benjamin Isaac, *The Invention of Racism in Classical Antiquity* (Princeton, NJ: Princeton University Press, 2004); idem, 'Proto-Racism in Graeco-Roman Antiquity', *World Archaeology* 28 (2006), pp. 32-47. Also useful are the essays in Daniel C. Harlow, *The 'Other' in Second Temple Judaism: Essays in Honor of John Collins* (Grand Rapids, MI: Eerdmans, 2011).

49. On the possible sectarian conflict reflected, see Paul D. Hanson, *The Dawn of Apocalyptic: The Historical and Sociological Roots of Jewish Apocalyptic Eschatology* (Philadelphia, PA: Fortress Press, 1979), pp. 92-97.

Similarly, Yahweh issues a list of horrific punishments applicable to the entire Israelite nation if they do not obey his commandments. Note these curses: 'And the LORD will scatter you among all peoples, from one end of the earth to the other; and there you shall serve other gods, of wood and stone, which neither you nor your fathers have known' (Deut. 28.64). Such punishments outlined in Deuteronomy 28 were viewed as in effect in many Second Temple texts, such as in Daniel:

> We have sinned and done wrong and acted wickedly and rebelled, turning aside from thy commandments and ordinances; we have not listened to thy servants the prophets, who spoke in thy name to our kings, our princes, and our fathers, and to all the people of the land. To thee, O LORD, belongs righteousness, but to us confusion of face, as at this day, to the men of Judah, to the inhabitants of Jerusalem, and to all Israel, those that are near and those that are far away, in all the lands to which thou hast driven them, because of the treachery which they have committed against thee...
>
> As it is written in the law of Moses, all this calamity has come upon us, yet we have not entreated the favor of the LORD our God, turning from our iniquities and giving heed to thy truth (Dan. 9.5-13).

New Testament texts continued such ideas of collective punishment. One illustration is in Acts 2, where Peter speaks in Jerusalem to 'Jews, devout men from every nation under heaven' (v. 5) assembled for the feast of Pentecost. These Jews come from Mesopotamia, Asia Minor, Egypt and Rome, among other places. Yet, Peter considers them responsible for the death of Jesus: 'Let all the house of Israel therefore know assuredly that God has made him both Lord and Christ, this Jesus whom you crucified ['Ιησοῦν ὃν ὑμεῖς ἐσταυρώσατε]' (Acts 2.36). The use of the second person plural (ὑμεῖς) pronoun as the subject of the Greek clause shows that Peter had no trouble attributing Jesus' death even to those who may not even have been present at the crucifixion.

Given such a continued belief in collective characterizations and punishments, why couldn't any historical Jesus think that Judaism was just as described in Jn 8.44? Why is it rhetorical, metaphorical or exaggerated language rather than descriptive of his actual beliefs? If Jesus is following polemic or theological Jewish traditions advocating collective punishment and characterizations, then such characterizations would not be outside of his tradition at all. And if Jesus is simply continuing such ideas of collective culpability and punishment, then Fredriksen's historical scheme is fundamentally flawed.

Summary

If there was an historical Jesus, then there is no reason why Jesus could not have said any of the anti-Jewish statements attributed to him in the Gospels.

That does not mean he did say those things, but the core of my argument is that the standard arguments offered for denying that Jesus did say those things are fundamentally flawed. It is not true, for example, that such abusive language was so routine that it was deemed acceptable or just another way of identifying opponents. It is not necessarily true that it would have been seen the way that in-group ethnic humor is viewed today. None of the ethicists discussed here even contemplate the very real possibility that Jesus was perpetuating the type of ethnic and collective culpability and characterizations that these ethicists otherwise accept as real phenomena in the Hebrew Bible, as well as at the time of Jesus. The refusal to admit that anti-Judaism may be attributed to Jesus, even if he was Jewish, is more the product of Christian theological apologetics than it is the result of rigorous critical scholarship.

Chapter 8

THE UNECONOMIC JESUS AS ENEMY OF THE POOR

Open almost any book on New Testament ethics or the historical Jesus, and somewhere you will find a reference or allusion to Jesus being a friend of the poor.[1] In fact, the movement called liberation theology views salvation itself as part of Jesus' radical anti-poverty program.[2] Gustavo Gutiérrez, perhaps the most prominent voice of liberation theology, affirmed: 'the salvation of Christ is a radical liberation from all misery, exploitation, and alienation'.[3] For John Dominic Crossan:

> The historical Jesus was *a peasant Jewish Cynic...* His strategy, implicitly for himself and explicitly for his followers, was the combination of *free healing and common eating*, a religious and economic egalitarianism that negated alike and at once the hierarchical and patronal normalcies of Jewish religion and Roman power.[4]

---

1. For some studies of poverty in the Bible, see Douglas E. Oakman, *Jesus, Debt, and the Lord's Prayer: First-Century Debt and Jesus' Intentions* (Eugene, OR: Cascade Books, 2014); Albino Barrera, *Biblical Economic Ethics: Sacred Scripture's Teachings on Economic Life* (Lanham, MD: Lexington Books, 2013); Bruce W. Longenecker, *Remember the Poor: Paul, Poverty, and the Greco-Roman World* (Grand Rapids, MI: Eerdmans, 2010); Leslie J. Hoppe, *There Shall be No Poor among you: Poverty in the Bible* (Nashville, TN: Abingdon Press, 2004); Louise Schottroff and Wolfgang Stegemann, *Jesus and the Hope of the Poor* (trans. Matthew O'Connell; Maryknoll, NY: Orbis Books, 1986); Wolfgang Stegemann, *The Gospel and the Poor* (Philadelphia, PA: Fortress Press, 1984); Bruce Malina, 'Wealth and Poverty in the New Testament and its World', *Int* 41 (1987), pp. 354-67; Albert Gelin, *The Poor of Yahweh* (Collegeville, MN: Liturgical Press, 1964). For an African context, see Pieter Verster, *Good News for the Poor and the Sick* (Acta Theologica Supplementum, 16; Bloemfontein: SUN MeDia, 2012).

2. See Tombs, *Latin American Liberation Theology*; Avalos, 'Liberation Theology', II, pp. 435-37.

3. Gustavo Gutiérrez, *Teología de la liberación: Perspectivas* (Salamanca: Ediciones Sigueme, 1987), p. 240: 'la salvación de Cristo es una liberación radical de toda miseria, de todo despojo, de toda alienación'. My translation.

4. John Dominic Crossan, *Jesus: A Revolutionary Biography* (New York: HarperCollins, 1995), p. 198; Crossan's italics. See also Douglas E. Oakman, *Jesus and the Peasants* (Matrix: The Bible in Mediterranean Context, 4; Eugene, OR: Wipf & Stock,

Speaking principally of Luke, Richard Burridge notes how 'Jesus begins his ministry by preaching good news to the poor'.[5]

While the idea that Jesus was primarily concerned with the poor has always had ample representation in Christian history, the rise of the so-called 'Social Gospel' movement, particularly in the Anglophonic world, marked a historical milestone for that idea.[6] The theme of Jesus as friend of the poor became very central with the onset of decolonization and the reconfiguration of global economics after World War II. For Gustavo Gutiérrez, it was the overly optimistic economic promises of the 1950s that set the stage for the outcry about economic inequities in the 1960s.[7] During the era of Ronald Reagan one finds renewed attention to whether capitalism was Christian, as reflected in Franky Schaeffer's anthology *Is Capitalism Christian?*[8] The role of Christianity in capitalism, of course, was the subject of serious attention from at least the time of Max Weber's *The Protestant Ethic and the Spirit of Capitalism* (1905).[9] Other scholars were very

---

2008). For studies of Paul and poverty, see Longenecker, *Remember the Poor*; Dieter Georgi, *Remembering the Poor: The History of Paul's Collection for Jerusalem* (Nashville, TN: Abingdon Press, 1965). For other studies of poverty, see Mark D. Mathews, *Riches, Poverty and the Faithful: Perspectives on Wealth in the Second Temple Period and the Apocalypse of John* (SNTSMS, 154; Cambridge: Cambridge University Press, 2013).

5. Burridge, *Imitating Jesus*, p. 261.

6. Primary exponents of the Social Gospel included Walter Rauschenbusch, A *Theology for the Social Gospel* (New York: Macmillan, 1917) and Shailer Matthews, *Jesus on Social Institutions* (New York: Macmillan, 1928). See also Susan Curtis, *A Consuming Faith: The Social Gospel in Modern American Culture* (Baltimore, MD: The Johns Hopkins University Press, 1991); Paul M. Minus, *Walter Rauschenbusch: American Reformer* (New York: Macmillan, 1988); Jacob H. Dorn (ed.), *Socialism and Christianity in Early 20th Century America* (Westport, CT: Greenwood Press, 1998). For the role of biblical scholarship, see Steven Cassedy, 'Walter Rauschenbusch, the Social Gospel Movement, and How Julius Wellhausen Unwittingly Helped Create American Progressivism in the Twentieth Century', in *Sacred History, Sacred Literature: Essays on Ancient Israel, the Bible, and Religion in Honor of R.E. Friedman on his Sixtieth Birthday* (ed. Shawna Dolansky; Winona Lake, IN: Eisenbrauns, 2008), pp. 315-24.

7. Gutiérrez, *Teología de la liberación*, especially pp. 114-17.

8. Franky Schaeffer (ed.), *Is Capitalism Christian?* (Westchester, IL: Crossway Books, 1985). For Catholic responses to poverty in the 1980s, see also Charles R. Strain (ed.), *Prophetic Visions and Economic Realities: Protestants, Jews, and Catholics Confront the Bishops' Letter on the Economy* (Grand Rapids, MI: Eerdmans, 1989); Craig L. Blomberg, *Neither Poverty Nor Riches: A Biblical Theology of Possessions* (New Studies in Biblical Theology, 7; Downers Grove, IL: InterVarsity Press, 1999). For a continental European perspective, see Vincenzo Petracca, *Gott oder das Geld. Die Besitzethik des Lukas* (Text und Arbeiten zum neutestamentlichen Zeitalter, 39; Tübingen: Francke, 2003).

9. See further, Michael H. Lesnoff, *The Spirit of Capitalism and the Protestant*

specific about their work on Jesus being a response to the economic policies of George W. Bush and the entire American republican party.[10]

At the same time, there were scholars who questioned whether Jesus encouraged poverty and whether he favored any one economic system. As early as 1902, Orello Cone, who served as the Richardson Professor of Biblical Theology and Ethics at St Lawrence University (New York), challenged those who viewed Jesus as a socialist revolutionary. Cone expressed great doubts about the historical Jesus. In his *Rich and Poor in the New Testament* (1902), Cone preferred to see in the Gospels a more general 'spirit to the social problems of every age, and thus hasten the advent of the kingdom of brotherhood and peace'.[11]

Today Christianity is nearly irrelevant in terms of economists who appeal to it to solve global issues of poverty. Reviewers of Thomas Piketty's *Capital in the Twenty-First Century* (2014), a recent massive treatise on poverty and inequality, often miss the fact that it has no indexed references to Christianity, and only one mention of Christianity overall.[12] Phil Zuckerman, a scholar of religion, has amassed evidence that secularized countries have better standards of living than those with higher degrees of religiosity.[13] Christian ethics, in other words, seem to have little to do with how well people live economically.

This chapter will show how much Christian New Testament ethics is preoccupied with portraying Jesus as a champion of the poor despite the existence of texts that can be reasonably interpreted to show the opposite. New Testament ethicists often claim that Jesus' economics program seeks to address a stark binary between the rich and the poor in Galilee.[14] I will show

---

Ethic (Aldershot: Edward Elgar, 1994); Sascha O. Becker and Ludger Wössmann, 'Was Weber Wrong? Human Capital Theory of Protestant Economics History', Munich Discussion Paper No. 2007-7 (Munich: University of Munich, 2007). Online: http://epub. ub.uni-muenchen.de/1366/1/weberLMU.pdf; Alan Richardson, *The Biblical Doctrine of Work* (London: SCM Press, 1952).

10. Examples include Hendricks, *The Politics of Jesus*.

11. Orello Cone, *Rich and Poor in the New Testament: A Study of the Primitive Doctrine of Earthly Possessions* (New York: Macmillan, 1902), p. 232.

12. Thomas Piketty, *Capital in the Twenty-First Century* (trans. Arthur Goldhammer; Cambridge, MA: Harvard University Press, 2014). Piketty (*Capital*, p. 530) mentions Christianity together with Islam briefly as examples of religions who have restricted usury.

13. Phil Zuckerman, *Society without God: What the Least Religious Nations can Tell us about Contentment* (New York: New York University Press, 2010). Similarly, Pippa Norris and Ronald Inglehart, *Sacred and Secular: Religion and Politics* (Cambridge Series in Social Theory, Religion and Politics; Cambridge: Cambridge University Press, 2012).

14. See James G. Crossley, *Why Christianity Happened: A Sociohistorical Account of Christian Origins (26–50 CE)* (Louisville, KY: Westminster/John Knox Press, 2006),

how apologetics permeates the interpretations of passages where Jesus' teachings seem to be inimical to escaping a life of poverty. In fact, sometimes Jesus' reported actions and teachings not only would have impoverished families, but they show how the biblical authors used the poor, sick and hungry as props for Jesus' own imperialistic theocratic agenda. If this is any reflection on an historical Jesus, then his teachings and practices betray a man who was egotistical, delusional or economically inept. The effort to salvage Jesus' image as a friend of the poor says more about the ethics of New Testament scholarship.

Jesus as Radical Egalitarian

Gustavo Gutiérrez and many others who see Jesus as a friend of the poor often cite these words in Luke as proof:

> The Spirit of the Lord is upon me, because he has anointed me to preach good news to the poor. He has sent me to proclaim release to the captives and recovering of sight to the blind, to set at liberty those who are oppressed, to proclaim the acceptable year of the Lord (Lk. 4.18-19).

This sounds very liberatory and egalitarian to Gutiérrez, but it is far from innovative.[15] As it is, Jesus is citing Isa. 61.1-2, which shows that the concept of bringing good news to the poor was there hundreds of years before Jesus.

Nor are such liberatory concepts absent from non-biblical religions. The emphasis on helping those less fortunate can be traced at least as far back as Hammurabi. Consider this passage in the prologue of his famous Code of Hammurabi (CH):

> When the supreme Anu, King of the Anunnaki, and Bel, the master of Heaven and Earth, who decrees the fate of the land, assigned to Marduk, the firstborn son of Ea, God of righteousness, dominion over earthly man, and exalted him among the Igigi, they called Babylon by his illustrious name, made it great on earth, and founded an everlasting kingdom in it... then Anu and Bel called by name me, Hammurabi, the exalted prince, who feared God, to make justice shine forth in the land, to destroy the wicked and the evil-doers; so that the strong should not harm the weak; so that I

especially pp. 73-74. For a critique of stark and exaggerated binaries between the rich and the poor, see Walter Scheidel and Steven J. Friesen, 'The Size of the Economy and the Distribution of Income in the Roman Empire', *JRS* 99 (2009), pp. 61-91 (90). See also Walter Scheidel, 'In Search of Roman Economic Growth', *Journal of Roman Archaeology* 22 (2009), pp. 46-70. A more general study of the economics of Christianity in the first millennium is found in Robert B. Eklund and Robert D. Tolleson, *Economic Origins of Roman Christianity* (Chicago, IL: University of Chicago Press, 2011).

15. Gutiérrez, *Teología de la liberación*, p. 225.

should rule over the black-headed people like Shamash, and illuminate the land, to further the well-being of mankind.[16]

Thus, the CH clearly enunciates these principles for the laws:

(1) to make justice shine forth in the land,
(2) to destroy the wicked and the evil-doers;
(3) so that the strong should not harm the weak;
(4) so that I should rule over the black-headed people like Shamash, and illuminate the land,
(5) to further the well-being of humankind
(6) 'to protect widows and orphans' (Epilogue).

An Akkadian prophetic text predicts that 'a king will arise in Uruk who will provide justice [di-i-na] in the land and will give the right decisions for the land'.[17] In fact, these ideals are part and parcel of some crucial liturgies in Mesopotamia. In the Mesopotamian incantation series known as Šurpu, one finds a list of blessings expected from the Babylonian god, Marduk: 'To extirpate sin, to remove crime/to make good error/to heal the sick/to lift up the fallen/to take the weak by the hand/to change fate...'.[18] Yet, one does not hear many Christian scholars praising such texts as 'good news' for the fallen, sick and downtrodden. Indeed, Jesus is a latecomer to this sort of rhetoric.

If one wishes to witness a truly radical program of egalitarianism and anti-poverty sentiments, one can also read the Sibylline Oracles. Note the following vision for the future:

> The earth will belong equally to all, undivided by walls or fences. It will then bear more abundant fruits spontaneously. Lives will be in common and wealth will have no division. For there will be no poor man there, no rich, and no tyrant. Further, no one will be either great or small anymore. No kings, no leaders. All will be on a part together (SibOr. 2.229-324).[19]

Although this section of the Sibylline Oracles may date after the time of Jesus, the point is that New Testament scholars don't often praise the author of these texts for being some radical innovator or friend of the poor despite

16. My adapted translation of the cuneiform text in Roth, *Law Collections*, pp. 76 and 133.

17. Following Hermann Hunger and Stephen A. Kaufman, 'A New Akkadian Prophecy Text', *JAOS* 95 (1975), pp. 371-75 (372, line 11).

18. Erica Reiner, *Šurpu: A Collection of Sumerian and Akkadian Incantations* (AfO, 11; Graz: Selbstverlage des Herausgebers, 1958), p. 25, Tablet IV, lines 14-19: ár-ni šu-su-ḫu gil-la-[ti] šu-us-su-ú/ḫi-ti-tu šul-lu-mu/LÚ.GIG bul-lu-ṭu/ma-aq-tú šu-ut-bu-ú/ ŠUᴵᴵ en-ši ṣa-ba-tu. I use slashes to represent the line divisions.

19. Following, *OTP*, I, p. 353. See also John J. Collins, 'Sibylline Oracles', *NIDB*, V, p. 247; idem, *The Sibylline Oracles of Egyptian Judaism* (SBLDS, 13; Missoula, MT: Scholars Press, 1974).

the clearly egalitarian nature of the future envisioned. On the other hand, New Testament ethicists labor enormously to extract some faint egalitarian sentiment out of Jesus from even more opaque biblical texts.

Heroic Disciples or Deadbeat Dads?

The call of the twelve disciples is nearly universally praised as a story of faith displayed by men who were willing to follow Jesus. One version of this call is found in Mark:

> And passing along by the Sea of Galilee, he saw Simon and Andrew the brother of Simon casting a net in the sea; for they were fishermen. And Jesus said to them, 'Follow me and I will make you become fishers of men'. And immediately they left their nets and followed him. And going on a little farther, he saw James the son of Zebedee and John his brother, who were in their boat mending the nets. And immediately he called them; and they left their father Zebedee in the boat with the hired servants, and followed him (Mk 1.16-20).

In another instance, Jesus seems to make an equally outrageous demand:

> Now when Jesus saw great crowds around him, he gave orders to go over to the other side. And a scribe came up and said to him, 'Teacher, I will follow you wherever you go'. And Jesus said to him, 'Foxes have holes, and birds of the air have nests; but the Son of man has nowhere to lay his head'. Another of the disciples said to him, 'Lord, let me first go and bury my father'. But Jesus said to him, 'Follow me, and leave the dead to bury their own dead' (Mt. 8.18-22).

Imagine if a group of twelve men today left their families to follow a man they just met or barely knew. What sorts of questions would arise? For starters, one might ask what happened to their families? How are these families supposed to make a living after being abandoned by their main or only breadwinners? Who will assume the burden of the burial that the scribe abandoned? Is it morally right for someone to abandon a family in the first place?

However, these are hardly the sorts of questions asked by New Testament ethicists. For example, two major treatments of the family in early Christianity by Carolyn Osiek and David L. Balch show no interest in these questions.[20] Leslie J. Hoppe, who wrote an entire book on poverty in the Bible, also has no serious discussion of how Jesus' demands on his disciples probably impoverished their families. As far as Hoppe is concerned,

---

20. See Carolyn Osiek and David L. Balch (eds.), *Families in the New Testament World* (Louisville, KY: Westminster/John Knox Press, 1997); David L. Balch and Carolyn Osiek (eds.), *Early Christian Families in Context: An Interdisciplinary Dialogue* (Grand Rapids, MI: Eerdmans, 2003).

the disciples already 'shared the lot of the poor'.[21] Burridge simply notes that following Jesus 'involves leaving everything at Jesus' command, as Peter later reminds him' (cf. Mk 10.28//Mt. 19.27).[22] Burridge offers no further moral reflection on how the disciples 'leaving everything' might have affected their families.

The main reason is that Christian ethicists assume that Jesus' call is praiseworthy, and his rewards are real and better than what the followers could have gained by feeding their families. So the disciples are viewed as heroic. Verhey cites Mk 1.16-20 in a section titled 'Mark: Heroic Discipleship in the Counter-Empire'.[23] Alan Matera tells readers that '[e]mbracing the Kingdom of God entails a new way of thinking that often contradicts the values and standards of this age'.[24] Of course, Matera assumes that contradicting those values is a good thing on the part of Jesus and the disciples. Hoppe tells readers that 'the tradition is unanimous in asserting that material, economic poverty is an outrage'.[25] Yet, Hoppe also says that 'Jesus was able to disassociate himself from possessions because they accounted for nothing in terms of the reign of God that he was called to announce'.[26] What is so outrageous about poverty if possessions account for nothing in terms of the reign of God?

Once one begins to think more seriously about what Jesus wanted the disciples to do, it becomes very clear to anyone who studies basic economics that abandonment would impoverish the corresponding families almost immediately. If that family has infants, then those infants may be left without much food. Any wives are now left more vulnerable. Any hired servants may go unpaid. There was seemingly no notice given to every affected family by these disciples, but the anxiety of such an abandonment is hardly ever the subject of any compassion or sympathy by New Testament scholarship. These disciples are never labeled as deadbeat dads, cruel or irresponsible.

The Gospels provide some economic data, even if some of it is embellished for literary and theological effect. The situations described must have had some verisimilitude for the stories to work. In the story of the miraculous draught of fish in John 21, the narrator tells us that some of the disciples 'went out and got into the boat; but that night they caught nothing' (Jn 21.3). That means that some fishermen might have returned empty handed

---

21. Hoppe, *There Shall be No Poor among you*, p. 144.
22. Burridge, *Imitating Jesus*, p. 219.
23. Verhey, *Remembering Jesus*, p. 420.
24. Matera, *New Testament Ethics*, p. 22.
25. Hoppe, *There Shall be No Poor among you*, p. 171.
26. Hoppe, *There Shall be No Poor among you*, p. 144.

to their families.[27] John 21.11 reports that Peter's catch totaled 153 fish, and that was considered a miracle. The story tells us that some of the catch was eaten for breakfast by the fishermen, who worked all night (Jn 21.10-11), and so one has to subtract that from what the rest of the family would eat from that catch. The Lukan variant of that story tells readers that one of the boats belonged to Simon, and that he had partners to help him (Lk. 5.3-7). As Victor Matthews observes 'The forming of fishing cooperatives allowed families to work together and share the risks and burdens of the sea.'[28] Those risks would be magnified if these fishermen left their families.

The Fragrance of Poverty

If Jesus is a friend of the poor, then the story of his anointing by a woman at Bethany presents many challenges for New Testament ethicists. The Markan version is as follows:

> And while he was at Bethany in the house of Simon the leper, as he sat at table, a woman came with an alabaster flask of ointment of pure nard, very costly, and she broke the flask and poured it over his head. But there were some who said to themselves indignantly, 'Why was the ointment thus wasted? For this ointment might have been sold for more than three hundred denarii, and given to the poor'. And they reproached her. But Jesus said, 'Let her alone; why do you trouble her? She has done a beautiful thing to me. For you always have the poor with you, and whenever you will, you can do good to them; but you will not always have me. She has done what she could; she has anointed my body beforehand for burying. And truly, I say to you, wherever the gospel is preached in the whole world, what she has done will be told in memory of her' (Mk 14.3-9).

From a modern or non-Christian ethical perspective, one could argue that Jesus here is uncaring toward the poor, as well as self-centered and hypocritical. Jesus is uncaring because it is true that the three hundred denarii spent on the ointments could have been given to the poor. Jesus does not deny that this money could have been of use to the poor. Instead, Jesus' response is simply that 'you always have the poor with you...but you will not always have me'. This is not a very good ethical rationale to deny help to the poor.

---

27. For the labor and economics of fishing, see Mendel Nun, 'Cast your Net upon the Waters: Fish and Fishermen in Jesus' Time', *BARev* 19 (1993), pp. 46-56, 70; for the economics and construction of boats on the Sea of Galilee, see Winkler and Frankel, *The Boat and the Sea of Galilee*; Elizabeth Struthers Malbon, 'The Jesus of Mark and the Sea of Galilee', *JBL* 103 (1984), pp. 363-77.

28. Victor H. Matthews, 'Fishermen', *NIDB*, II, p. 460. Sean Freyne (*Jesus, a Jewish Galilean: A New Reading of the Jesus-Story* [London: T. & T. Clark, 2004], p. 52) argues that fishing was more lucrative than one might think, though losing fishermen in a family would probably still be economically harmful.

In fact, Jesus relies on a false analogy. Jesus' false analogy compares the discontinued presence of an individual (Jesus) to the continual presence of a class of people (the poor). Jesus' argument can be schematized as follows: If Individual X will not continue to exist, then you can deny members of Group Y the benefits given to X because Group Y will continue to exist. Yet, this moral reasoning could be reduced to absurdity because that characterization could apply to any individual whose life is limited. For example, the rich man in Mark 10 could also justify the retention of his riches because he will not always exist, while the category of the poor will outlive him. If one says that it is inappropriate to compare the unmeasured wealth of the rich man against the 300 denarii spent on Jesus, then one can still make the case that anyone who will not always exist is entitled to at least 300 denarii that could have been given to the poor.

Furthermore, Jesus presents a false analogy because the benefits he receives may not be the same as what the poor will receive. The benefit Jesus receives is that his body will avoid the smell of death. On the other hand, 300 denarii could feed thousands of starving children. The two are not analogous benefits. The benefit that Jesus receives does not maintain life, while the benefit of food for starving children does maintain life. Ultimately, the issues definitely center on the importance of having a corpse smell good over maintaining the life of living human beings.

Mark 6 provides us a means to calculate how much food one could purchase with 300 denarii. In that chapter, there are 5,000 men (Mk 6.44) who ate five loaves of bread and two fishes miraculously multiplied by Jesus. However, before the miraculous multiplication, the disciples asked: 'Shall we go and buy two hundred denarii worth of bread, and give it to them to eat?' (Mk 6.37). If the disciples expected to feed 5,000 with 200 denarii, then, as James Jeffers remarks, 'one denarius would buy enough bread for twenty-five lunches'.[29] Accordingly, 300 denarii would have bought 7,500 lunches. A entire day's wage could be paid with one denarius according to Mt. 20.2, and so Jesus could have paid the wages of 300 poor laborers for one day. Overall, Jeffers calculates that 300 denarii is the equivalent of 5,000 dollars.[30]

For Jesus to say that keeping his body from stinking is equivalent to preventing the starvation of thousands of children might be held to be morally reprehensible today if anyone else made the same equivalence. Indeed, Jesus is self-centered because he believes that his dead corpse is more valuable than that of the living bodies of the poor that could have been fed with that money. Jesus is hypocritical because he has instructed the rich on other

---

29. James S. Jeffers, *The Greco-Roman World of the New Testament Era: Exploring the Background* (Downers Grove, IL: InterVarsity Press, 1999), p. 153.

30. Jeffers, *Greco-Roman World*, p. 153.

occasions to sell what they have and give it to the poor (Mk 10.21; Mt. 19.21; Lk. 14.33, 18.22). But the woman is not similarly instructed here. It looks as if giving your possessions away to the poor is a good thing unless Jesus needs them.

Some New Testament ethicists don't bother to give a defense for Jesus, as they apparently assume that there are no ethical problems with what Jesus said or did. For Hoppe it is ethically acceptable that Jesus spend that money on himself because Mark 'likely sees the anointing is a token of Jesus' messiahship'.[31] Burridge only mentions the passage in a discussion of a similar story in Lk. 7.36-50. Burridge notices that Luke has the anointing long before Jesus' death, while Mark places it right before Jesus' death. Otherwise, Burridge evades the more serious issues by remarking: 'Rather than getting into the awkward issue of the waste of something which could have been given in alms... The little story of the Two Debtors sums up both passages: those who have been forgiven much show the greater love.'[32]

Allen Verhey does offer a more elaborate defense of Jesus' statement: 'For you always have the poor with you.'[33] Verhey's main premise is that '[t]o help the poor with a self-forgetful generosity is to welcome God's coming reign (Lk. 19.8-9)'. By 'self-forgetful' Verhey refers to giving 'without looking for a return', or to giving selflessly and altruistically.[34] Verhey explains:

> So Jesus rebuked the disciples with these words, not for being concerned about the poor, but for self-righteously singling out this woman, for presumptuously condemning her when the presence of poverty condemned the whole community. The disciples were casting stones at the woman in Israel's glass house.[35]

To show how the presence of the poor 'condemned the whole community', Verhey points to Jesus' allusion to Deuteronomy: 'For the poor will never cease out of the land; therefore I command you, You shall open wide your hand to your brother, to the needy and to the poor, in the land' (Deut. 15.11). Verhey links that verse to this conditional statement earlier in the chapter:

> But there will be no poor among you (for the LORD will bless you in the land which the LORD your God gives you for an inheritance to possess), if only you will obey the voice of the LORD your God, being careful to do all this commandment which I command you this day (Deut. 15.4-5).

Verhey understands the lack of poverty as a promise that is dependent on Israel's obedience. If poverty exists, then there must have been some

---

31. Hoppe, *There Shall be No Poor among you*, p. 147.
32. Burridge, *Imitating Jesus*, p. 266.
33. Verhey, *Remembering Jesus*, p. 272.
34. Verhey, *Remembering Jesus*, p. 272.
35. Verhey, *Remembering Jesus*, pp. 273-74.

violation of God's covenant. Verhey admits that 'it is true that Jesus focuses attention on himself'.[36] But Verhey insists that Jesus' words are more about calling attention to how 'the presence of poverty called forth judgment on Israel and demonstrated that it is not yet God's unchallenged reign'.[37]

Verhey's defense of Jesus relies on his poor exegesis of Deuteronomy 15. While it is true that Deuteronomy 15 makes the prosperity of Israel conditional on their obedience, it is another thing to affirm that the statement about the continued presence of the poor 'becomes not only a judgment but also the occasion for the continuing invitation to repent of tight-fistedness and to "open the hand to the poor and needy neighbor in your land" (Deut. 15.11)'.[38] Indeed, even if the presence of poverty in Israel signals a judgment by God, the continued presence of that judgment does not remove the obligation to help the poor as long as the poor remain in the land. The whole lesson of Deuteronomy 15 is that a continued presence of the poor demands a continued assistance to them.

However, Jesus does not acknowledge any continuing assistance at all in his logion. Jesus' truncated quotation amounts to a distortion of the lesson of Deut. 15.11. If Jesus had included the rest of the verse, it would be clear that he was in violation of it. The verse demanded continued assistance to the poor, and he denied assistance to the poor. Note that Deut. 15.11 does not say, as Jesus implies, that one can deny help to the poor because one will not always be around. But that is precisely how Jesus justifies his denial of helping the poor when he says 'you will not always have me'. Neither Verhey nor any other major New Testament ethicist critically examines or interrogates Jesus' own exegesis of Deuteronomy 15 to see if it is sound.

Metaethically, both Verhey and Jesus use dubious and even unethical premises to justify Jesus' actions. The premise seems to be this in schematic form: If Person X calls attention to poverty as a judgment of God, then X is justified in retaining resources that could go to the poor. That means that the value of calling attention to God's judgment is more valuable than feeding the hungry. Verhey never addresses the metaethics of Jesus' claim that his limited existence justifies his denial of aid to the poor. Nor does Verhey explain why any judgment upon Israel justifies denying aid to the poor or the hungry. In fact, Verhey contradicts himself as Deut. 15.11-12 demands precisely that aid continue to the poor regardless of whether there is a judgment and regardless of whether someone else will not always exist

36. Verhey, *Remembering Jesus*, p. 273.
37. Verhey, *Remembering Jesus*, p. 273.
38. Verhey, *Remembering Jesus*, p. 273. For other understandings of the mandate in Deuteronomy, see Hoppe, *There Shall be No Poor among you*, especially p. 31; E.O. Nwaoru, 'Poverty Eradication: A Divine Mandate', *African Ecclesial Review* 46 (2004), pp. 198-213.

as an individual. And given that the disciples were supposed to be poor, it is unclear how they were supposed to help the poor.

Verhey misrepresents Jesus' answer to the disciples. It may be true that Jesus did not rebuke the disciples for being concerned about the poor. But a case can be made that he rebuked them for not being more concerned about his impending absence than about the poor. A case can also be made that Jesus is not calling attention to Israel's judgment for having poverty. Nothing in the text indicates such a reading. On the contrary, Jesus gives two explicit reasons for why the needs of the poor should be denied in this instance:

A. Whenever you will, you can do good to them;
B. but you will not always have me.

The contrast Jesus makes is clear here, and it has nothing to do with exposing the presence of the poor as a judgment. Because of the limited time Jesus has, resources should go to his body instead of to the poor. Once you compare an individual poor person who is denied assistance to Jesus as an individual who wishes his corpse to smell good (the proper symmetry is comparing an individual to an individual, not Jesus to a class of people), then the moral absurdity of Jesus' request becomes more pointed.

Elaine Wainwright's defense of Jesus uses a feminist ecological orientation.[39] For Wainwright, the woman who anoints Jesus is acting as a healer, and thus transgressing into the domain of male healers. Wainwright further alleges that the identification of the *alabastron* as the component of the flask with the costly substances 'turns our attention toward the Earth... Earth has given of it resources to provide the woman with an appropriate container for the costly ointment and perfumed oil.'[40] Since it is a gift from the earth, the disciples ought to appreciate it. Instead they scold the woman.[41] As Wainwright remarks:

39. Elaine Wainwright, 'Healing Ointment/Healing Bodies: Gift and Identification in a Ecofeminist Reading of Mark 14.3-9', in *Exploring Ecological Hermeneutics* (ed. Norman C. Habel and Peter Trudinger; Atlanta, GA: Society of Biblical Literature, 2008), pp. 131-39. For Wainwright's previous studies of this passage, see Elaine M. Wainwright, *Women Healing/Healing Women: The Genderization of Healing in Early Christianity* (London: Equinox, 2006), pp. 131-38; idem, 'The Pouring Out of Healing Ointment: Rereading Mark 14.3-9', in *Toward a New Heaven and a New Earth: Essays in Honor of Elisabeth Schüssler Fiorenza* (ed. Fernando F. Segovia; Maryknoll, NY: Orbis Books, 2003), pp. 157-78.

40. Wainwright, 'Healing Ointment/Healing Bodies', p. 134.

41. For the role of women in death and burial activities, see Kathleen E. Corley, 'Women and the Crucifixion and Burial of Jesus', *Forum: A Journal of the Foundations and Facets of Western Culture*, New Series 1 (1998), pp. 181-225. For the perfume industry, see Ehud Netzer, 'Did Any Perfume Industry Exist at 'Ein Feshkha?', *Israel Exploration Journal* 55.1 (2005), pp. 97-100.

[T]hey name the gift or the giving of the gift as waste, and they reproach the giver (verse 5). They negate the gift and the life-enhancing aspect of the gift. They name it as a 'destruction' and in their very act of naming they cause a destruction of their relationship to the *muron*... At the heart of not only this gifting that is the central focus of this Markan account but of all gifting is 'dependence'... A denial of dependence means an inability to recognize dependence on the Earth and its gifts in a web of relationships, contrary to what the woman and Jesus knew.[42]

Wainwright accuses the disciples of commodifying the *muron* because for them '[i]t is a means of exchange and it is into this web of exchange that they draw giving to the poor'.[43]

For Wainwright, Jesus is actually revealing the flaws of this commodity-exchange view of the gift. As Wainwright remarks, 'Jesus, however, rescues the giving to the poor from the commodity-exchange model that the indignant ones signify'.[44] Jesus' reprimand of the disciples should be seen as an encouragement to move away from this commodity-exchange model and see 'a new mode of gifting: Whenever they "will" they are able to do good for the poor, just as the woman did a good thing for Jesus.'[45]

Wainwright's proposal has many infirmities. First, her characterization of what was objectionable about the woman's actions contradicts the plain sense of the text. The woman is not called a healer nor is there any indication in the text that her healing activity is objectionable to the disciples. Not only does the plain text not describe the woman as performing a healing, but Jesus explicitly says that 'she has anointed my body beforehand for burying'. According to Rachel Hachlili's study of Second Temple Jewish burial customs, the preparation of the body for burial was 'usually the duty of women'.[46] If the woman is engaged in burial rituals, then the woman was not transgressing any domain of male healers at all.[47] Moreover, the plain text says that the question asked by those who complained was 'Why was

42. Wainwright, 'Healing Ointment/Healing Bodies', pp. 136-37.

43. Wainwright, 'Healing Ointment/Healing Bodies', p. 137.

44. Wainwright, 'Healing Ointment/Healing Bodies', p. 138. For the view that the activities of the historical Jesus were materially political in aim (and later religionized by disciples), see Douglas E. Oakman, *The Political Aims of Jesus* (Minneapolis: Fortress Press, 2012), especially p. 4.

45. Wainwright, 'Healing Ointment/Healing Bodies', p. 138.

46. Rachel Hachlili, *Jewish Funerary Customs, Practice and Rites in the Second Temple Period* (Supplements for the Journal for the Study of Judaism, 94; Leiden: E.J. Brill, 2005), p. 480. See also Angela Standhartinger, 'What Women were Supposed to Do for the Dead Beloved by them (*Gospel of Peter* 12.50): Traces of Laments and Mourning Rituals in Early Easter Passion, and Lord's Supper Traditions', *JBL* 129.3 (2010), pp. 559-74.

47. Elisabeth Moltmann-Wendel (*The Women around Jesus* [New York: Crossroad, 1987], pp. 96-97) regards it as an error to think that anointing 'is a strictly feminine

the ointment thus wasted?', not 'Why is this woman healing?' or 'Why is a woman healing you?'

Second, Wainwright places too much weight on the Greek phrase, καλὸν ἔργον ἠργάσατο ἐν ἐμοί, which she translates as '"a good work" has been done "in me"', to support a therapeutic interpretation.[48] Jesus, according to Wainwright, is referencing 'healing in the very materiality of his body, to his very heart, the place of deep anxiety "in [him]" (ἐν ἐμοί)'.[49] But the phrase, ἐν ἐμοί, is probably best translated as a dative expression, 'for/to me', as does Adela Collins ('She has done a good deed to me').[50] The same understanding is shared by the NRSV, REB, NAB and NJB versions, as well as by Wainwright herself.[51] Therefore, there is also no healing or interiority (e.g., inner anxiety to be healed) necessarily designated by ἐν ἐμοί. John Charles Doudna collects examples from the papyri of where the verb ἐρ-γάζεσθαι uses a dative, instead of an accusative, to describe 'benefiting and harming'.[52] But the benefits need not be healing. Matthew Black suggests an Aramaism that need not involve healing.[53]

Third, Wainwright's idea that the ointments are a 'gift' of the earth is arbitrary. Wainwright tries to redeem Jesus and the woman by claiming that she is offering Jesus a gift from the Earth.[54] But one could just as well describe the removal of those medicinal resources as 'robbing' the Earth. After all, why does Wainwright characterize these ointments as a gift but not coal or oil? How is taking coal from the earth different from taking ointments from nature?

Fourth, Wainwright's metaethical premises are selective and/or unclear. For example, what does it mean to say that in calling the *muron* a waste, the objectors 'cause a destruction of their relationship to the *muron*'? That is akin to saying that calling the use of coal a waste 'causes a destruction of a relationship to the *coal*'. Why should calling something a waste not affirm the objectors' connection and relationship with the poor, which is what they explicitly mentioned? Why is it not Jesus who is severing his relationship

practice', but she neither carefully distinguishes funerary from other types of anointing, nor does she cite any extra-biblical archaeological evidence for her statement.

48. Wainwright, *Women Healing/Healing Women*, p. 135.

49. Wainwright, 'The Pouring Out of Healing Ointment', p. 168.

50. Collins, *Mark: A Commentary*, p. 620.

51. Wainwright ('Healing Ointment/Healing Bodies', p. 138) translates the phrase at least once as 'good work in/for Jesus'.

52. John Charles Doudna, *The Greek of the Gospel of Mark* (Journal of Biblical Literature Monograph Series, 12; Philadelphia, PA: Society of Biblical Literature and Exegesis, 1961), pp. 14-15.

53. Matthew Black, *An Aramaic Approach to the Gospels* (New York: Oxford University Press, 3rd edn, 1967), p. 301.

54. Wainwright, *Women Healing/Healing Women*, p. 134.

with the poor? Wainwright apparently critically accepts that what Jesus regards as a 'gift' to him should also be regarded as a gift to the poor by everyone else. But why privilege Jesus' valuation of this substance, and not that of assistance to the poor or those standing up for the poor?

Fifth, it is ethically meaningless to describe Jesus as rejecting a commodity-exchange model, and announcing a 'new mode of gifting'.[55] Whatever type of exchange model one uses, and whatever mode of gifting one uses, will not change the fact that Jesus admits that money could have been 'gifted' to the poor. That money could have served the real biological and material needs of human beings. Using the money to feed the hungry provides a much clearer biological and material alleviation of suffering than any money spent on alleviating any inner anxiety that Wainwright attempts to retrieve from the text. Indeed, Wainwright never explains why Jesus' need for relief should be placed above that of thousands of hungry children who might also have been relieved in a real way.

Sermon on the Mount of Debts and Merits

Matthew 5–7 contain what is commonly known as the Sermon on the Mount, which contains some of the best known teachings of Jesus. According to Wayne A. Meeks, '[t]he Sermon on the Mount serves as the epitome of Jesus' teaching'.[56] J.L. Houlden tells readers that '[c]lassically and popularly, the Sermon on the Mount has been regarded as the quintessence of the moral teaching of Jesus'.[57] Others are more cautious in attributing that Sermon to Jesus himself, and attribute it to Matthew or some other source. Burridge praises Verhey for challenging Houlden and recognizing that the Sermon 'is rather the quintessence of Matthew's ethics'.[58]

---

55. For the argument that Roman patronage did not have a significant effect on Judaism and almsgiving, see Erlend D. MacGillivray, 'Re-evaluating Patronage and Reciprocity in Antiquity and New Testament Studies', *Journal of Greco-Roman Christianity and Judaism* 6 (2009), pp. 37-81. For another view, see Zeba A. Crook, *Reconceptualizing Conversion: Patronage, Loyalty, and Conversion in the Religions of the Ancient Mediterranean* (Berlin: W. de Gruyter, 2004).

56. Meeks, *The Origins of Christian Morality*, p. 200.

57. J.L. Houlden, *Ethics and the New Testament* (Edinburgh: T. & T. Clark, 1992), p. 53.

58. Burridge, *Imitating Jesus*, p. 206. It is rather obvious that Burridge (*Imitating Jesus*, p. 206) did not consult Houlden directly, but rather through the representation of Allen Verhey (*The Great Reversal: Ethics and the New Testament* [Grand Rapids, MI: Eerdmans, 1984], p. 85). Houlden (*Ethics and the New Testament*, p. 54) recognizes the Sermon does not represent the words of Jesus, and he remarks 'the Sermon on the Mount at least presents the ethics, or part of the ethics, in which Matthew believed'.

Although most New Testament ethicists defend that Sermon as an example of Christian ethics, there have been dissenters. According to W.D. Davies, the Sermon on the Mount has been considered by some to be a 'pernicious document, which, by presenting an impossible ethic, has wrought incalculable harm in personal, social, and international life'.[59] Davies quotes Sir James Fitzjames Stephen, the distinguished English jurist, as regarding that Sermon as 'not only impudent but unjust'.[60]

The aim of this section is not to rehearse all the arguments about the sources and redaction of the Sermon.[61] For the moment, I agree that the beatitudes in Matthew and Luke are a variant of widespread Jewish traditions that can be found in the Dead Sea Scrolls and also in other cultures.[62] For example, the Qumran text designated as 4Q525 has a concatenation of beatitudes addressed in the third person and beginning with אשרי, which would correspond to *makarios* in the Sermon on the Mount. Note this chain:

> Blessed are those who adhere to his laws,
> and do not adhere to perverted paths.
> Blessed are those who rejoice in her
> and do not explore insane paths.
> Blessed are those who search for her with pure hands
> and do not importune her with treacherous heart.[63]

Given such widespread traditions that pre-existed Jesus, it is difficult to ever reconstruct what he actually said, as any editor or writer could easily mix and match preexisting collections or add new ones. I agree that at least

---

59. W.D. Davies, *The Setting of the Sermon on the Mount* (Cambridge: Cambridge University Press, 1963), p. 1.

60. Davies, *The Setting of the Sermon on the Mount*, p. 1.

61. For an exhaustive study of the Sermon, see Hans Dieter Betz, *The Sermon on the Mount* (Hermeneia; Minneapolis: Fortress Press, 1995). See also Frank Matera, *The Sermon on the Mount: The Perfect Measure of the Christian Life* (Collegeville, MN: Liturgical Press, 2013); Hans-Ulrich Weidemann (ed.), *Er stieg auf der Berg... und lehre sie (Mt. 5, 1f.): Exegetische und rezeptiongeschichtliche Studien zur Bergpredigt* (Stuttgarter Bibelstudien, 226; Stuttgart: Katholischen Bibelwerk, 2012); Charles H. Talbert, *Reading the Sermon on the Mount: Character Formation and Decision Making in Mattthew 5–7* (Columbia: University of South Carolina Press, 2004); Benedict T. Viviano, 'The Sermon on the Mount in Recent Study', *Bib* 78 (1997), pp. 255-65.

62. For Egyptian beatitudes, see Jacques Dupont, 'Béatitudes egyptiennes', *Bib* 47 (1966), pp. 185-222.

63. Following Martínez, *The Dead Sea Scrolls Translated*, p. 395. For the first publication, see Émile Puech, '4Q525 et les péricopes des beatitudes en Ben Sira et Matthieu', *RB* 98 (1991), pp. 80-106. For a more popular report, see Benedict T. Viviano, 'Beatitudes Found among Dead Sea Scrolls', *BARev* 18 (1992), pp. 53-55, 66. For the links with Proverbs, see Elisa Uusimäki, 'Use of Scripture in 4QBeatitudes: A Torah-Adjustment to Proverbs 1–9', *Dead Sea Discoveries* 20 (2013), pp. 71-97.

the first few beatitudes of the Sermon on the Mount may have been inspired by Isa. 61.1-4.[64]

Instead, the objective is to explore how the beatitude concerning the poor in Mt. 5.3 has been used to uphold Jesus' care for the poor despite the fact that the meaning of this beatitude is unclear. Indeed, the very meaning of the Greek words Μακάριοι, πτωχοί and πτωχοὶ τῷ πνεύματι (usually translated as 'blessed', 'poor' and 'poor in spirit', respectively) has been hotly contested.[65] So, instead of providing a definitive conclusion about the 'real' original meaning of these words and the entire beatitude, I seek to show how the meanings that Christian New Testament scholars themselves give are usually permeated by an effort to portray Jesus in a better light. I will show that alternative meanings, which show Jesus in a poorer light, are just as plausible.

The Sermon on the Mount (SM) in Matthew 5 is related to the Sermon on the Plain (SP) in Luke 6, which both share the same first macarism, or 'blessing'.[66] The Matthean and Lucan versions of the first beatitude or macarism are as follows:

> Blessed are the poor in spirit, for theirs is the kingdom of heaven/Μακά-ριοι οἱ πτωχοὶ τῷ πνεύματι ὅτι αὐτῶν ἐστιν ἡ βασιλεία τῶν οὐρανῶν (Mt. 5.3)

> Blessed are you poor, for yours is the kingdom of God/Μακάριοι οἱ πτωχοὶ ὅτι ὑμετέρα ἐστὶν ἡ βασιλεία τοῦ Θεοῦ (Lk. 6.20).

In both cases, many New Testament ethicists use the beatitude as evidence that Jesus is a friend of the poor.[67]

The macarism is ethically problematic because it raises the question of how one could possibly consider the poor to be blessed. In his massive commentary on the Sermon, Hans Dieter Betz explains the problem:

> The term 'the poor' has unquestionably always referred to persons living in social and economic misery. Therefore, it is important to realize that the SM does *not* regard the condition of poverty as a blessing. At this point, the SM differs from some strands of Greek philosophy critical of external wealth... Indeed, praising the condition of poverty as such would hardly be conceivable in antiquity, unless it were done as an act of folly or cynicism.

---

64. For others who have elaborated on this connection, see Martin Hengel, 'Zur matthäischen Bergpredigt und ihrem jüdischen Hintergrund', *Theologische Rundschau* 52 (1987), pp. 327-400; Betz, *The Sermon on the Mount*, p. 121; Ulrich Luz, *Matthew 1–7: A Commentary* (Minneapolis: Fortress Press, 2007), p. 193.

65. The literature on these terms alone is enormous, but some representative studies include Korinna Zamfir, 'Who are (the) Blessed? Reflections on the Relecture of the Beatitudes in the New Testament and Apocrypha', *Sacra Scripta* 5 (2007), pp. 75-100.

66. I follow the abbreviations of Betz, *The Sermon on the Mount.*

67. See Burridge, *Imitating Jesus*, p. 261.

> Also, praising the poor simply because they are poor economically would
> be equally cynical because experience indicates that poor people may be
> good or bad like everyone else.[68]

Note how Betz, who elsewhere praises Jesus for radical innovation, cannot
seem to fathom that Jesus might break with tradition and praise what is not
regarded as praiseworthy in Greco-Roman or Jewish culture.

Nonetheless, it is true that the poor need not be viewed as virtuous. For
example, the author of 1 Timothy does not seem to view the poor or young
widows as morally virtuous just because of any need for assistance (cf.
1 Tim. 5.15) or poverty:

> But refuse to enroll younger widows; for when they grow wanton against
> Christ they desire to marry, and so they incur condemnation for having vio-
> lated their first pledge. Besides that, they learn to be idlers, gadding about
> from house to house, and not only idlers but gossips and busybodies, saying
> what they should not (1 Tim. 5.11-13).

Early Christians believed that some unemployed people may abuse the
charity of others (2 Thess. 3.11).[69] The *Didache* identified as false those
prophets who sought more than two days of lodging or money. An apostle
was supposed to ask only for bread (εἰ μὴ ἄρτον) until reaching the night's
lodging.[70]

On the other hand, one also must be sensitive to broader literary conventions. For example, Arkady Kovelman, the Russian rabbinic scholar, has
called attention to how the dichotomy of poor and rich was increasingly
used as a trope in Hellenistic and post-New Testament literature.

> But the second-fourth centuries witnessed the generalization and typifica-
> tion of every conflict: the author was always a 'moderate', honest, and poor
> man, while the offender was always a 'powerful' man. The virtues of the
> 'poor' and the vices of the 'rich' were invariably enumerated; references to
> abstract law and morality were ubiquitous.[71]

For Kovelman, however, these trends began already by the time of Jesus,
and so it is difficult to attribute to Jesus some innovative mentality about
rich/poor relations when it is probably part of a larger literary trend that
Gospel writers might have utilized.

---

68. Betz, *The Sermon on the Mount*, p. 114; SM = Sermon on the Mount for Betz.

69. On the role of work in early Christianity, see Ben Witherington, *Work: A Kingdom
Perspective on Labor* (Grand Rapids, MI: Eerdmans, 2011).

70. *Didache* 11.3-6 (Lake, LCL). See also Huub Van de Sandt (ed.), *Matthew and the
Didache: Two Documents from the Same Jewish-Christian Milieu?* (Minneapolis: Fortress Press, 2005).

71. Arkady Kovelman, 'Continuity and Change in Hellenistic Jewish Exegesis and in
Early Rabbinic Literature', *Review of Rabbinic Literature* 7 (2004), pp. 123-61 (124).

Given the problems of declaring the poor to be 'blessed', there is no shortage of proposed solutions that are often internally contradictory. For example, Ulrich Luz, a prominent Matthean scholar, in one instance rejects the notion of a present blessing when he remarks that '[t]he background of these three beatitudes is instead the apocalyptic hope for a total reversal of conditions'.[72] Yet, Luz also states that 'these beatitudes are not designed to give comfort by making promises about the next life; they are an authoritative language act that pronounces people happy in the here and now'.[73] Otherwise, Luz seems to follow a hybrid approach wherein the beatitude is descriptive of both the present and the future.

Mark Allan Powell believes that the poor here 'are people who have no reason for hope in this world, period'.[74] But how can they possibly be called 'blessed' if they have no hope in this world? Powell proposes dividing Mt. 5.3-10 into two stanzas:

> Acceptance of a two-stanza structure allows for a compromise solution to the reversal-reward debate: the first stanza (5.3-6) speaks of reversals for the unfortunate, and the second stanza (5.7-10) describes rewards for the virtuous.[75]

Powell then elaborates:

> The real sense of the apodosis of this beatitude (see also 5.10; 19.14) may be brought out by taking the two genitive constructions as objective and subjective complements of a verbal noun. The phrase then reads simply, 'heaven rules them'. According to Matthew's Gospel, the rule of heaven (or God) implies the accomplishment of God's will (6.10). When Jesus says the poor in spirit are blessed because heaven rules them, he means that the accomplishment of God's will is going to be a blessing to those who are poor in spirit.[76]

Powell provides no detailed linguistic defense for turning what are normally understood as possessive genitives (i.e., 'theirs is the kingdom of heaven'/ αὐτῶν ἐστιν ἡ βασιλεία τῶν οὐρανῶν) into 'two genitive constructions

---

72. Luz, *Matthew 1–7*, p. 189. For Luz's own perspective on what type of 'history' Matthew is writing, and for his rejection of the idea that Matthew was following any type of fictional writing, see Ulrich Luz, 'Geschichte und Wahrheit im Matthäusevangelium: Das Problem der narrativen Fiktionen', *EvT* 69 (2009), pp. 194-208. For studies of the reversal of fortune theme in pre-Christian literature, see Abraham Winitzer, 'The Reversal of Fortune Theme in Esther: Israelite Historiography in its Ancient Near Eastern Context', *Journal of Ancient Near Eastern Religions* 11 (2011), pp. 170-218.

73. Luz, *Matthew 1–7*, p. 190.

74. Mark Allan Powell, 'Matthew's Beatitudes: Reversals and Rewards of the Kingdom', *CBQ* 58 (1996), pp. 460-79 (464).

75. Powell, 'Matthew's Beatitudes', p. 462.

76. Powell, 'Matthew's Beatitudes', p. 465.

as objective and subjective complements of a verbal noun'. Powell gives no examples of where else such a construction is found, especially in Matthew.

If one looks at ancient translations of Mt. 5.3, one finds that those genitives are uniformly translated as possessive genitives:

Latin: ipsorum est regnum caelorum
Gothic: izwara ist thiudangardi himine
Syriac: dlhwn hy mlkwt' dšmy'

If anything, I would expect the Gothic version to translate it in the manner that Powell envisions.[77] One might also expect the Syriac to agree with Powell as it is simply another form of Aramaic, the supposed language of Jesus.

The only semblance of an argument for this reading by Powell is as follows:

According to Matthew's Gospel, the rule of heaven (or God) implies the accomplishment of God's will (6.10). When Jesus says the poor in spirit are blessed because heaven rules them, he means that the accomplishment of God's will is going to be a blessing to those who are poor in spirit. The assumption is that God does not want anyone to be poor in spirit and that when God's will is accomplished no one will be poor in spirit any longer. Whether they know it or not, those who have no reason for hope in the world, who may be on the verge of giving up, are blessed, for the rule of heaven has drawn near (4.17), and their situation is about to change.[78]

But the fact that the rule of heaven implies the accomplishment of God's will does not mean that Mt. 5.3 should be translated as 'heaven rules them' instead of as 'theirs is the Kingdom of heaven'.

Overall, Powell is unsuccessful in showing that the poor are not regarded as being blessed now, as Luz proposed at least in one instance. By Powell's account, the poor should be regarded as blessed or should regard themselves as blessed because a future reward awaits them. After all, even Powell's own proposal entails that 'the rule of heaven has drawn near', and so why can't the macarism be promising the poor both rewards and a reversal of their condition? Despite any suffering they endure now, as long as the poor have a future reward, then they are counted as blessed and fortunate now.

---

77. The Gothic version, translated by Ulfilas, the apostle to the Goths in the fourth century, is often underutilized because most biblical scholars do not know the language or think it a minor version. However, the Gothic version displays one very important attribute, namely its severe literalness. As Bruce Metzger and Bart Ehrman (*The Text of the New Testament: Its Transmission, Corruption and Restoration* [New York: Oxford University Press, 4th edn, 2005], p. 116) observe, 'Ulfilas' translation is remarkably faithful to the original, frequently to the point of being literalistic'.

78. Powell, 'Matthew's Beatitudes', p. 465.

Given the undesirability of saying that the poor should be regarded as blessed, there is also an effort to deny that Luke meant just 'the poor', as its text plainly states. But that 'the poor' in Luke is more original and/or is meant more literally may be the reason one finds 'the poor in spirit' in Matthew.[79] Perhaps Matthew also saw how odd it would be to say that the poor are blessed now, and so he has 'the poor in spirit' instead of just 'the poor' as does Luke. Betz denies any difference between Matthew and Luke and insists there was no softening by Matthew. Betz evaluates Matthew and Luke as follows:

> There is no stark contrast between them; rather, the SM simply spells out what the SP suggests. The SM wards off the misunderstanding that salvation is promised to the poor simply because they are in economic straits. Such a misconception could lead to questions like, What about a poor crook? The shift from suggestion to definition touches on the further question, What does poverty mean? Who is to be considered poor? Moreover the juxtaposition of poor and rich as social types conforms more to the Hellenistic mentality, while 'the poor in Spirit' (SM) describes Jewish notions of piety.[80]

Perhaps so, but why can't Jesus in Luke mean that he regards the poor, crooked or straight, as blessed? Jesus ate with sinners and prostitutes, and so why is calling the poor blessed that much more transgressive?

That apologetics rather than strict philology is the reason for Betz's view can be detected by how he uses Epiphanius of Salamis (ca. 310–403) to support his contention that 'the expression "poor in (the) spirit" points to an intellectual insight into the human condition. The attitude corresponding to this insight is "humility", a virtue highly prized in antiquity'.[81] Betz refers readers to Epiphanius' explanation for the name of Ebion, the leader of the famous heretical sect of the Ebionites. As quoted by Betz, Epiphanius says that Ebion is so named 'for he is truly poor in his intellect, in his hope and in his work'.[82] The key phrase in Greek is πτωχὸς...τῇ διανοια...τῇ ἐλπίδι...τῷ ἔργῳ, which all have datives modifying 'poor' and so similar to the construction (οἱ πτωχοὶ τῷ πνεύματι) in Mt. 5.3. However, as used by Epiphanius, this construction has no reference to anything relating

---

79. For example, Georg Strecker, 'Die Makarismen der Bergpredigt', *NTS* 17 (1971), pp. 255-75 (257): 'Die Urtradition wird durch Lk. vi. 20-3 (Mt. v.3 f., 6, 11 f.) bezeugt'. For the view that the poor were a major socioeconomic group in Galilee, see M. Thompson, '"Blessed are the Poor": What Did Jesus Mean by These Words?', *Friends Quarterly* 35 (2006), pp. 58-63. See also, David A. Fiensy and Ralph K. Hawkins (eds.), *The Galilean Economy in the Time of Jesus* (Atlanta, GA: Society of Biblical Literature, 2013).

80. Betz, *The Sermon on the Mount*, p. 576.

81. Betz, *The Sermon on the Mount*, pp. 115-16 and n. 173.

82. Betz, *The Sermon on the Mount*, p. 115 n. 173.

to humility because Epiphanius is describing features he finds contempt-ible in a heretic group.[83] So Epiphanius' use of 'poor' with modifiers other than 'in spirit' still does not tell us what 'poor in spirit' means in Matthew.

Despite Betz's denials, Mt. 5.3 can plausibly be considered a softening of Lk. 6.20. After all, Luke had no qualms about demanding that people give up everything they owned. Already in 1908 Karl Kautsky (1854–1938), the Czech-German Marxist writer, argued that Matthew was softening an ear-lier and more radical socialist program of Jesus.[84] If so, Luke may preserve the earlier and more 'original' belief that being poor was a good thing as long as you were following Jesus or as long as you believed one day Jesus would help you reverse your situation.[85]

Kenneth C. Hanson offers a solution based on so-called Mediterranean social values of honor and shame.[86] Hanson distinguishes a 'blessing' from a 'macarism' as follows.

> [M]akarisms are fundamentally different from blessings in a variety of ways. (1) Makarisms are not 'words of power'. (2) They are not limited to pronouncements by God or cultic mediators. (3) They only refer to humans, and never to God or non-human objects. (4) They do not have their setting in ritual. And (5) one does not pray for a makarism, or refer to oneself with a makarism.[87]

Hanson thinks that this proposal will avoid any thought that Jesus is declar-ing the poor to be blessed in the sense of 'happy' or the like. As he remarks:

---

83. Epiphanius, *Panarion* 30.17: 'For he is indeed poor, in understanding, hope and actual fact, since he takes Christ for a mere man, and thus hopes in him with poverty of faith.' Following the edition of Frank Williams, *The Panarion of Epiphanius* (2 vols.; Leiden: E.J. Brill, 1994), I, p. 133. For the Greek text cited by Betz, see Karl Holl, *Die griechischen christliche Schriftsteller der ersten drei Jahrhunderte* (2 vols.; Leipzig: J.C. Hinrichs, 1915), I, p. 355.

84. Karl Kautsky, *Der Ursprung des Christentums: Eine historische Untersuchung* (Stuttgart: Dietz, 1908), pp. 345-47: 'Hier fand sie "Stürmische und Revolutionäre des urchristlichen Enthusiasm und Sozialismus so moderiert zur richtigen Mitte eines kirchlichen Opportunismus, dass es für den Bestand einer mit der menschlichen Gesell-schaft sich auf Friedensfuss stellenden organisierten Kirche nicht mehr bedrohlich schien."' Kautsky is here quoting and approving of the statement of Otto Pfleiderer, *Das Urchristentum: Seine Schriften und Lehren in geschichtlichem Zusammenhang* (2 vols.; Berlin: Georg Reimer, 2nd edn, 1902), I, p. 613.

85. Note again, Luz (*Matthew 8–20*, p. 112), where he says that 'the original saying was formulated in a more radical, viz., in an antithetical way: "Whoever does not hate father and mother…"'.

86. Kenneth C. Hanson, '"How Honorable! How Shameful!" A Cultural Analysis of Matthew's Makarisms and Reproaches', *Semeia* 68 (1996), pp. 81-112.

87. Hanson, 'How Honorable!', p. 93.

But if ־רשׁא and μακάριος do not refer to a ritual blessing, neither do they mean 'happy'. They are not expressions of positive human emotion. One does not feel good who fears Yahweh (Ps 112.1), or walks in Yahweh's law (Ps 119.1), or is reproved and chastened by Yahweh (Job 5.17)! Similarly, one does not feel good who mourns or is persecuted (Mt. 5.4, 10). So 'happy' is a profoundly misleading translation and interpretation of the makarism.[88]

To support this argument, Hanson points to the following example in Sirach:

Nine considerations have I honored (ἐμακάρισα) in my heart, and the tenth I will utter with my tongue...

O how honorable (μακάριος) is the one who lives with an understanding wife... O how honorable (μακάριος) is the one who has found prudence... (Sir. 25.7-9).[89]

Given that *makarios* can be 'honorable', he proposes that this is how it should be read in Mt. 5.3, which has the following structure:

I. Makarism proper
   A. Value judgment: μακάριοι ('How honored')
   B. Subject (plural substantive)

II. Grant of honor
   A. Conjunction: ὅτι ('for')
   B. Present or future status.[90]

Hanson has a stronger philological argument than Powell, but it will not help mitigate the ethical problems with this macarism. Hanson does not explain why being poor in itself should be an honor. I have already cited examples of where being poor is not synonymous with being virtuous or honorable, which is what Hanson assumes.

The first macarism does not render Jesus a friend of the poor. If the poor are honorable or 'blessed' because of some future status, then one is again lapsing into a reward system that substitutes a lofty self-image (being 'honorable') for concrete help to alleviate the poverty. And why seek to change your poor status if it is such a blessing or an honor? Calling the poor 'honorable' because of some future reward will not feed the poor today. Calling the poor 'honorable' or 'blessed' will not solve the problem that is causing the poverty. If the imminent or future Kingdom of Heaven is supposed to remedy that poverty, then Jesus' entire program has failed or has allowed poverty to endure for more than two thousand years. It is perfectly reasonable to propose that Jesus was trying to raise hope in the midst of the Roman

88. Hanson, 'How Honorable!', p. 89.
89. Hanson, 'How Honorable!', p. 90.
90. Hanson, 'How Honorable!', pp. 99-100.

occupation. But that is also no reason to praise his ethics if what he promises is no more real than what any other religion promised its followers.

Jesus as Junk Bond Salesman

What most New Testament ethicists either deny or attempt to sanitize is that Jesus is actually more akin to a modern junk bond salesman. He is offering a spiritual version of Wall Street. But what he offers is worse than Wall Street because the returns and rewards promised can never be verified to exist, and historically they have never been fulfilled. Indeed, almost any modern financial counselor or professor of business ethics would ridicule investors for giving all their money to a Wall Street trader who promises heavenly rewards. Wall Street traders have gone to prison for less than that. It is usually held to be unethical to promise rewards that don't exist, or rewards that are completely unverifiable. Things are different in modern New Testament ethics. An illustrative case is found in the story of the rich man. The Markan version is as follows:

> And as he was setting out on his journey, a man ran up and knelt before him, and asked him, 'Good Teacher, what must I do to inherit eternal life?' And Jesus said to him, 'Why do you call me good? No one is good but God alone. You know the commandments: "Do not kill, Do not commit adultery, Do not steal, Do not bear false witness, Do not defraud, Honor your father and mother"'. And he said to him, 'Teacher, all these I have observed from my youth'. And Jesus looking upon him loved him, and said to him, 'You lack one thing; go, sell what you have, and give to the poor, and you will have treasure in heaven; and come, follow me'. At that saying his countenance fell, and he went away sorrowful; for he had great possessions. And Jesus looked around and said to his disciples, 'How hard it will be for those who have riches to enter the kingdom of God!' And the disciples were amazed at his words. But Jesus said to them again, 'Children, how hard it is to enter the kingdom of God! It is easier for a camel to go through the eye of a needle than for a rich man to enter the kingdom of God'. And they were exceedingly astonished, and said to him, 'Then who can be saved?' Jesus looked at them and said, 'With men it is impossible, but not with God; for all things are possible with God'. Peter began to say to him, 'Lo, we have left everything and followed you'. Jesus said, 'Truly, I say to you, there is no one who has left house or brothers or sisters or mother or father or children or lands, for my sake and for the gospel, who will not receive a hundredfold now in this time, houses and brothers and sisters and mothers and children and lands, with persecutions, and in the age to come eternal life. But many that are first will be last, and the last first' (Mk 10.17-31).

New Testament ethicists usually characterize this story as one where avarice is stronger than faith. Jesus' requests are seen as just and righteous. Jesus is a friend of the poor because he encourages the rich man to give his possessions to the poor. In his study of the ethics of Mark's Gospel, Dan O. Via tells readers:

> [T]he poor figure in the statement of the ethical norm: *whatever you have sell and give to the poor*. But it is tacit in this passage and clear in the next one that Mark has more interest in the consequences of possessions for the ethical agent who might give than he has in the consequences for the other/neighbor/poor to whom the money might be given. His question is: can the *rich* man enter the kingdom of God. Giving to the poor, as Mark implicitly interprets it by means of this story about the rich man, is intentioned by self-interest... But the self-interest which is served by gaining eternal life is a paradoxical one, for eternal life here as interpreted by the story, is freedom from the self, from self-interest, which enables one to give to the poor. The pattern of radical concern for the poor intentioned by the desire for eternal life for oneself may have a christological parallel and basis in Mark.[91]

Via goes on to explain the specific reasons for Jesus' actions. For Via, Jesus accepts giving his life as a ransom for many (Mk 10.45) because he 'wants to be obedient to the necessity (8.31) which has been written for him in Scripture (14.21) and grounded in the will of God (14.36)'.[92]

Via's interpretation of this passage cannot be sustained by a plain reading of the text. It is true that Jesus is testing the rich man's willingness to give up his possessions. But is not true that Jesus' response is not premised on self-interest. The explanation Jesus gives to his disciples confirms that he sees giving up earthly possessions as a sort of investment in the rewards offered by the Kingdom of God. When Peter laments how he has given up everything to follow Jesus, the latter specifically says that those who give up their earthly possessions will 'receive a hundredfold now in this time, houses and brothers and sisters and mothers and children and lands, with persecutions, and in the age to come eternal life' (Mk 10.30). The Matthean version goes further, 'Truly, I say to you, in the new world, when the Son of man shall sit on his glorious throne, you who have followed me will also sit on twelve thrones, judging the twelve tribes of Israel' (Mt. 19.28).

Moreover, nothing in the plain text indicates, as Via argues, that 'eternal life here as interpreted by the story, is freedom from the self, from self-interest, which enables one to give to the poor'. Eternal life is a commodity consisting of the ability to live eternally. Jesus says that you achieve eternal life by giving up earthly possessions, and so Via's sequence of causes and consequences is completely wrong. Via's sequence is: Eternal life/Freedom

---

91. Dan O. Via, *The Ethics of Mark's Gospel: In the Middle of Time* (Philadelphia, PA: Fortress Press, 1985), p. 136. All chapters and verses here are from Mark.

92. Via, *The Ethics of Mark's Gospel*, p. 136. On providence and the will of God, see also Wolfgang Schrage, *Vorsehung Gottes? Zur Rede von der providentia Dei in der Antike und im Neuen Testament* (Neukirchen–Vluyn: Neukirchener Verlag, 2005).

from the self > Giving to the poor. Jesus' instructions signal an opposite relationship between causes and consequences: Giving to the poor > Eternal life.

Jesus repeatedly asserts that there would be rewards for following him, and the greatest ones were called salvation and eternal life. In John we find this description of the benefits for believers: 'that whoever believes in him may have eternal life. For God so loved the world that he gave his only Son, that whoever believes in him should not perish but have eternal life' (Jn 3.15-16). Note that the text does not say that we ought to believe in Jesus so that believers will be more willing to give to the poor or kinder to one's neighbor. Rather, giving to the poor and being kinder to one's neighbor are usually placed in the context of attaining what Jesus thinks to be a greater reward. The reward may be 'spiritual' or 'heavenly' but it is no less a reward—that is, an item that should be valued or has greater value than what one expends.

The idea of reward permeates the entire rhetoric of the Gospels from start to finish. The Gospel of Mark, for example, begins with the announcement of the Good News by John the Baptist, who is described as 'preaching a baptism of repentance for the forgiveness of sins' (Mk 1.4). Forgiveness is a reward. Those who repent will be allowed to enter the Kingdom of God at hand, and that is a reward (Mk 1.15). Entering the kingdom of God is nearly synonymous with salvation, as shown by the disciples' question after Jesus remarks that it is difficult for a rich man to enter the Kingdom of God: 'Then who can be saved?' (Mk 10.26). Salvation, in turn, is a commodity that may include physical deliverance from human enemies and perils, as well as deliverance from real physical and material harm that can be caused by God himself when he judges sinners (Mk 13.20).

Recent work by Gary Anderson shows even more clearly that in certain texts Jesus works within a larger tradition of special heavenly rewards for charity to the poor.[93] Anderson is partly responding to Ed P. Sanders, who argued quite forcefully against the idea that Jewish theology worked by accumulating merits in heaven that could be transferred from one party to another in the final judgment. As Anderson phrases it: '[I]n making the point he [Sanders] went too far in saying that early rabbinic sources did not understand the transfer of merits in financial terms at all.'[94] There was a Jewish tradition wherein those keeping the commandments were rewarded equally

---

93. Gary Anderson, *Charity: The Place of the Poor in the Biblical Tradition* (New Haven, CT: Yale University Press, 2013). See also Carol Newsom, 'The Economics of Sin: A Not So Dismal Science', *HTR* 103 (2010), pp. 365-71; Alyssa M. Gray, 'Redemptive Almsgiving and the Rabbis of Late Antiquity', *Jewish Studies Quarterly* 18 (2011), pp. 144-84.

94. Anderson, *Charity*, p. 174.

(e.g., with a prolonged life and a promise to inherit the land), and another tradition where some commandments received special rewards. Giving to the poor fell into the latter category. Anderson thinks he can detect both traditions in the Talmud, and more specifically in this Mishna:

> He who performs one precept is well rewarded. His days are prolonged, and he inherits the land. But he who does not perform one precept, good is not done to him. His days are not prolonged, and he does not inherit the land (Qiddushin 39a).[95]

The Gemara corresponding to this passage says:

> But a contradiction is shewn. These are the things the fruit of which man eats in this world, while the principal [הקרן] remains for him in the future world. Viz., honouring one's parents, the practice of loving deeds, hospitality to wayfarers, and making peace between man and his neighbour; and the study of Torah surpasses them all.[96]

The 'contradiction' is what is being quoted (i.e., 'These are the things the fruit...the study of Torah surpasses them all') from another Talmudic tractate, *Peah* 1a. In other words, the discussion in the Gemara attempts to reconcile the view of rewards in Qiddushin and Peah by dividing actions into those that: (1) have a reward only in this world (as in *Qiddushin*); and (2) have a reward in both this world and the next (as in *Peah*).

Giving to the poor is one of those that fall into the latter case. As Anderson remarks concerning Jesus' injunction to sell possessions to the poor in Mk 10.21: 'This text clearly ascribes special powers to the act of giving money to the poor; it is precisely these expenditures that generate a treasury in heaven.'[97] Indeed, what Jesus said to the rich man makes much more sense. Jesus declared that there were special heavenly rewards and giving to the poor was how you acquired them. However, in giving away possessions to the poor, one also becomes poor.

To address the problem of Talmudic sources being later than Jesus, Anderson traces the tradition to sources dating to the Second Temple period. According to Anderson, the following Second Temple texts 'declare that it is charity and charity *alone* that can fund a treasury in heaven'.[98]

---

95. Following Freedman and Epstein (eds.), *Hebrew-English Edition of the Babylonian Talmud*.

96. Michael Sokoloff (*A Dictionary of Jewish Babylonian Aramaic of the Talmudic and Geonic Periods* [Baltimore, MD: The Johns Hopkins University Press, 2002], p. 1044b), also translates the word, קרנא, as 'principal'.

97. Anderson, *Charity*, p. 133. See also Gary A. Anderson, 'A Treasury in Heaven: The Exegesis of Proverbs 10:2 in the Second Temple Period', *Hebrew Bible and Ancient Israel* 1 (2012), pp. 351-67.

98. Anderson, *Charity*, p. 133. Anderson's italics.

> If you have many possessions, make your gift from them in proportion; if few, do not be afraid to give according to the little you have. So you will be laying up a good treasure for yourself against the day of necessity (Tob. 4.9-10).

> Lose your silver for the sake of a brother or a friend, and do not let it rust under a stone and be lost. Lay up your treasure according to the commandments of the Most High, and it will profit you more than gold (Sir. 29.10-11).

In 2 Baruch (Syriac) one also finds a possible key to explaining the first macarism in Matthew:

> For we all have been made like breath. For as breath ascends without human control and vanishes, so it is with the nature of men, who do not go away according to their own will, and who do not know what will happen to them in the end. For the righteous justly have good hope for the end and go away from this habitation without fear because they possess a store of good works which is preserved in treasuries. Therefore, they leave the world without fear and are confident of the world which they have promised to them with an expectation full of joy (2 Bar. 14.10-14).[99]

Given the tradition of special heavenly rewards for charity to the poor, Jesus' words in Matthew 6, which is part of the Sermon on the Mount, become much clearer:

> Do not lay up for yourselves treasures on earth, where moth and rust consume and where thieves break in and steal, but lay up for yourselves treasures in heaven, where neither moth nor rust consumes and where thieves do not break in and steal. For where your treasure is, there will your heart be also (Mt. 6.19-21).

Therefore, another possibility is that 'the poor' who are blessed with the Kingdom of Heaven are not 'the poor in general', but rather are precisely that set of poor people who have been impoverished by giving away their possessions to the poor and so are themselves voluntarily poor.[100] That explains both why they are blessed and why their reward is the Kingdom of Heaven. As in the case of the righteous in 2 Baruch, those who have been impoverished by giving away their possessions are also supposed to be happy because they are aware of how much they have saved up in the heavenly bank. As an aside, the notion of voluntary poverty for serving a god can be found in Hittite religions at least twelve hundred years before Jesus.[101]

---

99. Following *OTP*, I, p. 626.

100. For an attitudinal interpretation (the poor in spirit are those who show 'humble dependence on God's grace') that rejects a meaning of voluntary poverty, see Douglas R.A. Hare, *Matthew* (Louisville, KY: Westminster/John Knox Press, 1993), p. 37.

101. See Harry A. Hoffner, 'The Institutional "Poverty" of Hurrian Diviners and

To understand how differently New Testament ethicists treat Jesus' reward system from others who operate a similar system today, consider the case of Harold Camping (1921–2013), the American Christian broadcaster who told his followers that the rapture would occur on May 21, 2011. As far as most people could tell, Camping truly believed that he was right. Many of his followers also sincerely believed what he preached. Many sold or gave away their houses and possessions.[102] When the end did not come as predicted, they were left in poverty. Some committed suicide. But I don't see many defenders of Camping among New Testament scholars. In fact, many think of him as a crank or misguided individual, no matter how sincerely he held those beliefs.[103] Many feel sorry for his naïve flock.

The Myth of Altruistic Giving

The denial that heavenly rewards *are* rewards is one reason why Allen Verhey's appeal to Mt. 6.44 and Lk. 6.35 will not help him prove that Jesus encourages a system of completely uninterested giving. Verhey characterizes Jesus as follows: 'He calls people to give without looking for a return, to give "in secret" (Mt. 6.4), to lend "expecting nothing in return" (Lk. 6.35)'.[104] But Verhey does not quote the whole of Mt. 6.4, which says: 'so that your alms may be in secret; and your Father who sees in secret will reward you'. Neither does Verhey quote the whole of that verse which says: 'But love your enemies, and do good, and lend, expecting nothing in return; and your reward will be great, and you will be sons of the Most High; for he is kind to the ungrateful and the selfish' (Lk. 6.35). Both texts clearly indicate that the rewards are not to be expected from human beings, but from God. But rewards from God are still rewards.

Verhey detects the conflict between his claim and the offer of rewards by Jesus, and so he subsequently attempts to redefine 'rewards' in the following explanation: 'It is true that such generosity looks for a reward "at the resurrection of the righteous" (Lk. 14.14), but not by way of

---

entanni-Women', in *Pax Hethitica: Studies on the Hittites and their Neighbours in Honour of Itamar Singer* (ed. Yoram Cohen, Amir Gilan and Jared L. Miller; Wiesbaden: Harrasowitz, 2010), pp. 214-24.

102. See Dan Margolis, 'Followers of Rapture Evangelist Lost Millions', *People's World* (23 May 2011). Online: http://peoplesworld.org/followers-of-rapture-evangelist-lost-millions/

103. A discussion of Camping by an evangelical Christian may be found in J.G. Sheryl, 'Can the Date of Jesus' Return be Known?', *BSac* 169 (2012), pp. 20-32. A documentary of Harold Camping before, during, and after his prediction of the rapture on May 21, 2011 is found in *Apocalypse Later: Harold Camping vs. The End of the World* (Documentary film directed by Zeke Piestrup; Venice, CA: 15Trucks Productions, 2014).

104. Verhey, *Remembering Jesus*, p. 272.

calculation—as though one might succeed in making God one's client. Rather, God is acknowledged as the benefactor...'.[105] Verhey proceeds to argue that '[e]quality, not deliberate inequality, marks the giving of gifts in the new community'.[106] The 'economic world of the peasantry' is where Jesus operates, so that even the heavenly dinners are simply figurative insofar as they 'image that heavenly joy by hospitality to those on the margin of village life'.[107]

Verhey is working with a false dichotomy insofar as he thinks these texts can't express both a system of rewards for good works and identification of God as the benefactor. Why can't it be that the author is expressing the idea that those who do good works will receive rewards, as well as expressing the idea that God is the benefactor because he is the one who bestows those rewards?[108] Whether it is by calculation or not is irrelevant to the question of whether Jesus offered rewards for good works and for service to him. Verhey's denial that God is operating a sort of patronage system is not only contradicted by the tradition of rewards illuminated by Anderson's work, but also by the parables where God is depicted as a landowner, who rewards his servants as he deems appropriate (e.g., Mt. 20.1-15).[109]

Nor did Jesus introduce the idea that one should seek freedom from the self and freedom from possessions to follow God's will. One finds it in Epictetus:

> And how shall I free myself?—Have you not heard over and over again that you ought to eradicate desire utterly, direct your aversion towards the things that lie within the sphere of the moral purpose, and these things only, that you ought to give up everything, your body, your property, your reputation, your books, turmoil, office, freedom from office? For if once you swerve aside from this course, you are a slave, you are a subject, you have become liable to hindrance and to compulsion, you are entirely under the control of others. Nay, the word of Cleanthes is ready at hand, 'Lead thou me, O Zeus, and Destiny'. Will ye have me to go Rome. I will go to Rome... To Prison? I go to prison...[110]

---

105. Verhey, *Remembering Jesus*, p. 272. According to Crook (*Reconceptualizing Conversion*, p. 64), 'patronage and benefaction are two types of general reciprocity'. On benefaction and doing good works in pre-Christian Judaism, see Gregg Gardner, 'Jewish Leadership and Hellenistic Civic Benefaction in the Second Century B.C.E.', *JBL* 126 (2007), pp. 327-43.

106. Verhey, *Remembering Jesus*, p. 272.

107. Verhey, *Remembering Jesus*, pp. 272-73.

108. For the idea that ancient Mediterranean religons, including Christianity, expressed themselves in language involving patronage and benefaction, see Crook, *Reconceptualizing Conversion*.

109. See further, B.Z. Rosenfeld and H. Perlmutter, 'Landowners in Roman Palestine 100–300 CE: A Distinct Group', *Journal of Ancient Judaism* 2 (2011), pp. 327-52.

110. Epictetus, *Discourses* 4.4.33-34 (Oldfather, LCL).

Here, Epictetus is making very similar demands to Jesus.[111] To do the will
of God is what one should do, no matter what sort of suffering it may
entail.

Earlier, Epictetus affirmed that, for philosophers, 'desire is for things
good and aversion is for things evil' (cf. Amos 5.15).[112] In other words, one
should seek what is morally good, and not possessions.

Compared to Epictetus, Jesus sounds very much like a modern Wall
Street salesman, who promises fantastic rewards for a lot of work and suffering on the part of his investors. Indeed, Jesus receives actual labor and
services from his followers, but they may never see any heavenly rewards
or thrones, and so on. The only palpable outcome is that following Jesus left
many people penniless and their families without breadwinners.

Of course, one can argue that in the time of Jesus, there was a different
and eschatological world-view. Indeed, an eschatological view of possessions can be found at Qumran, where one must give them up to a common
pool at the appropriate stage of membership (1QS 6.22, 9.22).[113] One can
trace it as far back as the *Epic of Gilgamesh*. In that case, the impending
destruction of the world by a flood results in this directive: 'Abandon riches
and seek survival' ([m]a-ak-ku-ru ze-er-ma na-piš-ti bul-liṭ).[114] If Jesus
really did believe in what he was selling, the objections would be the same
as they would be for any modern sales person. Just as is the case today, it is
deemed unethical to not deliver the promised rewards for labor received. It
is economically foolish to expend real labor for rewards that may not exist
at all (unlike Wall Street returns on investments, which may exist). And is
it ever ethical to ask people to suffer for commodities or rewards that you
cannot prove to exist at all? Would we praise someone who had similar
beliefs today and sincerely held them, or would we still proclaim them to be
morally challenged and economically foolish?

Summary

Jesus cannot be called a friend of the poor if judged by any modern standard of economic equality, ethics, or basic business practices. John Kloppenborg admits that '[t]he early Christian tradition is saturated by sayings

---

111. A comparison of Epictetus and Paul may be found in Niko Huttunen, *Paul and
Epictetus on Law: A Comparison* (Library of New Testament Studies, 405, Early Christianity in Context; London: T. & T. Clark, 2009).

112. Epictetus, *Discourses* 1.4.1 (Oldfather, LCL): ἡ ὄρεξις ἀγαθῶν ἐστίν, ἡ δ'
ἔκκλισις πρὸς κακά.

113. See further, Ernst Bammel, 'πτωχός', *TDNT*, VI, p. 898.

114. *Epic of Gilgamesh* 11.26, following the edition of George, *The Babylonian Gilgamesh Epic*, I, pp. 704-705.

that privilege poverty over wealth'.[115] Although he is usually grouped with those who see Jesus as a friend of the poor, Kloppenborg may unwittingly be admitting that Jesus actually prefers an impoverished lifestyle, which is not necessarily beneficial to the poor. Although alternate interpretations are possible, the texts that I have examined can plausibly be interpreted to mean that Jesus is portrayed as actively encouraging the poverty of his disciples. Worse yet, Jesus actively and *knowingly* encouraged impoverishing the families of his followers, including children who could not have consented to having their parents follow him in the first place. The hungry that Jesus feeds are more like props to help him promote his status as a prophet. If he really could miraculously feed the poor, then why not feed all who are hungry in the world without demanding that they follow his vision of what God wanted?

The excuse that Jesus demanded 'radical discipleship' because it was part of some eschatological set of ethics is about as sound as praising Harold Camping's economics or those of the author of the *Epic of Gilgamesh*. I do not see many New Testament ethicists praising Harold Camping's followers for being examples of 'radical discipleship' or praising Camping for demanding belief in a future that did not come about. So why is Jesus any different simply because he may have believed that his rewards existed even if seeking them impoverished his followers for the moment? The answer is simple: Such New Testament ethicists assume Camping's theology was misguided, but the theology of Jesus was sound. It is a theological and religiocentric evaluation, not a historico-critical one.

The better way to understand the economics of any historical Jesus is to see him as a cult leader who demanded the type of loyalty that was well known among ancient despotic emperors. Just as cult leaders in ancient or modern times seek to transfer loyalty from family to themselves, so Jesus wanted to transfer loyalty from families to him regardless of how it might have destroyed their function and viability. In terms of economics, Karl Marx never had a better example of a cold-hearted or foolhardy religious capitalist who profited from real labor and gave nothing but empty or unverifiable heavenly promises for wages. The fact that so many New Testament ethicists praise Jesus as friend of the poor says more about the ethics of New Testament ethics than it does about Jesus.

---

115. John Kloppenborg, *The Tenants in the Vineyard: Ideology, Economics, and Agrarian Conflict in Jewish Palestine* (WUNT, 2.195; Tübingen: Mohr Siebeck, 2006), p. 351.

Chapter 9

THE MISOGYNISTIC JESUS:
CHRISTIAN FEMINISM AS MALE ANCESTOR WORSHIP

Among all the trends in biblical studies, the rise of feminist biblical studies stands as one of the most significant achievements. As Daphne Hampson, a post-Christian theologian, remarks, 'Feminism represents a revolution. It is not in essence a demand that women should be allowed to join the male world on equal terms. It is a different view of the world.'[1] Most Christian feminist theologians see Jesus and the 'true' Christianity as liberatory and as good news for women.[2] For such Christian feminists, the liberatory nature of biblical texts has been obscured by patriarchal and androcentric scholarship.[3] As Elisabeth Schüssler Fiorenza argues, 'a Christian feminist apologetics asserts that the Bible, correctly understood does not prohibit but rather authorizes the equal rights and liberation of women'.[4]

Some feminists are very open about Christology being the center of their lives and scholarly agenda, as is the case with Isabel Carter Heyward:

> Christology has become important to me for two primary reasons: (1) First, I am hooked on Jesus. I could no more pretend that the Jesus-figure, indeed

1. Daphne Hampson, *Theology and Feminism* (Oxford: Basil Blackwell, 1990), p. 1.
2. See, for example, Rebecca Merrill Groothuis, *Good News for Women: A Biblical Picture of Gender Equality* (Grand Rapids, MI: Baker Books, 1997); Letty M. Russell (ed.), *The Liberating Word: A Guide to Non-Sexist Interpretation of the Bible* (Philadelphia, PA: Westminster Press, 1976). For the supposed socio-economic benefits for women in early Christianity, see James Malcolm Arlandson, *Women, Class and Society in Early Christianity: Models from Luke–Acts* (Peabody, MA: Hendrickson, 1997), especially pp. 120-50. See also Richard H. Hiers, *Women's Rights and the Bible: Implications for Christian Ethics and Social Policy* (Eugene, OR: Pickwick, 2012). Protestant evangelical perspectives are offered in Ronald W. Pierce and Rebecca M. Groothuis, *Discovering Biblical Equality: Complementarity without Hierarchy* (Downers Grove, IL: InterVarsity Press, 2004); Wayne Grudem, *Evangelical Feminism and Biblical Truth: An Analysis of 118 Disputed Truths* (Downers Grove, IL: InterVarsity Press, 2004).
3. For the charge that the standard Greek editions of the New Testament have been reconstructed with androcentric biases, see Ray R. Schultz, 'Twentieth-Century Corruption of Scripture', *ExpTim* 119 (2008), pp. 270-74.
4. Elisabeth Schüssler Fiorenza, 'Feminist Hermeneutics', *ABD*, II, pp. 783-91 (789).

the Jesus Christ of the kerygma, is unimportant to me than I could deny
the significance of my parents and my past in the shaping of my future.
As a 'cradle Christian'—a person who came to know the storybook Jesus
long before I sat down and thought about God—I have no sane or creative
choice but to take very seriously this Jesus Christ who is written indelibly
in my own history… (2) The second reason christology is important to me
is that there is no more fundamental and problematic an issue for feminists
than the person of Jesus.[5]

Christian feminist scholarship, therefore, often resembles an enterprise centered on explaining the personal significance of a man who died two thousand years ago.

At the same time, other feminists see Christianity as a main instigator
of oppression against women. Daphne Hampson has argued that '[w]omen
theologians who try to read positive feminist messages, who tease out female
role models from biblical texts, are barking up the wrong tree'.[6] Hampson
credits Mary Daly with being 'the person who first gave voice, in a way
that received wide attention, to the conclusion that feminism and Christianity were never going to be reconcilable'.[7] Indeed, Mary Daly is important because she gave substantial attention to the problems that Christology
posed for women in a way that previous feminists had not.[8] Daly argues, as
I do, that '[a] great deal of Christian doctrine has been docetic, that is, it has
not seriously accepted the fact that Jesus was a limited human being'.[9] However, neither Daly nor Hampson are much interested in feminist biblical exegesis and scholarship per se. Annie Laurie Gaylor, a thorough secularist,
does give substantial attention to biblical texts.[10] Although Gaylor is not a
biblical scholar, her interpretations are often far more reasonable than what
Christian feminists propose.

While one can find important instances of what can be called feminist
interpretation of the Bible prior to the twentieth century, 1895 is a good

5. Isabel Carter Heyward, *The Redemption of God: A Theology of Mutual Relation*
(Washington, DC: University Press of America, 1982), p. 196.

6. 'A Faith that Crucifies Women', *Times Higher Education*, 21 April 1997. Online:
http://www.timeshighereducation.co.uk/features/a-faith-that-crucifies-women/101241.
article. See further Hampson, *Theology and Feminism*; idem, *After Christianity* (London:
SCM Press, 2nd edn, 2002).

7. Hampson, *Theology and Feminism*, p. 108.

8. See Daly, *Beyond God the Father*, especially pp. 78-81; idem, *Gyn/Ecology: The
Metaethics of Radical Feminism* (Boston, MA: Beacon Press, 1978). See also April D.
DeConick, *Holy Misogyny: Why the Sex and Gender Conflicts in the Early Church Still
Matter* (New York: Continuum, 2011).

9. Daly, *Beyond God the Father*, p. 69.

10. Annie Laurie Gaylor, *Woe to the Women—The Bible Tells Me So: The Bible,
Female Sexuality and the Law* (Madison, WI: Freedom from Religion Foundation,
2004).

starting point in feminist biblical studies.[11] In that year Elizabeth Cady Stanton (1815–1902) and her colleagues published *The Woman's Bible*, which challenged androcentric interpretations of the Bible from Genesis through Revelation.[12] Cady Stanton is frank about her departure from traditional views about the Bible when she speaks about how her 'reason had repudiated its divine authority'.[13] She explains that she does not believe that 'any man ever saw or talked with God'.[14] For Cady Stanton, 'all religions on the face of the earth degrade her' [i.e., woman].[15]

Other contemporaries of Cady Stanton were even more radical in their assault on biblical authority, and included Jesus specifically in their critiques. For example, Matilda Joslyn Gage (1826–1898), in responding to *The Woman's Bible*, remarked: 'From Adam's plaint "The woman gave me and I did eat", down to Christ's "Woman what do I have to do with thee?" the tendency of the Bible has been degradation of the divinest half of humanity—woman.'[16] In short, by the 1890s, one finds women who had advanced beyond the view that Jesus was the epitome of ethics, especially in the case of women's issues.

Academic feminist biblical scholarship remained dormant for much of the twentieth century. But the 1970s witnessed new efforts to make it part

11. For studies of pre-modern feminists, see Michael Graves, 'The Biblical Scholarship of a Fourth-Century Woman: Marcella of Rome', *ETL* 87.4 (2011), pp. 375-91; Christiana De Groot and Marion Ann Taylor (eds.), *Recovering Nineteenth Century Women Interpreters of the Bible* (Leiden: E.J. Brill, 2007); Nancy Calvert-Koyzis and Heather E. Weir (eds.), *Strangely Familiar: Protofeminist Interpretations of Patriarchal Biblical Texts* (Atlanta, GA: Society of Biblical Literature, 2009). See also Annie Besant, *Woman's Position According to the Bible* (London: Annie Besant and C. Bradlaugh, 1885).

12. See further, Kathi Kern, *Mrs. Stanton's Bible* (Ithaca, NY: Cornell University Press, 2001); Carolyn De Swarte Gifford, 'Politicizing the Sacred Texts: Elizabeth Cady Stanton and the Woman's Bible', in *Searching the Scriptures: A Feminist Commentary* (ed. Elisabeth Schüssler Fiorenza; 2 vols.; New York: Crossroad, 1994), I, pp. 52-63; Claudia Setzer, 'A Jewish Reading of *The Woman's Bible*', *Journal of Feminist Studies in Religion* 27 (2011), pp. 71-84; Emily R. Mace, 'Feminist Forerunners and a Usable Past: A Historiography of Elizabeth Cady Stanton's *The Woman's Bible*', *Journal of Feminist Studies in Religion* 25 (2009), pp. 5-23.

13. Elizabeth Cady Stanton, *The Woman's Bible* (repr., Boston, MA: Northeastern University Press, 1993 [1895]), p. 12.

14. Stanton, *The Woman's Bible*, p. 12.

15. Stanton, *The Woman's Bible*, p. 12.

16. Matilda Joslyn Gage's remarks are in the Appendix of Stanton, *The Woman's Bible*, p. 209. For a study of Gage, see Leila R. Brummer, *Excluded from Suffrage History: Matilda Joslyn Gage, Nineteenth Century American Feminist* (Westport, CT: Greenwood Press, 2000). See also Matilda Joslyn Gage, *Woman, Church and State: A Historical Account of the Status of Woman throughout the Christian Ages: With Reminiscences from the Matriarchate* (repr., Amherst, NY: Humanity Books, 2002 [1893]).

of the academy. Some of the Christian feminists in the 1970s were involved in what are largely issues of polity, insofar as there was an effort to respond to Catholic policies that excluded women from the priesthood. This concern with polity is illustrated by a whole volume responding to the Vatican's *Declaration on the Question of the Admission of Women to the Ministerial Priesthood* approved by Pope Paul VI in 1976.[17]

Elisabeth Schüssler Fiorenza, Carolyn Osiek and Rosemary Radford Ruether are among many Catholic feminists whose interpretation of scripture was closely tied to the question of whether Jesus would have allowed female priests.[18]

In 1976, Letty M. Russell, Elisabeth Schüssler Fiorenza, Sharon Ringe and Joanna Dewey published *The Liberating Word: A Guide to Non-Sexist Interpretation of the Bible* (1976). Unlike the views expressed by Cady Stanton or Gage, the plea in that volume was frankly Christian in its overall orientation. *The Liberating Word* seeks to protect Jesus from criticism. In the Introduction to that volume, Letty M. Russell declares that 'God is a feminist', and she speaks of how '[t]he Word of God is living and liberating to those who hear it with faith and live it out in faith'.[19] Her frankly Christian orientation is expressed when she points out how her volume 'dares to invite Christians everywhere to join in a risky task: Liberating the Word of God from sexist interpretations that continue to dominate our thoughts and actions'.[20] In an essay in the same volume, Elisabeth Schüssler Fiorenza remarks:

> It is quite remarkable that the canonical literature of the New Testament does not transmit a single androcentric statement or sexist story of Jesus, although he lived and preached in a patriarchal culture and society.[21]

The volume hardly showed any consciousness of Jewish feminist scholarship, and it evinced a heterosexist orientation throughout.[22] Jesus was presented as the heroic paradigm of non-sexist men found in the Bible despite

---

17. Leonard Swidler and Arlene Swidler (eds.), *Women Priests: A Catholic Commentary on the Vatican Declaration* (New York: Paulist Press, 1977). The text of the Declaration is found on pp. 37-49.

18. See, for example, Eugene C. Bianchi and Rosemary Radforth Ruether (eds.), *A Democratic Catholic Church: The Reconstruction of Roman Catholicism* (New York: Crossroad, 1992).

19. Letty M. Russell, 'Introduction', in Russell (ed.), *The Liberating Word*, pp. 13-22 (18 and 14, respectively).

20. Russell, 'Introduction', in Russell (ed.), *The Liberating Word*, p. 15.

21. Elisabeth Schüssler Fiorenza, 'Interpreting Patriarchal Traditions', in Russell (ed.), *The Liberating Word*, pp. 39-61 (52).

22. Russell (ed.), *The Liberating Word*, pp. 86-87, where the volume offers concrete suggestions for more gender-neutral language in Christianity, and still only speaks of 'women and men' without any consciousness of LGBTQI issues.

Schüssler Fiorenza's characterization of a patriarchal culture and society all around Jesus.

By 1989, *The Women's Bible Commentary* evidenced a slightly more interdenominational and inclusive approach.[23] The critiques of Jewish feminists, who pointed out the anti-Judaism of many Christian feminists, had begun to have an effect.[24] African American, Asian, Latina and Jewish feminist scholars were represented, but the vast majority continued to be Euroamerican feminists, though white Spanish feminist scholarship continued to be largely ignored by the Anglophonic world.[25] At the same time, many non-white scholars were beginning to point out the racist and ethnocentric biases of Euroamerican feminists.[26]

Typical of the feminist biblical scholarship of the 1990s was an influential two-volume compendium, *Searching the Scriptures*, which was published in 1994.[27] This work is notable for expanding its feminist approach to works beyond the canonical scriptures, including the *Gospel of Thomas* and *Pistis Sophia*. It also included historical and reflective essays on African American and Latina feminism. At the same time, there was an upsurge in literary approaches to feminist interpretation of the Bible, as exemplified by J. Cheryl Exum, who mainly works in Hebrew Bible. Exum also was more critical of the ethics of the biblical authors and the biblical god than one sees among feminists working primarily with the New Testament.[28]

---

23. Carol A. Newsom, Sharon H. Ringe and Jacqueline E. Lapsley (eds.), *The Women's Bible Commentary* (Louisville, KY: Westminster/John Knox Press, 2nd edn, 2012).

24. See Judith Plaskow, 'Christian Feminism and Anti-Judaism', *Cross Currents* 33 (1978), pp. 306-309. For a Christian feminist who acknowledges anti-Judaism among Christian feminists, see Elisabeth Schüssler Fiorenza, *Jesus: Miriam's Child, Sophia's Prophet* (New York: Crossroad, 1995), pp. 67-96.

25. See also Michael J. Brown, *Blackening the Bible: The Aims of African American Biblical Scholarship* (Harrisburg, PA: Trinity International Press, 2004). For an example of a Spanish feminist scholar, see Elisa Estévez López, *Qué se sabe de... Las mujeres en los orígenes del cristianismo* (Estella [Navarra]: Verbo Divino, 2012). A similar parochialism may be seen in Giuseppe Barbaglio, *Pace e violenza nella Bibbia* (Bologna: EDB, 2011), whose thin bibliography in the sparse footnotes restricts itself mostly to European and Italian scholarship, and cites nearly nothing from Anglophonic scholars.

26. See Jackelyn Grant, *White Women's Christ and Black Women's Jesus: Feminist Christology and Womanist Response* (American Academy of Religion Academy Series, 64; Atlanta, GA: Scholars Press, 1989).

27. Elisabeth Schüssler Fiorenza (ed.), *Searching the Scriptures: A Feminist Commentary* (2 vols.; New York: Crossroad, 1994).

28. One example is her analysis of the Jephthah narratives where she notes the disparity between how God intervened in the case of Isaac but not in the case of Jepththah's daughter. See further, Exum, 'Feminist Criticism', pp. 65-89; J. Cheryl Exum, *Tragedy and Biblical Narrative: Arrows of the Almighty* (Cambridge: Cambridge University Press, 1992), especially pp. 52-53.

By the dawn of the twenty-first century, a well-known group of feminist scholars had consolidated within the Society of Biblical Literature, the largest organization of biblical scholars in the world. By and large, works published since 2000 continue the globalization and inclusion of non-Euroamerican voices that one sees in the 1990s, but some authors are the same.[29] In particular, Barbara Reid's *Taking Up the Cross: New Testament Interpretations through Latina and Feminist Eyes* (2007) actually assimilates interpretations proposed by Euroamerican scholars, and seemingly represents them as views Latina feminists should adopt.[30] Training future feminists and the development of feminist pedagogy has also become increasingly important, though one can argue that pedagogy was always a centerpiece of liberation theology.[31] Translations that reflect an egalitarian attitude, which began to proliferate in the 1980s and 1990s, became more explicitly 'egalitarian' versions of the Bible.[32]

At the same time, the start of the twenty-first century saw the ascendance of those questioning heterosexism, and not just the racism of much of Christian feminist scholarship.[33] Some question whether the term 'feminist biblical studies' is itself overly parochial and narrow. Thus, Deryn Guest recently has proposed moving 'beyond feminist biblical studies' to 'gender criticism' that would be more inclusive of voices of the LGBTQI communities. According to Guest:

29. One example of a non-EuroAmerican feminist scholar in the new millennium is Seong Hee Kim, *Mark, Women, and Empire: A Korean Postcolonial Perspective* (The Bible and the Modern World, 20; Sheffield: Sheffield Phoenix Press, 2010). One finds Elisabeth Schüssler Fiorenza and Rosemary R. Ruether in many major anthologies in the 1970s, 1980s, 1990s and after 2000, including in Kathleen O. Wicker, Althea S. Miller and Musa W. Dube (eds.), *Feminist New Testament Studies: Global and Future Perspectives* (New York: Palgrave Macmillan, 2005). See also Stephanie Feder, 'Neue Perspektiven von Frauen: Exegesen afrikanischer Bibelwissenschaft-lerinnen aus westlicher Sicht', *Bibel und Kirche* 67 (2012), pp. 154-59; Anthony E. Nachef, *Women in the Eyes of Jesus: Yesterday, Today, and Forever* (Staten Island, NY: St Pauls, 2004); Sandra H. Polaski, *A Feminist Introduction to Paul* (St. Louis, MO: Chalice Press, 2005).

30. Barbara E. Reid, *Taking Up the Cross: New Testament Interpretations through Latina and Feminist Eyes* (Minneapolis: Ausburg Fortress Press, 2007). One case is her discussion of the atonement (Reid, *Taking Up the Cross*, pp. 33-35), where she adopts uncritically the explanations of René Girard and Joanna Dewey, which I critique in this book.

31. Julie B. Miller, 'Forming Future Feminists: Elisabeth Schüssler Fiorenza, Conscientization and the College Classroom', *Journal of Feminist Studies in Religion* 25 (2009), pp. 99-123. See also Ahida E. Pilarski, 'The Past and Future of Feminist Biblical Hermeneutics', *BTB* 41 (2011), pp. 16-23.

32. One example, is Priests for Equality, *The Inclusive Bible: The First Egalitarian Translation* (Lanham, MD: Rowman & Littlefield, 2007).

33. See Susanne Scholz, 'A Third Kind of Feminist Reading: Toward a Feminist Sociology of Biblical Hermeneutics', *Currents in Biblical Research* 9 (2010), pp. 9-32.

> Gender criticism is interested in how the author of the text, consciously or unconsciously constructs sex, gender, and sexualities (legitimized and ostracized) for the characters and in so doing grants them a solidity of sorts.[34]

Mary Daly had already begun to remodel her vocabulary, rejecting such words as 'homosexuality' and 'androgyny' in the preface to her *Gyn/Ecology* in 1978.[35] The work of Britanny Wilson, among others, illustrates how biblical scholarship is applying such ideas to specific New Testament texts.[36]

Indeed, some modern biologists believe that human beings can exhibit five sexes rather than two.[37] Others have questioned whether the categories of sex and gender are themselves to be interrogated, and so 'Queer Theory' has arisen to address that issue. As Ken Stone comments, 'queer theory highlights not simply the social construction, but also the instability of categories used to interpret sex, gender, and sexuality, including such categories as male and female, heterosexual, and so forth'.[38]

This chapter will show that for all the liberatory goals of feminist scholarship, the fact remains that much of it is still permeated by a protectionist attitude towards one man, and his name is Jesus. For these feminists, Jesus is not a misogynist but rather the bearer of a new radical philosophy that will benefit women. This chapter demonstrates that many feminist biblical scholars strive to show that Jesus was more friendly to women's rights and status than the textual evidence allows. Most feminists also don't see themselves as part of the Christian empire. Promoting a Christian view of the Bible still remains dominant and pervasive. I will show that much of Christian feminist scholarship is very much like its androcentric counterpart insofar as it still deploys a bibliolatrous apologetic approach that is

---

34. Deryn Guest, *Beyond Feminist Biblical Studies* (The Bible in the Modern World, 47; Sheffield: Sheffield Phoenix Press, 2012), p. 20. See also J.V. Brownson, *Bible, Gender, Sexuality: Reframing the Church's Debate on Same-Sex Relationships* (Grand Rapids, MI: Eerdmans, 2013); Aída B. Spencer, 'Does God Have a Gender?', *Priscilla Papers* 24 (2010), pp. 5-12.

35. Daly, *Gyn/Ecology*, p. xi.

36. Brittany E. Wilson, '"Neither Male nor Female": The Ethiopian Eunuch in Acts 8.26-40', *NTS* 60 (2014), pp. 403-422.

37. See Anne Fausto-Sterling, *Sexing the Body: Gender, Politics, and the Construction of Sexuality* (New York: Basic Books, 2000).

38. Ken Stone, 'Gender Criticism: The Un-Manning of Abimelech', in *Judges and Method: New Approaches in Biblical Studies* (ed. Gale A. Yee; Minneapolis: Fortress Press, 2nd edn, 2007), pp. 183-201 (189). See also Ken Stone (ed.), *Queer Commentary and the Hebrew Bible* (New York: Pilgrim Press, 2002); idem, *Practicing Safer Text: Food, Sex and Bible in Queer Perspective* (London: T. & T. Clark, 2005); Eve Kosofsky Sedgwick, 'Gender Criticism: What Isn't Gender', in *Redrawing the Boundaries: The Transformation of English and American Literary Studies* (ed. Stephen Greenblat and Giles Gunn; New York: Modern Language Association of America, 1992), pp. 271-301.

itself anti-feminist, heterosexist, ethnocentric, theological and traditional in many ways.

Mark 7/Matthew 15: The Misogynistic Jesus

A recurrent theme in feminist interpretation is the idea of subversive readings. Texts that seem to endorse androcentric ideologies are revealed to undermine them. In the case of narratives involving Jesus, many feminists insist that androcentrism is responsible for seeing Jesus as misogynistic or sexist. One such example is the case of the Canaanite or Syrophoenician woman, which is found in Mark 7 and Matthew 15.[39] I begin with the Matthean version:

> And behold, a Canaanite woman from that region came out and cried, 'Have mercy on me, O Lord, Son of David; my daughter is severely possessed by a demon'. But he did not answer her a word. And his disciples came and begged him, saying, 'Send her away, for she is crying after us'. He answered, 'I was sent only to the lost sheep of the house of Israel'. But she came and knelt before him, saying, 'Lord, help me'. And he answered, 'It is not fair to take the children's bread and throw it to the dogs'. She said, 'Yes, Lord, yet even the dogs eat the crumbs that fall from their masters' table'. Then Jesus answered her, 'O woman, great is your faith! Be it done for you as you desire'. And her daughter was healed instantly (Mt. 15.22-28).

The story depicts Jesus as resorting to abusive language to support his reticence to help this woman. This makes Jesus look uncompassionate, ethnocentric and misogynistic.

---

39. For a detailed study of this pericope, and one that is in full dialogue with feminist approaches, see Glenna Jackson, *'Have Mercy on Me': The Story of the Canaanite Woman in Matthew 15.21-28* (Sheffield: Sheffield Academic Press, 2002). For other studies, see Jennifer A. Glancy, 'The Syrophoenician Woman and Other First Century Bodies', *BibInt* 18 (2010), pp. 342-63; L.D. Hart, 'The Canaanite Woman: Meeting Jesus as Sage and Lord: Matthew 15:21-28 & Mark 7:24-30', *ExpTim* 122.1 (2010), pp. 20-25; J.M.C. Scott, 'Matthew 15.21-28: A Test-Case for Jesus' Manners', *JSNT* 63 (1996), pp. 21-44; John P. Meier, 'Matthew 15:21-28', *Int* 40 (1986), pp. 397-402; Jean-Paul Michaud and Pierrette Daviau, 'Jésus au-delà des frontières de Tyr: Analyse de Marc 7,24-31', in *De Jésus et des femmes: Lectures sémiotiques. Suivies d'un entretien avec A.J. Greimas* (ed. Adèle Chené *et al.*; Recherches, nouvelle série, 14; Paris: Cerf, 1987), pp. 35-57; Anita J. Monro, 'Alterity and the Canaanite Woman: A Postmodern Feminist Theological Reflection on Political Action', *Colloquium* 26 (1994), pp. 264-78; G. Schwartz, 'ΣΥΡΟΦΟΙΝΙΚΙΣΣΑ-ΧΑΝΑΝΑΙΑ (Markus 7.26/Matthäus 15.22)', *NTS* 30 (1984), pp. 626-28; E.A. Russell, 'The Canaanite Woman in the Gospels (Mt 15.21-28)', in *Studia Biblica 1978 II. Papers on the Gospels* (ed. Elizabeth A. Livingstone; JSNTSup, 2; Sheffield: JSOT Press, 1980), pp. 263-300.

Jesus' riposte, which equates non-Jews or women with 'dogs', uses a virulently degrading epithet in the ancient Near East.[40] Referring to someone as a 'dog' can dehumanize the addressee. Josephus provides a good example in his retelling of the story of David and Goliath, whose entourage derided David for using weapons that were meant to fight animals, not men. Goliath's warriors ask whether David took Goliath 'for a dog and not a man'.[41] David promises to defeat Goliath, and issues the following threat: 'For I will this day cut off thine head and fling thy carcass to the dogs, thy fellows [τοῖς ὁμοφύλοις]...'.[42] Clearly, this epithet is meant to dehumanize and humiliate Goliath. Imagine translations today placing the word 'bitches' on Jesus' lips to convey more faithfully the more degrading force of his rhetoric. Jesus uses the Greek word, κυνάριον, which is neuter, but my point is that the application of 'dynamic equivalence', which is often used to mitigate some of Jesus' statements, also may be used to justify a more degrading term in English. As Tom A. Burkill observes: 'And, as in English, so in other languages, to call a woman "a little bitch" is no less abusive than to call her "a bitch" without qualification.'[43]

The Woman's Bible already called Jesus' response 'ungracious' in 1895, though Stanton thought 'dogs' referred to the Jews.[44] Sharon Ringe observes that 'to compare a woman and her daughter to dogs is insulting in the extreme'.[45] She adds, 'I continue to be troubled by the harshness of the language attributed to Jesus, regardless of its political comprehensibility'.[46] One feminist who admits that there are attempts to mitigate any bad

40. For a study of dogs specifically related to Mt. 15.21-28, see Jackson, *'Have Mercy on Me'*, pp. 54-58. For studies of the socio-literary use of dogs in the Hebrew Bible and Near East, see Juan Antonio-Mayoral, 'El uso simbólico de los animals en los profetas del exilio', *EstBib* 53 (1995), pp. 317-63 (347-48); Gilbert Brunet, 'L'Hebreu Keleb', *VT* 35 (1985), pp. 485-88; D. Winton Thomas, 'Kelebh "Dog": Its Origins and Some Usages of it in the Old Testament', *VT* 10 (1960), pp. 410-27. On Roman attitudes towards their dogs, see Michael MacKinnon, '"Sick as a Dog": Zooarchaeological Evidence for Pet Dog Health and Welfare in the Roman World', *World Archaeology* 42 (2010), pp. 290-309.

41. Josephus, *Ant.* 6.186 (Thackeray and Marcus, LCL): μὴ αὐτὸν ἀντὶ ἀνθρώπου κύνα εἶναι δοκεῖ.

42. Josephus, *Ant.* 6.187 (Thackeray and Marcus, LCL).

43. Tom A. Burkill, 'The Historical Development of the Story of the Syrophoenician Woman (Mark VII:24-31)', *NovT* 9 (1967), pp. 161-77 (173). Sharon H. Ringe ('A Gentile Woman's Story', in Russell [ed.], *Feminist Interpretation of the Bible*, pp. 65-72 [69]) adopts Burkill's characterization of Jesus' insult.

44. Stanton, *The Woman's Bible*, p. 121.

45. Ringe, 'A Gentile Woman's Story, Revisited: Reading Mark 7.24-31', in Levine and Blickenstaff (eds.), *A Feminist Companion to Mark*, pp. 79-100 (89).

46. Ringe, 'A Gentile Woman's Story, Revisited', p. 97.

impressions about Jesus in this story is Ranjini Wickramatra Rebera, a Sri Lankan scholar:

> Many scholars, theologians and preachers attempt to minimize the impact of Jesus' response to her, since the image of Jesus one sees in this incident does not fit the inherited image we have of him as the 'kind, understanding, ever-helpful savior'.[47]

Indeed, I don't know of many Christian ethicists who characterize Jesus as dehumanizing, racist or misogynistic on the basis of this text.[48] On the contrary, many Christian ethicists, feminist or not, see this story as an example of Jesus' inclusiveness and caring attitude towards those outside of his ethnic group, and don't mention anything negative at all about Jesus' response. Thus, Richard Burridge's discussion of the Syrophoenician woman never even mentions Jesus' denigrating riposte.[49] Among the feminists defending Jesus is Elaine Wainwright, who remarks:

> As a result of our feminist critique and rereading, it has become clear that female power once again endured against all the barriers the patriarchal culture erected against it, and the words of Jesus recognize and celebrate this. The woman's great faith makes possible a life free of oppressive restrictions for herself and for her daughter. The subversive power of this story goes far beyond the traditional boundary breaking with which it is associated— namely, Gentile mission.[50]

After all, Jesus scolds the disciples for asking him to send this woman away. Jesus demonstrates that non-Jews are welcome in the Kingdom of God. The woman argues her case and convinces Jesus, and so it shows how empowered she is. But, as with many other cases, Wainwright's view of Jesus only shows the imperialistic nature of white Christian feminist interpretation

---

47. Ranjini Wickramatra Rebera, 'The Syrophoenician Woman: A South Asian Feminist Perspective', in Levine and Blickenstaff (eds.), *A Feminist Companion to Mark*, pp. 101-110 (103).

48. Herman C. Waetjen [*Reordering Power: A Socio-Political Reading of Mark* [Philadelphia, PA: Fortress Press, 1989], p. 135) uses the term 'racist' here, but he makes it clear that 'it is not a racism that is to be ascribed to Jesus, for it does not arise out of a pollution system'. Daniel Patte ('The Canaanite Woman and Jesus: Surprising Models of Discipleship (Matt. 15:21-28)', in *Transformative Encounters: Jesus and Women Re-Viewed* [ed. Ingrid Rosa Kitzberger; Atlanta, GA: Society of Biblical Literature, 2000], pp. 33-53 [44]) refers to Jesus using 'cruel metaphors', but he ultimately defends Jesus. John Nolland (*The Gospel of Matthew* [NIGTC; Grand Rapids, MI: Eerdmans, 2005], p. 630) seems critical when he remarks that the rationale used by Jesus 'loses its cogency: to help such a one takes nothing away from Israel'.

49. Burridge, *Imitating Jesus*, pp. 192-93.

50. Elaine Wainwright, 'The Gospel of Matthew', in Schüssler Fiorenza (ed.), *Searching the Scriptures*, II, pp. 635-77 (653).

insofar as it is still centered on showing the benign nature of the Christian empire with which it is often associated.

The fact is that this story shows not only Jesus' own misogyny, but also the imperialistic nature of his actions. First, what Wainwright regards as expanding inclusiveness and breaking of boundaries is actually what empires do. For example, the Roman empire was, in fact, a multicultural entity which continuously sought to expand the number of non-Roman peoples into its orbit.[51] Josephus understood this when he posed this rhetorical question to Apion, the anti-Jewish writer, who questioned how Jews could be called both Jews and Alexandrians: 'Have not the Romans in their generosity [φιλανθρωπία], imparted their name to wellnigh all of mankind, not to individuals only but to great nations as a whole?'[52] For Josephus, the Romans were being philanthropic, not imperialist, as he was a lackey for Rome.

Similarly, Jesus, as the agent of the empire known as the Kingdom of God, was expanding his orbit. The aim of the Kingdom of God is not simply to make Jews its subjects (or to reconfirm Jews as subjects), but also non-Jews. How is this any different from what Romans sought to do? In fact, one must again read the goals of the Yahwistic empire expressed in Isaiah 14.

> But the LORD will have compassion on Jacob and will again choose Israel, and will set them in their own land; and aliens will join them and will cleave to the house of Jacob. And the peoples will take them and bring them to their place, and the house of Israel will possess them in the LORD's land as male and female slaves; they will take captive those who were their captors, and rule over those who oppressed them (Isa. 14.1-2).

Jesus' so-called radical inclusivity is really a continuation of an imperial Yahwistic program that will assimilate many non-Jews.

Second, Jesus' acceptance of the woman was contingent on her declaring his dominion. She calls him 'Lord, Son of David' and repeats the title of 'Lord' after he refuses to help her the first time. Daniel Patte recognizes this feature when he remarks that the woman's use of those terms can be 'read as an example of the basic condition of discipleship: an acknowledgment of and submission to the authority of Jesus'.[53] John Nolland remarks that 'The explanation of Jesus that emerges here is of a firmly Jewish "Son of David"

---

51. See further Michael Erdrich, *Rom und die Barbaren: Das Verhältnis Zwischen dem Imperium Romanum und den germanischen Stämmen vor seiner Nordwestgrenze von der späten römischen Republik bis zum gallischen Sonderreich* (Mainz: Von Zabern, 2001).

52. Josephus, *Against Apion* 2.40 (Thackeray, LCL).

53. Patte, 'The Canaanite Woman and Jesus', p. 48. The woman's acceptance of Jesus' lordship is completely missed by Mark A. Chinen, 'Crumbs from the Table: The

whose status as Lord is nonetheless recognized in worshipful reverence by even a Canaanite woman.'[54]

Glenna Jackson's study of the Matthean pericope concludes:

> The story of the Canaanite Woman, therefore, is not merely a description of the rewards of faith, as it has been viewed in tradition history, but it is a reinforcement of Jewish law for the purpose of attaining membership in the Matthean community.[55]

To be accepted, the Syrophoenician woman has to adopt the cultural premises of Jesus. She is not accepted as she is, nor can she remain as she was (a non-believer in Jesus' messiahship, power, etc.). If so, Jesus follows imperialistic practices. An empire may help you as long as you acknowledge its sovereignty, which this woman did by addressing him with those Messianic titles. The argument that the vocative (κύριε) in Mt. 15. 25 and 27//Mk 7.28 is merely an honorific title (i.e., 'sir') is not borne out by the text or by parallels.[56] In the story of the two blind men healed by Jesus on his exit from Jericho in Mt. 20.29-34, one also finds the pairing of 'Son of David' (v. 31) and 'Lord' (v. 33), as if they were meant to be parallel expressions.

The story of the Syrophoenician/Canaanite woman is akin to that of Ruth, which many scholars see as an example of Hebrew inclusiveness.[57] However, Laura Donaldson, who identifies with Native American peoples in the United States, reads Ruth as a case where a woman must reject her Moabite identity and religion to be accepted into the Hebrew community.[58] For Donaldson, Ruth's story is not really about altruistic acceptance, but rather another story of cultural imperialism. Her study reveals that benign interpretations of cultural assimilation in the book of Ruth may reflect the privileged social position of Christian feminists who have not experienced forced assimilation and integration into another culture.

Syrophoenician Woman and International Law', *Journal of Law and Religion* 27 (2011–12), pp. 1-57.

54. Nolland, *The Gospel of Matthew*, p. 630.

55. Jackson, *'Have Mercy on Me'*, p. 141.

56. Ringe ('A Gentile Woman's Story, Revisited', pp. 87-88, especially 88 n. 17) raises the possibility of an honorific meaning, but then declares it to be unclear whether the word here has messianic or simply an honorific meaning.

57. See L. Juliana M. Claassens, 'Resisting Dehumanization: Ruth, Tamar and the Quest for Human Dignity', *CBQ* 74 (2012), pp. 659-74.

58. See Laura E. Donaldson, 'The Sign of Orpah: Reading Ruth through Native Eyes', in *Ruth and Esther: A Feminist Companion to the Bible* (ed. Athalya Brenner; Second Series; Sheffield: Sheffield Academic Press, 1999), pp. 130-44. For the continuation of the tradition that praises Ruth's conversion without any attention to how she had to assimilate to be accepted, see Christian M.M. Brady, 'The Conversion of Ruth in Targum Ruth', *Review of Rabbinic Judaism* 16 (2013), pp. 133-46.

Sharon Ringe proposes another way to explain Jesus' actions, and it centers on the woman's elite status. Despite her misgivings about Jesus' harsh rhetoric, Ringe argues that 'the woman's privileged place relative to the poorer Jewish peasants of the region around her city earns her a label of contempt ("dog") in light of Jesus' agenda elsewhere in Mark of bringing "good news to the poor"'.[59] Ringe denies that the word 'dogs' was applied by the Jews to Gentiles in general, and affirms that the term was reserved only for 'groups overtly hostile to God's people or to God's law'.[60] She presents the following evidence for the woman's status:

> The wealthy Gentile dwellers of Tyre certainly fit the description of 'enemies' relative to the poorer Jewish residents of the surrounding region in a context of chronic scarcity (limited 'bread'), and their exploitative behavior would have counted as hostility to the divine mandates of justice that Jesus' ministry and Jewish law alike affirmed.[61]

Ringe adds that Jesus' hesitant reaction can be explained if one realizes that the Syrophoenician woman's request is inappropriate 'in light of the disproportionate share of the region's resources that her people had been exploiting'.[62] Since Jesus' healing power is also a limited resource, his response merely implies that only at 'this time, priority would go to those who always wait at the end of the line'.[63]

Ringe's defense of Jesus is flawed on many levels. There is nothing explicit in the text itself that points to any exalted socioeconomic status for the woman. In an earlier essay, Ringe had argued for a lower socioeconomic status for this same Syrophoenician woman because she was alone and because she sought an itinerant healer instead of an established healing center.[64] Her evidence to support her change of mind is no better because nothing about being from Syrophoenicia necessarily entails some privileged position. We really don't know enough of the comparative economics of Tyre and Galilee at the time of Jesus to determine who was exploiting whom. Thus, Richard S. Hanson's study of the Galilean economy indicates many uncertainties about how much Tyre exploited or was involved

59. Ringe, 'A Gentile Woman's Story, Revisited', p. 97.

60. Ringe, 'A Gentile Woman's Story, Revisited', p. 89.

61. Ringe, 'A Gentile Woman's Story, Revisited', pp. 89-90.

62. Ringe, 'A Gentile Woman's Story, Revisited', pp. 89-90. Ringe is followed by a number of non-Euroamerican scholars, such as Poling Sun, 'Naming the Dog: Another Asian Reading of Mark 7:24-30', *Review & Expositor* 107 (2010), pp. 381-94; Hisako Kinukawa, 'The Story of the Syrophoenician Woman (Mark 7:24-30)', *In God's Image* 23 (2004), pp. 50-53.

63. Ringe, 'A Gentile Woman's Story, Revisited', p. 90.

64. Ringe, 'A Gentile Woman's Story', pp. 65-72.

in Galilean economics.[65] Eric M. Meyers and J. Andrew Overman have decisively critiqued the approaches of Richard Horsley and John Dominic Crossan, who are the main advocates of peasant revolt theories and urban–countryside conflicts.[66]

In fact, Acts indicates that the Tyrians were poor enough during the reign of Herod Agrippa (41–44 CE) to ask for food: 'Now Herod was angry with the people of Tyre and Sidon; and they came to him in a body, and having persuaded Blastus, the king's chamberlain, they asked for peace, because their country depended on the king's country for food' (Acts 12.20). Indeed, Ringe inexplicably assumes that poor women did not live in Tyre or its regions. Nor does Ringe explain why this woman should be held responsible for any exploitation that was being engineered by the Tyrian elite. Instead, the extent of her explicit identification and characterization in the text is as a Canaanite woman or as a Syrophoenician woman with a sick daughter at home. Such an identification shows that it is her ethnicity or geographical origin that matters in the story and not her wealth.[67]

Focus on the Syrophoenician woman's ethnicity is an important point because the Gospel writers elsewhere explicitly mention a person's socio-economic status when it matters to the story.[68] In Mt. 19.23, Jesus explicitly refers to the young man as a 'rich man' ($\pi\lambda o\acute{u}\sigma\iota o\varsigma$) and the narrator

65. Richard S. Hanson, *Tyrian Influence in the Upper Galilee* (Meiron Excavation Project, 2; Cambridge, MA: ASOR, 1980).

66. See Eric C. Meyers, 'Jesus and his Galilean Context', in *Archaeology and the Galilee: Texts and Contexts in the Graeco-Roman and Byzantine Periods* (ed. Douglas R. Edwards and C. Thomas McCullough; South Florida Studies in the History of Judaism, 143; Atlanta, GA: Scholars Press, 1997), pp. 57-66; J. Andrew Overman, 'Jesus of Galilee and the Historical Peasant', in Edwards and McCullough (eds.), *Archaeology and the Galilee*, pp. 67-73. See also Jürgen Zangenberg, Harold W. Attridge and Dale B. Martin (eds.), *Religion, Ethnicity, and Identity in Ancient Galilee: A Region in Transition* (WUNT, 2.210; Tübingen: Mohr Siebeck, 2007); Mark Chancey, *Greco-Roman Culture and the Galilee of Jesus* (SNTSMS, 134; Cambridge: Cambridge University Press, 2005). For a challenge to the claim that economic upheavals or ecological crises explain the rise of the Jesus movement, see Morten H. Jensen, 'Climate, Droughts, Wars and Famines in Galilee as a Background for Understanding the Historical Jesus', *JBL* 131 (2012), pp. 307-24; idem, 'Rural Galilee and Rapid Changes: An Investigation of the Socio-Economic Dynamics and Developments in Roman Galilee', *Bib* 93 (2012), pp. 43-67. For a critique of the idea of a distinctive Galilean form of Judaism, see Birger A. Pearson, 'A Q Community in Galilee?', *NTS* 50 (2004), pp. 476-94. For the argument that Q was Judean, not Galilean, see Joseph, *Jesus, Q and the Dead Sea Scrolls*.

67. A study of the ability to retain local identities in the Roman empire is offered by Louise Revell, *Roman Imperialism and Local Identities* (Cambridge: Cambridge University Press, 2010).

68. On the variant identifications of this woman as 'Syrophoenician' in Mark, and 'Canaanite' in Matthew, see Schwarz, 'ΣΥΡΟΦΟΙΝΙΚΙΣΣΑ-ΧΑΝΑΝΑΙΑ'.

tells us in Mt. 19.22 that this young man had abundant possessions (ἦν γὰρ ἔχων κτήματα πολλά). The point is that the rich are hesitant to give up their possessions to follow a man who requires that one give up possessions. In Mt. 27.57, the narrator informs readers that Joseph of Arimathea was 'a rich man' (ἄνθρωπος πλούσιος), which explains why he was able to secure a tomb. In Mk 12.41, Jesus sits down in front of the temple treasury, and watches 'many rich people [πολλοὶ πλούσιοι] put in large sums'.

More importantly, Ringe's solution yields an even more sexist Jesus than she might realize. To understand this sexism, one should compare Jesus' response to the Syrophoenician woman with his response to the Roman centurion in Matthew:

> As he entered Capernaum, a centurion came forward to him, beseeching him and saying, 'Lord, my servant is lying paralyzed at home, in terrible distress'. And he said to him, 'I will come and heal him' (Mt. 8.5-7).

Unlike in the case of the Syrophoenician woman, this story does tell us the social status of the petitioner. He is a Roman centurion, and so part of the single greatest imperial exploitative machine in the entire world of Jesus. There is no question that the Roman empire took Jewish resources, and there is no question that this man is not part of some lower peasant class. Given that the very definition of sexism entails a different treatment on the basis of sex, then Jesus is treating that woman differently from the way he treated the centurion.[69] Jesus makes the Syrophoenician woman beg for healing, while he acts promptly upon the centurion's request. Jesus is sexist here.

Ringe's analysis is also sexist. Ringe does not even consider how Jesus is treating men versus women who come for healing.[70] She does not seem even interested in comparing men to women who come to seek healing from Jesus. Protecting Jesus from sexism seems to have been more important to this feminist interpreter than looking at the inequality of male and female petitioners in the New Testament. Ringe's analysis is itself imperialistic because she does not consider the Kingdom of God as an empire which seeks to help only those people who acknowledge its supremacy.

Nor does Ringe delve sufficiently into Greco-Roman medical practices to understand another possibly sexist dimension of the story. There were

---

69. For how gender affects health care today, see Carolyn F. Sargent and Caroline B. Brettell (eds.), *Gender and Health: An International Perspective* (Upper Saddle River, NJ: Prentice–Hall, 1996).

70. Susan Miller (*Women in Mark's Gospel* [JSNTSup, 259; London: T. & T. Clark, 2004], p. 96) does notice a contrast with how Jesus responded to some men seeking healing for loved ones (e.g., Jairus in Mk 5.22-24) but does not elaborate on any sexism.

female healers in the Greco-Roman world, and they often specialized in the medical problems of women.[71] As Elisa Estévez López observes, Galen of Pergamon (ca. 129–200 CE), one of the most prominent medical writers of the time, claims that female patients sometimes came to him when female healers/midwives could not deal with a problem.[72] Galen's claim serves to devalue female healers, and exalt his authority and skill.[73] Similarly, the story of Jesus healing this woman may be meant to contrast Jesus' effectivity with that of other healers, perhaps including female healers who would likely specialize in problems such as this.[74]

A brief analysis of the healing stories associated with Vespasian is instructive in showing how other aspects of the Syrophoenician pericope mimic healing stories attributed to Roman emperors. According to Tacitus, while Vespasian waited in Alexandria to assume his full imperial power, two men came to beg him for healing. One was blind, and the other had a disabled hand. Tacitus states:

> Vespasian at first ridiculed [*inridere*] these appeals and treated them with scorn [*aspernari*]; then, when the men persisted, he began at one moment to fear the discredit of failure, at another to be inspired with the hopes of success by the appeals of the suppliants and the flattery of his courtiers.[75]

Tacitus explains that Vespasian consulted physicians to ensure that the healings would be seen as genuine. After those consultations, Tacitus continues:

> So, Vespasian, believing that his good fortune was capable of anything and that nothing was any longer incredible, with a smiling countenance and amid intense excitement on the part of the bystanders, did as he was asked to do. The hand was instantly restored to use, and the day again shone for the blind man. Both facts are told by eye-witnesses even now when falsehood brings no reward.[76]

71. Rebecca Flemming, 'Women, Writing, and Medicine in the Classical World', *ClQ* 57.1 (2007), pp. 257-59.

72. On the prominence of midwives and their association with physicians, see Christian Laes, 'Midwives and Greek Inscriptions in Hellenistic and Roman Antiquity', *ZPE* 176 (2011), pp. 154-62.

73. See Elisa Estévez López, *El poder de una mujer creyente: Cuerpo, identidad y discipulado en Mc 5,24b-34, un estudio desde las ciencias sociales* (Estella, Spain: Editorial Verbo Divino, 2003), p. 160 n. 42. See also Holt N. Parker, 'Galen and the Girls: Sources for Women Medical Writers Revisited', *ClQ* 62 (2012), pp. 359-86.

74. On how early Christianity sought to show its superiority over other health care systems, see Avalos, *Health Care and the Rise of Christianity*.

75. Tacitus, *Histories* 4.81 (Moore, LCL). For a study of these healings, and their versions, see Eric Eve, 'Spit in your Eye: The Blind Man of Bethsaida and the Blind Man of Alexandria', *NTS* 54 (2008), pp. 1-17.

76. Tacitus, *Histories* 4.81 (Moore, LCL).

Vespasian heals common local non-Roman Alexandrians (*plebe Alexand-rina*), just as Jesus heals a non-Jew. Vespasian at first treats the petitioners with scorn just as Jesus initially treated the Syrophoenician woman with scorn. Vespasian shows reluctance, but then is convinced, at least in part, by the persistence of the petitioners. Jesus initially shows reluctance, and then the woman convinces him to reverse it.

While there are many differences, a good Vespasian apologist could just as well make Vespasian a paradigm of inclusiveness. Vespasian also empow-ered the sick because they convinced him to change his mind. One could for-give Vespasian for ridiculing someone who needed help (though none of the versions tell us what specific derogatory language he used). Perhaps he saw those people as elitists, and his reluctance was just to make the point that he should help other people first. But the entire story is meant to validate Vespa-sian's claim to the emperorship, just as miracle stories are meant to validate Jesus' imperialistic Kingdom of God. So is Vespasian's story ultimately egal-itarian or imperialistic? Is it a story about the value of faith, which the version in Suetonius mentions?[77] Surely, most Christian ethicists don't see Vespasian as paragon of egalitarianism or inclusiveness. But one can transform Vespa-sian into one of the greatest humanitarians in the world by using the same her-meneutic moves that New Testament ethicists apply to Jesus.

Mark 8: Training Willing Victims

One of the recurrent themes in feminist biblical studies in general is vio-lence against women. In the case of Christianity, Joanne Carlson Brown and Rebecca Parker phrased the problem succinctly: 'Christianity is an abusive theology that glorifies suffering.'[78] Brown and Parker argue that violence against women, especially in North America, can be attributed, as least in part, to the fact that 'Christianity has been a primary—in many women's lives *the* primary force in shaping our acceptance of abuse'.[79] Although their work centered on the violent atonement of Christ, they saw the endorsement of violence and the redeeming value of suffering in many biblical texts.

For most Christian feminists, any thought that Jesus might have encour-aged victimhood would be antithetical to feminist, or even general ethical standards. Thus, Julie M. Hopkins remarks:

---

77. Suetonius, *Vespasian* 7.3 (Rolfe, LCL): 'Cum vix fides esset ullo modo rem suc-cesuram.'

78. Joanne C. Brown and Rebecca Parker, 'For God So Loved the World?', in *Chris-tianity, Patriarchy, and Abuse: A Feminist Critique* (ed. Joanne C. Brown and Carole R. Bohn; New York: Pilgrim Press, 1989), pp. 1-30 (26).

79. Brown and Parker, 'For God So Loved the World?', p. 2.

> It is morally abhorrent to claim that God the Father demanded the self-sacrifice of his only Son to balance the scales of justice. A god who punishes through pain, despair, and violent death is not a god of love but a sadist and a despot.[80]

Although Hopkins was mainly voicing objections against the substitutionary atonement, she and other feminists have critiqued any views of Jesus as encouraging suffering, self-sacrifice and passivity.[81]

Mark 8.34 has been particularly troublesome for many feminists who view Jesus as discouraging victimhood, and so I quote the relevant context in full:

> And he began to teach them that the Son of man must suffer many things, and be rejected by the elders and the chief priests and the scribes, and be killed, and after three days rise again. And he said this plainly. And Peter took him, and began to rebuke him. But turning and seeing his disciples, he rebuked Peter, and said, 'Get behind me, Satan! For you are not on the side of God, but of men'. And he called to him the multitude with his disciples, and said to them, 'If any man would come after me, let him deny himself and take up his cross and follow me. For whoever would save his life will lose it; and whoever loses his life for my sake and the gospel's will save it. For what does it profit a man, to gain the whole world and forfeit his life? For what can a man give in return for his life? For whoever is ashamed of me and of my words in this adulterous and sinful generation, of him will the Son of man also be ashamed, when he comes in the glory of his Father with the holy angels' (Mk 8.31-38).

The passage certainly seems to encourage victimhood in v. 34, where disciples are instructed to 'take up the cross', a known instrument of Roman torture and execution.

However, Joanna Dewey, a pioneer in feminist biblical interpretation, thinks it is androcentric readings that are responsible for viewing Jesus as encouraging victimhood. According to Dewey,

> [W]hen read in the context of the first-century cultural world and the larger narrative of Mark, Mk 8.34 is not an exhortation to suffering and victimage in general. It is an exhortation to remain faithful to Jesus and the rule of God in the face of persecution, even execution, by political authorities.[82]

---

80. Julie M. Hopkins, *Towards a Feminist Christology: Jesus of Nazareth, European Women, and the Christological Crisis* (Grand Rapids, MI: Eerdmans, 1995), p. 50.

81. For other examples, see Dorothee Soelle, *Suffering* (London: Darton, Longman & Todd, 1975), especially pp. 9-32; Rita Nakashima Brock, *Journeys by the Heart: A Chistology of Erotic Power* (New York: Crossroad, 1988). A more general treatment of suffering is that of Richard W. Miller, *Suffering and the Christian Life* (Maryknoll, NY: Orbis Books, 2013).

82. Joanna Dewey, "'Let them Renounce Themselves and Take up their Cross'": A

Dewey promises that new literary and sociological readings will correct any misperception that Jesus is encouraging victimhood.

Dewey argues that '[a]ncients viewed suffering as a normal if unpleasant part of life rather than an interruption to normal human existence'.[83] She contends that Mark distinguishes two types of suffering: '[G]eneral human suffering which is to be cured or alleviated with Jesus' inauguration of God's rule, and persecution, which is the lot of those who persevere in following the way of god as long as this age endures.'[84] Dewey points to how Jesus repeatedly is alleviating suffering by exorcizing demons, healing the sick and feeding multitudes. So why would Jesus alleviate the suffering of the ill and the hungry if he wished to encourage it?

Another argument relies, by her own admission, mostly on Bruce Malina's conclusions about personhood in the ancient Mediterranean.[85] In an effort to deny that the phrase 'let him deny himself' refers to individuals, Dewey claims:

> Today many do tend to read it as a denial of the individual self, a call to give up one's will, always to put oneself last. I suggest that this is not what it would have conveyed to a first-century audience. First, their sense of self was different; they had little idea of any individual identity. Second, the demand is in parallel with taking up one's cross and so is to be interpreted in the context of persecution.[86]

Jesus' instruction to 'take up the cross' refers to 'the inevitability of persecution' that will test the faith of disciples.[87] Given that individuals were so closely identified with their kinship group, rather than as individuals, Dewey concludes that '[t]o deny self, then, is to deny's one kin'.[88] She outlines the chiastic structure of Mk 8.34 as follows:

Feminist Reading of Mark 8.34 in Mark's Social and Narrative World', in Levine and Blickenstaff (eds.), *A Feminist Companion to Mark*, pp. 23-36 (35-36). For her other studies of Mark, see Joanna Dewey, 'The Survival of Mark's Gospel: A Good Story?', *JBL* 123 (2004), pp. 495-507. For a more general survey of women in Mark, see Miller, *Women in Mark's Gospel*.

83. Dewey, '"Let them Renounce Themselves"', p. 30.
84. Dewey, '"Let them Renounce Themselves"', p. 31.
85. Dewey ('"Let them Renounce Themselves"', p. 33 n. 29), states: 'This section is strongly indebted to Malina', and cites these particular studies: Bruce J. Malina, 'Understanding New Testament Persons', in *The Social Sciences and the New Testament* (ed. Richard Rohrbaugh; Peabody, MA: Hendrickson, 1996), pp. 41-61; idem, '"Let Him Deny Himself" (Mark 8:34 & Par): A Social Psychological Model of Self-Denial', *BTB* 24 (1994), pp. 106-119.
86. Dewey, '"Let them Renounce Themselves"', p. 33.
87. Dewey, '"Let them Renounce Themselves"', p. 33.
88. Dewey, '"Let them Renounce Themselves"', p. 35.

A If any want to follow me,
   B let them renounce themselves [that is, deny kin]
   C and take up their cross [that is, risk persecution]
A and follow me.[89]

According to Dewey, these arguments are sufficient to show that Jesus is not encouraging disciples to accept suffering or victimhood.

One major problem with Dewey's arguments is that they rest on an uncritical acceptance of Malina's claims about the nature of 'individuality' and 'person' in ancient Mediterranean societies. Malina's own conclusions about the ancient Mediterranean rest on sparse data and inappropriate retrojections from modern studies. For example, Malina makes the bald assertion that 'there simply were no individualistic cultures before the sixteenth century'.[90]

For his evidence, Malina cites only a book by Daniel Bell, a Harvard sociologist who is almost completely concerned with modern capitalism, and who supplies no data for the ancient Mediterranean views of personhood or individualism.[91] In that book, Bell remarks: 'The fundamental assumption of modernity, the thread that has run through Western Civilization since the sixteenth century, is that the social unit of society is not the group, but the guild, the tribe, or the city, but the person.'[92] Bell offers no detailed analysis to support this sweeping statement, nor does he really show interest in ancient Mediterranean societies. Moreover, Bell is opposed by many other historians who argue that the nation state is the mark of modernity, and nation states center on creating a group identity that can be just as powerful or more powerful than anything found in the ancient world.[93]

Although Malina complains of modern scholars using an 'anachronistic ethnocentric projection' when discussing ancient Mediterranean societies, the fact is that most of Malina's data comes from modern Mediterranean societies.[94] In particular, important aspects of Malina's view of what he calls 'Mediterranean society' are based primarily on modern anthropological stud-

89. Dewey, '"Let them Renounce Themselves"', p. 35. For the argument that Mk 8.31-33 goes back to the historical Jesus, see Michael V. Zolondek, 'The Authenticity of the First Passion Prediction and the Origin of Mark 8.31-33', *Journal for the Study of the Historical Jesus* 8 (2010), pp. 237-53.

90. Malina, 'Understanding New Testament Persons', p. 55.

91. Daniel Bell, *The Cultural Contradictions of Capitalism* (New York: Basic Books, 1976).

92. Bell, *The Cultural Contradictions of Capitalism*, p. 16.

93. See Liah Greenfield, *Nationalism: Five Roads to Modernity* (Cambridge, MA: Harvard University Press, 1992); Philip S. Gorski, 'The Mosaic Moment: An Early Modernist Critique of Modernist Theories of Nationalism', *American Journal of Sociology* 105.5 (March 2000), pp. 1428-68; Anthony W. Marx, *Faith in Nation: Exclusionary Origins of Nationalism* (New York: Oxford University Press, 2003).

94. Malina, 'Understanding New Testament Persons', p. 45.

ies, such as those of David D. Gilmore and George R. Saunders.[95] Neither of those scholars actually focuses on ancient Mediterranean societies.[96]

As it is, Malina's data about how persons saw themselves are questionable and yield unsupported and gross overgeneralizations. One problem is the definition of 'individualism' presented by Malina:

> Individualism may be described as the belief that persons are each and singly an end in themselves, and as such ought to realize their 'self' and cultivate their own judgment not withstanding the push of pervasive social pressures in the direction of conformity.[97]

Perhaps so, but that is not the only definition of 'individualism' in the anthropological literature. In a substantive meta-analysis of studies of individualism and collectivism from around the globe, Daphna Oyserman and her colleagues discuss the difficulty in finding precise metrics for 'individualism' cross-culturally. As Oyserman observes, the definition of individualism differs widely:

> Hofstede (1980) defined *individualism* as a focus on rights above duties, a concern for oneself and immediate family, an emphasis on personal autonomy and self-fulfillment, and the basing of one's identity on one's personal accomplishments. Waterman (1984) defined *normative individualism* as a focus on personal responsibility and freedom of choice, living up to one's potential, and respecting the integrity of others. Schwartz (1990) defined *individualistic societies* as fundamentally contractual, consisting of narrow primary groups and negotiated social relations, with specific obligations and expectations focusing on achieving status.[98]

---

95. For example, Malina ('Understanding New Testament Persons', p. 43) says that David Gilmore and George Saunders 'offer excellent comparative models describing modern eastern Mediterraneans [*sic*] and their traditional cultures'. See further David D. Gilmore, 'Anthropology of the Mediterranean Area', *Annual Review of Anthropology* 11 (1982), pp. 175-205; David D. Gilmore (ed.), *Honor and Shame and the Unity of the Mediterranean* (Washington, DC: American Anthropological Association, 1987); George R. Saunders, 'Men and Women in Southern Europe: A Review of Some Aspects of Cultural Complexity', *Journal of Psychoanalytic Anthropology* 4 (1981), pp. 435-66. For another 'Mediterraneanist' approach, see Stephen Clark, *Ancient Mediterranean Philosophy: An Introduction* (London: Bloomsbury, 2013).

96. See also L.J. Lawrence and M.I. Aguilar (eds.), *Anthropology and Biblical Studies: Avenues of Approach* (Leiden: Deo, 2004).

97. Malina, 'Understanding New Testament Persons', p. 46.

98. Daphna Oyserman, Heather M. Coon and Markus Kemmelmeier, 'Rethinking Individualism and Collectivism: Evaluation of Theoretical Assumptions and Meta-analyses', *Psychological Bulletin* 128 (2002), pp. 3-72 (4-5); Geert Hofstede, *Culture's Consequences* (Beverly Hills, CA: Sage, 1980); Alan S. Waterman, *The Psychology of Individualism* (New York: Praeger, 1984); Shalom H. Schwartz, 'Individualism-Collectivism: Critique and Proposed Refinements', *Journal of Cross-Cultural Psychology* 21 (1990), pp. 139-57.

If so, it is very difficult to develop metrics to study individualism cross-culturally. It is even more difficult to generalize about the extent of individualism in the ancient world.

Perhaps the weakest aspect of Malina's methodology is his heavy dependence on the work of Harry C. Triandis and his collaborators. In his study of Mk 8.34, Malina cites two of Triandis's articles.[99] If one looks at the methodology of Triandis, one finds that the manner in which he measures independence is both simplistic and would be very difficult to detect in the ancient Mediterranean world. Consider this metric used by Triandis:

> Independence: This factor is defined by loadings on 'I would rather struggle through a personal problem by myself than discuss it with my friends' and 'One should live one's life independently of others, as much as possible' and negative loading on 'I enjoy meeting and talking to my neighbors everyday'.[100]

Given such differing definitions, the metrics for identifying and measuring degrees of individualism and collectivism have been equally variant and problematic. For example, how would one measure whether ancient Mediterranean people enjoyed meeting and talking to neighbors every day? How do we measure the extent to which ancient Mediterranean people kept problems to themselves instead of talking to others? Would Mary fit this criterion for individualism when we are told that she 'kept all these things in her heart' about Jesus in Lk. 2.51?

Malina homogenizes American culture when he remarks that 'Americans live in an individualistic culture that centers on the value of self-reliance'.[101] Actual sociological studies record much diversity and nuance in American 'individualism'. The mere fact that millions of Americans use Facebook and have smartphones undermines the idea that Americans, in Malina's words, 'cultivate their own judgment not withstanding the push of pervasive social pressures in the direction of conformity'.[102] Other studies repeatedly show supposedly individualistic Americans succumbing to peer pressure and conformity for all sorts of anti-social behaviors.[103]

99. Harry C. Triandis *et al.*, 'Cross-Cultural Studies of Individualism and Collectivism', in *Nebraska Symposium on Motivation 1989* (ed. Richard A. Dienstbier *et al.*; Lincoln, NE: University of Nebraska Press, 1989), pp. 41-133; idem, 'An Etic-Emic Analysis of Individualism and Collectivism', *Journal of Cross-Cultural Psychology* 24 (1993), pp. 366-83.

100. Triandis, 'An Etic-Emic Analysis', p. 372.

101. Malina, 'Understanding New Testament Persons', p. 46.

102. Malina, 'Understanding New Testament Persons', p. 46.

103. For example, Margo Gardner and Laurence Steinberg, 'Peer Influence on Risk Taking, Risk Preference, and Risky Decision Making in Adolescence and Adulthood: An Experimental Study', *Developmental Psychology* 41 (2005), pp. 625-35; Donna Rae

In her analyses of multiple surveys of individualism, Oyserman summarized the findings as follows:

> European Americans were found to be both more individualistic—valuing personal independence more—and less collectivistic—feeling duty to ingroups less—than others. However, European Americans were not more individualistic than African Americans, or Latinos, and not less collectivistic than Japanese or Koreans. Among Asians, only Chinese showed large effects, being both less individualistic and more collectivistic.[104]

In other words, one has to have a much more nuanced and careful view of any stark individualistic/collectivist dichotomy for Americans, especially when comparing them to ancient societies for which our sociological data are comparatively sparse and diverse.

More importantly, Malina (and, by extension, Dewey) provides no detailed surveys of ancient Mediterranean concepts of individualism or collectivism. Dewey seems unaware that some question the extent to which Jews were part of a Mediterranean society.[105] In fact, such surveys are not even possible, given the gaps in the data we possess for ancient societies. Even the data we do have for ancient societies cannot approximate what we have for modern societies. That is a significant gap, and should dissuade us from characterizing any entire society as strictly 'individualist' or 'collectivist' even when we have such surveys.

Nonetheless, some recent scholarship has sought to overturn this idea that individualism was nearly non-existent in the ancient Mediterranean.[106] Jorg Rüpke, for example, has proposed the existence of five types (practical, moral, competitive, representative and reflexive) of individuality that would account for the range of individuation one sees in the ancient Mediterranean

---

Clasen and B. Bradford Brown, 'The Multidimensionality of Peer Pressure in Adolescence', *Journal of Youth and Adolescence* 14 (1985), pp. 451-68.

104. Oyserman, Coon and Kemmelmeier, 'Rethinking Individualism and Collectivism', p. 3.

105. See the discussion in Seth Schwartz, *Were the Jews a Mediterranean Society? Reciprocity and Solidarity in Ancient Judaism* (Princeton, NJ: Princeton University Press, 2012). For a response, see Steven Weitzman, 'Mediterranean Exchanges: A Response to Seth Schwartz's Were the Jews a Mediterranean Society?', *JQR* 102 (2012), pp. 491-512.

106. See Larry Siedentop, *Inventing the Individual:The Origins of Western Liberalism* (Cambridge, MA: Harvard University Press, 2014); Jörg Rüpke (ed.), *The Individual in the Religions of the Ancient Mediterranean* (New York: Oxford University Press, 2013); Maria Michela Luiselli, 'La partecipazione dell'individuo alla religione: rituali personali tra norma e individualità', *Aegyptus* 85 (2006), pp. 13-31; Andrea Purvis, *Singular Dedications: Founders and Innovators of Private Cults in Classical Greece* (London: Routledge, 2009); Michael Trapp, *Philosophy in the Roman Empire: Ethics, Politics, and Society* (Aldershot: Ashgate, 2007).

data, including in the thousands of votives dedicated by individuals and on behalf of individuals.[107] One finds plenty of evidence that individuals competed with each other for individual glory and status. Indeed, how does one explain works devoted to individuals (e.g., Plutarch's *Lives*) if individual identity was as moribund as Dewey claims?

Nor does Dewey seem to be cognizant of the scholarship and vast biblical evidence for the existence and development of individualism in ancient Judaism. Already by 1991, for example, Baruch Halpern had written an important essay on the rise of individualism in the seventh century BCE.[108] While it is true that one can find collectivist ideologies in the biblical texts, it is also true that one can find authors who stressed individual responsibility and identity.[109] The very act of naming a child could affirm both his individual and corporate identity (e.g., Moses in Exod. 2.10). Even though Esau and Jacob were twins, the biblical author stressed their radically contrasting personalities: 'When the boys grew up, Esau was a skillful hunter, a man of the field, while Jacob was a quiet man, dwelling in tents' (Gen. 25.27). In the so-called Deuteronomistic History, one finds this plea: 'The fathers shall not be put to death for the children, nor shall the children be put to death for the fathers; every man shall be put to death for his own sin' (Deut. 24.16).

On a purely linguistic-contextual level, the equation of 'to deny oneself' (ἀπαρνησάσθω ἑαυτὸν) with 'to deny one's kin' is flawed. Dewey specifically argues that the Greek word ἀπαρνέομαι means to deny kinship here and in Peter's renunciation of Jesus (Mk 14.30, 31, 72). However, there is no reason to read any direct object of ἀπαρνέομαι as a reference to a kinship group rather than to an individual. Dewey does not offer any detailed or rigorous study of that Greek word to reach her conclusion. Jesus in Mark had the linguistic means to speak collectively if he wished to do so. For example, Jesus could have used the Greek word, οἶκος (cf. 1 Cor. 1.16, Tit. 1.11), or listed kin as in Lk. 14.26 ('hate his own father and mother and wife and children and brothers and sisters yes, and even his own life...'). Dewey cites Lk. 14.26 as supporting her understanding, but the passage actually confirms that Jesus differentiates the family from an individual by a similar use of a reflexive pronoun (...καὶ τὴν ψυχὴν ἑαυτοῦ; cf. ἀπαρνησάσθω ἑαυτόν in Mk 8.34).

---

107. Jörg Rüpke, 'Individualization and Individuation as Concepts for Historical Research', in Rüpke (ed.), *The Individual in the Religions of the Ancient Mediterranean*, pp. 3-40 (12-14).

108. Baruch Halpern, 'Jerusalem and the Lineages in the Seventh Century BCE: Kinship and the Rise of Individual Moral Liability', in *Law and Ideology in Monarchic Israel* (ed. Baruch Halpern and Deborah W. Hobson; Sheffield: Sheffield Academic Press, 1991), pp. 11-107.

109. See Carol A. Newsom, 'Models of the Moral Self: Hebrew Bible and Second Temple Judaism', *JBL* 131 (2012), pp. 5-25.

Even if the basic unit of social organization is a kinship group, it does not follow that individuals could not be rejected or denied *as individuals*. While Peter's denial of Jesus may have entailed rejection of all of Jesus' followers (Peter's new kinship group), there is no reason why we cannot read the text as also expressing Peter's denial of Jesus as an individual. Denial is not an either-or proposition here, but rather one where the denial of an individual can entail the denial of some larger group. Dewey confuses the issue by wrongly presuming that any actions that entail consequences for one's family must mean that only families are being identified as the objects of any action. That is a false dichotomy because it is logically possible to identify individuals as individuals while being mindful of any consequences of their behavior for the larger kinship group.

There is supporting linguistic evidence for my individualistic understanding of ἀπαρνέομαι in another instance where Jesus promises to reciprocate such denials: 'but he who denies me before men will be denied before the angels of God' (ὁ δὲ ἀρνησάμενός με ἐνώπιον τῶν ἀνθρώπων ἀπαρνηθήσεται ἐνώπιον τῶν ἀγγέλων τοῦ θεοῦ, Lk. 12.9). The Greek use of the masculine singular pronoun/article is consistent with restricting this reciprocation to the individuals who commit the act of denying (ἀρνησάμενος) Jesus. And those individuals who commit that act will, in turn, be denied (ἀπαρνηθήσεται), presumably by Jesus, before the angels. Note that both ἀπαρνέομαι and ἀρνέομαι seem to be used synonymously and in parallel. If so, according to Dewey's logic, Jesus will 'deny' the entire kinship group of the one denying his kinship group. This would be an absurd reading by most standards. For example, if other members of the Jesus-denialist's family are followers of Jesus, will he deny them as well?

Dewey's distinction between 'general human suffering' and 'persecution' does not salvage Jesus from the charge that he is encouraging victimhood. Dewey fails to see that Jesus is not alleviating general human suffering at all. He is alleviating the suffering only of those who will help him make his point and display his power and authority, something unwittingly admitted by some scholars.[110] The sick and hungry are props in the stories of miracle healings and feedings. If Mark believed Jesus had this sort of power, he certainly did not have Jesus heal all the sick people in the world or feed all the hungry in the world. Jesus' selective healings and feedings are mainly for marketing the benefit of his kingdom and hegemony.

In practical terms, Jesus believed the coming persecution to be quite general. Note these warnings by Jesus:

---

110. For example, many scholars admit that Jesus healed specific people as a sign, and so imply that he would not have healed that person unless it provided a sign. See, Stephen S. Kim, 'The Significance of Jesus' Healing the Blind Man in John 9', *BSac* 167 (2010), pp. 307-318.

> But take heed to yourselves; for they will deliver you up to councils; and
> you will be beaten in synagogues; and you will stand before governors and
> kings for my sake, to bear testimony before them…and you will be hated
> by all for my name's sake. But he who endures to the end will be saved
> (Mk 13.9, 13).

Although Jesus says that God will shorten the days for the sake of the elect,
there is no hint that God or Jesus will directly intervene in any beatings
before they happen, or heal victims as soon as they are beaten. Rather, the
goal of the victims of persecution is to 'endure to the end'. How does suffering inflicted by persecution differ from 'general human suffering' and
how does the instruction to endure until the end not encourage victimhood
and suffering?

To avoid the obvious and plain meaning of Jesus' instructions, Dewey
seeks to challenge the Revised Standard Version's rendition of Mk 8.31,
which states: 'And he began to teach them that the Son of man must suffer
many things, and be rejected by the elders and the chief priests and the
scribes, and be killed, and after three days rise again' (Mk 8.31). But according to Dewey,

> The phrase translated 'suffer many things' or 'undergo great suffering' is
> better translated simply 'undergo many things'. The emphasis is not on
> suffering per se but specifically on rejection and persecution for living the
> life of the age to come, already in this age… So suffering in general is *not*
> being exalted.[111]

Again, Dewey offers no detailed exegesis of the Greek text or any comparative materials to reach her conclusion.

Dewey's proposed rendition, 'undergo many things', does not reflect
faithfully the Greek expression, πολλὰ παθεῖν, because the latter is almost
uniformly treated as a negative experience. Although BDAG identifies
some usages of πάσχω that are positive, it rightly affirms that 'in all other
places, as always in the LXX, in an unfavorable sense, **suffer, endure**'.[112]
In Markan usage, it is particularly negative, as in the case of the woman
with a longtime blood flow. Mark 5.26 says that the woman 'had suffered
much [πολλὰ παθοῦσα] under many physicians, and had spent all that she
had, and was no better but rather grew worse'. Saying that the woman had
merely 'undergone many things' erases the woman's significant suffering
that the author seeks to convey (cf. the use of 'scourge'/μάστιγος in v. 29),
and also the parallel Mark presents with Jesus.[113] In other words, Dewey's

---

111. Joanna Dewey, 'The Gospel of Mark', in Schüssler Fiorenza (ed.), *Searching the Scriptures*, II, pp. 470-509 (488).

112. BDAG, 'πάσχω', 785a; bold emphasis in BDAG.

113. For the narratological significance of this parallel usage in Mk 5.26 and 8.31, see Dogmar Oppel, *Heilsam erzählen-erzählend heilen: Die Heilung der Blutflüssigen und*

proposal would be decidedly anti-feminist, as it diminishes the plight of a suffering woman.[114]

One final issue to consider in Dewey's treatment of Mk 8.31 is her appeal to a version of the Greater Good theory, as follows:

> While the inbreaking of God's rule on earth gives Jesus and his follow-
> ers power over sickness and nature—the power to use force against them.
> During the overlap of the ages, human freedom is maintained. Humans are
> free to reject the rule of God and oppose its agents, and most of those who
> hold power in the old age do reject God's rule.[115]

Apparently, all of these sufferings are not so objectionable because there will be a better world coming, and people have freedom to accept or reject the kingdom of God.

But this reasoning is as imperialistic and hegemonic as anything one sees in the rhetoric of empires in history. All empires ask for sacrifice from their followers, whether it be American soldiers fighting in Iraq or ancient vassals of Assyrian kings. The fact that such empires don't call for general human suffering does not lessen the ethical objections to suffering on behalf of some empire, whether one calls it the Assyrian empire, the Roman empire, or the Kingdom of God. All empires are based on a vision for the future that is supposed to compensate for the suffering endured now. Behind Dewey's defense of Jesus is the premise that the Kingdom of God is a good empire, and so any request by its monarch (Jesus or God) to endure suffering on its behalf must be ethically acceptable.

In the end, Dewey exemplifies another feminist theologian protecting a man: Jesus. Dewey's defense of Jesus' words, which do encourage followers to endure beatings and other sufferings 'for my name's sake', relies on facile generalizations of what 'individual' or 'person' meant in the ancient Mediterranean. Her conclusions rely on bald assertions about the meaning of Greek words for which she offers no further comparative examples or detailed linguistic analysis. But more disturbingly, her entire defense of Jesus relies on the lack of any reflection on whether asking people to endure any persecution for the Kingdom of God is ethical in the first place.

---

die Erweckung der Jairustochter in Mk 5, 21-43 als Beispiel markinischer Erzählsfer-
tigkeit (BBB, 102; Weinheim: Beltz Athenäum Verlag, 1995), p. 167.

114. Ironically, Dewey completely misses the similar Greek usage despite the fact that she published a study (Joanna Dewey, 'Jesus' Healings of Women: Conformity and Non-conformity to Dominant Cultural Values as Clues for Historical Reconstruction', *BTB* 24 [1994], pp. 122-31) of healings that included the woman with the hemorrhage. Perhaps the most thorough recent study of this pericope is that of López, *El poder de una mujer creyente.*

115. Dewey, '"Let them Renounce Themselves"', p. 31.

Mark 10/Matthew 19: Divorcing Equality

The rights of women form a basic theme in feminist theory and scholarship. In the ancient world, the rights and obligations of women within the family, the basic unit of organization, has received much attention.[116] Jesus did voice some significant comments about marriage and divorce that have become the basis of much debate about marriage and divorce throughout Christian history.[117] Of particular importance are Jesus' teachings found in Mark 10 and Matthew 19. I begin with the version in Mark:

> And Pharisees came up and in order to test him asked, 'Is it lawful for a man to divorce his wife?' He answered them, 'What did Moses command you?' They said, 'Moses allowed a man to write a certificate of divorce, and to put her away'. But Jesus said to them, 'For your hardness of heart he wrote you this commandment. But from the beginning of creation, "God made them male and female". "For this reason a man shall leave his father and mother and be joined to his wife, and the two shall become one flesh". So they are no longer two but one flesh. What therefore God has joined together, let not man put asunder'. And in the house the disciples asked him again about this matter. And he said to them, 'Whoever divorces his wife and marries another, commits adultery against her; and if she divorces her husband and marries another, she commits adultery' (Mk 10.2-12).

Richard Hays uses a series of hyperbolic adjectives to convey Jesus' supposedly revolutionary advances on marriage and divorce. He refers to a 'fundamental redefinition of divorce' insofar as Jesus speaks about divorce being an offense against the wife, instead of against her father or household. Hays believes Jesus made some 'bold hermeneutical moves', issues a 'stunning reversal of convention', and 'changes the rules of the game in one bold stroke'.[118]

Many feminists similarly see Jesus' teachings as a great advance for women and for humanity. Amy-Jill Levine believes that Jesus' forbidding divorce and remarriage to both husband and wife was an 'egalitarian move' and an 'innovation'.[119] A more elaborate defense of Jesus' innovation is that of Joanna Dewey, who describes the social advances in this text as follows:

---

116. See Leo G. Perdue *et al.* (eds.), *Families in Ancient Israel* (Louisville, KY: Westminster/John Knox Press, 1997).

117. See Amy-Jill Levine, 'Jesus, Divorce, and Sexuality: A Jewish Critique', in *The Historical Jesus through Catholic and Jewish Eyes* (ed. Bryan F. LeBeau, Leonard Greenspoon and Dennis Hamm; London: Bloomsbury/T. & T. Clark, 2000), pp. 113-29.

118. Hays, *The Moral Vision*, pp. 350, 352.

119. Levine, 'Jesus, Divorce, and Sexuality', p. 118. For another study praising Jesus for innovative egalitarianism, see Maria-Luisa Rigato, *Discepoli di Gesù* (Studi biblici, 61; Bologna: Dehoniane, 2011).

According to Jewish law, a man could divorce his wife if she displeased him (Deut. 24.1); a woman had no such right. Jews and pagans alike understood women (and children) basically as property. Jesus' response to the Pharisees' question invalidates the one-sided privilege of the male to end the marriage at whim, increasing the woman's protection in a culture in which a woman without a man (husband or father) was exceedingly vulnerable and marginal. Not an unconditional prohibition of divorce for all times, the statement rather makes marriage a more equal institution in its first century context... Once again, the Markan Jesus treats the behavior of men and women equally: for both men and women divorce and remarriage are adultery. Christianity has tended to stress the prohibition of divorce, but in its own social context what was most radical about the teaching on divorce was equal treatment of women and men.[120]

Elisabeth Schüssler Fiorenza also sees Jesus' teachings as beneficial for women, but she concedes that 'as long as patriarchy is operative, divorce is commanded out of necessity... However, Jesus insists, God did not create or intend patriarchy but created persons as male and female human beings.'[121] Again, we see an apologetic strategem found in the work of other Christian ethicists. First is the claim that Jewish and pagan cultures are somehow morally retrogressive or inferior compared to Jesus' teachings. Second, it is affirmed that Jesus brought some sort of radical social innovation.

Other scholars are not so certain that this passage represents an innovation. Richard Horsley is less enthusiastic about any supersession of patriarchy:

The marriage and family Jesus was reinforcing with this principle were still patriarchal. We can hardly claim that Jesus had anticipated modern concerns for the equality of women. Yet the formulation of the principle [it] addresses to both men and women is striking in the context of a patriarchal society and tradition.[122]

Perhaps the most serious challenge comes from the work of Mary Rose D'Angelo, whose careful examination of Roman marriage and divorce law reveals that Mark is actually conforming to imperial law rather than resisting it. As D'Angelo phrases it:

The picture I have drawn is a less heartening one than Schüssler Fiorenza's reconstruction of the Jesus movement. In my reading, Mk 10.2-31 emerges from early Christian attempts to meet the demands of the gospel while reading biblical texts in a world whose political and moral exigencies were defined at least in part by the imperial order. Mark's divorce sayings match

---

120. Dewey, 'The Gospel of Mark', in p. 491.
121. Schüssler Fiorenza, *In Memory of Her*, p. 143.
122. Horsley, *Jesus and Empire*, p. 122. Horsley's text actually reads: '...principle in addresses...', and I have the presumed intended reading in brackets.

and outdo Roman claims of a founder who protected morality with an originally indissoluble form of marriage claiming as a protection for marriage
the order of creation.[123]

Indeed, the claims of these feminist Christian apologists cannot be sustained because they overlook ancient Near Eastern and Greco-Roman legal
history.

It is patently false to claim that, when compared to pagan or Jewish cultures, Jesus brought a radical innovation in the ability for women to divorce
men.[124] In the eighteenth century BCE, the Code of Hammurabi already man-
ifests such an ability for women to divorce in Law 142:

> If a woman repudiates her husband, and declares, 'You will not have mar-
> ital relations with me'—her circumstances will be investigated by the
> authorities of her city quarter, and if she is circumspect and without fault,
> but her husband is wayward and disparages her greatly, that woman will not
> be subject to any penalty. She shall take her dowry and she shall depart to
> her father's house.[125]

In contrast to what Hays claims about Jesus' revolutionary advances insofar divorce could count as an offense against the wife, the CH shows that a
woman could be viewed as the directly aggrieved party. The woman seems
to have individual standing in this marital lawsuit. There is no father fighting on her behalf, and she is said to be able to go to her father's house if she
wins. Even Simone de Beauvoir, who was not a biblical scholar, knew in the
1950s that the CH recorded at least some advances for women.[126]

Law 59 of the Laws of Eshnunna dictates that if a man who sired children
with one woman remarries another woman, then 'he shall be expelled from
the house...'.[127] The law seems to assume that the woman is the offended
party, and has the right to keep the house. It is not her father's house or the
house of her kin as far as one can tell from the text. It is her house. The man

---

123. Mary Rose D'Angelo, 'Roman Imperial Family Values and the Gospel of Mark:
The Divorce Sayings (Mark 10:2-12)', in *Women and Gender in Ancient Religions* (ed.
Stephen P. Ahearne-Kroll, Paul A. Holloway and James A. Kelhoffer; WUNT, 2.263;
Tübingen: Mohr Siebeck, 2010), pp. 59-84 (79). For a survey of Roman marriage law,
see Susan Treggiari, *Roman Marriage: Iusti Coniuges from the Time of Cicero to the
Time of Ulpian* (New York: Oxford University Press, 1991).

124. See Lipinski, 'The Wife's Right to Divorce', pp. 9-27. On Matthew evidencing
the earliest attested divorce for a broken engagement, see Peter Zaas, 'Matthew's Birth
Story: An Early Milepost in the History of Jewish Marriage Law', *BTB* 39.3 (2009), pp.
125-28.

125. Roth, *Law Collections*, p. 108.

126. Simone de Beauvoir, *The Second Sex* (trans. H.M. Parshley; New York: Vintage
Books, 1952), p. 96: 'In Babylon the Laws of Hammurabi acknowledged certain rights
of women...'.

127. Roth, *Law Collections*, p. 68.

must go and live with the second woman. So, at least indirectly, one can find evidence that women could be seen as the aggrieved party and had the ability to seek redress without help from one's kin.

At the Jewish colony of Elephantine, one finds parity between men and women in terms of divorce four centuries prior to Jesus. One example is found in the aforementioned *TAD* B2.6, which outlines the agreement concerning the marriage of Eshor, a royal builder or architect, and Miptahiah, the daughter of Mahseiah, an Aramean from Syene in Egypt. Again, the crucial portion reads:

> Tomorrow o[r] (the) next day, should Miptahiah stand up in an assembly and say: 'I hated Eshor my husband', silver of hatred is on her head. She shall PLACE UPON the balance-scale and weigh out to Eshor silver, 6[+1] (= 7) shekels, 2 q(uarters), and all that she brought in her hand she shall take out, from straw to string, and go away wherever she desires without suit or without process.

> Tomorrow or (the) next day, should Eshor stand up in an assembly and say: 'I *hated* my [wif]e Miptahiah', her mohar [will be] lost (= forfeit) and all that she brought in her hand she shall take out, from straw to string, on one day in one stroke and go away wherever she desires without suit or without process (*TAD* B2.6.22-29).

Note the parity in the procedure for the husband and wife. Both are able to stand up in the assembly. Both can voice the same divorce motivation formula ('I hate my spouse'). The woman can take her property, and go wherever she wishes regardless of who divorced whom. Jesus is not saying anything new relative to Elephantine in terms of the mere ability to divorce.

Mary Rose D'Angelo traces the equation of remarriage with adultery in Mk 10.11-12 to an increasingly rigorous definition of adultery initiated by Caesar Augustus. These laws, usually known as the *lex Iulia de adulteriis coercendis* or *de adulteriis et pudicitia*, are dated to 18 BCE.[128] Suetonius mentions these developments in his biography of Augustus: 'He revised existing laws and enacted some new ones, for example, on extravagance; on adultery and chastity [*de adulteriis et de pudicitia*], on bribery, and on the encouragement of marriage among various classes of citizens.'[129] According to D'Angelo, '[t]his law criminalized adultery, and lending aid to adultery, including by a husband who could be charged with pimping (*lenoncinium*)'.[130]

D'Angelo further observes that Philo, the Jewish philosopher of the first century, seems to be assimilating some of the Roman legal rhetoric when he discusses the divorce and remarriage statutes in Deut. 24.1-4. Philo, too,

---

128. See D'Angelo, 'Roman Imperial Family Values', p. 64.
129. Suetonius, *Augustus* 34.2 (Rolfe, LCL).
130. D'Angelo, 'Roman Imperial Family Values', p. 65.

pairs 'adultery and pandering' (μοιχείαν τε καὶ προαγωγειαν), which seems to integrate the charge of pimping (*lenoncinium*) that a husband could incur if he allowed adultery in a wife.[131] Such a concept is not found in Deuteronomy 24. D'Angelo argues that Mark is following a similar trend to match, and even outdo, Roman strictness on marriage and divorce. As D'Angelo phrases it: 'The equation of marriage with adultery in Mk 10.10-12 may have been suggested by the language and provisions of the Julian adultery law.'[132]

Although it is difficult to prove Mark's direct adoption or dependence on these Roman laws, it is the case that one can find a parallel rationale for Jesus' teachings on divorce in Greco-Roman literature. In his *Roman Antiquities*, Dionsyius of Halicarnassus (60 BCE–7 BCE), the Greek chronicler of Rome, described divorce as antithetical to Roman culture.[133] Just as Jesus traced the origins of marriage back to the founding father of humanity, Dionysius traced the origins of Roman marriage customs to the instructions of Romulus, the founder of Rome. Dionysius argues that in the earliest part of Roman history there was no divorce. In fact, Dionysius alleges that the first divorce did not occur until 231 BCE, and that was because of the barrenness of the wife of a man named Spurius Carvilius, who was widely denounced for his action.[134] Marriage, especially at the elite level (confarreate marriage), 'forged the compelling bond of an indissoluble union, and there was nothing that could annul these marriages'.[135]

While it is difficult to prove that Mark directly imitated Dionysius, one can argue for the currency of the following concepts at the time of Jesus: The placement of the institution of marriage in the time of the founders of the respective cultures, the emphasis on the indissolubility of marriage, and the equation of remarriage with a condemnatory sin. Celia Schultz also observes that in the Roman republic the *flamen Dialis*, the priest devoted to the cult of Jupiter, 'was permitted to be married only once and…was required to resign office if his wife should die' (cf. 1 Tim. 3.2; Tit. 1.6).[136] In

131. Philo, *Spec. Leg.* 3.31 (Colson, LCL).

132. D'Angelo, 'Roman Imperial Family Values', p. 79.

133. For another study of Dionysius and the New Testament, see Chrys C. Caragounis, 'Dionysius Halikarnasseus: The Art of Composition and the Apostel Paul', *Journal of Greco-Roman Christianity and Judaism* 1 (2000), pp. 25-54.

134. See D'Angelo, 'Roman Imperial Family Values', p. 73.

135. Dionysius of Halicarnassus, *Roman Antiquities* 2.25.3 (Carry, LCL): σύνδεσμον δ'ἀναγκαῖον οἰκειότητος ἔφερεν ἀδιαλύτου καὶ τὸ διαρῆσον τοὺς γάμους τούτους οὐδὲν ἦν.

136. Celia Schultz, *Women's Religious Activity in the Roman Republic* (Chapel Hill, NC: University of North Carolina Press, 2006), p. 141. See also Mary R. Lefkowitz and Maureen B. Fant, *Women's Life in Greece and Rome: A Source Book in Translation* (Baltimore, MD: The Johns Hopkins University Press, 3rd edn, 2005).

any case, rather than being some egalitarian innovation, the Markan Jesus may be following Roman trends.

Dewey arbitrarily declares part of Jesus' instructions to be temporary. Note again her representation of Jesus' teachings about divorce: 'Not an unconditional prohibition of divorce for all times, the statement rather makes marriage a more equal institution in its first century context.'[137] But there is nothing in the text that tells the reader that this is not meant 'for all times'. Perhaps one can say that since Jesus believed that the eschaton was approaching, then such laws would no longer be needed. That is a fair point. But that would mean that Jesus' instructions would be in force until the eschaton, which has not arrived yet for most Christians.

While many Christian apologists praise Jesus for any supposed radical social innovations, they don't balance that with a repudiation of any conformity he expresses with oppressive rules. Schüssler Fiorenza, for instance, regards patriarchy as oppressive, but seeks to explain away why Jesus did not simply repudiate all patriarchal marriage customs. According to her, 'as long as patriarchy is operative, divorce is *commanded* out of necessity'.[138] By that logic, as long as patriarchy is operative, then many other oppressive rules can be maintained and 'commanded out of necessity'.

In fact, while Dewey attempts to situate Jesus' instructions within his program to better the lives of women and bring equality, the text shows that this is not why he taught what he did on divorce. Jesus did not say that divorce was now restricted or enhanced in order to protect women. What he said is that Gen. 2.24 taught that God made humans male and female, and that what God had joined together should not be separated. And then Jesus contradicts himself. For he did allow separation of married people. He did allow divorce when the whole point of his response to the Pharisees is that human beings could not separate a bond that was divinely instituted.

At the same time, Dewey and Schüssler Fiorenza, among many other feminist scholars, don't see a problem with Jesus' heterosexism, which Jesus enthusiastically and emphatically reaffirms. In fact, Schüssler Fiorenza goes on to say that Gen. 2.24, which Jesus uses as his prooftext, 'does not allude to the myth of an androgynous primal man but to the equal partnership of man and woman in human marriage intended and made possible by the creator God'.[139] Jesus could have radically broken this insistence on heterosexism, but he perpetuated a system that has oppressed any human beings who would correspond to what we call members of the LGBTQI communities today.

137. Dewey, 'The Gospel of Mark', p. 491.
138. Schüssler Fiorenza, *In Memory of Her*, p. 143. Schüssler Fiorenza's italics.
139. Schüssler Fiorenza, *In Memory of Her*, p. 143.

Another arbitrary and selective feature of Christian ethicists who extol Jesus' view on divorce is how they choose Mark over Matthew. Consider the version of Jesus' response to the Pharisees in Matthew:

> He said to them, 'For your hardness of heart Moses allowed you to divorce your wives, but from the beginning it was not so. And I say to you: whoever divorces his wife, except for unchastity, and marries another, commits adultery'. The disciples said to him, 'If such is the case of a man with his wife, it is not expedient to marry' (Mt. 19.8-10).

In this version, Jesus does not have a corresponding instruction for women. It assumes that only men can divorce women. So, why is the Markan version assumed to be one that Jesus really voiced? For the most part, scholars adduce circular redactional arguments. They are circular because the arguments require that scholars know what Jesus thought in the first place in order to know what has been added.[140] As Jacquelyn Grant admits, 'there is a direct relationship between our perception of Jesus and our perception of ourselves'.[141]

The Womanless Twelve Apostles

According to Victoria Phillips, '[o]ne of the achievements of feminist biblical criticism has been establishing that Jesus included in his circle of disciples both men and women'.[142] Yet, the claim that Jesus had female disciples or had an egalitarian sense of discipleship is still debated. Birger Gerhardsson phrases the problem as follows:

> What we see in the New Testament is that women are invited without more ado to the Jesus movement and the Church, women as well as men: the Kingdom of God belongs to children, and even to women and to men. But I think we are building on wishful thinking rather than on historical truth if we believe that in the beginning, in the circle around Jesus and the very first days of the Church, women were given the same position and thus totally lifted up above the restrictions put on the female part of society in Palestine in this time.[143]

---

140. See further my critique of circularity in determining what Jesus said or taught in Avalos, *The End of Biblical Studies*, pp. 198-209, which includes a critique of the criteria for determining Jesus' words and language used by Jesus presented in Porter, *The Criteria for Authenticity in Historical-Jesus Research*.

141. Grant, *White Women's Christ*, p. 63.

142. Victoria Phillips, 'Full Disclosure: Towards a Complete Characterization of the Women who Followed Jesus in the Gospel According to Mark', in Kitzberger (ed.), *Transformative Encounters*, pp. 13-32 (13).

143. Birger Gerhardsson, 'Mark and the Female Witnesses', in *Dumu E$_2$-Dub-ba-a: Studies in Honor of Åke W. Sjöberg* (ed. Åke W. Sjöberg, Hermann Behrens, Darlene

One reason for Gerhardsson's negative view of Jesus' egalitarianism is the dearth of named women in Mark, considered by many feminist scholars to preserve the earliest traditions about Jesus and women.[144] As Julie Hopkins remarks: 'I assume that Mark as the earliest gospel, reflects the most authentic traditions of the Jesus movement.'[145]

But when one looks at Mark, it is difficult to find Jesus proclaiming any equality for women disciples. According to Winsome Munro,

> Prior to 15.40 Mark mentions no women by name except Mary the mother of Jesus in a pejorative context (see 6.3-4), and Herodias, who receives more attention than any other particular woman in the Gospel, in a legendary tale which makes her responsible for Herod's execution of John the Baptist (6.14-28). (Her daughter is not named.)[146]

Munro's statistical analysis also shows zero women characters, named or unnamed, in what is called Q, though admittedly there are only a total of four men.[147] John has twelve named male characters, but only four females.[148] In a study of Luke, Barbara E. Reid noted how no women 'share in the mission of healing', nor are they shown participating 'in the ministry of exorcism'.[149]

The lack of females among the twelve apostles was crucially important for feminists, and especially for Catholic feminists, to debunk because the Vatican *Declaration* of 1976 cited, as a reason for exclusion of women from the priesthood, the fact that 'Jesus did not call any women to become part of the Twelve'.[150]

Loding and Martha T. Roth; OPSNKF, 11; Philadelphia, PA: Samuel Noah Kramer Fund, University Museum, 1989), pp. 217-26 (226).

144. Hopkins, *Towards a Feminist Christology*, p. 38.

145. Hopkins, *Towards a Feminist Christology*, p. 38. See also K.W. Larsen, 'The Structure of Mark's Gospel: Current Proposals', *Currents in Biblical Research* 3 (2004), pp. 140-60.

146. Winsome Munro, 'Women Disciples in Mark?', *CBQ* 44 (1982), pp. 225-41 (226). Note a qualification for the statistics by Munro ('Women Disciples in Mark?', p. 226): 'Excluding genealogies, lists of authorities, undifferentiated groups, and characters in parabolic and other teaching material, the following comparisons can be made.'

147. Munro, 'Women Disciples in Mark?', p. 226.

148. Munro, 'Women Disciples in Mark?', p. 226.

149. Barbara E. Reid, *Choosing the Better Part: Women in the Gospel of Luke* (Collegeville, MN: Liturgical Press, 1996), pp. 44-45. A more positive view of Luke's feminism is that of Eben H. Scheffler, 'Towards Gender Equality in Luke's Gospel', *Acta Patristica et Byzantina* 19 (2008), pp. 185-206. See also F. Scott Spencer, *Salty Wives, Spirited Mothers, and Savvy Widows: Capable Women of Purpose and Persistence in Luke's Gospel* (Grand Rapids, MI: Eerdmans, 2012).

150. Quoting the text of the Vatican *Declaration* in Swidler and Swidler (eds.), *Women Priests*, p. 39.

To understand the challenge facing feminists who portray Jesus as a man valuing men and women equally as disciples, one can start with Mark's specific list of twelve disciples commissioned by Jesus:

> And he went up on the mountain, and called to him those whom he desired; and they came to him. And he appointed twelve, to be with him, and to be sent out to preach and have authority to cast out demons: Simon whom he surnamed Peter; James the son of Zebedee and John the brother of James, whom he surnamed Boanerges, that is, sons of thunder; Andrew, and Philip, and Bartholomew, and Matthew, and Thomas, and James the son of Alphaeus, and Thaddaeus, and Simon the Cananaean, and Judas Iscariot, who betrayed him (Mk 3.13-19).

As most feminist scholars recognize, none on this list are women. The text also states that Jesus called 'those whom he desired', which presumes that he could have chosen women but did not. Their commission contained here evinces two principal elements: (1) to preach and (2) have authority to cast out demons.

The problem becomes more acute because it looks as if all or most of the markers used to identify the earliest Jesus traditions point to a tradition of twelve disciples as being pre-Markan. It is already found 1 Cor. 15.5: 'he appeared to Cephas, then to the twelve'. Ed P. Sanders, among others, attempts to show that any arguments for a later invention fail to account for why the tradition of twelve disciples is so constant and widely attested, despite the fact that different sets of specific names may be given.[151] For Sanders, 'What seems virtually certain is that the conception of the twelve goes back to Jesus himself (though his closest companions at any given moment may not have consisted precisely of twelve men)'.[152]

On the other hand, Ann Brock uses the *Gospel of Mary* (ca. second century), an extracanonical work preserved in Coptic and Greek, to establish the apostolic stature of Mary Magdalene in Jesus' circle.[153] According to Brock, it was Luke who first formulated the tradition of the twelve and their

---

151. See Ed P. Sanders, *Jesus and Judaism* (Philadelphia, PA: Fortress Press, 1985), pp. 98-106. Sanders specifically challenges Phillip Vielhauer ('Gottesreich und Menschensohn in der Verkündigung Jesu', in Wilhelm Schneemelchert [ed.], *Festschrift für Gunther Dehn* [Neukirchen–Vluyn: Neukirchen Verlag, 1957], pp. 51-79), who argues for the invention of the tradition of the twelve.

152. Sanders, *Jesus and Judaism*, p. 106.

153. Ann Graham Brock, *Mary Magdalene, the First Apostle: The Struggle for Authority* (Harvard Theological Studies, 51; Cambridge, MA: Harvard University Press, 2002); Bruce D. Chilton, *Mary Magdalene: A Biography* (New York: Doubleday, 2005); Bart D. Ehrman, *Peter, Paul, and Mary Magdalene: The Followers of Jesus in History and Legend* (New York: Oxford University Press, 2006). See also Karen King, *The Gospel of Mary of Magdala: Jesus and the First Woman Apostle* (Santa Rosa, CA: Polebridge Press, 2003). I follow King's edition and abbreviation, *GMary*, when citing this work.

connection with Peter. Mary Magdalene, however, was probably already vying with Peter for authority in pre-Pauline and pre-Gospel traditions. It is true that the *Gospel of Mary* reflects some sort of conflict over male and female authority in Jesus' circle. For example, Peter challenges Mary's claims to be receiving teachings from Jesus: 'Did he then, speak with a woman in private without our knowing about it? Are we to turn around and listen to her? Did he choose her over us?' (*GMary* 10).[154]

However, the *Gospel of Mary* cannot be used to establish what Jesus thought any more than the canonical Gospels can be so used. As Karen King notes, 'it is unlikely that the Gospel of Mary was among the earliest Christian works'.[155] Moreover, the arguments depicted in the *Gospel of Mary* are principally between Peter and Mary. Jesus says little or nothing about who truly is the leader of his group or about gender relations in general, though Mary certainly seems to be a primary apostle. So, until more evidence can be adduced that shows the still incomplete Gospel of Mary (or similar extra-canonical gospels) to reflect the actual teachings of Jesus, then the historical Jesus' views on gender are at best contestable and uncertain.

In any case, the powers bestowed by Jesus on 'the twelve' in the canonical Gospels are quite impressive. For example,

> Jesus said to them, 'Truly, I say to you, in the new world, when the Son of man shall sit on his glorious throne, you who have followed me will also sit on twelve thrones, judging the twelve tribes of Israel. And every one who has left houses or brothers or sisters or father or mother or children or lands, for my name's sake, will receive a hundredfold, and inherit eternal life. But many that are first will be last, and the last first' (Mt. 19.28-30).

Sanders believes that Mt. 19.28 is 'authentic'.[156] It is important to observe that Jesus sets up a hierarchy here. Not all followers are treated equally. The twelve apostles will sit on twelve thrones, but all other followers will not, even if they receive a hundred times more than they lost and eternal life.

I want to reiterate that I am not arguing that Sanders or any other scholar should be certain about the authenticity for 'the twelve' tradition or the 'thrones' tradition, as I don't think any tradition, canonical or extracanonical, about Jesus can be held as 'virtually certain' at all. What I am affirming is that, if we use the criteria accepted by most Christian scholars, including feminist ones, then those so-called authentic and early traditions do not support a gender egalitarian Jesus.

Later in Matthew, one learns that Mary Magdalene and 'the other Mary' went to the tomb, where an angel, and then redundantly Jesus himself, tells

---

154. King, *The Gospel of Mary*, p. 17.
155. King, *The Gospel of Mary*, p. 117.
156. Sanders, *Jesus and Judaism*, p. 102.

them to go tell the disciples in Galilee about the resurrection (Mt. 28.10).[157] If anything the redundancy of Jesus' instructions shows that it is Jesus' appearance here that is added later. First, note that Mark does not have this appearance by Jesus to the women. Second, in Mk 16.7 an angel tells the women to go notify 'his disciples' (τοῖς μαθηταῖς αὐτοῦ), which implies that these women were not counted as 'his disciples'. Otherwise, it makes no sense for Jesus to repeat in Mt. 28.10 what the angels have already told the women in Mt. 28.7.

But for the sake of argument, I will assume that Jesus did first appear to the women in Matthew. One would think this was an opportune time for Jesus to thank these women for their services, and proclaim their equality with the other disciples. But Jesus instead tells the women to serve as his errand girls to inform, as Jesus phrased it, 'my brethren' (τοῖς ἀδελ-φοῖς μου), which again serves to exclude the women from any inner circle.[158] Jesus could not have meant a more gender inclusive 'brothers and sisters' here. 'My brethren' refers only to the eleven men that he had chosen because Jesus proceeds as follows:

> Now the eleven disciples went to Galilee, to the mountain to which Jesus had directed them. And when they saw him they worshiped him; but some doubted. And Jesus came and said to them, 'All authority in heaven and on earth has been given to me. Go therefore and make disciples of all nations, baptizing them in the name of the Father and of the Son and of the Holy Spirit, teaching them to observe all that I have commanded you; and lo, I am with you always, to the close of the age' (Mt. 28.16-20).

Jesus uses these women to run the errand of conveying the important message, which is for the male disciples to meet him so that he can give them his final commission. The women do not receive that message themselves, but only serve to tell the disciples that that climactic message is coming.

Jesus seems particularly ungrateful towards women because it is the males who are shown as less than ideal disciples at times in Matthew (as they are in Mark). Peter denies Jesus (Mt. 26.72), and the male disciples were asleep when Jesus needed their support (Mt. 26.40). Some even doubted Jesus even after he was resurrected directly before he commissioned them (Mt. 28.17). Yet, it is these men, and not the more faithful female followers, who are present at the climax of the book. The women, in other words, are portrayed as fulfilling a traditional role of being faithful, loyal and dutiful to

---

157. See William Hendriksen, *Exposition of the Gospel According to Matthew* (NTC; Grand Rapids, MI: BakerAcademic, 1973), p. 993; Paul S. Minear, 'Matthew 28:1-10', *Int* 38 (1984), pp. 59-63.

158. See Philip A. Harland, 'Familial Dimensions of Group Identity: "Brothers" ('Αδελφοί) in Associations of the Greek East', *JBL* 124.3 (2005), pp. 491-513.

a man (cf. Prov. 31.10-31).[159] Dorothy Lee, who tries to salvage some sort of egalitarian Jesus, admits that 'Matthew's Gospel leaves us in the final analysis with a disturbing and irresolvable tension between male and female presence and absence, authority and disenpowerment'.[160]

Winsome Munro's study of disciples in Mark emphasizes their negative portrayal almost throughout. However, she openly acknowledges that the female followers do not receive praise for their contrasting faithfulness. As she phrases it:

> Can it be that, having been spared the Marcan polemic against the disciples, the women are now put forward to take the place of the discredited and absent Twelve? The possibility is appealing but untenable, first, because of the distance Mark places between Jesus on the cross and the women, whereas the Fourth Gospel puts them close enough for conversation (19.25-26).[161]

Munro points to the use of 'from a distance' (ἀπὸ μακρόθεν) in Mk 15.40 (//Mt. 27.55) to contrast Mark with John, who has them right by Jesus at the Cross.

Marla J. Selvidge, however, believes that Munro is herself falling into an androcentric trap. Selvidge remarks:

> According to Munro women are relatively invisible in Mark because of the androcentric bias of the writer's culture and the language used by the Gospel. The primary problem is not the androcentric culture of Mark. The problem lies with a 1900-year-old androcentric approach to the text.[162]

Selvidge believes she can close the distance between the women and Jesus in Mk 15.40 by retranslation. According to Selvidge: 'The translation could read, "But there were even women from afar watching" (15.40). The emphasis in this translation is upon the place from which they originated.'[163]

Linguistically, Selvidge's proposal is not convincing. The construction consisting of a verb indicating 'to see' (e.g., ὁράω or θεωρέω) + ἀπὸ μακρόθεν ('from a distance') can be perfectly understood as reflecting the distance of the observer from the entity or person being observed.[164] Thus, Adela Y. Collins translates the crucial phrase as 'women observing from a

---

159. For comments by a pioneer of feminist cultural criticism on how traditional roles of women are perceived in the Bible, see de Beauvoir, *The Second Sex*, pp. 95-96.

160. Dorothy A. Lee, 'Presence or Absence? The Question of Women Disciples and the Last Supper', in *Biblical Studies Alternatively: An Introductory Reader* (ed. Susanne Scholz; Upper Saddle River, NJ: Prentice–Hall, 2003), pp. 121-36 (131).

161. Munro, 'Women Disciples in Mark?', p. 235.

162. Marla J. Selvidge, '"And Those Who Followed Feared" (Mark 10:32)', *CBQ* 45 (1983), pp. 396-400 (400).

163. Selvidge, '"And Those Who Followed Feared"', p. 400.

164. See BDAG, 'μακρόθεν', p. 612b.

distance'.[165] Elsewhere, Mk 5.6 ('When he saw Jesus from afar'/ἰδὼν τὸν
Ἰησοῦν ἀπὸ μακρόθεν) and Mk 11.13 ('seeing in the distance a fig tree'/
ἰδὼν συχῆν ἀπὸ μακρόθεν) use a participular form of a verb of seeing
(e.g., ὁράω or θεωρέω) + ἀπὸ μακρόθεν, just as in Mk 15.40. Selvidge
offers no linguistic reason to suppose that ἀπὸ μακρόθεν θεωροῦσαι in Mk
15.40 is different. So, it is best to read it as Collins translates it.

The Last Supper: Guess Who's not Coming to Dinner

In chapter fifty-eight of his sensational novel, *The Da Vinci Code*, Dan
Brown has Robert Langdon, the Harvard symbologist and hero of the novel,
making the case that Leonardo Da Vinci's *Last Supper* includes a woman.
Sophie, Langdon's interlocutor, is skeptical because she accepts the standard notion that the painting has thirteen men, and no women. But Langdon
patiently explains that the figure to Jesus' immediate right is not John. That
figure has 'flowing red hair, delicate folding hands, and the hint of a bosom.
It was without a doubt…female.[166] Langdon then asserts that that woman is
none other than Mary Magdalene, Jesus' lover and wife.

Brown was excoriated by many historians and biblical scholars. Entire
books were written to refute Brown's historical blunders and misrepresentations.[167] However, what Dan Brown was asserting is precisely what many
reputable Christian scholars have argued. It was not only feminists who first
asserted the inclusion of women in the Last Supper but rather otherwise
very traditional scholars. Joachim Jeremias had already argued briefly for
the inclusion of women in his *The Eucharistic Words of Jesus*:

> According to Mark 14.17 (par. 26.20) Jesus celebrated the last Supper with
> the Twelve. It is not possible, however, to assume from this that the women
> mentioned in Mark 15.40; Luke 23.49, 55 were excluded. In Eastern texts
> the argument from silence is inadmissible in such cases.[168]

---

165. Collins, *Mark: A Commentary*, p. 772.

166. Dan Brown, *The Da Vinci Code* (New York: Doubleday, 2003), p. 243.

167. Examples include Ben Witherington, *The Gospel Code: Novel Claims about
Jesus, Mary Magdalene and Da Vinci* (Downers Grove, IL: InterVarsity Press, 2004);
Mary R. Thompson, *Mary of Magdala: What the Da Vinci Code Misses* (Mahwah, NJ:
Paulist Press, 2006); D.J. Kennedy and J. Newcombe, *The Da Vinci Myth versus the
Gospel Truth* (Wheaton, IL: Crossway, 2006); Mark Shea and Edward Sri and the Edi-
tors of Catholic Exchange, *The Da Vinci Deception: 100 Questions about the Facts
and Fiction of the Da Vinci Code* (West Chester, PA: Ascension Press, 2006); G. Jones,
Beyond Da Vinci (New York: Seabury, 2004); Robert M. Price, 'The Da Vinci Fraud',
Fourth R 17 (2004), pp. 7-12. See also R. Burnet, *Marie-Madeleine (1er-XXIe siècle). De
la pécheresse repentie à l'espouse de Jesus. Histoire de la reception d'une figure bibique*
(Lire la Bible, 140; Paris: Cerf, 2004).

168. Joachim Jeremias, *The Eucharistic Words of Jesus* (London: SCM Press, 3rd edn,

In 1983, Quentin Quesnell raised the issue in his essay 'The Women in Luke's Supper'.[169] Quesnell principally relies on the fact that the term 'disciples' (μαθηταί) can include women. For example, Luke–Acts explicitly includes women:

> But Saul, still breathing threats and murder against the disciples of the Lord, went to the high priest and asked him for letters to the synagogues at Damascus, so that if he found any belonging to the Way, men or women [ἄνδρας τε καὶ γυναῖκας], he might bring them bound to Jerusalem (Acts 9.1-2).

In Luke, the two angels issue the following reminder to the women at the tomb:

> Remember how he told you, while he was still in Galilee, that the Son of man must be delivered into the hands of sinful men, and be crucified, and on the third day rise. And they remembered his words (Lk. 24.6-8).

However, the particular 'words' that the women were supposed to remember were issued to 'the disciples' (οἱ μαθηταί) in Lk. 9.18, where it says 'Now it happened that as he was praying alone the disciples were with him.' While Quesnell's evidence shows that the term 'disciples' could include women, it still does not demonstrate definitively that women were in the Last Supper. In fact, Acts 9.1-2 shows that Luke has no trouble saying 'men and women' (ἄνδρας τε καὶ γυναῖκας) when he wanted to indicate the presence of both genders.

Another piece of evidence for Quesnell is the use of the Greek word *hypostrephō* (ὑποστρέφω; 'return') to describe the action of the women in Lk. 24.9: 'and returning from the tomb they told all this to the eleven and to all the rest' (καὶ ὑποστρέψασαι ἀπὸ του μνημείου ἀπήγγειλαν ταῦτα πάντα τοῖς ἕνδεκα καὶ πᾶσιν τοῖς λοιποῖς). Quesnell argues that 'in all 30 instances Luke uses *hypostrephō* to mean return in the strict sense of going back to a place from which one earlier departed'.[170] Quesnell suggests that the women returned 'to the place they had been the night before the crucifixion'.[171] That place is where the Last Supper was held, and shows

---

1966), p. 46. For another view, see Gerd Theissen and Annette Merz, *The Historical Jesus: A Comprehensive Guide* (trans. John Bowden; Minneapolis: Fortress Press, 1998), p. 426.

169. Quentin Quesnell, 'The Women in Luke's Supper', in *Political Issues in Luke–Acts* (ed. Richard J. Cassidy and Philip J. Scharper; Maryknoll, NY: Orbis Books, 1983), pp. 59-79. For his earlier discussion of the Last Supper, see Quentin Quesnell, *The Mind of Mark: Interpretation and Method through the Exegesis of Mark 6, 52* (Rome: Pontifical Biblical Institute, 1969), especially pp. 20 and 205.

170. Quesnell, 'The Women in Luke's Supper', p. 70.

171. Quesnell, 'The Women in Luke's Supper', p. 70.

that the women were present at that event. But nothing in the text of Luke says that they returned to where the Last Supper was held.

Linguistically, Quesnell mischaracterizes how Luke uses *hypostrephō*. Luke most often uses *hypostrephō* + εἰς to specify a return to the place from which one had earlier departed. Note 'And when those who had been sent returned to the house' [ὑποστρέψαντες εἰς τὸν οἶκον] in Lk. 7.10, and 'And Jesus returned in the power of the Spirit into Galilee' (ὑπέστρεψεν... εἰς τὴν Γαλιλαίαν) in Lk. 4.14. However, when Luke uses *hypostrephō* + ἀπό, the only place named is usually where they are before they leave. Thus, it is best to translate as 'leave X' or 'withdraw from X'. For instance, in Lk. 4.1 one finds 'Jesus, full of the Holy Spirit, returned from the Jordan' (ὑπέστρεψεν...ἀπὸ τοῦ Ἰορδάνου) in the RSV. But it makes little sense to have Jesus return to the Jordan where he was presumably present already (Lk. 3.21). It makes better sense to translate it as 'When Jesus left the Jordan' or 'When Jesus withdrew from the Jordan', as the next place mentioned is the wilderness in Lk. 4.2.

The Last Supper was held in a room of the house of a man that the disciples were supposed to encounter in the city (Lk. 22.10-12). That place seems to have been used only for that supper, and not as a permanent place to which disciples were to return or stay. As it is, it looks as if the disciples had begun to disperse by the time of the crucifixion (Lk. 22.54-62; Mk 14.50). The women watched the crucifixion 'from afar' (Lk. 23.49). The preparation of funerary spices in which the women were engaged (Lk. 23.56) before they were told to 'return' in Lk. 24.9 does not seem to point to the same place where they had supper. Preparing spices for the dead can be a laborious task, and it would not likely take place in the same home that was used for the Last Supper.[172] So, at best, it is very difficult to know where the women went.

Dorothy Lee continues this effort to include women in the Last Supper. Lee asserts that 'at the Last Supper there is no reason to deny women's presence alongside the men'.[173] For Lee, it was in the Gospel of John where one could best make the case. She proposes that John diminishes the role of 'the twelve', which renders him more inclusive. As she phrases it: 'Unlike the Synoptics, John does not list the twelve, although he is familiar with the tradition and names several of them.'[174] What Lee means is that there is no specific list of all twelve apostles.

But, as Lee herself notes, John certainly does use the phrase 'the twelve' at least four times (Jn 6.67, 70, 71 and 20.24). While it is true that we cannot

172. See further, Craig A. Evans, 'Jewish Burial Traditions and the Resurrection of Jesus', *Journal for the Study of the Historical Jesus* 3 (2005), pp. 233-48.

173. Lee, 'Presence or Absence?', p. 132.

174. Lee, 'Presence or Absence?', p. 131.

say that all twelve are men on the basis of John, there is little reason to read it as anything but a tradition of twelve male disciples attested in every other Gospel. Thomas is specifically called 'one of the twelve' in Jn 20.24. Judas is specifically called 'one of the twelve' in Jn 6.71, and Peter is certainly included as one of the twelve in Jn 6.68. These are included in all the lists of the twelve disciples, and never does John name a woman as one of the twelve.

Lee makes the point that Jesus often includes more than the twelve. True enough, but that would not mean that he treats the women as equally as he does the men or that the women are included in the Last Supper. For example, there were women followers in Matthew and there were more than twelve followers in all the Gospels, but that did not prevent Jesus from giving the twelve special privileges such as having twelve thrones in Mt. 19.28 or receiving the great commission in Mt. 28.16-20.

Having women followers does not preclude having a hierarchy, any more than having all men followers precludes a hierarchy among them. That is to say, there can be many followers, but some may be more special than others. Thus, Jesus is said to have a beloved disciple who is more beloved than others (Jn 21.20-24). Likewise, there may be many followers, including women, in John but that fact will not render them as beloved as this particular male disciple. By the same token, the fact that there are many followers, including women, does not constitute evidence that Jesus believes that all of them should dine with him at the Last Supper.

Lee cites at best some very forced evidence. She argues that the Last Supper was a 'fellowship meal' that reflects hospitality.[175] She then appeals to a number of texts recording 'stories which include women in table sharing (e.g., Mk 14.3-9/Mt. 26.6-13; Lk. 7.36-50)'.[176] Yet, it is these very texts that undermine her case because she elsewhere admits that 'Matthew is clear about the exclusive presence of the twelve at the Last Supper'.[177] Therefore, she has just proved that Matthew can treat the Last Supper differently from other instances of table sharing in which Jesus has engaged. The fact that Matthew can show a wide range of people in some meals with Jesus does not mean that the Gospel will show the same range at the Last Supper.

Given that the texts do not support the claim that any female followers or disciples are given a status equal to the twelve or inclusion in the Last Supper, Lee resorts to circular reasoning. She claims:

---

175. Lee, 'Presence or Absence?', p. 134. See also Dennis E. Smith, 'Table Fellowship as a Literary Motif in the Gospel of Luke', *JBL* 106 (1987), pp. 616-38.

176. Lee, 'Presence or Absence?', p. 134.

177. Lee, 'Presence or Absence?', p. 130.

It is hard to conclude from this that, on the critical occasion of his final meal, Jesus excluded disciples such as these. It is hard to believe that Jesus departed from the radical inclusiveness so characteristic of his ministry.[178]

One can reduce her statements to a circular rationale: Jesus must have included women in the Last Supper because he was radically inclusive; Jesus is radically inclusive because he included women in the Last Supper, among other meals. Yet, Lee has not shown that Jesus is any more radically inclusive than many other people we can mention. She still has not shown that Jesus including people in other meals must mean that he includes women in every meal.

To support her notion of Jesus' 'inclusive wholeness', Lee cites pages 118-30 of Schüssler Fiorenza's *In Memory of Her*.[179] But Schüssler Fiorenza will not help Lee. In those pages, Schüssler Fiorenza cites texts (e.g., Mt. 22.1-14, Lk. 14.16-24) that show that Jesus wanted to include everyone in the Kingdom of God (or, as Schüssler Fiorenza, dubs it, 'the *basileia* of God'). Those particular texts are parables where the banquet is explicitly equated with the Kingdom of God. These parables cannot be used to prove whom Jesus would invite to an actual meal because not every meal is meant to illustrate the Kingdom of God. Meals can be used to illustrate other points, including his power to multiply food (Mt. 15.32-39).

Most of the time, Jesus consumes a meal simply because he is hungry. He may eat alone or with whomever is around him at the time (cf. Mt. 4.2; 12.1). When Jesus went to eat a fig because he was hungry (Mt. 21.18), he did not make it a point to invite everyone just to liken that meal to the Kingdom of God. He did the opposite. He cursed the fig tree to death, and so now no one else would partake of any meal from that tree. Likewise, the fact that Jesus wants to include everyone in the Kingdom of God does not show that he included women in any particular meal any more than it shows that he appointed women among the twelve apostles. The fact that Jesus wanted to encompass a range of poor or destitute people in his Kingdom does not preclude a hierarchy among those subjects of his empire who might have special privileges over others.

Lee's final principal argument appeals to an equation between the Last Supper and the Jewish Passover. According to Lee, Jesus would not have excluded women from the Last Supper because 'Passover was a time of family celebration which included men, women, and children, each of whom had a vital role to play in the ritual'.[180] This claim flies in the face of the social context of the Gospel of Matthew, which many

178. Lee, 'Presence or Absence?', p. 134.
179. Lee, 'Presence or Absence?', p. 134 n. 69.
180. Lee, 'Presence or Absence?', p. 134.

scholars characterize as substantially interested in Jewish observance.[181] Again, Lee admits that Matthew speaks of an exclusive male presence at the Last Supper, and that seems odd if he saw Passover in the same way as Lee claims. It is probably more the case, as Jonathan Klawans argues, that many scholars erroneously conflate later traditions of the Seder meal with the Passover of Jesus' time.[182]

Even if Jesus' meal was a Passover meal, Jonathan Klawans shows that we don't really know how Jews celebrated Passover in the home in the first century. The main non-biblical sources we have are Philo and Josephus. For Josephus, the main interests in the Passover are the activities at the temple, not in the home. He does not describe a Passover meal in a home in any detail. As it is, Josephus says that menstruating women (γυναιξὶν ἐπεμμήνοις) and lepers were not allowed to partake of the Passover sacrifice.[183] Philo (*Spec.* 2.145-148) does describe the Passover meal as a domestic one, but a domestic setting seems opposed by the author of Jubilees (cf. Jub. 49.22-23).[184] And why couldn't it be that Jesus was not following any female-inclusive part of Jewish tradition? Here is a case where

181. See Levine and Brettler (eds.), *The Jewish Annotated New Testament*, p. 1; Amy-Jill Levine, 'The Gospel of Matthew', in Newsom, Ringe and Lapsley (eds.), *The Women's Bible Commentary*, p. 465.

182. See Jonathan Klawans, 'Was Jesus' Last Supper a Seder?', *BR* 17 (2001), pp. 24-33, 47. Klawans is challenging specifically Joachim Jeremias, who argues for greater conformity between the Last Supper and the Jewish Passover as envisioned by Lee. See also Baruch Bokser, *The Origins of the Seder* (Berkeley: University of California Press, 1984); Christine Schlund, *'Kein Knochen soll gebrochen werden': Studien zu Bedeutung und Funktion des Pesachfests in Texten des frühen Judentums und im Johannesevangelium* (WMANT, 107; Neukirchen–Vluyn: Neukirchener, 2005).

183. Josephus, *War* 6.426 (Thackeray, LCL). See also Tarja S. Philip, *Menstruation and Childbirth in the Bible: Fertility and Impurity* (Studies in Biblical Literature, 88; New York: Peter Lang, 2006).

184. See Joel Marcus, 'Passover and Last Supper Revisited', *NTS* 59 (2013), pp. 303-324 (308). Marcus believes that the Last Supper does preserve aspects of the pre-70 Seder. See also Martin D. Stringer, *Rethinking the Origins of the Eucharist* (London: SCM Press, 2011). A variety of theories of origin, together with modern religious perspectives, are surveyed in the essays in Thomas R. Schreiner and Matthew R. Crawford, *The Lord's Supper: Remembering and Proclaiming Christ until He Comes* (Nashville, TN: B & H Academic, 2010). The recently discovered Katumuwa Stele may push the prehistory of the Last Supper to eighth-century BCE funerary meals in the Levant. See further, Seth L. Sanders, 'The Appetites of the Dead: West Semitic Linguistics and Ritual Aspects of the Katumuwa Stele', *BASOR* 369 (2013), pp. 35-55. Neither Marcus nor Sanders mentions the connections with the Last Supper, but these are briefly referenced in Virginia Rimmer Herrmann and J. David Schloen (eds.), *In Remembrance of me: Feasting with the Dead in the Ancient Middle East* (Oriental Institute Museum Publications, 37; Chicago, IL: Oriental Institute of the University of Chicago, 2014), especially p. 23 n. 3.

some Christian feminists want to have Jesus conform to Jewish tradition, while everywhere else they praise him for breaking radically from Jewish tradition.

Theology is the last refuge when the plain text cannot clearly support Lee's claims. Lee admits the difficulty of finding explicit references to women in the Last Supper, but she finds them by 'sometimes reading "against the grain", sometimes reading in harmony with the narrative as a whole—a different perspective emerges'.[185] In other words, one simply picks and chooses the evidence that fits our theory even if it goes against the plain sense of the text.[186]

Given what we do know about the inclusion of women in meals in non-Christian cultures, I can easily argue that Jesus represents a retrogression in terms of including women in such crucial meals. In her study of Greco-Roman meal practices, Rachel M. McRae observes: 'That women also participated in the distribution of honor through banquet iconography is seen in funerary monuments.'[187] In a treatise on Roman banquets, Katherine M.D. Dunbabin notes radical differences she detects in some Etruscan practices: 'The most striking difference lies in the presence and position of women. Although many scenes show all-male participants in the banquet, on others women appear, reclining alongside the men on the same couch.'[188] Perhaps we should praise those Etruscans for such 'radical inclusivity'. Indeed, Jesus was extremely androcentric and retrograde judging by such precedents.

The Egalitarian Golden Age under Jesus

Although not often noticed by critics of Christian feminism, the devotion to a feminist Jesus creates one of the oddest pictures of the first century that one can encounter. To understand this historical oddity, one only needs to examine how some prominent Christian feminists describe what came before and after Jesus. One example is Elisabeth's Schüssler Fiorenza's essay on 'Interpreting Patriarchal Traditions' where she discusses the increasing patriarchalization of Christianity after Jesus.[189] According

185. Lee, 'Presence or Absence?', p. 136.
186. A similar charge may be made against Rigato, *Discepoli di Gesù*.
187. Rachel M. McRae, 'Eating with Honor: The Corinthian Lord's Supper in the Light of Voluntary Association Meal Practices', *JBL* 130 (2011), pp. 165-81 (173). See also David W. Pao, 'Waiters or Preachers: Acts 6:1-7 and the Lukan Table Fellowship Motif', *JBL* 130 (2011), pp. 127-44.
188. Katherine M.D. Dunbabin, *The Roman Banquet: Images of Conviviality* (Cambridge: Cambridge University Press, 2003), p. 27. See also John S. Kloppenborg and Stephen G. Wilson (eds.), *Voluntary Associations in the Graeco-Roman World* (London and New York: Routledge, 1996).
189. Schüssler Fiorenza, 'Interpreting Patriarchal Traditions', pp. 39-61.

to Schüssler Fiorenza, 'The Hebrew and Christian Scriptures originated in a patriarchal society and perpetuated the androcentric traditions (male-centered) of their culture.'[190] She reiterates that 'the patriarchal nature of Hebrew culture is undisputed'.[191]

However, once Jesus arrives, there is a radical change. As previously noted, Schüssler Fiorenza claims in that same essay that 'the canonical literature of the New Testament does not transmit a single androcentric statement or sexist story of Jesus'.[192] After Jesus, one begins to see the 'patriarchalization of the early Church'.[193] This implies that such patriachalization was not there before, which would mean at the time of Jesus and/or shortly thereafter. She elaborates on this idea as follows:

> From a sociological perspective, the gradual institutionalization and adaption of the Christian movement to the patriarchal structures of the time was unavoidable if the Christian community was to expand and to survive. At the same time, this structural solidification meant a patriachalization of the Christian leadership functions that gradually eliminated women from roles of leadership and relegated them to subordinate feminine roles.[194]

If so, then Schüssler Fiorenza's history of Christian patriarchalism is as follows: Pre-Christian Jewish and Pagan patriarchalism > Radical egalitarian interlude under Jesus > (Re)patriarchalization by the Church. If one were to be more chronologically precise, then it would be something like this:

1000 BCE–30 CE	29–30 CE?	30 CE–present day
Hebrew patriarchalism	Radical gender egalitarianism under Jesus	(Re)Patriarchalization by the Church

Under this historiography of patriarchalism, Christian gender egalitarianism apparently survived only for the year or so of Jesus' ministry. Christianity then resumed the patriarchal nature of pre-Jesus Hebrew society or developed its own version of patriarchy, which apparently forgot the golden age of egalitarianism under Jesus.

All this is very odd historically. Indeed, no non-Christian contemporary knew of such radical interlude in patriarchy under Jesus nor is there any mention of it in contemporary records (the Gospels and epistles are certainly not contemporary with Jesus). Those who believe in such a scheme cannot document women who speak of such a Golden Age or appeal to Jesus' words to make their case for inclusion. Even the extant portions of the *Gospel of Mary*, which certainly reflects a conflict around female

---

190. Schüssler Fiorenza, 'Interpreting Patriarchal Traditions', p. 39.
191. Schüssler Fiorenza, 'Interpreting Patriarchal Traditions', p. 41.
192. Schüssler Fiorenza, 'Interpreting Patriarchal Traditions', p. 52.
193. Schüssler Fiorenza, 'Interpreting Patriarchal Traditions', p. 54.
194. Schüssler Fiorenza, 'Interpreting Patriarchal Traditions', pp. 54-55.

leadership, does not have Jesus making definitive pronouncements about gender equality for leadership. But if we accept Schüssler Fiorenza's history of patriarchy, then there must have been a very brief Golden Age of gender egalitarianism under Jesus that no one else then was talking about.

Women in Pre-Christian Religions

Much of the discussion by Christian feminists involves the idea that Jesus brought something new or radical to gender relations. This is a continuation of the apologetics one sees among Christian scholars in general, and so Christian feminists are not departing from tradition at all here. Instead of progress, I can argue that Jesus was retrogressive in many aspects of gender relations. To understand this point, it is necessary to take a brief look at what women had accomplished before Jesus came on the scene. I've already mentioned a few areas, such as meals, but it is instructive to provide a few more examples.

While many Christian feminists search for equality where Jesus never expressly said anything about the equality of male and female leaders, one does find instances where equality was given explicitly in non-Christian cultures. In 1983, John Huehnergard, the prominent semitic philologist, published some Akkadian texts, probably dating to the Late Bronze Age, from the vicinity of Emar, an ancient city in what is now Syria.[195] At least two of the texts were wills that gave a daughter the rights of a man, and also classified her as both male and female. Here is an example:

> From this day, Zikrī-Dagan son of Ibni-Dagan, in good health, seated his 'brothers'. He said as follows: Now then, I have established my daughter Unara as female and male [ana MUNUS ù NITAḪ aš-ʳkuʰ-un-ši]. She may call upon my gods and *my dead*(?). Now then, my three sons—now then, let Adda, the eldest son, Dagan-Baʿlu, and Baʿlu-lī-mi support their mother Unara. Whoever among my three sons does not support his mother will not receive his inheritance. As long as their mo[th]er lives, the inheri[tance] will not be claimed.[196]

Unara is declared to have the legal powers of both males and females, and male relatives are subjected to her.

In another testament published in the same collection of texts, one finds this declaration:

> From this day, Muzazu son of Šamana, in good health, has decreed the disposition of his estate. He said as follows: Now then, my wife Ḫebate is

195. John Huehnergard, 'Five Tablets from the Vicinity of Emar', *RA* 77 (1983), pp. 11-43.

196. Huehnergard, 'Five Tablets', p. 15, Text 1, lines 1-16. The transliterated Akkadian text is on p. 13. Huehnergard's italics.

father and mother of my estate [abu ù AMA [ša] E-ia]. Now then, I have
established my daughter Al-ḫāṭī as female and male. She may call upon my
gods and my dead(?).[197]

In both of these texts the newly declared female/male daughter may call
upon the dead or the gods, which may refer to exercising a religious function within the family.[198] If I were a Mesopotamian feminist apologist I
would be hailing this as a monumental socio-religious achievement not
only for feminism, but also for Queer Theory because it seems that gender
has been transcended and/or erased. One such case for Mesopotamian feminism has been made by Julian Reade, an Assyriologist who argues that Sennacherib, the Assyrian king (705–681 BCE), could be regarded as a feminist.
Among other things, Sennacherib acknowledged the role of women in his
reign far more than any previous monarch. Reade remarks:

> We are obliged to look on Sennacherib, at one time or another, either as a
> doting husband or as a perceptive man with the confidence to break free
> from tradition and acknowledge to some extent that women sustained him
> in his public role.[199]

So, where are the Christian feminists applauding Sennacherib? For the most
part, Christian feminism, like its more traditional male-dominated New
Testament scholarship, is permeated by a religiocentric and ethnocentric
approach to the accomplishments for women by other cultures.

In her study of women in Neo-Assyrian society, Sherry Lou Macgregor
catalogs all the female functionaries that she could document.[200] Neo-Assyria
was no gender egalitarian paradise. But Macgregor observes that, while all
of scholars were men, 'the majority of known prophets were women' in
the extant Neo-Assyrian records.[201] She adds that '[t]here is no evidence
that there was any differentiation made between female and male prophets.
Seemingly a prophet was a prophet.'[202] Compare this Neo-Assyrian situation to that of the Gospels, where Christian feminists have to expend enormous labor to recover meager traces of female prophets commissioned by
Jesus.

---

197. Huehnergard, 'Five Tablets', p. 19, Text 2, lines 1-10; Akkadian on p. 17.

198. See also Katarzyna Grosz, 'Daughters as Adopted Sons at Nuzi and Emar', in *La Femme dans le Proche-Orient Antique, Compte Rendu de la XXXIIIe rencontre assyri-ologique internationale (Paris, 7-10 juillet 1986)* (ed. Jean Marie Durand; Paris: Edi-tions Recherche sur le Civilisations, 1987), pp. 81-86.

199. Julian Reade, 'Was Sennacherib a Feminist?', in Durand (ed.), *La Femme dans le Proche-Orient Antique*, pp. 139-45 (145).

200. Sherry Lou Macgregor, *Beyond Hearth and Home: Women in the Public Sphere in Neo-Assyrian Society* (SAA, 21; Helsinki: Neo-Assyrian Corpus Text Project, 2012).

201. Macgregor, *Beyond Hearth and Home*, p. 18.

202. Macgregor, *Beyond Hearth and Home*, p. 27.

Celia E. Schultz's study of women's religious activity in the Roman Republic shows how much women had accomplished before Christianity. Again, much of the Christian feminist effort has sought to explain why Jesus did not choose any women in his group of twelve apostles. But in Republican Rome at least some priesthoods required a female–male pair, or married couple, for its function. According to Schultz, the flaminate, the priesthood devoted to Jupiter, 'should be viewed as a single priesthood that required the services of a married couple' and she posits the same for at least one other priesthood.[203] This approach reflects the respect for gender balance that one does not find in the Jesus group at all. Jesus did not balance his twelve men with twelve women. Much less did he seem willing to share his own self-appointed office with a woman.[204]

Bernadette Brooten's studies of Jewish female leaders in the synagogues shows a more active religious life for Jewish women than many Christian feminists have asserted. In Brooten's own words:

> It is my thesis that women served as leaders in a number of synagogues during the Roman and Byzantine periods. The evidence for this consists of nineteen Greek and Latin inscriptions in which women bear the titles 'head of the synagogue', 'leader', 'elder', 'mother of the synagogue', and 'priestess'. These inscriptions date from 27 BCE to perhaps the sixth century CE and provenance from Italy to Asia Minor, Egypt, and Palestine.[205]

In other words, all of the sorts of leadership offices that Christian feminists are trying to find in the biblical texts by forced inferences and theological claims can be found in actual data in non-Christian religions.

203. Schultz, *Women's Religious Activity*, p. 81. For the role of women in war, see Pasi Loman, '"No Women, No War", Women's Participation in Ancient Greek Warfare', *Greece & Rome* 51 (2004), pp. 34-54; Leif E. Vaage (ed.), *Religious Rivalries in the Early Roman Empire and the Rise of Christianity* (Studies in Christianity and Judaism, 18; Waterloo, Ontario: Wilfrid Laurier University Press, 2006). On the admiration of the rhetorical abilities of elite women, see Bradley Buszard, 'The Speech of Greek and Roman Women in Plutarch's *Lives*', *Classical Philology* 105 (2010), pp. 83-115.

204. A recently discovered inscription from Akmoneia, a small central Phrygian town in the Roman province of Asia, shows a corporate body of women issuing a decree to honor a woman. This apparently unprecedented development could be hailed as a 'radical' innovation for women by Greek culture by any good apologist for Greek religion. See further, Peter Thonemann, 'The Women of Akmoneia', *JRS* 100 (2010), pp. 163-78.

205. Bernadette J. Brooten, *Women Leaders in the Ancient Synagogue* (Brown Judaic Studies, 36; Atlanta, GA: Scholars Press, 1982), p. 1. For other recent studies of Jewish women, see Isaac Sassoon, *The Status of Women in Jewish Tradition* (Cambridge: Cambridge University Press, 2011); Cecilia Wassen, *Women in the Damascus Document* (SBL Academia Biblica, 21; Atlanta, GA: Society of Biblical Literature, 2005).

Sometimes these facts are known even by feminists who are not biblical scholars or Christians. As mentioned, Simone de Beauvoir observed that '[i]n Babylon the Laws of Hammurabi acknowledged certain rights of women'.[206] Yet, most Christian feminists either ignore these pre-Christian developments or baldly contradict their own claims about non-Christian societies in order to place Jesus in a better light on gender issues. One example will suffice. In her book, *When Women were Priests*, Karen Jo Torjesen attempts to show the existence of female leadership among early Christians. Torjesen specifically argues:

> There seems to be no doubt that women figured prominently in Jesus' life and ministry, both during his lifetime and after his resurrection when the first communities were formed and his message began to spread... But because such independence and prominence on the part of women conflicted directly with the view of women's roles that pervaded Greco-Roman society, these traditions were ignored and submerged as much as possible in order to conform Christian teaching and practice to social convention.[207]

Torjesen's ethnocentric generalization of Greco-Roman society is contradicted by her own earlier statement: 'Even religious authority in Greek and Roman worship was not limited by gender. Women as well as men functioned as prophets and priests.'[208] It could be that Greco-Roman conventions did not prompt later Christians to suppress any gender equality in Jesus stories. Rather, it could be that Jesus was not really as 'advanced' as Greco-Roman religion on gender equality in the first place. Perhaps it was his later followers who sought conformity with the more gender egalitarianism found in the Greco-Roman world.

Summary

Christian feminist biblical scholarship paradoxically is still heavily invested in maintaining the elevated ethical status of a man named Jesus. The examples I have reviewed show that many feminist Christian scholars are actually quite traditional in their apologetic strategies. Like their androcentric counterparts, feminists often devalue non-Christian cultures to make Jesus appear innovative, radically inclusive, and an anti-hierarchical paragon of feminism. Like their androcentric counterparts, Christian feminists don't normally see themselves as part of a Christian

206. De Beauvoir, *The Second Sex*, p. 96.
207. Karen Jo Torjesen, *When Women were Priests: Women's Leadership in the Early Church and the Scandal of their Subordination in the Rise of Christianity* (New York: HarperCollins, 1995), p. 37.
208. Torjesen, *When Women were Priests*, p. 13.

empire that uses benign language to justify its expansionist ends. Christian feminists will sometimes throw ancient women under the proverbial bus to ensure that Jesus was good—for example, Sharon Ringe turns the Syrophoenician woman into a victimizer instead of the victim of Jesus' verbal abuse.

When evidence from linguistics and socio-religious context fails to salvage a gender egalitarian Jesus, Christian feminists often resort to theological and circular rationales, which is something more traditional male interpreters also use to elevate Jesus' ethics.[209] When the textual evidence fails to make her point, Lee tells us that women must have been included in the Last Supper because Jesus is radically inclusive. This presumes that Jesus is radically inclusive in the first place. Schüssler Fiorenza tells readers: 'Biblical revelation and truth about women are found, I would suggest, in those texts which transcend and criticize their patriarchal culture and religion.'[210] This is just as circular as affirming: 'Biblical revelation and truth about women are found, I would suggest, in those texts which affirm and promote their patriarchal culture and religion.'

The diminished role of women in the Gospels could have many reasons, and certainly one of them is later androcentric redaction. But what if later redactors who did favor an expanded role for women were actually departing from Jesus' teachings? What if later redactors were conforming more to the Gentile world, where females did have more roles than Christian feminists often acknowledge? Christian feminists either ignore or dismiss such non-Christian advances for women, but praise them as a radical social breakthrough when there is even a slight glimmer that Jesus might have done something similar over a thousand years later.

More importantly, Christian feminism still has not adequately explained why anyone should invest so much time in finding out what a man named Jesus thought about anything. *That is the crucial metaethical question.* Christian feminists have either ignored or inadequately addressed the metaethics of why any modern behavior should look back at a man named Jesus. As Daphne Hampson phrased it: 'What was I doing, in the late twentieth century, arguing that what happened in the first century was of relevance to whether or not I could be a deacon.'[211] It is the lack of interest in that question that confirms that much of modern Christian feminism is part of an

---

209. For example, when commenting on the Canaanite woman pericope, John P. Meier ('Matthew 15.21-28', *Int* 40 [1986], pp. 397-402 [397]) states: 'Hermeneutics is possible because, by the light of faith, believers can perceive surprising structural similarities in different encounters between human need and divine grace—even across the gaping chasm of cultural shifts.' But 'the light of faith' is not a tool of hermeneutics when studying any other type of ancient literature (e.g., Greek, Mesopotamian, etc.) in secular academia.

210. Schüssler Fiorenza, 'Interpreting Patriarchal Traditions', p. 61.

211. Hampson, *Theology and Feminism*, p. 31.

ecclesial-academic empire whose main goal is the protection of the status and authority of their founder, a man who supposedly lived and died two thousand years ago. These Christian feminists are fully engaged in very traditional male ancestor worship, but they call it critical scholarship.

Chapter 10

THE ANTI-DISABLED JESUS: LESS THAN FULLY HUMAN

New Testament ethics often lauds how the loving nature of Jesus extended to the ill and disabled. The title of Christopher W. Bogosh's *Compassionate Jesus: Rethinking the Christian's Approach to Modern Medicine* (2013) is evidence of the persistence of this idea.[1] At the same time, other scholars seek to refute any notion that Jesus was cruel or unjust to disabled persons. Thus, when speaking of the scholarship which recognizes the use of the disabled as pawns in God's demonstration of power in John 9, John C. Poirier refers to it as 'the monstrous thesis that God struck a man with disability *from birth* just for the sake of allowing Jesus to make a public display of God's healing power at an obscenely later time in his life'.[2] For Poirier and like-minded scholars, Jesus must have had as enlightened a view of disability as we do today.

In my own, *Health Care and the Rise of Christianity* (1999), I argued that early Christian health care did present some advantageous features that may have attracted many converts.[3] For example, even if Christian rituals or the procedures used by Jesus did not heal any more effectively than those in non-Christian traditions, there was at least the concept that one should not charge for providing health care (Mt. 10.8). The emphasis on the role of faith over pharmaceuticals, which could be expensive, may also have attracted those disillusioned by Greco-Roman medical traditions (e.g., Mk 5.24-25).

Nevertheless, Jesus exhibits many attitudes toward the sick and disabled that may be regarded as wrong or disrespectful by modern standards. One modern standard is represented by the *American with Disabilities Act* (1990), which ushered in a new era in integrating the disabled into modern

---

1. Christopher W. Bogosh, *Compassionate Jesus: Rethinking the Christian's Approach to Modern Medicine* (Grand Rapids, MI: Reformation Heritage Books, 2013).

2. John C. Poirier, 'Another Look at the Man Born Blind', *Journal of Religion, Disability and Health* 11 (2007), pp. 60-65 (62). Poirier is reacting to the work of, among others, John M. Hull, *In the Beginning There was Darkness: A Blind Person's Conversation with the Bible* (Harrisburg, PA: Trinity Press International, 2001).

3. Avalos, *Health Care and the Rise of Christianity*. See also Ilka Isserman, 'Did Christian Ethics have Any Influence on the Conversion to Christianity', *Zeitschrift für Antikes Christentum/Journal of Ancient Christianity* 16.1 (2012), pp. 99-112.

American society. The ADA recognizes the plight of the disabled in its introductory remarks:

> [I]ndividuals with disabilities are a discrete and insular minority who have been faced with restrictions and limitations, subjected to a history of purposeful unequal treatment, and relegated to a position of political powerlessness in our society, based on characteristics that are beyond the control of such individuals and resulting from stereotypic assumptions not truly indicative of the individual ability of such individuals to participate in, and contribute to, society.[4]

Although there are a variety of illness theodicies in the New Testament, Jesus' supposition that sin can be linked to disability is not only scientifically wrong, but also serves to marginalize and blame those in a disadvantaged physical state.[5] In addition, there are examples where Jesus subscribes to the idea that those who are blind or deaf have to be healed to be viewed as proper worshippers of God or Jesus. As such, Jesus is perpetuating 'normate' and stereotypical views of the body and human abilities on those who have physical features that are different from the statistical norm.

Disability Studies

To understand why Jesus can be considered as antagonistic to disabled people, it is necessary to understand a burgeoning field called 'disability studies'. The differential valuation of persons, based on presumed or real mental and physical features and 'abilities', is the principal subject matter of what is called 'disability studies'. As an academic discipline, disability studies emerged in the British social sciences in the 1980s, while in North America disability studies developed primarily within the humanities in the 1990s.[6] Its spectacular growth is reflected in the sheer number of volumes devoted to disability studies since 1995.[7]

---

4. *American with Disabilities Act of 1990-ADA-42, US Code, Chapter 126*, Section 12101, 'Findings and Purpose'. Online: http://finduslaw.com/americans-disabilities-act-1990-ada-42-us-code-chapter-126.

5. Robert M. Price ('Illness Theodicies in the New Testament', *Journal of Religion and Health* 25 [1986], pp. 309-315) identifies at least six different explanations for the origin of illness, but sin is one of them.

6. For general and historical perspectives, see Gary L. Albrecht, Katherine D. Seelman and Michael Bury (eds.), *Handbook of Disability Studies* (Thousand Oaks, CA: Sage, 2001); Lennard J. Davis (ed.), *The Disability Studies Reader* (New York: Routledge, 1997); Henri Jaques-Stiker, *A History of Disability* (trans. William Sayers and David T. Mitchell; Ann Arbor, MI: University of Michigan Press, 2002). If one ventures outside of scholarship per se, then Tod Browning's *Freaks* (1932) is perhaps one of the most significant filmic representations of how wrongly the normate world perceives the abilities of those who lack entire limbs or some significant sensory ability.

7. A few titles include Nancy Eiesland and Don Saliers (eds.), *Human Disability*

Prior to the rise of disability studies, the study of disability within biblical studies focused on medical diagnosis. This focus is easily illustrated by reference works, which measure the status of the field. For example, in the article titled, 'Lame, Lameness' in *The Interpreter's Dictionary of the Bible* (1962), Roland K. Harrison tells us that the man in Acts 3.2 suffered from 'weakness of the astragalus and metatarsus bones of the foot', and the person healed at Lystra (Acts 14.8) probably 'suffered from some form of cyllosis'.[8]

The recent publication of *Diagnoses in Assyrian and Babylonian Medicine* by JoAnn Scurlock and Burton R. Andersen shows that such diagnostic approaches have not disappeared. Scurlock and Andersen's massive tome purports to provide precise diagnoses ranging from Parkinson's disease to conditions related to individual 'cranial nerves'.[9] However, increasingly replacing these diagnostic approaches are those interested in how illnesses were experienced by patients and how illnesses are represented in the literature of the ancient Near East.[10] In general, such scholars study how socio-religious frameworks interact with health care and with the valuation of persons.

All scholarly disciplines have landmark events within their history. In the study of disabilities within religious studies, 20 November 1995 is a landmark date. It was on that day that the first session of the 'Religion and Disability Studies Consultation' was held at the American Academy of Religion/Society of Biblical Literature Annual Meeting in Philadelphia.

and the Service of God: Reassessing Religious Practice (Nashville, TN: Abingdon Press, 1998); J.Z. Abrams, *Judaism and Disability: Portrayals of Ancient Texts from the Tanach through the Bavli* (Washington, DC: Gallaudet University Press, 1998); Hector Avalos, Sarah Melcher and Jeremy Schipper (eds.), *This Abled Body: Rethinking Disabilities in Biblical Studies* (SBLSS, 55; Atlanta, GA: Society of Biblical Literature, 2007); J.H.W. Dorman, 'The Blemished Body: Deformity and Disability in the Qumran Scrolls' (PhD dissertation; Rijksuniversiteit Groningen, 2007); Rebecca Raphael, *Biblical Corpora: Representations of Disability in Hebrew Biblical Literature* (London: T. & T. Clark, 2008); Saul Olyan, *Disability in the Hebrew Bible: Interpreting Mental and Physical Differences* (Cambridge: Cambridge University Press, 2008); Deborah B. Creamer, *Disability and Christian Theology: Embodied Limits and Constructive Possibilities* (New York: Oxford University Press, 2009); Jeremy Schipper, *Disability and Isaiah's Suffering Servant* (New York: Oxford University Press, 2011); Candida R. Moss and Jeremy Schipper (eds.), *Disability Studies and Biblical Literature* (New York: Palgrave Macmillan, 2011).

8. Roland K. Harrison, 'Lame, Lameness', *IDB*, III, pp. 59-60.

9. JoAnn Scurlock and Burton R. Andersen, *Diagnoses in Assyrian and Babylonian Medicine* (Champaign, IL: University of Illinois Press, 2005), especially pp. 336-37 and 399-402.

10. See, for example, Maria Häusl, 'Verkörpertes Leben: Körperbilder und-konzepte im Alten Testament', *BK* 67 (2012), pp. 10-15.

Nine years later, at the 2004 Annual Meeting in San Antonio, the Biblical Scholarship and Disabilities Consultation within the Society of Biblical Literature made its debut. According to Darla Schumm and Michael Stoltzfus, editors of a comparative study of disability in the Abrahamic religions, 'the emergence of these two consultations (now official groups or units in both the AAR and SBL) ushered in a new era for discussion of disability and religion in the academy'.[11] Now, biblical scholarship in North America has popularized disability studies so successfully that even German scholarship is adopting the English terms 'disability' and 'disability studies'.[12]

And as is the case with most nascent fields, it often does not take long to see opposing or complementary approaches emerge. In the case of the study of disabilities by biblical scholars, we can see at least three approaches that represent our modern attitudes toward biblical ideas about disability. Identifying these three approaches does not mean that there are no mixtures, but only that they can be held independently. Yet, in some ways, they are still concerned with exploring whether religion or the Bible have been positive and/or negative in helping people with disabilities define themselves.

Those types of issues, of course, inevitably involve New Testament ethics. Although standard treatments of New Testament ethics have yet to integrate the full implications of disability studies, one can recognize different approaches emerging in disability studies that bear ethical implications.[13]

One approach that is emerging is what I would denominate as a 'redemptionist' approach because it seeks to redeem the biblical text, despite any negative stance on disabilities, by recontextualizing it for modern application. In general, this has been the main approach used in New Testament ethics even if works in that field have not always been conscious of disability studies. One reason this approach is used is that ethicists are becoming very aware of the social ill effects that linking sin and disability/illness has for the treatment of the disabled (e.g., the claim that AIDS is God's punishment for a sinful lifestyle).[14]

---

11. Darla Schumm and Michael Stoltzfus (eds.), *Disability in Judaism, Christianity, and Islam: Sacred Texts, Historical Traditions, and Social Analysis* (New York: Palgrave Macmillan, 2011), p. xvi.

12. For example, see Wolfgang Gründstäudl and Markus Schiefer Ferrari (eds.), *Gestörte Lektüre: Disability als hermeneutische Leitkategorie biblischer Exegese* (Stuttgart: W. Kohlhammer, 2012), p. 7: 'In Laufe der letzten Jahrzehnte wurden zahlreiche neue hermeneutische Begriffe und Konzepte… Eine vergleichweise neue, ebenso herausfordernde wie bereichernde Anregung erwächst der biblischen Exegese seit einigen Jahren durch die Etablierung der sogenannten Disability Studies…'

13. See further Hector Avalos, 'Redemptionism, Rejectionism, and Historicism as Emerging Approaches in Disability Studies', *PRSt* 34 (2007), pp. 61-75.

14. The claim that AIDS is God's punishment for homosexuality is most famously attributed to Jerry Falwell (1933–2007), the fundamentalist American preacher and

An opposing approach may be described as 'rejectionist' because it would argue that the Bible has negative portrayals of disability that should be rejected in modern society.[15] The aim of such an approach is not to recontextualize, but to repudiate. A variant of the rejectionist approach is perhaps best termed a 'post-scripturalist approach', which argues that we should not use any ancient text at all, whether it has positive or negative portrayals, to provide normative values today. A third approach may be called 'historicist', because it undertakes historical examinations of disabilities in the Bible and its subsequent interpretation, sometimes in comparison with neighboring ancient cultures, without any overt interest in the consequences of the conclusions for today.

In terms of New Testament ethics, the redemptionist approach will be the focus of this chapter. A redemptionist approach seeks to rescue the text from the misinterpretations of modern scholars with normate views of the body. The normate body, for example, is supposed to have all its limbs or functions to be regarded as optimal or perfect. A non-normate view of the body explores the extent to which people who don't have all their body parts or functions can still be deemed as valuable human beings. Most importantly, the redemptionist approach often centers on showing that Jesus was as compassionate and understanding of disabled people as modern norms would expect him to be.

John 5 and 9: Redeeming Jesus

An example of a redemptionist approach can be found in an article titled, 'Johannine Healings and the Otherness of Disability', by Kerry Wynn, who attempts to 'redeem' two passages in the Gospel of John (5.1-18 and 9.3) that have played an important role in the study of disabilities in the Bible.[16] As Wynn phrases it, 'Those who would liberate disability from such normate hermeneutics struggle to make sense of the healing passages found in

founder of Liberty University. See Robert S. McElvaine, *Grand Theft Jesus: The Hijacking of Religion in America* (New York: Crown, 2009), p. 35.

15. See James A. Metzger, 'Reclaiming a "Dark and Malefic Sacred" for a Theology of Disability', *Journal of Religion, Disability and Health* 15 (2011), pp. 296-316 (312); idem, 'Disability and the Marginalization of God in the Parable of the Snubbed Host (Luke 14.15-24)', *The Bible and Critical Theory* 6 (2010), pp. 23.1-23.15. Online: http://novaojs.newcastle.edu.au/ojsbct/index.php/bct/article/view/308

16. Kerry Wynn, 'Johannine Healings and the Otherness of Disability', *PRSt* 34 (2007), pp. 61-75. See also Alois Stimpfle, '"Von Geburt an Blind" (John 9, 1): Disability und Wirklichkeitskonstruktion', in Gründstäudl and Ferrari (eds.), *Gestörte Lektüre*, pp. 98-126; Dorothy A. Lee, 'The Gospel of John and the Five Senses', *JBL* 129 (2010), pp. 115-27.

the gospels.'[17] Wynn begins by clearly outlining two ideas in 'popular the-ology' that he wishes to dissect: '(1) disability is caused by sin, and (2) if one has enough faith one will be healed'.[18] The entire article concludes that '[s]in in the Johannine healing narratives is not a cause of disability' and that 'faith is not a prerequisite to healing'.[19]

Wynn's conclusions are partly derived from an examination of Jn 5.1-18. Briefly, in that episode a man with an apparently musculo-skeletal disabil-ity was lying amidst 'a multitude of invalids, blind, lame, and paralyzed' (Jn 5.3). He had been ill for thirty-eight years, but the large crowds had pre-vented him from reaching the healing waters, and no one would help him do so. So Jesus heals him on a Sabbath day. Towards the end of the story, Jesus tells him, 'Do not sin anymore, so that nothing worse happens to you' (Jn 5.14; NRSV). It is this latter statement that has led some scholars to con-clude that Jesus did make a link between sin and disability that can be traced back to the Hebrew Bible. For example, Warren Carter remarks that 'Jesus' warning frames the man's disabling 38 year illness as a reflection and pun-ishment for his sinful character'.[20]

Wynn rejects that interpretation, and specifically as defended by Col-leen Grant, as a case of normate hermeneutics.[21] According to Wynn, read-ing the Bible from a normate viewpoint has caused Grant to attribute to Jesus the belief that sin can cause illness. Wynn apparently sees Jesus as not advocating a view that today would be considered to be not only scientifi-cally wrong but also perhaps cruel because it blames the victim, or because it views the disabled as somehow morally tainted. Indeed, prior to the rise of disability studies it was far more common to find scholarship on healing that routinely assumed that illness and sin were connected in the New Tes-tament. Thus, in 1981 Borgen says: '[T]he connection between sin and sick-ness is still maintained. Sickness is seen as one aspect of the fallen state that man is in despite being God's creature.'[22]

However, Wynn's argument uses some very problematic premises, not least of which is Wynn's claim that '[d]isability is a phenomenon of nature, not punishment throughout the Hebrew Bible'.[23] In fact, he says that 'we look in vain' for a Hebrew tradition making a link between sin and dis-

17. Wynn, 'Johannine Healings', p. 61.
18. Wynn, 'Johannine Healings', p. 61.
19. Wynn, 'Johannine Healings', p. 74.
20. Warren Carter, 'The Blind, Lame and Paralyzed', in Moss and Schipper (eds.), *Disability Studies and Biblical Literature*, pp. 127-50 (130).
21. Colleen C. Grant, 'Reinterpreting the Healing Narratives', in Eiesland and Saliers (eds.), *Human Disability and the Service of God*, pp. 72-87.
22. Peder Borgen, 'Miracles of Healing in the New Testament: Some Observations', *ST* 35 (1981), pp. 91-106 (99).
23. Wynn, 'Johannine Healings', p. 62.

ability.[24] To buttress his point, Wynn cites Lev. 21.17-23 to argue that the passage 'applies only to Levites and restricts their priestly service on the basis of purity issues and identifies no cause for disability'.[25]

Wynn's entire argument is premised on the idea that 'purity issues' do not entail valuations of disability. Yet, purity is not a 'phenomenon of nature', but rather a social construct.[26] In fact, 'purity' is an expression of power relations that may be used to describe all sorts of conditions not valued by those in power. As such, certain physical conditions may be classified as 'impure' if the normate society does not value them. Thus, Lev. 21.18-21 includes all sorts of physical features ('blind or lame…limb too long…injured foot or an injured hand…hunchback, or a dwarf').[27] It could also be that they are considered impure precisely because it is assumed that they reflect some sort of sin on the part of their parents. Otherwise, Wynn's definition of 'purity' leaves unexplained why such physical conditions are considered 'impure' in the first place.

Moreover, all this seems to assume that Leviticus 21 is the only or strongest passage used to argue that the Hebrew Bible does link sin with disability. In fact, Wynn does not mention the single most important text, which is Deuteronomy 28. In that passage there is an elaborate catalog of conditions associated with those that keep the covenant, and those that do not keep the covenant. Note the preface to the curses in Deut. 28.15: 'But if you will not obey the voice of the LORD your God or be careful to do all his commandments…'. If sin is defined as any act that violates God's commandments or moral order, then some of the punishments in Deuteronomy 28 do come in the form of illnesses and disabilities:

> The LORD will make the pestilence cleave to you until he has consumed you off the land which you are entering to take possession of it. The LORD will smite you with consumption, and with fever, inflammation, and fiery heat, and with drought, and with blasting, and with mildew; they shall pursue you until you perish… The LORD will smite you with the boils of Egypt, and with the ulcers and the scurvy and the itch, of which you cannot be

24. Wynn, 'Johannine Healings', p. 62.
25. Wynn, 'Johannine Healings', p. 62.
26. For a comparative study of purity rhetoric in the ancient Near East, see Christian Frevel and Christoph Nihan (eds.), *Purity and the Forming of Religious Traditions in the Ancient Mediterranean World and Ancient Judaism* (Dynamics in the History of Religion, 3: Leiden: E.J. Brill, 2013); Roger P. Booth, *Jesus and the Laws of Purity: Tradition History and Legal History in Mark 7* (JSNTSup, 13; Sheffield: JSOT Press, 1986).
27. A discussion of similar physical requirements for being a diviner in Mesopotamia is offered by Wilfred G. Lambert, 'The Qualifications of Babylonian Diviners', in *Festschrift für Rykle Borger zu seinem 65. Geburtstag am 24. Mai 1994: tikip santakki mala bašmu* (ed. Stefan M. Maul; Cuneiform Monographs, 10; Groningen: Styx, 1998), pp. 141-58.

healed. The LORD will smite you with madness and blindness and confusion
of mind; and you shall grope at noonday, as the blind grope in darkness,
and you shall not prosper in your ways; and you shall be only oppressed
and robbed continually, and there shall be no one to help you (Deut. 28.21-
22, 27-29).

This helplessness describes the very situation of the man at Bethesda, who
says no one would help him (Jn 5.7). Similarly, the link between sin and illness is placed on the lips of Yahweh himself:

If you will diligently hearken to the voice of the LORD your God, and do
that which is right in his eyes, and give heed to his commandments and
keep all his statutes, I will put none of the diseases upon you which I put
upon the Egyptians; for I am the LORD, your healer (Exod. 15.26).

Within John itself, one finds the author has no problem believing that
God strikes people blind, even if only in a spiritual sense. Thus, Jn 12.40
quotes Isa. 6.10 as follows: 'He has blinded their eyes and hardened their
heart, lest they should see with their eyes and perceive with their heart, and
turn for me to heal them.' Striking people with spiritual blindness is even
worse than striking them with physical blindness, as the former can result
in a lost eternal life. Thus, Yahweh does send diseases as punishment or to
accomplish other ends. The fact that New Testament scholars can see striking people with spiritual blindness as acceptable, and striking people with
physical blindness as unacceptable, shows a flaw in the ethical premises of
those modern scholars.

When one considers the specific Greek word used for the man at Bethesda,
one finds that he is described as having an ἀσθένεια. In the Greek version
of 1 Sam. 2.10, ἀσθένεια is the very word used to describe how God will
afflict his adversaries, although the English translation, such as the RSV,
does not reflect it so well ('The adversaries of the Lord shall be broken to
pieces'). In short, there is plenty of evidence to show that the Hebrew Bible
does make disability a 'punishment' for sin, if that means any action that
violates God's commandments or moral order.[28]

All of this brings us to Jn 5.14, which Wynn claims 'is not a general
statement about sin'. Instead, Wynn links this statement to one uttered
by Yahweh in Gen. 4.7 after Cain killed Abel: 'If you do well, will you
not be accepted? And if you do not do well, sin is lurking at the door; its
desire is for you, but you must master it' (NRSV). However, the relevance
of this passage for interpreting Jesus' words in Jn 5.14 is not explained
very clearly.

---

28. See further Karel van der Toorn, *Sin and Sanction in Israel and Mesopotamia: A
Comparative Study* (Assen: Van Gorcum, 1985); Gary Anderson, *Sin: A History* (New
Haven, CT: Yale University Press, 2010).

More relevant is to study what the Greek word χεῖρόν means in Jn 5.14. It certainly can be used in the sense of becoming sicker, as in Mk 5.26 when it describes the sufferings of the woman with the twelve-year hemorrhage who 'had suffered much under many physicians, and had spent all that she had, and was no better but rather grew worse' (εἰς τὸ χεῖρον ἐλθοῦσα). Many early church interpreters, such as Irenaeus, certainly understood this text to refer to the relationship between sin and punishment.[29]

Wynn's redemptionist approach might be contrasted with the 'rejection-ist' approach of John M. Hull's *In The Beginning There was Darkness: A Blind Person's Conversations with the Bible* (2001). John M. Hull is an unsighted biblical scholar, and so he writes as a disabled person about the sick people at the pool of Bethesda.[30] For Hull, Jn 5.14 makes sense if 'Jesus shared the belief that they were all there because of some sin'.[31] In fact, Jesus nowhere denies that sin is the cause of the invalid's plight. Rather, Jesus sees the invalid as an opportunity to show his own authority on the Sabbath. Once that was accomplished, he warns the same invalid not to sin again because something worse might come upon him, something consis-tent with Deuteronomy 28. Thus, Jesus nowhere denies, and rather reaf-firms, a clear connection between sin and disability.

A similar problem is found in Wynn's exegesis of Jn 9.2-3, which I will discuss more fully below. In this episode, the disciples are characterized by Wynn as asking a foolish question. However, Jesus does not call the disci-ples foolish, something Jesus has not hesitated to do on other occasions (Lk. 24.25). Given Deuteronomy 28, there is no reason to characterize the disci-ples' supposition as foolish at all. Rather, Jesus can be interpreted to mean that this disabled individual is *an exception to the rule*, and then Jesus gives a very specific reason for the exception: 'he was born blind so 'that God's works might be made manifest in him' (Jn 9.3).

Wynn's redemptionist approach can again be contrasted with Hull's eval-uation, 'the man has been born blind in order to provide a sort of photo opportunity for Jesus'.[32] But Hull's rejectionism is most clearly outlined in this statement concerning John: 'the symbolism made me feel uneasy and I soon came to realize that this book was not written for people like me, but for sighted people. No other book of the Bible is so dominated by

29. See Irenaeus, *Against Heresies* 4.36.6 (ANF, I, p. 517). For a discussion of early Christian understandings of this text, see also Michael Mees, 'Die Heilung des Kranken vom Bethesdateich aus Joh 5.1-18 in frühchristlicher Sicht', *NTS* 32 (1986), pp. 596-608 (602-603). For the argument that v. 14 is meant to mark the original ending of the story, see L. Th. Witkamp, 'The Use of Traditions in John 5.1-18', *JSNT* 25 (1985), pp. 19-47 (27).

30. Hull, *In the Beginning There was Darkness*, p. 49.

31. Hull, *In the Beginning There was Darkness*, p. 49.

32. Hull, *In the Beginning There was Darkness*, p. 49.

the contrast between light and darkness, and blindness is the symbol of darkness.'[33]

Amos Yong's Redemptionism

Amos Yong, currently a professor of Theology at Fuller Theological Seminary, follows Wynn in an attempt to redeem Jesus' views of disability. In his book, *The Bible, Disability and the Church: A New Vision for the People of God* (2011), Amos Yong tells readers that he believes that 'the Bible remains applicable to our modern lives'.[34] Yong explicitly aligns himself with a 'redemptionist' approach when he remarks, 'I also believe that the Bible is redemptive for the experience of disability'.[35] He emphasizes that,

> [p]eople with disabilities are created in the image of God that is measured according to the person of Christ, not by any Mr. Universe or Ms. America... Disabilities are not necessarily evil or blemishes to be eliminated.[36]

The latter claims are particularly problematic when addressing many instances where Jesus heals disabled people in order to make them 'better'.

Yong explicitly denies that Jesus links sin and blindness in John 9, and he likewise denies that Jesus views the blindness as an inferior physical status. A crucial portion of the narrative in John 9 reads as follows:

> As he passed by, he saw a man blind from his birth. And his disciples asked him, 'Rabbi, who sinned, this man or his parents, that he was born blind?' Jesus answered, 'It was not that this man sinned, or his parents, but that the works of God might be made manifest in him. We must work the works of him who sent me, while it is day; night comes, when no one can work. As long as I am in the world, I am the light of the world'. As he said this, he spat on the ground and made clay of the spittle and anointed the man's eyes with the clay, saying to him, 'Go, wash in the pool of Siloam' (which means Sent). So he went and washed and came back seeing. The neighbors and those who had seen him before as a beggar, said, 'Is not this the man who used to sit and beg?' Some said, 'It is he'; others said, 'No, but he is like him'. He said, 'I am the man'. They said to him, 'Then how were your eyes opened?'

> He answered, 'The man called Jesus made clay and anointed my eyes and said to me, "Go to Siloam and wash"; so I went and washed and received my sight' (Jn 9.1-11).

---

33. Hull, *In the Beginning There was Darkness*, pp. 49-50.

34. Amos Yong, *The Bible, Disability and the Church: A New Vision for the People of God* (Grand Rapids, MI: Eerdmans, 2011), p. 6; for his earlier work in disability studies, see Amos Yong, *Theology and Down Syndrome: Reimagining Disability in Late Modernity* (Waco, TX: Baylor University Press, 2007).

35. Yong, *The Bible, Disability and the Church*, pp. 6-7.

36. Yong, *The Bible, Disability and the Church*, p. 13.

Overall, Yong attributes to 'ableism' and 'normate readings' any notion that Jesus viewed the disabled as inferior. As Yong himself phrases it:

> [C]lassical interpretations of this passage presume the normate, sighted, and ableist salvation history which rejects blindness and disability as aberrant… It is sighted presuppositions, not the text itself, that canonize God in terms of light and sightedness, thus condemning darkness and blindness as blots within the created order that must finally be eliminated.[37]

Indeed, Yong tells readers that 'the Johannine text is important for a contemporary theology because it clearly records Jesus rejecting the assumption that this man's congenital disorder was due to ancestral sin'.[38] Briefly, Yong outlines his redemptionist rationale as follows:

> First, the blind man was not as pitiable or dependent a case as might be assumed from a normate point of view. After all, he seemed to be able to find his way around just fine, without the help of others… Second, the man clearly understood his sighted identity as continuous with his blind identity. Yes, he did say 'I was blind but now I see' (v. 25), but this difference didn't mean that he wasn't the same person. Thus, in his response to the debate among the townspeople about whether this sighted man was the same as the one born blind, 'He kept saying, "I am the man"' (v. 9)…his newfound capacity to see physically (precisely what the Pharisees were overly concerned about from a normate vantage point) was less important than his new spiritual vision (which the ableism of the Pharisees completely prevented them from recognizing).[39]

Yong's interpretation depends on a number of questionable assumptions, and it does not address what the text actually says at certain points.

First, Yong assumes that the blind man was able 'to find his way around just fine' and independently on the strength of this description: 'So he went and washed and came back seeing' (Jn 9.7). Yet, nowhere does Yong address another case where Jesus indicates that the blind cannot move about independently: 'He also told them a parable: "Can a blind man lead a blind man? Will they not both fall into a pit?"' (Lk. 6.39). Of course, Jesus himself once helped a blind man find his way around: 'And he took the blind man by the hand, and led him out of the village' (Mk 8.23).

Even if we restrict ourselves to the Johannine text, the fact that the blind man may have walked unassisted to the pool of Siloam does not have any relevance to whether Jesus saw him as having an inferior physical status. Today, many blind men are able to find their way around with walking sticks and other aides, but that does not mean that modern society sees the blind as having a normative status. The modern environment is also relatively more

---

37. Yong, *The Bible, Disability and the Church*, pp. 55.
38. Yong, *The Bible, Disability and the Church*, pp. 6-7.
39. Yong, *The Bible, Disability and the Church*, pp. 50-51.

friendly for the blind (e.g., use of braille in elevators, and sound to help the blind at crosswalks). It would be more difficult to understand how someone in the ancient world could navigate 'just fine' without assistance. In fact, the legal codes understood this problem, as is indicated by this law: 'You shall not curse the deaf or put a stumbling block before the blind, but you shall fear your God: I am the LORD' (Lev. 19.14).

Second, Yong confuses the issue of identity with the issue of devaluation of the blind man. The very text to which Yong points for his evidence ('I am the man' in v. 9) refers more precisely to his status as a sedentary beggar. Indeed, this statement is an answer to the specific question posed in v. 8: 'Is not this the man who used to sit and beg?' If so, the newly healed man is pointing to his former and pitiable condition as a blind man, and not to some satisfied and independent life as a blind man. The answer given reflects the fact that the blind man was not 'able to find his way around just fine', but rather he was identified by his stationary and beggarly lifestyle. The amazement of the onlookers consisted precisely of contrasting his former predominantly immobile lifestyle to his newly mobile one.

Furthermore, Yong erroneously assumes that continuity in identity and devaluation were incompatible in biblical ethics. Conversely, Yong seems to assume that continuity in identity of a person is evidence that the valuation of the person remains the same. But that is clearly not the case. Thus, Adam was still identified as Adam in his prelapsarian and postlapsarian state, which is usually deemed inferior in Christian theology. Most of the disciples were identified the same way (e.g., 'Philip of Bethsaida' in Jn 1.44) before and after their rise to the status of Jesus' disciples or followers. Nathanael was still identified as 'Nathanael of Cana in Galilee' (Jn 21.2), even after he upgraded his spiritual status by recognizing Jesus' true identity in Jn 1.46-51.

Other criticisms of ableist readings reveal retrojections of modern views of the disabled into the first century. For example, Yong argues:

> [T]he assumption that equates darkness and blindness presumes to know, from a sighted perspective, that blind people know only darkness and don't recognize the difference between darkness and light. In point of fact, most blind people can distinguish between the two and even are able to appreciate how such metaphors work without being offended by them.[40]

For his evidence, Yong cites no real scientific studies of blindness, but only appeals to a work by Susan Wendell, who reflects philosophically on blindness.[41] Yet, Wendell is not speaking for blind people, but rather making a

40. Yong, *The Bible, Disability and the Church*, p. 56.
41. Yong (*The Bible, Disability and the Church*, p. 56) cites Susan Wendell, *The Rejected Body: Feminist Philosophical Reflections on Disability* (New York: Routledge, 1996), pp. 80-81.

plea that we not eliminate all metaphors equating blindness with some deficiency (e.g., the question, 'Are you blind?', directed to someone who lacks
understanding). As Wendell remarks, 'Metaphors of these abilities must
sometimes hurt the people who lack them, but we would impoverish language if we stopped using metaphors of all abilities that some people lack.'[42]

Moreover, the question is not what modern science has determined to be
true about the perception of light and darkness in blind people. The question
is what did the author of John and his cultural background believe about the
ability of blind people to perceive the difference between light and darkness. The biblical texts indicate that blind people could be seen as utterly
helpless, as shown in Deut. 28.29: 'and you shall grope at noonday, as the
blind grope in darkness, and you shall not prosper in your ways; and you
shall be only oppressed and robbed continually, and there shall be no one to
help you'. Similarly, when Saul was struck blind, it is said: 'Saul arose from
the ground; and when his eyes were opened, he could see nothing; so they
led him by the hand and brought him into Damascus' (Acts 9.8).

The Ethics of Punctuation

The effort to disassociate Jesus from any linkage between sin and illness
includes a plea from John C. Poirier to repunctuate Jn 9.3-4, which he renders as follows according to what he calls the 'traditional punctuation':[43]

> Neither this man nor his parents sinned so that he was born blind, but in
> order that the works of God might be made manifest in him. We must work
> the works of him who sent me while it is day; night is coming when no one
> can work (Jn 9.3-4).[44]

Poirier's ethical struggle with this punctuation is clear when he remarks:
'The old punctuation presents us with the monstrous thesis that God struck
a man with disability *from birth* just for the sake of allowing Jesus to make a
public display of God's healing power at an obscenely later time in his life.'[45]
Accordingly, Poirier proposes that we repunctuate Jn 9.3-4 as follows:

> Neither this man nor his parents sinned so that he was born blind. But in
> order that the works of God might be made manifest in him, we must work
> the works of him who sent me while it is day; night is coming when no one
> can work.[46]

---

42. Wendell, *The Rejected Body*, p. 80.
43. Poirier, 'Another Look', p. 61.
44. See also J. Duncan M. Derrett, 'The True Meaning of Jn 9, 3-4', *Filología Neotestamentaria* 16 (2003), pp. 103-106.
45. Poirier, 'Another Look', p. 62. Poirer's italics.
46. Poirier, 'Another Look', p. 61.

Poirier explains what he hopes to achieve by such repunctuation: 'The more likely punctuation of these verses lends an altogether different meaning to Jesus' words in vv. 3-4, and absolves him (at least in this context) of expressing a connection between disability and sin.'[47]

Poirier argues that repunctuation serves the literary function better than the usual punctuation. As he phrases it:

> Putting a full stop at the end of 'Neither this man nor his parents sinned so that he was born blind' functions literarily to negate the Pharisees' supposition that the man was born in sin. Its literary function is already fulfilled, and does not call for an explanation as to *why* the man was born blind.[48]

Yet, his own repunctuated translation violates this supposed lack of a need to explain why the man was healed. After all, is Jesus' answer in v. 3 ('But in order that the works of God might be made manifest in him...') not an explanation?

The main problem with Poirier's repunctuation is that it is grammatically implausible. To understand what Poirier proposes, one needs to look at the Greek text of Jn 9.3-4:

> ἀπεκρίθη Ἰησοῦς, Οὔτε οὗτος ἥμαρτεν οὔτε οἱ γονεῖς αὐτοῦ, ἀλλ' ἵνα φανερωθῇ τὰ ἔργα τοῦ Θεοῦ ἐν αὐτῷ. ἡμᾶς δεῖ ἐργάζεσθαι τὰ ἔργα τοῦ πέμψαντός με ἕως ἡμέρα ἐστίν. ἔρχεται νὺξ ὅτε οὐδεὶς δύναται ἐργάζεσθαι.

Note that both the RSV and Poirier's translation insert another verb (γεννηθῇ; '...he was born [blind]') borrowed from v. 2 that is not in the actual Greek text of v. 3. This inserted verb reflects the fact that Johannine grammar has a tendency to omit the principal verb before ἵνα.[49]

In any case, the main grammatical issue centers on whether the Greek expression, ἀλλ' ἵνα φανερωθῇ, refers to what precedes or to what follows. Poirier rightly observes that there are other clauses beginning with ἀλλ' ἵνα in John (e.g., 1.8, 31; 3.17; 11.52; 12.9, 47; 13.18; 15.25; 17.15), along with three occurrences of ἵνα φανερωθῇ (Jn 1.31; 3.21; 9.3).[50] For Poirier, the closest analogy is between 1.31 and 9.3. As he phrases it: 'John 1.31's parallel to the wording of 9.3 supports my interpretation of 9.3, in that it functions exactly in the way I have suggested for 9.3.'[51]

---

47. Poirier, 'Another Look', p. 61.
48. Poirier, 'Another Look', p. 62.
49. See Abbott, *Johannine Grammar*, pp. 119-20.
50. Poirier, 'Another Look', p. 63.
51. Poirier, 'Another Look', p. 63.

John 1.31 reads: 'I myself did not know him; but for this I came baptizing with water, that he might be revealed to Israel' (κἀγὼ οὐκ ἤδειν αὐτόν ἀλλ' ἵνα φανερωθῇ τῷ 'Ισραὴλ διὰ τοῦτο ἦλθον ἐγὼ ἐν ὕδατι βαπτίζων). More specifically, Poirier claims, 'the Baptist's declaration, "I myself did not know him", is materially separate from what follows, and the clause introduced by *all' hina* modifies what follows rather than what precedes'.[52] But Poirier offers no grammatical reason why John the Baptist's declaration is 'materially separate' from what follows. In addition, Poirier does not address the Johannine use of the prepositional phrase διὰ τοῦτο in Jn 1.31, which finds no equivalent in Jn 9.3. As Edwin Abbott observes, 'Διὰ τοῦτο, "for this cause", "consequently", is almost always placed by John at the beginning of a sentence'.[53]

As to Jn 1.31, Abbott adds: 'Here, however, there is probably an ellipsis, as in other cases, before ἵνα, and the rendering should be "But [it came to pass] in order that he should be made manifest to Israel. *For this cause* came I etc"'.[54] If so, then Jn 1.31 does not constitute an example where ἀλλ' ἵνα φανερωθῇ modifies what follows. BDAG similarly remarks that '[t]he use of ἀλλά in Johannine lit[erature] is noteworthy, in that the parts contrasted are not always of equal standing grammatically'.[55] Accordingly, BDAG translates Jn 9.3 as 'neither this man has sinned nor his parents (he was born blind) that...might be revealed'.[56]

Indeed, Poirier seems unaware of the routine Johannine omission of the principal verb before ἵνα. Note the example in Jn 1.8, which occurs in the list that Poirier provided above: 'He was not the light, but came to bear witness to the light' (οὐκ ἦν ἐκεῖνος τὸ φῶς, ἀλλ' ἵνα μαρτυρήσῃ περὶ τοῦ φωτός). In this case, the RSV has supplied the principal verb (ἦλθεν; 'came') from the preceding v. 7. As mentioned, Poirier's own translation also adds a verb ('was born') that is not in the Greek text, though he positions it before ἀλλ'.

Once one recognizes that John routinely omits the principal verb before ἵνα, then one understands that there should be a principal verb between ἀλλ' and ἵνα φανερωθῇ. That verb is most plausibly 'born [blind]' ([τυφλὸς] γεννηθῇ). Accordingly, ἵνα φανερωθῇ completes the sense of the principal verb (γεννηθῇ), and should be translated as Abbott suggests: 'Neither did this man sin nor his parents, but on the contrary [he was born blind] in order that the works of God should be manifested.'[57]

---

52. Poirier, 'Another Look', p. 63.
53. Abbott, *Johannine Grammar*, p. 288.
54. Abbott, *Johannine Grammar*, pp. 288-89. Abbott's italics.
55. BDAG, 'ἀλλα', p. 45a.
56. BDAG, 'ἀλλα', p. 45a.
57. Abbott, *Johannine Grammar*, p. 120.

Paralyzed by Sin

Separating healing from the forgiveness of sins forms another argument against the claim that Jesus linked sin and disability. According to Yong, '[a] disability perspective, however, counters that Jesus' forgiveness and healing are two distinct acts'.[58] Yong appeals to Wynn's claim that [f]orgiveness was for the sake of the faithful person with a disability; the healing was a sign for unbelieving religious leaders'.[59] However, there is not warrant for separating sin and forgiveness especially when biblical texts repeatedly make these connections.

A key narrative at issue is that of the paralytic whose sins are forgiven by Jesus in Mark 2. When a paralytic man was presented to Jesus, the latter proceeded as follows:

> And when Jesus saw their faith, he said to the paralytic, 'My son, your sins are forgiven'. Now some of the scribes were sitting there, questioning in their hearts, 'Why does this man speak thus? It is blasphemy! Who can forgive sins but God alone?' And immediately Jesus, perceiving in his spirit that they thus questioned within themselves, said to them, 'Why do you question thus in your hearts? Which is easier, to say to the paralytic, "Your sins are forgiven", or to say, "Rise, take up your pallet and walk"? But that you may know that the Son of man has authority on earth to forgive sins'—he said to the paralytic—'I say to you, rise, take up your pallet and go home'. And he rose, and immediately took up the pallet and went out before them all; so that they were all amazed and glorified God, saying, 'We never saw anything like this!' (Mk 2.5-12).

Separating forgiveness and healing in the fashion suggested by Yong is not viable. The text does not indicate that 'forgiveness was for the sake of the faithful person with a disability; the healing was a sign for unbelieving religious leaders'. In fact, Jesus' acts of forgiveness and healing seem to be for the benefit of *both* the audience and the paralytic.

The fact that the forgiveness of sins was a sign for unbelievers is suggested very clearly by Mk 2.5: 'when Jesus saw their faith, he said to the paralytic, "My son, your sins are forgiven"'. The use of the plural ('their faith'; τὴν πίστιν αὐτῶν) shows that Jesus is acting because of the lack of belief of his audience. And just prior to uttering the command for the paralytic to be healed, the text says: 'Jesus, perceiving in his spirit that they thus questioned within themselves' (Mk 2.8). So, both the actions pertaining to the forgiveness of sins and the healing are meant for all onlookers to witness.[60]

---

58. Yong, *The Bible, Disability and the Church*, p. 61.

59. Yong, *The Bible, Disability and the Church*, p. 61, quoting Kerry H. Wynn, 'Disability versus Sin: A Rereading of Mark 2.1-12', an unpublished paper presented to the American Academy of Religion Annual Meeting (1999).

60. See also Duane F. Watson (ed.), *Miracle Discourse in the New Testament* (Atlanta,

Jesus then links forgiveness and healing more closely in Mk 2.10-11: '"But that you may know [ἵνα δὲ εἰδῆτε] that the Son of man has authority on earth to forgive sins"—he said to the paralytic—"I say to you, rise, take up your pallet and go home".' Note the use of the plural in Greek that reinforces the claim that both the forgiveness of sins and the healing are meant for the benefit or contemplation of unbelievers. Otherwise, Jesus preached that sin can be caused by specific body parts, including the eyes: 'And if your eye causes you to sin, pluck it out; it is better for you to enter the kingdom of God with one eye than with two eyes to be thrown into hell' (Mk 9.47).

These linkages between sin and illness follow a long tradition found in the Hebrew Bible, as in Psalm 32:

> Blessed is the man to whom the LORD imputes no iniquity, and in whose spirit there is no deceit. When I declared not my sin, my body wasted away through my groaning all day long. For day and night thy hand was heavy upon me; my strength was dried up as by the heat of summer. [Selah] I acknowledged my sin to thee, and I did not hide my iniquity; I said, 'I will confess my transgressions to the LORD'; then thou didst forgive the guilt of my sin (Ps. 32.2-5).

Similarly, in Psalm 38, one finds his plea:

> O LORD, rebuke me not in thy anger, nor chasten me in thy wrath! For thy arrows have sunk into me, and thy hand has come down on me. There is no soundness in my flesh because of thy indignation; there is no health in my bones because of my sin (Ps. 38.1-3).

If Jesus believed he was fulfilling the scripture (e.g., Jn 12.38; 13.18; 15.25; 17.12) then it is inexplicable why he could not have retained such concepts.[61]

Did Jesus Subvert Physiognomy?

Another approach to trumpeting the supposed ethical superiority or advances in the New Testament involves physiognomy, which studies the relationship between physical appearance and moral character.[62] According to Aristotle's

---

GA: Society of Biblical Literature, 2012); Daniel Johansson, '"Who can Forgive Sins but God Alone?": Human and Angelic Agents and Divine Forgiveness in Early Judaism', *JSNT* 33 (2011), pp. 351-74.

61. See also Thomas R. Blanton IV, 'Saved by Obedience: Matthew 1.21 in Light of Jesus' Teaching on the Torah', *JBL* 132 (2013), pp. 393-413 (411), where Blanton traces Jesus' views back to Deuteronomy, among other texts in the Hebrew Bible.

62. Elizabeth C. Evans (*Physiognomics in the Ancient World* [Transactions of the American Philosophical Society, 59, part 5; Philadelphia, PA: American Philosophical Society, 1969], p. 5) refers to physiognomy as '[t]he study of the relation of the features of a man to his inner character'. See also Mikeal Parsons, *Body and Character in Luke*

Prior Analytics: 'It is possible to judge men's character from their physical appearance, if one grants that body and soul change together in all natural affections.'[63] Hippocrates, the putative father of Greek medicine, engaged in physiognomic analysis when observing that 'those with a large head, large black eyes, and a wide, snub nose are honest'.[64] Negative characteristics could also be attributed on the basis of physical appearance as in the case of Didymus the Blind's assessment of black Africans: 'Ethiopians... share in the devil's evil and sin, getting their name from his blackness'.[65] Elizabeth Evans, a major scholar of ancient physiognomy, argues that many Greco-Roman authors displayed a 'physiognomic consciousness'.[66]

Generalizations about character inferred from physical attributes are not viewed as ethical or proper under the guidelines of the *Americans with Disabilities Act* or other modern western codes affecting the disabled. Accordingly, many Christian ethicists affirm that Jesus came to undermine this sort of physiognomic thinking. In particular, Mikeal Parsons, author of *Body and Character in Luke and Acts: The Subversion of Physiognomy in Early Christianity* (2006), argues:

> Luke at times employs physiognomic categories in his literary presentation of certain characters, usually for the purpose of subverting them. This is especially true of those texts that seek to establish Luke's vision of the eschatological community established around the person of Jesus Christ and grounded in the Abrahamic covenant (Genesis 12). For Luke this is a radically inclusive community, comprised not only of sinners and social outcasts but also of the physically disabled and disfigured who, on the basis of the appearance of their physical body, have been ostracized as misfit from the body politic (or religious).[67]

Parsons devotes much of his effort to the stories of the bent woman (Lk. 13.10-17), Zacchaeus (Lk. 19.1-10), the lame man from birth (Acts 3.1-10) and the Ethiopian eunuch (Acts 8.26-40).

For my purposes, I will analyze the story of the so-called bent woman in order to show how apologetics intrudes into otherwise very fine analyses of

and Acts: The Subversion of Physiognomy in Early Christianity (Grand Rapids, MI: Baker Academic, 2006), p. 17.

63. Aristotle, *Prior Analytics* 2.27.7-10 (Cooke and Tredennick, LCL): Τὸ δὲ φυσιογνωμονεῖν δυνατόν ἐστιν εἴ τις δίδωσιν ἅμα μεταβάλλειν τὸ σῶμα καὶ τὴν ψυχὴν ὅσα φυσικά ἐστι παθήματα.

64. Hippocrates, *Epidemics* 2.6.1 as quoted in Parsons, *Body and Character in Luke and Acts*, p. 18.

65. Didymus the Blind, *Commentary on Zechariah* (trans. Robert C. Hill; The Fathers of the Church, 111; Washington, DC: Catholic University of America Press, 2006), p. 313.

66. See Evans, *Physiognomics in the Ancient World*, p. 6.

67. Parsons, *Body and Character in Luke and Acts*, pp. 14-15.

these stories. The story of the bent woman is found in Luke 13, and reads as follows:

> Now he was teaching in one of the synagogues on the sabbath. And there was a woman who had had a spirit of infirmity for eighteen years; she was bent over [συγκύπτουσα] and could not fully straighten herself. And when Jesus saw her, he called her and said to her, 'Woman, you are freed from your infirmity'. And he laid his hands upon her, and immediately she was made straight, and she praised God. But the ruler of the synagogue, indignant because Jesus had healed on the sabbath, said to the people, 'There are six days on which work ought to be done; come on those days and be healed, and not on the sabbath day'. Then the Lord answered him, 'You hypocrites! Does not each of you on the sabbath untie his ox or his ass from the manger, and lead it away to water it? And ought not this woman, a daughter of Abraham whom Satan bound for eighteen years, be loosed from this bond on the sabbath day?' As he said this, all his adversaries were put to shame; and all the people rejoiced at all the glorious things that were done by him (Lk. 13.10-17).

For Parsons, this narrative shows how the bent woman was part of an agenda of inclusivity principally because 'at the end of the story, when challenged by the ruler of the synagogue, Jesus declares that the woman is a "daughter of Abraham", and here we may find another clue to Luke's strategy of introducing physiognomic concerns in order to subvert them'.[68]

There are a number of problems with Parsons's arguments. First, the entire case for the integration of physiognomic concerns by Luke assumes that Luke is thinking of the specific physiognomic texts or physiognomic relationships that Parsons identifies. In particular, Parsons identifies 'the physiognomic tractates that address the phenomenon of being "bent" or "crooked"' as consisting of three quotations from two authors: (a) pseudo-Aristotle, author of *Physiognomics* (thirdrd century BCE) and (b) Polemo of Laodicea, author of *De Phsyiognomica* (second century CE).[69] In the case of pseudo-Aristotle, Parsons quotes two texts as follows:

> Those whose back is very large and strong are of strong character; witness the male. Those which have a narrow, weak back are feeble; witness the female.

> Those who have a large, fleshy and well-jointed back are strong in character; witness the male; those in whom it is weak, fleshless, and badly jointed are weak in character; witness the female. Those in whom the back is very bent with the shoulders driven into the chest are of evil disposition; this is appropriate, because the parts in front which should be visible disappear.[70]

---

68. Parsons, *Body and Character in Luke and Acts*, p. 87.
69. Parsons, *Body and Character in Luke and Acts*, pp. 85-86.
70. Parsons, *Body and Character in Luke and Acts*, p. 85.

From Polemo, Parsons chose this extract:

> If you see the back is broad, it is an indication of mighty and strong men, and it indicates great anger. If it is the opposite of that, it indicates weakness and the contrary of what the broad and strong back indicated.[71]

While it may be possible that the bent woman's community saw her the same way as is indicated in these physiognomic texts, the fact is that nothing in the text of Luke indicates this to be the case. As it is, the quotes from Pseudo-Aristotle seem to apply to all women ('witness the female'), and not just to women who are bent over. The quote from Polemo actually addresses 'a broad back' (dorsum latum), which is not quite the same as a bent back. Note that the Vulgate (Lk. 13.11) describes her as 'inclinata'.[72]

It is true that pseudo-Aristotle also says that '[t]hose in whom the back is very bent...are of evil disposition', but one could just as well quote Deut. 28.59 ('the LORD will bring on you and your offspring extraordinary afflictions, afflictions severe and lasting, and sicknesses grievous and lasting') to show that Luke or Jesus was thinking of the woman's sin as the cause of any problem. So why assume that Luke or Jesus is thinking of subverting Greco-Roman physiognomy when one could just as well conclude that Jesus is upholding Deuteronomistic relationships between sin and physical affliction? Again, Luke does not really specify what the evil or sinful character of the woman was in the view of any audience members, and Luke does not say that he is thinking of those particular physiognomic texts or ideas.

Second, Parsons does not explore more closely the Greek verb συγκύπτω, which takes the form of a feminine singular present participle in the nominative case (συγκύπτουσα).[73] The usual supposition that it relates to some sort of spinal or back pathology certainly is reasonable, but there are other possibilities that Parsons never addresses. As Annette Weissenrieder observes, the use of συγκύπτειν/ἀνακύπτειν by Soranus of Ephesus, author of a treatise on gynecology, 'points us toward a state of "being drawn

---

71. Parsons, *Body and Character in Luke and Acts*, p. 86. Parsons does not provide the original Latin text, which reads as follow in the edition of R. Foerster, *Scriptores Physiognomonici* (repr., Leipzig: Teubner, 1994 [1893]), I, p. 208: 'Ubi dorsum latum robustum vides, ide heroes fortissimos notat et vehementem iracundiam indicat. Cum vero contrarie comparatum est, debilitatem indicat ei quote latum robustam notat opposite.'

72. For a catalogue of deformities in the biblical texts, see Lynn Holden, *Forms of Deformity* (JSOTSup, 131; Sheffield: Sheffield Academic Press, 1991). Holden does not include this woman in her section on 'The Back and Shoulders' (*Forms of Deformity*, pp. 168-75).

73. On participles, see Margaret Sim, 'Underdeterminacy in Greek Participles: How Do we Assign Meaning?', *BT* 55.3 (2004), pp. 348-59.

into oneself" in the sense of paralysis'.[74] In Job 9.27 (LXX), συγκύπτω seems to be applied to one's countenance: 'If I say, "I will forget my complaint, I will put off my sad countenance [συγκύψας τῷ προσώπῳ], and be of good cheer".'[75] Accordingly, συγκύπτουσα may not have to do specifically with a spinal ailment or bent back, and so Parsons's physiognomical analysis may need to change accordingly.

Third, Parsons points to Jesus calling the woman a 'daughter of Abraham' to buttress the notion of some radical approach to inclusivity on the part of the Lukan Jesus, and yet Parsons fails to see that the woman was *already* included in her Jewish community because the narrative suggests that she was present *in the synagogue* when Jesus encountered her. Clearly, she was not ejected from her Jewish synagogue because of her infirmity.[76] The same applies to the man with the withered hand (Lk. 6.1-6) and to the demon-possessed man (Lk. 4.33-36) who are in the synagogue when Jesus encounters them. The bent woman's presence in the synagogue also makes it unlikely that her fellow Jews thought of the bent woman as 'evil', as removal of evil people was one of the directives of both Jewish and Christian authors (e.g., Deut. 13.5; 1 Cor. 5.9-13).

Overall, this is not a case of some radical inclusivism because the afflicted woman seems already included in her synagogue. At the same time, the afflicted woman serves as a prop in the Lukan effort to establish Jesus' authority to heal on the Sabbath, as is indicated by v. 16: 'And ought not this woman, a daughter of Abraham whom Satan bound for eighteen years, be loosed from this bond on the sabbath day?' Subverting physiognomy or advocating radical inclusivism has little to do with subverting the Sabbath here. On the contrary, we have a case where 'daughter of Abraham' can signal exclusivism, as Jesus' genealogical identification identifies her as a Jewish woman, and not just any woman from any other religious or ethnic community. After all, Jesus does not heal every afflicted woman, regardless of ethnicity, on the Sabbath out of the sheer joy of helping the disabled. That would be 'radical inclusivism'. Rather, Jesus arbitrarily chooses whom to heal on the basis of whether that disabled person suits his purposes.

74. Annette Weissenrieder, *Images of Illness in the Gospel of Luke* (Tübingen: Mohr Siebeck, 2003), p. 301. See also William Kirk Hobart, *The Medical Language of St. Luke* (London: Longmans, Green & Co., 1882), p. 21.

75. Clines (*Job 1–20*, p. 214) translates the corresponding Hebrew portion (אעזבה פני) as 'I will lay aside my sadness', and more literally as 'I will forsake my face' (Clines, *Job 1–20*, p. 219).

76. For similar observations, see Weissenrieder, *Images of Illness*, p. 327.

Summary

There is sufficient evidence to demonstrate that Jesus did consider disability and illness to be the result of sin (e.g., Mk 2.10-11; Jn 5.14). There is also sufficient evidence to demonstrate that Jesus considered disability and illness as opportunities to showcase his personal religious agenda (e.g., Lk. 6.21-22) rather than to empower the disabled in a normate society.[77] Jesus is generally working with the Deuteronomistic moral universe that equated illness with sin, and well-being with sinlessness. John 9.3 ('It was not that this man sinned, or his parents, but that the works of God might be made manifest in him') represents an exception that confirms the rule. In many cases where Jesus makes no moral judgments about the disabled, there is none recorded by his opponents either (e.g., the woman in Lk. 13.10-17).

Historically, the consequences of Jesus' perpetuation of the connection between sin and disability have been very negative. First, it made it permissible for Christians to marginalize and even persecute the disabled. This is the case, especially in sixteenth and seventeenth centuries, with those suffering mental illnesses that were sometimes interpreted as demon possession or reflective of the practice of witchcraft.[78] Second, the connection between sin and illness delayed the scientific study of illness because it was tantamount to contradicting the etiologies of disease that Jesus advocated. Otherwise, the disabled usually are valued to the extent that they will become Jesus' worshippers or showcase his messianic agenda. The fact that Jesus heals the disabled shows that he does not generally regard the optimal worshippers to be disabled people. He does not see the disabled as fully human because he needs to correct their deficiencies. Thus, the disabled are part of Jesus' imperialistic agenda to have the entire world under the dominion of the Kingdom of God with worshippers who have normative bodies and health.

---

77. The idea of empowering patients can be found in Mesopotamia, as is argued by Daniel Schwermer, 'Empowering the Patient: The Opening Section of the Ritual *Maqlû*', in *Pax Hethitica: Studies on the Hittites and their Neighbours in Honour of Itamar Singer* (ed. Yoram Cohen, Amir Gilan and Jared L. Miller; Wiesbaden: Harrasowitz, 2010), pp. 312-39.

78. See H.C. Erik Midelfort, *A History of Madness in Sixteenth-Century Germany* (Stanford, CA: Stanford University Press, 1999), especially p. 227; idem, *Witchcraft, Madness, Society, and Religion in Early Modern Germany: A Ship of Fools* (Aldershot: Ashgate, 2013). Otherwise, Midelfort (*A History of Madness*, p. 19) urges caution in attributing all madness to demonological causes in the sixteenth century.

Chapter 11

THE MAGICALLY ANTI-MEDICAL JESUS

Medical ethics addresses subjects ranging from the morality of life support systems for those who are brain dead to the propriety of faith healing.[1] The ethics of faith healing are important because there are Christians who insist that faith is sufficient to cure an illness. This view can become very problematic, especially when children die because their parents withhold medical treatment for religious reasons. In 1998, the prestigious medical journal, *Pediatrics*, counted 172 faith-related medical fatalities over a twenty-year span.[2] More recently, Shawn Francis Peters has argued that such cases are more numerous than official statistics may indicate.[3] Because of the potential for harm, any practices that may be labeled as magical, religious or non-scientific are generally regarded as improper or unethical by modern medicine. In fact, Christopher Bogosh goes so far as to say that modern medicine is 'radically anti-biblical' and adds, 'modern medicine has chosen to build its science on the pillars of naturalism, humanism, agnosticism, and evolution'.[4]

1. For general surveys of medical ethics, see Tom L. Beauchamp and James Childress, *Principles of Biomedical Ethics* (New York: Oxford University Press, 6th edn, 2008); Albert R. Jonsen, Mark Siegler and William J. Winslade, *Clinical Ethics: A Practical Approach to Ethical Decisions in Clinical Medicine* (New York: McGraw-Hill Medical, 7th edn, 2010). For religious perspectives, see Christopher Tollefsen, *Artificial Nutrition and Hydration: A New Catholic Debate* (Dordrecht: Springer, 2010); Robert Orr, *Medical Ethics and the Faith Factor: A Handbook for Clergy and Health Care Professionals* (Grand Rapids, MI: Eerdmans, 2009); John F. Kilner, Nigel M. de S. Cameron and David L. Schiedemeyer (eds.), *Bioethics and the Future of Medicine: A Christian Appraisal* (Grand Rapids, MI: Eerdmans, 1995).

2. Seth Asser and Rita Swan, 'Child Fatalities from Religion-Motivated Medical Neglect', *Pediatrics* 101 (1998), pp. 625-29. For the argument that emphasis on the positive health benefits of religion reflects a distorted commercialization of Christianity, see Joel James Shuman and Keith G. Meador, *Heal Thyself: Spirituality, Medicine, and the Distortion of Christianity* (New York: Oxford University Press, 2003).

3. Shawn Francis Peters, *When Prayer Fails: Faith Healing, Children, and the Law* (New York: Oxford University Press, 2008).

4. Christopher W. Bogosh, *Compassionate Jesus: Rethinking the Christian's Approach to Modern Medicine* (Grand Rapids, MI: Reformation Heritage Books, 2013),

Given that Jesus himself emphasized the role of faith in healing in at least some narratives, faith healing poses a challenge for New Testament ethicists who believe that Jesus' life and teachings are a model for today. As Chistopher S. Mann notes concerning the rising critical scholarship of the nineteenth century: 'Even if the assumed closed system of the universe here and there admitted of some puzzling variations, there was widespread discomfort and embarrassment among many Christians with respect to miracles.'[5] Yet, a case for Jesus' portrayal as an exorcist or magician can be made even if we grant that different Gospels had different emphases or presentations of this aspect of Jesus' healings.[6]

Aside from regarding healing stories as simply being literary inventions or part of a unique ministry, New Testament ethicists have followed two complementary strategies that seek to reconcile Jesus' healings with modern medicine and medical ethics.[7] One is to reject the notion that Jesus practiced anything akin to magical or even religious healing.[8] The other strategy is to assert that Jesus did heal people with techniques that are compatible with modern scientific findings.[9] Thus, when commenting on Jesus'

pp. 4-5. Bogosh distinguishes 'modern medicine' from 'medical science', which he believes is legitimate and compatible with Christianity.

5. Christopher S. Mann, *Mark: A New Translation with Introduction and Commentary* (AB, 27; New York: Doubleday, 1986), p. 50.

6. For a study of how Matthew differed in its emphasis and presentation of healing miracles, see Dieter Trunk, *Der messianische Heiler: Eine redactions- und religionsgeschichtliche Studie zu den Exorzismen im Matthäusevangelium* (Freiburg: Herder, 1994). Although Trunk evidences interest in comparing biblical materials to those of non-Christian religions in the Greco-Roman period, he is still primarily focused on redaction and form criticism. See also Joseph A. Comber, 'The Verb *Therapeuō* in Matthew's Gospel', *JBL* 97 (1978), pp. 431-34; John Paul Heil, 'Significant Aspects of the Healing Miracles in Matthew', *CBQ* 41 (1979), pp. 274-87.

7. For the view that Jesus' exorcisms were real, but were also part of a unique ministry that has no direct application today, see Keith Warrington, *Jesus the Healer: Paradigm or Unique Phenomenon?* (Carlisle: Paternoster Press, 2000). Warrington (*Jesus the Healer*, p. 162) concludes: 'Rather than assuming a direct line between Jesus' practice and contemporary healing, the uniqueness of his ministry is to be recognized and affirmed.'

8. For a brief but useful sketch of the different positions on how scholarship up to the 1990s has viewed Jesus' healings, see Bernd Kollmann, *Jesus und die Christen als Wundertäter: Studien zu Magie, Medizin und Schmanismus in Antike und Christentum* (Göttingen: Vandenhoeck & Ruprecht, 1996), pp. 31-54. See also Graham H. Twelftree, *Jesus the Exorcist: A Contribution to the Study of the Historical Jesus* (Peabody, MA: Hendrickson, 1993), pp. 1-12. For older treatments, see Anton Fridrichsen, *The Problem of Miracle in Primitive Christianity* (trans. Roy Harrisville and John S. Hanson; Minneapolis: Ausburg, 1972); F.C. Conybeare, *Myth, Magic, and Morals: A Study of Christian Origins* (London: Watts, 1910).

9. The idea of Christianity as a 'medical religion' in modern scholarship reaches at

use of saliva to heal the blind man in Jn 9.1-7, John Wilkinson, who is a medical doctor and a missionary, tells readers:

> There are indications that in the ancient world, saliva was believed to possess healing power, but this is usually of a magical nature which is not appropriate in the gospel record... Tacitus records how the Roman emperor Vespasian was credited with the restoration of a man's sight at Alexandria in Egypt by moistening the eyes with his saliva on the instructions of the god Serapis, the Egyptian god of healing. However, this can hardly be compared with the healing activity of a humble Galilean peasant teacher.[10]

Thus, even when the ingredients and basic procedures are ostensibly the same or similar, what Jesus is doing cannot be called 'magic' while that of Vespasian and others should be so designated by Wilkinson's logic.[11] David Aune evinces a more ambivalent position in declaring that 'the wonders performed by Jesus are magical because they occur within a context of social deviance... However, it does not seem appropriate to regard Jesus as a magician.'[12] Aune prefers to see Jesus as a Messianic prophet who engages in magical activities.

More recently, Maurice Casey emphasized that 'Jesus was not a magician' and chastises Morton Smith for poor scholarship on this issue.[13] In a highly controversial book titled, *Jesus the Magician* (1978), Morton Smith argued that '"Jesus the magician" was the figure seen by most ancient opponents of Jesus; "Jesus the son of God" was the figure seen by that party of followers which eventually triumphed'.[14] Casey adds that Morton's 'accusation that Jesus was a magician appears to be due to malicious hostility

---

least as far back as Adolf Harnack, *Medicinisches aus der ältesten Kirchengeschichte* (Leipzig: Hinrichs, 1892). Note especially this statement by Harnack (*Medicinisches*, p. 132): 'Das Christentum ist medicinische Religion: das ist seine Stärke, in manchen Ausgestaltungen auch seine Schwäche.'

10. John Wilkinson, *The Bible and Healing: A Medical and Theological Commentary* (Grand Rapids, MI: Eerdmans, 1998), p. 117. For a study of Vespasian's healing, see Eric Eve, 'Spit in your Eye: The Blind Man of Bethsaida and the Blind Man of Alexandria', *NTS* 54 (2008), pp. 1-17. For study of another blind man healed by Jesus with saliva, see E.S. Johnson, 'Mark VIII.22-26: The Blind Man from Bethsaida', *NTS* 25 (1979), pp. 370-83. For Greek attitudes toward the supernatural, see E.R. Dodds, *The Greeks and the Irrational* (Berkeley, CA: University of California Press, 2004).

11. For a positive assessment of Wilkinson's view, see Frederick J. Gaiser, *Healing in the Bible: Theological Insight for Christian Ministry* (Grand Rapids, MI: Baker Academic, 2010), p. 154 n. 11.

12. David E. Aune, 'Magic in Early Christianity', *ANRW*, II, 23.2, pp. 1507-57 (1539).

13. Maurice Casey, *Jesus of Nazareth: An Independent Historian's Account of His Life and Teaching* (London and New York: T. & T. Clark, 2010), p. 275. For another denial that Jesus used magic, see Borgen, 'Miracles and Healing', pp. 91-106.

14. Morton Smith, *Jesus the Magician* (repr., New York: Barnes and Noble, 1993 [1978]), p. vii.

to Christianity. His misinterpretation of the primary sources is so gross as to be virtually fraudulent.'[15] Yet, an evaluation of Jesus as a magician need not depend on Smith's more controversial claims, and the idea that Jesus worked as an exorcist or magician has widespread scholarly support.[16]

Much of this debate involves the thorny issue of the definition of 'magic', especially as it is contrasted with science and religion. I will not enter into any detailed discussion here on the definition of magic. For the moment, I still value the utility in separating how ancient people defined magic and how we, as bearers of a scientific method, see religion and magic. I will define *magic as any practice that uses supernatural forces and/or beings in order to effect changes in the universe.*[17] Perhaps one may view religion and magic as analogous to theory and practice. Religion refers to an entire set of ideas that center on the human relationship with transcendent forces and beings. Magic refers to all acts by which those religious ideas are effected in the world.[18]

15. Casey, *Jesus of Nazareth*, p. 278.

16. So, for example, Franz Annen (*Heil für die Heiden: Zur Bedeutung und Geschichte der Tradition von besessenen Gerasene (Mk 5, 1-20 parr.)* [Frankfurt: Josef Knecht, 1976], p. 199) declares: 'Jesus hat sicher als Exorzist gewirkt, mit grosser Wahrscheinlichkeit auch ausserhalb des jüdischen Gebietes und an Heiden.' Twelftree (*Jesus the Exorcist*, p. 225) states: 'we are able unhesitatingly to support the view that Jesus was an exorcist'. Though Twelftree prefers the term 'exorcist' he grants that Jesus was using what can be otherwise called 'magical' procedures, as when he remarks '[t]he short authoritative commands of Jesus to demons in the Gospel narratives are formulas of magical adjuration' (*Jesus the Exorcist*, p. 153). On the other hand Xabier Pikaza Ibarrondo ('Exorcismo, poder y evangelio: Transfondo histórico y ecclesial de Mc 9, 38-40', *EstBib* 57 [1999], pp. 539-64 [563]) emphasizes that 'exorcism is not magic' ('el exorcismo no es magia'); my translation.

17. For general discussions of the issues surrounding magic, including the history of its definitions, see M. Labahn and B.J. Lietaert Peterbolte (eds.), *A Kind of Magic: Understanding Magic in the New Testament and its Religious Environment* (Library of New Testament Studies, 306; London: T. & T. Clark, 2007); Sulochana R. Asirvatham, Corinne Ondine Pache and John Watrous (eds.), *Between Magic and Religion: Interdisciplinary Studies in Ancient Mediterranean Religion and Society* (Lanham, MD: Rowman & Littlefield, 2001); Fritz Graf, *Magic in the Ancient World* (trans. Franklin Philip; Cambridge, MA: Harvard University Press, 1997); Jacob Neusner, Ernest S. Frerichs and Paul Virgil McCracken Flesher (eds.), *Religion, Science, and Magic: In Concert and in Conflict* (New York: Oxford University Press, 1989); Howard Clark Kee, *Medicine, Miracle and Magic in New Testament Times* (Cambridge: Cambridge University Press, 1988); Aune, 'Magic in Early Christianity', pp. 1507-57; John M. Hull, *Hellenistic Magic and the Synoptic Tradition* (London: SCM Press, 1974).

18. Compare Aune ('Magic in Early Christianity', p. 1516): 'Magic is a phenomenon which exists only within the matrix of particular religious traditions; magic is not religion in the sense that the species is not a genus.' See also Georg Luck, *Arcana Mundi: Magic and the Occult in the Greek and Roman Worlds* (Baltimore, MD: The Johns Hopkins University Press, 1985), pp. 3-60; Harold Remus, *Pagan-Christian over Miracle in the Second Century* (Cambridge, MA: Philadelphia Patristic Foundation, 1983).

Thus, all therapeutic rituals are part of the magical aspect of a religion. What Hebrew and Christian prophets did when they effected healings is no less magical than what other Near Eastern healers were doing. Indeed, some of the procedures of Jesus reach back to ancient Mesopotamia.[19] Early Christianity's distinction from non-Christian religions did not reside in its emphasis on miracle over magic. Rather, Christianity evinces a simplification of its therapeutic ritual procedures. Simple utterances, prayers, and one or two adjuncts (e.g., oil, laying of hands) were the most complex rituals that we usually see in New Testament healings.[20]

Otherwise, I agree with Susan Garrett, who argues that the definition of 'magic' is really culture bound.[21] Accordingly, John D. Crossan says that 'religion is official and approved magic; magic is unofficial and unapproved religion'.[22] Aune remarks: 'magic is defined as that form of religious deviance whereby an individual or social goals are sought by means alternate to those normally sanctioned by the dominant religious institution'.[23] Michael Bailey, an historian specializing in European witchcraft, argues that it is more important to explore 'whether a society or some significant segment within it—usually but not necessarily intellectually or judicially powerful elites bent on condemning—would have considered a given set of beliefs or practices to be magical or superstitious'.[24]

The resistance to viewing Jesus as a magician has deeper historical roots than simply a perceived opposition to modern science. Magic has borne a bad name in Western culture and so Jesus cannot be viewed as practicing what may be called magic when others perform or use similar rituals and procedures. Most philological research agrees that 'magic' ultimately derives from Persian culture, with Herodotus (ca. 484–425 BCE), the Greek historian, being one of the first to use that term in Greek. Herodotus applied it to a very select and elite group of Persian religious personnel: 'no sacrifice can be offered without a Magian'.[25]

---

19. For the magical aspects of Mesopotamian healing, see Cynthia Jean, *Le Magie Neó-assyrienne en Contexte: recherches sure le métier d'exorciste et le concept d'ašipūtu* (Helsinki: Neoassyrian Text Corpus Project, 2006).

20. See Avalos, *Health Care and the Rise of Christianity*; Aune, 'Magic in Early Christianity', p. 1531.

21. Susan R. Garrett, *The Demise of the Devil: Magic and the Demonic in Luke's Gospel* (Minneapolis: Fortress Press, 1989), pp. 4-5.

22. Crossan, *The Historical Jesus*, p. 305.

23. Aune, 'Magic in Early Christianity', p. 1515.

24. Michael D. Bailey, *Magic and Superstition in Europe: A Concise History from Antiquity to the Present* (Lanham, MD: Rowman & Littlefield, 2007), p. 5.

25. Herodotus 1.32 (Godley, LCL): 'ἄνευ γὰρ δὴ Μάγου οὔ σφι νόμος ἐστὶ θυσίας ποιέεσθαι'.

After Herodotus, 'magic' slowly expanded its meaning. According to Bailey, 'the first appearance of a truly generalized concept of "magic" in Roman usage' is found toward the end of the [first] century BCE (e.g., Virgil's *Eclogues*).[26] During the Julio-Claudian dynasties, Roman culture became increasingly hostile toward magic, which was viewed as harmful and increasingly distinguished from legitimate religious practices.[27] However, one already finds an analogous distinction between magical and naturalistic poisoning in Plato:

> A division in our treatment of poisoning cases is required by the fact that, following the nature of mankind, they are of two different types. The type that we have now expressly mentioned is that in which injury is done to bodies by bodies according to nature's laws. Distinct from this is the type which, by means of sorceries [μαγγανείαις] and incantations and spells (as they are called), not only convinces those who attempt to cause injury that they really can do so, but convinces also their victims that they are certainly being injured by those who possess the power of bewitchment.[28]

Plato endorsed the death penalty for those who used these sorts of procedures to cause harm. Likwise, a biblical law states: 'You shall not permit a sorceress to live' (Exod. 22.18).

When one detects a distinction between the 'magical' procedures of non-Hebrews and Hebrews, the distinction is one of the degree of power and not necessarily the presence or absence of power in causing a particular effect. For example, note the distinction in Moses's contest with Pharaoh's magicians:

> When Pharaoh says to you, 'Prove yourselves by working a miracle', then you shall say to Aaron, 'Take your rod and cast it down before Pharaoh, that it may become a serpent'. So Moses and Aaron went to Pharaoh and did as the LORD commanded; Aaron cast down his rod before Pharaoh and his servants, and it became a serpent. Then Pharaoh summoned the wise men and the sorcerers; and they also, the magicians of Egypt, did the same by their secret arts. For every man cast down his rod, and they became serpents. But Aaron's rod swallowed up their rods (Exod. 7.9-12).

So, what may be called 'magic' is not as powerful as what Moses and Aaron are able to do, but the biblical author does not deny the Egyptian ability to turn a rod into a serpent. The Egyptian gods are presumed to have power, but not to be as powerful as Yahweh (Exod. 15.11).

In early Christian history, the negative Roman (and biblical) views of 'magicians' persists, and there also began the pervasive use of the Greek

---

26. Bailey, *Magic and Superstition*, p. 19.

27. For the change in attitudes in the Julio-Claudian period, see Graf, *Magic in the Ancient World*, p. 56.

28. Plato, *Laws* 11.933a (Bury, LCL).

and Latin words for 'magic/magician' that are precisely cognate with our English words. Already in Acts 8.9-24, one sees a negative view of a man named Simon who practiced magic (v. 9, μαγεύων) in a story that contrasts his power with those of the apostles. Later, Origen devoted some of his prodigious energy to refuting Celsus, an anti-Christian writer who charged that Jesus was a magician.[29] Origen remarked:

> Indeed Scripture also makes clear that demons exist, but it opposes their being worshipped and prayed to. Rightly then it forbids the use of magic [*magica*] too, since the ministers of magic [*magorum ministri*] are renegade angels and evil spirits and unclean demons; for none of the holy spirits obey a magician. A magician [*magus*] cannot invoke Michael, Raphael, or Gabriel; how much more can a magician not invoke the Almighty God or his Son Jesus Christ our Lord or his Holy Spirit.[30]

For Origen, the efficacy of the procedure is not really where the distinction lies. Origen's distinction ultimately centers on which entities are responsible for any efficacy of the procedure. Magicians operate by the agency of demonic powers, while Christians use God, Jesus, and his angels.[31] From the early Christian viewpoint, generally magic referred to practices and supposed miracles that relied on non-Christian deities, real or illusory. From the non-Christian viewpoint, the healing acts of Christians were performed by trickery or by some demon, as was argued in the Beelzebul episode (Mk 3.22).

29. See, for example, Origen, *Against Celsus* 2.48 (ANF, IV, p. 449): 'Celsus moreover, unable to resist the miracles which Jesus is recorded to have performed, has already on several occasions spoken of them slanderously as works of sorcery'; PG 11.869: 'Πολλάκις δ' ὁ Κέλσος ἤδη μὴ δυνάμενος ἀντιβλέπειν αἷς ἀναγέγραπται πεποιηκέναι δυνάμεσιν ὁ Ἰησοῦς διαβάλλει αὐτὰς ὡς γοητείας'. *Against Celsus* 2.51 (ANF IV, p. 451/PG 11.877) describes Celsus as accusing Jesus of both 'μαγείαν καὶ γοητείαν'. On the γόης see Graf, *Magic in the Ancient World*, pp. 24-28. For an older, but still useful, discussion, see P. Samain, 'L'Accusation de magie contre le Christ dans les Evangelies', *ETL* 15 (1938), pp. 449-90.

30. Origen, *Homilies on Numbers* 13.5. I follow the edition of Origen, *Homilies on Numbers* (ed. Christopher A. Hall, trans. Thomas P. Scheck; Downers Grove, IL: InterVarsity Press, 2009), p. 76. For the Latin text, I depend on PG 12.672: 'Nam et daemones Scriptura esse designat, sed coli cos et exorari vetat. Recte ergo etiam magica uti prohibet, quia magorum ministri angeli sunt refugae, et spiritus maligni, et daemonia immunda. Nullus enim sanctorum spirituum obtemperat mago. Non potest invocare magus Michaelem, non potest invocare Raphaelem, neque Gabrielem; muto magis magus invocare non potest omnipotentem Deum, nec Filium ejus Dominum nostrum Jesum Christum, nec sanctum Spiritum ejus.'

31. Origen, *Against Celsus* 2.50 (ANF IV, p. 451/PG 11.876): 'For the power of the Egyptian magicians was not similar to the divinely bestowed grace of Moses, but the issue clearly showed that the acts of the former were the effect of magic [μαγγανείας], while those of Moses were wrought by divine power.'

Hostility towards magico-medical approaches to healing could be so intense that some Church fathers advised Christians to prefer death over using magical therapy even if it does work. One example is Chrysostom (ca. 347–407), who admits that magical therapy can work: 'If any demon-fearing pagan has medical knowledge, will he also find it easy to win you over to worship the pagan gods? They, too, have often cured many diseases and brought the sick back to health.'[32] Later, he advises Christians more specifically to forego magical therapy for fever even if it results in death: 'It is better to die the way that I am than to betray my faith and the godly life.'[33]

This entire distinction between a legitimate religious practice and magic was reproduced in the late nineteenth and early twentieth centuries in a then nascent field now known as anthropology.[34] In particular, Sir James George Frazer's *Golden Bough*, a massive compendium of folklore from around the world, sought to distinguish magic, religion and science in a way that privileged Christianity and modern science.[35] The difference between religion and magic was that the former entailed submission to supernatural powers, while the latter sought to use those powers for personal or practical gain in some way. For Frazer, humanity progressed from magic to religion, and science formed the ultimate stage of human thinking.[36] A variant of Frazer's evolutionary theory was developed by Edward Burnett Tylor (1832–1917), who saw the development as progressing from animism to polytheism, and finally to monotheism.[37] Yet, the whole debate in modern

32. Chrysostom, *Discourses Against Judaizing Christians* 1.7.7. I follow the translation of Saint John Chrysostom, *Discourses Against Judaizing Christians* (trans. Paul W. Harkins; Washington, DC: Catholic University of America, 1979), p. 29.

33. Chrysostom, *Discourses* 8.7.5 (p. 231).

34. The literature on this debate is enormous, and so I will only refer to some selected treatments. Pamela A. Moro and James E. Myers (eds.), *Magic, Witchcraft, and Religion: A Reader in the Anthropology of Religion* (New York: McGraw-Hill, 2010); Christopher I. Lehrich, *The Occult Mind: Magic in Theory and Practice* (Ithaca, NY: Cornell University Press, 2009); James McClenon, *Wondrous Healing: Shamanism, Human Evolution, and the Origin of Religion* (DeKalb, IL: Northern Illinois University Press, 2002).

35. For an edition, see Sir James George Frazer, *The Golden Bough: A Study of Magic and Religion* (12 vols.; London: Macmillan, 3rd edn, 1913–1920).

36. For discussions of the debate in anthropology, see Graf, *Magic in the Ancient World*, pp. 12-19. For Frazer's life and work, see also Robert Ackerman, *J.G. Frazer: His Life and Work* (Cambridge: Cambridge University Press, 1991); idem, *The Myth and Ritual School: J.G. Frazer and the Cambridge Ritualists* (New York: Routledge, 2002). For the view that the religion–magical dichotomy in anthropological debates can be traced back to Protestant–Catholic polemics, see Keith Thomas, *Religion and the Decline of Magic* (New York: Charles Scribner's Sons, 1971), especially pp. 51-77 and 540 n. 1.

37. See Edward B. Tylor, *Primitive Culture: Researches into the Development of*

anthropology about the difference between magic and religion was a reprise of ancient debates, and one clearly detects an effort to place Christianity on a superior footing.

Miracles, not Magic?

Howard Clark Kee has argued that Christianity's distinction in healing was its emphasis on miracle over magic and science.[38] I have already argued elsewhere that the distinctive aspects of Christianity rest on a combination of features in its health care system relative to other non-Christian traditions, with the magical vs. miracle distinction being quite minimal.[39] In order to understand why Kee's typology is not the key to Christianity's distinctiveness in health care, let us begin with his definitions of medicine, miracle and magic:

> Medicine is a method of diagnosis of human ailments and prescription for them based on a combination of theory about and observation of the body, its functions and malfunctions.

> Miracle embodies the claim that healing can be accomplished through appeal to, and subsequent action by the gods, either directly or through a chosen intermediary agent.

> Magic is a technique, through word or act, by which a desired end is achieved, whether that end lies in the solution to the seeker's problem or in damage to the enemy who has caused the problem.[40]

Mythology, Philosophy, Religion, Art, and Custom (2 vols.; London: John Murray, 1871). For a recent discussion of Tylor, see Ivan Strenski, *Thinking about Religion: An Historical Introduction to Theories of Religion* (Malden, MA: Blackwell, 2006), pp. 91-116. For a famous example of a similar evolutionary scheme in biblical studies, see William F. Albright, *From the Stone Age to Christianity: Monotheism and Historical Progress* (Garden City, NY: Doubleday, 1957). For a recent critique of this unilineal view, see Fiona Bowie, *The Anthropology of Religion* (Oxford: Blackwell, 2000), pp. 14-16. See also Y. Tzvi Langerman (ed.), *Monotheism and Ethics: Historical and Contemporary Intersections among Judaism, Christianity and Islam* (Studies on the Children of Abraham, 2; Leiden and Boston: Brill, 2012). For how assimilation of foreign cults was negotiated and provided stability for the Roman empire, see Eric M. Orlin, *Foreign Cults in Rome: Creating a Roman Empire* (New York: Oxford University Press, 2010). The idea of a secular vacuum created by Caesar Augustus and subsequently filled by foreign cults has been discussed by Hans D. Betz, 'New Testament and Roman Religions', *JR* 90.3 (2010), pp. 377-81.

38. For Kee's basic exposition on these issues, see Kee, *Medicine, Miracle and Magic*; *Miracle in the Early Christian World: A Study in Sociohistorical Method* (New Haven, CT: Yale University Press, 1983). For previous critiques of Kee's distinctions, see Crossan, *The Historical Jesus*, p. 306.

39. Avalos, *Health Care and the Rise of Christianity*, pp. 85-87.

40. Kee, *Medicine, Miracle and Magic*, p. 3.

Kee's distinction between miracle and magic is misguided and unsuccessful in explaining the distinctiveness of Christian health care.

First, some of Kee's defining features of magic can be found in Christianity. For example, there is no reason why Christian prayer cannot be seen as a 'technique, through word or act by which a desired end is achieved'. Praying is a technique, insofar as it involves a set of acts that are supposed to be undertaken in a proper manner for them to work (cf. Mt. 6.5-15//Lk. 11.2-4). Prayer involves uttering words. Prayer centers on the utterance of words to achieve ends.

If we apply Kee's definition, prayers for healing may also involve 'damage to the enemy who has caused the problem'. Thus, the words uttered by Jesus in the case of demon possession can be seen as intending to damage the demons. In Mk 5.7 the demons ask Jesus not to torment them, indicating a fear of damage. In the Beelzebul episode (Mk 3.20-30), Jesus is accused of casting out demons by using the power of Beelzebul, the prince of demons. Jesus' counter argument is that Beelzebul would not be a party to an act that damages his dominion by dividing it. In short, the casting out of Satan is implied to be an act that is damaging to his power.

Nor will it do much good to argue that magic centers on coercing a supernatural being to do one's will. Prayer can also be seen as an attempt to persuade and coerce the deity to do one's will. The idea that the Christian god can be coerced or persuaded through the utterance of words (e.g., prayer) is encapsulated by Jesus himself:

> So I say to you, Ask, and it will be given you; search, and you will find; knock, and the door will be opened for you. For everyone who asks receives, and everyone who searches finds, and for everyone who knocks, the door will be opened. Is there anyone among you who, if your child asks for a fish, will give a snake instead of a fish? Or if the child asks for an egg, will give a scorpion? If you then, who are evil, know how to give good gifts to your children, how much more will the heavenly Father give the Holy Spirit to those who ask him! Now he was casting out a demon that was mute; when the demon had gone out, the one who had been mute spoke, and the crowds were amazed. But some of them said, 'He casts out demons by Beelzebul, the ruler of the demons' (Lk. 11.9-15; NRSV).

Note that the discourse about the power of prayer is linked to an exorcism. In the discourse, Jesus asserts that the reason that a believer may expect his prayer to be answered is that God is analogous to a parent, who acts out of love for his children. That is to say, requests by God's children are expected to be fulfilled because the parent is constrained and susceptible to fulfilling requests out of sheer love. In sum, prayer can be seen as coercing the Christian deity to act on behalf of believers just as love coerces parents into fulfilling children's wishes.

Kee also claims that miracles are acts that focus on 'the divine will at work in human experience, concerned for human destiny and cosmic purpose'.[41] Of course, such a definition assumes that the absence of explicit references to cosmic purposes in non-Christian healing incantations means that none were assumed by the 'magician'. For example, Kee assumes that just because the magical papyri were not explicit about larger cosmic purposes, then none must have been in the minds of the magicians. But even Kee recognizes that procedures appearing to be completely medical may also be attributed to divine efficacy. As Kee himself remarks concerning the *Iamata* (miracle inscriptions) of Asclepius: '[T]he *Iamata* of Hellenistic times are striking: although the god is given ultimate credit for the cure, the therapy seems to have been largely self-administered.'[42]

Indeed, there is a long history of separating incantations and other ritual procedures from commentaries on larger cosmic purposes. Even as early as the time of Gula, the goddess of healing in the Near East attested from at least the early second millennium BCE, we have the following statement: 'May the sages apply the bandages! You (Gula) have brought about health and healing.'[43] If one looks at many healing incantations associated with Gula, one can erroneously conclude that the power of the healer resided solely in his manipulation of impersonal forces and technical skill in recitation. Yet, this text recognizes that all medical procedures are in fact directed by the will of the deity. This also may be the case with some healing stories in the Gospels that don't always elaborate further on the supernatural origin of an illness.[44] In sum, the lack of any explicit attribution of any healing efficacy to divine assistance does not mean that none was supposed.

---

41. Kee, *Medicine, Miracle and Magic*, p. 124.

42. Kee, *Miracle in the Early Christian World*, p. 89.

43. *AMT* 9.1.2.26-28: 'liddi Gula tē balāṭi enqūti ṣimdēti liqerribu atti taškuni balaṭ bulṭi'. The transcription and translation follows that of Benno Landsberger, 'Corrections to the Article: "An Old Babylonian Charm against Merḫu"', *JNES* 17 (1958), pp. 56-58 (57).

44. For example, Mk 1.30 speaks of Peter's mother-in-law having a fever. No explicit supernatural is posited, though fever certainly is believed to be of supernatural and demonic origin in other texts. See, for example, 'an amulet against fever' (קמיע לאשתה) from the late fourth to early fifth centuries CE published in C.T. McCollough and B. Glazier-McDonald, 'An Aramaic Bronze Amulet from Sepphoris', *Atiqot* 28 (1996), pp. 161-65 (162). See also Roy Kotansky, 'Two Amulets in the Getty Museum: A Gold Amulet for Aurelia's Epilepsy, an Inscribed Magical-Stone for Fever, "Chills", and a Headache', *J. Paul Getty Museum Journal* 8 (1980), pp. 181-87; David Lincicum, 'Greek Deuteronomy's "Fever" and "Chills" and their Magical Afterlife', *VT* 58 (2008), pp. 544-49.

The Bad Jesus

The Naturalistic Jesus

Given this background, it is no surprise to encounter biblical scholarship
that cannot seem to bear a portrayal of Jesus as engaging in magic. Instead,
Jesus is portrayed as using naturalistic medicine that would render him
more compatible with what is practiced today. One such example is offered
by Gary B. Ferngren in his *Medicine and Health Care in Early Christianity*.[45] Ferngren, a professor of history at Oregon State University, presents
this thesis: 'One might infer from reading the Gospels that religious healing
was normative among Christians in the New Testament... I shall try to correct this misapprehension.'[46]

Ferngren discusses how Christianity adopted mainstream Greco-Roman
ideas about the causes and cures for illnesses, but he emphasizes that demon-
ology played only a very marginal role in early Christian explanations for
illness.[47] Instead, early Christians seem to have accepted the natural explanations for illness found in the Greco-Roman world (e.g., imbalances of
bodily fluids). Ferngren's modern ethical concerns are apparent when he
remarks:

> It is equally mistaken to assert that early Christians encouraged the sick to
> seek miraculous healing for their diseases, and conversely that Christians
> always urged them to seek the aid of physicians. In fact, one finds medicine

45. Gary B. Ferngren, *Medicine and Health Care in Early Christianity* (Baltimore, MD:
The Johns Hopkins University Press, 2009). For other similar approaches, see Margaret
Lloyd Davies and T.A. Lloyd Davies, *The Bible: Medicine and Myth* (Cambridge: Silent
Books, 2nd edn, 1991). Other studies of Jesus' healing activities include: Lidija Novakovic, *Messiah, the Healer of the Sick: A Study of Jesus as the Son of David in the Gospel
of Matthew* (WUNT, 2.170; Tübingen: Mohr Siebeck, 2003); W. Kahl, *New Testament
Miracle Stories in their Religious-Historical Setting: A Religionsgeschichtliche Comparison from a Structural Perspective* (FRLANT, 163; Göttingen: Vandenhoeck & Ruprecht,
1994). For a somewhat different angle, which sees Jesus as a fully historical person who is
unaware of any divine or supernatural powers, see Raymond A. Martin, *Studies in the Life
and Ministry of the Historical Jesus* (Lanham, MD: University Press of America, 1995).

46. Ferngren, *Medicine and Health Care*, p. 1.

47. For general surveys of medicine in Greece and Rome, see Vivian Nutton, *Ancient
Medicine* (London: Routledge, 2004); Ralph Jackson, *Doctors and Diseases in the
Roman Empire* (Norman, OK: University of Oklahoma Press, 1988); Helen King (ed.),
Health in Antiquity (London: Routledge, 2005); G.E.R. Lloyd, 'The Transformation of
Ancient Medicine', *Bulletin of the History of Medicine* 66 (1992), pp. 114-32; Wesley D.
Smith, 'Notes on Ancient Medical Historiography', *Bulletin of the History of Medicine*
63 (1989), pp. 73-109. For other areas of the Near East, see Markham J. Geller, *Ancient
Babylonian Medicine* (Chichester: Wiley-Blackwell, 2010); H.F.J. Hortmanshoff and M.
Stol (eds.), *Magic and Rationality in Ancient Near Eastern and Graeco-Roman Medi-
cine* (Leiden: E.J. Brill, 2004); Irene Huber, *Rituale der Seuchen- und Schadensabwehr
im Vorderen Orient und Griechenland: Formen kollektiver Krisenbewältigung in der
Antike* (Wiesbaden: Franz Steiner, 2005).

and religion spoken of not only in harmonious but even in a mutually supportive fashion in the writings of the church fathers.[48]

At once we detect the effort to show how early Christianity and science are
compatible. To achieve this compatibilist view of science and early Christianity, Ferngren must explain away a lot of biblical material.

Indeed, Ferngren goes far beyond the evidence in denying that religious/
supernaturalistic healing was normative in the New Testament. Method-
ologically, Ferngren conflates 'religious', 'supernatural' and 'demonological' causes to support his argument. He sometimes assumes that disproving
a demonological cause is tantamount to disproving a 'religious' explanation. When discussing the death of Lazarus (Jn 11.1-44), Ferngren deems
it sufficient to show that demonological/supernatural explanations are supposedly absent, and so we can infer attribution to 'natural processes'.[49] But
Jn 11.4 suggests that Lazarus's illness and death are intended to showcase
the Son of God, and so 'religious' explanations are not really absent.[50]

Moreover, Ferngren's denial of demonological causes is highly circular. For example, he argues that the New Testament generally distinguishes
symptoms of physical ailments from 'the symptoms that are said typically to
accompany demonic possession, such as erratic or self-destructive behavior
(as in Mk 5.1-15 and Mt. 8.28-29)'.[51] Since erratic/self-destructive behavior is 'typically' associated with demonic possession, then other illnesses
probably are not demonic even when demons are associated with them.
But Ferngren ignores the fact that demonic ailments could assume diverse
forms, and not just erratic or self-destructive behavior. For example, Jesus
was suspected of being possessed just for disagreeing with various points
of traditional Jewish theology (Jn 10.20-21). There is no hint that Jesus was
convulsing or acting erratically.

The circularity is clearly apparent when Ferngren tries to explain Lk.
13.10-17, which speaks in v. 11 about 'a woman with a spirit that had crip-
pled her for eighteen years' (NRSV; γυνὴ πνεῦμα ἔχουσα ἀσθενείας ἔτη
δεκαοκτώ). Jesus later (v. 16) describes her as someone, 'whom Satan
bound for eighteen years' (ἣν ἔδησεν ὁ Σατανᾶς ἰδοὺ δέκα καὶ ὀκτὼ

---

48. Ferngren, *Medicine and Health Care*, p. 147. For other treatments of healing and
health care in early church history, see Véronique Boudon-Millot and Bernard Pouderon (eds.), *Les Péres de L'Èglise face à la science médicale de leur temps* (Paris:
Beauchesne, 2005).

49. Ferngren, *Medicine and Health Care*, p. 60.

50. For the argument that Jesus' miracles are meant to show that his powers were at
least equal to those of pagan savior/divine figures, see Charles Hedrick, 'Miracles in
Mark: A Study of Markan Theology and its Implication for Modern Religious Thought',
PRSt 34.3 (2007), pp. 297-313.

51. Ferngren, *Medicine and Health Care*, p. 46.

ἔτη). But, for Ferngren, the references to 'a spirit' and to Satan are not evidence of a demonological explanation. Instead Ferngren argues that these references 'ascribe to disease and physical disability to Satan as the source of evil, suggesting that disease results from the material effects of sin on the human race'.[52] Ferngren offers no evidence for the claim that Luke sees disease in this manner, and he seems to be following views similar to those of Wilkinson and Howard.[53] Indeed, Jesus did not say here that humanity was bound by Satan, but rather that *this particular woman was bound*. In fact, what is 'typical' for Luke is to view women as possessed.[54]

The phrase 'spirit of X', where X refers to an illness (as in πνεῦμα... ἀσθενείας, 'a spirit of infirmity', in Lk. 13.11), is a demonological formula known from the Dead Sea Scrolls (e.g., שחלניא רוח, 'spirit of purulence' in the Genesis Apocryphon 20.26) and elsewhere in Second Temple Jewish literature.[55] The Greek term (δέω), translated 'bind', had a clear equivalent (אסר/'asar) in Aramaic exorcistic/healing texts from late antiquity.[56] Similarly, Greek magical works often use κατάδεσμος/καταδέω ('bond'/'bind')

52. Ferngren, *Medicine and Health Care*, p. 60.

53. Wilkinson, *The Bible and Healing*, p. 141, says: 'Jesus' reference to the bond of Satan does not mean that this woman was demon-possessed. What it does mean is that her condition is due to the activity of Satan as the primary cause of sin and disease.' J. Keir Howard (*Medicine, Miracle and Myth in the New Testament* [Eugene, OR: Resource Publications, 2010], p. 58) remarks that 'the additional phrase about being bound by Satan is again no more than a general statement designed to make the contrast with the bonds of animals that could be released on the Sabbath day to allow them to drink'.

54. See Wainwright, *Women Healing/Healing Women*; Todd Klutz, *The Exorcism Stories in Luke–Acts: A Sociostylistic Reading* (SNTSMS, 129; Cambridge: Cambridge University Press, 2004); see also Dewey, 'Jesus' Healings of Women', pp. 122-31.

55. Daniel Machiela (*The Dead Sea Genesis Apocryphon: A New Text and Translation with Introduction and Special Treatment of Columns 13-17* [Leiden and Boston: E.J. Brill, 2009], p. 76) translates this as 'spirit of foulness'. García Martínez (*The Dead Sea Scrolls Translated*, p. 234) translates this as 'spirit of purulent evils'; Klaus Beyer (*Die aramäische Texte vom Toten Meer* [Göttingen: Vandenhoeck & Ruprecht, 1984], p. 177), as 'die Geschwüre...Geist'. See also Joseph A. Fitzmyer, *The Genesis Apocryphon of Qumran Cave 1 (1Q20): A Commentary* (Biblica et Orientalia, 18/B; Rome: Pontifical Biblical Institute Press, 3rd edn, 2004); Émile Puech, '11QPsApᵃ: Un rituel d'exorcismes. Essai de reconstruction', *RevQ* 14 (1990), pp. 377-408; Paul-Eugène Dion, 'Raphaël l'Exorciste', *Bib* 57 (1976), pp. 399-413; Craig A. Evans, 'Jesus and Psalm 91 in Light of the Exorcism Scrolls', in Flint, Duhaim and Baek (eds.), *Celebrating the Dead Sea Scrolls*, pp. 541-55; Peter Busch, *Das Testament Salomos: Die älteste christliche Dämonlogie, kommentiert und in deutscher Erstübersetzung* (TU, 153; Berlin: W. de Gruyter, 2005); William H.C. Propp, 'Exorcising Demons', *BR* 20 (2004), pp. 14-21, 47.

56. See, for example, Joseph Naveh and Shaul Shaked, *Amulets and Magic Bowls: Aramaic Incantations of Late Antiquity* (Jerusalem: Magnes Press, 1998), p. 266; Markham J.

in their formulary.[57] While it may be true that the biblical author does not see this woman as 'possessed', it would not be true to say that there is no demonological activity associated with the woman's condition.[58]

Ferngren also denies that Jas 5.14-16 refers to a religious ritual for bodily healing. As he remarks, '[t]he passage in James...speaks of healing from sin rather than physical healing, and it was so interpreted by its earliest commentators'.[59] Part of his evidence is that '[t]he juxtaposition of *sosei* (v. 15) and *iathete* (v. 16) might argue for a figurative interpretation of the passage in light of the frequently found pairing of salvation with health in biblical literature'.[60] Yet, judging by John Wilkinson's counts, the Greek word, σῴζω (*sozo*), is precisely one associated with healing in at least thirteen instances in the Gospels.[61] Note especially the narrative where Jesus heals the sick at Genessareth in Mk 6.53-56. It is clear that these individuals are physically ill because v. 55 states that some were brought 'on their pallets' (ἐπὶ τοῖς κραβάττοις). At the end of the narrative (Mk 6.56) it is said that 'as many as touched it were made well' (καὶ ὅσοι ἂν ἥψαντο αὐτοῦ ἐσῴζοντο).[62]

Religiocentrism plagues Ferngren's discussion of the *imago Dei* concept as the main cause of Christian healing philanthropy. Ferngren frequently speaks of non-Christians (he prefers the word 'pagans') as nearly devoid of human compassion toward the sick. Thus, he tells us that '[t]he classical world had no religious or ethical impulse for individual charity'.[63] Authentic love toward the sick had to await Christianity. He dismisses as unrepresentative any evidence of Greco-Roman philanthropy (e.g., the Hippocratic Oath), and he generalizes certain Greco-Roman positions that may not represent the majority either (e.g., Stoic attitudes toward suffering). He does

Geller, 'Jesus' Theurgic Powers: Parallels in the Talmud and Incantation Bowls', *JJS* 28 (1977), pp. 141-55.

57. See Graf, *Magic in the Ancient World*, pp. 121-22. For the idea that some biblical passages were intentionally ambiguous about the demonic nature of an illness, see John Granger Cook, 'In Defense of Ambiguity: Is There a Hidden Demon in Mark 1.29-31?', *NTS* 43 (1997), pp. 184-208. See also Pierre Guillemette, 'Mc 1, 24 est-il une formule de defense magique?', *Science et Esprit* 30 (1978), pp. 81-96.

58. For the distinction between demonic possession and demonic origin of this illness, see John Christopher Thomas, *The Devil, Disease and Deliverance: Origins of Illness in New Testament Thought* (Sheffield: Sheffield Academic Press, 1998), p. 226.

59. Ferngren, *Medicine and Health Care*, p. 147. For a scholar who considers miracles to be both historical and symbolic, see A.D. Baum, 'Die Heilungswunder Jesu als Symbolhandlungen—Ein Versuch', *European Journal of Theology* 13 (2004), pp. 5-15.

60. Ferngren, *Medicine and Health Care*, p. 67.

61. Wilkinson, *The Bible and Healing*, pp. 77, 80.

62. See also Martin Albl, 'Are Any among you Sick?: The Health Care System in the Letter of James', *JBL* 121 (2002), pp. 123-43.

63. Ferngren, *Medicine and Health Care*, p. 98.

not address the fact that Aelianus (ca. 175–235 CE), the Roman rhetori-
cian, called Asclepius the most philanthropic of the gods (θεῶν φιλανθρω-
πότατε) even after the arrival of Jesus.[64]

Ferngren also argues that the theological concept of creation in the image
of God (*imago Dei*) generated a revolution in human philanthropy that
prompted Christian resistance to everything from euthanasia to abortion.[65]
According to Ferngren, the *imago Dei* ('image of God') concept motivated
Christians to engage in a systematic healing ministry that eventually led to
hospitals and other medical institutions. However, the *imago Dei* is a highly
inconsistent ethical anchor even in the Bible. Other factors soon could
create differences that prompted God to command the enslavement, torture
or killing of the infants of 'pagan' people who presumably also were made
in the *imago Dei* (Lev. 25.44; Deut. 7.1-7; 1 Sam. 15.1-3).[66] In short, Ferngren engages in Christian apologetics rather than in rigorous historical and
linguistic analysis when it comes to Jesus' use of concepts and procedures
that are called 'magic' if used by non-Christian healers.

Psychosomatic Ethics

Ferngren is actually part of a wider set of scholars who affirm that Jesus'
healings were more scientific or at least more scientifically explainable than
commonly assumed. Usually, these scholars view Jesus as a master of healing psychosomatic illnesses. Psychosomatic illnesses bear accepted scientific
validity.[67] That is to say, it is scientifically accepted that how one thinks or
responds emotionally can affect the body. Worrying, for example, can cause
stress that changes our physiology and body chemistry in deleterious ways.[68]

However, the specific types of illnesses classified as psychosomatic in
the Gospels are either poorly documented or the modern samples are not
really large enough to make any conclusions about Jesus' healings. Consider the woman with the hemorrhage in Mark 5:

---

64. Aelianus, *De natura animalium* 11.33. I follow the Greek text of Emma J. Edelstein and Ludwig Edelstein, *Asclepius: Collection and Interpretation of Testimonies*
(repr., Baltimore, MD: The Johns Hopkins University Press, 1998 [1945]), p. 220.

65. Ferngren, *Medicine and Health Care*, pp. 97-98.

66. See further, Avalos, *Slavery*, pp. 57-59; Annette Schellenberg, *Der Mensch, das
Bild Gottes? Zum Gedanken einer Sonderstellung des Menschen im Alten Testament und
in weiteren altorientalischen Quellen* (Zürich: Theologischer Verlag, 2011); for an older
treatment, see David J.A. Clines, 'The Image of God in Man', *TynBul* 19 (1968), pp.
53-103.

67. For a general survey, see James L. Levenson, *Essentials of Psychosomatic Medicine* (Arlington, VA: American Psychiatric Publishing, 2006).

68. See, for example, Gaofeng Wang *et al.*, 'Anxiety and Adverse Coronary Artery
Disease Outcomes in Chinese Patients', *Psychosomatic Medicine* 75 (2013), pp. 530-36.

And there was a woman who had had a flow of blood for twelve years, and who had suffered much under many physicians, and had spent all that she had, and was no better but rather grew worse.

She had heard the reports about Jesus, and came up behind him in the crowd and touched his garment. For she said, 'If I touch even his garments, I shall be made well'. And immediately the hemorrhage ceased; and she felt in her body that she was healed of her disease. And Jesus, perceiving in himself that power had gone forth from him, immediately turned about in the crowd, and said, 'Who touched my garments?' And his disciples said to him, 'You see the crowd pressing around you, and yet you say, "Who touched me?"' And he looked around to see who had done it. But the woman, knowing what had been done to her, came in fear and trembling and fell down before him, and told him the whole truth.

And he said to her, 'Daughter, your faith has made you well; go in peace, and be healed of your disease' (Mk 5.25-34//Mt. 9.20-26//Lk. 8.43-48).

J. Keir Howard, who is both a physician and an Anglican priest, assesses this woman with the hemorrhage as follows:

The causes of such bleeding are many, although more serious forms of pathology, such as tumors, may be reasonably excluded in view of the chronic nature of the condition. However, apart from various physical causes, severe and excessive bleeding may arise from psychological factors.[69]

Yet, the problems with this assessment rest not just on medical disputes, but also on correctly evaluating the biblical text and its related culture.[70] As it is, Howard's medical diagnosis is definitely disputed by other physicians. John Wilkinson, who is a physician and missionary, remarks that 'the most probable cause of her chronic uterine hemorrhage was the presence of fibroid tumors (leiomyomata) in the uterus which although benign in nature may cause chronic vaginal bleeding'.[71] All of this shows the questionable practice of trying to diagnose someone in antiquity. Even if the bleeding is psychosomatic, Howard offers no scientific documentation that excessive bleeding lasting years has ever suddenly stopped after touching a garment

69. Howard, *Medicine, Miracle and Myth*, p. 28. For a critique of scholarship that views female bleeding as cause for marginalizing women in Judaism, see Amy-Jill Levine, 'Discharging Responsibility: Matthean Jesus, Biblical Law, and Hemorrhaging Woman', in *Treasures New and Old: Recent Contributions to Matthean Studies* (ed. David R. Bauer and Mark Allan Powell; Atlanta, GA: Scholars Press, 1996), pp. 379-97.

70. For a more complex view of the role of allusions to the Hebrew Bible in the story of the hemorrhaging woman, see J. Duncan M. Derrett, 'Mark's Technique: The Hemorrhaging Woman and Jairus' Daughter', *Bib* 63 (1982), pp. 474-505. For a comprehensive literary study of Mk 5.21-43, see Oppel, *Heilsam erzählen-erzählend heilen*.

71. Wilkinson, *The Bible and Healing*, p. 110.

or any other item that a patient believes belongs to some powerful healer. There are no scientific experiments referenced to show that bleeding of this magnitude ever stops instantaneously through the means described in Mark.

Overall, Howard displays a pick-and-choose attitude toward what to interpret literally and what to interpret non-literally in the story. For example, to mitigate the lack of scientific documentation for the instantaneous cessation of bleeding, and apparently to heighten the plausible scientific explanation, Howard posits that '[a]lthough Mark has undoubtedly compressed the time scale with his favorite word, "immediately", it may be assumed that the woman certainly began to feel her health had improved from the moment she touched Jesus'.[72] So, Jesus did not really heal as miraculously and instantaneously as Mark seems to relate, but rather Mark was simply indicating that she 'began to feel her health had improved'.

On the other hand, Howard takes literally the twelve years that this woman has suffered from a hemorrhage. But Greco-Roman healing stories sometimes exaggerate the time that a person has suffered an illness to maximize the miraculous powers of the healing god. For example, among the dozens of healing testimonia posted in an inscription at the temple of Asclepius at Epidaurus, one finds a patient named 'Cleo, who was with child five years' ([Κλ]εω πένθ' ἔτη ἐκύησε).[73] This length of a pregnancy certainly is not scientifically documented anywhere as far as I can determine. It also would be absurd to attribute such a pregnancy to psychosomatic processes that are no better attested than bleeding for that length of time, especially as literary imagination and religious propaganda can suffice to explain it.

Summary

Modern New Testament scholarship still maintains a tension between a supernatural Jesus and a Jesus that is not acceptable to modern medical ethics in crucial aspects. A Jesus who routinely assumes supernatural etiologies and cures would be a bad Jesus by modern medical standards, and so many New Testament scholars have sought to harmonize Jesus with modern medicine. In addition, many New Testament scholars who reject the magical Jesus apparently are still following ancient Christian definitions of magic that view it as harmful or idolatrous. While the word 'magic' is not native to Hebrew or Greek, it was adopted by early Christians to speak of unapproved supernatural practices, whether these had efficacy or not (e.g., Acts 8.9-24). Modern scholars who reject the magical Jesus ultimately reflect a combination of Greco-Roman attitudes and biblical ones toward magic.

---

72. Howard, *Medicine, Miracle and Myth*, p. 29.
73. See Edelstein and Edelstein, *Asclepius*, pp. 221, 229.

In any case, the negative ethical implications of a Jesus who assumes that illnesses can be the result of demonic powers appear to be the main reason for trying to naturalize Jesus. Recall Wilkinson's rejection of applying the term 'magic' for Jesus' practices because it would not be 'appropriate in the gospel record'.[74] Imitating such a supernatural Jesus today would mean that modern Christians can justify relying only on prayer or fasting to expel demons they believe to be the cause of their illnesses. But using supernatural means to cure illness can have dire consequences for health care today, especially among children who cannot make decisions for themselves.

Paradoxically, this naturalization of Jesus seems to run counter to my otherwise general argument that New Testament scholarship persists in divinizing Jesus. But, in fact, it is part of a modern agenda in New Testament scholarship to privilege Jesus' ethical teachings even when disavowing his divine or supernatural aspects. Thus, Thomas Jefferson constructed a Bible that eliminated all the supernatural narratives about Jesus, but left the best ethical teachings intact. Jefferson thought that the purest form of Jesus' teachings involved ethics, not any theological or supernatural pronouncements.[75] So, while naturalization is the reverse of the divinization of Jesus, it still reflects a Christology that seeks to promote the superiority of Jesus' ethics.

74. Wilkinson, *The Bible and Healing*, p. 117.
75. See further, Charles B. Sanford, *The Religious Life of Thomas Jefferson* (Charlottesville, VA: University Press of Virginia, 1984); Gilbert Chinard, *The Literary Bible of Thomas Jefferson: His Commonplace Book of Philosophers and Poets* (New York: Greenwood Press, 1928); Edgar J. Goodspeed, 'Thomas Jefferson and the Bible', *HTR* 40 (1947), pp. 71-75.

Chapter 12

THE ECO-HOSTILE JESUS

Environmental ethics addresses the moral relationship between human beings and the natural world.[1] The existence of any moral relationship between human beings and the natural world is itself contested within enviornmental ethics because some philosophers believe that only human relationships can be the subject of ethics, and non-human entities deserve no 'moral considerability'.[2] An important theme is a critique of anthropocentrism, especially as manifested by the idea of extending rights to animals. In this view, nature, and animals in particular, do not need to serve human beings in order to be valued.[3] According to the well-known Gaia hypothesis, the entire planet could be viewed as a living organism that has inherent rights.[4]

Many ethicists place the modern academic origins of environmental ethics in the 1970s. J. Baird Callicott, a prominent environmental ethicist states: 'In 1973, with the publication of three seminal papers, environmental ethics made its formal debut on the staid and conservative stage of professional philosophy.'[5] The journal, *Environmental Ethics*, a principal vehicle

1. There are variants of this definition. For example, Gretel van Wieren, *Restored to Earth: Christianity, Environmental Ethics and Ecological Restoration* (Washington, DC: Georgetown University Press, 2013), p. 6, states that environmental ethics 'refers to a far-ranging set of issues and questions related to the moral aspects of the human relationship with the natural world'. See also Kathryn D. Blanchard and Kevin J. O'Brien, *An Introduction to Christian Environmentalism: Ecology, Virtue, and Ethics* (Waco, TX: Baylor University Press, 2014); Dieter Hessel and Mary Radford Ruether (eds.), *Christianity and Ecology: Seeking the Welfare of the Earth and Humans* (Cambridge, MA: Harvard University Press, 2000).

2. See Kenneth Goodpaster, 'On Being Morally Considerable', *Journal of Philosophy* 75 (1978), pp. 308-325.

3. For example, Tom Regan, *The Case for Animal Rights* (Berkeley, CA: University of California Press, 1983).

4. See James Lovelock, *Gaia: A New Look at Life on Earth* (New York: Oxford University Press, 2000). The notion that nature has 'intrinsic value' is a distinctive aspect of what Bron Taylor (*Dark Green Religion: Nature, Spirituality, and the Planetary Future* [Berkeley, CA: University of California Press, 2010], p. 10) calls 'Dark Green Religion'.

5. J. Baird Callicott, 'Introduction', in *Environmental Philosophy: From Animal*

for this field, was founded only in 1979. In general, the modern academic study of environmental ethics grew out of the perception that our society was ruining the environment with its rampant industrialization and use of chemicals to solve problems. Thus, Aldo Leopold's *Sand County Alma-nac* spoke of the need for a land ethic in 1949.[6] Rachael Carson's *Silent Spring* (1962) raised concerns about the effects of the pesticide, DDT, on our environment.[7]

The novelty of environmental ethics in standard treatments of New Testament ethics is manifested by the lack of any chapters or substantive discussion devoted to Jesus' view of the environment in the works of Bur-ridge, Hays, Longenecker, Matera, Schnackenburg, Verhey, and many other prominent New Testament ethicists.[8] These scholars do not have any related terms, such as 'environment(al)', 'ecology/ecological', or 'nature' in their indices, though sometimes one can find 'natural theology', which usually does not refer to environmental ethics. Even a survey of biblical ethics in the twenty-first century, where one would expect the most up-to-date dis-cussion of major ethical issues, has no chapters devoted to environmen-tal ethics, nor any mention of 'ecology', 'environmental ethics' or 'animal rights' in its index.[9]

Nevertheless, there are now significant projects devoted to biblical envi-ronmental ethics. The Earth Bible Project, led by Norman C. Habel and based in Adelaide, Australia, is one example of a sustained examination of biblical environmental ethics. The Earth Bible Project already produced *The Earth Bible* (2000–2002), a five-volume multi-authored series.[10] Currently

Rights to Radical Ecology (cd. Michael E. Zimmerman, J. Baird Callicott, George Ses-sions, Karen J. Warren and John Clark; Englewood Cliffs, NJ: Prentice–Hall, 1993), pp. 3-11 (3). Similarly, the noted animal rights advocate, Peter Singer (*In Defense of Ani-mals* [New York: Basil Blackwell, 1985], p. 1), calls animal liberation a 'product of the 1970s'.

6. Aldo Leopold, *A Sand County Almanac, and Sketches Here and There* (New York: Oxford University Press, 1949).

7. Rachel L. Carson, *Silent Spring* (Boston, MA: Houghton Mifflin, 1962).

8. Burridge, *Imitating Jesus*; Hays, *The Moral Vision*; Longenecker, *New Testament Social Ethics*; Matera, *New Testament Ethics*; Schnackenburg, *The Moral Teaching of the New Testament*; Verhey, *Remembering Jesus*.

9. Chan and Keenan (eds.), *Biblical Ethics in the Twenty-First Century*.

10. Norman C. Habel (ed.), *Readings from the Perspective of the Earth* (Earth Bible, 1; Sheffield: Sheffield Academic Press, 2000); Norman C. Habel and S. Wurst (eds.), *The Earth Story in Genesis* (Earth Bible, 2; Sheffield: Sheffield Academic Press, 2000); Norman C. Habel and S. Wurst (eds.), *The Earth Story in Wisdom Traditions* (Earth Bible, 3; Sheffield: Sheffield Academic Press, 2000); Norman C. Habel, *The Earth Story in Psalms and the Prophets* (Earth Bible, 4; Sheffield: Sheffield Academic Press, 2001); Norman C. Habel and Vicky Balabanski (eds.), *The Earth Story in the New Testament* (Earth Bible, 5; Sheffield: Sheffield Academic Press, 2002). See also Norman Habel,

in preparation is an Earth Bible Commentary that treats both the Hebrew Bible and the New Testament.[11] Following the tradition of red-letter Bibles, *The Green Bible* (2008), based on the New Revised Standard Version, highlights in green those passages that have ecological significance.[12] In the Society of Biblical Literature, there is an entire unit, Ecological Hermeneutics, devoted to the topic.

Although one can trace environmental concerns back to the Bible and early Church fathers, any examination of those biblical scholars who do substantive work in environmental ethics often cite 1967 as a crucial year.[13] That year, Lynn White, a Medieval historian with a graduate degree from Union Theological Seminary, published an essay titled 'The Historical Roots of our Ecologic Crisis' in *Science*, perhaps the most respected journal in the entire scientific world.[14] Most of biblical scholarship on ecology today is in some form a response to Lynn White. As David G. Horrell observes: 'White's essay remains probably the most cited contribution to eco-theological debate.'[15]

'Introducing Ecological Hermeneutics', *Lutheran Journal of Theology* 46 (2012), pp. 97-105.

11. The volumes already published include Norman C. Habel, *The Birth, the Curse and the Greening of Earth: An Ecological Reading of Genesis 1–11* (Earth Bible Commentary, 1; Sheffield: Sheffield Phoenix Press, 2011); Michael Trainor, *About Earth's Child: An Ecological Listening to the Gospel of Luke* (Earth Bible Commentary, 2; Sheffield: Sheffield Phoenix Press, 2012). For ecological concerns in other areas of the ancient Near East, see Hervé Reculeau, *Climate, Environment and Agriculture in Assyria in the 2nd Half of the 2nd Millennium BCE* (Studia Chaburensia, 2; Wiesbaden: Harrasowitz, 2011).

12. Michael Maudlin and Marlene Baer (eds.), *The Green Bible* (New York: Harper-Collins, 2008). See also Stephen W. Pattemore, 'How Green is your Bible? Ecology and the End of the World in Translation', *BT* 58 (2007), pp. 75-85.

13. For a basic survey of concerns about nature in Christian history, see Jame Schaeffer, *Theological Foundations of Environmental Ethics: Reconstructing Patristic and Medieval Concepts* (Washington, DC: Georgetown University Press, 2009). For a survey of more recent work, especially among evangelicals, see Douglas Moo, 'Nature in the New Creation: New Testament Eschatology and the Environment', *JETS* 49 (2006), pp. 449-88. For an example of a feminist approach, see Anne F. Elvey, *An Ecological Feminist Reading of the Gospel of Luke: A Gestational Paradigm* (Lewiston, NY: Edwin Mellen Press, 2005). An emphasis on climate change is offered by Carol S. Robb, *Wind, Sun, Soil, Spirit: Biblical Ethics and Climate Change* (Minneapolis: Fortress Press, 2010).

14. Lynn White, Jr, 'The Historical Roots of our Ecologic Crisis', *Science* 155 (1967), pp. 1203-1207. For a recent assessment of White's thesis, see Elspeth Whitney, 'The Lynn White Thesis: Reception and Legacy', *Environmental Ethics* 35 (2013), pp. 313-31.

15. David G. Horrell, 'Introduction', in *Ecological Hermeneutics: Biblical, Historical, and Theological Perspectives* (ed. David G. Horrell *et al.*; London: T. & T. Clark,

White argued that our modern ecological crisis had its origin in the biblical attitudes toward human dominance over nature voiced from Genesis 1 onward. More recently, Peter Singer, perhaps the most prominent animal rights philosopher, also pointed to Genesis 1 and remarked, '[h]ere is a myth to make humans feel their superiority and their power'.[16] For White, 'Christianity bears a huge burden of guilt' for its anthropocentrism and application of biblical principles.[17] On the other hand, White also saw Christianity as the solution, and he ended his essay by proposing that our society adopt '[Saint] Francis as a patron saint for ecologists'.[18]

It was the seeming attack on Christianity that prompted many biblical scholars to pay attention to ecological issues in the Bible, and this fact betrays the apologetic origins or undertones of much of the biblical scholarship on environmental issues. Not surprisingly, some New Testament ethicists proclaim Jesus as the paradigm of environmental ethics. Michael S. Northcott claimed, for example, that in the New Testament 'Jesus is portrayed as one who lives in supreme harmony with the natural order'.[19] Northcott provides no sustained or detailed exegesis of any passage containing Jesus' actions or teachings that pertain to nature. Despite a diversity of Christian viewpoints on environmental ethics, Van Wieren affirms that:

> [T]here are some points of agreement among Christian environmental ethicists. Most basically perhaps is the belief that individuals should be *against* the unjustified destruction of nature and *for* the care of God's earth. Further, and more substantially, is the generally agreed-upon view that Christian environmental ethics should promote the flourishing of all earth's creatures and communities, human and nonhuman together.[20]

The Earth Bible Project has developed a set of six eco-justice principles that bear repeating in full:

2010), pp. 1-12 (2). For a response to White by a Christian theologian, see Alister E. McGrath, *The Reenchantment of Nature: The Denial of Religion and the Ecological Crisis* (New York: Doubleday, 2002). See also Raymond Grizzle, Paul E. Rothrock and Christopher B. Barrett, 'Evangelicals and Environmentalism: Past, Present, and Future', *Trinity Journal* 19 (1998), pp. 3-27. For an attempt to integrate spiritual and ecological concerns in policymaking, see Sean Esbjörn-Hargens and Michael E. Zimmerman, *Integral Ecology: Uniting Multiple Perspectives in the Natural World* (Boston, MA: Integral Books, 2009).

16. Singer, *In Defense of Animals*, p. 2.

17. White, 'The Historical Roots of our Ecologic Crisis', p. 1206.

18. White, 'The Historical Roots of our Ecologic Crisis', p. 1207.

19. Michael S. Northcott, *The Environment and Christian Ethics* (Cambridge: Cambridge University Press, 1996), p. 224. A similar view is voiced by Matthew Sculy, *Dominion: The Power of Man, the Suffering of Animals, and the Call to Mercy* (New York: St. Martin's Griffin, 2002), which displays no familiarity with the scholarly exegetical literature of any texts he discusses (e.g., Mk. 5 on p. 95).

20. Van Wieren, *Restored to Earth*, p. 25. Van Wieren's italics.

The principle of intrinsic worth: the universe, Earth and all its components have intrinsic worth/value.

The principle of interconnectedness: Earth is a community of interconnected living things that are mutually dependent on each other for life and survival.

The principle of voice: Earth is a subject capable of raising its voice in celebration and against injustice.

The principle of purpose: the universe, Earth and all its components are part of a dynamic cosmic design within which each piece has a place in the overall goal of that design.

The principle of mutual custodianship: Earth is a balanced and diverse domain where responsible custodians can function as partners with, rather than rulers over, Earth to sustain its balance and a diverse Earth community.

The principle of resistance: Earth and its components not only suffer from human injustices but actively resist them in the struggle for justice.[21]

Most of the publications by the Earth Bible team, though critical of many facile assumptions of the Bible's eco-friendliness, ultimately do affirm that biblical materials are compatible with a modern eco-friendly approach to the Earth.

This chapter will examine the validity of Northcott's claim, and investigate whether Jesus would satisfy the standards that Van Wieren represents as the consensus of modern Christian environmental ethics. This chapter will also examine the compatibility of Jesus' ethics with the principles of eco-justice enunciated by the Earth Bible Project. I shall do so by looking more closely at how these environmental ethicists address specific texts that may be problematic for the claim that Jesus championed harmony with nature. In general, ethicists either ignore problematic biblical texts or seek to mitigate their negative implications.[22]

Mark 5: Animal Rights and Deviled Ham

Within the broader scope of environmental ethics is a movement that views animals as worthy moral subjects. The advocacy of animal rights seeks to challenge those who deny the rights of animals based on the latter's lack

21. These principles have been published in various versions, but I am quoting the version in Norman C. Habel and Peter Trudinger (eds.), *Exploring Ecological Hermeneutics* (Atlanta, GA: Society of Biblical Literature, 2008), p. 2. My emphasis.

22. An earlier critique of using the Bible in moral argumentation about environmental ethics is found in James A. Nash, 'The Bible vs. Biodiversity: The Case against Moral Argument from Scripture', *Journal for the Study of Religon, Nature and Culture* 3 (2009), pp. 213-37.

of, among other human features, rationality, language, a divine image, or a soul.[23]

Aristotle famously believed that animals are, by nature, servants of human beings because lower orders of life and class are meant to serve the upper levels.[24] Many Christians saw animals as created by God to serve human needs because of what is stated in Gen. 1.28: 'and have dominion over the fish of the sea and over the birds of the air and over every living thing that moves upon the earth'.[25]

Instead of focusing on rationality or other distinguishing human features, some major animal rights advocates affirm that animals and human beings share inherent rights. The American philosopher Tom Regan, for example, proposes that both human beings and animals are each 'the experiencing subject of a life, a conscious creature having an individual welfare that has importance to us whatever our usefulness to others'.[26] He goes on to argue that '[i]nherent value, then, belongs equally to those who are the experiencing subjects of a life.[27] This premise leads Regan to advocate the abolition of all hunting, whether for food or sport. Regan also would abolish the use of animals in commercial agriculture or in science (e.g., as experimental subjects). Gary Francione, a legal theorist, goes further: '[W]e have a moral obligation to stop using animals for food, biomedical experiments, entertainment, or clothing, or for any other uses that assume that animals are merely resources, and that we prohibit the ownership of animals.'[28]

---

23. For a summary of the features that anthropocentrists use to justify the use of animals, see Andrew Linzey, *Why Animal Suffering Matters: Philosophy, Theology and Practical Ethics* (New York: Oxford University Press, 2009), pp. 9-42.

24. Aristotle, *Politics*, 1.2.12 (Rackham, LCL): '[T]ame animals are superior in their nature to wild animals, yet for all the former it is advantageous to be ruled by man, since this gives them security.'

25. Within recent biblical scholarship, Gen. 1.28 has sparked a debate about whether the author intended 'dominion' or 'stewardship' of nature. See Richard Bauckham, *The Bible and Ecology: Rediscovering the Community of Creation* (Waco, TX: Baylor University Press, 2010), especially pp. 1-36; Norman C. Habel, 'Geophany: The Earth Story in Genesis 1', in Habel and Wurst (eds.), *The Earth Story in Genesis*, pp. 34-48; idem, 'Playing with God or Playing Earth?' An Ecological Reading of Genesis 1.26-28', in *'And God Said that it was Good': Essays on Creation and God in Honor of Terence Fretheim* (ed. Frederick Gaiser and Mark Thronveit; St. Paul, MN: Luther Seminary, 2006), pp. 33-41.

26. Regan, 'The Case for Animal Rights', in Singer (ed.), *In Defense of Animals*, p. 22. See also Tom Regan, *The Case for Animal Rights Rights* (Berkeley, CA: University of California Press, 1983).

27. Regan, 'The Case for Animal Rights', p. 23.

28. Gary Francione, 'Animals—Property or Persons?', in *Animal Rights: Current Debates and New Directions* (ed. Cass R. Sustein and Martha C. Nussbaum; New York: Oxford University Press, 2005), pp. 108-142 (132). For a Christian perspective

Other philosophers ground the rights of animals in their 'sentience', which refers to the fact that animals are able to feel pain, even encompassing a more holistic emotional life similar to that of human beings. Martha Nussbaum remarks that '[s]entience is not the only thing that matters for basic justice, but it seems plausible to consider sentience a threshold condition for membership in the community of beings who have entitlements based on justice'.[29] Marc Bekoff goes beyond sentience, and ascribes to animals very rich emotional lives based on experiment and observation in the wild.[30]

Given the inclusion of animals within the community entitled to rights and moral considerability, it is useful to examine how Jesus' treatments of animals would fare ethically. Mark 5.1-20 (//Mt. 8.28-34//Lk. 8.26-39) contains the story of a demon-possessed man who haunted a cemetery. Upon confronting the demon(s) who possessed the man, Jesus proceeds as follows:

> And Jesus asked him, 'What is your name?' He replied, 'My name is Legion; for we are many'. And he begged him eagerly not to send them out of the country. Now a great herd of swine was feeding there on the hillside; and they begged him, 'Send us to the swine, let us enter them'. So he gave them leave. And the unclean spirits came out, and entered the swine; and the herd, numbering about two thousand, rushed down the steep bank into the sea, and were drowned in the sea (Mk 5.9-13).

This is a clear case of Jesus purposely allowing thousands of innocent animals to perish. The deaths were painful insofar as the pigs were probably physically traumatized by landing on rocks before drowning, which itself is a traumatic experience. In addition, the owners or caretakers of these herds were left in worse economic straits because they probably depended on the swine herd for their food or economic well-being. Jesus gave no thought to the effects of his actions for these swine or for the swine herd owners.

on animal experimentation, see Donna Yarri, *The Ethics of Animal Experimentation: A Critical Analysis and Constructive Christian Proposal* (New York: Oxford University Press, 2005).

29. Martha C. Nussbaum, 'Beyond "Compassion and Humanity"', in Sustein and Nussbaum (eds.), *Animal Rights*, pp. 299-320 (309). Clare Palmer (*Animal Ethics in Context* [New York: Columbia University Press, 2010]) argues that human beings don't owe the same rights to wild animals as we do to domestic animals, regardless of sentience.

30. Marc Bekoff, *The Emotional Lives of Animals: A Leading Scientist Explores Animal Joy, Sorrow, and Empathy—and Why They Matter* (Novato, CA: New World Library, 2007). For the relationship of animals and humans in Greco-Roman literature and some apocryphal texts, see Judith Perkins, 'Animal Voices', *Religion and Theology* 12 (2005), pp. 385-96.

More often than not, New Testament ethicists ignore this episode altogether. Thus, James Houlden and Frank Matera, in their respective treatises on New Testament ethics, do not even mention the passage in their scriptural indices.[31] Richard A. Burridge cites Mk 5.1-20 in a list of exorcisms performed by Jesus.[32] Allen Verhey mentions the political connotations of the exorcism in that passage, but nothing about the animals or their suffering.[33] Richard Hays cites it as an example of the signs of the imminent arrival of God's kingdom.[34] In other words, there is not even a consciousness among these New Testament ethicists that the swine deserved any ethical consideration.

As portrayed by the author of Mark, Jesus assumes that he has a right to use swine as vessels for demons regardless of how much suffering it may cause these animals. Jesus echoes the thoughts found in another New Testament author when comparing false prophets and their followers to animals: 'But these, like irrational animals [ἄλογα ζῷα], creatures of instinct, born to be caught and killed, reviling in matters of which they are ignorant, will be destroyed in the same destruction with them' (2 Pet. 2.12).

Augustine was one of the earliest Christian exegetes to understand correctly that the story in Mark 5 shows Jesus' willingness to marginalize and harm animals. In one of his treatises against the Manicheans, Augustine attacked their abstention from killing animals and plants as follows:

> And, in the first place, your abstaining from the slaughter of animals and from injuring plants is shown by Christ to be mere superstition; for, on the ground that there is no community of rights between us and brutes and trees, He both sent the devils into an herd of swine and withered by His curse a tree in which He had found no fruit. The swine assuredly had not sinned, nor had the tree.[35]

Augustine's last sentence emphasizes that the swine could not have possibly committed any sinful act that merited their destruction. Andrew Linzey, a famous Christian advocate of animal rights, seeks to mitigate the negative ecological implications of this episode, and he criticizes Augustine's interpretation of Jesus' ethics as follows:

31. Matera, *New Testament Ethics*, p. 313; Houlden, *Ethics and the New Testament*, p. 128.
32. Burridge, *Imitating Jesus*, p. 162.
33. Verhey, *Remembering Jesus*, p. 401.
34. Hays, *The Moral Vision*, p. 85.
35. Augustine, *On the Morals of the Manichaeans* 17.54 (NPNF[1], IV, p. 84); PL 32.54: 'Ac primum quidem quod ab animalium nece, et ab stirpium laceratione vos temperatis, superstitiosissimum Christus ostendit: qui nullam nobis cum belluis and aroribus societatem juris esse judicans, et in gregem percocum demones misit (Matt. viii, 32), et arborem in qua fructum non invenerat, maledicto aridam fecit (Matth. xxi, 19). Nihil certe porci, nihil arbor illa peccaverat.'

> The point is that Jesus does not *send* the demons into the pigs; demons by their very nature prey upon the defenceless, whether humans or animals. We have to face the fact that when it comes to determining Jesus' actual attitude to animals, in the records as we now have them at least, we have to work largely from hints and guesses. But these are on the whole certainly more positive than negative. The rejecting attitude toward animal sacrifice is, I judge, far more significant than most scholars have so far allowed.[36]

Note how Linzey allows himself the certainty to claim that Christianity is generally eco-friendly, while admitting that the founder's attitudes are unclear.[37]

Even Richard Bauckham, a conservative evangelical scholar, sees this episode as specifically contradicting Northcott's claim that Jesus 'lives in supreme harmony with the natural order'.[38] As I shall show below, it is not true that Jesus always rejected animal sacrifice.

Linzey's claim that Jesus did not send the demons into the pigs cannot be sustained, and overlooks some of the main emphases of Markan theology. The plain text of Mk 5.9-13 says that the demons begged [παρεκάλεσαν] Jesus for permission to go into the pigs, and that assumes that they would not have done so unless Jesus had authority over them. The specific Greek word, ἐπέτρεψεν, points to Jesus' authority and ability to prohibit or allow the demons to enter the pigs. The word is a form of ἐπιτρέπω, a verb commonly attributed to those in power.[39] Note these examples:

> Mk 10.4: Moses allowed [ἐπέτρεψεν] a man to write a certificate of divorce, and to put her away.

> Jn 19.38: After this Joseph of Arimathea, who was a disciple of Jesus, but secretly, for fear of the Jews, asked Pilate that he might take away the body of Jesus, and Pilate gave him leave [ἐπέτρεψεν]. So he came and took away his body.

Markan theology emphasizes Jesus' authority over demons.[40] Jesus can permit or prohibit demons from undertaking any particular action. Thus,

---

36. Andrew Linzey, *Christianity and the Rights of Animals* (New York: Crossroad, 1989), p. 48. Linzey's italics.

37. Linzey (*Christianity and the Rights of Animals*, p. 5) states: 'Christian theology provides some of the best arguments for respecting animal life and for taking seriously animals as partners with us within God's creation.'

38. See Richard Bauckham, 'Reading the Synoptic Gospels Ecologically', in Horrell *et al.* (eds.), *Ecological Hermeneutics*, pp. 70-82 (81).

39. See further, 'ἐπιτρέπω', BDAG, pp. 384b-385a.

40. For a detailed redactional study of Mk 5.1-20, see Annen, *Heil für die Heiden*, especially pp. 56-57; Otto Bauernfeind, *Die Worte der Dämonen im Markusevangelium* (Stuttgart: W. Kohlhammer, 1927), pp. 23-28. For the idea that the swine drowning story parallels that of the pharaoh's drowning army in Exodus, see Eric K. Wefald, 'The

Jesus does not permit demons even to speak in Mk 1.34. According to Mk 3.15, part of the mission of the twelve disciples is to 'have authority to cast out demons' (ἔχειν ἐξουσίαν ἐκβάλλειν τὰ δαιμόνια). Given the fact that Jesus allowed what he could have prohibited, one can say that Jesus is directly responsible for sending the demons into the pigs. Jesus is, at least, indirectly responsible for their subsequent pain and death.

Christopher S. Mann does take more seriously the ethical problem of the swine in his commentary on Mark.

> Difficulty has always been felt with the significance of the narrative as we have it now, especially with respect to the fate of the pigs. No amount of pleading that evil belongs to the abyss (represented in this story by the sea) and that swine were unclean animals removes the feeling that the whole incident as recorded represents gratuitous waste. Perhaps the only adequate hypothesis is that the man's reactions to exorcism were so terrified that his panic communicated itself to the herd of swine. Panic behavior in many species of animals is well attested, and our sources simply combine this panic behavior with an exorcism.[41]

Despite the attempt to see an ethical problem related to these animals, Mann does not ascribe to Jesus any responsibility for the fate of the pigs. After admitting that the loss of the pigs represents a 'gratuitous waste', Mann's next sentence seeks to explain why the pigs acted in the way that they did instead of seeking to explain why Jesus sent the demons into the pigs in the first place. Mann ascribes the swineherd's behavior to the 'man's reactions to exorcism', and so absolves Jesus of any responsibility. In her commentary on Mark, Camille Focant argues that the demons deceive Jesus because their destruction of the pigs resulted in his expulsion. Thus, it is the demons that Focant holds responsible for the pigs drowning, and not Jesus.[42]

As mentioned, the text indicates that it was Jesus who gave permission to these demons to enter the swine. In addition to his ability to reject the demons' request, Jesus also could have expressed some sympathy for the pigs just as he expressed sympathy for human beings who were afflicted in some manner (e.g., Mk 6.34). It was the possession of the pigs by the demons, not the man's reaction to the exorcism, that is most likely held to be the reason why the pigs ran over the cliffs. The distressed actions of the pigs parallel the distressed actions of the man when he was possessed. The

Separate Gentile Mission in Mark: A Narrative Explanation of Markan Geography, the Two Feeding Accounts and Exorcisms', *JSNT* 60 (1995), pp. 3-26 (15-16); J. Duncan M. Derrett, 'Contributions to the Study of the Gerasene Demoniac', *JSNT* 3 (1979), pp. 2-17 (5-6).

41. Mann, *Mark*, p. 278.

42. Camille Focant, *The Gospel According to Mark: A Commentary* (trans. Leslie Robert Keylock; Eugene, OR: Pickwick Press, 2012), pp. 195-204.

possessed man ran toward Jesus, and the possessed pigs ran away from Jesus. Just as the possessed man was 'bruising himself with stones', the possessed pigs ran toward the cliffs and probably hit rocks, bruising themselves on the rocks, until their final drowning deaths.

Otherwise, Jesus' actions follow an exorcistic technique well known in the ancient Near East. Demons and evil are transferred from a human patient to animals and/or to water. Thus, the scapegoat that is released into the wilderness (Lev. 16.22) carries away the sins of the people.[43] The wilderness often was the normal dwelling of evil spirits. A post-talmudic Aramaic incantation bears this command directed at demons: 'Flee and fall upon the mountains, and heights, and unclean beasts' (ותיזלון ותיפלון על טורי ועל ראמתא ועל בעירא מסאבא).[44] Mesopotamian exorcistic rituals frequently allude to letting water carry away any evil.[45] According to the Greek writer Pausanias, a dangerous ghost lost a fight against a man named Euthymus, and the ghost was 'driven out of the land and disappeared, sinking into the depth of the sea'.[46] Moreover, Mann does not explain why Jesus thought that transferring demons to a herd of swine, which did not even belong to him, was an ethical action in the first place.

The whole episode shows that the pigs have no inherent value for Jesus, but are rather convenient tools to display his authority over nature and demons. The episode also shows the weakness of van Wieren's description of the consensus of Christian attitude toward the environment: 'individuals should be *against* the unjustified destruction of nature'.[47] Moreover, if Jesus is allowed to justify the killing of these animals because his theology allowed it, then the term 'unjustified' becomes completely relative and practically meaningless. Since theological claims cannot be adjudicated by any objective means, then any theology that calls for the mass killing of animals has as much right to enact its view as Jesus' theological view.

Animal rights ethicists often speak of 'speciesism', which Peter Singer defines as a 'prejudice or attitude of bias in favor of the interests of members of one's own species and against those of members of other species'.[48]

43. For a more detailed discussion, see Milgrom, *Leviticus 1–16*, pp. 1041-46.

44. My translation. The text is published in Josef Wohlstein, 'Über einige aramäische Inschriften auf Thongefassen des Königlichen Musuems zu Berlin', *ZA* 8 (1893), pp. 313-40. My quote is from the Aramaic text on p. 328, lines 28-29. See also Trunk, *Der messianische Heiler*, p. 108.

45. For example, LKA 139.90-91 in van der Toorn, *Sin and Sanction*, p. 154, lines 90-91: 'When he had spoken these words, he shall throw into the river what he carried on his head and bow.'

46. Pausanias, *Description of Greece* 6.8 (Jones, LCL): ἐξηλαύνετο γὰρ ἐκ τῆς γῆς...ἀφαινίζεταί τε καταδοὺς ἐς θάλασσαν.

47. Van Wieren, *Restored to Earth*, p. 25.

48. Peter Singer, *Animal Liberation* (New York: Harper Collins, 2009 [1975]), p. 6.

However, Mark 5 also underlines the cultural speciesism one sees in the Hebrew Bible, where pigs are regarded as unclean, impure, and unworthy of domestication or even life (cf. Lev. 11.7). Jesus himself views dogs and pigs as dangerous and undesirable: 'Do not give dogs what is holy; and do not throw your pearls before swine, lest they trample them under foot and turn to attack you' (Mt. 7.6). While the episode with the pigs in Mark 5 may appear to be a singular event, I will show that Jesus supported a more continuous and systematic slaughter of animals in some texts.

Luke 22 and Matthew 8: Sacrificing Animal Rights

According to Andrew Linzey, 'there is no hint in the Gospels of Jesus' support for the practice of sacrifice itself; neither he nor his disciples practiced it'.[49] The fact is that Jesus and his disciples sometimes are portrayed as supporting animal sacrifice, and they seemingly practiced it or participated in it. For example, in the narrative about the Last Supper in Luke, Jesus is fully aware that sacrificing a lamb will be part of the Passover meal.

> Then came the day of Unleavened Bread, on which the passover lamb had to be sacrificed [ᾗ ἔδει θύεσθαι τὸ πάσχα]. So Jesus sent Peter and John, saying, 'Go and prepare the Passover [Πορευθέντες ἑτοιμάσατε ἡμῖν τὸ πάσχα] for us, that we may eat it' (Lk. 22.7-8).

Jesus is clearly referencing the sacrifice of the Passover lamb, which is itself referred to as τὸ πασχα in Exod. 12.21 (LXX: θύσατε τὸ πασχα).[50] In 1 Cor. 5.7, the author uses the word, τὸ πάσχα, when he remarks: 'For Christ, our paschal lamb, has been sacrificed' (καὶ γὰρ τὸ πάσχα ἡμῶν ἐτύθη Χριστός).

Not only does Jesus declare his intention to participate in a meal where the Passover lamb is sacrificed, but he commands his disciples to go prepare that meal.[51] According to I. Howard Marshall, '[t]he task of preparation for the Passover (πάσχα here means the meal as a whole) included…providing the lamb…and cooking the meal or arranging for helpers to do this'.[52] While it is true that Jesus says he cannot partake of the meal in this particular instance in Lk. 22.16 ('I shall not eat it until it is fulfilled in the kingdom

---

For a systematic treatment of this concept, see Joan Dunayer, *Speciesism* (Derwood, MD: Rice, 2004).

49. Linzey, *Christianity and the Rights of Animals*, p. 42.

50. For the classic study of the parallels between the Last Supper and the Passover, see Jeremias, *The Eucharistic Words of Jesus*, especially pp. 42-61. For a contrary view, see Klawans, 'Was Jesus' Last Supper a Seder?'

51. See further, Fitzmyer, *Luke X–XXIV*, pp. 1382-83.

52. Marshall, *The Gospel of Luke*, p. 791.

of God'), he says that eventually he will. Jesus does not reject, in principle, the sacrificing of lambs for the Passover meal by indicating that he cannot eat it at this point in time.

Contrary to Linzey's claim that Jesus rejects sacrifice, in Matthew 8 one finds Jesus endorsing sacrifice more systematically:

> When he came down from the mountain, great crowds followed him; and behold, a leper came to him and knelt before him, saying, 'Lord, if you will, you can make me clean'. And he stretched out his hand and touched him, saying, 'I will; be clean'. And immediately his leprosy was cleansed. And Jesus said to him, 'See that you say nothing to any one; but go, show yourself to the priest, and offer the gift that Moses commanded, for a proof to the people' (Mt. 8.1-4).

Jesus' reference to 'the gift that Moses commanded' harks back to Leviticus 14, where one finds these instructions:

> This shall be the law of the leper for the day of his cleansing. He shall be brought to the priest; and the priest shall go out of the camp, and the priest shall make an examination. Then, if the leprous disease is healed in the leper, the priest shall command them to take for him who is to be cleansed two living clean birds and cedarwood and scarlet stuff and hyssop; and the priest shall command them to kill one of the birds in an earthen vessel over running water. He shall take the living bird with the cedarwood and the scarlet stuff and the hyssop, and dip them and the living bird in the blood of the bird that was killed over the running water; and he shall sprinkle it seven times upon him who is to be cleansed of leprosy; then he shall pronounce him clean, and shall let the living bird go into the open field (Lev. 14.2-7).

Birds are not the only living things to be killed. Leviticus 14 continues as follows:

> And on the eighth day he shall take two male lambs without blemish, and one ewe lamb a year old without blemish, and a cereal offering of three tenths of an ephah of fine flour mixed with oil, and one log of oil. And the priest who cleanses him shall set the man who is to be cleansed and these things before the LORD, at the door of the tent of meeting. And the priest shall take one of the male lambs, and offer it for a guilt offering, along with the log of oil, and wave them for a wave offering before the LORD; and he shall kill the lamb in the place where they kill the sin offering and the burnt offering, in the holy place; for the guilt offering, like the sin offering, belongs to the priest; it is most holy (Lev. 14.10-13).

The Matthean Jesus has no problem with the sacrificial system, which could theoretically result in thousands of birds and sheep slaughtered in any given year just for these sorts of rituals.

Usually there is no mention of the ethics of sacrifice by New Testament ethicists when they discuss this text. Neither Verhey nor Burridge list Mt.

8.4 in their scriptural indices.[53] Matera cites it as an example of how 'Jesus' compassion and mercy do not stand in opposition to God's law'.[54] Matera's anthropocentrism is clear insofar as 'compassion and mercy' is what Jesus extends to human beings, and not to the animals that will be slaughtered by following Moses's commandment.

Jonathan Morgan does attempt to defend the sacrificial system of Leviticus more systematically.[55] By implication, it would also be a defense of Jesus' endorsement of that sacrificial system. As Morgan phrases his general defense:

> It is my proposal that, rather than being a cruel, wasteful practice emanating from the logic of human domination, animal sacrifice can be seen to function in priestly thought as an act of humility, deriving from a keen sense of human perpetuation of, and culpability for, violence and corruption. In the light of this, I also question traditional assumptions regarding the substitutionary function, passivity and victimhood of the sacrificial animal.[56]

To be fair, one also should note that Morgan's defense does admit that '[a] hierarchical structuring of creation with human beings at the apex is irrefutably part of the priestly vision'.[57]

For Morgan, sacrifice is a postdiluvial development meant to regulate human violence and to check human violence. In his own words:

> [C]areful attention to the precise role and function of the sacrificed animal serves to lead us still further from the conceptual paradigm wherein humans *use* other animals to rectify *their* problems. Not only is the world of Ancient Israelite priestly thought not ruled by these issues of utility, but it relies on and expounds a conception of reality in which humans, non-human animals and the earth itself are inextricably bound up in a set of relationships with Yhwh that require humans to commit to regulating the proliferation of violence, which is the result of human sin and require certain non-human animals to function as mediators and agents of purification on behalf of the whole community.[58]

Note Morgan's denial of any utilitarianism on the part of Israelite priestly sacrifice.

Otherwise, Morgan makes his argument in large part because he redefines crucial terms arbitrarily. Morgan has redefined sacrificial animals as 'agents' and 'mediators' instead of as victims. The words 'agents' and 'mediators', in the sense of entities who exercise a conscious and deliberate

53. Burridge, *Imitating Jesus*, p. 473; Verhey, *Remembering Jesus*, p. 518.
54. Matera, *New Testament Ethics*, p. 52.
55. Jonathan Morgan, 'Sacrifice in Leviticus: Eco-Friendly Ritual or Unholy Waste?', in Horrell *et al.* (eds.), *Ecological Hermeneutics*, pp. 32-45.
56. Morgan, 'Sacrifice in Leviticus', p. 33.
57. Morgan, 'Sacrifice in Leviticus', p. 35.
58. Morgan, 'Sacrifice in Leviticus', pp. 43-44.

choice about their function, nowhere appear in any corresponding Hebrew description of these animals in Leviticus. Whatever function the animals perform has been completely determined for them by human beings.

That sacrifice certainly is conceptualized in utilitarian and anthropocentric manner is clear from Leviticus itself. There are motive clauses that accompany some sacrificial laws.[59] For example, Lev. 22.29 states: 'And when you sacrifice a sacrifice of thanksgiving to the LORD, you shall sacrifice it so that you may be accepted' (cf. Lev. 19.5). The utilitarian aspect of sacrifice was also noted by other ancient Jewish writers. Philo devotes considerable space to explaining why certain animals were chosen for sacrifice. Note his explanation for the selection of the oxen, sheep and goats among the land animals:

> [T]hese are the gentlest and most docile. We see great herds and flocks of each kind led by a single person, it matters not who. He may even be not a grown man, but the merest child, and under his guidance they go out to the pasture and when required return back in order to their pens... Furthermore, in the whole animal kingdom they are the most serviceable for human life.[60]

In other words, the docility of some of these animals makes them excellent victims, as one does not need to be chasing after them to sacrifice them (cf. Isa. 53.7). They can be led in large numbers even by a child. While one could theoretically sacrifice hunted animals, the larger and continuous quantities required by the Levitical system made docile animals much more suitable. There is nothing here about choosing these animals because they were more valuable inherently, but rather because they serve human needs better.

In fact, some laws that were originally meant to be humane to animals in the Hebrew Bible have been interpreted in the New Testament to be for the benefit of human beings. Note Paul's explanation of a law in Deut. 25.4 that seemingly benefits oxen:

> For it is written in the law of Moses, 'You shall not muzzle an ox when it is treading out the grain'. Is it for oxen that God is concerned? Does he not speak entirely for our sake? It was written for our sake, because the plowman should plow in hope and the thresher thresh in hope of a share in the crop (1 Cor. 9.9-10).

One can thus argue that the New Testament may represent a regression in terms of animal rights in some cases.

59. For a utilitarian view of motive clauses in Hebrew law, see Rifat Sonsino, *Motive Clauses in Hebrew Law: Biblical Forms and Near Eastern Parallels* (Chico, CA: Scholars Press, 1980).
60. Philo, *Spec. Leg.* 1.163-65 (Colson, LCL).

Human violence is assumed to be permanent and recurrent, and so there is a continual need to atone in some way for bad actions. If anything, a sacrificial system can encourage corruption and violence because almost any sin or act of corruption can be removed by sacrifice, and so a perpetrator theoretically can continue to act sinfully as long as he or she knows there are means to remove the punishment. This sort of reasoning can actually result in killing more animals because one never could be sure of how many sins one had committed. Note what Job did on behalf of his sons:

> He would rise early in the morning and offer burnt offerings according to the number of them all; for Job said, 'It may be that my sons have sinned, and cursed God in their hearts'. Thus Job did continually (Job 1.5).

Similarly, Leviticus speaks of sacrificing for known and inadvertent sins:

> If any one commits a breach of faith and sins unwittingly in any of the holy things of the LORD, he shall bring, as his guilt offering to the LORD, a ram without blemish out of the flock, valued by you in shekels of silver, according to the shekel of the sanctuary; it is a guilt offering (Lev. 5.15).

Although there are various theories about the purpose of sacrifice, the biblical practice is best envisioned as part of the tribute or offering that a vassal owes to a lord in the ancient Near East.[61] For example, the Assyrian king Shalmaneser III (858–824 BCE) states: 'I received the tribute of Arame, man of Gusi (to wit); silver, gold, large [and small] cattle, wine, a couch of whitish gold'.[62] Such tributary animals were part of the economy in the reign of Solomon:

> Solomon ruled over all the kingdoms from the Euphrates to the land of the Philistines and to the border of Egypt; they brought tribute and served Solomon all the days of his life. Solomon's provision for one day was thirty cors of fine flour, and sixty cors of meal, ten fat oxen, and twenty pasture-fed cattle, a hundred sheep, besides harts, gazelles, roebucks, and fatted fowl. For he had dominion over all the region west of the Euphrates from Tiphsah to Gaza, over all the kings west of the Euphrates; and he had peace on all sides round about him (1 Kgs 4.21-24).

---

61. For a survey of theories about animal sacrifice, see Maria-Zoe Petropoulou, *Animal Sacrifice in Ancient Greek Religion, Judaism, and Christianity, 100 BC to AD 200* (New York: Oxford University Press, 2012); Jonathan Klawans, *Purity, Sacrifice, and the Temple: Symbolism and Supersessionism in the Study of Ancient Judaism* (New York: Oxford University Press, 2006); Moshe Halbertal, *On Sacrifice* (Princeton, NJ: Princeton University Press, 2012); Richard E. DeMaris, 'Sacrifice, an Ancient Mediterranean Ritual', *BTB* 43 (2013), pp. 60-73. For a general treatment of tribute in Mesopotamia, and other areas of the ancient Near East, see H. Klinkott, S. Kubisch and R. Müller-Wollermann (eds.), *Geschenke und Steuern, Zölle und Tribute: Antike Abgabenformen in Anspruch und Wirklichkeit* (Leiden: E.J. Brill, 2007).

62. *ANET*, p. 255.

Even if Solomon's kingdom and tribute are exaggerated, the story shows that biblical authors expected kings to receive tribute, including animals.

Yahweh, as the lord of the Israelites, receives his due tribute from the people in the form of their animals as do many other ancient kings. Note that Jesus himself refers to sacrifice as offering 'the gift' (τὸ δῶρον) in Mt. 8.4. Yahweh's priests, as his agents, can consume all or part of these goods.[63] Thus, one finds these instructions:

> And this shall be the priests' due from the people, from those offering a sacrifice, whether it be ox or sheep: they shall give to the priest the shoulder and the two cheeks and the stomach. The first fruits of your grain, of your wine and of your oil, and the first of the fleece of your sheep, you shall give him (Deut. 18.3-4).

This demonstrates that economic motives, rather than some benign attitude toward nature, is probably more important from the viewpoint of the priests who depend on these sacrifices for their livelihood.

Similarly, when Haggai enunciates Yahweh's reasons for why there is a drought and lack of agricultural productivity, he says that it is 'Because of my house that lies in ruins, while you busy yourselves each with his own house' (Hag. 1.9). The self-serving nature of this plea is evident once one realizes that most of the temple's income derives from agricultural production. It is in the interest of the priesthood that the land be productive because priests make their living from that land through this sacrificial taxation system.

Redefining terms is another strategy used to mitigate the ethical problems posed by animal sacrifice. For example, Linzey frankly admits: 'The only way forward in grappling with the rationale of the practice of sacrifice has to be to move away from the simple equation of sacrifice with the infliction of death.'[64]

Linzey goes on to affirm that the central issue is whether the essential feature of sacrifice was the 'death of the victim or the offering of lifeblood', and he makes his case as follows:

> First of all…all life was a gift from God and therefore belonged to him… Secondly, the act of return to the Creator was probably understood (by those who practiced it) as the offering of life. Thirdly, and perhaps more importantly, the practice of sacrifice thereby assumed that the life of the individual animal continued beyond mortal death. In these ways it is possible to understand the historic practice of sacrifice as affirming the value of the individuals slain and not simply as their gratuitous destruction.

---

63. The Deuteronomistic and Priestly traditions differ as to the extent to which priests can consume a sacrifice. See further William H. Propp, *Exodus 1–18* (AB, 2; New Haven, CT: Yale University Press, 1999), p. 455.

64. Linzey, *Christianity and the Rights of Animals*, p. 41.

> The tradition of sacrifice did not necessarily involve a low view of animal life.[65]

Perhaps unwittingly, Linzey here accepts a more patriarchal and imperialistic view of sacrifice when he says that 'all life was a gift from God and therefore belonged to him'. This is consistent with the view that vassals owe their lord the most precious commodities they possess.

On a metaethical level, Linzey affirms that 'Killing Animal X is justified if some larger symbolic purpose is achieved'. In other words, he holds to a Greater Good theory or utilitarian set of ethics. But for an ethicist like Regan, an animal has an inherent right to live and endowing the killing with some larger symbolic purpose is irrelevant. After all, it is human beings who made the decision about what sort of symbolism to inject into the killing, and so it is a completely anthropocentric way of looking at killing animals. Linzey also fails to explain why conferring some supposed higher value on the animal justifies killing it. Linzey seems to equate a higher value with a higher worthiness for death. Moreover, Linzey misses the utilitarian view of sacrifice expressed by Jesus himself. Note Jesus' instructions again: 'show yourself to the priest, and offer the gift that Moses commanded, for a proof to the people [εἰς μαρτύριον αὐτοῖς]' (Mt. 8.4). The animal killed is a tool to display Jesus' power, and not to exhibit any sort of compassion or benefit for the animal sacrificed.

Morgan's attempt to deny the victimization of animals is even more unclear compared to that of Linzey. As Morgan phrases it:

> The sacrificial animal *begins* as a victim...but, through enabling the cleansing of the sanctuary and the offender, ends by dissolving the very context of the victimhood of all concerned. The animal does not remain a victim in exactly the same way that the community as a whole is restored from a position of victimization.[66]

If I understand Morgan, his ethical premise may be simplified as follows: 'Animal X should not be viewed as a victim if the killing of X restores some greater benefit to the larger community to which X belongs.'

If so, victimhood has really nothing ultimately to do with whether an animal suffered or is killed, which is a sufficient condition for 'victimhood' by animal rights advocates and by many modern legal standards.[67] For example, consider the penal code of the American state of California, which after noting some exceptions, states:

65. Linzey, *Christianity and the Rights of Animals*, p. 41.

66. Morgan, 'Sacrifice in Leviticus', p. 42. Morgan's italics.

67. See further Andrew N. Ireland Moore, 'Defining Animals as Crime Victims', *Journal of Animal Law* 1 (2005), pp. 91-108.

> [E]very person who maliciously and intentionally maims, mutilates, tortures, or wounds a living animal, or maliciously and intentionally kills an animal, is guilty of a crime punishable pursuant to subdivision (d).[68]

Rather, Morgan is arguing for a more utilitarian view of victimhood. If the killing of Animal X confers a greater benefit, then it is not a victim. The obverse would apparently be that if the killing of animal X does not confer a greater benefit, then it is a victim. For Morgan, the animal has no inherent right to life, and its victimhood status depends on whether it serves human purposes.

Morgan makes much of the idea that the sacrificial animal belongs to the human community. He notes that in ancient Israel domesticated sheep, goats and cattle lived side by side with human beings.[69] Morgan then uses that fact to suggest that these animals were valued as much or more than human beings, who saw them as part of the family. Even if true, this does not make biblical ethics any better than what is found in many other ancient Near Eastern societies where the animals slaughtered were also domesticated ones. By that logic, one ought to praise the eco-friendliness of the Assyrian king Tiglat-Pileser (744–727 BCE) even more because his more inclusive tribute lists 'horses, mules, large and small cattle (male), female camels with their foals'.[70]

The concept of 'humility' is invoked by Morgan to mitigate the victimhood of the animals. According to Morgan, it is actually a privilege for the animal to be sacrificed, as opposed to the human being. Animal sacrifice involves 'the replacement of a less ritually capable and significant animal (the human) with the more ritually capable and significant one (the "holy" sheep/bull/goat/bird)'.[71] But where does Leviticus ever speak of humans as ritually less 'significant' than animals, and what does 'significant' mean in this context? By this logic, the larger the variety of species that a culture sacrifices, then the more eco-friendly we can assume that culture to be.

If anything, it is the opposite in the Bible. Because humans are so significant and important relative to animals, then animals should die instead of human beings. That is certainly the case in the story of Isaac, where God tested Abraham to see if he would kill his son. However, when Abraham showed his willingness, the angel responded: 'Do not lay your hand on the lad or do anything to him; for now I know that you fear God, seeing you have not withheld your son, your only son, from me' (Gen. 22.12). Instead,

---

68. Animal Protection Laws of California, §597 (2013), Cruelty to Animals, (a). Online: http://aldf.org/wp-content/themes/aldf/compendium-map/us/2013/CALIFORNIA.pdf.

69. Morgan, 'Sacrifice in Leviticus', p. 40.

70. *ANET*, p. 265.

71. Morgan, 'Sacrifice in Leviticus', p. 42.

a ram was substituted, and 'Abraham went and took the ram, and offered it up as a burnt offering instead of his son' (Gen. 22.13). How does the phrase, 'instead of his son' (תחת בנו), not refer to anything but a substitution indicating that Isaac is more significant than the animal?[72]

Similarly, Exodus 13 relates how the firstborn of domestic animals were to be God's tribute. Thus, Exod. 13.2: 'Consecrate to me all the first-born; whatever is the first to open the womb among the people of Israel, both of man and of beast, is mine.' The Hebrew expression, לי הוא ('it is mine'), leaves no doubt that Yahweh's ownership, rather than some cosmic balance, is the reason for sacrifice.[73] Any cosmic imbalances result from a vassal not giving his lord the due tribute. According to Exod. 13.13: 'Every first-born of man among your sons you shall redeem.' The redemption involved substituting an animal.[74] Exodus 13 certainly does not show that biblical authors killed animals because they saw the animals as more 'significant' compared to human beings. Rather, animals were substituted for human beings precisely because animals are deemed of lesser value and significance compared to humans. Saying an animal is 'more ritually significant' than a human being does not lessen the ethical problem of killing the animal in the first place. In general, a vassal is to give his lord what is most valuable among his possessions, but such a gift does not imply that the vassal is less valuable than what he gives.

According to Morgan, the need for social harmony (and a harmony between the divine and human realms) justifies sacrifice:

> The fundamental logic that the priestly instructions regarding sacrifice attest to, reinforce and indeed proceed from, is that regular, officially sanctioned sacrifice is a fundamental requirement for the proper functioning of Israelite society and this is because of the ever-present reality of human corruption.[75]

True enough, the priestly author does believe that sacrifice is necessary for the proper functioning of society and for maintaining the presence of Yahweh in the community. But nowhere in Leviticus does the author say that the purpose of sacrifice is to check human violence or to deter human corruption. The claim that animal sacrifice is fundamental to the society does not justify animal sacrifice any more than human sacrifice is justified

---

72. See further, Levenson, *The Death and Resurrection of the Beloved Son.*

73. See further, Stuart Lasine, 'Everything Belongs to me: Holiness, Danger, and Divine Kingship in the Post-Genesis World', *JSOT* 35 (2010), pp. 31-62.

74. On the debate of whether human sacrifice was replaced by animal sacrifice in Exodus 13, see Propp, *Exodus 1–18*, pp. 454-57. See also Karin Finsterbusch, Armin Lange and K.F. Diethard Römheld (eds.), *Human Sacrifice in Jewish and Christian Tradition* (Numen Book Series, 112; Leiden: E.J. Brill, 2007).

75. Morgan, 'Sacrifice in Leviticus', p. 38.

because the Aztecs of Mexico might have believed that it was fundamental to their society.

Morgan, in general, completely ignores the lord–vassal context of offering animals to a deity. Tribute serves to keep a good relationship between vassal and master because the vassal is giving the master what he deems valuable or is necessary to maintain his position and power. Yahweh is no different. Accordingly, any ascription to some benign and eco-friendly motivation for sacrifice is nothing more than a modern apologetic retrojection.

In addressing the argument that Levitical sacrifice is wasteful, Morgan undermines his entire major argument that animal sacrifice is necessary to regulate human violence and corruption after the Fall. Indeed, he affirms: 'The simple answer to the question as to why, for Leviticus, an animal has to die for a sacrifice to be performed, is that it does not.'[76] Morgan points to the fact that wheat, barley, wine, salt, and other non-animal resources can be offered. Of course, one finds some biblical authors who seemingly can dispense with sacrifice altogether. Thus, Hosea states: 'For I desire steadfast love and not sacrifice, the knowledge of God, rather than burnt offerings' (Hos. 6.6). There is also the possibility, even if not very plausible, that prayer came to be substituted for sacrifice at Qumran.[77]

Morgan's denial of the necessity of sacrifice only begs the question of why any animals were ever sacrificed at all, especially if we can use non-animal resources to achieve the same results. If, as Morgan argues, sacrifice serves to counter the 'ever present reality of human corruption', then why did other biblical authors (e.g., Isa. 1.11; Amos 5.20-25) not think it was necessary at all? Killing animals would definitely be wasteful if Morgan is admitting that they don't have to be killed for sacrifice in the first place. It is a needless killing and suffering for the animals.

In fact, some non-Christian authors had moved beyond sacrifice altogether. Apollonius of Tyana, who is believed to have lived in the first century, exemplifies such a position. Note this letter sent by Apollonius to the priests of Olympia:

> The gods do not need sacrifices [θυσιῶν οὐ δέονται]. Then what can one do to please them? Acquire wisdom, it seems to me, and do good to honorable men as far as one is able. That is what is dear to the gods; sacrifice is the occupation of the godless.[78]

76. Morgan, 'Sacrifice in Leviticus', p. 42.

77. Paul Heger, 'Did Prayer Replace Sacrifice at Qumran?', *RevQ* 22 (2005), pp. 213-33.

78. Robert J. Penella (ed.), *The Letters of Apollonus of Tyana: A Critical Text with Prolegomena, Translation and Commentary* (Leiden: E.J. Brill, 1979), pp. 46-47. On the rejection of animal sacrifice in Buddhist traditions, see Natalie D. Gummer, 'Sacrificial Sutras: Mahayana Literature and the South Asian Ritual Cosmos', *Journal of the American Academy of Religion* 82 (2014), pp. 1091-1126.

Apollonius has been able to move here to a completely non-sacrificial ethic that would automatically remove animals from this sort of torture and/or death.[79] So, why not praise Apollonius as much or more than Jesus, who is sometimes portrayed as clinging to the idea that animal sacrifice was good?

Matthew 6: The Eco-Apathetic Jesus

In a discourse on how disciples must devote their entire loyalty to Jesus or to the Kingdom of God of which he is an agent, Jesus strives to soothe the anxiety of those wondering how they will make a living. Jesus replies as follows:

> No one can serve two masters; for either he will hate the one and love the other, or he will be devoted to the one and despise the other. You cannot serve God and mammon. Therefore I tell you, do not be anxious about your life, what you shall eat or what you shall drink, nor about your body, what you shall put on. Is not life more than food, and the body more than clothing? Look at the birds of the air: they neither sow nor reap nor gather into barns, and yet your heavenly Father feeds them. Are you not of more value than they? And which of you by being anxious can add one cubit to his span of life? And why are you anxious about clothing? Consider the lilies of the field, how they grow; they neither toil nor spin; yet I tell you, even Solomon in all his glory was not arrayed like one of these. But if God so clothes the grass of the field, which today is alive and tomorrow is thrown into the oven, will he not much more clothe you, O men of little faith? Therefore do not be anxious, saying, 'What shall we eat?' or 'What shall we drink?' or 'What shall we wear?' For the Gentiles seek all these things; and your heavenly Father knows that you need them all. But seek first his kingdom and his righteousness, and all these things shall be yours as well (Mt. 6.24-33).

Jesus' attitude toward nature (not to mention his ethnocentric overgeneralization about Gentiles) could be judged negatively by modern ethical standards.[80] Jesus does not feel any sort of stewardship or 'mutual custodianship' as the Earth Bible Project describes it. Jesus seems to abdicate all human responsibility for the care of wildlife. God takes care of wild animals. There is also an empirical problem, as is expressed by James A. Metzger: 'What then does one do when one's reflective gaze wanders from healthy, well-fed birds (Mt 6.25-34; Lk. 12.22-34) to the myriad corpses of those who have died prematurely due to disease or drought?'[81]

---

79. For the idea that animal sacrifice was not part of an earlier idyllic past, see Daniel Ulluci, 'Before Animal Sacrifice, a Myth of Innocence', *Religion and Theology* 15 (2008), pp. 357-74.

80. See also Erich S. Gruen, *Rethinking the Other in Antiquity* (Martin Classical Lectures; Princeton, NJ: Princeton University Press, 2012).

81. Metzger, 'Reclaiming a "Dark and Malefic Sacred"', p. 312.

Jesus seemingly has no consciousness of how human beings can alter habitats or destroy food supplies for animals. Plants such as lilies don't always grow uninhibited in the wild. In the New World, the animals and other species brought by human beings altered the landscape.[82] Some indigenous plants could no longer compete with some of the invasive species, and some invasive species overran the native habitats. But rather than being an example of Jesus' understandable ecological naïveté or apathy toward nature, Northcott analyzes the remarks of Jesus as follows:

> The natural provision of the creation for animals, their dependence on seasons and natural foods, is contrasted with human greed and materialism. Humanity is enjoined to show the same dependence on God as the animal world already shows.[83]

Northcott does violence not only to the immediate context of Jesus' teachings, but also ignores the long history of animal extinctions that occurred even before human beings existed or could show signs of materialism and greed.

It is true that Jesus' instructions in vv. 25-33 follow up on the affirmation that one cannot serve both God and Mammon. The Greek prepositional phrase, διὰ τοῦτο ('therefore'), at the beginning of v. 25 suggests that those instructions are a logical consequence of that contrast between serving God and Mammon. However, v. 31 also indicates that the anxieties of the disciples are not focused on getting rich but rather on having the basic staples of life ('What shall we eat?' or 'What shall we drink?' or 'What shall we wear?'). Perhaps Northcott is led astray by the reference to Solomon, which is not directly related to the anxieties that Jesus is describing. The reference to Solomon functions to show that lilies left to their own devices will outshine Solomon's glory, and not that the disciples are yearning for Solomon's glory or riches.

Jesus has repeatedly instructed his disciples to leave all possessions behind (cf. Lk. 14.33). Jesus comments on his own penury: 'Foxes have holes, and birds of the air have nests; but the Son of man has nowhere to lay his head' (Mt. 8.20). Therefore, it seems reasonable for the disciples to wonder how they will find shelter, food, drink and clothing without employment or steady income. Jesus tells them that they will be just as fine as wild animals. Given that Jesus wants complete loyalty to him, rather than to the families of the disciples (cf. Mt. 10.34-37), these instructions can be seen as a self-serving directive, and not some magnanimous statement about environmental harmony.

---

82. See Alfred W. Crosby, *The Biological Expansion of Europe, 900–1900* (Cambridge: Cambridge University Press, 1986).

83. Northcott, *The Environment and Christian Ethics*, p. 225.

Supporting evidence that Jesus' discourse need not always have been tied with riches, but rather with the basic necessities of life, comes from the *Gospel of Thomas*, which bears a simpler form of these instructions:

> Jesus said, Do not fret, from morning to evening and from evening to morning, [about your food—what you're going to eat, or about your clothing—] what you are going to wear. [You're much better than the lilies, which neither card nor spin. As for you, when you have no garment, what will you put on? Who might add to your stature? That very one will give you a garment.][84]

Even if I am not arguing that the *Gospel of Thomas* preserves earlier or more 'authentic' versions of Jesus' teachings, it does attest to the fact that these sayings did not have to be associated with the contrast between greed for riches and serving God. They may have just as well originated with a very real anxiety for disciples about what they were going to eat and drink from day to day rather than with any accumulation of wealth.

Matthew 21: Fig-uratively Speaking

One of the most important concepts discussed in environmental ethics is anthropocentrism, or the idea that human beings are the center of all ethical interests and everything is judged by human standards. Lynn White called Christianity 'the most anthropocentric religion the world has seen'.[85] All of nature is meant to serve human needs and wants. How we treat nature is a product of how well we benefit from it. One example of Jesus' anthropocentrism is how he dealt with his own hunger in the following episode in Matthew 21:

> In the morning, as he was returning to the city, he was hungry. And seeing a fig tree by the wayside he went to it, and found nothing on it but leaves only. And he said to it, 'May no fruit ever come from you again!' And the fig tree withered at once. When the disciples saw it they marveled, saying, 'How did the fig tree wither at once?' And Jesus answered them, 'Truly, I say to you, if you have faith and never doubt, you will not only do what has been done to the fig tree, but even if you say to this mountain, "Be taken up and cast into the sea", it will be done. And whatever you ask in prayer, you will receive, if you have faith' (Mt. 21.18-22).

This story not only demonstrates Jesus' anthropocentrism, but also his egotism. After all, the fig tree might have served the needs of others, and not just his. Yet, he arrogates for himself the right to effectively destroy that tree so that no one else can use it. With his miraculous powers, he could

---

84. Funk, Hoover and the Jesus Seminar, *The Five Gospels*, p. 493.
85. White, 'The Historical Roots of our Ecologic Crisis', p. 1205.

just as well have made it productive and a tree whose fruit could be shared by many.

Mark 13: Eschatological Eco-Destruction

The eco-hostile attitudes of Jesus reach their widest scope in his eschatological teachings. The eschatology of Jesus outlined in Mark 13, which some scholars believe to witness the earliest version of Christian eschatology, calls not only for the destruction of sinners, but also for the destruction of nature as we know it.[86] Mark 13 certainly refutes Northcott's contention that Jesus is one 'who lives in supreme harmony with the natural order'.[87] Instead, Jesus seems to hate the natural world in which he lives.

According to Adela Yarbro Collins, '[a]lthough the Gospel of Mark is not history in the rational, empirical Greek sense or in the modern critical sense, it seems to have been such in an eschatological or apocalyptic sense and in the intention of the author'.[88] Anyone who reads Mark 13 literally would not be expected to care much about the environment. Indeed, if this world is going to be destroyed soon, then what is the use of trying to save it? If God will renovate the world, then why bother with any sort of restoration projects now? Jesus' teachings about the end of the world not only might encourage apathy, but encourage destruction of the world in order to hasten the new and improved utopia he promised.

The eschatology of Jesus has proved to be a formidable challenge to an eco-friendly view of the Bible, and some New Testament scholars admit as much. Mary Anne Tolbert, for example, remarks:

> The difficulty Mark furnishes for modern appropriation is not its negative assessment of the human situation but its solution to the problem. Mark argues that only direct divine intervention can preserve the elect from the mess this generation is making of the cosmos. While some even now may wish to continue affirming Mark's view, such acquiescence has unfortunately permitted this generation to keep increasing the mess for almost two thousand years.[89]

---

86. For example, Mann (*Mark*, p. 527) remarks: 'We have concluded that this chapter is an apocalypse which predates the composition of the gospels, and the wealth of Old Testament allusions serves to underline that conclusion.'

87. Northcott, *The Environment and Christian Ethics*, p. 224.

88. Adela Yarbro Collins, 'Narrative, History and Gospel', *Semeia* 43 (1988), pp. 143-53 (148). For the difference between eschatology and apocalypticism, see Thomas B. Slater, 'Apocalypticism and Eschatology: A Study of Mark 13:3-37', *PRSt* 40 (2013), pp. 7-18.

89. Mary Ann Tolbert, *Sowing the Gospel: Mark's World in Literary-Historical Perspective* (Minneapolis: Fortress Press, 1996), p. 310.

In a survey of the attitudes of evangelicals toward the environment, Al Truesdale observed:

> So long as evangelicals hold to an eschatology that understands the world to exist under a divinely imposed death sentence, we should expect no major change in their disposition toward the environment or the environmental movement.[90]

When speaking of the destruction of heaven and earth in 2 Pet. 3.7-13, Keith Dyer, who links that passage to Mark 13, also speaks of how 'the torching and dissolving of the heavens and the fiery melting of the elements presents irretrievable problems for an ethical response to the environment'.[91]

Despite such misgivings, there is no shortage of New Testament scholars, most of them writing from explicitly Christian viewpoints, who argue that Jesus' eschatology is not as destructive or frightening as it seems. In his defense of the eco-friendliness of Mark 13, Dyer says:

> A credible argument can be mounted, however, that the origin of the bleak apocalyptic outlook they have described is not to be found in the earliest Gospel and its setting—be it in Galilee, Syria or Rome in the late sixties or early seventies of the Common Era. Rather, we should search closer to home for the source of the heightened dualisms of apocalypticism: in nineteenth- and twentieth-century America, and wherever else we find that particular combination of modern Western science and fundamentalist Biblicism.[92]

In other words, any bleak reading of this passage is a modern construct, and not something found in Mark 13. In contrast to Dyer, I will show that any eco-friendly analysis of Jesus' eschatology rests on special pleading, and redefining what human transgressions against nature mean.

If Mark's narrative is the earliest form of Jesus' eschatological thinking, then it still looks very destructive. Note this portion:

> Pray that it may not happen in winter. For in those days there will be such tribulation as has not been from the beginning of the creation which God created until now, and never will be.

> And if the Lord had not shortened the days, no human being would be saved; but for the sake of the elect, whom he chose, he shortened the days...

90. Al Truesdale, 'Last Things First: The Impact of Eschatology on Ecology', *Perspectives on Science and Christian Faith* 46 (1994), pp. 116-22 (117).

91. Keith D. Dyer, 'When is the End Not the End? The Fate of the Earth in Biblical Eschatology', in Habel and Balabanski (eds.), *The Earth Story in the New Testament*, pp. 44-56 (56). See also Mark B. Stephens, *Annihilation or Renewal? The Meaning and Function of New Creation in the Book of Revelation* (WUNT, 2.307; Tübingen: Mohr Siebeck, 2011).

92. Dyer, 'When is the End Not the End?', p. 47.

> [A]nd the stars will be falling from heaven, and the powers in the heavens will be shaken. And then they will see the Son of man coming in clouds with great power and glory.
>
> And then he will send out the angels, and gather his elect from the four winds, from the ends of the earth to the ends of heaven (Mk 13.18-27).

This sort of rhetoric harkens back to the Divine Warrior theme that has been so well studied in the Hebrew Bible.[93]

In any case, rendering such passages as eco-friendly often relies on affirming that the language is figurative. Michael F. Bird offers one example:

> I find myself in agreement with a growing number of commentators who suggest Mark 13 concerns itself with the destruction of Jerusalem and not (directly at least) with the *parousia* of Jesus... The language of the heavens being shaken and the stars falling is not literal (like meteors crashing to earth) but it aims to introduce a transcendent perspective into the equation that the rise and demise of empires is not a matter of purely historical cause and effect (due to economic, political and social forces) but results from the radical intervention of God into the sphere of human empires, emperors, cities, and alliances. This is most aptly described as *religio-political cosmology*.[94]

Edward Adams reads Mark 13 similarly, but he is more frank about the apologetic intent when he remarks that '[r]eading the catastrophic and cosmic language in this way is an effective way of nullifying its apparent anti-environmental force'.[95]

In particular, Keith Dyer appeals to a figurative understanding of the imagery as follows:

> The cosmic events in Mk 13.24-25 can be understood...as reflecting the falling leaders and powers immediately preceding Mark's day. In this

93. For the adaptation of the Divine Warrior motif in the New Testament, see Tremper Longman, 'The Divine Warrior: The New Testament Use of an Old Testament Motif', *WTJ* 44 (1982), pp. 290-307; Thomas R. Yoder Neufeld, *Put on the Armour of God: The Divine Warrior from Isaiah to Ephesians* (Sheffield: Sheffield Academic Press, 1997); Willard M. Swartley, *Israel's Scripture and the Synoptic Gospels: Story Shaping Story* (Peabody, MA: Hendrickson, 1994), pp. 109-111. For more general basic surveys of the Divine Warrior tradition, see Millard Lind, *Yahweh is a Warrior: The Theology of Warfare in Ancient Israel* (Scottsdale, PA: Herald Press, 1980); Patrick D. Miller, *The Divine Warrior in Early Israel* (Harvard Semitic Monographs, 5; Cambridge, MA: Harvard University Press, 1973).

94. Michael F. Bird, 'Tearing the Heavens and Shaking the Heavenlies: Mark's Cosmology in its Apocalyptic Context', in *Cosmology and New Testament Theology* (ed. Jonathan T. Pennington and Seand M. McDonough; London: T. & T. Clark, 2008), pp. 45-59 (56-57); original emphasis.

95. Edward Adams, 'Retrieving the Earth from the Conflagration: 2 Peter 3.5-13 and the Environment', in Horrell *et al.* (eds.), *Ecological Hermeneutics*, pp. 108-120 (110).

setting they would be understood as the realignment of temporal powers in the East after the fall of Jerusalem and the establishment of the House of Flavian in Rome. These are the powers (the 'they' of Mk 13.26) who will witness the vindication of the human one before God in heaven, just as the High Priest will (Mk 14.62).[96]

Dyer gives no reason why we should understand the references to the darkened sun and moon, along with stars falling from heaven, as references to earthly powers that fell *immediately preceding* Mark's day, especially since other statements seem to indicate that these events had not yet taken place at the time Mark was writing (e.g., 'when you see these things taking place' in v. 29).

Dyer undertakes no close study of the Greek phraseology to support his point. For example, where else does Mark refer to earthly kings as 'the powers in the heavens'? BDAG translates the phrase, αἱ δυνάμεις τῶν οὐρανῶν σαλευθήσονται, as 'the armies of heaven will be shaken' in Mt. 24.29 (cf. Mk 13.25).[97] The movement of the heavens could be understood in a perfectly literal manner. For example, 1 Clement says that 'the heavens moving [οἱ οὐρανοὶ...σαλευόμενοι] at his appointment are subject to him in peace', and this is undoubtedly a reference to God moving the heavens physically, not some metaphor for earthly powers.[98] Indeed, Dyer does not give an instance where such a Greek expression is used for earthly powers in Mark or in the New Testament (cf. Eph. 6.12).

While it is certainly possible that the heavenly bodies are metaphors for earthly powers, the events in heaven don't seem to be less literal than the events that will occur on earth (e.g., earthquakes, famines, wars). The possibility that stars literally can fall from heaven seems perfectly reasonable in light of the cosmology of Lucretius, a Roman epicurean of the first century BCE. In his *De Rerum Natura*, Lucretius explains that the sun and moon cannot be larger than they appear because their size does not seem to change regardless of how close or far we are to them (e.g., whether on a high mountain or the floor of a valley). He concludes that 'so with all the fires of ether which you see from this earth...[they] can be only a very little indeed smaller or larger by a small and but trifling difference'.[99] Since stars are as small as one sees them, their fall to earth poses no insuperable problem

96. Dyer, 'When is the End Not the End?', p. 52.
97. See 'σαλεύω', BDAG, p. 911a.
98. 1 Clement 1.20 in *The Apostolic Fathers* (Lake, LCL).
99. Lucretius, *De Rerum Natura* 5.587-91 (Rouse and Smith, LCL). See also the comments in Cyril Bailey, *Lucretius: De Rerum Natura, Edited with Prolegomena, Critical Apparatus, Translation and Commentary* (3 vols.; New York: Oxford University Press, 1947), III, p. 1407. For a general survey of Lucretius scholarship, see Stuart Gillespie and Philip Hardie (eds.), *The Cambridge Companion to Lucretius* (Cambridge: Cambridge University Press, 2007).

in Greco-Roman cosmology. According to Seneca, 'after great earthquakes pestilence often occurs...because many deadly elements are concealed in the sky'.[100] Seneca shows that there was a real fear of literal earthquakes and associated heavenly phenomena, and so why is Mark 13 necessarily different?

Any plain reading seems to indicate that Jesus really believed that most of these destructive events were to happen literally and soon. Jesus warns his disciples to heed the signs and to flee to safer areas. It makes no sense for Jesus to wish that these events not happen in winter if he did not take them literally. It makes no sense to mix figurative events with a warning to the disciples to watch for other events that were known to occur literally (wars, earthquakes). If, as Bird and Dyer argue, the discourse is symbolic of what had already taken place, then there is no sense to the saying in v. 30: 'this generation will not pass away *before all these things* take place' (my italics). The whole point is that the Christians to whom Mark is writing should be watching for these events, and not just reflecting on past events. Clearly, there will be a cataclysmic destruction of life on earth. Angels are sent to save only those who follow Jesus, and the rest (including animals, women and children) will be destroyed by these cosmic events.

Although Dyer believes that Tolbert is characterizing Mark as eco-hostile, the fact is that Tolbert also tries to mitigate what Mark is affirming. Note, for example, Tolbert's remark that 'Mark argues that only direct divine intervention can preserve the elect from the mess this generation is making of the cosmos'.[101] But what 'mess' is Mark's generation making of the cosmos? Jesus indictment certainly does not point to his generation polluting the environment, or overtaxing its resources, or overpopulation. Rather the 'mess' of which Jesus complains is that his targets are not submitting to his imperialistic rule or that of the Kingdom of God of which he is the agent. Jesus concludes his entire discourse with the main lesson about a master and a slave: 'Watch therefore—for you do not know when the master of the house will come...' (Mk 13.35).

If one wishes to find texts that speak of environmental 'messes' that displease the gods, then one can find them in the inscriptions of Nabonidus, the last king (556–539 BCE) of the Neo-Babylonian empire. Note these divine instructions given to Nabonidus.

> E-ḫul-ḫul the temple of Sin which (is) in Harran quickly build (seeing that) the lands, all of them, to thy hands are verily committed. (But) the sons of Babylon, Borsippa, Nippur, Ur, Erech, Larsa, priests (and) people of the

---

100. Seneca, *Naturalis quaestiones* 6.27.2: 'solere post magnos terrarum motus pesti-lentiam fieri...multa enim mortifera in alto latent'. As quoted and translated in Bailey, *Lucretius*, III, p. 1651.

101. Tolbert, *Sowing the Gospel*, p. 310.

capitals of Akkad, against his great divinity offended, whenever (?) they sought after (anything) they did wickedly, they knew not the wrath (the resentment), of the king of the gods, even Nannar, they forgot their duty, whenever (?) they talked (it was) treason and not loyalty, like a dog they devoured one another; fever and famine in the midst of them they caused to be, it minished the people of the land.[102]

Here we do have at least the idea that 'the lands, all of them, to thy hands are verily committed' (mātāi (MEŠ) ka-la-ši-na ana qatâ(II)-ka lu-ták-la).[103] One encounters the idea that gods are displeased when people devour each other like dogs and cause disease and famine among them, perhaps by polluting and overtaxing their environments. Of course, one could also interpret the pestilence and famines as punishment by the gods, but the point remains that one can easily interpret this text as being about stewardship and eco-friendliness by applying the same hermeneutical maneuvers that New Testament ethicists apply to their favored texts.

Mark 13 places Jesus' discourse squarely within the long Near Eastern tradition of rulers who destroy the environments of those who don't obey their dominion. For example, when Shalmaneser III besieges Hazael, the king of Damascus, he says: '(There) I cut down his gardens (outside the city, and departed)'.[104] A later Assyrian king, Sennacherib (705–681 BCE), relates how he dealt with the lands of the Kassites and Yasubigalli, which had not submitted to his lordship: 'Their small cities, which are without number I destroyed, I devastated, I turned into ruins. The houses of the steppe, the tents, in which they dwell I burned with fire and turned them into ashes.'[105] Environmental destruction was both punitive and pragmatic, as it would deprive enemies of their resources and instill enough terror to ensure compliance.

Yahweh himself says that ecological destruction of the land of those who disobey him will be one of his punishments:

The LORD will bring a nation against you from afar, from the end of the earth, as swift as the eagle flies, a nation whose language you do not understand, a nation of stern countenance, who shall not regard the person of the old or show favor to the young, and shall eat the offspring of your cattle and the fruit of your ground, until you are destroyed; who also shall not leave you grain, wine, or oil, the increase of your cattle or the young of your flock, until they have caused you to perish (Deut. 28.49-51).

102. Nabonidus H2, A and B, lines 12-22, following the edition in C.J. Gadd, 'The Harran Inscriptions of Nabonidus', *Anatolian Studies* 8 (1958), pp. 35-92 (56-59).

103. Transliterated Akkadian in Gadd, 'The Harran Inscriptions of Nabonidus', p. 56, lines 13-14.

104. *ANET*, p. 257.

105. K. Lawson Younger, *Ancient Conquest Accounts: A Study in Ancient Near Eastern and Biblical History Writing* (Sheffield: JSOT Press, 1990), p. 113.

Yahweh's actions do not differ much from those of Assyrian campaigns, where destruction involves not just killing people, but also destroying the environment. In fact, some Near Eastern scholars have observed the similarities between Mesopotamian 'apocalyptic' prophecies and what one finds in the Bible.[106]

The destruction of Egypt's environment was certainly part of Yahweh's tools to motivate Pharaoh to liberate Israel: 'The hail struck down everything that was in the field throughout all the land of Egypt, both man and beast; and the hail struck down every plant of the field, and shattered every tree of the field' (Exod. 9.25).[107]

References to heavenly phenomena are also part of the Assyrian militaristic rhetoric. For example, note this prophetic oracle describing how the Assyrian god, Asshur, will help Essarhaddon defeat his enemies:

> I heard your cry and appeared in a fiery glow from the gate of heaven [*issu libbi abul šamê*], to throw down fire and have it devour them. As you were standing in their midst, I removed them from your presence, drove up to the mountains and rained fire and brimstone upon them. I slaughtered your enemies and filled the River with their blood.[108]

While it is true that some of this language is metaphorical and theological, there is no question that real physical violence and destruction is intended by this language. There is no question that Esarhaddon used real physical force to destroy his enemies and their territories literally. Metaphorical language does not nullify violent intentions or violent actions.

In the case of Sodom and Gomorrah, Yahweh described ecological destruction in language similar to that of Esarhaddon: 'Then the LORD rained on Sodom and Gomorrah brimstone and fire from the LORD out of heaven; and he overthrew those cities, and all the valley, and all the inhabitants of the cities, and what grew on the ground' (Gen. 19.24-25). Mark 13.24-25 derives part of its imagery from Isaiah 13, which states: 'For the stars of the heavens and their constellations will not give their light; the sun will be dark at its rising and the moon will not shed its light' (Isa. 13.10).

---

106. For example, Hector Avalos, 'Daniel 9:24-25 and Mesopotamian Temple Rededications', *JBL* 117 (1998), pp. 507-511; Hunger and Kaufman, 'A New Akkadian Prophecy Text', pp. 371-75; William W. Hallo, 'Akkadian Apocalypses', *IEJ* 16 (1966), pp. 231-42.

107. For a discussion that includes ecological perspectives, see Ziony Zevit, 'Three Ways to Look at the Ten Plagues', *BR* 6 (1990), pp. 16-23, 42.

108. SAA 9 3.3, lines 14-23, following the edition of Martin Nissinen, C.L. Seow and Robert Ritner, *Prophets and Prophecy in the Ancient Near East* (Writings of the Ancient World, 12; Atlanta, GA: Society of Biblical Literature, 2003), p. 120. See also Jonathan Stökl, *Prophecy in the Ancient Near East: A Philological and Sociological Comparison* (Culture and History of the Ancient Near East, 56; Leiden: E.J. Brill, 2012).

Yet, Isaiah 13 clearly shows that Yahweh sees himself as engaging in a military campaign: 'The LORD Almighty is mustering an army for war' (Isa. 13.4; NIV). Just as Esarhaddon destroyed environments while using metaphorical language, a Hebrew author could convey with metaphorical language the intention to destroy environments of enemies literally.

Another attempt to defend Jesus' eschatology from the charge of eco-hostility is perhaps the most ethically odious and puzzling of all. This attempt relies on the claim that the apocalyptic descriptions one sees in Mark 13 and elsewhere speak of transformation rather than complete destruction. In discussing eschatological references to the new earth that replaces the present earth (cf. Mk 13.31; Rev. 21.5; and 2 Pet. 3.3-13), Gale Heide remarks: 'I think it most likely that this creation is a transformed creation returned to a likeness of its original state.'[109] Heide emphasizes that destruction does not mean complete physical annihilation (e.g., of all atoms and their constituents), and makes similar arguments for the pre-Christian sources of this language in Isaiah 65.17 and elsewhere.[110] In particular, Heide argues the following concerning the meaning of λυθήσεται (a passive form of λύω) in 2 Pet. 3.10:

> It could also mean the breaking down into component parts or even the release from bondage. While it is certain that some form of physical alteration is meant by this word, it may be a process of refinement instead of a total eradication of all physical substance. The comparison Peter makes with the Flood is instructive here.[111]

Heide points to the fact that Noah's Flood 'did not destroy the earth completely'.[112] That is to say, there is no eradication of all physical substance, but

---

109. Gale Z. Heide, 'What is New about the New Heaven and the New Earth: A Theology of Creation from Revelation 21 to 2 Peter 3', *JETS* 40 (1997), pp. 37-56 (48).

110. Heide, 'What is New', p. 51 n. 42. For treatments of Isaiah 65, see Anne Gardner, 'Ecojustice or Anthropological Justice? A Study of the New Heavens and the New Earth in Isaiah 65.17', in Habel (ed.), *The Earth Story in Psalms and the Prophets*, pp. 204-218; Michael Chan, 'Isaiah 65–66 and the Genesis of Reorienting Speech', *CBQ* 72 (2010), pp. 445-63; Tremper Longman, 'Isaiah 65:17-25', *Int* 64 (2010), pp. 72-73; Konrad Schmid, 'Neue Schöpfung als Überbietung de neuen Exodus. Die tritojesajanische Aktualisierung der deuterojesajanischen Theologie und die Tora', in *Schriftgelehrte Traditionsliteratur: Fallstudien zur innerbiblischen Schriftauslegung im Alten Testament* (ed. Konrad Schmid; FAT, 77; Tübingen: Mohr Siebeck, 2011), pp. 185-205. See also John J. Collins, 'The Beginning and End of the World in the Hebrew Bible', in *Thus Says the Lord: Essays on the Former and Latter Prophets in Honor of Robert R. Wilson* (ed. John J. Ahn and Stephen L. Cook; Library of Hebrew Bible/Old Testament Studies, 502; London: T. & T. Clark, 2009), pp. 137-55.

111. Heide, 'What is New', p. 53.

112. Heide, 'What is New', p. 53.

rather a dissolution into constituent parts.[113] In fact, one can almost speak of 'recycling', which is usually an eco-friendly process in modern times. As Adams phrases it: 'For the writer of 2 Peter, matter is not to be dumped into eternal nothingness but *recycled*.'[114]

The reason that this approach is ethically odious is that it seems to suggest that the destruction of the present biosphere is morally acceptable so long as one does not eradicate the atomic components of the entire planet or the existence of the entire planet. To say that such texts speak of transformation and not destruction involves a false dichotomy because all destruction entails transformation. The act of transforming by itself tells us nothing about the moral worthiness of that action.

One could reduce this approach to absurdity by insisting on the moral acceptability of burning people alive or bombing civilians because one did not entirely destroy their atomic components. These people were only 'transformed' or dissolved into their component parts. Indeed, it assumes that 'transformation' is always morally unobjectionable. One need only point to Nazi Germany, where some Holocaust victims were infamously transformed and 'recycled' into lampshades, to understand that 'transformation' is not necessarily more laudable than total destruction or ontological annihilation.[115]

Biblically, this entire line of argument is unsupportable. Neither the biblical god nor Jesus viewed the Flood or other destructive actions as a good thing for those who were punished by them. In the case of the Flood, Jesus comments:

> As were the days of Noah, so will be the coming of the Son of man. For as in those days before the flood they were eating and drinking, marrying and giving in marriage, until the day when Noah entered the ark, and they did not know until the flood came and swept them all away, so will be the coming of the Son of man (Mt. 24.37-39).

Jesus does not see the Flood as a good thing for those who perished despite the fact that the earth was not completely destroyed or that the constituent matter still remained. The biocidal Flood was interpreted to be a real historical event by Jesus, and not some metaphorical narrative about the fall of earthly powers. Jesus envisions an even worse punishment for those who

---

113. A similar rationale is manifested by Gardner ('Ecojustice or Anthropological Justice?', pp. 217-18) for Isa. 65.17: '[D]evastation is not the equivalent of obliteration. In addition, Zion is to be renewed and assured of perpetuity as its only inhabitants will be those loyal to God... In conclusion, the context of Isa. 65.17 advocates both anthropological justice and ecojustice.'

114. Adams, 'Retrieving the Earth from the Conflagration', p. 117. Adams's italics.

115. On these Nazi atrocities, see Mark Jacobson, *The Lampshade: A Holocaust Detective Story from Buchenwald to New Orleans* (New York: Simon and Schuster, 2010).

did not obey his directives: 'And if any one will not receive you or listen to your words, shake off the dust from your feet as you leave that house or town. Truly, I say to you, it shall be more tolerable on the day of judgment for the land of Sodom and Gomorrah than for that town' (Mt. 10.14-15). So, if Jesus thought the punishment of Sodom and Gomorrah was historically literal, then why would a worse future punishment not be even more literally harsh or at least just as literally harsh (cf. 'the sign of Jonah' in Mt. 12.39-41)?[116]

It would be difficult to salvage any eco-friendly aspect of Mark 13 even if one reads it completely metaphorically. The fact is no metaphorical destruction needs to take place at all. According to Mark, Jesus was able to heal people without destroying them. He could restore paralyzed limbs and return lost senses without destroying the patient. There was no logical reason why the author of Mark could not conceive of a god who could heal the entire planet of its sin or transgressive behavior without destroying it. The fact that the Markan Jesus does not use destructive metaphors or language when speaking of healing people, and the fact that the Markan Jesus does use destructive language when speaking of reforming our larger world, is what makes Mark's Jesus eco-hostile and anthropocentric.

Summary

Jesus is not eco-friendly by any major definition developed by modern environmental ethicists. While one can find some instances where Jesus seems to care for animals (e.g., Mt. 12.11-12 where Jesus only confirms that people are more valuable than sheep), the Gospels repeatedly refute Northcott's claim that Jesus lives in harmony with nature, just as they refute the notion that not harming nature is a bedrock principle of Christian ethics. The depictions of Jesus in the Gospels reveal a blatant anthropocentrism and speciesism when he transfers demons to a herd of swine that end up drowning in the sea. He violently drove animals from the temple in Jn 2.15 instead of proclaiming their liberation. His egoism is revealed by his cursing of a fig tree when he could have made it produce more fruit that could be shared by everyone. His hatred of nature as we know it underlines the destruction of this world envisioned in Mark 13. If anything, Jesus is predominantly eco-hostile.

116. For an interpretation of 'the sign of Jonah' as a violent judgment, see George M. Landes, 'Matthew 12:40 as an Interpretation of "the Sign of Jonah" against its Biblical Background', in *The Word of the Lord Shall Go Forth: Essays in Honor of David Noel Freedman in Celebration of his Sixtieth Birthday* (ed. Carol L. Meyers and M. O'Connor; Winona Lake, IN: Eisenbrauns, 1983), pp. 665-84; R.A. Edwards, *The Sign of Jonah in the Theology of the Evangelists and Q* (London: SCM Press, 1971).

The metaethics of Christian ethicists in the case of animals have been shown to be internally inconsistent and ethically questionable in themselves. Attempts to deny the victimization of animals in the biblical sacrificial system flounder on admissions that such sacrifices were either unnecessary (so, Morgan) or that they redefine 'victimhood'. Even if one accepted the argument that some larger cosmic harmony was the reason for Israel's sacrificial system, that would not be much of an ethical justification for sacrifice. It becomes simply another version of the Greater Good theodicy and it is human beings who are doing the determining of what the Greater Good is.

It is also a vacuous exercise to render Jesus' eschatology more eco-friendly by calling it a transformation or merely figurative. Even if one accepts the argument that Jesus intended to speak of transforming the earth rather than obliterating it completely, one does not gain much in terms of motivating believers to be more eco-friendly. If belief that the earth will be destroyed is responsible for some of the apathy toward the environment, then how would belief that the earth will merely be transformed lessen the apathy? Why bother to seek restoration of damaged environments or stop eco-hostile behavior if one believes that God will soon transform the earth? By re-envisioning destruction as transformation or recycling one simply is 'kicking the can down the road' again.

Perhaps apologists can argue that Jesus is not expected to have any sort of sophistication about ecological systems or even the history of our earth. After all, if God takes such great care of wildlife, why have most species that have lived on our planet become extinct even before human beings arrived on the scene, especially since God promises to preserve all that he created (cf. Neh. 9.6)?[117] But if we exempt Jesus from any scientific knowledge of eco-systems, then one must also reject claims by Christian ethicists that he lived in perfect harmony with nature.

The fact is that Jesus could not do so without more sophisticated knowledge of how eco-systems work. So, either Christian ethicists need to cease making such claims or explain why we should ascribe some laudable environmental ethical concepts to Jesus while denying them to many other ancient sages who also might have lacked sophisticated knowledge of eco-systems. Equally important, one can use some of the same hermeneutical techniques (e.g., it is meant 'figuratively') used by Christian exegetes in biblical interpretation to render almost any ancient Near Eastern text just as eco-friendly regardless of how eco-destructive its language may seem.

---

117. See Peter Douglas Ward, *Under a Green Sky: Global Warming, the Mass Extinctions of the Past, and What they can Tell us about our Future* (New York: HarperCollins, 2007).

There is no doubt that much of what passes for New Testament ethics involves religiocentrism and special pleading. For example, if Christian ethicists appeal to the supernatural worldview to justify the sacrificing of animals, then they would encounter many other ethical problems. By that standard, any religion that wishes to slaughter any number of animals would be similarly justified. In her study of the role of animal sacrifice in Mesopotamia, JoAnn Scurlock concludes:

> In sum, animals played an important role in ancient Mesopotamia sacrifice; the regular offerings and covenant sacrifices that they made possible were as crucial to the maintenance of cordial relations between human and divine powers as treaty sacrifices were to cement alliances between human beings.[118]

A similar purpose can be attributed to all animal sacrifice in the ancient Near East, and it would only be religiocentrism that justified Hebrew sacrifice over that of other cultures. And if the religious premises of other cultures also justify killing animals, then I am not sure how that avoids anthropocentrism or utilitarianism on the part of any theistic animal ethics.

At the same time, Christian ethicists cannot claim that Jesus is in perfect harmony with nature unless they specify how they are defining 'nature', which, for modern ethicists, does not include the supernatural in any of its rationales. Thus, Baird Callicott affirms that '[t]he idea that God gave morals to man is ruled out in principle—as any supernatural explanation of a natural phenomenon is ruled out in principle in natural science'.[119] Jesus was a human being as ignorant and as eco-hostile or as eco-friendly any other human being in the ancient Near East. Attempting to make him something more than a human being of his time on questions of environmental ethics only betrays the modern apologetic intent of New Testament ethics.

118. JoAnn Scurlock, 'Animal Sacrifices in Ancient Mesopotamian Religion', in *A History of the Animal World in the Ancient Near East* (ed. Billie Jean Collins; Leiden: E.J. Brill, 2002), pp. 389-403 (403).

119. J. Baird Callicott, 'The Conceptual Foundations of the Land Ethic', in Zimmerman *et al.* (eds.), *Environmental Philosophy: From Animal Rights to Radical Ecology*, pp. 110-34 (113).

Chapter 13

THE ANTI-BIBLICAL JESUS: MISSED INTERPRETATIONS

In 2004, Mel Gibson released *The Passion of the Christ*, one of the most successful movies about Jesus ever made. In various interviews and literature provided by Icon, the film's production company, *The Passion* was promoted as an authentic and historically accurate depiction of the death of Jesus. To lend even more credibility to the film's claims of authenticity, the language spoken by the characters was entirely in Aramaic and/ or Latin, despite the fact that Koine Greek may have been more appropriate in many instances. Gibson, in fact, went so far as to hire a biblical scholar, William J. Fulco, to ensure that Jesus spoke the best Galilean Aramaic one could reconstruct.[1] Nonetheless, Gibson admits that much of what one finds in *The Passion* is inspired by the work of Anne Catherine Emmerich (1774–1824), who wrote meditations now widely regarded as permeated with anti-Judaism.[2]

Mel and Jesus: The Hypocrisy of New Testament Ethics

Despite its enormous popularity with the general public, Gibson's film was met with a barrage of criticisms from biblical scholars who pointed out how much he had misrepresented the Bible. Most critical responses came in the form of anthologies, and these included: *Jesus and Mel Gibson's The Passion of the Christ: The Film, the Gospels, and the Claims of History* (2004),

---

1. William J. Fulco describes his role as follows: 'Collaborator with Icon Productions (Mel Gibson) in the production of THE PASSION, a feature film based on the New Testament narratives of the Passion and Death of Christ. Specifically, translating the dialogues into reconstructed First Century AD Aramaic and other contemporaneous languages, and advising on historical and archaeological continuity' (Fulco's capitalization). See William J. Fulco, 'Curriculum Vitae' (online: http://myweb.lmu.edu/wfulco/CV.htm). See also Steven Fassberg, 'Which Semitic Languages did Jesus and Other Contemporary Jews Speak?', *CBQ* 74 (2012), pp. 263-80.

2. For an edition, see Noel L. Griese (ed.), *The Dolorous Passion of our Lord Jesus Christ after the Meditations of Anne Catherine Emmerich as Told to Clemens Brentano* (Atlanta, GA: Anvil, 2005). This edition is keyed to more than forty scenes in *The Passion of the Christ*.

Re-Viewing the Passion: Mel Gibson's Film and its Critics (2004), *After the Passion is Gone: American Religious Consequences* (2004), *Mel Gibson's Bible* (2006) and *On the Passion of the Christ: Exploring the Issues Raised by the Controversial Movie* (2006).[3] Many of the editors and contributors who criticized Gibson also are prominent discussants of New Testament ethics, and these included John Dominic Crossan, Craig A. Evans and Paula Fredriksen.

Most films about Jesus or the Bible are replete with flaws and anachronisms, but it was the ethical dimensions and implications of the film that most alarmed the biblical scholars who criticized it.[4] In particular, critics feared that the film would promote anti-Semitism because it gave more prominence to the role of the Jews in Jesus' execution than these scholars thought the New Testament records allowed or recorded. Paula Fredriksen stated:

3.   Kathleen E. Corley and Robert L. Webb (eds.), *Jesus and Mel Gibson's The Passion of the Christ: The Film, the Gospels, and the Claims of History* (London and New York: Continuum, 2004); S. Brend Plate (ed.), *Re-Viewing the Passion: Mel Gibson's Film and its Critics* (New York: Palgrave Macmillan, 2004); J. Shawn Landres and Michael Berenbaum, *After the Passion is Gone: American Religious Consequences* (Walnut Creek, CA: AltaMira Press, 2004); Timothy K. Beal and Todd Linafelt (eds.), *Mel Gibson's Bible* (Chicago, IL: University of Chicago Press, 2006); Paula Fredriksen, *On the Passion of the Christ: Exploring the Issues Raised by the Controversial Movie* (Berkeley, CA: University of California Press, 2006); S. Bouvier, 'La Passion: La ligne rouge de Mel Gibson', *Nova et Vetera* 79 (2004), pp. 103-112; Christian A. Eberhart, 'The "Passion" of Gibson: Evaluating a Recent Interpretation of Christ's Suffering and Death in Light of the New Testament', *Consensus* 30 (2005), pp. 37-74; Mary C. Boys, '"I Didn't See Any Anti-Semitism": Why Many Christians Don't Have a Problem with *The Passion of the Christ*', *Cross Currents* 54 (2004), pp. 8-15; Alan F. Segal, '"How I Stopped Worrying about Mel Gibson and Learned to Love the Quest for the Historical Jesus": A Review of Mel Gibson's *The Passion of the Christ*', *Journal for the Study of the Historical Jesus* 2 (2004), pp. 190-208.

4.   On the use of use and abuse of history in movies, see Ted Mico, John Miller-Monzon and David Rubel, *Past Imperfect: History According to the Movies* (New York: Henry Holt and Company, 1995). On the use of the Bible in modern film, see Adele Reinhartz (ed.), *Bible and Cinema: Fifty Key Films* (London and New York: Routledge, 2013); idem, 'History and Pseudo-History in the Jesus Film Genre', *BibInt* 14 (2006), pp. 1-17; Richard C. Stern, Clayton N. Jefford and Guerric Debona, *Savior on the Silver Screen* (New York: Paulist Press, 1999); W. Barnes Tatum, *Jesus at the Movies: A Guide to the First Hundred Years* (Santa Rosa, CA: Polebridge Press, 1997); Joel W. Martin and Conrad E. Oswalt (eds.), *Screening the Sacred: Religion, Myth, and Ideology in Popular American Film* (Boulder, CO: Westview Press, 1995); Bernard Brandon Scott, *Hollywood Dreams and Biblical Stories* (Minneapolis: Fortress Press, 1994); Bruce Babington and Peter William Evans, *Biblical Epics: Sacred Narrative in the Hollywood Cinema* (Manchester: Manchester University Press, 1993); Gerald E. Forshey, *American Religious and Biblical Spectaculars* (Westport, CT: Praeger, 1992). For the role of film in biblical apologetics, see Hector Avalos, 'Film and the Apologetics of Biblical Violence', *Journal of Religion and Film* 13 (April 2009). Online: http://www.unomaha.edu/jrf/vol13.no1/BiblicalViolence.htm.

[I]n a film as ideologically charged as Gibson's, presented with as much
historical pretense, the anachronisms can also be dangerous. In insisting
that the viewer was getting biblically authentic, intensely realistic, look
at the first century past and the execution of Jesus of Nazareth, Icon actually retailed the luridly violent and intrinsically anti-Jewish fiction of the
Middle Ages.[5]

Fredriksen added that *The Passion* 'is *not* a movie based on the Gospels.
And it is certainly not a movie about the historical Jesus.'[6]

Many of the specific errors cited certainly represent major contradictions
to the Gospels, but they also included these: (a) 'there was not a "Great
Hall" in proximity to the Holy of Holies where a Sanhedrin and a large
Jewish crowd could assemble for a nighttime trial of Jesus'; (b) 'There were
no pillars near the Holy of Holies'.[7] These architectural misrepresentations
allowed Gibson to portray the Jewish crowds in the temple as larger than
they were. When confronted with such historical inaccuracies and anachronisms, Gibson responded that 'it's a movie not a documentary', and he
appealed to his right to include artistic licenses in his interpretation.[8]

At the same time, Fredriksen and other critics felt that the emphasis on
the crucifixion in *The Passion* means that 'the significance of Jesus' life is
obscured' and that 'viewers learn virtually nothing about the ministry of
Jesus, of his teaching and preaching about God's reign, his distinctive table
companionship, his mediation of God's gracious mercy'.[9] Similarly, Margaret Miles complains that 'Christians could become better Christians, not
by viewing a Hollywood director's interpretation of Christ's sufferings, but
by participating in Christ's teachings and ministry'.[10] Of course, all of this
assumes that these activities are historically verified to be performed by
Jesus rather than the product of the Gospel writers' theological imagination. In any case, the main ethical premise behind such criticisms of Gibson
is that misrepresenting scripture is not only wrong, but anti-biblical and
dangerous.

Yet, when it comes to Jesus' misrepresentations of scripture, New Testament ethicists, many of whom criticized Gibson, are stonily silent. After
all, did Gibson do anything to the New Testament that Jesus did not do to

5. Paula Fredriksen, 'Preface', in Fredriksen (ed.), *On the Passion of the Christ*,
p. xxii.

6. Fredriksen, 'Gospel Truths', in Fredriksen (ed.), *On the Passion of the Christ*,
p. 32. Fredriksen's italics.

7. Fredriksen, 'Report of The Ad Hoc Scholars Group: Reviewing the Script of *The
Passion*', in Fredriksen (ed.), *On the Passion of the Christ*, pp. 225-54 (232).

8. Fredriksen, 'Gospel Truths', p. 32.

9. Fredriksen, 'The Ad Hoc Scholars Group', p. 233.

10. Margaret Miles, 'The Passion for Social Justice', in Beal and Linafelt (eds.), *Mel
Gibson's Bible*, pp. 121-27 (127).

the Hebrew Bible? Why, then, is Gibson so heavily censured while Jesus' scripture-twisting and scriptural illiteracy escapes unscathed in New Testament scholarship? The answer again lies in the fact that the criticisms of Gibson by these biblical scholars really involve a theological dispute, and not simply a dispute about historical accuracy. Nor is it truly a dispute about the dangers of misinterpretation because Jesus' misinterpretations of the Hebrew Bible have had consequences that make those of Gibson pale in comparison.

Behind all the anti-Gibsonian rhetoric is the assumption that there was an original intent to the biblical text that Gibson is not honoring. There is also an assumption that there are historical facts about Jesus that Gibson is not honoring.

Those assumptions are sound, but they should apply to Jesus just the same. After all, the existence of an original authorial intent that should be honored and respected is part of Jesus' culture, as well. Jesus assumed it when he told the Sadducees in Mt. 22.29: 'You are wrong, because you know neither the scriptures nor the power of God', and then proceeded to quote scripture to prove his point. The assumption is repeated every time Jesus or a Gospel author says that Jesus has fulfilled scripture by performing some act (cf. Mt. 5.17).

In any case, to understand this disparity in the way Gibson is treated by New Testament scholars as compared to Jesus, one should begin by categorizing the sorts of misrepresentations that Gibson allegedly committed. These basically consist of: (a) flatly contradicting scriptural accounts; (b) adding material that is not canonical and late compared to the Gospels; (c) interpreting scripture contrary to its original intent and context; and (d) inventing and promoting interpretations that, even if sound, are dangerous, especially to the Jewish community. The fact is that Jesus can be accused of every single one of these criticisms, but most New Testament ethicists simply ignore the facts or seek to justify what Jesus did in terms of biblical hermeneutics.

Mark 2.23-28: Jesus as Biblically Illiterate

Given the superior authority and divine status usually accorded to Jesus in New Testament ethics, it is not surprising that very few works on the ethics of Jesus mention what otherwise might be termed dangerous biblical illiteracy on the part of Jesus. Some of the works that focus on Jesus' use of scripture do not show much interest in any misuse of scripture by Jesus.[11] Indeed, Jesus makes statements about scripture that would be

---

11. For example, Steve Moyise, *Jesus and Scripture: Studying the New Testament Use of the Old Testament* (Grand Rapids, MI: Baker Academic, 2010); Emerson B.

judged as wrong and factually inaccurate if anyone else expressed them. One case involves Jesus' justification for allowing his disciples to pluck grain on the Sabbath in Mark 2:

> One sabbath he was going through the grainfields; and as they made their way his disciples began to pluck heads of grain. And the Pharisees said to him, 'Look, why are they doing what is not lawful on the sabbath?' And he said to them, 'Have you never read what David did, when he was in need and was hungry, he and those who were with him: how he entered the house of God, when Abiathar was high priest, and ate the bread of the Presence, which it is not lawful for any but the priests to eat, and also gave it to those who were with him?' And he said to them, 'The sabbath was made for man, not man for the sabbath; so the Son of man is lord even of the sabbath' (Mk 2.23-28).

Jesus is referring to the narrative in 1 Samuel 21, and the relevant verse of that narrative states: 'Then came David to Nob to Ahimelech the priest; and Ahimelech came to meet David trembling, and said to him, "Why are you alone, and no one with you?"' (1 Sam. 21.1).

In the Hebrew Bible (MT) the priest's name is given there as Ahimelech, and not as Abiathar. Abiathar is the son of Ahimelech according to 1 Sam. 30.7. The Lucianic Greek text also has Ahimelech, although Abimelech is found in the Greek text represented by the Codex Vaticanus. Most text critics agree that Ahimelech is probably the earlier reading, and Abimelech is incorrect.[12]

But whether the 'original' reading is Ahimelech or Abimelech, the reading is certainly not Abiathar. This much is admitted in Christopher S. Mann's commentary on Mark: 'The statement in Mark is incorrect, for Ahimelech his father was high priest at the time.'[13]

However, even when one can attribute any problem with the priest's name to the manuscript tradition rather than to what Jesus may have actually said, there remains another misrepresentation of that story. Jesus indicates that David 'entered the house of God' (Mk 2.26). However, the Hebrew text of 1 Sam. 21.1 indicates no such thing: 'Ahimelech came

Powery, *Jesus Reads Scripture: The Function of Jesus' Use of Scripture in the Synoptic Gospels* (Biblical Interpretation, 63; Leiden: E.J. Brill, 2003); Gregory K. Beale, *Handbook on the New Testament Use of Old Testament. Exegesis and Interpretation* (Grand Rapids, MI: Baker Academic, 2012); Mary Healy, 'The Hermeneutic of Jesus', *Communio/International Catholic Review* 37 (2010), pp. 477-95. On how the Gospel writers utilized the Hebrew Bible to construct their portraits of Jesus, see Richard B. Hays, *Reading Backwards: Figural Christology and the Fourfold Gospel Witness* (Waco, TX: Baylor University Press, 2014).

    12. See also P. Kyle McCarter, *1 Samuel: A New Translation with Introduction and Commentary* (AB, 8; Garden City, NY: Doubleday, 1980), p. 347.
    13. Mann, *Mark*, p. 238.

to meet David trembling' (וַיֶּחֱרַד אֲחִימֶלֶךְ לִקְרַאת דָּוִד). Similarly, the narrative in the Hebrew Bible never indicates that David was in the temple
after that. In 1 Sam. 21.6 it says that 'the priest gave him the holy bread'
(וַיִּתֶּן לוֹ הַכֹּהֵן קֹדֶשׁ), which could mean that the priest fetched it and then
gave it to David as the latter waited outside. As noted by *The Jewish
Annotated New Testament*, the text of 1 Sam. 21 also does not say explicitly that David was motivated by hunger at the moment that he took the
bread, and it may have been meant for later consumption.[14] So, either
Jesus added details that are not in the actual text or he willfully misrepresented the text to win his argument.

Steve Moyise, who wrote an entire book titled *Jesus and Scripture* completely ignores the discrepancy.[15] Mary Healy is one scholar who defends
Jesus' substitution of Abiathar for Ahimelech.[16] According to Healy, 'Jesus'
mention of Abiathar instead of his father Ahimelech may be a case of substituting the more important for the less'.[17] For her evidence she cites rabbinic texts (*b. Menah* 95b; *Yal.* 130) where David's words in 1 Sam. 21.5 are
interpreted, according to Healy, as follows: 'Of a truth women have been
kept from us as always when I go on an expedition; the vessels of the young
men are holy, even when it is a common journey; how much more today
will their vessels be holy?'[18] However, this explains nothing, and there is no
substitution of names at all.

Healy's next piece of evidence is even more difficult to understand
because she refers the reader to the commentary on Mark by Morna D.
Hooker.[19] But Hooker says that,

> The statement that this took place **in the time of Abiathar the high priest**
> is incorrect; the high priest at the time was Ahimelech father of Abiathar
> (1 Sam. 21.1-6) but, since the latter was better known, the mistake is a nat-
> ural one.[20]

14. Lawrence Wills, 'Mark', in Levine and Brettler (eds.), *The Jewish Annotated New
Testament*, pp. 55-95 (65). McCarter (*1 Samuel*, p. 349) also assumes that David and his
men are to eat of it, though he does not specify whether they are hungry at the moment
or whether they will eat it once they do become hungry.

15. Moyise, *Jesus and Scripture*, pp. 15-16, where 1 Sam. 21.1-6 is discussed.

16. Healy, 'The Hermeneutic of Jesus', pp. 477-95. Other studies defensive of Jesus'
use of Abimelech include John R. Donahue and Daniel J. Harrington, *The Gospel of
Mark* (Sacra Pagina; Collegeville, MN: Liturgical Press, 2002), p. 111; Ratzinger, *Jesus
of Nazareth*, pp. 106-112. Ratzinger actually does not even note Jesus' statement about
Abiathar as a problem at all.

17. Healy, 'The Hermeneutic of Jesus', p. 487.

18. Healy, 'The Hermeneutic of Jesus', p. 487 n. 25.

19. Healy, 'The Hermeneutic of Jesus', p. 487 n. 26.

20. Morna Hooker, *The Gospel According to St. Mark* (Black's New Testament Commentaries; New York: Continuum, 1991), p. 103. Hooker's bold emphasis.

While Healy represents Jesus as using a rabbinic hermeneutic rule wherein one can substitute a more important name for a less important one, Hooker attributes the change to a simple mistake. Clearly, nothing adduced by Healy refutes the charge that Jesus made a mistake or misrepresented scripture.

Was Jesus' gaffe or misrepresentation as dangerous as any of Gibson's gaffes or misrepresentations? If Jesus' desecration of the Sabbath was imitated by later Christians, then it certainly might have led to violence. On the other hand, a full decade after Gibson's movie there are no major incidents of anti-Jewish violence compared to what has been generated by Jesus' own words here and elsewhere in the New Testament (e.g., Jn 8.44). Jesus is portrayed as allowing at least some people to justify the ends through whatever means he thinks are necessary, and that includes desecrating the temple when it is necessary. Moreover, unlike the unclear motives of David in 1 Samuel 21, the ultimate motivation given by Jesus is for self-aggrandizement in Mk 2.27-28: 'The sabbath was made for man, not man for the sabbath; so the Son of man is lord even of the sabbath.'

Even if Jesus is historically correct, scholars could agree that his statements are inflammatory. This is important to observe because Gibson is sometimes being judged not on whether he is intentionally anti-Semitic, but on the mere fact that he is being inflammatory. Paula Fredriksen remarks:

> Is *The Passion of the Christ anti-Semitic*? The question is misconceived. The only thing that matters is that the film is inflammatory, and that its depiction of Jewish villainy—exaggerated well beyond what is in the Gospels and violating historical knowledge we have of early-first century Judea will give aid and comfort to anti-Semites everywhere… Real Jews have suffered for it.[21]

Fair enough, but by that standard, the words of Jesus have been far more inflammatory for the last two thousand years and created more suffering among Jews than Mel Gibson probably ever will.

Matthew 19: Jesus Adds his Own Twist on Divorce

On another occasion, Jesus injects his own rationales into Mosaic law and then attributes them to Moses. In particular, note Jesus' interpretation of Mosaic law of divorce in Matthew 19:

> And Pharisees came up to him and tested him by asking, 'Is it lawful to divorce one's wife for any cause?' He answered, 'Have you not read that he who made them from the beginning made them male and female', and said, '"For this reason a man shall leave his father and mother and be joined to his wife, and the two shall become one flesh"? So they are no longer two but one flesh. What therefore God has joined together, let not man put

---

21. Fredriksen, 'Gospel Truths', pp. 46-47.

asunder'. They said to him, 'Why then did Moses command one to give a certificate of divorce, and to put her away?' He said to them, 'For your hardness of heart Moses allowed you to divorce your wives, but from the beginning it was not so. And I say to you: whoever divorces his wife, except for unchastity, and marries another, commits adultery' (Mt. 19.3-9).

Jesus alludes to two specific texts in the Hebrew Bible: Gen. 2.24 and Deuteronomy 24. Leaving aside for the moment Jesus' questionable interpretation of Gen. 2.24, there is nothing in the text of Deuteronomy 24, which Jesus is referencing, that indicates that Moses allowed divorce '[f]or your hardness of heart'.[22] In fact, Deut. 24.4 states that one should observe this law so that 'you shall not bring guilt upon the land which the LORD your God gives you for an inheritance'. Apparently, Jesus gives himself license, just as Mel Gibson gave himself license, to add whatever material or rationale he feels is appropriate for his audience.[23] One cannot object that Gibson's license is artistic or purely for entertainment. After all, Gibson also insists that his film is aimed to be pedagogical and instructive.

Psalm 41: A Prophecy about Judas?

Mel Gibson uses supposed biblical prophecies to serve his agenda. Indeed, Gibson begins *The Passion* with a quote from Isa. 53.5 ('He was wounded for our transgressions, crushed for our iniquities; by His wounds we are healed'), which serves as the background for his entire vision of a tortured Christ.[24] Apparently, critics of Gibson think it a great violation to take an

---

22. I do not know of any scholarship that directly challenges Jesus' interpretation of Gen. 2.24, but recent treatments of Jesus' views of that passage include Levine, 'Jesus, Divorce, and Sexuality', Bryan F. LeBeau, Leonard Greenspoon and Dennis Hamm; London: pp. 113-29; Casey D. Elledge, '"From the Beginning it was Not So...": Jesus, Divorce and Remarriage in Light of the Dead Sea Scrolls', *PRSt* 37 (2010), pp. 371-90. For the view that Gen. 2.24 does not restrict marriage only to monogamy, see Peter J. Dorey, 'Genesis 2:24: *Locus classicus* van monogamie in die Ou Testament? 'n literêr-historiese ondersoek na perspektiewe op poligamie huwelike in die Ou Testament', *OTE* 17 (2004), pp. 15-29. See also Paul Krueger, 'Etiology or Obligation? Genesis 2:24 Reconsidered in the Light of Textual Linguistics', in *Thinking Towards New Horizons: Collected Communications to the XIXth Congress of the International Organization for the Study of the Old Testament, Ljubljana 2007* (ed. Matthias Augustin and Hermann Michael Niemann; Beiträge zur Erforschung des Alten Testaments und des antiken Judentums, 55: Frankfurt: Peter Lang, 2008), pp. 35-47.

23. Angelo Tosato ('On Genesis 2.24', *CBQ* 52 [1990], pp. 389-409) believes that Gen. 2.24 is itself a gloss added to the text in the Persian period to explain matrimonial legislation adopted in that period.

24. Following the translation of Isa. 53.5 in *The Passion*. See further Jeremy Schipper, *Disability and Isaiah's Suffering Servant*; Robert B. Chisholm, 'The Christological Fulfillment of Isaiah's Servant Songs', *BibSac* 163 (2006), pp. 387-404; Janowski and

isolated verse in the Hebrew Bible to build an entire narrative focused on the theme of that verse. Yet, Jesus also reads texts in the Hebrew Bible in a prophetic manner that modern New Testament scholars would probably regard as egregiously wrong if read in that manner by anyone else. Jesus' interpretations hold up only if one assumes that he has some privileged divine knowledge, which should not be the case for a mere human being.

A particularly offensive case is how Jesus uses Ps. 41.9 (Heb. 41.10) in the following passage from John:

> When he had washed their feet, and taken his garments, and resumed his place, he said to them, 'Do you know what I have done to you? You call me Teacher and Lord; and you are right, for so I am. If I then, your Lord and Teacher, have washed your feet, you also ought to wash one another's feet. For I have given you an example, that you also should do as I have done to you. Truly, truly, I say to you, a servant is not greater than his master; nor is he who is sent greater than he who sent him. If you know these things, blessed are you if you do them. I am not speaking of you all; I know whom I have chosen; it is that the scripture may be fulfilled, "He who ate my bread has lifted his heel against me". I tell you this now, before it takes place, that when it does take place you may believe that I am he. Truly, truly, I say to you, he who receives any one whom I send receives me; and he who receives me receives him who sent me'. When Jesus had thus spoken, he was troubled in spirit, and testified, 'Truly, truly, I say to you, one of you will betray me' (Jn 13.12-21).

Jesus, who identifies with the speaker of Ps. 41.9 (MT 41.10), seems to be applying the actions described by that speaker to Judas, who is presumably the traitorous meal companion who is being referenced prophetically in that Psalm.[25]

The problem, of course, is that Psalm 41 is not a prophecy in its original context, and Jesus has completely decontextualized the verse he quotes. To understand the extent to which Jesus has decontextualized his quote, it is useful to provide the entire psalm:

> Blessed is he who considers the poor! The LORD delivers him in the day of trouble; the LORD protects him and keeps him alive; he is called blessed in the land; thou dost not give him up to the will of his enemies. The LORD sustains him on his sickbed; in his illness thou healest all his infirmities. As for

Stuhlmacher (eds.), *The Suffering Servant*; Bellinger and Farmer (eds.), *Jesus and the Suffering Servant*.

25. For a general study of the use of the Psalms in the New Testament, see Jean-Luc Vesco, *Le psautier de Jésus: Les citations des psaumes dans le Nouveau Testament* (2 vols.; Paris: Cerf, 2012). For the literary structure of Psalm 41 and its role in the Psalter, see Pierre Auffret, 'En ceci j'ai su que tu m'as aimé: Étude structurelle du Psaume 41', *Theoforum* 35 (2005), pp. 267-78; Christoph Levin, 'Die Enstehung der Bücherteilung des Psalters', *VT* 54 (2004), pp. 83-90.

me, I said, 'O LORD, be gracious to me; heal me, for I have sinned against thee!' My enemies say of me in malice: 'When will he die, and his name perish?' And when one comes to see me, he utters empty words, while his heart gathers mischief; when he goes out, he tells it abroad. All who hate me whisper together about me; they imagine the worst for me. They say, 'A deadly thing has fastened upon him; he will not rise again from where he lies'. Even my bosom friend in whom I trusted, who ate of my bread, has lifted his heel against me. But do thou, O LORD, be gracious to me, and raise me up, that I may requite them! By this I know that thou art pleased with me, in that my enemy has not triumphed over me. But thou hast upheld me because of my integrity, and set me in thy presence for ever. Blessed be the LORD, the God of Israel, from everlasting to everlasting! Amen and Amen (Ps. 41.1-13).

The first thing to note is that this psalm appears to be a penitential prayer, and perhaps to be used by a royal figure who is ill and has enemies plotting against him while he is in a vulnerable state.[26] Indeed, there is a reference to the supplicant's sick bed (MT v. 4: על ערש דוי). More importantly, the supplicant indicates that he is ill because he has sinned (MT v. 5: רפאה נפשי כי חטאתי לך).

Therefore, to be exegetically consistent, Jesus should see himself as a sinner because there is no explicit change in the speaker when the psalm reaches v. 9 (MT v. 10), the verse Jesus quoted. Moreover, Jesus only quotes the second part of that verse, which in its entirety reads: 'Even my bosom friend in whom I trusted, who ate of my bread, has lifted his heel against me.' But the grammar poses another problem for Jesus' use of this as a prophecy. Jesus cites the LXX version, which understands the Hebrew verbs (בטחתי/ἤλπισα and הגדיל/ἐμεγάλυνεν) as in the past tenses at the time the speaker is uttering them. Logically, that would mean that the speaker has experienced at least some of the actions described already by the time the psalm was written. Whatever the date of the psalm, it was written before Jesus was born. So this psalm cannot be speaking about Jesus. Jesus is prone to as much anachronism as Gibson.

Of course, in Second Temple Judaism, texts in the Hebrew Bible were routinely understood to apply to contemporary situations.[27] Yet, there was also a tradition that tried to understand Psalm 41 historically, as is noted by Raymond E. Brown: 'The rabbis understood this passage in Ps xli 10(9)

26. On this psalm as a penitential psalm for a sick individual, see Klaus Seybold and Ulrich B. Mueller, *Sickness and Healing* (trans. Douglas W. Stott; Nashville, TN: Abingdon Press, 1981), pp. 46-47.

27. See A.T. Hanson, *The Prophetic Gospel: A Study of John and the Old Testament* (Edinburgh: T. & T. Clark, 2000); Andreas Obermann, *Die christologische Erfüllung der Schrift im Johannesevangelium: Eine Untersuchung zur johanneischen Hermeneutik anhand der Schriftzitate* (WUNT, 2.83; Tübingen: J.C.B. Mohr [Paul Siebeck], 1996).

to refer to Ahitophel's conspiracy with Absalom against David (II Sam xv 12).'[28] Even if the specific historical setting is wrong, such rabbinic interpretations show that it was perfectly possible to understand the plain meaning of Psalm 41 historically, and not necessarily as a prophecy to be fulfilled hundreds of years later.

Nevertheless, Brown himself does not censure Jesus for this sort of irresponsible exegesis, but he uses it to promote the Gospel of John as scripture, as he does in the following remarks:

> Because of the Johannine appropriation of Scripture, events in the story make the Scriptures relevant in the events of the life of Jesus (1.23; 6.31, 45; 10.34; 12.13; 13.18; 15.25); the reflections of the later community on the significance of events that took place in the life of Jesus renders the Gospel of John relevant as Scripture.[29]

Apparently all one needs to make something relevant as scripture is to use an ancient text and 'appropriate' it in the manner that John does. It is plausible that Jesus never gave this interpretation of Psalm 41, and it was the Johannine community that is responsible for any misreading or reappropriation. However, it always seems curious how often Jesus' misreadings are attributed to the authors of the New Testament texts, while benign or commendable readings of the Hebrew Bible are attributed to the historical Jesus.

Isaiah 6.9-10: Integrating Extrabiblical Materials

In Mark 4, Jesus completely decontextualizes a passage in Isaiah 6, and then adds extrabiblical material to promote his own message. The episode occurs after concluding the parable of the sower, which relates the fate of seeds sown in different types of soil. When asked to explain the meaning of parables, Mark relates the following answer from Jesus:

> And he said to them, 'To you has been given the secret of the kingdom of God, but for those outside everything is in parables; so that they may indeed see but not perceive, and may indeed hear but not understand; lest they should turn again, and be forgiven'. And he said to them, 'Do you not understand this parable? How then will you understand all the parables'? (Mk 4.11-13).

Of course, the whole idea that Jesus would purposely withhold information crucial to forgiveness contradicts other statements by Jesus in the Gospels,

---

28. Brown, *The Gospel According to John XII–XXI*, p. 554. See also Nicholas J. Zola, '"The One who Eats my Bread has Lifted his Heel against me":Psalm 41:10 in 1QH^a and John 13:18', *PRSt* 37 (2010), pp. 407-419.

29. Raymond E. Brown, *An Introduction to the Gospel of John* (New Haven, CT: Yale University Press, 2009), p. 137.

including that in Jn 3.16: 'For God so loved the world that he gave his only Son, that whoever believes in him should not perish but have eternal life.' If this were the goal of Jesus' mission, then intentionally leading people astray with parables would not seem to be compatible with that goal.

The conspiratorial nature of Jesus' understanding of God's communication program is exacerbated by his use of the particle, ἵνα, which normally expresses purpose.[30] Of course, there has been a long history in New Testament scholarship of explaining why Jesus kept a 'messianic secret'.[31] Yet, Christopher S. Mann notes that, in order to avoid the ethical problems with Jesus' approach to the parables, some scholars also have attempted to explain this particle as an imperative or as a mistranslation of 'an Aramaic particle which ought to have been translated as *hoi* (who)'.[32] Joachim Jeremias also suggests that the Aramaic דלמא should be rendered as 'unless' and so the final clause in Mk 4.12 should be 'unless they turn and God will forgive them'.[33] This would be understood as a promise that the Jews would be forgiven, and not that their understanding would be suppressed for the purpose of avoiding forgiveness on the part of God. Moreover, Jeremias argues that 'Mark, misled by the catchword παραβολή, which he erroneously understood as "parable", inserted our logion into the parable-chapter'.[34] This would also mean that Mark, not Jesus, is the one who did not understand Isaiah properly.

Yet, Mann adds: 'No suggestions mitigate the force of the Markan saying.'[35] Recently, Hiroaki Yoshimura has argued that Mk 4.11-12 should be attributed to Jesus, and not to the Gospel author or some later tradition.[36]

---

30. See BDF, p. 197, paragraph 390.

31. See Schuyler Brown, '"The Secret of the Kingdom of God" (Mark 4:11)', *JBL* 92 (1973), pp. 60-74. For the view that the parables can be better understood using Ludwig Wittgenstein's idea of language games, see Markus Locker, *The New World of Jesus' Parables* (Newcastle upon Tyne: Cambridge Scholars, 2008). Locker, however, concentrates on Matthew, not Mark.

32. Mann, *Mark*, p. 264. The Aramaic particle is *de* (ד) as part of דלמא. Thus, Joachim Jeremias, *The Parables of Jesus* (trans. S.H. Hooke; New York: Charles Scribner's Sons, 2nd edn, 1972), p. 17 n. 24, accepts the following as a possible translation: 'For those who are without, everything remains obscure, who "see and yet do not see".' For the use of the imperative, see Joseph D. Fantin, *The Greek Imperative Mood in the New Testament: A Cognitive and Communicative Approach* (Studies in Biblical Greek, 12; New York: Peter Lang, 2010).

33. Jeremias, *The Parables of Jesus*, p. 17.

34. Jeremias, *The Parables of Jesus*, p. 18. For Jeremias (*The Parables of Jesus*, p. 18 n. 31), 'Mark 4.10 was originally followed by v. 13'.

35. Mann, *Mark*, p. 264.

36. Hiroaki Yoshimura, *Did Jesus Cite Isa 6:9-10? Jesus' Saying in Mark 4:11-12 and the Isaianic Idea of Hardening and Remnant* (Åbo: Åbo Akademis Förlag/Åbo Akademi University Press, 2010). For earlier treatments, see Craig A. Evans, *To See and Not*

This opposes Jeremias's view that the Isaianic passage was added by the evangelist.

Otherwise, many New Testament ethicists ignore or blatantly misrepresent the implications of Mk 4.12. For example, Schrage does not cite this specific verse in his scriptural index at all.[37] Dan O. Via, who wrote an entire treatise on *The Ethics of Mark's Gospel: In the Middle of Time* (1985), does not significantly address the ethical problems generated by Jesus' explanation.[38] Burridge cites Mk 4.1-13 to show that Jesus 'is not understood by his hearers' rather than to show that Jesus communicated in order to avoid being understood by his hearers.[39] Frank Matera does note the fact that Jesus intends to avoid being understood, but issues no further comment or explanation on the ethics of such an approach.[40]

Regardless of whether Mark or Jesus used Isaiah's logion, it is clear that there is no discussion of the ethics of Jesus' reappropriation even by those who do believe that this Isaianic logion goes back to Jesus, and was not added by the evangelist. And to understand the extent of any decontextualization and misrepresentation of Isaiah 6 by Jesus, it is necessary to read the entire chapter:

> In the year that King Uzziah died I saw the LORD sitting upon a throne, high and lifted up; and his train filled the temple. Above him stood the seraphim; each had six wings: with two he covered his face, and with two he covered his feet, and with two he flew. And one called to another and said: 'Holy, holy, holy is the LORD of hosts; the whole earth is full of his glory'. And the foundations of the thresholds shook at the voice of him who called, and the house was filled with smoke. And I said: 'Woe is me! For I am lost; for I am a man of unclean lips, and I dwell in the midst of a people of unclean lips; for my eyes have seen the King, the LORD of hosts!' Then flew one of

---

Perceive: Isaiah 6.9-10 in Early Jewish and Christian Interpretation (JSOTSup, 64; Sheffield: Sheffield Academic Press, 1989); idem, 'A Note on the Function of Isaiah vi, 9-10 in Mark iv', *RB* 88 (1981), pp. 234-35; J.W. Bowker, 'Mystery and Parable: Mark 4:1-20', *JTS* 25 (1974), pp. 300-317; Bruce D. Chilton, *A Galilean Rabbi and his Bible: Jesus' Use of the Interpreted Scripture in His Time* (Wilmington, DE: Michael Glazier, 1984); Michael D. Goulder, 'Those Outside (Mk 4:10-12)', *NovT* 33 (1991), pp. 289-302; Joel Marcus, 'Mark 4:10-12 and Marcan Epistemology', *JBL* 103 (1984), pp. 557-74; Joachim Eck, 'Bilden Jes 6,1-11 und 1 Kön 22, 19-22 eine Gattung? Ein umfassender exegetischer Vergleich (*Teil I*)', *BN* (2009), pp. 57-65; Robert L. Cole, 'Isaiah 6 in its Context', *Southeastern Theological Review* 2 (2011), pp. 161-80; Eugene Ulrich, 'Isaiah for the Hellenistic World: The Old Greek Translator of Isaiah', in *Celebrating the Dead Sea Scrolls; A Canadian Collection* (ed. Peter W. Flint, Jeane Duhaime and Kyung S. Baek; SBLEJL, 30; Atlanta, GA: Society of Biblical Literature, 2011), pp. 119-33.

37. See Schrage, *The Ethics of the New Testament*, p. 357.

38. Via, *The Ethics of Mark's Gospel*, pp. 182-95.

39. Burridge, *Imitating Jesus*, p. 163.

40. Matera, *New Testament Ethics*, p. 21.

the seraphim to me, having in his hand a burning coal which he had taken with tongs from the altar. And he touched my mouth, and said: 'Behold, this has touched your lips; your guilt is taken away, and your sin forgiven'. And I heard the voice of the LORD saying, 'Whom shall I send, and who will go for us?' Then I said, 'Here am I! Send me'. And he said, 'Go, and say to this people: "Hear and hear, but do not understand; see and see, but do not perceive. Make the heart of this people fat, and their ears heavy, and shut their eyes; lest they see with their eyes, and hear with their ears, and understand with their hearts, and turn and be healed"'. Then I said, 'How long, O LORD?' And he said: 'Until cities lie waste without inhabitant, and houses without men, and the land is utterly desolate, and the LORD removes men far away, and the forsaken places are many in the midst of the land. And though a tenth remain in it, it will be burned again, like a terebinth or an oak, whose stump remains standing when it is felled'. The holy seed is its stump (Isa. 6.1-13).

As it stands in the MT, the passage begins with a commissioning scene set at the time of Uzziah, the king of Judah (eighth century BCE). The prophet Isaiah sees a vision, and receives his mission, which is to go and tell the people of Judah that their perception will be dulled until their land is destroyed. Their dulled perception enhances the disobedience that they have already shown. Historically, the writer seems to be aware of the tragedy of the Babylonian conquest and destruction of Jerusalem in 587/86 BCE, and retrojects his prophecy back to the days of Uzziah.[41] All this sets the stage for revelations about the future of Judah and Jerusalem in the following chapters of Isaiah.

In any case, the passage in Isaiah 6 has nothing to do with the general purpose of parables. It deals with a concrete historical situation and period.[42] Any dullness in perception is supposed to be removed after the destruction of the land. Jesus decontextualizes the passage by removing it from its originally intended relevance to the destruction of Jerusalem in the sixth century BCE. Jesus ignores that the terminus for any dullness was 'until cities lie waste without inhabitant…', which happened in the sixth century BCE. Not only does Jesus insist that such divine suppression of their perception continues into his day, but now he sees himself as the agent of that suppression in their perception. More importantly, Jesus here makes the consequences indicated in the original text much worse. In Isaiah, God acted so that they would not be healed, but only until they were destroyed by the Babylonians. Jesus continues that suppression indefinitely (cf. 2 Thess. 2.9-12).

---

41. For comments, see Otto Kaiser, *Isaiah 1–12* (trans. John Bowden; Old Testament Library; Philadelphia, PA: Westminster, 2nd edn, 1983), pp. 117-33.

42. For the argument that the passage should be read ironically as an encouragement to repent, see Gordon C.I. Wong, 'Make their Ears Dull: Irony in Isaiah 6:9-10', *Trinity Theological Journal* 16 (2008), pp. 23-34. See also Yoshimura, *Did Jesus Cite Isa 6:9-10?*

As it relates to the issue of adding extracanonical material to the original biblical text, the words 'be forgiven' (ἀφεθῇ αὐτοῖς in Mk 4.12 are certainly not from either the MT, which has ורפא לו, nor are they from the Septuagint, which has καὶ ἰάσομαι αὐτούς. Rather, the words that Jesus inserts are from the Aramaic targum, which has וישתביק להון.[43] The latter certainly matches closely to what Jesus has inserted into Isaiah's text. Jesus' rendition of Isaiah makes the situation for Jews and the world much worse. Jesus changes 'be healed' to 'be forgiven', and then offers no terminus for this divine conspiracy to prevent forgiveness.

So how is injecting material from a non-canonical targumic tradition by Jesus any worse than Mel Gibson using non-canonical sources, such as the visions of Emmerich, to enhance his understanding of the Gospels? As one can see, they are not much different at all. The only objection to Gibson must be theological, not historical. That is to say, Fredriksen, Crossan and others who dislike what Gibson did with Emmerich are simply arguing that they do not regard her writings as a theologically approved source to enhance or recontextualize anything in the scriptures. The targums bear theologically acceptable reinterpretations or misunderstandings of scripture, while Emmerich's reinterpretations or misunderstanding do not.

On the other hand, Fredriksen, Crossan and other anti-Gibsonians apparently think that using the non-canonical targums to recontextualize Isaiah is legitimate when Jesus does it. If one objects that the targums were a normal part of the Jewish hermeneutical strategy of the Second Temple period, then there is no reason to deny that Gibson should be free to use the hermeneutical strategies that also have been in use throughout Christianity, and that includes the integration of non-canonical materials into exegesis. After all, there are now extensive studies of how the Septuagintal translators can be viewed as storytellers, not just translators. J. Ross Wagner has specifically studied how the Septuagint was engaging in theological recontextualization of Isaiah.[44] Similarly, *The Passion of the Christ* can be viewed as another creative translation of the passion narratives.

Summary

Theology, not just historico-critical scholarship, is behind the difference in the way in which many modern scholars address the hermeneutical ethics

---

43. Following the edition of the Targum Jonathan in Alexander Sperber, *The Bible in Aramaic Based on Old Manuscripts and Printed Texts* (4 vols.; Leiden: E.J. Brill, 1992), III, p. 13.

44. See J. Ross Wagner, *Reading the Sealed Book: Old Greek and the Problem of Septuagint Hermeneutics* (Waco, TX: Baylor University Press, 2014). See also Timothy Michael Law, *When God Spoke Greek: The Septuagint and the Making of the Christian Bible* (New York: Oxford University Press, 2013); Beck, *Translators as Storytellers*.

of Gibson's *The Passion of the Christ* compared to the hermeneutical ethics of Jesus in the Gospels. Just as Corley and Webb can complain that *The Passion* 'is not accurate to either the Gospels or to history', one could just as well conclude that all of Jesus' interpretations are 'not accurate to either the Hebrew Bible or to history'.[45] Yet, when Jesus gets his scriptural facts wrong or blatantly misrepresents the original intent of texts, then it is usually viewed by New Testament ethicists as a normal part of his cultural context. When Gibson gets his facts wrong or blatantly misrepresents scripture, then it is an irresponsible and dangerous use of scripture. I've never seen Jesus' misuse of scripture characterized as dangerous or as a cause for censure.

Of course, I am well aware that Jesus was doing what others were doing in the Jewish context of his time.[46] However, this is not a good ethical argument, but another version of a *tu quoque* argument, which suggests that what I do is allowable because you do it, too. It is also another version of the 'is = ought' fallacy, which argues that something is ethically justified because that is the way it is.[47] But just because Jesus and others in his culture routinely recontextualized and reinterpreted scripture does not mean that recontextualization and reinterpretation are ethically justified. If the original intent of an author matters in historical interpretation, then both Jesus and Gibson should be condemned equally. If original intent does not matter, then one wonders if any of the scholars who criticize Gibson would deem acceptable any effort to interpret their own words and writings to mean the opposite of what they originally intended.

And one could just as well argue that Mel Gibson is simply doing what also is attested in his cultural context. So, is Gibson doing something wrong when he really did not do anything less 'reappropriational' than what Jesus did? Just as Gibson used unhistorical readings even when more historically accurate ones were available, Jesus chose to use less historically oriented readings even when more historically accurate readings might have been available in this time. Both Jesus and Gibson represented their conclusions as historically accurate at a time when the value of historical accuracy was understood to some extent. Otherwise, the foregoing discussion exposes how the hermeneutical ethics of anti-Gibsonian New Testament scholars need to be critically examined and censured where needed. New Testament ethicists repeatedly miss the bad biblical interpretations of Jesus.

45. See Corley and Webb, *Jesus and Mel Gibson's The Passion*, p. 177.
46. See Henze (ed.), *Biblical Interpretation at Qumran*.
47. The maxim that one cannot argue that is = ought is otherwise known as Hume's Law, on which see Noel Stewart, *Ethics: An Introduction to Moral Philosophy* (Cambridge: Polity, 2009), pp. 203-205.

Chapter 14

Conclusion

If Jesus was a human being, then he should have had flaws. This study has found many of Jesus' teachings and actions to be in contraposition to the most widely accepted standards of modern ethics. There is no ethical innovation with Jesus on almost anything claimed by New Testament ethicists, and his concept of love certainly is not in any way innovative. As preached by Jesus, *agapē* is a continuation of the covenantal relationship between Yahweh and his vassals. It can be violent, and it can be brutal. Loving Yahweh entails obedience to him just as loving an emperor entails obedience to him.

A literal reading of 'hate' in Lk. 14.26 is linguistically and contextually plausible, and so Jesus advocated hating one's father and mother, among other family members. Those are not actions that most ancient or modern people valued. Efforts to read Lk. 14.26 otherwise are flawed or no more plausible than a literal reading. This hate is best explained as Jesus' debt to passages such as Deut. 13.6-11, which calls for the destruction of family members who adopt another religion. That passage encourages the extinction of any love for apostate family members.

Jesus certainly is an advocate of violence in some texts (Mt. 10.34; Jn 2.15). Texts where Jesus seems to reject violence usually don't take into account his view of deferred violence against those who do not obey him or his disciples (Mt. 25.41-46). Jesus' self-descriptons of his mission (e.g., Mk 10.45) certainly is violent but it is violence against the self. The efforts to mitigate the violent premises of his atoning sacrifice fail on numerous levels, and ultimately depend on theological grounds rather than on any linguistic or historical grounds.

Jesus is not an egalitarian or an anti-imperialist. Replacing the Roman empire cannot count as being anti-imperialist if the goal is simply to replace it with another empire called the Kingdom of God. Jesus has a hierarchy among his disciples, and the fact that the last shall be first is simply a replacement of slots in the hierarchy, and not an abolition of hierarchy. Jesus certainly has no problem with slavery, and never spoke of it as being sinful or ethically abhorrent. As Jn 8.44 and other passages show, Jesus could be ethnocentric and as anti-Jewish as any other self-hating member of any ethnicity can be today.

Nor was Jesus always the friend of the poor, given that he demanded that disciples leave their families regardless of how those families were affected economically. He received the labor of his disciples in return for heavenly rewards or other future benefits that he could not deliver by any modern standard of verification. If anything, Jesus was akin to a modern Harold Camping to whom little sympathy is shown by biblical scholars regardless of how sincere he was in his beliefs, and regardless of how his 'eschatological worldview' explained the demands on his followers.

Jesus was as sexist, or even more so, than any other famous leader we can name in antiquity. All the Synoptic Gospels concur that he chose only twelve disciples all of whom were men. One has to exert significant leaps in exegetical logic to tease out any equal or larger participation by women, who often acted as loyal errand girls and servants to his cause, in his ministry. Even when the male disciples are disloyal, and the female ones loyal, he does not reward the women more than the men for that loyalty.

There is sufficient evidence to demonstrate that Jesus did consider disability and illness to be the result of sin (e.g., Mk 2.10-11; Jn 5.14). Jesus is generally working with the Deuteronomistic moral universe that equated illness with sin, and well-being with sinlessness. Jesus did not consider the disabled as fully human or as able to participate in the Kingdom of God in their current condition. Rather, the disabled needed to be 'fixed' or made normal to be viewed as legitimate members of the Kingdom of God. There is overwhelming evidence that Jesus believed that demons caused diseases, and supernatural therapy could cure them. There is also sufficient evidence to demonstrate that Jesus considered disability and illness as opportunities to showcase his personal religious agenda (e.g., Lk. 6.21-22; Jn 9.3). He did not heal all sick people, but only those that would further his agenda. The fact that Jesus heals the disabled shows that he does not accept them as they are, or value them unless they are in a normate body. The disabled are part of Jesus' imperialistic agenda to have the entire world under the dominion of the Kingdom of God with worshipers who have ideal bodies and health.

The consequences of Jesus' belief in magical therapy and his perpetuation of the connection between sin and disability have been very negative historically. First, it made it permissible for Christians to marginalize and even persecute the disabled. This is the case, especially in the sixteenth and seventeenth centuries, with those suffering mental illnesses that were sometimes interpreted as demon possession or reflective of the practice of witchcraft.[1] Second, the connection between sin and illness delayed the scientific

---

1. See H.C. Eric Midelfort, *A History of Madness in Sixteenth Century Germany* (Stanford, CA: Stanford University Press, 1999), especially p. 227; idem, *Witchcraft, Madness, Society, and Religion in Early Modern Germany: A Ship of Fools* (Aldershot:

study of illness because it was tantamount to contradicting the etiologies of disease that Jesus advocated.

Jesus could not care less about the environment in any modern sense. For him, animals mattered little compared to human beings, and he had no problem in having them die to showcase his power (Mk 5.11-13). He absolved human beings of responsibility for their care, and left it to God (Mt. 6.26). He had no trouble with slaughtering animals to appease his god (Mt. 8.1-4). Jesus had no trouble envisioning divine judgment that would devastate our biosphere (Mark 13; Matthew 24).

Finally, Jesus was as anti-biblical as Mel Gibson, who has become a poster boy for poor and dangerous biblical interpretation. But few ethicists ever even discuss Jesus' gaffes or misappropriations of the Hebrew Bible (1 Sam. 21.1-6; Ps. 41.9; Isa. 6.9-10). Much less do they discuss how his reappropriation of the Hebrew Bible has led to human tragedy that will forever eclipse anything Mel Gibson could ever do. Claims that Jesus is an authoritative interpreter of scripture are theological claims that are no more valid than those one can make on Mel Gibson's behalf.

The Ethics of New Testament Ethics

Given these problems, why is Jesus still considered a paradigm of ethics in the works of New Testament ethics? The main reason for such a disparity between the Jesus of the New Testament and that of modern New Testament ethics is that New Testament ethics is still predominantly part of an ecclesial-academic complex and an agent of the Christian empire. New Testament ethicists usually do not denounce any of Jesus' ethics because they have made a theological judgment that his ethics are sound. That is purely a theological, not an historical or critical judgment. Jesus' requests that disciples abandon their families is not viewed as unethical because it is assumed that his mission is authentic, while that of Harold Camping, who had imminent eschatological expectations, is not. Jesus' misuse of scripture is not regarded as such because his interpretations are assumed to be theologically sound, while those of Mel Gibson are not.

As is the case with all theistic ethics, the judgments made by Christian ethicists are circular and self-referential. Most or all claims about what God intends can be reduced to: 'I believe X is God's will because I believe X is God's will'. One example will do. Eric Seibert who, while claiming to show that Jesus reveals God's true nature, claimed, 'Jesus commands them to love their enemies because that's what God does'.[2] Seibert's claim is no

---

Ashgate, 2013). Otherwise, Middlefort (*A History of Madness*, p. 19) urges caution in attributing all madness to demonological causes in the sixteenth century.

2. Seibert, *Disturbing Divine Behavior*, p. 192.

better than any apologist for Judas Iscariot claiming that he betrayed Jesus 'because that is what God does'. There is no method to adjudicate or verify any claims about what 'God does', even if such a being exists. Since all faith claims are equal in their unverifiability, then anyone can say whatever they want about God. That is not scholarship. That is theology, which is itself a pseudo-scholarly discipline with no referent other than oneself because all views of God cannot be shown to be anything beyond one's own opinion. Any statement about God is an act of self-deification.

Thus, the claim that loving everyone equally conforms to God's will is simply a restatement of the claim that loving everyone equally conforms to God's will. The claim that God wants us to be stewards of the environment is a restatement of the claim that God wants us to be stewards of the environment. When judging Jesus' ethics New Testament ethicists simply substitute Jesus for God, and their own thoughts for those of both Jesus and God. Once this rationale is accepted, then if Jesus said or did something that is wrong upon plain reading, then the plain reading must be wrong because Jesus cannot possibly do anything wrong. The hermeneutics are entirely circular.

The reason that New Testament ethicists view Jesus as a moral authority is itself an ethical problem seldom discussed. Why should Jesus be a moral authority for the modern world at all? I return to Daphne Hampson's incisive question: 'What was I doing, in the late twentieth century, arguing that what happened in the first century was of relevance to whether or not I could be a deacon'.[3] Indeed, all theistic ethics are undemocratic because they are premised on information that is accessible to only a few (e.g., the biblical authors who are considered to have had a revelation from God; or Jesus who is said to be representing God). But true democracy depends on all citizens having the same potential access to verifiable information that will be used to determine their destiny.

That New Testament ethicists so regard Jesus as a paradigm of ethics betrays the fact that biblical scholarship is still largely operating as part of the detritus of Christian empires, which often used the Bible as their textual authority. It is that textual authority that Christian ethicists seek to retain and impose on the world. Jean Baudrillard, a keen observer of how imagery is ideologically manipulated, once remarked that 'Disneyland exists in order to hide that it is the "real country", all of "real" America, that is Disneyland (a bit like prisons are there to hide that it is the social life in its entirety, in its banal omnipresence, that is carcereal)'.[4] Similarly, anti-imperialist scholarship hides the fact that it itself is part of an imperialist program.

---

3. Hampson, *Theology and Feminism*, p. 31.

4. Jean Baudrillard, *Simulacra and Simulation* (trans. Sheira Faria Glaser; Ann Arbor, MI: University of Michigan Press, 1994), p. 12. French text in *Simulacres et*

The recent 'anti-imperialistic' orientation actually deflects attention from the fact that Christian biblical scholars are part of an empire. Empires, of course, usually frame their agendas as liberatory and benign. And like good propagandists for their Christian empires, many Christian biblical scholars often try to preserve biblical values and ideals, which are often framed benignly despite the genocidal and biocidal ideologies that the Bible can espouse. A better vision of liberation is one that rejects the role of any ancient text in determining modern ethics.[5] Ethics should not be based on textual authority or the authority of any particular individual. Ethics should be based on scientifically verifiable phenomena, and empathy is the core of all ethics. Empathy is a biological constituent of humanity, as it is of many other species.[6]

New Testament ethics does not deserve to be called fully 'critical scholarship' because any discipline engaged in propaganda for invisible entities should be deemed to be as pseudo-scholarly as creationism or defenses of the Greek god Zeus. Indeed, imagine if one argued for the validity of Zeus's commands or wishes in Homer's *Iliad*. In commenting on how conservative Christians scholars rely on faith in testimony to validate the Bible, John J. Collins observed, '[s]uch a hermeneutic of belief cannot be accepted as critical scholarship'.[7] J. Cheryl Exum also noted how those who use the Bible as a source of solace, assurance and empowerment 'have an agenda that is usually more pastoral than scholarly, and such a readerly position makes critical feminist scholarship as it is practiced elsewhere in the academy difficult'.[8]

New Testament ethics still has a few honorable options left if it desires to be considered a genuine part of the humanities in academia. First, it must relinquish its role as an advocate for any theological view or ecclesial affiliation. Second, it must refocus itself on describing the diversity of ethical and contradictory positions held by Jesus as portrayed in canonical

---

simulation (Paris: Èditions Galilée, 1981), pp. 25-26: 'Disneyland est là pour cacher que c'est le pays "réel", toute l'Amérique "réele" qui est Disneyland (un peu comme les prisons sont là pour cacher que c'est le social tout entier, dans son omniprésence banale, qui est carcéral.'

5. On the process of transforming texts into authoritative scriptures, see Russell Hobson, *Transforming Literature into Scripture: Texts as Cult Objects at Nineveh and Qumran* (Sheffield: Equinox, 2012); Mladen Popovic (ed.), *Authoritative Scriptures in Ancient Judaism* (Supplements to the Journal for the Study of Judaism, 141; Leiden: E.J. Brill, 2010).

6. On empathy as a key to ethics, see Frans de Waal, *The Age of Empathy: Nature's Lessons for a Kinder Society* (New York: Random House, 2009); *Primates and Philosophers: How Morality Evolved* (Princeton, NJ: Princeton University Press, 2006).

7. Collins, 'Faith, Scholarship, and the Society of Biblical Literature', p. 75.

8. Exum, 'Trusting in the God of their Fathers', p. 54.

and extra-canonical texts. Third, it must address the question of why anything Jesus says matters to the modern world any more than what any other
ancient figure may have said. Fourth, it must admit that it has been part of an
imperialist agenda wherein the authority of Jesus and the New Testament is
simply a cipher for the will of the Christian empire. Otherwise, New Testament ethics is a pseudoscholarly discipline that deserves to be ejected from
any institution that respects academic inquiry. If Jesus was a man, he should
have flaws. If is to be a credible historical-critical discipline, New Testament ethics needs to find both the Good and the Bad Jesus.

APPENDIX

Representation of Christian and non-Christian cultures in work on New Testament ethics as reflected in the indices of any works cited besides the Bible and Apocrypha.

Burridge, *Imitating Jesus*, pp. 488-90.
'Pseudepigrapha'
'Dead Sea Scrolls'
'Josephus and Philo'
'Christian Writings (Including Nag Hammadi)'
'Graeco-Roman Literature'

Green, *Dictionary of Scripture and Ethics*, pp. 861-89.
Nothing listed outside of Bible and Apocrypha

Hays, *Moral Vision*, p. 496.
'Apocrypha and Pseudepigrapha'
'Dead Sea Scrolls'
'Early Christian Literature'
'Rabbinic Literature'
'Other Ancient Writings'

Longenecker, *New Testament Social Ethics for Today.*
No citation index for any work

Matera, *New Testament Ethics*, pp. 311-19.
Nothing listed outside of Bible and Apocrypha

Sanders, *Ethics in the New Testament*, pp. 139-44.
Nothing listed outside of Bible and Apocrypha

Schnackenburg, *The Moral Teaching of the New Testament.*
No citation index for any work

Schüssler Fiorenza, *In Memory of Her*, pp. 353-57.
Nothing listed outside the Bible.

Verhey, *Remembering Jesus*, pp. 525-26.
'Early Christian Literature'

BIBLIOGRAPHY

Abbott, Edwin, *Johannine Grammar* (London: A. & C. Black, 1906).

Abernathy, Ralph David. *And the Walls Came Tumbling Down: An Autobiography* (New York: Harper & Row, 1989).

Abrams, J.Z., *Judaism and Disability: Portrayals of Ancient Texts from the Tanach through the Bavli* (Washington, DC: Gallaudet University Press, 1998).

Acevedo, Joaquim (ed.), *A Simplified Coptic Dictionary (Sahidic Dialect)* (Cachoeira, Brazil: Seminario Adventista Latino-Americano de Teologia, 2001).

Achenbach, Reinhard, and Martin Arneth (eds.), *'Gerechtigkeit und Recht zu üben' (Gen 18,19): Studien zur altorientalischen und biblischen Rechtsgeschichte, zur Religionsgeschichte Israels und zur Religionssoziologie. Festschrift für Eckart Otto zum 65. Geburtstag* (Beihefte zur Zeitschrift für Altorientalische and Biblische Rechtsgeschichte, 13; Wiesbaden: Harrassowitz Verlag, 2009).

Ackerman, Robert, *J.G. Frazer: His Life and Work* (Cambridge: Cambridge University Press, 1991).

—*The Myth and Ritual School: J.G. Frazer and the Cambridge Ritualists* (New York: Routledge, 2002).

Ackerman, Susan, 'The Personal is Political: Covenental and Affectionate Love [*'ĀHĒB, 'AHĂBÂ*] in the Hebrew Bible', *VT* 52 (2002), pp. 437-58.

Adam, Andrew K.M. *Faithful Interpretation: Reading the Bible in a Postmodern World* (Minneapolis: Fortress Press, 2006).

Adams, Edward, 'Retrieving the Earth from the Conflagration: 2 Peter 3.5-13 and the Environment', in Horrell*et al.* (eds.), *Ecological Hermeneutics*, pp. 108-120.

Adeney, Frances, 'Comparative Religious Ethics', in Green (ed.), *Dictionary of Scripture and Ethics*, pp. 152-57.

Adler, Eric, *Valorizing the Barbarians: Enemy Speeches in Roman Historiography* (Austin, TX: University of Texas Press, 2011).

Ahearne-Kroll, Stephen P., Paul A. Holloway and James A. Kelhoffer (eds.), *Women and Gender in Ancient Religions* (WUNT, 2.263; Tübingen: Morh Siebeck, 2010).

Ahn, John J., and Stephen L. Cook (eds.), *Thus Says the Lord: Essays on the Former and Latter Prophets in Honor of Robert R. Wilson* (Library of Hebrew Bible/Old Testament Studies, 502; London: T. & T. Clark, 2009).

Akurgal, Ekrem, Folke Josephson and Emmanuel Laroche (eds.), *Florilegium Anatolicum: Mélanges offerts à Emmanuel Laroche* (Paris: Boccard, 1979).

Albl, Martin, 'Are Any among you Sick?: The Health Care System in the Letter of James', *JBL* 121 (2002), pp. 123-43.

Albrecht, Gary L., Katherine D. Seelman and Michael Bury (eds.), *Handbook of Disability Studies* (Thousand Oaks, CA: Sage, 2001).

Albright, William F., *From the Stone Age to Christianity: Monotheism and Historical Progress* (Garden City, NY: Doubleday, 1957).

Aldrete, Gregory S., and Alicia Aldrete, *The Long Shadow of Antiquity: What Have the Greeks and the Romans Done for us?* (London: Continuum, 2012).

Alexander, Loveday, 'Luke's Political Vision', *Int* 66 (2012), pp. 283-93.

Alexander, Philip S., 'Rabbinic Judaism and the New Testament', *ZNW* 74 (1983), pp. 237-46.

Alexis-Baker, Andy, 'Violence, Nonviolence and the Temple Incident in John 2:13-15', *BibInt* 20 (2012), pp. 73-96.

Allison, Dale C., 'The Eschatology of Jesus', in J.J. Collins (ed.), *The Encylopedia of Apocalypticism: Volume 1*, pp. 267-302.

—'Rejecting Violent Judgment: Luke 9:52-56 and its Relatives', *JBL* 121 (2002), pp. 459-78.

—*The Testament of Abraham* (Commentaries on Early Jewish Literature; Berlin: W. de Gruyter, 2003).

Altman, Amnon, *The 'Historical Prologues' of Hittite Vassal Treaties: An Inquiry into the Concepts of Hittite Interstate Law* (Ramat-Gan: Bar-Ilan University Press, 2004).

—'How Many Treaty Traditions Existed in the Ancient Near East?', in Cohen, Gilan and Miller (eds.), *Pax Hethitica*, pp. 18-36.

American with Disabilities Act of 1990-ADA-42, US Code, Chapter 126, Section 12101, 'Findings and Purpose'. Online: http://www.eeoc.gov/laws/statutes/ada.cfm.

Ames, Frank Ritchel, and Charles William Miller (eds.), *Foster Biblical Scholarship: Essays in Honor of Kent Harold Richards* (Atlanta, GA: Society of Biblical Literature, 2010).

Anderson, Gary A., *Charity: The Place of the Poor in the Biblical Tradition* (New Haven, CT: Yale University Press, 2013).

—*Sin: A History* (New Haven, CT: Yale University Press, 2010).

—'A Treasury in Heaven: The Exegesis of Proverbs 10:2 in the Second Temple Period', *Hebrew Bible and Ancient Israel* 1 (2012), pp. 351-67.

Animal Protection Laws of California (2013). Online: http://aldf.org/wp-content/themes/aldf/compendium-map/us/2013/CALIFORNIA.pdf.

Annas, Julia, 'Epictetus on Moral Perspectives', in Scaltsas and Mason (eds.), *The Philosophy of Epictetus*, pp. 140-52.

Annen, Franz, *Heil für die Heiden: Zur Bedeutung und Geschichte der Tradition von besessenen Gerasene (Mk 5, 1-20 parr.)* (Frankfurt: Josef Knecht, 1976).

[Anonymous], 'A Faith that Crucifies Women', *Times Higher Education*, 21 April 1997. Online: http://www.timeshighereducation.co.uk/features/a-faith-that-crucifies-women/101241.article (accessed 16 September 2014).

Anselm of Canterbury, Saint, *Proslogium, Monlogium, in Behalf of the Fool by Gaunilon, and Cur Deus Homo* (Chicago, IL: Open Court, 1903).

Antonio-Mayoral, Juan, 'El uso simbólico de los animals en los profetas del exilio', *EstBib* 53 (1995), pp. 317-63.

Apocalypse Later: Harold Camping vs. The End of the World (Documentary film directed by Zeke Piestrup; Venice, CA: 15Trucks Productions, 2014).

Archi, Alfonso, 'L'humanité des Hittites', in Akurgal, Josephson and Laroche (eds.), *Florilegium Anatolicum*, pp. 37-48.

Arenciba, Agustín Caballero, *Psicoanálisis y Biblia: El psicoanálisis aplicado a la investigación de textos bíblicos* (Salamanca: Universidad Pontificia de Salamanca, 1994).

Aristotle, *The Nicomachean Ethics* (trans. H. Rackham; LCL; Cambridge, MA: Harvard University Press, 1926).

Arlandson, James Malcolm, *Women, Class and Society in Early Christianity: Models from Luke–Acts* (Peabody, MA: Hendrickson, 1997).

Arnal, William, 'Just How Radical were the First Followers of Jesus? Q and the Use of Jesus' Sayings', *Fourth R* 23.3 (2010), pp. 8-20.

—'What Branches Grow out of this Stony Rubbish? Christian Origins and the Study of Religion', *StudRel/SciRel* 39 (2010), pp. 549-72.

Asgeirsson, Jon M., April D. DeConick and Risto Uro (eds.), *Thomasine Traditions in Antiquity: The Social and Cultural World of the Gospel of Thomas* (Nag Hammadi and Manichean Studies, 59; Leiden: E.J. Brill, 2006).

Ashcroft, Bill, Gareth Griffiths and Helen Tiffin (eds.), *The Empire Writes Back: Theory and Practice in Postcolonial Literatures* (London: Routledge, 1989).

Asirvatham, Sulochana R., Corinne Ondine Pache and John Watrous (eds.), *Between Magic and Religion: Interdisciplinary Studies in Ancient Mediterranean Religion and Society* (Lanham, MD: Rowman & Littlefield, 2001).

Asser, Seth, and Rita Swan, 'Child Fatalities from Religion-Motivated Medical Neglect', *Pediatrics* 101 (1998), pp. 625-29.

Aster, Shawn Zelig, 'Transmission of Neo-Assyrian Claims of Empire to Judah in the Late Eighth Century B.C.E.', *HUCA* 79 (2007), pp. 1-44.

Atkinson, Kenneth, 'Anti-Roman Polemics in the Dead Sea Scrolls and Related Literatures: Their Later Use in John's Apocalypse', *Qumran Chronicle* 12.2-4 (2004), pp. 109-122.

Attridge, Harold W., 'Can We Trust the Bible?', *Reflections* 92 (2005), pp. 4-9.

Auffret, Pierre, 'En ceci j'ai su que tu m'as aimé: Étude structurelle du Psaume 41', *Theoforum* 35 (2005), pp. 267-78.

Augustin, Matthias, and Hermann Michael Niemann (eds.), *Thinking Towards New Horizons: Collected Communications to the XIXth Congress of the International Organization for the Study of the Old Testament, Ljubljana 2007* (Beiträge zur Erforschung des Alten Testaments und des antiken Judentums, 55; Frankfurt: Peter Lang, 2008).

Aulén, Victor, *Christus Victor: A Historical Study of the Three Main Types of Atonement* (trans. Jaroslav Pelikan; repr., New York: Macmillan, 1969 [1931]).

Aune, David E., 'Magic in Early Christianity', *ANRW*, II, 23.2, pp. 1507-57.

Aune, David E., Torrey Seland and Jarl Henning Ulrichsen (eds.), *Neotestamentica et Philonica: Studies in Honor of Peder Borgen* (Leiden: E.J. Brill, 2002).

Avalos, Hector, 'Daniel 9:24-25 and Mesopotamian Temple Rededications', *JBL* 117 (1998), pp. 507-511.

—*The End of Biblical Studies* (Amherst, NY: Prometheus, 2007).

—'The End of Biblical Studies as a Moral Obligation', in Boer (ed.), *Secularism and Biblical Studies*, pp. 85-100.

—*Fighting Words: The Origins of Religious Violence* (Amherst, NY: Prometheus, 2005).

—'Film and the Apologetics of Biblical Violence', *Journal of Religion and Film* 13 (April 2009). Online: http://www.unomaha.edu/jrf/vol13.no1/BiblicalViolence.htm.

—'The Gospel of Lucas Gavilán as Postcolonial Biblical Exegesis', *Semeia* 75 (1996), pp. 87-105.

—*Health Care and the Rise of Christianity* (Peabody, MA: Hendrickson, 1999).

—'The Hidden Enlightenment: Humanism among US Latinos', *Essays in the Philosophy of Humanism* 20 (2012), pp. 3-14.

—'The Ideology of the Society of Biblical Literature and the Demise of an Academic

Profession', *SBL Forum* (April 2006). Online: http://www.sbl-site.org/publica-
    tions/article.aspx?ArticleId=520.

—*Introduction to the U.S. Latina and Latino Religious Experience* (Leiden and Boston,
    MA: E.J. Brill, 2004).

—'Liberation Theology', in Stavans (ed.), *Encyclopedia Latina*, II, pp. 435-37.

—'In Praise of the Evil Kings: Latino Ethnic Identity and Biblical Scholarship', *Bible
    and Interpretation* (December 2013). Online: http://www.bibleinterp.com/articles/
    2013/12/ava378004.shtml.

—'Redemptionism, Rejectionism, and Historicism as Emerging Approaches in Disabil-
    ity Studies', *PRSt* 34 (2007), pp. 61-75.

—'Religion and Scarcity: A New Theory for the Role of Religion in Violence', in *The
    Oxford Handbook of Religion and Violence* (ed. Mark Juergensmeyer, Margo Kitts
    and Michael Jerryson; New York: Oxford University Press, 2013), pp. 554-70.

—'Six Anti-Secularist Themes: Deconstructing Religionist Rhetorical Weaponry', *Bible
    and Interpretation* (November 2010). Online: http://www.bibleinterp.com/opeds/
    anti358029.shtml

—*Slavery, Abolitionism, and the Ethics of Biblical Scholarship* (Sheffield: Sheffield
    Phoenix Press, 2011).

—*Strangers in our Own Land: Religion in U.S. Latina/o Literature* (Nashville, TN: Abing-
    don Press, 2007).

—'Yahweh is a Moral Monster', in *The Christian Delusion: Why Faith Fails* (ed. John
    Loftus; Amherst, NY: Prometheus, 2010), pp. 209-36.

Avalos, Hector, Sarah Melcher and Jeremy Schipper (eds.), *This Abled Body: Rethink-
    ing Disabilities in Biblical Studies* (SBLSS, 55; Atlanta, GA: Society of Biblical
    Literature, 2007).

Azize, Joseph, and Noel Weeks (eds.), *Gilgameš and the World of Assyria: Proceedings
    of the Conference at Mandelbaum House, The University of Sydney, 21-23 July
    2004* (Leuven: Peeters, 2007).

Babington, Bruce, and Peter William Evans, *Biblical Epics: Sacred Narrative in the
    Hollywood Cinema* (Manchester: Manchester University Press, 1993).

Baden, Joel, *The Historical David: The Real Life of an Invented Hero* (New York: Harp-
    erOne, 2013).

Bailey, Cyril, *Lucretius: De Rerum Natura, Edited with Prolegomena, Critical Appa-
    ratus, Translation and Commentary* (3 vols.; New York: Oxford University Press,
    1947).

Bailey, Michael D., *Magic and Superstition in Europe: A Concise History from Antiquity
    to the Present* (Lanham, MD: Rowman & Littlefield, 2007).

Bailey, Randall C., Tat-siong Benny Liew and Ferndando Segovia (eds.), *They were All
    Together in One Place: Toward Minority Biblical Criticism* (SBL Semeia Studies,
    57; Atlanta, GA: Society of Biblical Literature, 2009).

Bainton, Roland H., *Christian Attitudes toward War and Peace: A Historical Survey and
    Critical Re-evaluation* (Nashville, TN: Abingdon Press, 1960).

Balch, David L., and Carolyn Osiek (eds.), *Early Christian Families in Context: An
    Interdisciplinary Dialogue* (Grand Rapids, MI: Eerdmans, 2003).

Baltzer, Klaus, *The Covenant Formulary in Old Testament, Jewish, and Early Christian
    Writings* (trans. David E. Green; Philadelphia, PA: Fortress Press, 1971).

Bammel, Ernst, 'πτωχός', *TDNT*, VI, pp. 885-915.

Barbaglio, Giuseppe, *Pace e violenza nella Bibbia* (Bologna: EDB, 2011).

Barber, Bruce, and David J. Neville (eds.), *Theodicy and Eschatology* (Adelaide: ATF Press, 2005).

Barrera, Albino, *Biblical Economic Ethics: Sacred Scripture's Teachings on Economic Life* (Lanham, MD: Lexington Books, 2013).

Barton, John, *Understanding Old Testament Ethics: Approaches and Explorations* (Louisville, KY: Westminster/John Knox Press, 2003).

Baslez, Marie-Francoise, '*Hellenismus-Ioudaismos*: Cross-Approaches of Jewish- Greek Literature of Martyrdom', *Henoch* 32.1 (2010), pp. 19-33.

Bauckham, Richard, *The Bible and Ecology: Rediscovering the Community of Creation* (Waco, TX: Baylor University Press, 2010).

—'Reading the Synoptic Gospels Ecologically', in Horrell *et al.* (eds.), *Ecological Hermeneutics*, pp. 70-82.

Baudrillard, Jean, *Simulacra and Simulation* (trans. Sheira Faria Glaser; Ann Arbor, MI: University of Michigan Press, 1994).

—*Simulacres et simulation* (Paris: Èditions Galilée, 1981).

Bauer, David R., and Mark Allan Powell (eds.), *Treasures New and Old: Recent Contributions to Matthean Studies* (Atlanta, GA: Scholars Press, 1996).

Bauernfeind, Otto, *Die Worte der Dämonen im Markusevangelium* (Stuttgart: W. Kohlhammer, 1927).

Baum, A.D., 'Die Heilungswunder Jesu als Symbolhandlungen—Ein Versuch', *European Journal of Theology* 13 (2004), pp. 5-15.

Beal, Timothy K., *The Rise and Fall of the Bible: The Unexpected History of an Accidental Book* (Boston, MA: Houghton Mifflin, 2011).

Beal, Timothy K., and Todd Linafelt (eds.), *Mel Gibson's Bible* (Chicago, IL: University of Chicago Press, 2006).

Beale, Gregory K., *Handbook on the New Testament Use of Old Testament: Exegesis and Interpretation* (Grand Rapids, MI: Baker Academic, 2012).

Beasley-Murray, George R., *Jesus and the Kingdom of God* (Grand Rapids, MI: Eerdmans, 1986).

Beauchamp, Tom L., and James Childress, *Principles of Biomedical Ethics* (New York: Oxford University Press, 6th edn, 2008).

de Beauvoir, Simone, *The Second Sex* (trans. H.M. Parshley; New York: Vintage Books, 1952).

Beck, John A., *Translators as Storytellers: A Study in Septuagint Translation Technique* (Studies in Biblical Literature, 25; New York: Peter Lang, 2000).

Becker, Sascha O., and Ludger Wössmann, 'Was Weber Wrong? A Human Capital Theory of Protestant Economic History', Munich Discussion Paper No. 2007-7 (Munich: University of Munich: 2007). Online: http://epub.ub.uni-muenchen.de/ 1366/1/weberLMU.pdf.

Becking, Bob, 'Love Thy Neighbour...', in Achenbach und Arneth (eds.), '*Gerechtigkeit und Recht zu üben*', pp. 182-87.

Bekoff, Marc, *The Emotional Lives of Animals: A Leading Scientist Explores Animal Joy, Sorrow, and Empathy—and Why They Matter* (Novato, CA: New World Library, 2007).

Bell, Daniel, *The Cultural Contradictions of Capitalism* (New York: Basic Books, 1976).

Bellinger, William H., and William R. Farmer (eds.), *Jesus and the Suffering Servant: Isaiah 53 and Christian Origins* (Harrisburg, PA: Trinity Press International, 1998).

Belousek, Darrin W. Snynder, *Atonement, Justice, and Peace: The Message of the Cross and the Mission of the Church* (Grand Rapids, MI: Eerdmans, 2012).

Berlinerblau, Jacques, *How to be Secular: A Call to Arms for Religious Freedom* (New York: Houghton Mifflin Harcourt, 2012).

—*The Secular Bible: Why Nonbelievers Must Take Religion Seriously* (Cambridge: Cambridge University Press, 2005).

Besant, Annie, *Woman's Position according to the Bible* (London: Annie Besant and C. Bradlaugh, 1885).

Betz, Hans Dieter, 'New Testament and Roman Religions', *JR* 90.3 (2010), pp. 377-81.

—*The Sermon on the Mount* (Hermeneia; Minneapolis: Fortress Press, 1995).

Betz, Hans Dieter (ed.), *The Greek Magical Papyri in Translation including the Demotic Spells* (Chicago, IL: University of Chicago Press, 1992).

Beyer, Klaus, *Die aramäische Texte vom Toten Meer* (Göttingen: Vandenhoeck & Ruprecht, 1984).

Bianchi, Eugene C., and Rosemary Radforth Ruether (eds.), *A Democratic Catholic Church: The Reconstruction of Roman Catholicism* (New York: Crossroad, 1992).

Bieringer, Reimund, Didier Pollefeyt and Frederique Vandecasteele-Vanneuville, *Anti-Judaism and the Fourth Gospel* (Louisville, KY: Westminster/John Knox Press, 2001).

Biggar, Nigel, 'Specify and Distinguish! Interpreting the New Testament on "Non-Violence"', *Studies in Christian Ethics* 22 (2009), pp. 164-84.

Bilde, Per, *The Originality of Jesus: A Critical Discussion and Comparative Attempt* (Göttingen: Vandenhoeck & Ruprecht, 2013).

Birch, Bruce C., *Let Justice Roll Down: The Old Testament Ethics and Christian Life* (Louisville, KY: Westminster/John Knox Press, 1991).

Bird, Michael F., 'Jesus and the Gentiles after Jeremias: Patterns and Prospects', *Currents in Biblical Research* 4 (2005), pp. 83-105.

—'Tearing the Heavens and Shaking the Heavenlies: Mark's Cosmology in its Apocalyptic Context', in Pennington and McDonough (eds.), *Cosmology and New Testament Theology*, pp. 45-59.

Black, Matthew, *An Aramaic Approach to the Gospels* (New York: Oxford University Press, 3rd edn, 1967).

Blanchard, Kathryn D., and Kevin J. O'Brien, *An Introduction to Christian Environmentalism: Ecology, Virtue, and Ethics* (Waco, TX: Baylor University Press, 2014).

Blanton, Thomas R., 'Saved by Obedience: Matthew 1:21 in Light of Jesus' Teaching on the Torah', *JBL* 132 (2013), pp. 393-413.

Blassingame, John W., and John R. McKivigan (eds.), *The Frederick Douglass Papers: Series One—Speeches, Debates and Interviews* (5 vols.; New Haven, CT: Yale University Press, 1979–92).

Blau, Ludwig, *Die jüdische Ehescheidung und der jüdische Scheidebrief: Eine historische Untersuchung, Erster Teil* (Strasburg: K.J. Trübner, 1911).

Bledstein, Burton J., *The Culture of Professionalism: The Middle Class and the Development of Higher Education in America* (New York: Norton & Norton, 1976).

Block, Berthold, *Jesus und seine Jünger: Wege im Wahn: Beobachtungen zu Bibel, Kirche, Christenthum* (Forum Religionskritik, 9; Münster: LIT, 2009).

Block, Daniel I., *The NIV Application Commentary: Deuteronomy* (Grand Rapids, MI: Zondervan, 2012).

Blomberg, Craig L., *Neither Poverty Nor Riches: A Biblical Theology of Possessions* (New Studies in Biblical Theology, 7; Downers Grove, IL: InterVarsity Press, 1999).

Bock, Darrell L., *The NIV Application Commentary: Luke* (Grand Rapids, MI: Zondervan, 1996).

Boehmer, Elleke, *Colonial and Postcolonial Literature: Migrant Metaphors* (New York: Oxford University Press, 1995).

Boer, Roland, *Marxist Criticism of the Bible* (Sheffield: Sheffield Academic Press, 2003).

—*Rescuing the Bible* (Blackwell Manifestos; Malden, MA: Blackwell, 2007).

Boer, Roland (ed.), *Secularism and Biblical Studies* (London: Equinox, 2010).

Bogosh, Christopher W., *Compassionate Jesus: Rethinking the Christian's Approach to Modern Medicine* (Grand Rapids, MI: Reformation Heritage Books, 2013).

Bokser, Baruch, *The Origins of the Seder* (Berkeley, CA: University of California Press, 1984).

Booth, Roger P., *Jesus and the Laws of Purity: Tradition History and Legal History in Mark 7* (JSNTSup, 13; Sheffield: JSOT Press, 1986).

Borg, Marcus, *Jesus and Buddha: The Parallel Sayings* (Berkeley, CA: Seastone, 1999).

Borgen, Peder, 'Miracles of Healing in the New Testament: Some Observations', *ST* 35 (1981), pp. 91-106.

Bornhäuser, Karl, *Jesus imperator mundi (Phil. 3,17-21 und 2,5-12)* (Gütersloh: Bertelsmann, 1938).

Bosman, Tiana, 'A Critical Review of the Translation of the Hebrew Lexeme אהב', *Old Testament Essays* 18 (2005), pp. 22-34.

Böstrich, Christfried, *Eschatologie und Ethik im frühen Christentum: Festschrift für Günter Haufe zum 75. Geburstag* (Greifswalder theologische Forschungen, 11; New York: Peter Lang, 2006).

Bosworth, Albert B., and Elizabeth J. Baynham (eds.), *Alexander the Great in Fact and Fiction* (New York: Oxford University Press, 2000).

Bosworth, Brian, 'Augustus, the *Res Gestae*, and Hellenstic Theories of Apotheosis', *JRS* 89 (1999), pp. 1-18.

Botta, Alejandro F., *The Aramaic and Egyptian Legal Traditions at Elephantine: An Egyptological Approach* (New York: T. & T. Clark, 2009).

—'Hated by the Gods and your Spouse: Legal Use of שנא in Elephantine and its Ancient Near Eastern Context', in Hagedorn and Kratz (eds.), *Law and Religion in the Eastern Mediterranean*, pp. 105-128.

Boudon-Millot, Véronique, and Bernard Pouderon (eds.), *Les Pères de L'Èglise face à la science médicale de leur temps* (Paris: Beauchesne, 2005).

Bousset, Wilhelm, *Kyrios Christos* (trans. John E. Steely; Nashville, TN: Abingdon Press, 5th edn, 1970).

Bouvier, S., 'La Passion: La ligne rouge de Mel Gibson', *Nova et Vetera* 79 (2004), pp. 103-112.

Bowie, Fiona, *The Anthropology of Religion* (Oxford: Blackwell, 2000).

Bowker, J.W., 'Mystery and Parable: Mark 4:1-20', *JTS* 25 (1974), pp. 300-317.

Boys, M.C., '"I Didn't See Any Anti-Semitism": Why Many Christians Don't Have a Problem with *The Passion of the Christ*', *Cross Currents* 54 (2004), pp. 8-15.

Brady, Christian M.M., 'The Conversion of Ruth in Targum Ruth', *Review of Rabbinic Judaism* 16 (2013), pp. 133-46.

Braund, Susanna, and Glenn W. Most (eds.), *Ancient Anger: Perspectives from Homer to Galen* (Yale Classical Studies, 32; Cambridge: Cambridge University Press, 2003).

Bredin, Mark, *Jesus, Revolutionary of Peace: A Nonviolent Christology in the Book of Revelation* (Waynesboro, GA: Paternoster, 2003).

Brenner, Athalya (ed.), *Ruth and Esther: A Feminist Companion to the Bible* (Second Series; Sheffield: Sheffield Academic Press, 1999).

Bright, John, *The Kingdom of God* (Nashville, TN: Abingdon Press, 1953).

Brighton, Mark Andrew, *The Sicarii in Josephus's Judean War: Rhetorical Analysis and Historical Observations* (Early Judaism and its Literature, 27; Atlanta, GA: Society of Biblical Literature, 2009).

Brisson, Carson, 'Luke 14:25-27', *Int* 61 (2007), pp. 310-12.

Britt, Brian, *Biblical Curses and the Displacement of Tradition* (Sheffield: Sheffield Phoenix Press, 2011).

Broadhurst, Jace R., *What is the Literal Sense? Considering the Hermeneutic of John Lightfoot* (Eugene, OR: Pickwick, 2012).

Brock, Ann Graham, *Mary Magdalene, The First Apostle: The Struggle for Authority* (Harvard Theological Studies, 51; Cambridge, MA: Harvard University Press, 2002).

Brock, Rita Nakashima, *Journeys by the Heart: A Chistology of Erotic Power* (New York: Crossroad, 1988).

Brooten, Bernadette J., *Women Leaders in the Ancient Synagogue* (Brown Judaic Studies, 36; Atlanta, GA: Scholars Press, 1982).

Brown, Dan, *The Da Vinci Code* (New York: Doubleday, 2003).

Brown, Jerry Wayne, *The Rise of Biblical Criticism in America, 1800–1870: The New England Scholars* (Middletown, CT: Wesleyan University Press, 1969).

Brown, Joanne C., and Carole R. Bohn (eds.), *Christianity, Patriarchy, and Abuse: A Feminist Critique* (New York: Pilgrim Press, 1989).

Brown, Joanne C., and Rebecca Parker, 'For God So Loved the World?', in Brown and Bohn (eds.), *Christianity, Patriarchy, and Abuse*, pp. 1-30.

Brown, Michael J., *Blackening the Bible: The Aims of African American Biblical Scholarship* (Harrisburg, PA: Trinity Press International, 2004).

Brown, Raymond E., *An Introduction to the Gospel of John* (New Haven, CT: Yale University Press, 2009).

—*The Gospel According to John 1–XII* (AB, 29; Garden City, NY: Doubleday, 1983).

—*The Gospel According to John XII–XXI* (AB, 29A; New York: Doubleday, 1982).

Brown, Robert MacAfee, *Religion and Violence* (Philadelphia, PA: Westminster, 2nd edn, 1987).

Brown, Schuyler, '"The Secret of the Kingdom of God" (Mark 4:11)', *JBL* 92 (1973), pp. 60-74.

Brownson, J.V., *Bible, Gender, Sexuality: Reframing the Church's Debate on Same-Sex Relationships* (Grand Rapids, MI: Eerdmans, 2013).

Brummer, Leila R., *Excluded from Suffrage History: Matilda Joslyn Gage, Nineteenth Century American Feminist* (Westport, CT: Greenwood Press, 2000).

Brunet, Gilbert, 'L'Hebreu Keleb', *VT* 35 (1985), pp. 485-88.

Brunt, A., and J.M. Moore, *Res Gestae Divi Augusti: The Achievements of the Divine Augustus* (London: Oxford University Press, 1967).

Bryan, Christopher, *Render to Caesar: Jesus, The Early Church and the Roman Superpower* (New York: Oxford University Press, 2005).

Buell, Denise Kimber, and Caroline Johnson Hodge, 'The Politics of Interpretation: The Rhetoric of Race and Ethnicity in Paul', *JBL* 123 (2004), pp. 235-51.

Bultmann, Rudolf, *Theology of the New Testament* (trans. Kendrick Grobel; 2 vols.; New York: Charles Scribner's Sons, 1951–1955).

Burkett, Derbert, *The Son of Man Debate: A History and Evaluation* (SNTSMS, 107; Cambridge: Cambridge University Press, 1999).

Burkill, Tom A., 'The Historical Development of the Story of the Syrophoenician Woman (Mark VII:24-31)', *NovT* 9 (1967), pp. 161-77.

Burnet, R., *Marie-Madeleine (1er-XXIe siècle). De la pécheresse repentie à l'espouse de Jesus. Histoire de la reception d'une figure bibique* (Lire la Bible, 140; Paris: Cerf, 2004).

Burridge, Richard A., *Imitating Jesus: An Inclusive Approach to New Testament Ethics* (Grand Rapids, MI: Eerdmans, 2007).

Busch, Peter, *Das Testament Salomos: Die älteste christliche Dämonlogie, kommentiert und in deutscher Erstübersetzung* (TU, 153; Berlin: W. de Gruyter, 2005).

Buszard, Bradley, 'The Speech of Greek and Roman Women in Plutarch's *Lives*', *Classical Philology* 105 (2010), pp. 83-115.

Byron, J., 'Paul and the Background of Slavery: The Status Questionis in New Testament Scholarship', *Currents in Biblical Research* 3 (2004), pp. 116-39.

Cahill, Lisa Sowle, *Love your Enemies: Discipleship, Pacifism, and Just War Theory* (Minneapolis: Fortress Press, 1994).

—*Sex, Gender and Christian Ethics* (Cambridge: Cambridge University Press, 1996).

Callahan, Allen D., Richard A. Horsley and Abraham Smith (eds.), *Slavery in Text and Interpretation* (Semeia, 83/84; Atlanta, GA: Scholars Press, 1998).

Callicott, J. Baird, 'The Conceptual Foundations of the Land Ethic', in Zimmerman *et al.* (eds.), *Environmental Philosophy*, pp. 110-34.

—'Introduction', in Zimmerman *et al.* (eds.), *Environmental Philosophy*, pp. 3-11.

Calvert-Koyzis, Nancy, and Heather E. Weir (eds.), *Strangely Familiar: Protofeminist Interpretations of Patriarchal Biblical Texts* (Atlanta, GA: Society of Biblical Literature, 2009).

Cameron, Ron, and Merrill P. Miller (eds.), *Redescribing Christian Origins* (SBL Symposium, 28; Atlanta, GA: Scholars Press, 2004).

Caragounis, Chrys C., 'Dionysius Halikarnasseus: The Art of Composition and the Apostel Paul', *Journal of Greco-Roman Christianity and Judaism* 1 (2000), pp. 25-54.

Carrier, Richard, *On The Historicity of Jesus: Why we Might have Reason to Doubt* (Sheffield: Sheffield Phoenix Press, 2014).

Carson, Donald A., 'The Jewish Leaders in Matthew's Gospel: A Reappraisal', *JETS* 25 (1982), pp. 161-74.

Carson, Rachel L., *Silent Spring* (Boston, MA: Houghton Mifflin, 1962).

Carter, Warren, 'The Blind, Lame and Paralyzed', in Moss and Schipper (eds.), *Disability Studies and Biblical Literature*, pp. 127-50.

—*Matthew and Empire: Initial Explorations* (Harrisburg, PA: Trinity Press International, 2001).

—*Matthew at the Margins: A Sociopolitical and Religious Reading* (Maryknoll, NY: Orbis Books, 2000).

Casey, Maurice, *Jesus of Nazareth: An Independent Historian's Account of His Life and Teaching* (London and New York: T. & T. Clark, 2010).

—'The Role of Aramaic in Reconstructing the Teaching of Jesus', in Holmén and Porter (eds.), *Handbook for the Study of the Historical Jesus*, II, pp. 1343-75.

Cassedy, Steven, 'Walter Rauschenbusch, the Social Gospel Movement, and How Julius Wellhausen Unwittingly Helped Create American Progressivism in the Twentieth Century', in Dolansky (ed.), *Sacred History, Sacred Literature*, pp. 315-24.

Cassidy, Richard J., and Philip J. Scharper (eds.), *Political Issues in Luke–Acts* (Maryknoll, NY: Orbis Books, 1983).

Chan, Lúcás, and James F. Keenan (eds.), *Biblical Ethics in the Twenty-First Century: Developments, Emerging Consensus, and Future Directions* (Mahwah, NJ: Paulist Press, 2013).

Chan, Michael, 'Isaiah 65–66 and the Genesis of Reorienting Speech', *CBQ* 72 (2010), pp. 445-63.

Chancey, Mark, *Greco-Roman Culture and the Galilee of Jesus* (SNTSMS, 134; Cambridge: Cambridge University Press, 2005).

Chanikuzhy, Jacob (ed.), *Jesus, the Eschatological Temple: An Exegetical Study of Jn 2, 13-22 in the Light of pre-70 CE. Eschatological Temple Hopes and the Synoptic Temple Action* (Contributions to Biblical Exegesis and Theology, 58; Leuven: Peeters, 2012).

Charles, Ronald, *Paul and the Politics of Diaspora* (Paul in Critical Contexts; Minneapolis: Fortress Press, 2014).

—'Q as a Question from a Postcolonial Point of View', *Black Theology* 7 (2009), pp. 182-99.

Chené, Adèle, Pierrette Daviau, Marcel Dumais, Olivette Genest, Clément Légnaré, Louise Milot, Jean-Paul Michaud, Richard Rivard, Jean-Yves Thériault and Walter Vogels (eds.), *De Jésus et des femmes: Lectures sémiotiques. Suivies d'un entretien avec A. J. Greimas* (Recherches, nouvelle série, 14; Paris: Cerf, 1987).

Chennattu, Rekha M., *Johannine Discipleship as a Covenant Relationship* (Peabody, MA: Hendrickson, 2006).

Chilton, Bruce D., '[ὡς] φραγέλλιον ἐκ σχοινίων (John 2.15)', in Horbury (ed.), *Templum Amicitiae*, pp. 330-44.

—*A Galilean Rabbi and his Bible: Jesus' Use of the Interpreted Scripture in His Time* (Wilmington, DE: Michael Glazier, 1984).

—*The Kingdom of God in the Teaching of Jesus* (Philadelphia, PA: Fortress Press, 1984).

—*Mary Magdalene: A Biography* (New York: Doubleday, 2005).

Chilton, Bruce D., and Craig E. Evans (eds.), *Authenticating the Words of Jesus* (Boston and Leiden: E.J. Brill, 2002).

Chilton, Bruce D., and J.I.H. McDonald, *Jesus and the Ethics of the Kingdom* (Grand Rapids, MI: Eerdmans, 1987).

Chilton, Bruce D., and Jacob Neusner, *Classical Christianity and Rabbinic Judaism: Comparing Theologies* (Grand Rapids, MI: Baker, 2004).

Chinard, Gilbert, *The Literary Bible of Thomas Jefferson: His Commonplace Book of Philosophers and Poets* (New York: Greenwood Press, 1928).

Chinen, Mark A., 'Crumbs from the Table: The Syrophoenician Woman and International Law', *Journal of Law and Religion* 27 (2011–12), pp. 1-57.

Chisholm, Robert B., 'The Christological Fulfillment of Isaiah's Servant Songs', *BSac* 163 (2006), pp. 387-404.

Chrysostom, Saint John, *Discourses Against Judaizing Christians* (trans. Paul W. Harkins; Washington, DC: Catholic University of America, 1979).

Cicero, *De oratore* (trans. E.W. Sutton and H. Rackham; LCL; 2 vols.; Cambridge, MA: Harvard University Press, 1942).

Claassens, L. Juliana M., 'Resisting Dehumanization: Ruth, Tamar and the Quest for Human Dignity', *CBQ* 74 (2012), pp. 659-74.

Clark, Elizabeth A., 'Antifamilial Tendencies in Ancient Christianity', *Journal of the History of Sexuality* 5 (1995), pp. 356-80.

Clark, Stephen, *Ancient Mediterranean Philosophy: An Introduction* (London: Blooms-bury, 2013).

Clasen, Donna Rae, and B. Bradford Brown, 'The Multidimensionality of Peer Pressure in Adolescence', *Journal of Youth and Adolescence* 14 (1985), pp. 451-68.

Clauss, Manfred, *Kaiser und Gott: Herrscherkult im römischer Reich* (Stuttgart and Leipzig: Teubner, 1999).

Clines, David J.A., *I, He, We, and They: A Literary Approach to Isaiah 53* (JSOTSup, 1; Sheffield: JSOT Press, 1976).

—'The Image of God in Man', *TynBul* 19 (1968), pp. 53-103.

—*Job 1–20* (Word Biblical Commentary, 17; Nashville, TN: T. Nelson, 1989).

Cohen, Eran, 'Akkadian *–ma* in Diachronic Perspective', *ZA* 90 (2000), pp. 207-226.

Cohen, Yoram, Amir Gilan and Jared L. Miller (eds.), *Pax Hethitica: Studies on the Hit-tites and their Neighbours in Honour of Itamar Singer* (Wiesbaden: Harrasowitz, 2010).

Cole, Robert L., 'Isaiah 6 in its Context', *Southeastern Theological Review* 2 (2011), pp. 161-80.

Collins, Adela Yarbro, *Mark: A Commentary* (Hermeneia: Minneapolis: Fortress Press, 2007).

—'Narrative, History and Gospel', *Semeia* 43 (1988), pp. 143-53.

—'Son of Man', in *NIDB*, V, pp. 341-48.

Collins, Billie Jean (ed.), *A History of the Animal World in the Ancient Near East* (Leiden: E.J. Brill, 2002).

Collins, John J., 'The Beginning and End of the World in the Hebrew Bible', in Ahn and Cook (eds.), *Thus Says the Lord*, pp. 137-55.

—'Faith, Scholarship, and the Society of Biblical Literature', in Ames and Miller (eds.), *Foster Biblical Scholarship*, pp. 64-81.

—'The Kingdom of God in the Apocrypha and Pseudepigrapha', in Willis (ed.), *The Kingdom of God*, pp. 81-95.

—'Sibylline Oracles', *NIDB*, V, p. 247.

—'The Zeal of Phinehas: The Bible and the Legitimation of Violence', *JBL* 122 (2003), pp. 3-21.

Collins, John J. (ed.), *The Encylopedia of Apocalypticism: Volume 1. The Origins of Apocalypticism in Judaism and Christianity* (New York: Continuum, 1998).

—'Marriage, Divorce and Family in Second Temple Judaism', in Perdue *et al.* (eds.), *Families in Ancient Israel*, pp. 104-162.

—*The Sibylline Oracles of Egyptian Judaism* (SBLDS, 13; Missoula, MT: Scholars Press, 1974).

Collins, John N., *Diakonia: Re-interpreting the Ancient Sources* (New York: Oxford University Press, 1990).

Comber, Joseph A., 'The Verb *Therapeuō* in Matthew's Gospel', *JBL* 97 (1978), pp. 431-34.

Cone, Orello, *Rich and Poor in the New Testament: A Study of the Primitive Doctrine of Earthly Possessions* (New York: Macmillan, 1902).

Conybeare, F.C., *Myth, Magic, and Morals: A Study of Christian Origins* (London: Watts, 1910).

Conzelmann, Hans, *I Corinthians: A Commentary on the First Epistle to the Corin-thians* (trans. James Leitch; Hermeneia; Philadelphia, PA: Fortress Press, 1975).

Cook, Johann, 'The Translation of a Translation: Some Methodological Considerations on the Translation of the Septuagint', in Peters (ed.), *XII Congress*, pp. 29-40.

Cook, John Granger, 'In Defense of Ambiguity: Is there a Hidden Demon in Mark 1.29-31?', *NTS* 43 (1997), pp. 184-208.

Corley, Kathleen E., 'Women and the Crucifixion and Burial of Jesus', *Forum: A Journal of the Foundations and Facets of Western Culture, New Series*, 1 (1998), pp. 181-225.

Corley, Kathleen E., and Robert L. Webb (eds.), *Jesus and Mel Gibson's The Passion of the Christ: The Film, the Gospels, and the Claims of History* (London and New York: Continuum, 2004).

Cosgrove, Charles H., 'New Testament Ethics', in Green (ed.), *Dictionary of Scripture and Ethics*, pp. 548-52.

Cowdell, Scott, *René Girard and Secular Modernity: Christ, Culture and Crisis* (Notre Dame, IN: University of Notre Dame Press, 2013).

Cowley, A., *Aramaic Papyri of the Fifth Century B.C.* (repr., Osnabrück: Otto Zeller, 1967 [1923]).

Cox, D. Michael, 'The Gospel of Matthew and Resisting Imperial Theology', *PRSt* 36 (2009), pp. 25-48.

Craddock, Fred B., *Interpretation Bible Commentary: Luke* (Louisville, KY: John Knox Press, 1990).

Craffert, Peter, 'New Testament Studies—Preventing or Promoting Human Society?', *Religion and Theology* 14.3-4 (2007), pp. 161-205.

Crane, Richard D., 'Michael Legaspi's *The Death of Scripture and the Birth of Biblical Studies*: A Review Essay', *PRSt* 39.4 (2012), pp. 395-404.

Creamer, Deborah B., *Disability and Christian Theology: Embodied Limits and Constructive Possibilities* (New York: Oxford University Press, 2009).

Crook, Zeba A., 'On the Treatment of Miracles in New Testament Scholarship', *StudRel/SciRel* 40 (2011), pp. 461-78.

—*Reconceptualizing Conversion: Patronage, Loyalty, and Conversion in the Religions of the Ancient Mediterranean* (Berlin: W. de Gruyter, 2004).

Crosby, Alfred W., *The Biological Expansion of Europe, 900–1900* (Cambridge: Cambridge University Press, 1986).

Crossan, John Dominic, *The Historical Jesus: The Life of a Mediterranean Jewish Peasant* (New York: HarperCollins, 1991).

—*Jesus: A Revolutionary Biography* (New York: HarperCollins, 1995).

Crossley James G., 'Can John's Gospel be Used to Reconstruct a Life of Jesus? An Assessment of Recent Trends and a Defence of a Traditional View', in Thompson and Verenna (eds.), *'Is This Not the Carpenter?'*, pp. 163-84.

—*Jesus in an Age of Neoliberalism: Quests, Scholarship, and Ideology* (London: Equinox, 2012).

—*Jesus in an Age of Terror: Scholarly Projects for a New American Century* (London: Equinox, 2008).

—*Why Christianity Happened: A Sociohistorical Account of Christian Origins (26–50 CE)* (Louisville, KY: Westminster/John Knox Press, 2006).

Croy, N., Clayton. '"To Die is Gain" (Philippians 1.19-26): Does Paul Contemplate Suicide?', *JBL* 122 (2003), pp. 517-31

—'The Messianic Whippersnapper: Did Jesus Use a Whip on People in the Temple (John 2:15)?', *JBL* 128 (2009), pp. 555-68.

Crum, W.E., *A Coptic Dictionary* (Oxford: Clarendon Press, 1939).

Curtis, Susan, *A Consuming Faith: The Social Gospel in Modern American Culture* (Baltimore, MD: The Johns Hopkins University Press, 1991).

Dachs, Gisela, 'Otto Michel: Freund der Juden?', *Zeit Online* (22 January 2012). Online: http://www.zeit.de/2012/04/Judaistik-Theologe-Michel (accessed 15 September 2014).

Daly, Mary, *Beyond God the Father* (Boston, MA: Beacon Press, 1973).

—*Gyn/Ecology: The Metaethics of Radical Feminism* (Boston, MA: Beacon Press, 1978).

D'Angelo, Mary Rose, 'Roman Imperial Family Values and the Gospel of Mark: The Divorce Sayings (Mark 10:2-12)', in Ahearne-Kroll, Holloway and Kelhoffer (eds.), *Women and Gender in Ancient Religions*, pp. 59-84.

Darr, John A., 'Mimetic Desire, the Gospels, and Early Christianity', *BibInt* 1 (1993), pp. 357-67.

Dart, John, 'Scholars and Believers: Growing Pains at the SBL', *Christian Century* 128.7 (2011), pp. 34-38.

Davenport, Tracy, 'An Anti-Imperialist Twist to the Gilgameš Epic', in Azize and Weeks (eds.), *Gilgameš and the World of Assyria*, pp. 1-23.

Davies, Alan T., *Anti-Semitism and the Christian Mind: The Crisis of Conscience after Auschwitz* (New York: Paulist Press, 1969).

Davies, Margaret, 'Work and Slavery in the New Testament: Impoverishment of Traditions', in Rogerson, Davies and Carroll R. (eds.), *The Bible in Ethics*, pp. 315-47.

Davies, Margaret Lloyd, and T.A. Lloyd Davies, *The Bible: Medicine and Myth* (Cambridge: Silent Books, 2nd edn, 1991).

Davies, W.D., *The Setting of the Sermon on the Mount* (Cambridge: Cambridge University Press, 1963).

Davis, Frederick B., *The Jew and Deicide: The Origins of an Archetype* (Lanham, MD: University Press of America, 2003).

Davis, Lennard J. (ed.), *The Disability Studies Reader* (New York: Routledge, 1997).

Dawkins, Richard, *The God Delusion* (New York: Bantam, 2006).

DeConick, April D., *Holy Misogyny: Why the Sex and Gender Conflicts in the Early Church Still Matter* (New York: Continuum, 2011).

DeCosse, David E., 'The Danish Cartoons Reconsidered: Catholic Social Teaching and the Contemporary Challenge of Free Speech', *TS* 71 (2010), pp. 101-132.

De Groot, Christiana, and Marion Ann Taylor (eds.), *Recovering Nineteenth Century Women Interpreters of the Bible* (Leiden: E.J. Brill, 2007).

Deines, Roland, and Karl-Wilhelm Niebuhr (eds.), *Philo und das Neue Testament. Wechselseitige Wahrnehmungen. 1. Internationale Symposium zum Corpus Judeo-Hellenisticum. 1-4 Mai 2003, Eisenach/Jena* (WUNT, 2.172; Tübingen: Mohr Siebeck, 2004).

Deissmann, Adolf, *Light from the Ancient East: The New Testament Illustrated by Recently Discovered Texts of the Greco-Roman World* (trans. Lionel R. Strachan; repr., Peabody, MA: Hendrickson, 1995 [1927]).

DeMaris, Richard E., 'Sacrifice, an Ancient Mediterranean Ritual', *BTB* 43 (2013), pp. 60-73.

Denniston, J.D., *The Greek Particles* (Oxford: Clarendon Press, 2nd edn, 1959).

Denny, J., 'The Word "Hate" in Luke xiv.26', *ExpTim* 20 (1909), pp. 41-42.

Derrett, J., Duncan M. 'Contributions to the Study of the Gerasene Demoniac', *JSNT* 3 (1979), pp. 2-17.

—'Mark's Technique: The Hemorrhaging Woman and Jairus' Daughter', *Bib* 63 (1982), pp. 474-505.

—'The True Meaning of Jn 9, 3-4', *Filología Neotestamentaria* 16 (2003), pp. 103-106.

DeSilva, David A., 'The Strategic Arousal of Emotions in the Apocalypse of John: A

Rhetorical-Critical Investigation of the Oracles to the Seven Churches', *NTS* 54 (2008), pp. 90-114.

Dessau, Hermann, *Inscriptiones Latinae Selectae, Volume 2, Part 2* (Chicago, IL: Ares Publishers, 1979).

Dewey, Joanna, 'The Gospel of Mark', in Schüssler Fiorenza (ed.), *Searching the Scriptures*, II, pp. 470-509.

—'Jesus' Healings of Women: Conformity and Nonconformity to Dominant Cultural Values as Clues for Historical Reconstruction', *BTB* 24 (1994), pp. 122-31.

—'"Let them Renounce Themselves and Take up their Cross": A Feminist Reading of Mark 8.34 in Mark's Social and Narrative World', in Levine and Blickenstaff (eds.), *A Feminist Companion to Mark*, pp. 23-36.

—'The Survival of Mark's Gospel: A Good Story?', *JBL* 123 (2004), pp. 495-507.

Didymus the Blind, *Commentary on Zechariah* (trans. Robert C. Hill; The Fathers of the Church, 111; Washington, DC: Catholic University of America Press, 2006).

Diehl, Judith, 'Anti-Imperial Rhetoric in the New Testament', *Currents in Biblical Research* 10.1 (2011), pp. 9-52.

—'Anti-Imperial Rhetoric in the New Testament', in McKnight and Modica (eds.), *Jesus is Lord, Caesar is Not*, pp. 38-81.

Dienstbier, Richard A. *et al.* (eds.), *Nebraska Symposium on Motivation 1989* (Lincoln, NE: University of Nebraska Press, 1989).

Diodorus Siculus, *Historia* (trans. C.H. Oldfather, LCL; 12 vols.; Cambridge, MA: Harvard University Press, 1950).

Diogenes Laertius, *Lives of Eminent Philsophers* (trans. R.D. Hicks; LCL; 2 vols.; Cambridge, MA: Harvard University Press, 1931).

Dion, Paul-Eugène, 'Raphaël l'Exorciste', *Bib* 57 (1976), pp. 399-413.

Dionysius of Halicarnassus. *Roman Antiquities* (trans. Earnest Cary; LCL; 7 vols.; Cambridge, MA: Harvard University Press, 1937).

Dodds, E.R., *The Greeks and the Irrational* (Berkeley, CA: University of California Press, 2004).

Dolansky, Shawna (ed.), *Sacred History, Sacred Literature: Essays on Ancient Israel, the Bible, and Religion in Honor of R.E. Friedman on his Sixtieth Birthday* (Winona Lake, IN: Eisenbrauns, 2008).

Dole, Charles F., *What We Know about Jesus* (Chicago, IL: Open Court, 1908).

Donahue, John R., and Daniel J. Harrington, *The Gospel of Mark* (Sacra Pagina; Collegeville, MN: Liturgical Press, 2002).

Donaldson, Laura E., 'The Sign of Orpah: Reading Ruth through Native Eyes', in Brenner (ed.), *Ruth and Esther*, pp. 130-44.

Donoghue, Frank, *The Last Professors: The Corporate University and the Fate of the Humanities* (New York: Fordham University Press, 2008).

Dorey, Peter J., 'Genesis 2:24: *Locus classicus* van monogamie in die Ou Testament? 'n literêr-historiese ondersoek na perspektiewe op poligamie huwelike in die Ou Testament', *OTE* 17 (2004), pp. 15-29.

Dorman, Johanna H.W., 'The Blemished Body: Deformity and Disability in the Qumran Scrolls' (PhD dissertation; Rijksuniversiteit Groningen, 2007).

Dorn, Jacob H. (ed.), *Socialism and Christianity in Early 20th Century America* (Westport, CT: Greenwood Press, 1998).

Doudna, John Charles, *The Greek of the Gospel of Mark* (Journal of Biblical Literature Monograph Series, 12; Philadelphia, PA: Society of Biblical Literature and Exegesis, 1961).

Douglass, Frederick, 'Great Britain's Example is High, Noble, and Grand...6 August, 1885', in Blassingame and McKivigan (eds.), *The Frederick Douglass Papers*, V, p. 203.

Dowling, Elizabeth V., 'Luke–Acts: Good News for Slaves?', *Pacifica: Journal of the Melbourne College of Divinity* 24 (2011), pp. 123-40.

Drake, Harold A. (ed.), *Violence in Late Antiquity: Perceptions and Practices* (Burlington, VT: Ashgate, 2006).

Droge, Arthur J., and James D. Tabor, *A Noble Death: Suicide and Martyrdom among Christians and Jews in Antiquity* (New York: HarperCollins, 1992).

Duhaime, Jean, *The War Texts: 1QM and the Related Manuscripts* (Companion to the Qumran Scrolls, 6; New York: T. & T. Clark, 2007).

Duling, Dennis, 'Kingdom of God, Kingdom of Heaven', *ABD*, IV, pp. 49-69.

Dunayer, Joan. *Speciesism* (Derwood, MD: Rice Publishing, 2004).

Dunbabin, Katherine M.D., *The Roman Banquet: Images of Conviviality* (Cambridge: Cambridge University Press, 2003).

Dunn, James D.G., *Jesus Remembered: Christianity in the Making, Volume 1* (Grand Rapids, MI: Eerdmans, 2003).

—*Beginning from Jerusalem: Christianity in the Making, Volume 2* (Grand Rapids, MI: Eerdmans, 2008).

—*The Theology of Paul the Apostle* (Grand Rapids, MI: Eerdmans, 1998).

Dupont, Jacques, 'Béatitudes egyptiennes', *Bib* 47 (1966), pp. 185-222.

Durand, Jean Marie (ed.), *La Femme dans le Proche-Orient Antique, Compte Rendu de la xxxiiie recontre assyriologique internationale (Paris, 7-10 juillet 1986)* (Paris: Editions Recherche sur le Civilisations, 1987).

Dyer, Keith D., 'When is the End Not the End? The Fate of the Earth in Biblical Eschatology', in Habel and Balabanski (eds.), *The Earth Story in the New Testament*, pp. 44-56.

Eberhart, Christian A., 'The "Passion" of Gibson: Evaluating a Recent Interpretation of Christ's Suffering and Death in Light of the New Testament', *Consensus* 30 (2005), pp. 37-74.

—*The Sacrifice of Jesus: Understanding Atonement Biblically* (Minneapolis: Fortress Press, 2011).

Eck, Joachim, 'Bilden Jes 6,1-11 und 1 Kön 22, 19-22 eine Gattung? Ein umfassender exegetischer Vergleich *(Teil I)*', *BN* (2009), pp. 57-65.

Eckstein, Arthur M., *Mediterranean Anarchy, Interstate War, and the Rise of Rome* (Hellenstic Culture and Society, 48; Berkeley, CA: University of California Press, 2006).

Edelman, Diana V. (ed.), *You Shall Not Abhor an Edomite for he is your Brother: Edom and Seir in History and Tradition* (SBLABS, 3; Atlanta, GA: Scholars Press, 1995).

Edelstein, Emma J., and Ludwig Edelstein, *Asclepius: Collection and Interpretation of Testimonies* (repr., Baltimore, MD: The Johns Hopkins University Press, 1998 [1945]).

Edwards, J. Christopher, *The Ransom Logion in Mark and Matthew: Its Reception and its Significance for the Study of the Gospels* (WUNT, 2.327; Tübingen: Mohr Siebeck, 2012).

Edwards, Douglas R., and C. Thomas McCullough, *Archaeology and the Galilee: Texts and Contexts in the Graeco-Roman and Byzantine Periods* (South Florida Studies in the History of Judaism, 143; Atlanta, GA: Scholars Press, 1997).

Edwards, R.A., *The Sign of Jonah in the Theology of the Evangelists and Q* (London: SCM Press, 1971).

Efthimiades-Keith, Helen, *The Enemy Within: A Jungian Psychoanalytic Approach to the Book of Judith* (Biblical Interpretation, 67; Leiden: E.J. Brill, 2004).

Egger-Wenzel, Renate, and Jeremy Corley (eds.), *Emotions from Ben Sira to Paul* (Berlin and Boston, MA: W. de Gruyter, 2012).

Ehrman, Bart, *Did Jesus Exist?: The Historical Argument for Jesus of Nazareth Scholarship* (New York: HarperOne, 2013).

—*God's Problem: How the Bible Fails to Answer our Most Important Questions—Why we Must Suffer* (New York: HarperCollins, 2008).

—*Lost Christianities: The Battles for Scripture and the Faiths We Never Knew* (New York: Oxford University Press, 2005).

—*Peter, Paul, and Mary Magdalene: The Followers of Jesus in History and Legend* (New York: Oxford University Press, 2006).

Eiesland, Nancy L., and Don E. Saliers (eds.), *Human Disability and the Service of God: Reassessing Religious Practice* (Nashville, TN: Abingdon Press, 1998).

Eklund, Robert B., and Robert D. Tolleson, *Economic Origins of Roman Christianity* (Chicago, IL: University of Chicago Press, 2011).

Eliav, Yaron Z., 'The Matrix of Ancient Judaism: A Review Essay of Seth Schwartz's *Imperialism and Jewish Society 200 B.C.E. to 640 C.E.*', *Prooftexts* 24 (2004), pp. 116-28.

Elledge, Casey D., '"From the Beginning it was Not So...": Jesus, Divorce and Remarriage in Light of the Dead Sea Scrolls', *PRSt* 37 (2010), pp. 371-90.

Ellens, J. Harold, *The Destructive Power of Religion: Violence in Judaism, Christianity, and Islam* (4 vols.; Westport, CT: Praeger, 2004), III, pp. 15-37.

—'The Violent Jesus', in *The Destructive Power of Religion: Violence in Judaism, Christianity, and Islam* (ed. J. Harold Ellens; 4 vols.; Westport, CT: Praeger, 2004), III, pp. 15-37.

Ellens, J. Harold, and Wayne G. Rollins (eds.), *Psychology and the Bible: A New Way to Read the Scriptures* (4 vols.; Westport, CT: Praeger, 2004).

Ellingsworth, P., 'We Must Have Blood', *BT* 60.1 (2009), pp. 5-9.

Elvey, Anne F., *An Ecological Feminist Reading of the Gospel of Luke: A Gestational Paradigm* (Lewiston, NY: Edwin Mellen Press, 2005).

Engberg-Pedersen, Troels, *Cosmology and Self in the Apostle Paul: The Material Spirit* (New York: Oxford University Press, 2010).

Ensor, Peter, 'Justin Martyr and Penal Substitutionary Atonement', *EvQ* 83 (2011), pp. 217-32.

Epictetus (trans. W.A. Oldfather; LCL; 2 vols.; Cambridge, MA: Harvard University Press, 1928).

Erdrich, Michael, *Rom und die Barbaren: Das Verhältnis Zwischen dem Imperium Romanum und den germanischen Stämmen vor seiner Nordwestgrenze von der späten römischen Republik bis zum gallischen Sonderreich* (Mainz: Von Zabern, 2001).

Esau, Ken, 'Disturbing Divine Behavior: Seibert's Solution to the Problem of the Old Testament God', *Direction: A Mennonite Brethren Forum* 40 (2011), pp. 168-78. Online: http://www.directionjournal.org/40/2/disturbing-scholarly-behavior-seiberts.html.

Esbjörn-Hargens, Sean, and Michael E. Zimmerman, *Integral Ecology: Uniting Multiple Perspectives in the Natural World* (Boston, MA: Integral Books, 2009).

Eshel, Esther, 'Leviticus, Book of', in Schiffman and VanderKam (eds.), *Encyclopedia of the Dead Sea Scrolls*, I, pp. 488-93.

Evans, Abigail Rian, 'Review of Hector Avalos, *Health Care and the Rise of Christianity*', *Theology Today* 58 (2002), pp. 576-77.

Evans, Craig E., 'Jesus and Psalm 91 in Light of the Exorcism Scrolls', in Flint, Duhaime and Baek (eds.), *Celebrating the Dead Sea Scrolls*, pp. 541-55.

—'Jewish Burial Traditions and the Resurrection of Jesus', *Journal for the Study of the Historical Jesus* 3 (2005), pp. 233-48.

—'A Note on the Function of Isaiah vi, 9-10 in Mark iv', *RB* 88 (1981), pp. 234-35.

—*To See and Not Perceive: Isaiah 6.9-10 in Early Jewish and Christian Interpretation* (JSOTSup, 64; Sheffield: Sheffield Academic Press, 1989).

—*St. Luke* (TPI New Testament Commentaries; Philadelphia, PA: Trinity Press International, 1990).

Evans, Craig E., and Donald A. Hagner (eds.), *Anti-Semitism and Early Christianity: Issues of Polemic and Faith* (Minneapolis: Fortress Press, 1993).

Evans, Elizabeth C., *Physiognomics in the Ancient World* (Transactions of the American Philosophical Society, 59, part 5; Philadelphia, PA: American Philosophical Society, 1969).

Eve, Eric, 'Spit in your Eye: The Blind Man of Bethsaida and the Blind Man of Alexandria', *NTS* 54 (2008), pp. 1-17.

Exum, J. Cheryl, 'Feminist Criticism: Whose Interests are Being Served?', in Yee (ed.), *Judges and Method*, pp. 65-89.

—*Tragedy and Biblical Narrative: Arrows of the Almighty* (Cambridge: Cambridge University Press, 1992).

—'Trusting in the God of their Fathers: A Response to the Articles by Robert Knetsch and Amanda Benckhuysen', in *Strangely Familiar: Protofeminist Interpretations of Patriarchal Biblical Texts* (ed. Nancy Calvert-Koyzis and Heather E. Weir; Atlanta, GA: Society of Biblical Literature, 2009), pp. 49-55.

Fabien, Patrick, 'L'interprétation de la citation d'Is 53, 7-8 en Ac 8, 23-33', *RB* 117 (2010), pp. 550-70.

Falk, Harvey, *Jesus the Pharisee: A New Look at his Jewishness* (New York: Paulist Press, 1985).

Fantin, Joseph D., *The Greek Imperative Mood in the New Testament: A Cognitive and Communicative Approach* (Studies in Biblical Greek, 12; New York: Peter Lang, 2010).

—*The Lord of the Entire World: Lord Jesus, a Challenge to Lord Caesar?* (Sheffield: Sheffield Phoenix Press, 2011).

Faraone, Christopher A., 'The Wheel, the Whip and Other Implements of Torture: Erotic Magic in Pindar Pythian 4.213-29', *Classical Journal* 89 (1993), pp. 1-19.

Fassberg, Steven, 'Which Semitic Languages did Jesus and Other Contemporary Jews Speak?', *CBQ* 74 (2012), pp. 263-80.

Fausto-Sterling, Anne, *Sexing the Body: Gender, Politics, and the Construction of Sexuality* (New York: Basic Books, 2000).

Feder, Stephanie, 'Neue Perspektiven von Frauen: Exegesen afrikanischer Bibelwissenschaft-lerinnen aus westlicher Sicht', *Bibel und Kirche* 67 (2012), pp. 154-59.

Fernandez, Miguel Pérez, 'Rabbinic Texts in the Exegesis of the New Testament', *Review of Rabbinic Judaism* 7 (2004), pp. 95-120.

Ferngren, Gary B., *Medicine and Health Care in Early Christianity* (Baltimore, MD: The Johns Hopkins University Press, 2009).

Fiensy, David A., and Ralph K. Hawkins (eds.), *The Galilean Economy in the Time of Jesus* (Atlanta, GA: Society of Biblical Literature, 2013)

Finlan, Stephen, *Options on Atonement in Christian Thought* (Collegeville, MN: Liturgical Press, 2007).

—*Problems with Atonement: The Origins of, and Controversy about, the Atonement Doctrine* (Collegeville, MN: Liturgical Press, 2005).

Finsterbusch, Karin, Armin Lange and K.F. Diethard Römheld (eds.), *Human Sacrifice in Jewish and Christian Tradition* (Numen Book Series, 112; Leiden: E.J. Brill, 2007).

Fitzmyer, Joseph A., *The Genesis Apocryphon of Qumran Cave 1 (1Q20): A Commentary* (Biblica et Orientalia, 18/B; Rome: Pontifical Biblical Institute Press, 3rd edn, 2004).

—*The Letter to Philemon: A New Translation with Introduction and Commentary* (AB, 34C; New York: Doubleday, 2000).

—*The Gospel According to Luke X–XXIV* (AB, 28A; Garden City, NY: Doubleday, 1985).

—'A Re-Study of an Elephantine Marriage Contract (*AP* 15)', in Goedicke (ed.), *Near Eastern Studies in Honor of William Foxwell Albright*, pp. 137-68.

Flemming, Rebecca, 'Women, Writing, and Medicine in the Classical World', *ClQ* 57.1 (2007), pp. 257-59.

Flint, Peter W., Jeane Duhaime and Kyung S. Baek (eds.), *Celebrating the Dead Sea Scrolls: A Canadian Collection* (SBLEJL, 30; Atlanta, GA: Society of Biblical Literature, 2011).

Flood, Derek, 'Substitutionary Atonement and the Church Fathers: A Reply to the Authors of *Pierced for our Transgressions*', *EvQ* 82 (2010), pp. 142-59.

Focant, Camille, *The Gospel According to Mark: A Commentary* (trans. Leslie Robert Keylock; Eugene, OR: Pickwick Press, 2012).

Foerster, R., *Scriptores Physiognomonici*, I (repr., Leipzig: Teubner, 1994 [1893]).

Forshey, Gerald E., *American Religious and Biblical Spectaculars* (Westport, CT: Praeger, 1992).

Francione, Gary, 'Animals—Property or Persons?', in Sunstein and Nussbaum (eds.), *Animal Rights*, pp. 108-142.

Frank, Harry Thomas, and William L. Reed (eds.), *Translating and Understanding the Old Testament: Essays in Honor of Herbert Gordon May* (Nashville, TN: Abingdon Press, 1970).

Frazer, Sir James George, *The Golden Bough: A Study of Magic and Religion* (12 vols.; London: Macmillan & Co., 3rd edn, 1913–1920).

Fredriksen, Paula, 'Report of The Ad Hoc Scholars Group: Reviewing the Script of *The Passion*', in Fredriksen (ed.), *On the Passion of the Christ*, pp. 225-54.

—'The Birth of Christianity and the Origins of Christian Anti-Judaism', in Fredriksen and Reinhartz (eds.), *Jesus, Judaism, and Christian Anti-Judaism*, pp. 8-30.

—'Gospel Truths', in Fredriksen (ed.), *On The Passion of the Christ*, pp. 31-47.

—*On The Passion of the Christ: Exploring the Issues Raised by the Controversial Movie* (Berkeley, CA: University of California Press, 2006).

—'Preface', in Fredriksen (ed.), *On The Passion of the Christ*, pp. xi-xxiii.

Fredriksen, Paula (ed.), *On the Passion of the Christ: Exploring the Issues Raised by the Controversial Movie* (Berkeley, CA: University of California Press, 2006).

Fredriksen, Paula, and Adele Reinhartz (eds.), *Jesus, Judaism, and Christian Anti-*

Judaism: Reading the New Testament after the Holocaust (Louisville, KY: Westminster/John Knox Press, 2002).

Freedman, Harry, and Isidore Epstein *et al.* (eds.), *Hebrew-English Edition of the Babylonian Talmud* (repr., London: Soncino Press, 1988–1994 [1935–1962]).

Frevel, Christian, and Christoph Nihan (eds.), *Purity and the Forming of Religious Traditions in the Ancient Mediterranean World and Ancient Judaism* (Dynamics in the History of Religion, 3: Leiden: E.J. Brill, 2013).

Freyne, Sean, *Jesus, a Jewish Galilean: A New Reading of the Jesus-Story* (London: T. & T. Clark, 2004).

Fridrichsen, Anton, *The Problem of Miracle in Primitive Christianity* (trans. Roy Harrisville and John S. Hanson; Minneapolis: Ausburg, 1972).

Friesen, Philip E., *The Old Testament Roots of Nonviolence: Abraham's Personal Faith, Moses' Social Vision, Jesus' Fulfillment, and God's Work Today* (Eugene, OR: Wipf & Stock, 2010).

Fudge, Edward William, *A Biblical and Historical Study of the Doctrine of Final Punishment* (Eugene, OR: Wipf & Stock, 2011).

Fudge, Edward William, and Peter Cousins, *The Fire that Consumes: The Biblical Case for Conditional Immortality* (Carlisle: Paternoster Press, 1994).

Fudge, Edward William, and Robert A. Peterson, *Two Views of Hell: A Biblical and Theological Dialogue* (Downers Grove, IL: InterVarsity Press, 2000).

Funk, Robert, Roy W. Hoover and the Jesus Seminar, *The Five Gospels: What Did Jesus Really Say* (New York: HarperCollins, 1997).

Gadd, C.J., 'The Harran Inscriptions of Nabonidus', *Anatolian Studies* 8 (1958), pp. 35-92.

Gage, Matilda Joslyn, *Woman, Church and State: A Historical Account of the Status of Woman throughout the Christian Ages: With Reminiscences from the Matriarchate* (repr., Amherst, NY: Humanity Books, 2002 [1893]).

Gaiser, Frederick J., *Healing in the Bible: Theological Insight for Christian Ministry* (Grand Rapids, MI: Baker Academic, 2010).

Gaiser, Frederick J., and Mark Thronveit (eds.), *'And God Said that it was Good': Essays on Creation and God in Honor of Terence Fretheim* (St. Paul, MN: Luther Seminary, 2006).

Gardner, Anne, 'Ecojustice or Anthropological Justice? A Study of the New Heavens and the New Earth in Isaiah 65.17', in Habel (ed.), *The Earth Story in Psalms and the Prophets*, pp. 204-218.

Gardner, Gregg, 'Jewish Leadership and Hellenistic Civic Benefaction in the Second Century B.C.E.', *JBL* 126 (2007), pp. 327-43.

Gardner, Margo, and Laurence Steinberg, 'Peer Influence on Risk Taking, Risk Preference, and Risky Decision Making in Adolescence and Adulthood: An Experimental Study', *Developmental Psychology* 41 (2005), pp. 625-35.

Garrett, Susan R., *The Demise of the Devil: Magic and the Demonic in Luke's Gospel* (Minneapolis: Fortress Press, 1989).

Gaylor, Annie Laurie, *Woe to the Women—The Bible Tells me So: The Bible, Female Sexuality and the Law* (Madison, WI: Freedom from Religion Foundation, 2004).

Gelin, Albert, *The Poor of Yahweh* (Collegeville, MN: Liturgical Press, 1964).

Geller, Markham J., *Ancient Babylonian Medicine* (Chichester: Wiley-Blackwell, 2010).

—'The Elephantine Papyri and Hosea 2, 3', *JSJ* (1977), pp. 139-48.

—'Jesus' Theurgic Powers: Parallels in the Talmud and Incantation Bowls', *JJS* 28 (1977), pp. 141-55.

George, A.R., *The Babylonian Gilgamesh Epic: Introduction, Critical Edition and Cuneiform Text* (2 vols.; New York: Oxford University Press, 2003).

Georgi, Dieter, *Remembering the Poor: The History of Paul's Collection for Jerusalem* (Nashville, TN: Abingdon Press, 1965).

Gerdmar, Anders, *Roots of Theological Antisemitism: Biblical Interpretation and the Jews, from Herder and Semmler to Kittel and Bultmann* (Leiden: E.J. Brill, 2009).

Gerhardsson, Birger, 'Mark and the Female Witnesses', in Sjöberg *et al.* (eds.), *Dumu E₂-Dub-ba-a*, pp. 217-26.

Gericke, Jaco, 'A Fourth Paradigm? Some Thoughts on Atheism in Old Testament Scholarship', *OTE* 25 (2012), pp. 518-33.

Gifford, Carolyn De Swartem, 'Politicizing the Sacred Texts: Elizabeth Cady Stanton and the Woman's Bible', in Schüssler Fiorenza (ed.), *Searching the Scriptures*, I, pp. 52-63.

Gill, Robin (ed.), *The Cambridge Companion to Christian Ethics* (Cambridge: Cambridge University Press, 2nd edn, 2012).

Gillespie, Stuart, and Philip Hardie (eds.), *The Cambridge Companion to Lucretius* (Cambridge: Cambridge University Press, 2007).

Gilmore, David D., 'Anthropology of the Mediterranean Area', *Annual Review of Anthropology* 11 (1982), pp. 175-205.

Gilmore, David D. (ed.), *Honor and Shame and the Unity of the Mediterranean* (Washington, DC: American Anthropological Association, 1987).

Girard, René, *Job: The Victim of his People* (trans. Yvonne Freccero; Stanford, CA: Stanford University Press, 1987).

—*Things Hidden since the Foundation of the World* (trans. Stephen Bann and Michael Metter; Stanford, CA: Stanford University Press, 1978).

—'*Violence Renounced*: Response by René Girard', in Swartley (ed.), *Violence Renounced*, pp. 312-13.

—*Violence and the Sacred* (trans. Patrick Gregory; Baltimore, MD: The Johns Hopkins University Press, 1977).

—*La violence et le sacré* (Paris: Bernard Grasset, 1972).

Glancy, Jennifer A., 'Boastings of Beatings (2 Corinthians 11.23-25)', *JBL* 123 (2004), pp. 99-135.

—'The Syrophoenician Woman and Other First Century Bodies', *BibInt* 18 (2010), pp. 342-63.

Glazier-McDonald, Beth, *Malachi: The Divine Messenger* (SBLDS, 98; Atlanta, GA: Scholars Press, 1987).

Goedicke, Hans (ed.), *Near Eastern Studies in Honor of William Foxwell Albright* (Baltimore, MD: The Johns Hopkins University Press, 1971).

Goldhagen, Daniel Jonah, *Hitler's Willing Executioners: Ordinary Germans and the Holocaust* (New York: Vintage Books, 1997).

Goodpaster, Kenneth, 'On Being Morally Considerable', *Journal of Philosophy* 75 (1978), pp. 308-325.

Goodspeed, Edgar J., 'Thomas Jefferson and the Bible', *HTR* 40 (1947), pp. 71-75.

Gorringe, Tim, *God's Just Vengeance* (Cambridge: Cambridge University Press, 1996).

Gorski, Philip S., 'The Mosaic Moment: An Early Modernist Critique of Modernist Theories of Nationalism', *American Journal of Sociology* 105 (2000), pp. 1428-68.

Goulder, Michael D., 'Those Outside (Mk 4:10-12)', *NovT* 33 (1991), pp. 289-302.

Gouldner, Alvin W., *The Future of Intellectuals and the Rise of the New Class* (New York: Oxford University Press, 1979).

Graf, Fritz, *Magic in the Ancient World* (trans. Franklin Philip; Cambridge, MA: Harvard University Press, 1997).

Graff, Gerald, *Professing Literature: An Institutional History* (Chicago, IL: University of Chicago Press, 1987).

Grant, Colleen C., 'Reinterpreting the Healing Narratives', in Eiesland and Don Saliers (eds.), *Human Disability and the Service of God*, pp. 72-87.

Grant, Jackelyn, *White Women's Christ and Black Women's Jesus: Feminist Christology and Womanist Response* (American Academy of Religion Academy Series, 64; Atlanta, GA: Scholars Press, 1989).

Grassi, Joseph A., *Jesus is Shalom: A Vision of Peace from the Gospels* (Mahwah, NJ: Paulist Press, 2006).

Graves, Michael, 'The Biblical Scholarship of a Fourth-Century Woman: Marcella of Rome', *ETL* 87.4 (2011), pp. 375-91.

Gray, Alyssa M., 'Redemptive Almsgiving and the Rabbis of Late Antiquity', *Jewish Studies Quarterly* 18.2 (2011), pp. 144-84.

Green, Joel B. (ed.), *Dictionary of Scripture and Ethics* (Grand Rapids, MI: Baker Academic, 2011).

Greenberg, Moshe, *Ezekiel 1–20* (AB, 22; Garden City, NY: Doubleday, 1983).

Greenblat, Stephen, and Giles Gunn (eds.), *Redrawing the Boundaries: The Transformation of English and American Literary Studies* (New York: Modern Language Association of America, 1992).

Greenfield, Liah, *Nationalism: Five Roads to Modernity* (Cambridge, MA: Harvard University Press, 1992).

Greengus, Samuel, 'Some Issues Relating to the Comparability of Laws and Coherence of the Legal Tradition', in Levinson (ed.), *Theory and Method in Biblical and Cuneiform Law*, pp. 65-72.

Gregg, Brian H., *The Historical Jesus and the Final Judgment Sayings in Q* (WUNT, 2.207; Tübingen: Mohr Siebeck, 2006).

Griese, Noel L. (ed.), *The Dolorous Passion of our Lord Jesus Christ after the Meditations of Anne Catherine Emmerich as Told to Clemens Brentano* (Atlanta, GA: Anvil, 2005).

Griffith, Francis L., and Herbert Thompson, *The Demotic Magical Papyrus of London and Leiden* (3 vols.; London: H. Grevel, 1904).

Grimsrud, Ted, 'Scapegoating No More: Christian Pacifism and New Testament Views of Jesus' Death', in Swartley (ed.), *Violence Renounced*, pp. 49-69.

Grizzle, Raymond, Paul E. Rothrock and Christopher B. Barrett, 'Evangelicals and Environmentalism: Past, Present, and Future', *Trinity Journal* 19 (1998), pp. 3-27.

Groothius, Rebecca Merrill, *Good News for Women: A Biblical Picture of Gender Equality* (Grand Rapids, MI: Baker Books, 1997).

Grosz, Katarzyna, 'Daughters as Adopted Sons at Nuzi and Emar', in Durand (ed.), *La Femme dans le Proche-Orient Antique*, pp. 81-86.

Grotius, Hugo, *The Law of War and Peace* (trans. Francis W. Kelsey; Indianapolis: Bobb-Merrill Company, 1925).

Grudem, Wayne, *Evangelical Feminism and Biblical Truth: An Analysis of 118 Disputed Truths* (Downers Grove, IL: InterVarsity Press, 2004).

Gruen, Erich S., *Rethinking the Other in Antiquity* (Martin Classical Lectures; Princeton, NJ: Princeton University Press, 2012).

Gründstäudl, Wolfgang, and Markus Schiefer Ferrari (eds.), *Gestörte Lektüre: Disability als hermeneutische Leitkategorie biblischer Exegese* (Stuttgart: W. Kohlhammer, 2012).

Guest, Deryn, *Beyond Feminist Biblical Studies* (The Bible in the Modern World, 47; Sheffield: Sheffield Phoenix Press, 2012).

Guillemette, Nil, 'Mc 1, 24 est-il une formule de defense magique?', *Science et Esprit* 30 (1978), pp. 81-96.

Guillemette, Pierre, 'The Sermon on the Mount: Feasible Ethics?', *Landas* 9 (1995), pp. 209-236.

Guillory, John, *Cultural Capital: The Problem of Literary Canon Formation* (Chicago, IL: University of Chicago Press, 1993).

Gummer, Natalie D., 'Sacrificial Sutras: Mahayana Literature and the South Asian Ritual Cosmos', *Journal of the American Academy of Religion* 82 (2014), pp. 1091-1126

Gutiérrez, Gustavo, *Teología de la liberación: Perspectivas* (Salamanca: Ediciones Sigueme, 1987).

Habel, Norman C., *The Birth, the Curse and the Greening of Earth: An Ecological Reading of Genesis 1–11* (Earth Bible Commentary, 1; Sheffield: Sheffield Phoenix Press, 2011).

—*The Earth Story in Psalms and the Prophets* (Earth Bible, 4; Sheffield: Sheffield Academic Press, 2001).

—'Geophany: The Earth Story in Genesis 1', in Habel and Wurst (eds.), *The Earth Story in Genesis*, pp. 34-48.

—'Introducing Ecological Hermeneutics', *Lutheran Journal of Theology* 46 (2012), pp. 97-105.

—'Playing with God or Playing Earth? An Ecological Reading of Genesis 1.26-28', in Gaiser and Thronveit (eds.), *'And God Said that it was Good'*, pp. 33-41.

Habel, Norman C. (ed.), *Readings from the Perspective of the Earth* (Earth Bible, 1; Sheffield Sheffield Academic Press, 2000).

Habel, Norman C., and Vicky Balabanski (eds.), *The Earth Story in the New Testament* (Earth Bible, 5; Sheffield: Sheffield Academic Press, 2002).

Habel, Norman C., and Peter Trudinger (eds.), *Exploring Ecological Hermeneutics* (Atlanta, GA: Society of Biblical Literature, 2008).

Habel, Norman C., and S. Wurst (eds.), *The Earth Story in Genesis* (Earth Bible, 2; Sheffield: Sheffield Academic Press, 2000).

—*The Earth Story in Wisdom Traditions* (Earth Bible, 3; Sheffield: Sheffield Academic Press, 2000).

Hachlili, Rachel, *Jewish Funerary Customs, Practice and Rites in the Second Temple Period* (Supplements for the Journal for the Study of Judaism, 94; Leiden: E.J. Brill, 2005).

Hadas-Lebel, Mireille, *Philo of Alexandria: A Thinker in the Jewish Diaspora* (trans. Robyn Fréchet; Studies in Philo of Alexandria, 7; Leiden: E.J. Brill, 2012).

Hagedorn, Anselm, and Reinhard G. Kratz (eds.), *Law and Religion in the Eastern Mediterranean: From Antiquity to Early Islam* (New York: Oxford University Press, 2013).

Hägglund, Frederick, *Isaiah 53 in the Light of Homecoming after Exile* (FAT, 31; Tübingen: Mohr Siebeck, 2008).

Hahn, Scott Walker, and John Seitze Bergsma, 'What Laws were "Not Good"? A Canonical Approach to the Theological Problem of Ezekiel 20:25-26', *JBL* 123 (2004), pp. 201-218.

Halbertal, Moshe, *On Sacrifice* (Princeton, NJ: Princeton University Press, 2012).

Hallo, William W., 'Akkadian Apocalypses', *IEJ* 16 (1966), pp. 231-42.

Hallo, William W., Bruce Williams Jones and Gerald L. Mattingly (eds.), *The Bible in Light of Cuneiform Literature* (Scriptures in Context, III; Lewiston: Edwin Mellen Press, 1990).

Halpern, Baruch, *David's Secret Demons: Messiah, Murderer, Traitor, King* (Grand Rapids, MI: Eerdmans, 2001).

—'Jerusalem and the Lineages in the Seventh Century BCE: Kinship and the Rise of Individual Moral Liability', in Halpern and Hobson (eds.), *Law and Ideology in Monarchic Israel*, pp. 11-107.

Halpern, Baruch, and Deborah W. Hobson (eds.), *Law and Ideology in Monarchic Israel* (Sheffield: Sheffield Academic Press, 1991).

Hamilton, James M., 'N.T. Wright and Saul's Moral Bootstraps: New Light on "The New Perspective"', *Trinity Journal* 25 (2004), pp. 139-55.

Hamilton, Mark W., 'Review of Hector Avalos, *Health Care and the Rise of Christianity*', *ResQ* 43 (2001), pp. 125-26.

Hamm, Dennis, 'Paul's Blindness and its Healing: Clues to Symbolic Intent (Acts 9, 22 and 26)', *Bib* 71 (1990), pp. 64-65.

Hampson, Daphne, *Theology and Feminism* (Oxford: Basil Blackwell, 1990).

—*After Christianity* (London: SCM Press, 2nd edn, 2002).

Hanke, Lewis, *Aristotle and the American Indians: A Study in Race Prejudice in the Modern World* (Bloomington, IN: Indiana University Press, 1959).

Hanson, A.T., *The Prophetic Gospel: A Study of John and the Old Testament* (Edinburgh: T. & T. Clark, 2000).

Hanson, Kenneth C., '"How Honorable! How Shameful!" A Cultural Analysis of Matthew's Makarisms and Reproaches', *Semeia* 68 (1996), pp. 81-112.

Hanson, Paul D., *The Dawn of Apocalyptic: The Historical and Sociological Roots of Jewish Apocalyptic Eschatology* (Philadelphia, PA: Fortress Press, 1979).

Hanson, Richard S., *Tyrian Influence in the Upper Galilee* (Meiron Excavation Project, 2; Cambridge, MA: ASOR, 1980).

Hardin, Justin K., *Galatians and the Imperial Cult: A Critical Analysis of the First-Century Social Context of Paul's Letter* (Tübingen: Mohr Siebeck, 2008).

Hare, Douglas R.A., *Matthew* (Louisville, KY: Westminster/John Knox Press, 1993).

—*The Theme of Jewish Persecution of Christians in the Gospel According to St. Matthew* (Cambridge: Cambridge University Press, 1967).

Harland, Philip A., 'Familial Dimensions of Group Identity: "Brothers" (Ἀδελφοί) in Associations of the Greek East', *JBL* 124.3 (2005), pp. 491-513.

Harlow, Daniel C., *The 'Other' in Second Temple Judaism: Essays in Honor of John Collins* (Grand Rapids, MI: Eerdmans, 2011).

Harnack, Adolf, *Medicinisches aus der ältesten Kirchengeschichte* (Leipzig: Hinrichs, 1892).

Harrington, Daniel J., *Jesus, the Revelation of the Father's Love: What the New Testament Teaches us* (Huntington, IN: Our Sunday Visitor, 2010).

Harris, Sam, *The End of Faith: Religion, Terror, and the Future of Reason* (New York: W.W. Norton, 2004).

Harrison, Roland K., 'Lame, Lameness', *IDB* III, pp. 59-60.

Hart, L.D., 'The Canaanite Woman: Meeting Jesus as Sage and Lord: Matthew 15:21-28 & Mark 7:24-30', *ExpTim* 122.1 (2010), pp. 20-25.

Hartmann, R.R.K. (ed.), *Lexicography: Principles and Practice* (New York: Academic Press, 1983).

Hatina, Thomas R., 'Who Will See "The Kingdom of God Coming with Power" in Mark 9, 1—Protagonists or Antagonists?', *Bib* 86 (2005), pp. 20-34.

Häusl, Maria, 'Verkörpertes Leben: Körperbilder und -konzepte im Alten Testament', *BK* 67 (2012), pp. 10-15.

Hays, Christopher M., 'Hating Wealth and Wives? An Examination of Discipleship Ethics in the Third Gospel', *TynBul* 60 (2009), pp. 47-68.

Hays, Richard B., *The Moral Vision of the New Testament: A Contemporary Introduction to New Testament Ethics* (New York: HarperOne, 1996).

—*Reading Backwards: Figural Christology and the Fourfold Gospel Witness* (Waco, TX: Baylor University Press, 2014).

Healy, Mary, 'The Hermeneutic of Jesus', *Communio/International Catholic Review* 37 (2010), pp. 477-95.

Hedrick, Charles, 'Miracles in Mark: A Study of Markan Theology and its Implication for Modern Religious Thought', *PRSt* 34.3 (2007), pp. 297-313.

Heger, Paul, 'Did Prayer Replace Sacrifice at Qumran?', *RevQ* 22 (2005), pp. 213-33.

Heide, Gale Z., 'What is New about the New Heaven and the New Earth: A Theology of Creation from Revelation 21 to 2 Peter 3', *JETS* 40 (1997), pp. 37-56.

Heil, John Paul, 'Significant Aspects of the Healing Miracles in Matthew', *CBQ* 41 (1979), pp. 274-87.

Hendel, Ronald, 'Farewell to the SBL: Faith, Reason, and Biblical Studies', *BARev* 36 (2010), pp. 28, 74.

—'Mind the Gap: Modern and Postmodern Biblical Studies', *JBL* 133 (2014), pp. 422-43.

Hendricks, Obery, Jr, *The Politics of Jesus: Rediscovering the True Revolutionary Nature of Jesus' Teachings and How They Have Been Corrupted* (New York: Doubleday, 2006).

Hendriksen, William, *Exposition of the Gospel According to Matthew* (NTC; Grand Rapids, MI: Baker Academic, 1973).

Hengel, Martin, *The Use of the Septuagint as Scripture: Its Prehistory and the Problems of its Canon* (Grand Rapids, MI: Baker Academic, 2004).

—'Zur matthäischen Bergpredigt und ihrem jüdischen Hintergrund', *Theologische Rundschau* 52 (1987), pp. 327-400.

Henken, Louis, 'Religion, Religions, and Human Rights', *Journal of Religious Ethics* 26 (1998), pp. 229-39.

Hentschel, Anni, *Diakonia im Neuen Testament: Studien zur Semantik unter besonderer Berücksichtigung der Rolle von Frauen* (WUNT, 2.226; Tübingen: Mohr Siebeck, 2007).

Henze, Matthias (ed.), *Biblical Interpretation at Qumran: Studies in the Dead Sea Scrolls and Related Literature* (Grand Rapids, MI: Eerdmans, 2005).

Herodotus (trans. A.D. Godley; LCL; Cambridge, MA: Harvard University Press, 1920).

Herrmann, Virginia Rimmer, and J. David Schloen (eds.), *In Remembrance of me: Feasting with the Dead in the Ancient Middle East* (Oriental Institute Museum Publications, 37; Chicago, IL: Oriental Institute of the University of Chicago, 2014).

Hessel, Dieter, and Mary Radford Ruether (eds.), *Christianity and Ecology: Seeking the Welfare of the Earth and Humans* (Cambridge, MA: Harvard University Press, 2000).

de Heusch, Luc, *Sacrifice in Africa: A Structuralist Approach* (trans. Linda O'Brien and Alice Morton; Bloomington, IN: Indiana University Press, 1985).

Heyward, Isabel Carter, *The Redemption of God: A Theology of Mutual Relation* (Washington, DC: University Press of America, 1982).

Hiers, Richard H., *Women's Rights and the Bible: Implications for Christian Ethics and Social Policy* (Eugene, OR: Pickwick, 2012).

Hippocrates (trans. W.H.S. Jones; LCL; 4 vols.; Cambridge, MA: Harvard University Press, 1923).

Hitchens, Christopher, *god is Not Great: How Religion Poisons Everything* (New York: Twelve Books, 2007).

Hitler, Adolf, *Mein Kampf* (trans. Ralph Manheim; Boston, MA: Houghlin Mifflin, 1971).

—*Mein Kampf* (Münich: Zentralverlag der NSDAP/Franz Eher Nachfolger, 1938).

Hobart, William Kirk, *The Medical Language of St. Luke* (London: Longmans, Green & Co., 1882).

Hobson, Russell, *Transforming Literature into Scripture: Texts as Cult Objects at Nineveh and Qumran* (Sheffield: Equinox, 2012).

Hoffner, Harry A., 'The Institutional "Poverty" of Hurrian Diviners and *entanni*-Women', in Cohen, Gilan and Miller (eds.), *Pax Hethitica*, pp. 214-24.

—*The Laws of the Hittites: A Critical Edition* (Leiden: E.J. Brill, 1997).

Hofreiter, Christian, 'Genocide in Deuteronomy and Christian Interpretation', in *Interpreting Deuteronomy: Issues and Approaches* (ed. David G. Firth and Philip S. Johnston; Downers Grove, IL: InterVarsity Press, 2012), pp. 240-62.

Hofstede, Geert, *Culture's Consequences* (Beverly Hills, CA: Sage, 1980).

Holden, Lynn, *Forms of Deformity* (JSOTSup, 131; Sheffield: Sheffield Academic Press, 1991).

Holl, Karl, *Die griechischen christliche Schriftsteller der ersten drei Jahrhunderte* (2 vols.; Leipzig: J.C. Hinrichs, 1915).

Holmén, Tom, and Stanley E. Porter (eds.), *Handbook for the Study of the Historical Jesus* (4 vols.; Leiden: E.J. Brill, 2011).

Holt, Frank, 'Alexander the Great Today: In the Interest of Historical Accuracy?', *Ancient History Bulletin* 13 (1999), pp. 111-17.

Hooker, Morna, *The Gospel According to St. Mark* (Black's New Testament Commentaries; New York: Continuum, 1991).

Hopkins, Julie M., *Towards a Feminist Christology: Jesus of Nazareth, European Women, and the Christological Crisis* (Grand Rapids, MI: Eerdmans, 1995).

Hoppe, Leslie J., *There Shall be No Poor among you: Poverty in the Bible* (Nashville, TN: Abingdon Press, 2004).

Horbury, William (ed.), *Templum Amicitiae: Essays on the Second Temple Presented to Ernst Bammel* (JSOTSup, 48; Sheffield: Sheffield Academic Press, 1991).

Horn, Friedrich W., 'Ethik und Neuen Testaments 1993–2009: Teil I', *TRu* 76 (2011), pp. 1-36.

—'Ethik und Neuen Testaments 1993–2009: Teil II', *TRu* 76 (2011), pp. 180-221.

Horrell, David G., 'Introduction', in Horrell *et al.* (eds.), *Ecological Hermeneutics*, pp. 1-12.

Horrell, David G., Cheryl Hunt, Christopher Southgate and Francesca Stavrakopolou (eds.), *Ecological Hermeneutics: Biblical, Historical, and Theological Perspectives* (London: T. & T. Clark, 2010).

Horsley, Greg H.R., *New Documents Illustrating the History of Christianity, Volume 3: A Review of the Greek Inscriptions and Papyri Published in 1978* (Grand Rapids, MI: Eerdmans, 1983).

Horsley, Richard A., *Jesus and Empire: The Kingdom of God and the New World Disor-der* (Minneapolis: Fortress Press, 2003).

—*Jesus and the Spiral of Violence: Popular Jewish Resistance in Roman Palestine* (Minneapolis: Fortress Press, 1993).

—'Paul and Slavery: A Critical Alternative to Recent Readings', in Callahan, Horsley and Smith (eds.), *Slavery in Text and Interpretation*, pp. 153-200.

—'The Slave Systems of Classical Antiquity and their Reluctant Recognition by Modern Scholars', in Callahan *et al.* (eds.), *Slavery in Text and Interpretation*, pp. 19-66.

van der Horst, Pieter W., *Philo's Flaccus: The First Pogrom. Introduction, Translation, and Commentary* (Leiden: E.J. Brill, 2003).

Hortmanshoff, H.F.J., and M. Stol (eds.), *Magic and Rationality in Ancient Near Eastern and Graeco-Roman Medicine* (Leiden: E.J. Brill, 2004).

Houlden, J.L., *Ethics and the New Testament* (Edinburgh: T. & T. Clark, 1992).

Howard, J. Keir, *Medicine, Miracle and Myth in the New Testament* (Eugene, OR: Resource Publications, 2010).

Huber, Irene, *Rituale der Seuchen- und Schadensabwehr im Vorderen Orient und Griechenland: Formen kollektiver Krisenbewältigung in der Antike* (Wiesbaden: Franz Steiner, 2005).

Huehnergard, John, *A Grammar of Akkadian* (Atlanta, GA: Scholars Press, 1997).

—'Five Tablets from the Vicinity of Emar', *RA* 77 (1983), pp. 11-43.

Huizenga, Leroy A., 'The Confession of Jesus and the Curses of Peter: A Narrative-Christological Approach to the Text-Critical Problem of Mark 14:62', *NovT* 53 (2011), pp. 244-66.

—*The New Isaac: Tradition and Intertextuality in the Gospel of Matthew* (Supplements to Novum Testamentum, 131; Leiden: E.J. Brill, 2009).

Hull, John M., *In the Beginning There was Darkness: A Blind Person's Conversation with the Bible* (Harrisburg, PA: Trinity Press International, 2001).

—*Hellenistic Magic and the Synoptic Tradition* (London: SCM Press, 1974).

Hunger, Hermann, and Stephen A. Kaufman, 'A New Akkadian Prophecy Text', *JAOS* 95 (1975), pp. 371-75.

Hurtado, Larry W., *Lord Jesus Christ: Devotion to Jesus in Earliest Christianity* (Grand Rapids, MI: Eerdmans, 2003).

Hurtado, Larry W., and Paul L. Owen, *'Who is This Son of Man? The Latest Scholar-ship on a Puzzling Expression of the Historical Jesus* (London and New York: T. & T. Clark, 2011).

Huttunen, Niko, *Paul and Epictetus on Law: A Comparison* (Library of New Testament Studies, 405, Early Christianity in Context; London: T. & T. Clark, 2009).

Ibarrondo, Xabier Pikaza, 'Exorcismo, poder y evangelio: Transfondo histórico y eccle-sial de Mc 9, 38-40', *EstBib* 57 (1999), pp. 539-64.

Isaac, Benjamin, *The Invention of Racism in Classical Antiquity* (Princeton, NJ: Princ-eton University Press, 2004).

—'Proto-Racism in Graeco-Roman Antiquity', *World Archaeology* 28 (2006), pp. 32-47.

Isserman, Ilka, 'Did Christian Ethics have Any Influence on the Conversion to Christian-ity', *Zeitschrift für Antikes Christentum/Journal of Ancient Christianity* 16 (2012), pp. 99-112.

Izre'el, Shlomo, *The Amarna Tablets*. Online: http://www.tau.ac.il/humanities/semitic/EA115-162.html.

—*Amurru Akkadian: A Linguistic Study* (HSS, 41; 2 vols.; Atlanta, GA: Scholars Press, 1991).

Jackson, Bernard S. 'The "Institutions" of Marriage and the Divorce in the Hebrew Bible', *JSS* 56 (2011), pp. 221-51.

Jackson, Glenna, *'Have Mercy on Me': The Story of the Canaanite Woman in Matthew 15.21-28* (Sheffield: Sheffield Academic Press, 2002).

Jackson, Ralph, *Doctors and Diseases in the Roman Empire* (Norman, OK: University of Oklahoma Press, 1988).

Jacobson, Mark, *The Lampshade: A Holocaust Detective Story from Buchenwald to New Orleans* (New York: Simon and Schuster, 2010).

Jaffé, Dan, *Jésus sous le plume des historiens juifs du XXe siècle: Approche historique, perspectives historiographiques, analyses méthodologiques* (Paris: Cerf, 2009).

Janowski, Bernd, and Peter Stuhlmacher (eds.), *The Suffering Servant: Isaiah 53 in Jewish and Christian Sources* (trans. Daniel P. Bailey; Grand Rapids, MI: Eerdmans, 2004).

Japhet, Sarah (ed.), *Studies in Bible* (Scripta Hierosolymitana, 31; Jerusalem: Magnes Press, 1986).

Jaques-Stiker, Henri, *A History of Disability* (trans. William Sayers and David T. Mitchell; Ann Arbor, MI: University of Michigan Press, 2002).

Jassen, Alex P., 'The Dead Sea Scrolls and Violence: Sectarian Formation and Eschatological Imagination', *BibInt* 17 (2009), pp. 12-44.

Jastram, Nathan, 'Male as Male and Female: Created in the Image of God', *Concordia Theological Quarterly* 68.1 (2004), pp. 5-96.

Jastrow, Marcus, *A Dictionary of the Targumim, the Talmud Babli and Yerushalmi and the Midrashic Literature* (2 vols.; repr., Brooklyn, NY: Shalom, 1967 [1903]).

Jean, Cynthia, *Le Magie Neó-assyrienne en Contexte: recherches sure le métier d'exorciste et le concept d'ašipūtu* (Helsinki: Neoassyrian Text Corpus Project, 2006).

Jeffers, James S., *The Greco-Roman World of the New Testament Era: Exploring the Background* (Downers Grove, IL: InterVarsity Press, 1999).

Jeffrey, Steve, Michael Ovey and Andrew Sach, *Pierced for our Transgressions: Rediscovering the Glory of Penal Substitution* (Wheaton, IL: Crossway Books, 2007).

Jenni, E., 'שנא', *TLOT*, III, pp. 1277-79.

Jensen, Hans J.L., 'Desire, Rivalry and Collective Violence in the "Succession Narrative"', *JSOT* 55 (1992), pp. 39-59.

Jensen, Morten H., 'Climate, Droughts, Wars and Famines in Galilee as a Background for Understanding the Historical Jesus', *JBL* 131 (2012), pp. 307-324.

—'Rural Galilee and Rapid Changes: An Investigation of the Socio-Economic Dynamics and Developments in Roman Galilee', *Bib* 93 (2012), pp. 43-67.

Jeremias, Joachim, *The Eucharistic Words of Jesus* (London: SCM Press, 3rd edn, 1966).

—*Jesus' Promise to the Nations* (Naperville, IL: A.R. Allenson, 1958).

—*The Parables of Jesus* (trans. S.H. Hooke; New York: Charles Scribner's Sons, 2nd edn, 1972).

Johansson, Daniel, '*Kyrios* in the Gospel of Mark', *JSNT* 33 (2010), pp. 101-124.

—'"Who can Forgive Sins but God Alone?": Human and Angelic Agents and Divine Forgiveness in Early Judaism', *JSNT* 33.4 (2011), pp. 351-74.

Johnson, E.S., 'Mark VIII.22-26: The Blind Man from Bethsaida', *NTS* 25 (1979), pp. 370-83.

Johnson, Janet H., 'The Dialect of the Demotic Magical Papyrus of London and Leiden', in Johnson and Wente (eds.), *Studies in Honor of George R. Hughes*, pp. 105-132.

Johnson, Janet H., and Edward F. Wente (eds.), *Studies in Honor of George R. Hughes* (Ancient Oriental Civilization, 39; Chicago, IL: Oriental Institute, 1977).

Johnson, Luke Timothy, 'Anti-Judaism in the New Testament', in Holmén and Porter (eds.), *Handbook for the Study of the Historical Jesus*, II, pp. 1609-638.

—'The New Testament's Anti-Jewish Slander and the Conventions of Ancient Polemic', *JBL* 108 (1989), pp. 419-41.

—*The Real Jesus: The Misguided Quest for the Historical Jesus and the Truth of the Traditional Gospels* (New York: HarperSanFrancisco, 1996).

—*The Writings of the New Testament: An Introduction* (Philadelphia, PA: Fortress Press, 1986).

Johnson, Sarah Iles (ed.), *Religions of the Ancient World* (Cambridge, MA: Harvard University Press, 2004).

Johnston, J.W., *The Use of Πᾶς in the New Testament* (Studies in Biblical Greek, 11; New York: Peter Lang, 2004).

Jones, G., *Beyond Da Vinci* (New York: Seabury, 2004).

Jonsen, Albert R., Mark Siegler and William J. Winslade, *Clinical Ethics: A Practical Approach to Ethical Decisions in Clinical Medicine* (New York: McGraw-Hill Medical, 7th edn, 2010).

Joseph, Simon J., *Jesus, Q and the Dead Sea Scrolls: A Judaic Approach to Q* (WUNT, 2.333; Tübingen: Mohr Siebeck, 2012).

—'"Why Do you Call me 'Master'"? Q646, the Inaugural Sermon, and the Demands of Discipleship', *JBL* 132 (2013), pp. 955-72.

Josephus (trans. H.St.J. Thackeray *et al.*; LCL; 10 vols.; Cambridge, MA: Harvard University Press, 1926–65).

Kahl, W., *New Testament Miracle Stories in their Religious-Historical Setting: A Religionsgeschichtliche Comparison from a Structural Perspective* (FRLANT, 163; Göttingen: Vandenhoeck & Ruprecht, 1994).

Kaiser, Otto, *Isaiah 1–12* (trans. John Bowden; Old Testament Library; Philadelphia, PA: Westminster, 2nd edn, 1983).

Katz, Marilyn A., 'Problems of Sacrifice in Ancient Cultures', in Hallo, Jones and Mattingly (eds.), *The Bible in Light of Cuneiform Literature*, pp. 89-201.

Kaufman, Stephen A., 'Recent Contributions of Aramaic Studies to Biblical Hebrew Philology and the Exegesis of the Hebrew Bible', in Lemaire (ed.), *Congress Volume Basel 2001*, pp. 43-54.

Kautsky, Karl, *Der Ursprung des Christentums: Eine historische Untersuchung* (Stuttgart: Dietz, 1908).

Kazen, Thomas, 'The Coming Son of Man Revisited', *Journal for the Study of the Historical Jesus* 5 (2007), pp. 155-74.

Keck, Leander E., 'Rethinking "New Testament Ethics"', *JBL* 115 (1996), pp. 3-16.

Kee, Howard Clark, *Medicine, Miracle and Magic in New Testament Times* (Cambridge: Cambridge University Press, 1988).

—*Miracle in the Early Christian World: A Study in Sociohistorical Method* (New Haven, CT: Yale University Press, 1983).

Kee, Howard Clark, and Irvin J. Borowsky (eds.), *Removing the Anti-Judaism from the New Testament* (repr., Philadelphia, PA: American Interfaith Institute/World Alliance, 2000 [1998]).

Keener, Craig S., 'Jesus and Parallel Jewish and Greco-Roman Figures', in Porter and Pitts (eds.), *Christian Origins and Greco-Roman Culture*, pp. 85-111.

Kelly, Christopher, *Ruling the Later Roman Empire* (Cambridge, MA: Harvard University Press, 2004).

Kelso, Julie, 'Us versus Them: On Biblical (Studies) Identity Production', *The Bible and Critical Theory* 4 (2008), pp. 1-4.

Kennedy, D.J., and J. Newcombe, *The Da Vinci Myth versus the Gospel Truth* (Wheaton, IL: Crossway, 2006).

Kern, Kathi, *Mrs. Stanton's Bible* (Ithaca, NY: Cornell University Press, 2001).

Kierspel, Lars, *The Jews and the World in the Fourth Gospel: Parallelism, Function and Context* (WUNT, 2.220; Tübingen: Mohr Siebeck, 2006).

Kilgallen, John, 'Was Jesus Right to Eat with Sinners and Tax Collectors?', *Bib* 93 (2013), pp. 590-600.

Kilner, John F., Nigel M. de S. Cameron and David L. Schiedemeyer (eds.), *Bioethics and the Future of Medicine: A Christian Appraisal* (Grand Rapids, MI: Eerdmans, 1995).

Kim, Jintae, 'The Concept of Atonement in Early Rabbinic Thought and the New Testament', *Journal of Greco-Roman Christianity and Judaism* 2 (2001–2005), pp. 117-45.

—'The Concept of Atonement in Hellenistic Thought and 1 John', *Journal of Greco-Roman Christianity and Judaism* 2 (2001–2005), pp. 100-116.

—'The Concept of Atonement in the Qumran Literature and the New Covenant', *Journal of Greco-Roman Christianity and Judaism* 7 (2010), pp. 98-111.

Kim, Seong Hee, *Mark, Women, and Empire: A Korean Postcolonial Perspective* (The Bible and the Modern World, 20; Sheffield: Sheffield Phoenix Press, 2010).

Kim, Seyoon, *Christ and Caesar: The Gospel and the Roman Empire in the Writings of Paul and Luke* (Grand Rapids, MI: Eerdmans, 2008).

Kim, Stephen S., 'The Significance of Jesus' Healing the Blind Man in John 9', *BSac* 167 (2010), pp. 307-18.

Kindt, Julia, *Rethinking Greek Religion* (Cambridge: Cambridge University Press, 2012).

King, Helen (ed.), *Health in Antiquity* (London: Routledge, 2005).

King, Henry Churchill, *The Ethics of Jesus* (New York: Macmillan, 1910).

King, Karen, *The Gospel of Mary of Magdala: Jesus and the First Woman Apostle* (Santa Rosa, CA: Polebridge Press, 2003).

Kinukawa, Hisako, 'The Story of the Syrophoenician Woman (Mark 7:24-30)', *In God's Image* 23 (2004), pp. 50-53.

Kirk, Alan, '"Love your Enemies", the Golden Rule, and Ancient Reciprocity (Luke 6:27-35)', *JBL* 122 (2003), pp. 667-86.

Kitzberger, Ingrid Rosa (ed.), *Transformative Encounters: Jesus and Women Re-Viewed* (Atlanta, GA: Society of Biblical Literature, 2000).

Klassen, William, 'Love (NT and Early Jewish)', *ABD*, IV, pp. 381-96.

—*Love of Enemies: The Way to Peace* (Philadelphia, PA: Fortress Press, 1984).

—'"Love your Enemy": A Study of NT Teaching on Coping with an Enemy', *Mennonite Quarterly Review* 37 (1963), pp. 147-71.

Klawans, Jonathan, *Purity, Sacrifice, and the Temple: Symbolism and Supersessionism in the Study of Ancient Judaism* (New York: Oxford University Press, 2006).

—'Was Jesus' Last Supper a Seder?', *BR* 17 (2001), pp. 24-33, 47.

Klinkott, H., S. Kubisch and R. Müller-Wollermann (eds.), *Geschenke und Steuern, Zölle und Tribute: Antike Abgabenformen in Anspruch und Wirklichkeit* (Leiden: E.J. Brill, 2007).

Kloppenborg, John, *The Tenants in the Vineyard: Ideology, Economics, and Agrarian Conflict in Jewish Palestine* (WUNT, 2.195; Tübingen: Mohr Siebeck, 2006).

Kloppenborg, John S., and Stephen G. Wilson (eds.), *Voluntary Associations in the Graeco-Roman World* (London and New York: Routledge, 1996).

Klutz, Todd, *The Exorcism Stories in Luke–Acts: A Sociostylistic Reading* (SNTSMS, 129; Cambridge: Cambridge University Press, 2004).

Knight, Douglas A. (ed.), *Ethics and Politics in the Bible* (Semeia, 66; Atlanta, GA: Society of Biblical Literature, 1995).

—'Old Testament Ethics', *Christian Century* 99.2 (1982), pp. 55-59.

Knoblet, Jerry, *Herod the Great* (Lanham, MD: University Press of America, 2004).

Knudtzon, J.A., *Die El-Amarna Tafeln mit Einleitung un Erläuterungen* (2 vols.; repr., Osnabruck: Otto Zeller, 1964 [1915]).

Kollmann, Bernd, *Jesus und die Christen als Wundertäter: Studien zu Magie, Medizin und Schmanismus in Antike und Christentum* (Göttingen: Vandenhoeck & Ruprecht, 1996).

Kotansky, Roy, 'Two Amulets in the Getty Museum: A Gold Amulet for Aurelia's Epilepsy, an Inscribed Magical-Stone for Fever, "Chills", and a Headache', *J. Paul Getty Museum Journal* 8 (1980), pp. 181-87.

Kovelman, Arkady, 'Continuity and Change in Hellenistic Jewish Exegesis and in Early Rabbinic Literature', *Review of Rabbinic Literature* 7 (2004), pp. 123-61.

Kraeling, Emil G., *The Brooklyn Museum Aramaic Papyri: New Documents from the Fifth Century B.C. from the Jewish Colony at Elephantine* (New Haven, CT: Yale University Press, 1953).

Krueger, Paul, 'Etiology or Obligation? Genesis 2:24 Reconsidered in the Light of Textual Linguistics', in Augustin and Niemann (eds.), *Thinking Towards New Horizons*, pp. 35-47.

Krüger, Thomas, *Das Menschliche Herz und die Weisung Gottes* (Zürich: Theologischer Verlag Zürich, 2009).

Kuma, Hermann V.A., *The Centrality of* Αἷμα *(Blood) in the Theology of the Epistle to the Hebrews: An Exegetical and Philological Study* (Lewiston, NY: Edwin Mellen Press, 2012).

Kurzban, Robert, *Why Everyone (Else) is a Hypocrite: Evolution and the Modular Mind* (Princeton, NJ: Princeton University Press, 2012).

Labahn, M., and B.J. Lietaert Peterbolte (eds.), *A Kind of Magic: Understanding Magic in the New Testament and its Religious Environment* (Library of New Testament Studies, 306; London: T. & T. Clark, 2007).

Lachs, Samuel Tobias, 'Hebrew Elements in the Gospels and Acts', *JQR* 71 (1980), pp. 31-43.

Laes, Christian, 'Midwives and Greek Inscriptions in Hellenistic and Roman Antiquity', *ZPE* 176 (2011), pp. 154-62.

Lambert, David, 'Did Israel Believe that Redemption Awaited its Repentance? The Case of Jubilees 1', *CBQ* 68 (2006), pp. 631-50.

Lambert, Wilfred G., *Babylonian Wisdom Literature* (Oxford: Clarendon Press, 1960).

—'Morals in Ancient Mesopotamia', *JEOL* 15 (1955–58), pp. 184-96.

—'The Qualifications of Babylonian Diviners', in Maul (ed.), *Festschrift für Rykle Borger*, pp. 141-58.

Landes, George M., 'Matthew 12:40 as an Interpretation of "the Sign of Jonah" against its Biblical Background', in Meyers and O'Connor (eds.), *The Word of the Lord Shall Go Forth*, pp. 665-84.

Landres, J. Shawn, and Michael Berenbaum, *After the Passion is Gone: American Religious Consequences* (Walnut Creek, CA: AltaMira Press, 2004).

Landsberger, Benno, 'Corrections to the Article: "An Old Babylonian Charm against Merḫu"', *JNES* 17 (1958), pp. 56-58.

Landsberger, Benno (ed.), *Die Serie ana ittišu* (Rome: Pontifical Biblical Institute, 1937).

Langerman, Y. Tzvi (ed.), *Monotheism and Ethics: Historical and Contemporary Intersections among Judaism, Christianity and Islam* (Studies on the Children of Abraham, 2; Leiden and Boston, MA: E.J. Brill, 2012).

Langlands, Rebecca, 'Roman *exempla* and Situation Ethics: Valerius Maximus and Cicero *de Officis*', *JRS* 101 (2011), pp. 100-122.

Lapsley, Jacqueline E., 'Feeling our Way: Love for God in Deuteronomy', *CBQ* 65 (2003), pp. 350-69.

Larsen, K.W., 'The Structure of Mark's Gospel: Current Proposals', *Currents in Biblical Research* 3 (2004), pp. 140-60.

Lasine, Stuart, 'Everything Belongs to me: Holiness, Danger, and Divine Kingship in the Post-Genesis World', *JSOT* 35 (2010), pp. 31-62.

Lataster, Raphael C., *There was No Jesus, There is No God: A Scholarly Examination of the Scientific, Historical, and Philosophical Evidence and Arguments for Monotheism* (Charleston, SC: CreateSpace Independent Publishing Platform, 2013).

Law, Timothy Michael, *When God Spoke Greek: The Septuagint and the Making of the Christian Bible* (New York: Oxford University Press, 2013).

Lawrence, L.J., and M.I. Aguilar (eds.), *Anthropology and Biblical Studies: Avenues of Approach* (Leiden: Deo, 2004).

LeBeau, Bryan F., Leonard Greenspoon and Dennis Hamm (eds.), *The Historical Jesus through Catholic and Jewish Eyes* (London: Bloomsbury/T. & T. Clark, 2000).

Le Donne, Anthony, 'The Quest for the Historical Jesus: A Revisionist History through the Lens of Jewish-Christian Relations', *Journal for the Study of the Historical Jesus* 10 (2012), pp. 63-86.

Lee, Dorothy A., 'The Gospel of John and the Five Senses', *JBL* 129 (2010), pp. 115-27.

—'Presence or Absence? The Question of Women Disciples and the Last Supper', in *Biblical Studies Alternatively: An Introductory Reader* (ed. Susanne Scholz; Upper Saddle River, NJ: Prentice–Hall, 2003), pp. 121-36.

Lefebure, Leo, 'Violence in the New Testament and the History of Interpretation', in Rennard (ed.), *Fighting Words*, pp. 75-100.

Lefkowitz, Mary R., and Maureen B. Fant, *Women's Life in Greece and Rome: A Source Book in Translation* (Baltimore, MD: The Johns Hopkins University Press, 3rd edn, 2005).

Legaspi, Michael C., *The Death of Scripture and the Rise of Biblical Studies* (New York: Oxford University Press, 2010).

Lehrich, Christopher I., *The Occult Mind: Magic in Theory and Practice* (Ithaca, NY: Cornell University Press, 2009).

Leigh, David J., 'Forgiveness, Pity, and Ultimacy in Ancient Greek Culture', *Ultimate Reality and Meaning* 27 (2004), pp. 152-61.

Leigh, Matthew, 'Quintilian on the Emotions [Institutio Oratoria 6 preface and 1-2)', *JRS* 94 (2004), pp. 123-40.

Leiner, Martin, 'Neutestamentliche Exegese zwischen "Psycholatrie" und "Psychophobie"', *EvT* 65 (2005), pp. 148-54.

Lelyveld, Joseph, *Great Soul: Mahatma Gandhi and his Struggle with India* (New York: Alfred A. Knopf, 2011).

Lemaire, André (ed.), *Congress Volume Basel 2001* (VTSup, 80; Leiden and Boston, MA: E.J. Brill, 2002).

Lendon, Jon E., *Empire of Honor: The Art of Government in the Roman World* (New York: Oxford University Press, 1997).

Leopold, Aldo, *A Sand County Almanac, and Sketches Here and There* (New York: Oxford University Press, 1949).

Lesnoff, Michael H., *The Spirit of Capitalism and the Protestant Ethic* (Aldershot: Edward Elgar, 1994).

Levenson, James L., *Essentials of Psychosomatic Medicine* (Arlington, VA: American Psychiatric Publishing, 2006).

Levenson, Jon, *The Death and Resurrection of the Beloved Son: The Transformation of Child Sacrifice in Judaism and Christianity* (New Haven, CT: Yale University Press, 1993).

Levering, Matthew, 'God and Greek Philosophy in Contemporary Scholarship', *Journal of Theological Interpretation* 4 (2010), pp. 169-85.

Levey, Geoffrey B., and Tariq Modood, 'Liberal Democracy, Multicultural Citizenship, and the Danish Cartoon Affair', in Levey and Modood (eds.), *Secularism, Religion and Multicultural Citizenship*, pp. 216-42.

Levey, Geoffrey B., and Tariq Modood (eds.), *Secularism, Religion and Multicultural Citizenship* (Cambridge: Cambridge University Press, 2009).

Levin, Christoph, 'Die Enstehung der Bücherteilung des Psalters', *VT* 54 (2004), pp. 83-90.

Levin, Jack, and Gordana Rabrenovic, *Why we Hate* (Amherst, NY: Prometheus, 2004).

Levine, Amy-Jill, 'The Gospel of Matthew', in Newsom, Ringe and Lapsley (eds.), *The Women's Bible Commentary*, pp. 465-77.

—'Jesus, Divorce, and Sexuality: A Jewish Critique', in LeBeau, Greenspoon and Hamm (eds.), *The Historical Jesus through Catholic and Jewish Eyes*, pp. 113-29.

—'Discharging Responsibility: Matthean Jesus, Biblical Law, and Hemorrhaging Woman', in Bauer and Powell (eds.), *Treasures New and Old*, pp. 379-97.

Levine, Amy-Jill, and Marianne Blickenstaff (eds.), *A Feminist Companion to Mark* (Sheffield: Sheffield Academic Press, 2001).

Levine, Amy-Jill, and Marc Zvi Brettler (eds.), *The Jewish Annotated New Testament* (New York: Oxford University Press, 2011).

Levine, Baruch A., 'On the Origins of the Aramaic Legal Formulary at Elephantine', in Neusner (ed.), *Christianity, Judaism, and Other Greco-Roman Cults*, pp. 37-54.

—'René Girard and Job: The Question of the Scapegoat', *Semeia* 33 (1985), pp. 125-33.

Levine, Lee I., *Jerusalem: Portrait of the City in the Second Temple Period (538 B.C.E.– 70 C.E.)* (Philadelphia, PA: Jewish Publication Society, 2002).

Levinson, Bernard M. (ed.), *Theory and Method in Biblical and Cuneiform Law: Revision, Interpolation, and Development* (Sheffield: Sheffield Academic Press, 1994).

Lewy, Guenter, *The Catholic Church and Nazi Germany* (New York: McGraw-Hill, 1964).

Lichtheim, Miriam, *Ancient Egyptian Literature* (3 vols.; Berkeley, CA: University of California Press, 1976).

Liddell, Henry George, and Robert Scott, *Greek-English Lexicon* (repr., London: Oxford University Press, 1968 [1889]).

Lieu, Judith M., *Christian Identity in the Jewish and Greco-Roman World* (New York: Oxford University Press, 2006).

Liew, Tat-siong Benny, *Politics of Parousia: Reading Mark Inter(con)textually* (Leiden: E.J. Brill, 1999).

Lincicum, David, 'Greek Deuteronomy's "Fever" and "Chills" and their Magical After-life', *VT* 58 (2008), pp. 544-49.

Lind, Millard, *Yahweh is a Warrior: The Theology of Warfare in Ancient Israel* (Scotts-dale, PA: Herald Press, 1980).

Linzey, Andrew, *Christianity and the Rights of Animals* (New York: Crossroad, 1989).

—*Why Animal Suffering Matters: Philosophy, Theology and Practical Ethics* (New York: Oxford University Press, 2009).

Lipinski, Edward, 'שׂנא', *TDOT*, XIV, pp. 164-74.

—'The Wife's Right to Divorce in the Light of an Ancient Near Eastern Tradition', *Jewish Law Annual* 8 (1981), pp. 9-27.

Livingstone, Elizabeth A. (ed.), *Studia Biblica 1978 II. Papers on the Gospels* (JSNT-Sup, 2; Sheffield: JSOT Press, 1980).

Lloyd, G.E.R., 'The Transformation of Ancient Medicine', *Bulletin of the History of Medicine* 66 (1992), pp. 114-32.

Locker, Markus, *The New World of Jesus' Parables* (Newcastle upon Tyne: Cambridge Scholars, 2008).

Lohse, Eduard, *Die Texte aus Qumran: Hebräisch und Deutsch* (Munich: Kösel, 2nd edn, 1981).

Loman, Pasi, '"No Women, No War": Women's Participation in Ancient Greek War-fare', *Greece & Rome* 51 (2004), pp. 34-54.

Long, Adrian, *Paul and Human Rights: A Dialogue with the Father of the Corinthian Community* (Sheffield: Sheffield Phoenix Press, 2009).

Longenecker, Bruce W., *Remember the Poor: Paul, Poverty, and the Greco-Roman World* (Grand Rapids, MI: Eerdmans, 2010).

Longenecker, Richard N., *New Testament Social Ethics for Today* (Grand Rapids, MI: Eerdmans, 1984).

Longman, Tremper, 'The Divine Warrior: The New Testament Use of an Old Testament Motif', *WTJ* 44 (1982), pp. 290-307.

—'Isaiah 65:17-25', *Int* 64 (2010), pp. 72-73.

López, Elisa Estévez, *El poder de una mujer creyente: Cuerpo, identidad y discipulado en Mc 5,24b-34, un estudio desde las ciencias sociales* (Estella, Spain: Editorial Verbo Divino, 2003).

—*Qué se sabe de...Las mujeres en los orígenes del cristianismo* (Estella [Navarra]: Verbo Divino, 2012).

Lovelock, James, *Gaia: A New Look at Life on Earth* (New York: Oxford University Press, 2000).

Lucas, Shirley, *The Concept of the Messiah in the Scriptures of Judaism and Christianity* (Library of Second Temple Studies, 78; London: T. & T. Clark, 2011).

Luck, Georg, *Arcana Mundi: Magic and the Occult in the Greek and Roman Worlds* (Baltimore, MD: The Johns Hopkins University Press, 1985).

Lucretius, *De Rerum Natura* (trans. W.H.D. Rouse and M.F. Smith; LCL; Cambridge, MA: Harvard University Press, 1975).

Lüdemann, Gerd, *Intolerance and the Gospel: Selected Texts from the New Testament* (Amherst, NY: Prometheus, 2008).

Luiselli, Maria Michela, 'La partecipazione dell'individuo alla religione: rituali person-ali tra norma e individualità', *Aegyptus* 85 (2006), pp. 13-31.

Luz, Ulrich, 'Geschichte und Wahrheit im Matthäusevangelium: Das Problem der narrativen Fiktionen', *EvT* 69.3 (2009), pp. 194-208.

—*Matthew 1–7: A Commentary* (Minneapolis: Fortress Press, 2007).

—*Matthew 8–20: A Commentary* (trans. James E. Crouch; Hermeneia; Minneapolis: Fortress Press, 2001).

Lynch, Chloe, 'How Convincing is Walter Wink's Interpretations of Paul's Language of the Powers?', *EvQ* 83.3 (2011), pp. 251-66.

Mace, Emily R., 'Feminist Forerunners and a Usable Past: A Historiography of Elizabeth Cady Stanton's *The Woman's Bible*', *Journal of Feminist Studies in Religion* 25 (2009), pp. 5-23.

MacGillivray, Erlend D., 'Re-evaluating Patronage and Reciprocity in Antiquity and New Testament Studies', *Journal of Greco-Roman Christianity and Judaism* 6 (2009), pp. 37-81.

Macgregor, Sherry Lou, *Beyond Hearth and Home: Women in the Public Sphere in Neo-Assyrian Society* (SAA, 21; Helsinki: Neo-Assyrian Corpus Text Project, 2012).

Machiela, Daniel, *The Dead Sea Genesis Apocryphon: A New Text and Translation with Introduction and Special Treatment of Columns 13-17* (Leiden and Boston, MA: E.J. Brill, 2009).

Machinist, Peter, 'Assyria and its Image in the First Isaiah', *JAOS* 103 (1983), pp. 719-37.

MacKinnon, Michael, '"Sick as a Dog": Zooarchaeological Evidence for Pet Dog Health and Welfare in the Roman World', *World Archaeology* 42.2 (2010), pp. 290-309.

MacMullen, Ramsey, 'The Power of the Roman Empire', *Historia* 55.4 (2006), pp. 471-81.

Malbon, Elizabeth Struthers, 'The Jesus of Mark and the Sea of Galilee', *JBL* 103 (1984), pp. 363-77.

Malina, Bruce J., 'Wealth and Poverty in the New Testament and its World', *Int* 41 (1987), pp. 354-67.

—'"Let Him Deny Himself" (Mark 8:34 & Par): A Social Psychological Model of Self-Denial', *BTB* 24 (1994), pp. 106-19.

—'Understanding New Testament Persons', in Rohrbaugh (ed.), *The Social Sciences and the New Testament*, pp. 41-61.

Mann, Christopher S., *Mark: A New Translation with Introduction and Commentary* (AB, 27; New York: Doubleday, 1986).

Marcus, Joel, 'Mark 4:10-12 and Marcan Epistemology', *JBL* 103 (1984), pp. 557-74.

—'Passover and Last Supper Revisited', *NTS* 59 (2013), pp. 303-324.

Margolis, Dan, 'Followers of Rapture Evangelist Lost Millions', *People's World* (23 May 2011). Online: http://peoplesworld.org/followers-of-rapture-evangelist-lost-millions/.

Marks, John H., and Robert M. Good (eds.), *Love and Death in the Ancient Near East: Essays in Honor of Marvin H. Pope* (Guilford, CT: Four Quarters, 1987).

Marshall, I. Howard, *Beyond the Bible: Moving from Scripture to Theology* (Grand Rapids, MI: Baker Academic, 2004).

—*The Gospel of Luke: A Commentary on the Greek Text* (New International Greek Testament Commentary; Exeter: Paternoster Press, 1978).

Marshall, Mary J., 'Jesus: Glutton and Drunkard?', *Journal for the Study of the Historical Jesus* 3 (2005), pp. 47-60.

Martin, Joel W., and Conrad E. Oswalt (eds.), *Screening the Sacred: Religion, Myth, and Ideology in Popular American Film* (Boulder, CO: Westview Press, 1995).

Martin, Ralph P., *Ephesians, Colossians, and Philemon* (Atlanta, GA: John Knox Press, 1991).

Martin, Raymond A., *Studies in the Life and Ministry of the Historical Jesus* (Lanham, MD: University Press of America, 1995).

Martin, Roger, *R.A. Torrey: Apostle of Certainty* (Murfreesboro, TN: Sword of the Lord, 1976).

Martínez, Florentino García, *The Dead Sea Scrolls Translated: The Qumran Texts in English* (Leiden: E.J. Brill, 1994).

Marucci, P., *Parole di Gesù sul divorzio* (Aloisiana, 16; Pubblicazioni della Pontificia Facoltà Teologica dell' Italia Meridonale, Sezione S. Luigi; Naples: Morcelliana, 1982).

Marx, Anthony W., *Faith in Nation: Exclusionary Origins of Nationalism* (New York: Oxford University Press, 2003).

Mason, Steve, 'Jews. Judaeans, Judaizing, Judaism: Problems of Categorization in Ancient History?', *Journal for the Study of Judaism* 38 (2007), pp. 457-512.

Matera, Frank, *New Testament Ethics: The Legacies of Jesus and Paul* (Louisville, KY: Westminster/John Knox Press, 1996).

—*The Sermon on the Mount: The Perfect Measure of the Christian Life* (Collegeville, MN: Liturgical Press, 2013).

Mathews, Mark D., *Riches, Poverty and the Faithful: Perspectives on Wealth in the Second Temple Period and the Apocalypse of John* (SNTSMS, 154; Cambridge: Cambridge University Press, 2013).

Matson, Thomas B., *Biblical Ethics: A Guide to the Ethical Message of the Scriptures from Genesis through Revelation* (repr., Macon, GA: Mercer University Press, 1991 [1967]).

Matthews, Shailer, *Jesus on Social Institutions* (New York: Macmillan, 1928).

Matthews, Shelly, and E. Leigh Gibson (eds.), *Violence in the New Testament* (New York: T. & T. Clark, 2005).

Matthews, Victor H., 'Fishermen', *NIDB*, II, p. 460.

Maudlin, Michael, and Marlene Baer (eds.), *The Green Bible* (New York: HarperCollins, 2008).

Maul, Stefan M. (ed.), *Festschrift für Rykle Borger zu seinem 65. Geburtstag am 24. Mai 1994: tikip santakki mala bašmu* (Cuneiform Monographs, 10; Groningen: Styx, 1998).

McCarter, P. Kyle, *1 Samuel: A New Translation with Introduction and Commentary* (AB, 8; Garden City, NY: Doubleday, 1980).

McClenon, James, *Wondrous Healing: Shamanism, Human Evolution, and the Origin of Religion* (DeKalb, IL: Northern Illinois University Press, 2002).

McCollough, C.T., and Beth Glazier-McDonald, 'An Aramaic Bronze Amulet from Sepphoris', *Atiqot* 28 (1996), pp. 161-65.

McDonald, J. Ian H., *The Crucible of Christian Morality: Religion in the First Christian Centuries* (New York: Routledge, 1998).

McElvaine, Robert S., *Grand Theft Jesus: The Hijacking of Religion in America* (New York: Crown, 2009).

McGee, J. Vernon, *Thru the Bible with J. Vernon McGee* (5 vols.; Pasadena, CA: Thru the Bible Radio, 1988).

McGrath, Alister E., *The Reenchantment of Nature: The Denial of Religion and the Ecological Crisis* (New York: Doubleday, 2002).

McGrath, James F., *The Burial of Jesus: History and Faith* (Englewood, CO: Patheos Press, 2011).

McIver, R.K., *Mainstream or Marginal? The Matthean Community in Early Christianity* (Friedensauer Schriftenreihe, Reihe A: Theologie, 12; Frankfurt: Peter Lang, 2012).

McKenna, Andrew J. (ed.), 'René Girard and Biblical Studies', *Semeia* 33 (1985).

McKnight, Scot, 'A Loyal Critic: Matthew's Polemic with Judaism in Theological Perspective', in Evans and Hagner (eds.), *Anti-Semitism and Early Christianity*, pp. 55-79.

—*Jesus and His Death: Historiography, the Historical Jesus, and Atonement Theory* (Waco, TX: Baylor University Press, 2005).

McKnight, Scot, and Joseph B. Modica (eds.), *Jesus is Lord, Caesar is Not: Evaluating Empire in New Testament Studies* (Downers Grove, IL: InterVarsity Press, 2013).

McKnight, Scot, and Grant R. Osborn (eds.), *The Face of New Testament Studies: A Survey of Recent Research* (Grand Rapids, MI: Baker, 2004).

McRae, Rachel M., 'Eating with Honor: The Corinthian Lord's Supper in the Light of Voluntary Association Meal Practices', *JBL* 130 (2011), pp. 165-81.

Meeks, Wayne A., *The Origins of Christian Morality: The First Two Centuries* (New Haven, CT: Yale University Press, 1993).

—'Why Study the New Testament?', *NTS* 51 (2005), pp. 155-70.

Mees, Michael, 'Die Heilung des Kranken vom Bethesdateich aus Joh 5.1-18 in Frühchristlicher Sicht', *NTS* 32 (1986), pp. 596-608.

Meier, John P., *A Marginal Jew: Rethinking the Historical Jesus, Volume 4: Law and Love* (New Haven, CT: Yale University Press, 2009).

—'Matthew 15.21-28', *Int* 40 (1986), pp. 397-402.

Meiser, Martin (ed.), *The Torah in the Ethics of Paul* (Library of New Testament Studies, 473, European Studies on Christian Origins; London: T. & T. Clark, 2012).

Mellor, Ronald, *Tacitus' Annals* (Oxford Approaches to Classical Literature; New York: Oxford University Press, 2011).

Menkens, Maarten J.J., and Steve Moyise (eds.), *Deuteronomy in the New Testament* (Library of New Testament Studies, 358; London: T. & T. Clark, 2007).

Mettinger, Arthur. *Aspects of Semantic Opposition in English* (New York: Oxford University Press, 1994).

Metzger, Bruce M., *A Textual Commentary on the Greek New Testament* (New York: United Bible Societies, 1975)

Metzger, Bruce M., and Bart Ehrman, *The Text of the New Testament: Its Transmission, Corruption and Restoration* (New York: Oxford University Press, 4th edn, 2005).

Metzger, James A., 'Disability and the Marginalization of God in the Parable of the Snubbed Host (Luke 14.15-24)', *The Bible and Critical Theory* 6 (2010), pp. 23.1-23.15. Online: http://novaojs.newcastle.edu.au/ojsbct/index.php/bct/article/view/308.

—'Reclaiming a "Dark and Malefic Sacred" for a Theology of Disability', *Journal of Religion, Disability and Health* 15 (2011), pp. 296-316.

—'Where has Yahweh Gone? Reclaiming Unsavory Images of God in New Testament Studies', *Horizons in Biblical Theology* 31 (2009), pp. 51-76.

Meyer, Marvin, and Richard Smith, *Ancient Christian Magic: Coptic Texts of Ritual Power* (New York: HarperCollins, 1994).

Meyers, Carol L., and M. O'Connor (eds.), *The Word of the Lord Shall Go Forth: Essays in Honor of David Noel Freedman in Celebration of his Sixtieth Birthday* (Winona Lake, IN: Eisenbrauns, 1983).

Meyers, Eric C., 'Jesus and his Galilean Context', in Edwards and McCullough (eds.), *Archaeology and the Galilee*, pp. 57-66.

Meyers, Susan E. (ed.), *Portraits of Jesus: Studies in Christology* (WUNT, 2.321; Tübingen: Mohr Siebeck, 2012).

Michaud, Jean-Paul, and Pierrette Daviau, 'Jésus au-delà des frontières de Tyr: Analyse de Marc 7,24-31', in Chené *et al.* (eds.), *De Jésus et des femmes*, pp. 35-57.

Michel, Otto, 'μισέω', *TDNT* IV, pp. 683-94.

Mico, Ted, John Miller-Monzon and David Rubel, *Past Imperfect: History According to the Movies* (New York: Henry Holt and Company, 1995).

Midelfort, H.C. Erik, *A History of Madness in Sixteenth-Century Germany* (Stanford, CA: Stanford University Press, 1999).

—*Witchcraft, Madness, Society, and Religion in Early Modern Germany: A Ship of Fools* (Aldershot: Ashgate, 2013).

Miguens, Emanuel, '1 Corinthians 13:8-13 Reconsidered', *CBQ* 37 (1975), pp. 76-97.

Miles, Margaret, 'The Passion for Social Justice', in Beal and Linafelt (eds.), *Mel Gibson's Bible*, pp. 121-27.

Milgrom, Jacob, *Leviticus 1–16* (AB, 3; New York: Doubleday, 1991).

Millard, Ann V., and Jorge Chapa, *Apple Pie and Enchiladas: Latino Newcomers in the Rural Midwest* (Austin, TX: University of Texas Press, 2001).

Miller, Julie B., 'Forming Future Feminists: Elisabeth Schüssler Fiorenza, Conscientization and the College Classroom', *Journal of Feminist Studies in Religion* 25 (2009), pp. 99-123.

Miller, Patrick D., *The Divine Warrior in Early Israel* (Harvard Semitic Monographs, 5; Cambridge, MA: Harvard University Press, 1973).

Miller, Richard C., 'Mark's Empty Tomb and Other Translation Fables in Classical Antiquity', *JBL* 129 (2010), pp. 759-76.

Miller, Richard W., *Suffering and the Christian Life* (Maryknoll, NY: Orbis Books, 2013).

Miller, Susan, *Women in Mark's Gospel* (JSNTSup, 259; London: T. & T. Clark, 2004).

Mills, Mary E., *Biblical Morality: Moral Perspectives in Old Testament Narratives* (Burlington, VT: Ashgate, 2001).

Minear, Paul S., 'Matthew 28:1-10', *Int* 38 (1984), pp. 59-63.

Minus, Paul M., *Walter Rauschenbusch: American Reformer* (New York: Macmillan, 1988).

Mitchell, David C., 'Firstborn *Shor* and *Rem*: A Sacrificial Josephite Messiah in 1 Enoch 90.37-38 and Deuteronomy 33.17', *JSP* 15.3 (2006), pp. 211-28.

Moltmann, Jürgen, *The Crucified God: The Cross of Christ as the Foundation and Criticism of Christian Theology* (trans. R.A. Wilson and John Bowden; New York: Harper & Row, 1974).

Moltmann-Wendel, Elisabeth, *The Women around Jesus* (New York: Crossroad, 1987).

Mondrego, Angel Gil, 'Estudio de lēb/āb en el Antiguo Testamento: análisis sintagmático y paradigmático' (Doctoral dissertation; 2 vols.; Madrid: Universidad Complutense de Madrid, 1990).

Monro, Anita J., 'Alterity and the Canaanite Woman: A Postmodern Feminist Theological Reflection on Political Action', *Colloquium* 26 (1994), pp. 264-78.

Moo, Douglas, 'Nature in the New Creation: New Testament Eschatology and the Environment', *JETS* 49 (2006), pp. 449-88.

Moore, Andrew N. Ireland, 'Defining Animals as Crime Victims', *Journal of Animal Law* 1 (2005), pp. 91-108.

Moore, Daniel F., *Jesus, an Emerging Jewish Mosaic: Jewish Perspectives, Post Holocaust* (Jewish and Christian Texts in Contexts and Related Studies, 2; London: T. & T. Clark, 2011).

Moore, Stephen D., and Yvonne Sherwood, 'After "After Theory", and Other Apocalyptic Conceits', *BibInt* 18 (2010), pp. 1-27.

—'Biblical Studies "after" Theory: Onwards Towards the Past. Part Three: Theory in the First and Second Waves', *BibInt* 18 (2010), pp. 191-225.

—*The Invention of the Biblical Scholar: A Critical Manifesto* (Minneapolis: Fortress Press, 2011).

—'The Secret Vices of the Biblical God', *BibInt* 8 (2010), pp. 87-113.

Moran, William L., 'The Ancient Near Eastern Background of the Love of God in Deuteronomy', *CBQ* 25 (1963), pp. 77-87.

—*Les Lettres d'El Amarna* (trans. Dominique Collon and Henri Cazelles; Paris: Cerf, 1987).

Moran, William L. (ed.), *The Amarna Letters* (Baltimore, MD: The Johns Hopkins University Press, 1992).

Morgan, Jonathan, 'Sacrifice in Leviticus: Eco-Friendly Ritual or Unholy Waste?', in Horrell *et al.* (eds.), *Ecological Hermeneutics*, pp. 32-45.

Morgenthau, Hans, *Politics among Nations: The Struggle for Power and Peace* (ed. Kenneth Thompson; New York: McGraw-Hill, 1993).

Moro, Pamela A., and James E. Myers (eds.), *Magic, Witchcraft, and Religion: A Reader in the Anthropology of Religion* (New York: McGraw-Hill, 2010).

Morrow, Glenn R., *Plato's Laws of Slavery in its Relation to Greek Law* (repr., New York: Arno Press, 1976 [1939]).

Moss, Candida R., and Jeremy Schipper (eds.), *Disability Studies and Biblical Literature* (New York: Palgrave Macmillan, 2011).

Moxnes, Halvor, *The Economy of the Kingdom: Social Conflict and Economic Relations in Luke's Gospel* (Philadelphia, PA: Fortress Press, 1988).

Moyise, Steve, *Jesus and Scripture: Studying the New Testament Use of the Old Testament* (Grand Rapids, MI: Baker Academic, 2010).

Muffs, Yochanan, 'Joy and Love as Metaphorical Expressions of Willingness and Spontaneity in Cuneiform, Ancient Hebrew, and Related Literatures: Investitures in the Midrash in the Light of Neo-Babylonian Royal Grants', in Neusner (ed.), *Christianity, Judaism, and Other Greco-Roman Cults*, pp. 1-36.

Munro, Winsome, 'Women Disciples in Mark?', *CBQ* 44 (1982), pp. 225-41.

Murphy, Nancey, 'When Jesus Said "Love your Enemies" I Think He Probably Meant Don't Kill Them', *PRSt* 40 (2013), pp. 123-29.

Nachef, Anthony E., *Women in the Eyes of Jesus: Yesterday, Today, and Forever* (Staten Island, NY: St Pauls, 2004).

Nash, James A., 'The Bible vs. Biodiversity: The Case against Moral Argument from Scripture', *Journal for the Study of Religion, Nature and Culture* 3 (2009), pp. 213-37.

Naveh, Joseph, and Shaul Shaked, *Amulets and Magic Bowls: Aramaic Incantations of Late Antiquity* (Jerusalem: Magnes Press, 1998).

Neff, David, 'Jesus through Jewish Eyes', *Christianity Today* (April 2012), pp. 52-54.

Nelson-Pallmeyer, Jack. 'Another Inconvenient Truth: Violence within the "Sacred Texts"', *Fourth R* 20.1 (2007), pp. 9-15.

—*Jesus against Christianity: Reclaiming the Missing Jesus* (Harrisburg, PA: Trinity Press International, 2001).

Netzer, Ehud, *The Architecture of Herod the Great Builder* (Grand Rapids, MI: Baker Academic, 2008).

—'Did Any Perfume Industry Exist at 'Ein Feshkha?', *IEJ* 55.1 (2005), pp. 97-100.

Neufeld, Thomas R. Yoder, *Killing Enmity: Violence and the New Testament* (Grand Rapids, MI: Baker Academic, 2011).

—*Put on the Armour of God: The Divine Warrior from Isaiah to Ephesians* (Sheffield: Sheffield Academic Press,1997).

Neusner, Jacob (ed.), *Christianity, Judaism, and Other Greco-Roman Cults: Studies for Morton Smith at Sixty. Part 3, Judaism before 70* (Leiden: E.J. Brill, 1975).

Neusner, Jacob, Ernest S. Frerichs and Paul Virgil McCracken Flesher (eds.), *Religion, Science, and Magic: In Concert and in Conflict* (New York: Oxford University Press, 1989).

Neville, David J., *A Peaceable Hope: Contesting Violent Eschatology in the New Testament Narratives* (Grand Rapids, MI: Baker Academic, 2013).

—'Moral Vision and Eschatology in Mark's Gospel: Coherence or Conflict?', *JBL* 127 (2008), pp. 359-84.

Newsom, Carol A., 'The Economics of Sin: A Not So Dismal Science', *HTR* 103 (2010), pp. 365-71.

—'Models of the Moral Self: Hebrew Bible and Second Temple Judaism', *JBL* 131 (2012), pp. 5-25.

Newsom, Carol A., Sharon H. Ringe and Jacqueline E. Lapsley (eds.), *The Women's Bible Commentary* (Louisville, KY: Westminster/John Knox Press, 2nd edn, 2012).

Nicklas, Tobias, 'Die johanneische "Tempelreinigung" (Joh 2, 12-22) für Leser der Synoptiker', *Theologie und Philosophie* 80 (2005), pp. 1-16.

Nietzsche, Friedrich, *Beyond Good and Evil* (trans. Helen Zimmern; Amherst, NY: Prometheus, 1989).

Nissinen, Martin, C.L. Seow and Robert Ritner, *Prophets and Prophecy in the Ancient Near East* (Writings of the Ancient World, 12; Atlanta, GA: Society of Biblical Literature, 2003).

Noll, Kurt L., 'Investigating Earliest Christianity without Jesus', in Thompson and Verenna (eds.), *'Is This Not the Carpenter?'*, pp. 163-84.

Nolland, John, *The Gospel of Matthew* (NIGTC; Grand Rapids, MI: Eerdmans, 2005).

Norris, Pippa, and Ronald Inglehart, *Sacred and Secular: Religion and Politics* (Cambridge Series in Social Theory, Religion and Politics; Cambridge: Cambridge University Press, 2012).

Northcott, Michael S., *The Environment and Christian Ethics* (Cambridge: Cambridge University Press, 1996).

Novakovic, Lidijam, *Messiah, the Healer of the Sick: A Study of Jesus as the Son of David in the Gospel of Matthew* (WUNT, 2.170; Tübingen: Mohr Siebeck, 2003).

Nun, Mendel, 'Cast your Net upon the Waters: Fish and Fishermen in Jesus' Time', *BARev* 19 (1993), pp. 46-56, 70.

Nussbaum, Martha C., 'Beyond "Compassion and Humanity"', in Sunstein and Nussbaum (eds.), *Animal Rights*, pp. 299-320.

Nutkowicz, Hélène, 'Concerning the Verb *SN'* in Judaeo-Aramaic Contracts from Elephantine', *JSS* 52 (2007), pp. 211-25.

Nutton, Vivian, *Ancient Medicine* (London: Routledge, 2004).

Nwaoru, E.O., 'Poverty Eradication: A Divine Mandate', *African Ecclesial Review* 46 (2004), pp. 198-213.

Nygren, Anders, *Agape and Eros* (trans. Philip S. Watson; Philadelphia, PA: Westminster Press, 1953).

Oakman, Douglas E., *Jesus, Debt, and the Lord's Prayer: First-Century Debt and Jesus' Intentions* (Eugene, OR: Cascade Books, 2014).

—*The Political Aims of Jesus* (Minneapolis: Fortress Press, 2012).

—*Jesus and the Peasants* (Matrix: The Bible in Mediterranean Context, 4; Eugene, OR: Wipf & Stock, 2008).

—Obermann, Andreas. *Die christologische Erfüllung der Schrift im Johannesevangelium: Eine Untersuchung zur johanneischen Hermeneutik anhand der Schriftzitate* (WUNT, 2.83; Tübingen: J.C.B. Mohr [Paul Siebeck], 1996).

Olyan, Saul, *Disability in the Hebrew Bible: Interpreting Mental and Physical Differences* (Cambridge: Cambridge University Press, 2008).

Oppel, Dogmar, *Heilsam erzählen-erzählend heilen: Die Heilung der Blutflüssigen und die Erweckung der Jairustochter in Mk 5, 21-43 als Beispiel markinischer Erzählfertigkeit* (BBB, 102; Weinheim: Beltz Athenäum Verlag, 1995).

Origen, *Commentary on the Gospel According to John, Books 1–10* (trans. Ronald E. Heine; The Fathers of the Church: A New Translation; Washington, DC: Catholic University of America Press, 1989).

—*Homilies on Numbers* (ed. Christopher A. Hall; trans. Thomas P. Scheck; Downers Grove, IL: InterVarsity Press, 2009).

Orlin, Eric M., *Foreign Cults in Rome: Creating a Roman Empire* (New York: Oxford University Press, 2010).

Orlinsky, Harry M., 'Nationalism-Universalism and Internationalism in Ancient Israel', in Frank and Reed (eds.), *Translating and Understanding the Old Testament*, pp. 206-236.

Orr, Robert, *Medical Ethics and the Faith Factor: A Handbook for Clergy and Health Care Professionals* (Grand Rapids, MI: Eerdmans, 2009).

Osiek, Carolyn, and David L. Balch (eds.), *Families in the New Testament World* (Louisville, KY: Westminster/John Knox Press, 1997).

Otto, Eckart, 'The History of the Legal-Religious Hermeneutics of the Book of Deuteronomy from the Assyrian to the Hellenistic Period', in Hagedorn and Kratz (eds.), *Law and Religion in the Eastern Mediterranean*, pp. 211-50.

—'Of Aims and Methods in Hebrew Bible Ethics', in Knight (ed.), *Ethics and Politics in the Bible*, pp. 161-71.

—'Law and Ethics', in Johnson (ed.), *Religions of the Ancient World*, pp. 84-97.

—*Theologische Ethik des Alten Testaments* (Stuttgart: Kohlhammer, 1994).

Outka, Gene, *Agape: An Ethical Analysis* (New Haven, CT: Yale University Press, 1972).

Overman, J. Andrew, 'Jesus of Galilee and the Historical Peasant', in Edwards and McCullough (eds.), *Archaeology and the Galilee*, pp. 67-73.

Oyserman, Daphna, Heather M. Coon and Markus Kemmelmeier, 'Rethinking Individualism and Collectivism: Evaluation of Theoretical Assumptions and Meta-analyses', *Psychological Bulletin* 128 (2002), pp. 3-72.

Pabst, Adrian, and Angus Addison (eds.), *The Pope and Jesus of Nazareth: Christ, Scripture and the Church* (London: SCM Press, 2009).

Palachuvattil, Mathew, *'The One who Does the Will of the Father': Distinguishing Character of Disciples According to Matthew: An Exegetical and Theological*

Study (Tesi Gregoriana, Serie Teologia, 154: Rome: Editrice Pontificia Università Gregoriana, 2007).

Palmer, Clare, *Animal Ethics in Context* (New York: Columbia University Press, 2010).

Pamment, M., 'The Kingdom of Heaven According to the First Gospel', *NTS* 27 (1981), pp. 211-32.

Pao, David W., 'Waiters or Preachers: Acts 6:1-7 and the Lukan Table Fellowship Motif', *JBL* 130 (2011), pp. 127-44.

Parker, B., 'The Nimrud Tablets, 1952: Business Documents', *Iraq* 16 (1954), pp. 29-58.

Parker, H.N., 'Galen and the Girls: Sources for Women Medical Writers Revisited', *ClQ* 62 (2012), pp. 359-86.

Parpola, Simo, and Kazuko Watanabe, *Neo-Assyrian Treaties and Loyalty Oaths* (SAA, 2; Helsinki: Helsinki University Press, 1988).

Parsons, Mikeal, *Body and Character in Luke and Acts: The Subversion of Physiognomy in Early Christianity* (Grand Rapids, MI: Baker Academic, 2006).

Patrick, Dale, 'The Kingdom of God in the Old Testament', in Willis (ed.), *The Kingdom of God*, pp. 67-79.

Patte, Daniel, 'The Canaanite Woman and Jesus: Surprising Models of Discipleship (Matt. 15:21-28)', in Kitzberger (ed.), *Transformative Encounters*, pp. 33-53.

Pattemore, Stephen W., 'How Green is your Bible? Ecology and the End of the World in Translation', *BT* 58.2 (2007), pp. 75-85.

Pausanias, *Description of Greece* (trans. W.H.S. Jones; LCL; 4 vols.; Cambridge, MA: Harvard University Press, 1933).

Paz, Octavio, *Sor Juan* (Cambridge, MA: Harvard University Press, 1988).

Pearson, Birger A. 'A Q Community in Galilee?', *NTS* 50 (2004), pp. 476-94.

Penella, Robert J. (ed.), *The Letters of Apollonus of Tyana: A Critical Text with Prolegomena, Translation and Commentary* (Leiden: E.J. Brill, 1979).

Pennington, Jonathan T., and Seand M. McDonough (eds.), *Cosmology and New Testament Theology* (London: T. & T. Clark, 2008).

Peppard, Michael, 'The Eagle and the Dove: Roman Imperial Sonship and the Baptism of Jesus (Mark 1.9-11)', *NTS* 56.4 (2010), pp. 431-51.

Perchansky, David, and Paul Redditt (eds.), *Shall Not the Judge of the Earth Do What is Right? Studies in the Nature of God in Tribute to James L. Crenshaw* (Winona Lake, IN: Eisenbrauns, 2000).

Perdue, Leo G., Joseph Blenkinsopp, John J. Collins and Carol Meyers (eds.), *Families in Ancient Israel* (Louisville, KY: Westminster/John Knox Press, 1997).

Perkins, Judith, 'Animal Voices', *Religion and Theology* 12.3-4 (2005), pp. 385-96.

Perrin, Nicholas, *Jesus and the Language of the Kingdom* (Philadelphia, PA: Fortress Press, 1976).

—*Jesus the Temple* (Grand Rapids, MI: Baker Academic, 2010).

Pestman, P.W., *Marriage and Matrimonial Property in Ancient Egypt* (Papyrologica Lugdono-Batava, 39; Leiden: E.J. Brill, 1961).

Peters, Melvin K.H. (ed.), *XII Congress of the International Organization for Septuagint and Cognate Studies, Leiden 2004* (Septuagint and Cognate Studies, 54; Atlanta, GA: Society of Biblical Literature, 2006).

Peters, Shawn Francis, *When Prayer Fails: Faith Healing, Children, and the Law* (New York: Oxford University Press, 2008).

Petracca, Vincenzo, *Gott oder das Geld. Die Besitzethik des Lukas* (Text und Arbeiten zum neutestamentlichen Zeitalter, 39; Tübingen: Francke, 2003).

Petropoulou, Maria-Zoe, *Animal Sacrifice in Ancient Greek Religion, Judaism, and Christianity, 100 BC to AD 200* (New York: Oxford University Press, 2012).

Pfleiderer, Otto, *Das Urchristentum: Seine Schriften und Lehren in geschichtlichem Zusammenhang* (2 vols.; Berlin: Georg Reimer, 2nd edn, 1902).

Philip, Tarja S., *Menstruation and Childbirth in the Bible: Fertility and Impurity* (Studies in Biblical Literature, 88; New York: Peter Lang, 2006).

Phillips, Victoria, 'Full Disclosure: Towards a Complete Characterization of the Women who Followed Jesus in the Gospel According to Mark', in Kitzberger (ed.), *Transformative Encounters*, pp. 13-32.

Philo (trans. F.H. Colson *et al.*; LCL; 11 vols.; Cambridge, MA: Harvard University Press, 1935).

Pierce, Ronald W., and Rebecca M. Groothuis, *Discovering Biblical Equality: Complementarity without Hierarchy* (Downers Grove, IL: InterVarsity Press, 2004).

Piketty, Thomas, *Capital in the Twenty-First Century* (trans. Arthur Goldhammer; Cambridge, MA: Harvard University Press, 2014).

Pilarski, Ahida E., 'The Past and Future of Feminist Biblical Hermeneutics', *BTB* 41 (2011), pp. 16-23.

Pippin, Tina, *Apocalyptic Bodies: The Biblical End of the World in Text and Image* (London: Routledge, 1999).

Placher, William C., 'Christ Takes our Place: Rethinking Atonement', *Int* 53 (1999), pp. 5-20.

Plaskow, Judith, 'Christian Feminism and Anti-Judaism', *Cross Currents* 33 (1978), pp. 306-309.

Plate, S. Brend (ed.), *Re-Viewing the Passion: Mel Gibson's Film and its Critics* (New York: Palgrave Macmillan, 2004).

Plato, Laws (trans. R.G. Bury; LCL; 2 vols.; Cambridge, MA: Harvard University Press, 1926).

Plisch, Uwe-Karsten, *The Gospel of Thomas: Original Text with Commentary* (Stuttgart: Deutsche Bibelgesellschaft, 2008).

Plutarch. *Plutarch's Lives* (trans. Bernadotte Perrin; LCL; 11 vols.; Cambridge, MA: Harvard University Press, 1914).

Poirier, John C., 'Another Look at the Man Born Blind', *Journal of Religion, Disability and Health* 11 (2007), pp. 60-65.

Polaski, Sandra H., *A Feminist Introduction to Paul* (St. Louis, MO: Chalice Press, 2005).

Popovic, Mladen (ed.), *Authoritative Scriptures in Ancient Judaism* (Supplements to the Journal for the Study of Judaism, 141; Leiden: E.J. Brill, 2010).

Porten, Bezalel, 'Elephantine', in Westbrook (ed.), *A History of Ancient Near Eastern Law*, II, pp. 863-81.

Porten, Bezalel, and Ada Yardeni, *Textbook of Aramaic Documents from Ancient Egypt* (4 vols.; Jerusalem: Hebrew University of Jerusalem, 1989–1999).

Porter, Stanley, *The Criteria for Authenticity in Historical-Jesus Research: Previous Discussions and New Proposals* (Sheffield: Sheffield Academic Press, 2000).

Porter, Stanley E., and Andrew W. Pitts (eds.), *Christian Origins and Greco-Roman Culture: Social and Literary Contexts for the New Testament* (Texts and Editions for New Testament Study, 9; Leiden: E.J. Brill, 2012).

Postgate, J.N., *Fifty Neo-Assyrian Legal Documents* (Warminster: Aris and Phillips, 1976).

Powell, Mark Allan, 'Matthew's Beatitudes: Reversals and Rewards of the Kingdom', *CBQ* 58 (1996), pp. 460-79.

Powery, Emerson B., *Jesus Reads Scripture: The Function of Jesus' Use of Scripture in the Synoptic Gospels* (Biblical Interpretation, 63; Leiden: E.J. Brill, 2003).

Pregeant, Russell, *Knowing Truth, Doing Good: Engaging New Testament Ethics* (Minneapolis: Fortress Press, 2008).

Price, Robert M., 'The Da Vinci Fraud', *Fourth R* 17 (2004), pp. 7-12.

—'Illness Theodicies in the New Testament', *Journal of Religion and Health* 25 (1986), pp. 309-315.

Price, S.R.F., 'Gods and Emperors: The Greek Language of the Roman Imperial Cult', *Journal of Hellenic Studies* 104 (1984), pp. 79-95.

—*Rituals of Power: The Roman Imperial Cult in Asia Minor* (Cambridge: Cambridge University Press, 1985).

Priests for Equality. *The Inclusive Bible: The First Egalitarian Translation* (Lanham, MD: Rowman & Littlefield, 2007).

Propp, William H.C., *Exodus 1–18* (AB, 2; New Haven, CT: Yale University Press, 1999).

—'Exorcising Demons', *Bible Review* 20 (2004), pp. 14-21, 47.

Provan, Iain, *Seriously Dangerous Religion: What the Old Testament Says and Why it Matters* (Waco, TX: Baylor University Press, 2014).

Pryke, Louise M., 'The Many Complaints of Rib Addi of Byblos', *JAOS* 131 (2011), pp. 411-22.

Puech, Émile, '4Q525 et les péricopes des beatitudes en Ben Sira et Matthieu', *RB* 98 (1991), pp. 80-106.

—'*11QPsAp*ᵃ: Un rituel d'exorcismes. Essai de reconstruction', *RevQ* 14 (1990), pp. 377-408.

—'Le diable, homicide, menteur et père du mensonge en Jean 8, 44', *RevBib* 112.2 (2005), pp. 215-52.

Purvis, Andrea, *Singular Dedications: Founders and Innovators of Private Cults in Classical Greece* (London: Routledge, 2009).

Quesnell, Quentin, *The Mind of Mark: Interpretation and Method through the Exegesis of Mark 6, 52* (Rome: Pontifical Biblical Institute, 1969).

—'The Women in Luke's Supper', in Cassidy and Scharper (eds.), *Political Issues in Luke–Acts*, pp. 59-79.

Rahlfs, Alfred, *Septuaginta... Editio minor* (Stuttgart: Deutsche Bibelgesellschaft, 1979).

Ramsey, Paul, 'Justice in War', in *The Essential Paul Ramsey: A Collection* (ed. William Werpehowski and Stephen D. Crocco (eds.), New Haven, CT: Yale University Press, 1994), pp. 60-67.

Raphael, Rebecca, *Biblical Corpora: Representations of Disability in Hebrew Biblical Literature* (London: T. & T. Clark, 2008).

Rasimus, Tuomas, Troels Engberg-Pedersen and Ismo Dunderberg (eds.), *Stoicism and Early Christianity* (Grand Rapids, MI: Baker, 2010).

Ratzinger, Joseph, and Pope Benedict XVI, *Jesus of Nazareth: Part 2. Holy Week. From the Entrance into Jerusalem to the Resurrection* (trans. P.J. Whitmore; San Francisco: Ignatius, 2011).

—*Jesus of Nazareth: From the Baptism in the Jordan to the Transfiguration* (trans. Adrian Walker; New York: Doubleday, 2007).

—*Jesus von Nazareth. I. Von der Taufe im Jordan zur Verklärung* (Freiburg: Herder, 2007).

Rausch, Jerome, 'The Principle of Nonresistance and Love of Enemy in Mt 5, 38-48',
    CBQ 28 (1966), pp. 31-41.
Rauschenbusch, Walter, *A Theology for the Social Gospel* (New York: Macmillan, 1917).
Reade, Julian, 'Was Sennacherib a Feminist?', in Durand (ed.), *La Femme dans le
    Proche-Orient Antique*, pp. 139-45.
Rebera, Ranjini Wickramatra, 'The Syrophoenician Woman: A South Asian Feminist
    Perspective', in Levine and Blickenstaff (eds.), *A Feminist Companion to Mark*,
    pp. 101-110.
Reculeau, Hervé, *Climate, Environment and Agriculture in Assyria in the 2nd Half of
    the 2nd Millennium BCE* (Studia Chaburensia, 2; Wiesbaden: Harrasowitz, 2011).
Redditt, Paul, 'The God who Loves and Hates', in Perchansky and Redditt (eds.), *Shall
    Not the Judge of the Earth Do What is Right?*, pp. 175-90.
Reed, David, 'How Semitic was John? Rethinking the Hellenistic Background to John
    1:1', *Anglican Theological Review* 85 (2004), pp. 709-726.
Reed, Randall, *A Clash of Ideologies: Marxism, Liberation Theology and Apocalyp-
    ticism* (Princeton Theological Monograph Series; Eugene, OR: Pickwick Press,
    2009).
Reeder, Caryn A., *The Enemy in the Household: Family Violence in Deuteronomy and
    Beyond* (Grand Rapids, MI: Baker Academic, 2012).
Regan, Tom, *The Case for Animal Rights* (Berkeley, CA: University of California Press,
    1983).
—'The Case for Animal Rights', in Singer (ed.), *In Defense of Animals*, pp. 13-26.
Reid, Barbara E., *Choosing the Better Part: Women in the Gospel of Luke* (Collegeville,
    MN: Liturgical Press, 1996).
—*Taking Up the Cross: New Testament Interpretations through Latina and Feminist
    Eyes* (Minneapolis: Ausburg Fortress Press, 2007).
Reiner, Erica, *Šurpu: A Collection of Sumerian and Akkadian Incantations* (AfO, 11;
    Graz: Selbstverlage des Herausgebers, 1958).
Reinhartz, Adele, *Bible and Cinema: Fifty Key Films* (London and New York: Rout-
    ledge, 2013).
—'The Gospel of John: How "The Jews" Became Part of the Plot', in Fredriksen and
    Reinhartz (eds.), *Jesus, Judaism, and Christian Anti-Judaism*, pp. 99-116.
—'History and Pseudo-History in the Jesus Film Genre', *BibInt* 14 (2006), pp. 1-17.
—'Love, Hate, and Violence in the Gospel of John', in Matthews and Gibson (eds.),
    Violence in the New Testament, pp. 109-123.
Reiser, Marius, 'Love of Enemies in the Context of Antiquity', *NTS* 47 (2001), pp.
    411-27.
Remus, Harold, *Pagan-Christian over Miracle in the Second Century* (Cambridge, MA:
    Philadelphia Patristic Foundation, 1983).
Rennard, John (ed.), *Fighting Words: Religion, Violence, and the Interpretation of Sacred
    Texts* (Berkeley, CA: University of California Press, 2012).
Rensberger, David, *The Epistles of John* (Louisville, KY: Westminster/John Knox Press,
    2001), pp. 58-59.
Revell, Louise, *Roman Imperialism and Local Identities* (Cambridge: Cambridge Uni-
    versity Press, 2010).
Richardson, Alan, *The Biblical Doctrine of Work* (London: SCM Press, 1952).
Richey, Lance B., *Roman Imperial Ideology and the Gospel of John* (Catholic Biblical
    Quarterly Monograph Series, 283; Washington, DC: Catholic Biblical Association
    of America, 2007).

Ridley, Ronald T., *The Emperor's Retrospect: Augustus' Res Gestae in Epigraphy, Historiography, and Commentary* (Dudley, MA: Peeters, 2003).

Rieger, Joerg, *Christ and Empire: From Paul to Postcolonial Times* (Minneapolis: Fortress Press, 2007).

Riga, P.J., 'Christ and Nonviolence', *Emmanuel* 118 (2012), pp. 301-305.

Rigato, Maria-Luisa, *Discepoli di Gesù* (Studi biblici, 61; Bologna: Dehoniane, 2011).

Rigby, Paul, and Paul O'Grady, '*Agape* and Altruism: Debates in Theology and Social Psychology', *JAAR* 57 (1989), pp. 719-37.

Ringe, Sharon H., 'A Gentile Woman's Story', in Russell (ed.), *Feminist Interpretation of the Bible*, pp. 65-72.

—'A Gentile Woman's Story, Revisited', in Levine and Blickenstaff (eds.), *A Feminist Companion to Mark*, pp. 87-88.

Robb, Carol S., *Wind, Sun, Soil, Spirit: Biblical Ethics and Climate Change* (Minneapolis: Fortress Press, 2010).

Robertson, A.T., *A Grammar of the Greek New Testament in the Light of Historical Research* (Nashville, TN: Broadman Press, 1934).

Robinson, James M., Paul Hoffmann and John S. Kloppenborg (eds.), *The Critical Edition of Q* (Louvain: Peeters, 2000).

Rock, Ian E., *Paul's Letter to the Romans and Roman Imperialism: An Ideological Analysis of the Exordium (Romans 1:1-17)* (Eugene, OR: Pickwick Press, 2012).

Rodriguez, Rafael, 'Authenticating Criteria: The Use and Misuse of a Critical Method', *Journal for the Study of the Historical Jesus* 7 (2009), pp. 152-67.

Rogerson, John W., Margaret Davies and M. Daniel Carroll R. (eds.), *The Bible in Ethics: The Second Sheffield Colloquium* (JSOTSup, 207; Sheffield: Sheffield Academic Press, 1995).

Rohrbaugh, Richard (ed.), *The Social Sciences and the New Testament* (Peabody, MA: Hendrickson, 1996).

Rosenfeld, B.Z., and H. Perlmutter, 'Landowners in Roman Palestine 100–300 CE: A Distinct Group', *Journal of Ancient Judaism* 2 (2011), pp. 327-52.

Roth, Martha T., *Law Collections from Mesopotamia* (Atlanta, GA: Scholars Press, 2nd edn, 1997).

—*Babylonian Marriage Agreements 7th–3rd Centuries B.C.* (Neukirchen–Vluyn: Butzon & Bercker Kevelaer, 1989).

Rowe, C. Kavin, 'God, Greek Philosophy, and the Bible: A Response to Matthew Levering', *Journal of Theological Interpretation* 5.1 (2011), pp. 69-80.

—'New Testament Theology: The Revival of a Discipline. A Review of Recent Contributions to the Field', *JBL* 125 (2006), pp. 393-410.

—*The World Turned Upside Down: Reading Acts in the Graeco-Roman Age* (New York: Oxford University Press, 2009).

Runesson, Anna (ed.), *Exegesis in the Making: Postcolonialism and New Testament Studies* (Biblical Interpretation, 103; Leiden: E.J. Brill, 2011).

Rüpke, Jörg, 'Individualization and Individuation as Concepts for Historical Research', in Rüpke (ed.), *The Individual in the Religions of the Ancient Mediterranean*, pp. 3-40.

—*Von Jupiter zu Christus: Religionsgeschichte im römischer Zeit* (Darmstadt: Wissenschaftliche Buchgesellschaft, 2011).

Rüpke, Jörg (ed.), *The Individual in the Religions of the Ancient Mediterranean* (New York: Oxford University Press, 2013).

Russell, E.A., 'The Canaanite Woman in the Gospels (Mt 15.21-28)', in Livingstone (ed.), *Studia Biblica 1978*, pp. 263-300.

Russell, Letty M. (ed.), *Feminist Interpretation of the Bible* (Philadelphia, PA: Westminster Press, 1985).

—'Introduction', in Russell (ed.), *The Liberating Word*, pp. 13-22.

—*The Liberating Word: A Guide to Non-Sexist Interpretation of the Bible* (Philadelphia, PA: Westminster Press, 1976).

Rütersworden, Udo, 'Die Liebe zu Gott im Deuteronomium', in Witte *et al.* (eds.), *Die deuteronomistischen Geschichtswerke*, pp. 229-38.

Saggs, H.W.F., *The Encounter with the Divine in Mesopotamia and Israel* (London: Athlone Press, 1978).

Sahlins, Marshall, *Stone Age Economics* (Chicago, IL: Aldine, 1972).

Said, Edward, *Orientalism* (New York: Vintage Books, 1978).

Salles, Ricardo, ''Εκπύρωσις and the Goodness of God in Cleanthes', *Phronesis* 50 (2005), pp. 56-78.

Samain, P., 'L'Accusation de magie contre le Christ dans les Evangelies', *ETL* 15 (1938), pp. 449-90.

Samuel, Simon, *A Postcolonial Reading of Mark's Story* (Library of New Testament Studies, 340; London: T. & T. Clark, 2007).

Samuelsson, Gunnar, *Crucifixion in Antiquity: An Inquiry into the Background and Significance of the New Testament Terminology of Crucifixion* (WUNT, 2.310; Tübingen: Mohr Siebeck, 2011).

Sanders, E.P., 'Jesus, Ancient Judaism, and Modern Christianity: The Quest Continues', in Fredriksen and Reinhartz (eds.), *Jesus, Judaism, and Christian Anti-Judaism*, pp. 31-55.

—*Jesus and Judaism* (Philadelphia, PA: Fortress Press, 1985).

—*Paul and Palestinian Judaism: A Comparison of Patterns of Religion* (Philadelphia, PA: Fortress Press, 1977).

Sanders, Jack T., *Ethics in the New Testament* (London: SCM Press, 1986).

Sanders, James A., 'The Hermeneutics of Translation', in Kee and Borowsky (eds.), *Removing the Anti-Judaism from the New Testament*, pp. 43-62.

Sanders, Seth L., 'The Appetites of the Dead: West Semitic Linguistics and Ritual Aspects of the Katumuwa Stele', *BASOR* 369 (2013), pp. 35-55.

van de Sandt, Huub (ed.), *Matthew and the Didache: Two Documents from the Same Jewish-Christian Milieu?* (Minneapolis: Fortress Press, 2005).

Sanford, Charles B., *The Religious Life of Thomas Jefferson* (Charlottesville, VA: University Press of Virginia, 1984).

Sargent, Carolyn F., and Caroline B. Brettell (eds.), *Gender and Health: An International Perspective* (Upper Saddle River, NJ: Prentice–Hall, 1996).

Sassoon, Isaac, *The Status of Women in Jewish Tradition* (Cambridge: Cambridge University Press, 2011).

Sauer, J., 'Traditionsgeschichtliche Erwägungen zu den synoptischen und paulinischen Aussagen über Feindesliebe und Wiedervergeltungsverzicht', *ZNW* 76 (1985), pp. 102-125.

Saunders, Ernest W., *Searching the Scriptures: A History of the Society of Biblical Literature, 1880–1980* (Chico, CA: Scholars Press, 1982).

Saunders, George R., 'Men and Women in Southern Europe: A Review of Some Aspects of Cultural Complexity', *Journal of Psychoanalytic Anthropology* 4 (1981), pp. 435-66.

Sawicki, Marianne, 'Review of Jesus of Nazareth by Joseph Ratzinger', *Fourth R* 20 (2007), pp. 20-22.

Scaltsas, Theodore, and Andrew S. Mason (eds.), *The Philosophy of Epictetus* (New York: Oxford University Press, 2007).

Schaeffer, Franky (ed.), *Is Capitalism Christian?* (Westchester, IL: Crossway Books, 1985).

Schaeffer, Jame, *Theological Foundations of Environmental Ethics: Reconstructing Patristic and Medieval Concepts* (Washington, DC: Georgetown University Press, 2009).

Scheffler, Eben H. 'Towards Gender Equality in Luke's Gospel', *Acta Patristica et Byzantina* 19 (2008), pp. 185-206.

Scheidel, Walter, 'In Search of Roman Economic Growth', *Journal of Roman Archaeology* 22 (2009), pp. 46-70.

Scheidel, Walter, and Steven J. Friesen, 'The Size of the Economy and the Distribution of Income in the Roman Empire', *JRS* 99 (2009), pp. 61-91.

Schellenberg, Annette, *Der Mensch, das Bild Gottes? Zum Gedanken einer Sonderstellung des Menschen im Alten Testament und in weiteren altorientalischen Quellen* (Zürich: Theologischer Verlag, 2011).

Scherer, Lester B., *Slavery and the Churches in Early America* (Grand Rapids, MI: Eerdmans, 1976).

Schiffman, Lawrence, and James VanderKam (eds.), *Encyclopedia of the Dead Sea Scrolls* (2 vols.; New York: Oxford University Press, 2000).

Schipper, Jeremy, *Disability and Isaiah's Suffering Servant* (New York: Oxford University Press, 2011).

Schlaifer, Robert, 'Greek Theories of Slavery from Homer to Aristotle', *Harvard Studies in Classical Philology* 47 (1936), pp. 165-204.

Schlund, Christine, *'Kein Knochen soll gebrochen werden': Studien zu Bedeutung und Funktion des Pesachfests in Texten des frühen Judentums und im Johannesevangelium* (WMANT, 107; Neukirchen–Vluyn: Neukirchener, 2005).

Schmid, Konrad (ed.), 'Neue Schöpfung als Überbietung de neuen Exodus. Die tritojesajanische Aktualisierung der deuterojesajanischen Theologie und die Tora', in Schmid (ed.), *Schriftgelehrte Traditionsliteratur*, pp. 185-205.

—*Schriftgelehrte Traditionsliteratur: Fallstudien zur innerbiblischen Schriftauslegung im Alten Testament* (FAT, 77; Tübingen: Mohr Siebeck, 2011).

Schmiechen, Peter, *Saving Power: Theories of Atonement and Forms of the Church* (Grand Rapids, MI: Eerdmans, 2005).

Schmitt, Rüdiger, *Magie im Alten Testament* (AOAT, 313; Münster: Ugarit-Verlag, 2004).

Schnackenburg, Rudolf, *The Johannine Epistles: Introduction and Commentary* (trans. Reginald Fuller and Ilse Fuller; New York: Crossroad, 1992).

—*The Moral Teaching of the New Testament* (trans. J. Holland-Smith and W.J. O'Hara; London: Burns and Oates, 1975).

Schneemelchert, Wilhelm (ed.), *Festschrift für Gunther Dehn* (Neukirchen–Vluyn: Neukirchener Verlag, 1957).

Schoenfeld, Eugen, 'An Illusive Concept in Christianity', *Review of Religious Research* 30 (1989), pp. 236-45.

Scholz, Susanne, 'A Third Kind of Feminist Reading: Toward a Feminist Sociology of Biblical Hermeneutics', *Currents in Biblical Research* 9.1 (2010), pp. 9-32.

Schottroff, Louise, and Wolfgang Stegemann, *Jesus and the Hope of the Poor* (trans. Matthew O'Connell; Maryknoll, NY: Orbis Books, 1986).

Schrage, Wolfgang, *The Ethics of the New Testament* (trans. David E. Green; Philadelphia, PA: Fortress Press, 1988).

—*Das Verhältnis des Thomas-Evangeliums zur synoptischen Tradition und zu den koptischen Evangeliensübersetzungen* (BZNW, 29; Berlin: Alfred Topelmann, 1964).

—*Vorsehung Gottes? Zur Rede von der providentia Dei in der Antike und im Neuen Testament* (Neukirchen–Vluyn: Neukirchener Verlag, 2005).

Schreiner, Thomas R., and Matthew R. Crawford, *The Lord's Supper: Remembering and Proclaiming Christ until He Comes* (Nashville, TN: B & H Academic, 2010).

Schultz, Celia, *Women's Religious Activity in the Roman Republic* (Chapel Hill, NC: University of North Carolina Press, 2006).

Schultz, Ray R., 'Twentieth-Century Corruption of Scripture', *ExpTim* 119.6 (2008), pp. 270-74.

Schumm, Darla, and Michael Stoltzfus (eds.), *Disability in Judaism, Christianity, and Islam: Sacred Texts, Historical Traditions, and Social Analysis* (New York: Palgrave Macmillan, 2011).

Schüssler Fiorenza, Elisabeth. *In Memory of Her: A Feminist Reconstruction of Christian Origins* (New York: Crossroad, 1983).

—'Interpreting Patriarchal Traditions', in Russell (ed.), *The Liberating Word*, pp. 39-61.

—'Feminist Hermeneutics', *ABD*, II, pp. 783-91.

—*Jesus: Miriam's Child, Sophia's Prophet* (New York: Crossroad, 1995).

Schüssler Fiorenza, Elisabeth (ed.), *Searching the Scriptures: A Feminist Commentary* (2 vols.; New York: Crossroad, 1994).

Schwartz, D.R., 'Philo and Josephus on the Violence in Alexandria in 38 C.E.', *Studia Philonica Annual* 24 (2012), pp. 149-66.

Schwarz, G., 'ΣΥΡΟΦΟΙΝΙΚΙΣΣΑ-ΧΑΝΑΝΑΙΑ (Markus 7.26/Matthäus 15.22)', *NTS* 30 (1984), pp. 626-28.

Schwartz, Seth, *Imperialism and Jewish Society, 200 B.C.E. to 640 C.E.* (Princeton, NJ: Princeton University Press, 2001).

—*Were the Jews a Mediterranean Society? Reciprocity and Solidarity in Ancient Judaism* (Princeton, NJ: Princeton University Press, 2012).

Schwartz, Shalom H., 'Individualism-Collectivism: Critique and Proposed Refinements', *Journal of Cross-Cultural Psychology* 21 (1990), pp. 139-57.

Schwermer, Daniel, 'Empowering the Patient: The Opening Section of the Ritual *Maqlû*', in Cohen, Gilan and Miller (eds.), *Pax Hethitica*, pp. 312-39.

Scott, Bernard Brandon, *Hollywood Dreams and Biblical Stories* (Minneapolis: Fortress Press, 1994).

Scott, J.M.C., 'Matthew 15.21-28: A Test-Case for Jesus' Manners', *JSNT* 63 (1996), pp. 21-44.

Sculy, Matthew, *Dominion: The Power of Man, the Suffering of Animals, and the Call to Mercy* (New York: St. Martin's Griffin, 2002).

Scurlock, JoAnn, 'Animal Sacrifices in Ancient Mesopotamian Religion', in Collins (ed.), *A History of the Animal World in the Ancient Near East*, pp. 389-403.

Scurlock, JoAnn, and Burton R. Andersen, *Diagnoses in Assyrian and Babylonian Medicine* (Champaign, IL: University of Illinois Press, 2005).

Sedgwick, Eve Kosofsky, 'Gender Criticism: What Isn't Gender', in Greenblat and Gunn (eds.), *Redrawing the Boundaries*, pp. 271-301.

Segal, Alan F., '"How I Stopped Worrying about Mel Gibson and Learned to Love the Quest for the Historical Jesus": A Review of Mel Gibson's *The Passion of the Christ*', *Journal for the Study of the Historical Jesus* 2 (2004), pp. 190-208.

Segert, Stanislav, 'Live Coals Heaped on the Head', in Marks and Good (eds.), *Love and Death in the Ancient Near East*, pp. 159-64.

Segovia, Fernando F., *Love Relationships in the Johannine Tradition: Agapē/Agapan in 1 John and the Fourth Gospel* (SBLDS, 58: Chico, CA: Society of Biblical Literature, 1982).

Segovia, Fernando F. (ed.), *Toward a New Heaven and a New Earth: Essays in Honor of Elisabeth Schüssler Fiorenza* (Maryknoll, NY: Orbis Books, 2003).

Segovia, Fernando, and Stephen D. Moore, *Postcolonial Biblical Criticism: Interdisciplinary Intersections* (Bible and Postcolonialism; London: T. & T. Clark, 2005).

Segovia, Fernando F., and R.S. Sugirtharajah (eds.), *A Postcolonial Commentary on the New Testament Writings* (The Bible and Postcolonialism, 13; London: T. & T. Clark, 2007).

Seibert, Eric A., *Disturbing Divine Behavior: Troubling Old Testament Images of God* (Minneapolis: Fortress Press, 2009).

Selvidge, Marla J., '"And Those who Followed Feared" (Mark 10:32)', *CBQ* 45 (1983), pp. 396-400.

Sen, Amartya, *Inequality Reexamined* (New York: Oxford University Press, 1992).

Setzer, Claudia, 'A Jewish Reading of *The Woman's Bible*', *Journal of Feminist Studies in Religion* 27 (2011), pp. 71-84.

Seybold, Klaus, and Ulrich B. Mueller, *Sickness and Healing* (trans. Douglas W. Stott; Nashville, TN: Abingdon Press, 1981).

Sharma, Arvind, 'Universal Declaration of Human Rights by the World's Religions', *Journal of Religious Ethics* 27 (1999), pp. 539-44.

Sharp, Douglas S., *Epictetus and the New Testament* (London: Charles H. Kelley, 1914).

Shaver, J.R., 'Christian Anti-Semitism: Tracing the Roots to the Gospel', *Church* 20 (2004), pp. 15-19.

Shea, Mark, Edward Sri and the Editors of Catholic Exchange, *The Da Vinci Deception: 100 Questions about the Facts and Fiction of the Da Vinci Code* (West Chester, PA: Ascension Press, 2006).

Shelton, W. Brian, '[Review of] Hector Avalos, *Health Care and the Rise of Christianity*', *JECS* 9 (2001), pp. 286-87.

Shepherd, David, '"Do you Love me?" A Narrative-Critical Reappraisal of ἀγαπάω and φιλέω in John 21.15-17', *JBL* 129 (2010), pp. 777-92.

Sheridan, Ruth, 'Issues in the Translation of οἱ Ἰουδαῖοι in the Fourth Gospel', *JBL* 132 (2013), pp. 671-95.

Sheryl, J.G., 'Can the Date of Jesus' Return be Known?', *BSac* 169 (2012), pp. 20-32.

Shotter, David, *Augustus Caesar* (London: Routledge, 2nd edn, 2005).

Shuman, Joel James, and Keith G. Meador, *Heal Thyself: Spirituality, Medicine, and the Distortion of Christianity* (New York: Oxford University Press, 2003).

Sider, Ronald, *Christ and Violence* (repr., Eugene, OR: Wipf & Stock, 2001 [1979]).

Siedentop, Larry, *Inventing the Individual:The Origins of Western Liberalism* (Cambridge, MA: Harvard University Press, 2014).

Sim, Margaret, 'Underdeterminacy in Greek Participles: How Do We Assign Meaning?', *BT* 55.3 (2004), pp. 348-59.

Singer, Peter, *Animal Liberation* (New York: HarperCollins, 2009 [1975]).

Singer, Peter (ed.), *In Defense of Animals* (New York: Basil Blackwell, 1985).

Sjöberg, Åke W., Hermann Behrens, Darlene Loding and Martha T. Roth (eds.), *Dumu E₂-Dub-ba-a: Studies in Honor of Åke W. Sjöberg* (OPSNKF, 11; Philadelphia, PA: Samuel Noah Kramer Fund, University Museum, 1989).

Sjöberg, Mikael, *Wrestling with Textual Violence: The Jephthah Narrative in Antiquity and Modernity* (The Bible in the Modern World, 4; Sheffield: Sheffield Phoenix Press, 2006).

Slater, Thomas B., 'Apocalypticism and Eschatology: A Study of Mark 13:3-37', *PRSt* 40 (2013), pp. 7-18.

Smith, Barry D., *Jesus' Twofold Teaching about the Kingdom of God* (New Testament Monographs, 54; Sheffield: Sheffield Phoenix Press, 2009).

Smith, Christian, *The Bible Made Impossible: Why Biblicism is Not Truly Evangelical Reading of Scripture* (Grand Rapids, MI: Brazos, 2011).

Smith, Dennis E., 'Table Fellowship as a Literary Motif in the Gospel of Luke', *JBL* 106 (1987), pp. 616-38.

Smith, Michael G., 'The Empire of Theory and the Empire of History—A Review Essay', *Christian Scholar's Review* 39.3 (2010), pp. 305-322.

Smith, Morton, *Jesus the Magician* (repr., New York: Barnes and Noble, 1993 [1978]).

Smith, Wesley D., 'Notes on Ancient Medical Historiography', *Bulletin of the History of Medicine* 63 (1989), pp. 73-109.

Soelle, Dorothee, *Suffering* (London: Darton, Longman & Todd, 1975).

Sokoloff, Michael, *A Dictionary of Jewish Babylonian Aramaic of the Talmudic and Geonic Periods* (Baltimore, MD: The Johns Hopkins University Press, 2002).

Sonsino, Rifat, *Motive Clauses in Hebrew Law: Biblical Forms and Near Eastern Parallels* (Chico, CA: Scholars Press, 1980).

Spencer, Aída B., 'Does God Have a Gender', *Priscilla Papers* 24.2 (2010), pp. 5-12.

Spencer, F. Scott, *Salty Wives, Spirited Mothers, and Savvy Widows: Capable Women of Purpose and Persistence in Luke's Gospel* (Grand Rapids, MI: Eerdmans, 2012).

Sperber, Alexander, *The Bible in Aramaic Based on Old Manuscripts and Printed Texts* (4 vols.; Leiden: E.J. Brill, 1992).

Spicq, Ceslas, *Agape in the New Testament* (trans. Sister Marie Aquinas McNamara, OP and Sister Mary Honoria Richter, OP; 3 vols.; St. Louis, MO: B. Herder Book Company, 1963–66).

—*Agapè: Prolégomènes a une étude de théologie néo-testamentaire* (Leiden: E.J. Brill, 1955).

—*Théologie morale du Nouveau Testament* (2 vols.; Paris: J. Gabalda, 1965).

Spilsbury, Paul, *The Image of the Jew in Flavius Josephus' Paraphrase of the Bible* (Texte un Studien zum antiken Judentum; Tübingen: Mohr Siebeck, 1998).

Standhartinger, Angela, 'What Women were Supposed to Do for the Dead Beloved by them (*Gospel of Peter* 12.50): Traces of Laments and Mourning Rituals in Early Easter Passion, and Lord's Supper Traditions', *JBL* 129 (2010), pp. 559-74.

Stanton, Elizabeth Cady, *The Woman's Bible* (repr., Boston, MA: Northeastern University Press, 1993 [1895]).

Stassen, Glen H., 'The Fourteen Triads of the Sermon on the Mount (Matthew 5:21–7:12)', *JBL* 122 (2003), pp. 267-308.

Stavans, Ilan (ed.), *Encyclopedia Latina: History, Culture and Society in the United States* (4 vols.; Danbury, CT: Grolier, 2005).

Stegemann, Wolfgang, *The Gospel and the Poor* (Philadelphia, PA: Fortress Press, 1984).

Steigmann-Gall, Richard, *The Holy Reich: Nazi Conceptions of Christianity, 1919–1945* (Cambridge: Cambridge University Press, 2003).

Steinhauser, Michael G., 'The Violence of Occupation: Matthew 5:40-41 and Q', *Toronto Journal of Theology* 8 (1992), pp. 28-37.

Stendahl, Krister, 'Hate, Non-Retaliation, and Love: 1QS x. 17-20 and Rom. 12:19-21', *HTR* 55 (1962), pp. 343-55.

Stenger, Victor, *The New Atheism: Taking a Stand for Science and Reason* (Amherst, NY: Prometheus, 2009).

Stephens, Mark B., *Annihilation or Renewal? The Meaning and Function of New Creation in the Book of Revelation* (WUNT, 2.307; Tübingen: Mohr Siebeck, 2011).

Stern, Richard C., Clayton N. Jefford and Guerric Debona, *Savior on the Silver Screen* (New York: Paulist Press, 1999).

Stewart, Noel, *Ethics: An Introduction to Moral Philosophy* (Cambridge: Polity, 2009).

Stimpfle, Alois, '"Von Geburt an Blind" (John 9, 1): Disability und Wirklichkeitskonstruktion', in Gründstäudl and Ferrari (eds.), *Gestörte Lektüre*, pp. 98-126.

Stökl, Jonathan, *Prophecy in the Ancient Near East: A Philological and Sociological Comparison* (Culture and History of the Ancient Near East, 56; Leiden: E.J. Brill, 2012).

Stoltz, Fritz, 'לב', *TLOT*, II, pp. 638-42.

Stone, Ken, 'Gender Criticism: The Un-Manning of Abimelech', in Yee (ed.), *Judges and Method*, pp. 183-201.

—*Practicing Safer Text: Food, Sex and Bible in Queer Perspective* (London: T. & T. Clark, 2005).

Stone, Ken (ed.), *Queer Commentary and the Hebrew Bible* (New York: Pilgrim Press, 2002).

Strain, Charles R. (ed.), *Prophetic Visions and Economic Realities: Protestants, Jews, and Catholics Confront the Bishops' Letter on the Economy* (Grand Rapids, MI: Eerdmans, 1989).

Strecker, Georg, 'Die Makarismen der Bergpredigt', *NTS* 17 (1971), pp. 255-75.

Streiker, Lowell D., 'The Christian Understanding of Platonic Love: A Critique of Anders Nygren's *Agape and Eros*', *Chicago Studies* 47 (1964), pp. 331-40.

Strenski, Ivan, *Thinking about Religion: An Historical Introduction to Theories of Religion* (Malden, MA: Blackwell, 2006).

Stringer, Martin D., *Rethinking the Origins of the Eucharist* (London: SCM Press, 2011).

Stuhlmacher, Peter, *Die Geburt des Immanuel: Die Weihnachtsgeschichten aus dem Lukas- und Matthäusevangelium* (Göttingen: Vandenhoeck & Ruprecht, 2005).

Sugirtharajah, R.S., *The Bible in Asia: From the Pre-Christian Era to the Postcolonial Age* (Cambridge, MA: Harvard University Press, 2013).

—*Postcolonial Criticism and Biblical Interpretation* (New York: Oxford University Press, 2002).

Sun, Poling, 'Naming the Dog: Another Asian Reading of Mark 7:24-30', *Review & Expositor* 107 (2010), pp. 381-94.

Sunstein, Cass R., and Martha C. Nussbaum (eds.), *Animal Rights: Current Debates and New Directions* (New York: Oxford University Press, 2005).

Sutcliffe, Edmund, 'Hatred at Qumran', *RevQ* 2 (1960), pp. 345-56.

Swartley, Willard M., *Covenant of Peace: The Missing Peace in New Testament Theology and Ethics* (Grand Rapids, MI: Eerdmans, 2006).

—*Israel's Scripture and the Synoptic Gospels: Story Shaping Story* (Peabody, MA: Hendrickson, 1994).

Swartley, Willard M. (ed.), *Violence Renounced: René Girard, Biblical Studies and Peacemaking* (Telford, PA: Pandora Press; Scottdale, PA: Herald Press, 2000).

Swidler, Leonard, and Arlene Swidler (eds.), *Women Priests: A Catholic Commentary on the Vatican Declaration* (New York: Paulist Press, 1977).

Szubin, H.Z., and B. Porten, 'The Status of a Repudiated Spouse: A New Interpretation of Kraeling 7 (TAD B3.8)', *Israel Law Review* 35 (2001), pp. 46-78.

Tacitus, *Agricola* (trans. M. Hutton and R.M. Ogilvie; LCL; Cambridge, MA: Harvard University Press, 1970).

—*The Histories and the Annals* (trans. Clifford H. Moore; LCL; 4 vols.; Cambridge, MA: Harvard University Press, 1921).

Talbert, Charles H., *The Development of Christology during the First Hundred Years and Other Essays in Early Christian Christology* (Supplements to Novum Testamentum, 140; Leiden: E.J. Brill, 2011).

—*Reading the Sermon on the Mount: Character Formation and Decision Making in Mattthew 5–7* (Columbia, SC: University of South Carolina Press, 2004).

Tarn, William W., *Alexander the Great* (Cambridge: Cambridge University Press, 1948).

Tatum, W. Barnes, *Jesus at the Movies: A Guide to the First Hundred Years* (Santa Rosa, CA: Polebridge Press, 1997).

Taylor, Bron, *Dark Green Religion: Nature, Spirituality, and the Planetary Future* (Berkeley, CA: University of California Press, 2010).

Taylor, Joan E., 'Pontius Pilate and the Imperial Cult in Roman Judaea', *NTS* 52 (2006), pp. 555-82.

Tebes, Juan Manuel, '"You shall not abhor an Edomite for he is your brother": The Tradition of Esau and the Edomite Genealogies from an Anthropological Perspective', *Journal of Hebrew Scriptures* 6 (2006), pp. 2-30.

Telscher, Guido, *Opfer aus Barmherzigkeit: Hebr 9, 11-28 im Kontext biblischer Sühnetheologie* (Forschung zur Bibel, 112; Würzburg: Echter, 2007).

Tempest, Kathryn, *Cicero: Politics and Persuasion in Ancient Rome* (New York: Continuum, 2011).

Theissen, Gerd, and Annette Merz, *The Historical Jesus: A Comprehensive Guide* (trans. John Bowden; Minneapolis: Fortress Press, 1998).

Thiroux, Jacques P., and Keith W. Krasemann, *Ethics: Theory and Practice* (Upper Saddle River, NJ: Prentice–Hall, 2009).

Thomas, D. Winton, 'Kelebh "Dog": Its Origins and Some Usages of it in the Old Testament', *VT* 10 (1960), pp. 410-27.

Thomas, John Christopher, *The Devil, Disease and Deliverance: Origins of Illness in New Testament Thought* (Sheffield: Sheffield Academic Press, 1998).

—'The Fourth Gospel and Rabbinic Judaism', *ZNW* 82 (1991), pp. 159-82.

Thomas, Keith, *Religion and the Decline of Magic* (New York: Charles Scribner's Sons, 1971).

Thompson, J.A., 'The Significance of the Verb *Love* in the David-Jonathan Narratives in 1 Samuel', *VT* 24 (1974), pp. 334-38.

Thompson, M., '"Blessed are the Poor": What Did Jesus Mean by These Words?', *Friends Quarterly* 35 (2006), pp. 58-63.

Thompson, Mary R., *Mary of Magdala: What the Da Vinci Code Misses* (Mahwah, NJ: Paulist Press, 2006).

Thompson, Thomas L., and Thomas S. Verenna (eds.), *'Is This Not the Carpenter?' The Question of the Historicity of the Figure of Jesus* (London: Equinox, 2012).

Thonemann, Peter, 'The Women of Akmoneia', *JRS* 100 (2010), pp. 163-78.

Thornsteinsson, Runar M., *Roman Christianity and Roman Stoicism: A Comparative Study of Ancient Morality* (New York: Oxford University Press, 2010).

Thucydides (trans. C.F. Smith; LCL; Cambridge, MA: Harvard University Press, 1975).

Tidball, Derek, David Hilborn and Justin Thacker (eds.), *The Atonement Debate: Papers from the London Symposium on the Theology of the Atonement* (Grand Rapids, MI: Zondervan, 2008).

van Tillborg, Sjef, *The Jewish Leaders in Matthew* (Leiden: E.J. Brill, 1972).

Tolbert, Mary Ann, *Sowing the Gospel: Mark's World in Literary-Historical Perspective* (Minneapolis: Fortress Press, 1996).

Tollefsen, Christopher, *Artificial Nutrition and Hydration: A New Catholic Debate* (Dordrecht: Springer, 2010).

Tombs, David, *Latin American Liberation Theology* (Leiden: E.J. Brill, 2003).

van der Toorn, Karel, *Sin and Sanction in Israel and Mesopotamia* (Assen: Van Gorcum, 1985).

Torjesen, Karen Jo, *When Women were Priests: Women's Leadership in the Early Church and the Scandal of their Subordination in the Rise of Christianity* (New York: HarperCollins, 1995).

Torrey, Reuben A., *Difficulties in the Bible: Alleged Errors and Contradictions* (Chicago, IL: Moody Press, n.d.).

Tosato, Angelo, 'On Genesis 2.24', *CBQ* 52 (1990), pp. 389-409.

Tov, Emanuel. '4QLev ᶜ·ᵉ·ᵍ (4Q25, 26a, 26b)', in Wright, Freedman and Hurvitz (eds.), *Pomengranates and Golden Bells*, pp. 257-66.

Trainor, Michael, *About Earth's Child: An Ecological Listening to the Gospel of Luke* (Earth Bible Commentary, 2; Sheffield: Sheffield Phoenix Press, 2012).

Trapp, Michael, *Philosophy in the Roman Empire: Ethics, Politics, and Society* (Aldershot: Ashgate, 2007).

Treggiari, Susan, 'Domestic Staff at Rome in the Julio-Claudian Period, 27 B.C. to A.D. 68', *Histoire Sociale* 3 (1973), pp. 241-55.

—*Roman Marriage: Iusti Coniuges from the Time of Cicero to the Time of Ulpian* (New York: Oxford University Press, 1991).

Triandis, Harry C., Christopher McCusker, Hector Betancourt, Sumiko Iwao, Kowk Leung, Bernadette Setiadi, Jai B. Sinha, Hubert Touzard and Zbignew Zaleski, 'Cross-Cultural Studies of Individualism and Collectivism', in Dienstbier *et al.* (eds.), *Nebraska Symposium on Motivation 1989*, pp. 41-133.

—'An Etic-Emic Analysis of Individualism and Collectivism', *Journal of Cross-Cultural Psychology* 24 (1993), pp. 366-83.

Trible, Phyllis, 'Wrestling with Scripture [interview with Hershel Shanks]', *BARev* 32 (2006), pp. 46-52, 76-77.

Trompf, Garry W., *Early Christian Historiography: Narratives of Retribution* (London: Equinox, 2007).

Truesdale, Al, 'Last Things First: The Impact of Eschatology on Ecology', *Perspectives on Science and Christian Faith* 46 (1994), pp. 116-22.

Trunk, Dieter, *Der messianische Heiler: Eine redactions- und religionsgeschichtliche Studie zu den Exorzismen im Matthäusevangelium* (Freiburg: Herder, 1994).

Tso, M.K.M., *Ethics in the Qumran Community: An Interdisciplinary Investigation* (WUNT, 2.292; Tübingen: Mohr Siebeck, 2010).

Twelftree, Graham H., *Jesus the Exorcist: A Contribution to the Study of the Historical Jesus* (Peabody, MA: Hendrickson, 1993).

Tylor, Edward B., *Primitive Culture: Researches into the Development of Mythology, Philosophy, Religion, Art, and Custom* (2 vols.; London: John Murray, 1871).

Ulluci, Daniel, 'Before Animal Sacrifice, a Myth of Innocence', *Religion and Theology* 15 (2008), pp. 357-74.

Ulrich, Eugene, *The Biblical Qumran Scrolls: Transcriptions and Textual Variants* (Leiden: E.J. Brill, 2010).

—'Isaiah for the Hellenistic World: The Old Greek Translator of Isaiah', in Flint, Duhaime and Baek (eds.), *Celebrating the Dead Sea Scrolls*, pp. 119-33.

Ulrichsen, Jarl Henning, 'Jesus—Der neue Tempel? Ein kritischer Blick auf Die Auslegung von Joh 2, 313-22', in Aune, Seland and Ulrichsen (eds.), *Neotestamentica et Philonica: Studies in Honor of Peder Borgen*, pp. 202-214.

United Nations, *Convention on the Prevention and Punishment of the Crime of Genocide*. Online: https://treaties.un.org/doc/Publication/UNTS/Volume%2078/volume-78-I-1021-English.pdf.

—*The Universal Declaration of Human Rights, 1948*. Online: http://www.un.org/en/documents/udhr/ (accessed 14 September 2014).

Upson-Saia, Kristi, 'Holy Child or Holy Terror? Understanding Jesus' Anger in the Infancy Gospel of Thomas', *Church History* 82.1 (2013), pp. 1-39.

Uusimäki, Elisa, 'Use of Scripture in 4QBeatitudes: A Torah-Adjustment to Proverbs 1–9', *Dead Sea Discoveries* 20.1 (2013), pp. 71-97.

Vaage, Leif E. 'En otra casa: El discipulado en Marcos como asceticismo domestico', *EstBib* 63.1 (2005), pp. 21-42.

Vaage, Leif E. (ed.), *Religious Rivalries in the Early Roman Empire and the Rise of Christianity* (Studies in Christianity and Judaism, 18; Waterloo, Ontario: Wilfrid Laurier University Press, 2006).

Verhey, Allen, 'The Gospels and Christian Ethics', in *The Cambridge Companion to Christian Ethics* (ed. Robin Gill; Cambridge: Cambridge University Press, 2nd edn, 2012), pp. 41-53.

—*Remembering Jesus: Christian Community, Scripture and the Moral Life* (Grand Rapids, MI: Eerdmans, 2002).

— *The Great Reversal: Ethics and the New Testament* (Grand Rapids, MI: Eerdmans, 1984).

Vermes, Geza, *Jesus, the Jew: A Historian's Reading of the Gospels* (London: William Collins Sons & Co., 1973).

Verster, Pieter, *Good News for the Poor and the Sick* (Acta Theologica Supplementum, 16; Bloemfontein: SUN MeDia, 2012).

Vesco, Jean-Luc, *Le psautier de Jésus: Les citations des psaumes dans le Nouveau Testament* (2 vols.; Paris: Cerf, 2012).

Via, Dan O., *The Ethics of Mark's Gospel: In the Middle of Time* (Philadelphia, PA: Fortress Press, 1985).

Vielhauer, Phillip, 'Gottesreich und Menschensohn in der Verkündigung Jesu', in Schneemelchert (ed.), *Festschrift für Gunther Dehn*, pp. 51-79.

Vines, Matthew, *God and the Gay Christian: The Biblical Case in Support of Same-Sex Relationships* (New York: Convergent Books, 2014).

Viviano, Benedict T., 'Beatitudes Found among Dead Sea Scrolls', *BARev* 18 (1992), pp. 53-55, 66.

—'The Sermon on the Mount in Recent Study', *Bib* 78 (1997), pp. 255-65.

Vogel, Manuel, *Herodes: König der Juden, Freund der Römer* (Biblische Gestalten, 5; Leipzig: Evangelische Verlangstalt, 2002).

Voorwinde, Stephen, *Jesus' Emotions in the Gospels* (London: T. & T. Clark, 2011).

de Vries, Hent, *Religion and Violence: Philosophical Perspectives from Kant to Derrida* (Baltimore, MD: The Johns Hopkins University Press, 2002).

de Waal, Frans, *The Age of Empathy: Nature's Lessons for a Kinder Society* (New York: Random House, 2009).

—*Primates and Philosophers: How Morality Evolved* (Princeton, NJ: Princeton University Press, 2006).

Waetjen, Herman C., *Reordering Power: A Socio-Political Reading of Mark* (Philadelphia, PA: Fortress Press, 1989).

Wagemakers, Bart, 'Incest, Infanticide, and Cannibalism: Anti-Christian Imputations in the Roman Empire', *Greece and Rome* 57 (2010), pp. 337-54.

Wagner, J. Ross, *Reading the Sealed Book: Old Greek and the Problem of Septuagint Hermeneutics* (Waco, TX: Baylor University Press, 2014).

Wainwright, Elaine, 'The Gospel of Matthew', in Schüssler Fiorenza (ed.), *Searching the Scriptures*, II, pp. 635-77.

—'Healing Ointment/Healing Bodies: Gift and Identification in a Ecofeminist Reading of Mark 14.3-9', in Habel and Trudinger (eds.), *Exploring Ecological Hermeneutics*, pp. 131-39.

—'The Pouring out of Healing Ointment: Rereading Mark 14.3-9', in Segovia (ed.), *Toward a New Heaven and a New Earth*, pp. 157-78.

—*Women Healing/Healing Women: The Genderization of Healing in Early Christianity* (London: Equinox, 2006).

Wallace, Daniel B., *The Basics of New Testament Syntax: An Intermediate Greek Grammar* (Grand Rapids, MI: Zondervan, 2000).

Wallerstein, Immanuel, *The Capitalist World Economy* (Cambridge: Cambridge University Press, 1979).

—*The Modern World System: Capitalist Agriculture and its Origin in the European World-Economy in the Sixteenth Century* (New York: Academic Press, 1974).

Waltke, Bruce K., and M. O'Connor, *An Introduction to Biblical Hebrew Syntax* (Winona Lake, IN: Eisenbrauns, 1990).

Wang, Gaofeng *et al.*, 'Anxiety and Adverse Coronary Artery Disease Outcomes in Chinese Patients', *Psychosomatic Medicine* 75 (2013), pp. 530-36.

Ward, Keith, *The Word of God? The Bible after Modern Scholarship* (London: SPCK, 2010).

Ward, Peter Douglas, *Under a Green Sky: Global Warming, the Mass Extinctions of the Past, and What they can Tell us about our Future* (New York: HarperCollins, 2007).

Wardle, Timothy, *The Jerusalem Temple and Early Christian Identity* (WUNT, 2.291; Tübingen: Mohr Siebeck, 2010).

Warraq, Ibn, *Defending the West: A Critique of Edward Said's Orientalism* (Amherst, NY: Prometheus Books, 2007).

Warrington, Keith, *Jesus the Healer: Paradigm or Unique Phenomenon?* (Carlisle: Paternoster Press, 2000).

Wassen, Cecilia. *Women in the Damascus Document* (SBL Academia Biblica, 21; Atlanta, GA: Society of Biblical Literature, 2005).

Waterman, Alan S., *The Psychology of Individualism* (New York: Praeger, 1984).

Watson, Duane F. (ed.), *Miracle Discourse in the New Testament* (Atlanta, GA: Society of Biblical Literature, 2012).

Watson, Robert N., 'Bottom Line Shows Humanities Really Do Make Money', *Chronicle of Higher Education* (21 March 2010). Online: http://newsroom.ucla.edu/stories/bottom-line-shows-humanities-really-155771 (accessed 2 October 2014).

Watt, Jan G. van der, and Ruben Zimmerman (eds.), *Rethinking the Ethics of John:*

'*Implicit Ethics' in the Johannine Writings* (Kontexte und Normen neutesta-mentlicher Ethik/Contexts and Norms for New Testament Ethics, 3; WUNT, 2.291; Tübingen: Mohr Siebeck, 2012).

Wattles, Jeffrey, *The Golden Rule* (New York: Oxford University Press, 1996).

Weaver, J. Denny, *The Nonviolent Atonement* (Grand Rapids, MI: Eerdmans, 2001).

Weaver, P.R.C., *Familia Caesaris: A Social Study of the Emperor's Freedmen and Slaves* (Cambridge: Cambridge University Press, 1972).

Weaver, Simon, *The Rhetoric of Racist Humor: US, UK, and Global Race Joking* (Burlington, VT: Ashgate, 2011).

Weber, Manfred, 'Ein koptischer Zaubertexte aus der Kölner Papyrussamlung', *Enchoria* 2 (1972), pp. 55-63.

Wedderburn, Alexander J.M., *The Death of Jesus: Some Reflections on Jesus-Traditions and Paul* (WUNT, 2.299; Tübingen: Mohr Siebeck, 2013).

Wefald, Eric K., 'The Separate Gentile Mission in Mark: A Narrative Explanation of Markan Geography, the Two Feeding Accounts and Exorcisms', *JSNT* 60 (1995), pp. 3-26.

Weidemann, Hans-Ulrich (ed.), *Er stieg auf der Berg... und lehre sie (Mt. 5, 1f.): Exegetische und rezeptiongeschichtliche Studien zur Bergpredigt* (Stuttgarter Bibelstudien, 226; Stuttgart: Katholischen Bibelwerk, 2012).

Weissenrieder, Annette, *Images of Illness in the Gospel of Luke* (Tübingen: Mohr Siebeck, 2003).

Weitzman, Steven, 'Mediterranean Exchanges: A Response to Seth Schwartz's Were the Jews a Mediterranean Society?', *JQR* 102.4 (2012), pp. 491-512.

Wells, Bruce, 'The Hated Wife in Deuteronomic Law', *VT* 60 (2010), pp. 131-46.

—'Sex, Lies, and Virginal Rape: The Slandered Bride and False Accusation in Deuteronomy', *JBL* 124 (2005), pp. 41-72.

Wendell, Susan, *The Rejected Body: Feminist Philosophical Reflections on Disability* (New York: Routledge, 1996).

Wengst, Klaus, *Pax Romana and the Peace of Jesus Christ* (trans. John Bowden; Philadelphia, PA: Fortress Press, 1987).

Wénin, André, 'Coeur et affectivité humaine dans le premier Testament', *Theologica* 36 (2011), pp. 31-46.

Werpehowski, William, and Stephen D. Crocco (eds.), *The Essential Paul Ramsey: A Collection* (New Haven, CT: Yale University Press, 1994).

Westbrook, Raymond (ed.), *A History of Ancient Near Eastern Law* (2 vols.; Leiden: E.J. Brill, 2003).

—'Old Babylonian Period', in Westbrook (ed.), *A History of Ancient Near Eastern Law*, I, pp. 361-430.

—'The Prohibition on Restoration of Marriage in Deuteronomy 24:1-14', in Japhet (ed.), *Studies in Bible*, pp. 386-405.

Westcott, Brooke Foss, *The Gospel According to St. John* (repr., Grand Rapids, MI: Eerdmans, 1971 [1881]).

Whewell, William (ed.), *Hugonis Grottii De Jure Belli et Pacis Libri Tres* (Cambridge: Cambridge University Press, 1853).

White, Lynn, Jr, 'The Historical Roots of our Ecologic Crisis', *Science* 155 (1967), pp. 1203-1207.

Whitney, Elspeth, 'The Lynn White Thesis: Reception and Legacy', *Environmental Ethics* 35 (2013), pp. 313-31.

Whybray, R. Norman, 'The Immorality of God: Reflections on Some Passages in Genesis, Job, Exodus and Numbers', *JSOT* 21 (1996), pp. 89-120.

—'"Shall Not the Judge of the Earth Do What is Just?" God's Oppression of the Innocent in the Old Testament', in *Shall Not the Judge of the Earth Do What is Right? Studies in the Nature of God in Tribute to James L. Crenshaw* (ed. David Perchansky and Paul L. Redditt; Winona Lake, IN: Eisenbrauns, 2000), pp. 1-19.

Wicker, Kathleen O., Althea S. Miller and Musa W. Dube (eds.), *Feminist New Testament Studies: Global and Future Perspectives* (New York: Palgrave Macmillan, 2005).

van Wieren, Gretel, *Restored to Earth: Christianity, Environmental Ethics and Ecological Restoration* (Washington, DC: Georgetown University Press, 2013).

Wilkinson, John, *The Bible and Healing: A Medical and Theological Commentary* (Grand Rapids, MI: Eerdmans, 1998).

Williams, Frank, *The Panarion of Epiphanius* (2 vols.; Leiden: E.J. Brill, 1994).

Williams, James G., *The Bible, Violence and the Sacred: Liberation from the Myth of Sanctioned Violence* (New York: HarperCollins, 1991).

—'King as Servant, Sacrifice as Service: Gospel Transformations', in Swartley (ed.), *Violence Renounced*, pp. 178-99.

Williams, Michael James, *Deception in Genesis: An Investigation into the Morality of a Unique Biblical Phenomenon* (Studies in Biblical Literature, 32; Frankfurt: Peter Lang, 2001).

Willis, Wendell (ed.), *The Kingdom of God in 20th-Century Interpretation* (Peabody, MA: Hendrickson, 1987).

Willitts, Joel, *Matthew's Messianic Shepherd-King: In Search of the Lost Sheep of the House of Israel* (Beihefte für die neutestamentliche Wissenschaft und die Kunde der alteren Kirche, 147; Berlin: W. de Gruyter, 2007).

Wills, Lawrence, 'Mark', in Levine and Brettler (eds.), *The Jewish Annotated New Testament*, pp. 55-95.

Wilson, Brittanny, 'The Blinding of Paul and the Power of God: Masculinity, Sight, and Self-Control in Acts 9', *JBL* 133 (2014), pp. 367-87.

—'"Neither Male nor Female": The Ethiopian Eunuch in Acts 8.26-40', *NTS* 60 (2014), pp. 403-422.

Wimbush, W.L. (ed.), *Theorizing Scripture: New Critical Orientations to a Cultural Phenomenon* (New Brunswick, NJ: Rutgers University Press, 2008).

Wink, Walter, *Engaging the Powers: Discernment and Resistance in a World of Domination* (Minneapolis: Fortress Press, 1992).

—*Jesus and Nonviolence: A Third Way* (Minneapolis: Fortress Press, 2003).

—'Neither Passivity nor Violence: Jesus' Third Way (Matt 5:38-42//Luke 6:29-30)', *Forum* 7 (1991), pp. 5-28.

Winitzer, Abraham, 'The Reversal of Fortune Theme in Esther: Israelite Historiography in its Ancient Near Eastern Context', *Journal of Ancient Near Eastern Religions* 11 (2011), pp. 170-218.

Winkler, Lea Lofenfeld, and Ramit Frankel, *The Boat and the Sea of Galilee* (trans. Ora Cummings; New York: Gefen, 2007), pp. 65-70.

Wischmeyer, Oda, 'Traditiongeschichtliche Untersuchung der Paulinischen Aussagen über die Liebe (*Agape*)', *ZNW* 74 (1983), pp. 222-36.

—'Vorkommen und Bedeutung von *Agape* in der Ausserliche Antike', *ZNW* 69 (1978), pp. 212-38.

Wiseman, Donald J., *The Alalakh Tablets* (London: British Institute of Archaeology at Ankara, 1953).

—'Supplementary Copies of Alalakh Tablets', *JCS* 8 (1954), pp. 1-30.

—*The Vassal Treaties of Esarhaddon* (London: British School of Archaeology in Iraq, 1958).

Witherington, Ben, *The Gospel Code: Novel Claims about Jesus, Mary Magdalene and Da Vinci* (Downers Grove, IL: InterVarsity Press, 2004).

—*The Letters to Philemon, the Colossians, and Ephesians: A Socio-Rhetorical Commentary on the Captivity Epistles* (Grand Rapids, MI: Eerdmans, 2007).

—*Work: A Kingdom Perspective on Labor* (Grand Rapids, MI: Eerdmans, 2011).

Wisse, Ruth, *No Joke: Making Jewish Humor* (Princeton, NJ: Princeton University Press, 2013).

Witkamp, L. Th., 'The Use of Traditions in John 5.1-18', *JSNT* 25 (1985), pp. 19-47.

Witte, Markus, Konrad Schmid, Dorish Prechel, Jan Christian Gertz and Johannes F. Diehl (eds.), *Die deuteronomistischen Geschichtswerke: Redaktions und religiongeschichtliche Perspektiven zu 'Deuteronomismus'—Diskussion in Tora und Vorderen Propheten* (BZAW, 365; Berlin: W. de Gruyter, 2006).

Wohlstein, Josef, 'Über einige aramäische Inschriften auf Thongefassen des Königlichen Musuems zu Berlin', *ZA* 8 (1893), pp. 313-40.

Wollstonecraft, Mary, *A Vindication of the Rights of Women* (repr., Köln: Könneman, 1998 [1792]).

Wong, Gordon C.I., 'Make their Ears Dull: Irony in Isaiah 6:9-10', *Trinity Theological Journal* 16 (2008), pp. 23-34.

Wong, Solomon Hong-fai, *The Temple Incident in Mark 11, 15-10: The Disclosure of Jesus and the Marcan Faction* (New Testament Studies in Contextual Exegesis, 5; Frankfurt: Peter Lang, 2009).

Woodman, Anthony J., 'Tiberius and the Taste of Power: The Year 33 in Tacitus', *ClQ* 56 (2006), pp. 175-89.

Wortmann, Dierk, 'Neue magische Texte', *Bonner Jahrburcher* 168 (1968), pp. 85-102.

Wright, David P., *Inventing God's Law: How the Covenant Code of the Bible Used and Revised the Code of Hammurabi* (New York: Oxford University Press, 2009).

Wright, David P., David N. Freedman and Avi Hurvitz (eds.), *Pomengranates and Golden Bells: Studies in Biblical, Jewish, and Near Eastern Ritual, Law, and Literature in Honor of Jacob Milgrom* (Winona Lake, IN: Eisenbrauns, 1995).

Wright, N.T., *How God Became King: The Forgotten Story of the Gospels* (New York: Harper One, 2012).

—*Paul: In Fresh Perspective* (Minneapolis: Fortress Press, 2005).

Wunsch, Cornelia, *Urkunden zum Ehe-, Vermögens- und Erbrecht aus verschiedenen neubabylonischen Archiven* (Dresden: Islet, 2003).

Wynn, Kerry H., 'Disability versus Sin: A Rereading of Mark 2.1-12' (Unpublished paper presented to the American Academy of Religion Annual Meeting, 1999).

—'Johannine Healings and the Otherness of Disability', *PRSt* 34 (2007), pp. 61-75.

Yaron, Reuven, *The Laws of Eshnunna* (Jerusalem: Magnes Press, 2nd edn, 1988).

Yarri, Donna, *The Ethics of Animal Experimentation: A Critical Analysis and Constructive Christian Proposal* (New York: Oxford University Press, 2005).

Yee, Gale A. (ed.), *Judges and Method: New Approaches in Biblical Studies* (Minneapolis: Fortress Press, 2nd edn, 2007).

Yoder, John Howard, *The Politics of Jesus* (Grand Rapids, MI: Eerdmans, 1972).

Yoffee, Norman, 'Mesopotamian Interaction Spheres', in Yoffee and Clark (eds.), *Early Stages in the Evolution of Mesopotamian Civilization*, pp. 257-70.

Yoffee, Norman, and Jeffrey J. Clark (eds.), *Early Stages in the Evolution of Mesopotamian Civilization: Soviet Excavations in Northern Iraq* (Tucson, AZ: University of Arizona Press, 1993).

Yong, Amos, *The Bible, Disability and the Church: A New Vision for the People of God* (Grand Rapids, MI: Eerdmans, 2011).

—*Theology and Down Syndrome: Reimagining Disability in Late Modernity* (Waco, TX: Baylor University Press, 2007).

Yoshimura, Hiroaki, *Did Jesus Cite Isa 6:9-10? Jesus' Saying in Mark 4:11-12 and the Isaianic Idea of Hardening and Remnant* (Åbo: Åbo Akademis Förlag/Åbo Akademi University Press, 2010).

Younger, K. Lawson, *Ancient Conquest Accounts: A Study in Ancient Near Eastern and Biblical History Writing* (Sheffield: JSOT Press, 1990).

Zaas, Peter, 'Matthew's Birth Story: An Early Milepost in the History of Jewish Marriage Law', *BTB* 39.3 (2009), pp. 125-28.

Zahn, Gordon, *German Catholics and Hitler's Wars: A Study in Social Control* (New York: Sheed and Ward, 1962).

Zamfir, Korinna, 'Who are (the) Blessed? Reflections on the Relecture of the Beatitudes in the New Testament and Apocrypha', *Sacra Scripta* 5 (2007), pp. 75-100.

Zangenberg, Jürgen, Harold W. Attridge and Dale B. Martin (eds.), *Religion, Ethnicity, and Identity in Ancient Galilee: A Region in Transition* (WUNT, 2.210; Tübingen: Mohr Siebeck, 2007).

Zerbe, Gordon M., *Non-Retaliation in Early Jewish and New Testament Texts: Ethical Themes and Social Contexts* (Sheffield: JSOT Press, 1993).

Zevit, Ziony, 'Three Ways to Look at the Ten Plagues', *BR* 6 (1990), pp. 16-23, 42.

Zimmerman, Michael E., J. Baird Callicott, George Sessions, Karen J. Warren and John Clark (eds.), *Environmental Philosophy: From Animal Rights to Radical Ecology* (Englewood Cliffs, NJ: Prentice–Hall, 1993).

Zimmermann, Ruben, Jan G. van der Watt, and Susanne Luther (eds.), *Moral Language in the New Testament: The Interrelatedness of Language and Ethics in Early Christian Writings* (WUNT 2.296; Tübingen: Morh Siebeck, 2010).

Zola, Nicholas J., '"The One who Eats my Bread has Lifted his Heel against me": Psalm 41:10 in 1QH[a] and John 13:18', *PRSt* 37 (2010), pp. 407-419.

Zolondek, Michael V., 'The Authenticity of the First Passion Prediction and the Origin of Mark 8.31-33', *Journal for the Study of the Historical Jesus* 8 (2010), pp. 237-53.

Zuckerman, Phil, *Society without God: What the Least Religious Nations can Tell us about Contentment* (New York: New York University Press, 2010).

INDEX OF REFERENCES

HEBREW BIBLE/OLD TESTAMENT

OTHER ANCIENT REFERENCES

Index of Authors

Abbott, E. 120, 121, 294, 295
Abernathy, R.D. 3
Abrams, J.Z. 283
Acevedo, J. 82
Ackerman, R. 310
Ackerman, S. 40
Adam, A.K.M. 25
Adams, E. 348
Addison, A. 16
Adeney, F. 10
Adler, E. 157
Aguilar, M.I. 248
Albl, M. 317
Albrecht, G.L. 282
Albright, W.F. 311
Aldrete, A. 33
Aldrete, G.S. 33
Alexander, L. 162
Alexander, P.S. 114
Alexis-Baker, A. 113, 116
Allison, D.C. 100, 101, 105
Altman, A. 39
Andersen, B.R. 283
Anderson, G.A. 221, 222, 288
Anderson, H. 137
Annas, J. 58
Annen, F. 306, 330
Antonio-Mayoral, J. 236
Archi, A. 149
Arenciba, A.C. 5
Arlandson, J.M. 228
Arnal, W. 9, 83
Asgeirson, J.M. 81
Ashcroft, B. 152, 154
Asirvatham, S.R. 306
Asser, S. 303
Aster, S.Z. 40
Atkinson, K. 171
Attridge, H.W. 9, 241
Auffret, P. 366
Aulén, V. 130, 144

Aune, D.E. 305-307
Avalos, H. 1, 3, 8, 9, 11, 14, 15, 20, 23,
    28, 91, 106, 149, 151, 153, 154, 162,
    182, 196, 243, 261, 281, 283, 284, 307,
    311, 318, 352, 359

Babington, B. 359
Baden, J. 3
Baer, M. 324
Bailey, C. 349, 350
Bailey, M.D. 307, 308
Bailey, R.C. 28
Bainton, R.H. 92
Balabanski, V. 323
Balch, D.L. 201
Baltzer, K. 40
Bammel, E. 226
Barbaglio, G. 232
Barber, B. 105
Barrera, A. 196
Barrett, C.B. 325
Barton, J. 21
Baslcz, M.-F. 135
Bauckham, R. 327, 330
Baudrillard, J. 377
Bauernfiend, O. 330
Baum, A.D. 317
Baynham, E.J. 2
Beal, T.K. 17, 359
Beale, G.K. 362
Beasley-Murray, G.R. 166
Beauchamp, T.L. 303
Beauvoir, S. de 257, 266, 278
Beck, J.A. 61, 372
Becker, S.O. 198
Becking, B. 33
Bekoff, M. 328
Bell, D. 247
Bellinger, W.H. 138, 366
Belousek, D.W.S. 96, 129
Berenbaum, M. 359

CPSIA information can be obtained
at www.ICGtesting.com
Printed in the USA
BVHW04s1644160318
510798BV00003B/43/P